THE GOLDEN BOUGH

The Golden Bough, by Turner. A sybil holding up the golden bough in the sanctuary at Nemi.

THE
GOLDEN BOUGH
THE ROOTS OF
RELIGION AND FOLKLORE

BY

JAMES G. FRAZER, M.A.
FELLOW OF TRINITY COLLEGE, CAMBRIDGE

TWO VOLUMES
IN ONE

WITH A NEW FOREWORD

AVENEL BOOKS
NEW YORK

This book was originally published in 1890 in two
volumes as *The Golden Bough: A Study in Comparative Religion*.

Copyright © 1981 by Crown Publishers, Inc.
All rights reserved.

This edition is published by Avenel Books,
distributed by Crown Publishers, Inc.
  b c d e f g h
1981 EDITION

Manufactured in the United States of America

The illustrations opposite pages (in Volume I) 1, 72,
(and in Volume II) 112, 132, 140, and 194, are by
H. M. Brock, and appeared in *Leaves from the Golden Bough*,
by Lady Frazer, published in 1924. Reprinted by
permission of The MacMillan Company, Ltd., London.

Library of Congress Cataloging in Publication Data

Frazer, James George, Sir, 1854–1941.
    The golden bough.

    Reprint. Originally published: London : Mac-
millan, 1890.
    Includes index.
    1. Mythology.   2. Religion, Primitive.
3. Magic.   4. Superstition.   I. Title.
BL310.F7   1981   291   81-925
ISBN 0-517-336332   AACR2

TO

MY FRIEND

WILLIAM ROBERTSON SMITH

IN

GRATITUDE AND ADMIRATION

FOREWORD

The Golden Bough has been a magical book for many people in the ninety-plus years since its first edition appeared in 1890. Its impact on culture and literature, far beyond its own field of anthropology, has been enormous. But the name of Sir James George Frazer is not on our lips as much as the names of other cultural revolutionaries of the nineteenth century, like Darwin and Marx and Freud.

What is this book and what was it to its first readers? Frazer's original purpose was modest—to explain an ancient Italian folk custom. A runaway slave, if successful in pulling down a bough from a special golden tree, won the right to fight to the death the king of the sacred forest grove at Nemi and perhaps to become the next king of the woods. An interesting custom but not startling, you might think. But Frazer pondered the similarity of this golden bough of Nemi and the golden bough which, in Virgil's epic poem the *Aeneid*, allowed the hero Aeneas to enter the underworld and gave him access to its secrets. Following this lead, on his way to explaining what the golden bough, the king and his fight for survival, his death and replacement all meant, Frazer opened up the whole world of myth and ritual, from the far reaches of the legendary past to the practices of primitive peoples of his day. It was an astounding revelation to Frazer's culture-bound world that the customs and superstitions of civilized society were in many ways comparable to the beliefs and practices of primitive peoples.

For the first time, in language that was both understandable and stylistically beautiful as well, Frazer presented the random remarks of travelers in a world then beginning to grow smaller, and expanded upon the notations of the increasing number of scientific observers returning from isolated corners of the earth. The result was one of the first triumphs of the new science of anthropology. What Frazer suggested to the cultured readers of his world was that the doings of backward and primitive peoples were comprehensible, even rational by their own lights. But more revolutionary than this was Frazer's message that we can learn from "savages" and that the study of primitive institutions can throw light on our own society.

Frazer lived the uneventful private life of an English university scholar. He didn't even teach for long. He married late, at the age of forty-five, to a widow. They had no children and were an exceedingly close couple. Though Frazer corresponded with a great number of people all around the globe, he never traveled farther from England than Greece. His personal history is monotonous to the extent that his biographer and former secretary wrote: "The facts of his life consist essentially of a list of books."

But those books and especially this book, *The Golden Bough*, were earth-shaking. Sigmund Freud was influenced by Frazer's writing and so was T. S. Eliot, though Frazer refused to read Freud and found *The Waste Land* impossible to understand.

What we have here, with the addition of illustrations, many from sources contemporary with Frazer, is the two-volume first edition of 1890, unabridged and with Frazer's original footnotes. This edition contains the clearest statement of Frazer's approach to other cultures, before he overburdened the book with volumes of illustrative examples which tended to hide the thread of his argument.

The essence of Frazer's achievement was that he saw the need to stand outside his own culture to understand other cultures. This goal he did not fully achieve—sometimes he failed and resorted to moralistic ridicule of the "savage and his ways." But then we haven't yet achieved this goal either. Frazer helps us to come closer to understanding that what sometimes seem like baseless superstitions in other cultures, are to the people who hold them matters of fact, parts of complex systems of belief. And the reverse—that our most cherished beliefs may seem to others foolish self-deception.

Frazer sums up his views in this way: "When all is said and done our resemblances to the savage are still far more numerous than our differences from him; and what we have in common with him, and deliberately retain as true and useful, we owe to our savage forefathers."

PREFACE

For some time I have been preparing a general work on primitive superstition and religion. Among the problems which had attracted my attention was the hitherto unexplained rule of the Arician priesthood; and last spring it happened that in the course of my reading I came across some facts which, combined with others I had noted before, suggested an explanation of the rule in question. As the explanation, if correct, promised to throw light on some obscure features of primitive religion, I resolved to develop it fully, and, detaching it from my general work, to issue it as a separate study. This book is the result.

Now that the theory, which necessarily presented itself to me at first in outline, has been worked out in detail, I cannot but feel that in some places I may have pushed it too far. If this should prove to have been the case, I will readily acknowledge and retract my error as soon as it is brought home to me. Meantime my essay may serve its purpose as a first attempt to solve a difficult problem, and to bring a variety of scattered facts into some sort of order and system.

A justification is perhaps needed of the length at which I have dwelt upon the popular festivals observed

by European peasants in spring, at midsummer, and at
harvest.   It can hardly be too often repeated, since it
is not yet generally recognised, that in spite of their
fragmentary character the popular superstitions and
customs of the peasantry are by far the fullest and
most trustworthy evidence we possess as to the primitive religion of the Aryans.   Indeed the primitive
Aryan, in all that regards his mental fibre and texture,
is not extinct.   He is amongst us to this day.   The
great intellectual and moral forces which have revolu-
tionised the educated world have scarcely affected
the peasant.   In his inmost beliefs he is what his
forefathers were in the days when forest trees still
grew and squirrels played on the ground where Rome
and London now stand.

Hence every inquiry into the primitive religion of
the Aryans should either start from the superstitious
beliefs and observances of the peasantry, or should at
least be constantly checked and controlled by reference
to them.   Compared with the evidence afforded by
living tradition, the testimony of ancient books on the
subject of early religion is worth very little.   For
literature accelerates the advance of thought at a
rate which leaves the slow progress of opinion by
word of mouth at an immeasurable distance behind.
Two or three generations of literature may do more
to change thought than two or three thousand years
of traditional life.   But the mass of the people who
do not read books remain unaffected by the mental
revolution wrought by literature ; and so it has come
about that in Europe at the present day the superstitious beliefs and practices which have been handed

down by word of mouth are generally of a far more archaic type than the religion depicted in the most ancient literature of the Aryan race.

It is on these grounds that, in discussing the meaning and origin of an ancient Italian priesthood, I have devoted so much attention to the popular customs and superstitions of modern Europe. In this part of my subject I have made great use of the works of the late W. Mannhardt, without which, indeed, my book could scarcely have been written. Fully recognising the truth of the principles which I have imperfectly stated, Mannhardt set himself systematically to collect, compare, and explain the living superstitions of the peasantry. Of this wide field the special department which he marked out for himself was the religion of the woodman and the farmer, in other words, the superstitious beliefs and rites connected with trees and cultivated plants. By oral inquiry, and by printed questions scattered broadcast over Europe, as well as by ransacking the literature of folk-lore, he collected a mass of evidence, part of which he published in a series of admirable works. But his health, always feeble, broke down before he could complete the comprehensive and really vast scheme which he had planned, and at his too early death much of his precious materials remained unpublished. His manuscripts are now deposited in the University Library at Berlin, and in the interest of the study to which he devoted his life it is greatly to be desired that they should be examined, and that such portions of them as he has not utilised in his books should be given to the world.

Of his published works the most important are, first, two tracts, *Roggenwolf und Roggenhund*, Danzig 1865 (second edition, Danzig, 1866), and *Die Korndämonen*, Berlin, 1868. These little works were put forward by him tentatively, in the hope of exciting interest in his inquiries and thereby securing the help of others in pursuing them. But, except from a few learned societies, they met with very little attention. Undeterred by the cold reception accorded to his efforts he worked steadily on, and in 1875 published his chief work, *Der Baumkultus der Germanen und ihrer Nachbarstämme*. This was followed in 1877 by *Antike Wald- und Feldkulte*. His *Mythologische Forschungen*, a posthumous work, appeared in 1884.[1]

Much as I owe to Mannhardt, I owe still more to my friend Professor W. Robertson Smith. My interest in the early history of society was first excited by the works of Dr. E. B. Tylor, which opened up a mental vista undreamed of by me before. But it is a long step from a lively interest in a subject to a systematic study of it ; and that I took this step is due to the influence of my friend W. Robertson Smith. The debt which I owe to the vast stores of his knowledge, the abundance and fertility of his ideas, and his unwearied kindness, can scarcely be overestimated. Those who know his writings may form some, though a very inadequate, conception of the extent to which I have been influenced by him. The views of sacrifice set forth in his article " Sacrifice " in the *Encyclopaedia*

---

[1] For the sake of brevity I have sometimes, in the notes, referred to Mannhardt's works respectively as *Roggenwolf* (the references are to the pages of the first edition), *Korndämonen*, *B. K.*, *A. W. F.*, and *M. F.*

Britannica, and further developed in his recent work, *The Religion of the Semites*, mark a new departure in the historical study of religion, and ample traces of them will be found in this book. Indeed the central idea of my essay—the conception of the slain god—is derived directly, I believe, from my friend. But it is due to him to add that he is in no way responsible for the general explanation which I have offered of the custom of slaying the god. He has read the greater part of the proofs in circumstances which enhanced the kindness, and has made many valuable suggestions which I have usually adopted; but except where he is cited by name, or where the views expressed coincide with those of his published works, he is not to be regarded as necessarily assenting to any of the theories propounded in this book.

The works of Professor G. A. Wilken of Leyden have been of great service in directing me to the best original authorities on the Dutch East Indies, a very important field to the ethnologist. To the courtesy of the Rev. Walter Gregor, M.A., of Pitsligo, I am indebted for some interesting communications which will be found acknowledged in their proper places. Mr. Francis Darwin has kindly allowed me to consult him on some botanical questions. The manuscript authorities to which I occasionally refer are answers to a list of ethnological questions which I am circulating. Most of them will, I hope, be published in the *Journal of the Anthropological Institute*.

The drawing of the Golden Bough which adorns the cover is from the pencil of my friend Professor J. H. Middleton. The constant interest and sympathy which he has shown in the progress of the book have been a great help and encouragement to me in writing it.

The Index has been compiled by Mr. A. Rogers, of the University Library, Cambridge.

J. G. FRAZER.

TRINITY COLLEGE, CAMBRIDGE,
8th March 1890.

CONTENTS

VOLUME I

CHAPTER I

THE KING OF THE WOOD, pp. 1-108

CHAPTER II

THE PERILS OF THE SOUL, pp. 109-212

CHAPTER III

KILLING THE GOD, pp. 213-409

VOLUME II

CHAPTER III (*continued*)

KILLING THE GOD, pp. 1-222

CHAPTER IV

THE GOLDEN BOUGH, pp. 223-371

NOTE

VOLUME I

Aeneas finds the Golden Bough.

CHAPTER I

THE KING OF THE WOOD

> " The still glassy lake that sleeps
> Beneath Aricia's trees—
> Those trees in whose dim shadow
> The ghastly priest doth reign,
> The priest who slew the slayer,
> And shall himself be slain."
>
> MACAULAY.

§ 1.—*The Arician Grove*

WHO does not know Turner's picture of the Golden Bough? The scene, suffused with the golden glow of imagination in which the divine mind of Turner steeped and transfigured even the fairest natural landscape, is a dream-like vision of the little woodland lake of Nemi, " Diana's Mirror," as it was called by the ancients. No one who has seen that calm water, lapped in a green hollow of the Alban hills, can ever forget it. The two characteristic Italian villages which slumber on its banks, and the equally Italian palazzo whose terraced gardens descend steeply to the lake, hardly break the stillness and even the solitariness of the scene. Dian herself might still linger by this lonely shore, still haunt these woodlands wild.

In antiquity this sylvan landscape was the scene of a strange and recurring tragedy. On the northern shore of the lake, right under the precipitous cliffs on which the modern village of Nemi is perched, stood the sacred grove and sanctuary of Diana Nemorensis, or Diana of the Wood.[1] The lake and the grove were sometimes known as the lake and grove of Aricia.[2] But the town of Aricia (the modern La Riccia) was situated about three miles off, at the foot of the Alban Mount, and separated by a steep descent from the lake, which lies in a small crater-like hollow on the mountain side. In this sacred grove there grew a certain tree round which at any time of the day and probably far into the night a strange figure might be seen to prowl. In his hand he carried a drawn sword, and he kept peering warily about him as if every instant he expected to be set upon by an enemy.[3] He was a priest and a murderer; and the man for whom he looked was sooner or later to murder him and hold the priesthood in his stead. Such was the rule of the sanctuary. A candidate for the priesthood could only succeed to office by slaying the priest, and having slain him he held office till he was himself slain by a stronger or a craftier.

This strange rule has no parallel in classical antiquity, and cannot be explained from it. To find an explanation we must go farther afield. No one will probably deny that such a custom savours of a barbar-

---

[1] The site was excavated in 1885 by Sir John Savile Lumley, English ambassador at Rome. For a general description of the site and excavations, see the *Athenaeum*, 10th October 1885. For details of the finds see *Bulletino dell' Instituto di Corrispondenza Archeologica*, 1885, pp. 149 *sqq.*, 225 *sqq.*

[2] Ovid, *Fasti*, vi. 756; Cato quoted by Priscian, see Peter's *Historic. Roman. Fragmenta*, p. 52 (lat. ed.); Statius, *Sylv.* iii. 1, 56.

[3] ξιφήρης οὖν ἐστιν ἀεί, περισκοπῶν τὰς ἐπιθέσεις, ἕτοιμος ἀμύνεσθαι, is Strabo's description (v. 3, 12), who may have seen him "pacing there alone."

ous age and, surviving into imperial times, stands out
in striking isolation from the polished Italian society of
the day, like a primeval rock rising from a smooth-
shaven lawn.   It is the very rudeness and barbarity of
the custom which allow us a hope of explaining it.
For recent researches into the early history of man
have revealed the essential similarity with which, under
many superficial differences, the human mind has
elaborated its first crude philosophy of life.   Accordingly if we can show that a barbarous custom, like that
of the priesthood of Nemi, has existed elsewhere ; if we
can detect the motives which led to its institution ; if
we can prove that these motives have operated widely,
perhaps universally, in human society, producing in
varied circumstances a variety of institutions specifically
different but generically alike ; if we can show, lastly,
that these very motives, with some of their derivative
institutions, were actually at work in classical antiquity ;
then we may fairly infer that at a remoter age the same
motives gave birth to the priesthood of Nemi.   Such
an inference, in default of direct evidence as to how the
priesthood did actually arise, can never amount to
demonstration.   But it will be more or less probable
according to the degree of completeness with which it
fulfils the conditions indicated above.   The object of
this book is, by meeting these conditions, to offer a
fairly probable explanation of the priesthood of Nemi.

I begin by setting forth the few facts and legends
which have come down to us on the subject.   According
to one story the worship of Diana at Nemi was instituted by Orestes, who, after killing Thoas, King of the
Tauric Chersonese (the Crimea), fled with his sister to
Italy, bringing with him the image of the Tauric Diana.
The bloody ritual which legend ascribed to that goddess

is familiar to classical readers; it is said that every stranger who landed on the shore was sacrificed on her altar. But transported to Italy, the rite assumed a milder form. Within the sanctuary at Nemi grew a certain tree of which no branch might be broken. Only a runaway slave was allowed to break off, if he could, one of its boughs. Success in the attempt entitled him to fight the priest in single combat, and if he slew him he reigned in his stead with the title of King of the Wood (*Rex Nemorensis*). Tradition averred that the fateful branch was that Golden Bough which, at the Sibyl's bidding, Aeneas plucked before he essayed the perilous journey to the world of the dead. The flight of the slave represented, it was said, the flight of Orestes; his combat with the priest was a reminiscence of the human sacrifices once offered to the Tauric Diana. This rule of succession by the sword was observed down to imperial times; for amongst his other freaks Caligula, thinking that the priest of Nemi had held office too long, hired a more stalwart ruffian to slay him.[1]

Of the worship of Diana at Nemi two leading features can still be made out. First, from the votive-offerings found in modern times on the site, it appears that she was especially worshipped by women desirous of children or of an easy delivery.[2] Second, fire seems

---

[1] Virgil, *Aen.* vi. 136 *sqq.*; Servius, *ad l.*; Strabo, v. 3, 12; Pausanias, ii. 27; Solinus, ii. 11; Suetonius, *Caligula*, 35. For the title "King of the Wood," see Suetonius, *l.c.*; and compare Statius, *Sylv.* iii. 1, 55 *sq.*—
"*Jamque dies aderat, profugis cum regibus aptum*
Fumat Aricinum Triviae nemus;"
Ovid, *Fasti*, iii. 271, "Regna *tenent fortesque manu, pedibusque fugaces;*" *id. Ars am.* i. 259 *sq.*—

"*Ecce suburbanae templum nemorale Dianae,*
Partaque per gladios regna nocente manu."

[2] *Bulletino dell' Instituto*, 1885, p. 153 *sq.*; *Athenaeum*, 10th October 1885; Preller, *Römische Mythologie*,[3] i. 317. Of these votive offerings some represent women with children in their arms; one represents a delivery, etc.

Diana, Roman goddess of forests and groves, who was worshipped at the sanctuary in the wood at Nemi.

Diana and her nymphs. Diana was considered the protectress of women.

to have played a foremost part in her ritual.   For
during her annual festival, celebrated at the hottest time
of the year, her grove was lit up by a multitude of
torches, whose ruddy glare was reflected by the waters
of the lake ; and throughout the length and breadth of
Italy the day was kept with holy rites at every domestic
hearth.[1]   Moreover, women whose prayers had been
heard by the goddess brought lighted torches to the
grove in fulfilment of their vows.[2]   Lastly, the title of
Vesta borne by the Arician Diana[3] points almost
certainly to the maintenance of a perpetual holy fire in
her sanctuary.

At her annual festival all young people went through
a purificatory ceremony in her honour ; dogs were
crowned ; and the feast consisted of a young kid, wine,
and cakes, served up piping hot on platters of leaves.[4]

But Diana did not reign alone in her grove at
Nemi.   Two lesser divinities shared her forest sanctuary.   One was Egeria, the nymph of the clear water
which, bubbling from the basaltic rocks, used to fall in
graceful cascades into the lake at the place called Le
Mole.[5]   According to one story the grove was first
consecrated to Diana by a Manius Egerius, who was
the ancestor of a long and distinguished line.   Hence
the proverb "There are many Manii at Ariciae."
Others explained the proverb very differently.   They
said it meant that there were a great many ugly and

---

[1] Statius, *Sylv.* iii. 1, 52 *sqq.*   From
Martial, xii. 67, it has been inferred
that the Arician festival fell on the 13th
of August.   The inference, however,
does not seem conclusive.   Statius's
expression is :—

" *Tempus erat, caeli cum ardentissimus
      axis
  Incumbit terris, ictusque Hyperione
      multo
  Acer anhelantes incendit Sirius agros.*"

[2] Ovid, *Fasti*, iii. 269 ; Propertius,
iii. 24 (30), 9 *sq.* ed. Paley.
[3] *Inscript. Lat.* ed. Orelli, No. 1455.
[4] Statius, *l.c.* ; Gratius Faliscus, *v.*
483 *sqq.*
[5] *Athenaeum*, 10th October 1885.
The water was diverted a few years
ago to supply Albano.   For Egeria,
compare Strabo, v. 3, 12 ; Ovid,
Fasti, iii. 273 *sqq.* ; *id. Met.* xv. 487
sqq.

deformed people, and they referred to the word *Mania* which meant a bogey or bugbear to frighten children.[1]

The other of these minor deities was Virbius. Legend had it that Virbius was the youthful Greek hero Hippolytus, who had been killed by his horses on the sea-shore of the Saronic Gulf. Him, to please Diana, the leech Aesculapius brought to life again by his simples. But Jupiter, indignant that a mortal man should return from the gates of death, thrust down the meddling leech himself to Hades ; and Diana, for the love she bore Hippolytus, carried him away to Italy and hid him from the angry god in the dells of Nemi, where he reigned a forest king under the name of Virbius. Horses were excluded from the grove and sanctuary, because horses had killed Hippolytus.[2] Some thought that Virbius was the sun. It was unlawful to touch his image.[3] His worship was cared for by a special priest, the Flamen Virbialis.[4]

Such then are the facts and theories bequeathed to us by antiquity on the subject of the priesthood of Nemi. From materials so slight and scanty it is impossible to extract a solution of the problem. It remains to try whether the survey of a wider field may not yield us the clue we seek. The questions to be answered are two : first, why had the priest to slay his predecessor ? and second, why, before he slew him, had he to pluck the Golden Bough ? The rest of this book will be an attempt to answer these questions.

---

[1] Festus, p. 145, ed. Müller ; Schol. on Persius, vi. 56 *ap.* Jahn on Macrobius, i. 7, 35.

[2] Virgil, *Aen.* vii. 761 *sqq.*; Servius, *ad l.*; Ovid, *Fasti*, iii. 265 *sq.*; *id. Met.* xv. 497 *sqq.*; Pausanias, ii. 27.

[3] Servius on Virgil, *Aen.* vii. 776.

[4] *Inscript. Lat.* ed. Orelli, Nos. 2212, 4022. The inscription No. 1457 (Orelli) is said to be spurious.

§ 2.—*Primitive man and the supernatural*

The first point on which we fasten is the priest's title. Why was he called the King of the Wood? why was his office spoken of as a Kingdom?[1]

The union of a royal title with priestly duties was common in ancient Italy and Greece. At Rome and in other Italian cities there was a priest called the Sacrificial King or King of the Sacred Rites (*Rex Sacrificulus* or *Rex Sacrorum*), and his wife bore the title of Queen of the Sacred Rites.[2] In republican Athens the second magistrate of the state was called the King, and his wife the Queen; the functions of both were religious.[3] Many other Greek democracies had titular kings, whose duties, so far as they are known, seem to have been priestly.[4] At Rome the tradition was that the Sacrificial King had been appointed after the expulsion of the kings in order to offer the sacrifices which had been previously offered by the kings.[5] In Greece a similar view appears to have prevailed as to the origin of the priestly kings.[6] In itself the view is not improbable, and it is borne out by the example of Sparta, the only purely Greek state which retained the kingly form of government in historical times. For in Sparta all state sacrifices were offered by the kings as descendants of the god.[7] This combination of priestly functions with royal authority is familiar to every one. Asia Minor, for example, was the seat of various great religious capitals peopled

---

[1] See above, p. 4, note 1.
[2] Marquardt, *Römische Staatsver-waltung*, iii.[2] 321 *sqq.*
[3] G. Gilbert, *Handbuch der griechi-schen Staatsalterthümer*, i. 241 *sq.*
[4] Gilbert, *op. cit.* ii. 323 *sq.*

[5] Livy, ii. 2, 1; Dionysius Halic. iv. 74, 4.
[6] Demosthenes, *contra Neaer.* § 74, p. 1370. Plutarch, *Quaest. Rom.* 63.
[7] Xenophon, *Repub. Lac.* c. 15, cp. *id.* 13; Aristotle, *Pol.* iii. 14, 3.

by thousands of "sacred slaves," and ruled by pontiffs who wielded at once temporal and spiritual authority, like the popes of mediaeval Rome. Such priest-ridden cities were Zela and Pessinus.[1] Teutonic kings, again, in the old heathen days seem to have stood in the position, and exercised the powers of high priests.[2] The Emperors of China offer public sacrifices, the details of which are regulated by the ritual books.[3] It is needless, however, to multiply examples of what is the rule rather than the exception in the early history of the kingship.

But when we have said that the ancient kings were commonly priests also, we are far from having exhausted the religious aspect of their office. In those days the divinity that hedges a king was no empty form of speech but the expression of a sober belief. Kings were revered, in many cases not merely as priests, that is, as intercessors between man and god, but as themselves gods, able to bestow upon their subjects and worshippers those blessings which are commonly supposed to be beyond the reach of man, and are sought, if at all, only by prayer and sacrifice offered to superhuman and invisible beings. Thus kings are often expected to give rain and sunshine in due season, to make the crops grow, and so on. Strange as this expectation appears to us, it is quite of a piece with early modes of thought. A savage hardly conceives the distinction commonly drawn by more advanced peoples between the natural and the supernatural. To him the world is mostly worked by supernatural agents, that is, by personal beings

---

[1] Strabo, xii. 3, 37. 5, 3 ; cp. xi. 4, 7. xii. 2, 3. 2, 6. 3, 31 *sq.* 3, 34. 8, 9. 8, 14. But see *Encyc. Brit.*, art. "Priest," xix. 729.

[2] Grimm, *Deutsche Rechtsalterthümer*, p. 243.

[3] See the *Lî-Kî* (Legge's translation), *passim.*

acting on impulses and motives like his own, liable like him to be moved by appeals to their pity, their fears, and their hopes.   In a world so conceived he sees no limit to his power of influencing the course of nature to his own advantage.   Prayers, promises, or threats may secure him fine weather and an abundant crop from the gods ; and if a god should happen, as he sometimes believes, to become incarnate in his own person, then he need appeal to no higher power ; he, the savage, possesses in himself all the supernatural powers necessary to further his own well-being and that of his fellow men.

This is one way in which the idea of a man-god is reached.   But there is another.   Side by side with the view of the world as pervaded by spiritual forces, primitive man has another conception in which we may detect a germ of the modern notion of natural law or the view of nature as a series of events occurring in an invariable order without the intervention of personal agency.   The germ of which I speak is involved in that sympathetic magic, as it may be called, which plays a large part in most systems of superstition. One of the principles of sympathetic magic is that any effect may be produced by imitating it.   To take a few instances.   If it is wished to kill a person an image of him is made and then destroyed ; and it is believed that through a certain physical sympathy between the person and his image, the man feels the injuries done to the image as if they were done to his own body, and that when it is destroyed he must simultaneously perish. Again, in Morocco a fowl or a pigeon may sometimes be seen with a little red bundle tied to its foot.   The bundle contains a charm, and it is believed that as the charm is kept in constant motion by the bird a corresponding restlessness is kept up in the mind of him or her against whom the charm is directed.[1]   In Nias when a wild pig has fallen into the pit prepared for it, it is taken out and its back is rubbed with nine fallen leaves, in the belief that this will make nine more wild pigs fall into the pit just as the nine leaves fell from the tree.[2]   When a Cambodian hunter has set his nets and taken nothing, he strips himself naked, goes some way off, then strolls up to the net as if he did not see it, lets himself be caught in it and cries, "Hillo! what's this? I'm afraid I'm caught."   After that the net is sure to catch game.[3]   In Thüringen the man who sows flax carries the seed in a long bag which reaches from his shoulders to his knees, and he walks with long strides, so that the bag sways to and fro on his back. It is believed that this will cause the flax crop to wave in the wind.[4]   In the interior of Sumatra the rice is sown by women who, in sowing, let their hair hang loose down their back, in order that the rice may grow luxuriantly and have long stalks.[5]   Again, magic sympathy is supposed to exist between a man and any severed portion of his person, as his hair or nails; so that whoever gets possession of hair or nails may work his will, at any distance, upon the person from whom they were cut.   This superstition is world-wide. Further, the sympathy in question exists between friends and relations, especially at critical times. Hence, for example, the elaborate code of rules which

[1] A. Leared, *Morocco and the Moors,* p. 272.

[2] J. W. Thomas, "De jacht op het eiland Nias," in *Tijdschrift voor Indische Taal-Land-en Volkenkunde,* xxvi. 277.

[3] E. Aymonier, "Notes sur les coutumes et croyances superstitieuses des Cambodgiens," in *Cochinchine Française, Excursions et Reconnaissances,* No. 16, p. 157.

[4] Witzschel, *Sagen, Sitten und Gebräuche aus Thüringen,* p. 218, No. 36.

[5] Van Hasselt, *Volksbeschrijving van Midden-Sumatra,* p. 323.

regulates the conduct of persons left at home while a party of their friends is out fishing or hunting or on the war-path. It is thought that if the persons left at home broke these rules their absent friends would suffer an injury, corresponding in its nature to the breach of the rule. Thus when a Dyak is out head-hunting, his wife or, if he is unmarried, his sister, must wear a sword day and night in order that he may always be thinking of his weapons; and she may not sleep during the day nor go to bed before two in the morning, lest her husband or brother should thereby be surprised in his sleep by an enemy.[1] In Laos when an elephant hunter is setting out for the chase he warns his wife not to cut her hair or oil her body in his absence; for if she cut her hair the elephant would burst the toils, if she oiled herself it would slip through them.[2]

In all these cases (and similar instances might be multiplied indefinitely) an action is performed or avoided, because its performance is believed to entail good or bad consequences of a sort resembling the act itself. Sometimes the magic sympathy takes effect not so much through an act as through a supposed resemblance of qualities. Thus some Bechuanas wear a ferret as a charm because, being very tenacious of life, it will make them difficult to kill.[3] Others wear a certain insect, mutilated but living, for a similar purpose.[4] Other Bechuana warriors wear the hair of an ox among their own hair and the skin of a frog on their mantle, because a frog is slippery and the ox from

---

[1] J. C. E. Tromp, "De Rambai en Se-broeang Dajaks," *Tijdschrift voor Indische Taal-Land-en Volkenkunde*, xxv. 118.

[2] E. Aymonier, *Notes sur le Laos*, p. 25 *sq.*

[3] J. Campbell, *Travels in South Africa* (second journey), ii. 206; Barnabas Shaw, *Memorials of South Africa*, p. 66.

[4] Casalis, *The Basutos*, p. 271 *sq.*

which the hair has been taken has no horns and is
therefore hard to catch ; so the warrior who is provided
with these charms believes that he will be as hard to
hold as the ox and the frog.[1]

Thus we see that in sympathetic magic one event
is supposed to be followed necessarily and invariably
by another, without the intervention of any spiritual or
personal agency.   This is, in fact, the modern conception of physical causation ; the conception, indeed, is
misapplied, but it is there none the less.   Here, then,
we have another mode in which primitive man seeks to
bend nature to his wishes.   There is, perhaps, hardly
a savage who does not fancy himself possessed of this
power of influencing the course of nature by sympathetic magic ; a man-god, on this view, is only an
individual who is believed to enjoy this common power
in an unusually high degree.   Thus, whereas a man-
god of the former or inspired type derives his divinity
from a deity who has taken up his abode in a tabernacle
of flesh, a man-god of the latter type draws his supernatural power from a certain physical sympathy with
nature.   He is not merely the receptacle of a divine
spirit.   His whole being, body and soul, is so delicately
attuned to the harmony of the world that a touch of his
hand or a turn of his head may send a thrill vibrating
through the universal framework of things ; and conversely his divine organism is acutely sensitive to such
slight changes of environment as would leave ordinary
mortals wholly unaffected.   But the line between these
two types of man-god, however sharply we may draw
it in theory, is seldom to be traced with precision in
practice, and in what follows I shall not insist on it.

To readers long familiarised with the conception of

---

[1] Casalis, *The Basutos*, p. 272.

natural law, the belief of primitive man that he can rule
the elements must be so foreign that it may be well to
illustrate it by examples.   When we have seen that in
early society men who make no pretence at all of being
gods do nevertheless commonly believe themselves to
be invested with supernatural powers, we shall have
the less difficulty in comprehending the extraordinary
range of powers ascribed to individuals who are actually
regarded as divine.

Of all natural phenomena there are perhaps none
which civilised man feels himself more powerless to
influence than the rain, the sun, and the wind.   Yet
all these are commonly supposed by savages to be in
some degree under their control.

To begin with rain-making.   In a village near
Dorpat in Russia, when rain was much wanted, three
men used to climb up the fir-trees of an old sacred
grove.   One of them drummed with a hammer on a
kettle or small cask to imitate thunder; the second
knocked two fire-brands together and made the sparks
fly, to imitate lightning; and the third, who was called
"the rain-maker," had a bunch of twigs with which he
sprinkled water from a vessel on all sides.[1]   This is an
example of sympathetic magic; the desired event is
supposed to be produced by imitating it.   Rain is often
thus made by imitation.   In Halmahera (Gilolo), a
large island to the west of New Guinea, a wizard
makes rain by dipping a branch of a particular kind of
tree in water and sprinkling the ground with it.[2]   In
Ceram it is enough to dedicate the bark of a certain
tree to the spirits and lay it in water.[3]   In New Britain

[1] W. Mannhardt, *Antike Wald-und*
Feldkulte, p. 342, *note*.
[2] C. F. H. Campen "De Godsdienstbegrippen der Halmaherasche Alfoeren," in *Tijdschrift voor Indische*
Taal-Land-en Volkenkunde, xxvii. 447.
[3] Riedel, *De sluik-en kroesharige ras-*
sen tusschen Selebes en Papua, p. 114.

the rain-maker wraps some leaves of a red and green striped creeper in a banana-leaf, moistens the bundle with water and buries it in the ground ; then he imitates with his mouth the plashing of rain.[1] Amongst the Omaha Indians of North America, when the corn is withering for want of rain, the members of the sacred Buffalo Society fill a large vessel with water and dance four times round it. One of them drinks some of the water and spirts it into the air, making a fine spray in imitation of a mist or drizzling rain. Then he upsets the vessel, spilling the water on the ground ; whereupon the dancers fall down and drink up the water, getting mud all over their faces. Lastly they spirt the water into the air, making a fine mist. This saves the corn.[2] Amongst the Australian Wotjobaluk the rain-maker dipped a bunch of his own hair in water, sucked out the water and squirted it westward, or he twirled the ball round his head making a spray like rain.[3] Squirting water from the mouth is also a West African way of making rain.[4] Another mode is to dip a particular stone in water or sprinkle water on it. In a Samoan village a certain stone was carefully housed as the representative of the rain-making god ; and in time of drought his priests carried the stone in procession, and dipped it in a stream.[5] In the Ta-ta-thi tribe of New South Wales the rain-maker breaks off a piece of quartz crystal and spits it towards the sky ; the rest of the crystal he wraps in emu feathers, soaks both crystal and feathers in water, and carefully hides them.[6]

[1] R. Parkinson, *Im Bismarck Archipel*, p. 143.

[2] J. Owen Dorsey, " Omaha Sociology," in *Third Annual Report of the Bureau of Ethnology* (Washington), p. 347. Cp. Charlevoix, *Voyage dans l'Amérique septentrionale*, ii. 187.

[3] *Journal of the Anthropological Institute*, xvi. 35. Cp. Dawson, *Australian Aborigines*, p. 98.

[4] Labat, *Relation historique de l'Ethiopie occidentale*, ii. 180.

[5] Turner, *Samoa*, p. 145.

[6] *Journ. Anthrop. Inst.* xiv. 362.

In the Keramin tribe of New South Wales the wizard retires to the bed of a creek, drops water on a round flat stone, then covers up and conceals it.[1] The Fountain of Baranton, of romantic fame, in the forest of Brécilien, used to be resorted to by peasants when they needed rain; they caught some of the water in a tankard and threw it on a slab near the spring.[2] When some of the Apache Indians wish for rain, they take water from a certain spring and throw it on a particular point high up on a rock; the clouds then soon gather and rain begins to fall.[3] There is a lonely tarn on Snowdon called Dulyn or the Black Lake, lying "in a dismal dingle surrounded by high and dangerous rocks." A row of stepping stones runs out into the lake; and if any one steps on the stones and throws water so as to wet the farthest stone, which is called the Red Altar, "it is but a chance that you do not get rain before night, even when it is hot weather."[4] In these cases it is probable that, as in Samoa, the stone is regarded as in some sort divine. This appears from the custom sometimes observed of dipping the cross in the Fountain of Baranton, to procure rain; for this is plainly a substitute for the older way of throwing the water on the stone.[5] In Mingrelia, to get rain they dip a holy image in water daily till it rains.[6] In Navarre the image of St. Peter was taken to a river, where some prayed to him for rain, but others called out to duck him in the water.[7] Here the dipping in

---

[1] *Journ. Anthrop. Inst. l.c.* Cp. Curr, *The Australian Race*, ii. 377.

[2] Rhys, *Celtic Heathendom*, p. 184; Grimm, *Deutsche Mythologie*[4] i. 494. Cp. San-Marte, *Die Arthur Sage*, pp. 105 *sq.*, 153 *sqq.*

[3] *The American Antiquarian*, viii. 339.

[4] Rhys, *Celtic Heathendom*, p. 185 *sq.*

[5] *Ib.* p. 187. So at the fountain of Sainte Anne, near Gevezé, in Brittany. Sébillot, *Traditions et Superstitions de la Haute Bretagne*, i. 72.

[6] Lamberti, "Relation de la Colchide ou Mingrélie," *Voyages au Nord*, vii. 174 (Amsterdam, 1725).

[7] Le Brun, *Histoire critique des pratiques superstitieuses* (Amsterdam, 1733), i. 245 *sq.*

the water is used as a threat; but originally it was probably a sympathetic charm, as in the following instance. In New Caledonia the rain-makers blackened themselves all over, dug up a dead body, took the bones to a cave, jointed them, and hung the skeleton over some taro leaves. Water was poured over the skeleton to run down on the leaves. "They supposed that the soul of the departed took up the water, made rain of it, and showered it down again."[1] The same motive comes clearly out in a mode of making rain which is practised by various peoples of South Eastern Europe. In time of drought the Servians strip a girl, clothe her from head to foot in grass, herbs, and flowers, even her face being hidden with them. Thus disguised she is called the Dodola, and goes through the village with a troop of girls. They stop before every house; the Dodola dances, while the other girls form a ring round her singing one of the Dodola songs, and the housewife pours a pail of water over her.

One of the songs they sing runs thus—

" We go through the village ;
The clouds go in the sky ;
We go faster,
Faster go the clouds ;
They have overtaken us,
And wetted the corn and the vine."

A similar custom is observed by the Greeks, Bulgarians, and Roumanians.[2] In such customs the leaf-dressed girl represents the spirit of vegetation, and drenching her with water is an imitation of rain. In Russia, in the Government of Kursk, when rain is much wanted, the women seize a passing stranger and

[1] Turner, *Samoa*, p. 345 *sq.*
[2] Mannhardt, *Baumkultus*, p. 329 *sqq.* ; Grimm, *D. M.*[4] i. 493 *sq.* ; W. Schmidt, *Das Jahr und seine Tage in* *Meinung und Brauch der Romänen Siebenbürgens*, p. 17 ; E. Gerard, *The Land beyond the Forest*, ii. 13.

throw him into the river, or souse him from head to foot.[1]   Later on we shall see that a passing stranger is often, as here, taken for a god or spirit. Amongst the Minahassa of North Celebes the priest bathes as a rain-charm.[2]   In the Caucasian Province of Georgia, when a drought has lasted long, marriageable girls are yoked in couples with an ox-yoke on their shoulders, a priest holds the reins, and thus harnessed they wade through rivers, puddles, and marshes, praying, screaming, weeping, and laughing.[3]   In a district of Transylvania, when the ground is parched with drought, some girls strip themselves naked, and, led by an older woman, who is also naked, they steal a harrow and carry it across the field to a brook, where they set it afloat. Next they sit on the harrow and keep a tiny flame burning on each corner of it for an hour. Then they leave the harrow in the water and go home.[4]   A similar rain-charm is resorted to in India ; naked women drag a plough across the field by night.[5]   It is not said that they plunge the plough into a stream or sprinkle it with water.   But the charm would hardly be complete without it.

Sometimes the charm works through an animal. To procure rain the Peruvians used to set a black sheep in a field, poured *chica* over it, and gave it nothing to eat till rain fell.[6]   In a district of Sumatra all the women of the village, scantily clad, go to the river, wade into it, and splash each other with the water. A black cat is thrown into the water and made to swim about for a while, then allowed to escape to the

[1] Mannhardt, *B. K.* p. 331.

[2] J. G. F. Riedel, "De Minahasa in 1825," *Tijdschrift v. Indische Taal-Land-en Volkenkunde*, xviii. 524.

[3] J. Reinegg, *Beschreibung des Kaukasus*, ii. 114.

[4] Mannhardt, *B. K.* p. 553 ; Gerard, *The Land beyond the Forest*, ii. 40.

[5] *Panjab Notes and Queries*, iii. Nos. 173, 513.

[6] Acosta, *History of the Indies*, bk. v. ch. 28.

bank, pursued by the splashing of the women.[1] In these cases the colour of the animal is part of the charm ; being black it will darken the sky with rain-clouds. So the Bechuanas burn the stomach of an ox at evening, because they say, "the black smoke will gather the clouds, and cause the rain to come."[2] The Timorese sacrifice a black pig for rain, a white or red one for sunshine.[3] The Garos offer a black goat on the top of a very high mountain in time of drought.[4]

Sometimes people try to coerce the rain-god into giving rain. In China a huge dragon made of paper or wood, representing the rain-god, is carried about in procession ; but if no rain follows, it is cursed and torn in pieces.[5] In the like circumstances the Feloupes of Senegambia throw down their fetishes and drag them about the fields, cursing them till rain falls.[6] Some Indians of the Orinoco worshipped toads and kept them in vessels in order to obtain from them rain or sunshine as might be required ; when their prayers were not answered they beat the toads.[7] Killing a frog is a European rain-charm.[8] When the spirits withhold rain or sunshine, the Comanches whip a slave ; if the gods prove obstinate, the victim is almost flayed alive.[9] Here the human being may represent the god, like the leaf-clad Dodola. When the rice-crop is endangered by long drought, the governor of

---

[1] A. L. van Hasselt, *Volksbeschrijving van Midden-Sumatra*, p. 320 *sq.*

[2] *South African Folk-lore Journal*, i. 34.

[3] J. S. G. Gramberg, "Eene maand in de binnenlanden van Timor," in *Verhandelingen van het Bataviansch Genootschap van Kunsten en Wetenschappen*, xxxvi. 209.

[4] Dalton, *Ethnology of Bengal*, p. 88.

[5] Huc, *L'empire chinois*, i. 241.

[6] Bérenger-Féraud, *Les peuplades de la Sénégambie*, p. 291.

[7] *Colombia, being a geographical etc. account of that country*, i. 642 *sq.*; A. Bastian, *Die Culturländer des alten Amerika*, ii. 216.

[8] A. Kuhn, *Sagen, Gebräuche und Mährchen aus Westfalen*, ii. p. 80 ; Gerard, *The Land beyond the Forest*, ii. 13.

[9] Bancroft, *Native Races of the Pacific States*, i. 520.

The sacred Buffalo Society Indians performing a dance. *Illustrated by Frederic Remington.*

In China, a huge dragon, representing the rain-god, is carried about in procession to invoke rain.

Battambang, a province of Siam, goes in great state to a certain pagoda and prays to Buddha for rain. Then accompanied by his suite and followed by an enormous crowd he adjourns to a plain behind the pagoda. Here a dummy figure has been made up, dressed in bright colours, and placed in the middle of the plain. A wild music begins to play; maddened by the din of drums and cymbals and crackers, and goaded on by their drivers, the elephants charge down on the dummy and trample it to pieces. After this, Buddha will soon give rain.[1]

Another way of constraining the rain-god is to disturb him in his haunts. This seems the reason why rain is supposed to be the consequence of troubling a sacred spring. The Dards believe that if a cowskin or anything impure is placed in certain springs, storms will follow.[2] Gervasius mentions a spring into which if a stone or a stick were thrown, rain would at once issue from it and drench the thrower.[3] There was a fountain in Munster such that if it were touched or even looked at by a human being, it would at once flood the whole province with rain.[4] Sometimes an appeal is made to the pity of the gods. When their corn is being burnt up by the sun, the Zulus look out for a "heaven-bird," kill it, and throw it into a pool. Then the heaven melts with tenderness for the death of the bird; "it wails for it by raining, wailing a funeral wail."[5] In times of drought the Guanches of Teneriffe led their sheep to sacred ground, and there

---

[1] Brien, "Aperçu sur la province de Battambang," in *Cochinchine française, Excursions et Reconnaissances*, No. 25, p. 6 *sq.*

[2] Biddulph, *Tribes of the Hindoo Koosh*, p. 95.

[3] Gervasius von Tilburg, ed. Liebrecht, p. 41 *sq.*

[4] Giraldus Cambrensis, *Topography of Ireland*, ch. 7. Cp. Mannhardt, *A. W. F.* p. 341 *note.*

[5] Callaway, *Religious System of the Amazulu*, p. 407 *sq.*

they separated the lambs from their dams, that their plaintive bleating might touch the heart of the god.[1] A peculiar mode of making rain was adopted by the heathen Arabs. They tied two sorts of bushes to the tails and hind-legs of their cattle, and setting fire to the bushes drove the cattle to the top of a mountain, praying for rain.[2] This may be, as Wellhausen suggests,[3] an imitation of lightning on the horizon. But it may also be a way of threatening the sky; as some West African rain-makers put a pot of inflammable materials on the fire and blow up the flames, threatening that if heaven does not soon give rain they will send up a flame which will set the sky on fire.[4] The Dieyerie of South Australia have a way of their own of making rain. A hole is dug about twelve feet long and eight or ten broad, and over this hole a hut of logs and branches is made. Two men, supposed to have received a special inspiration from Mooramoora (the Good Spirit), are bled by an old and influential man with a sharp flint inside the arm; the blood is made to flow on the other men of the tribe who sit huddled together. At the same time the two bleeding men throw handfuls of down, some of which adheres to the blood, while the rest floats in the air. The blood is thought to represent the rain, and the down the clouds. During the ceremony two large stones are placed in the middle of the hut; they stand for gathering clouds and presage rain. Then the men who were bled carry away the stones for about fifteen miles and place them as high as they can in the tallest tree. Meanwhile, the other men gather gypsum, pound

---

[1] Reclus, *Nouvelle Géographie Universelle*, xii. 100.

[2] Rasmussen, *Additamenta ad historiam Arabum ante Islamismum*, p. 67 *sq.*

[3] *Reste arabischen Heidentumes*, p. 157.

[4] Labat, *Relation historique de l'Ethiopie occidentale*, ii. 180.

it fine, and throw it into a water-hole. This the Moora-moora is supposed to see, and at once he causes the clouds to appear in the sky. Lastly, the men surround the hut, butt at it with their heads, force their way in, and reappear on the other side, repeating this till the hut is wrecked. In doing this they are forbidden to use their hands or arms ; but when the heavy logs alone remain, they are allowed to pull them out with their hands. "The piercing of the hut with their heads symbolises the piercing of the clouds ; the fall of the hut, the fall of rain."[1] Another Australian mode of rain-making is to burn human hair.[2]

Like other peoples the Greeks and Romans sought to procure rain by magic, when prayers and processions [3] had proved ineffectual. For example, in Arcadia, when the corn and trees were parched with drought, the priest of Zeus dipped an oak branch into a certain spring on Mount Lycaeus. Thus troubled, the water sent up a misty cloud, from which rain soon fell upon the land.[4] A similar mode of making rain is still practised, as we have seen, in Halmahera near New Guinea. The people of Crannon in Thessaly had a bronze chariot which they kept in a temple. When they desired a shower they shook the chariot and the shower fell.[5] Probably the rattling of the chariot was meant to imitate thunder ; we have already seen that in Russia mock thunder and lightning form part of a rain-charm. The mythical Salmoneus of Thessaly made mock thunder by dragging bronze kettles behind his chariot or by driving over a bronze bridge, while

---

[1] S. Gason, "The Dieyerie tribe," in *Native Tribes of S. Australia*, p. 276 *sqq.*

[2] W. Stanbridge, "On the Aborigines of Victoria," in *Trans. Ethnol. Soc. of London*, i. 300.

[3] Marcus Antoninus, v. 7 ; Petronius, 44 ; Tertullian, *Apolog.* 40 ; cp. *id.* 22 and 23.

[4] Pausanias, viii. 38, 4.

[5] Antigonus, *Histor. Mirab.* 15 (*Script. mirab. Graeci*, ed. Westermann, p. 65).

he hurled blazing torches in imitation of lightning. It was his impious wish to mimic the thundering car of Zeus as it rolled across the vault of heaven.[1] Near a temple of Mars, outside the walls of Rome, there was kept a certain stone known as the *lapis manalis*. In time of drought the stone was dragged into Rome and this was supposed to bring down rain immediately.[2] There were Etruscan wizards who made rain or discovered springs of water, it is not certain which. They were thought to bring the rain or the water out of their bellies.[3] The legendary Telchines in Rhodes are described as magicians who could change their shape and bring clouds, rain, and snow.[4]

Again, primitive man fancies he can make the sun to shine, and can hasten or stay its going down. At an eclipse the Ojebways used to think that the sun was being extinguished. So they shot fire-tipped arrows in the air, hoping thus to rekindle his expiring light.[5] Conversely during an eclipse of the moon some Indian tribes of the Orinoco used to bury lighted brands in the ground; because, said they, if the moon were to be extinguished, all fire on earth would be extinguished with her, except such as was hidden from her sight.[6] In New Caledonia when a wizard desires to make sunshine, he takes some plants and corals to the burial-ground, and makes them into a bundle, adding two locks of hair cut from a living child (his own child if

---

[1] Apollodorus, *Bibl.* i. 9, 7; Virgil, *Aen.* vi. 585 *sqq.;* Servius on Virgil, *l.c.*

[2] Festus, *svv. aquaelicium* and *manalem lapidem*, pp. 2, 128, ed. Müller; Nonius Marcellus, *sv. trullum*, p. 637, ed. Quicherat; Servius on Virgil, *Aen.* iii. 175; Fulgentius, *Expos. serm. antiq., sv. manales lapides, Mythogr. Lat.* ed. Staveren, p. 769 *sq.*

[3] Nonius Marcellus, *sv. aquilex*, p.

69, ed. Quicherat. In favour of taking *aquilex* as rain-maker is the use of *aquaelicium* in the sense of rain-making. Cp. K. O. Müller, *Die Etrusker*, ed. W. Deecke, ii. 318 *sq.*

[4] Diodorus, v. 55.

[5] Peter Jones, *History of the Ojebway Indians*, p. 84.

[6] Gumilla, *Histoire de l'Orénoque*, iii. 243 *sq.*

possible), also two teeth or an entire jawbone from the skeleton of an ancestor. He then climbs a high mountain whose top catches the first rays of the morning sun. Here he deposits three sorts of plants on a flat stone, places a branch of dry coral beside them, and hangs the bundle of charms over the stone. Next morning he returns to this rude altar, and at the moment when the sun rises from the sea he kindles a fire on the altar. As the smoke rises, he rubs the stone with the dry coral, invokes his ancestors and says : "Sun ! I do this that you may be burning hot, and eat up all the clouds in the sky." The same ceremony is repeated at sunset.[1] When the sun rises behind clouds—a rare event in the bright sky of Southern Africa—the Sun clan of the Bechuanas say that he is grieving their heart. All work stands still, and all the food of the previous day is given to matrons or old women. They may eat it and may share it with the children they are nursing, but no one else may taste it. The people go down to the river and wash themselves all over. Each man throws into the river a stone taken from his domestic hearth, and replaces it with one picked up in the bed of the river. On their return to the village the chief kindles a fire in his hut, and all his subjects come and get a light from it. A general dance follows.[2] In these cases it seems that the lighting of the flame on earth is supposed to rekindle the solar fire. Such a belief comes naturally to people who, like the Sun clan of the Bechuanas,

---

[1] Glaumont, "Usages, mœurs et coutumes des Néo-Calédoniens," in *Revue d Ethnographie*, vi. 116.

[2] Arbousset et Daumas, *Voyage d'exploration au Nord-est de la Colonie du Cap de Bonne-Espérance*, p. 350 *sq.*

For the kinship with the sacred object (tchem) from which the clan takes its name, see *ib.* pp. 350, 422, 424. Other people have claimed kindred with the sun, as the Natchez of North America (*Voyages au Nord*, v. 24) and the Incas of Peru.

deem themselves the veritable kinsmen of the sun. The Melanesians make sunshine by means of a mock sun. A round stone is wound about with red braid and stuck with owl's feathers to represent rays; it is then hung on a high tree. Or the stone is laid on the ground with white rods radiating from it to imitate sunbeams.[1] Sometimes the mode of making sunshine is the converse of that of making rain. Thus we have seen that a white or red pig is sacrificed for sunshine, as a black one is sacrificed for rain.[2] Some of the New Caledonians drench a skeleton to make rain, but burn it to make sunshine.[3]

In a pass of the Peruvian Andes stand two ruined towers on opposite hills. Iron hooks are clamped into their walls for the purpose of stretching a net from one tower to the other. The net is intended to catch the sun.[4]

On the top of a small hill in Fiji grew a patch of reeds, and travellers who feared to be belated used to tie the tops of a handful of reeds together to detain the sun from going down.[5] The intention perhaps was to entangle the sun in the reeds, just as the Peruvians try to catch him in the net. Stories of men who have caught the sun in a noose are widely spread.[6] Jerome of Prague, travelling among the heathen Lithuanians early in the fifteenth century, found a tribe who worshipped the sun and venerated a large iron hammer. The priests told him that once the sun had been invisible for several months, because a powerful

---

[1] Codrington, in *Journ. Anthrop. Instit.* x. 278.

[2] Above, p. 18.

[3] Turner, *Samoa*, p. 346. See above, p. 16.

[4] Bastian, *Die Völker des östlichen Asien*, iv. 174. The name of the place is Andahuayllas.

[5] Th. Williams, *Fiji and the Fijians*, i. 250.

[6] Schoolcraft, *The American Indians*, p. 97 *sqq.* ; Gill, *Myths and Songs of the South Pacific*, p. 61 *sq.* ; Turner, *Samoa*, p. 200 *sq.*

king had shut it up in a strong tower; but the signs
of the zodiac had broken open the tower with this very
hammer and released the sun. Therefore they adored
the hammer.[1] When an Australian blackfellow wishes
to stay the sun from going down till he gets home, he
places a sod in the fork of a tree, exactly facing the
setting sun.[2] For the same purpose an Indian of
Yucatan, journeying westward, places a stone in a tree
or pulls out some of his eyelashes and blows them
towards the sun.[3] South African natives, in travelling,
will put a stone in a branch of a tree or place some
grass on the path with a stone over it, believing that
this will cause their friends to keep the meal waiting
till their arrival.[4] In these, as in previous examples,
the purpose apparently is to retard the sun. But why
should the act of putting a stone or a sod in a tree be
supposed to effect this? A partial explanation is
suggested by another Australian custom. In their
journeys the natives are accustomed to place stones in
trees at different heights from the ground in order to
indicate the height of the sun in the sky at the moment
when they passed the particular tree. Those who
follow are thus made aware of the time of day when
their friends in advance passed the spot.[5] Possibly
the natives, thus accustomed to mark the sun's progress,
may have slipped into the confusion of imagining that
to mark the sun's progress was to arrest it at the point
marked. On the other hand, to make it go down
faster, the Australians throw sand into the air and
blow with their mouths towards the sun.[6]

---

[1] Aeneas Sylvius, *Opera* (Bâle, 1571),
p. 418 [wrongly numbered 420].
[2] Brough Smyth, *Aborigines of
Victoria*, ii. 334; Curr, *The Australian
Race*, i. 50.
[3] Fancourt, *History of Yucatan*, p. 118.

[4] *South African Folk-lore Journal*,
i. 34.
[5] E. J. Eyre, *Journals of Expeditions
of Discovery into Central Australia*,
ii. 365.
[6] Curr, *The Australian Race*, iii. 145.

Once more, the savage thinks he can make the wind to blow or to be still. When the day is hot and a Yakut has a long way to go, he takes a stone which he has chanced to find in an animal or fish, winds a horse-hair several times round it, and ties it to a stick. He then waves the stick about, uttering a spell. Soon a cool breeze begins to blow.[1] The Wind clan of the Omahas flap their blankets to start a breeze which will drive away the mosquitoes.[2] When a Haida Indian wishes to obtain a fair wind, he fasts, shoots a raven, singes it in the fire, and then going to the edge of the sea sweeps it over the surface of the water four times in the direction in which he wishes the wind to blow. He then throws the raven behind him, but afterwards picks it up and sets it in a sitting posture at the foot of a spruce-tree, facing towards the required wind. Propping its beak open with a stick, he requests a fair wind for a certain number of days; then going away he lies covered up in his mantle till another Indian asks him for how many days he has desired the wind, which question he answers.[3] When a sorcerer in New Britain wishes to make a wind blow in a certain direction, he throws burnt lime in the air, chanting a song all the time. Then he waves sprigs of ginger and other plants about, throws them up and catches them. Next he makes a small fire with these sprigs on the spot where the lime has fallen thickest, and walks round the fire chanting. Lastly, he takes the ashes and throws them on the water.[4] On the altar of Fladda's chapel, in the island of Fladdahuan (one of

[1] Gmelin, *Reise durch Sibirien*, ii. 510.

[2] *Third Annual Report of the Bureau of Ethnology* (Washington), p. 241.

[3] G. M. Dawson, "On the Haida Indians of the Queen Charlotte Islands," *Geological Survey of Canada, Report of progress for* 1878-1879, p. 124 B.

[4] W. Powell, *Wanderings in a Wild Country*, p. 169.

the Hebrides), lay a round bluish stone which was always moist. Windbound fishermen walked sunwise round the chapel and then poured water on the stone, whereupon a favourable breeze was sure to spring up.[1] In Finnland wizards used to sell wind to storm-staid mariners. The wind was enclosed in three knots; if they undid the first knot, a moderate wind sprang up ; if the second, it blew half a gale ; if the third, a hurricane.[2] The same thing is said to have been done by wizards and witches in Lappland, in the island of Lewis, and in the Isle of Man.[3] A Norwegian witch has boasted of sinking a ship by opening a bag in which she had shut up a wind.[4] Ulysses received the winds in a leather bag from Aeolus, King of the Winds.[5] So Perdoytus, the Lithuanian wind-god, keeps the winds enclosed in a leather bag; when they escape from it he pursues them, beats them, and shuts them up again.[6] The Motumotu in New Guinea think that storms are sent by an Oiabu sorcerer ; for each wind he has a bamboo which he opens at pleasure.[7] But here we have passed from custom (with which alone we are at present concerned) into mythology. Shetland seamen still buy winds from old women who claim to rule the storms. There are now in Lerwick old women who live by selling wind.[8] When the Hottentots wish to make the wind drop, they take one of their fattest skins and hang it on the end of a pole,

---

[1] Miss C. F. Gordon Cumming, *In the Hebrides*, p. 166 *sq.* ; Martin, " Description of the Western Islands of Scotland," in Pinkerton's *Voyages and Travels*, iii. 627.

[2] Olaus Magnus, *Gentium Septentr. Hist.* iii. 15.

[3] Scheffer, *Lapponia*, p. 144 ; Gordon Cumming, *In the Hebrides*, p. 254 *sq.* ; Train, *Account of the Isle of Man*, ii. 166.

[4] C. Leemius, *De Lapponibus Finmarchiae etc. commentatio*, p. 454.

[5] *Odyssey*, x. 19 *sqq.*

[6] E. Veckenstedt, *Die Mythen, Sagen, und Legenden der Zamaiten* (*Litauer*), i. 153.

[7] J. Chalmers, *Pioneering in New Guinea*, p. 177.

[8] Rogers, *Social Life in Scotland*, iii. 220 ; Sir W. Scott, *Pirate*, note to ch. vii. ; Shaks. *Macbeth*, Act i. Sc. 3, l. 11.

believing that by blowing the skin down the wind will lose all its force and must itself fall.[1]   In some parts of Austria, during a heavy storm, it is customary to open the window and throw out a handful of meal, chaff, or feathers, saying to the wind, "There, that's for you, stop!"[2]   Once when north-westerly winds had kept the ice long on the coast, and food was getting scarce, the Eskimos of Alaska performed a ceremony to make a calm.   A fire was kindled on the shore and the men gathered round it and chanted. An old man then stepped up to the fire and in a coaxing voice invited the demon of the wind to come under the fire and warm himself.   When he was supposed to have arrived, a vessel of water, to which each man present had contributed, was thrown on the fire by an old man, and immediately a flight of arrows sped towards the spot where the fire had been. They thought that the demon would not stay where he had been so badly treated.   To complete the effect, guns were discharged in various directions, and the captain of a European vessel was asked to fire on the wind with cannon.[3]   When the wind blows down their huts, the Payaguas in South America snatch up fire-brands and run against the wind menacing it with the blazing brands, while others beat the air with their fists to frighten the storm.[4]   When the Guaycurus are threatened by a severe storm the men go out armed, and the women and children scream their loudest to intimidate the demon.[5]   During a tempest the inhabitants of a Batta village in Sumatra have been seen to

---

[1] Dapper, *Description de l'Afrique* (Amsterdam, 1686), p. 389.

[2] A. Peter, *Volksthümliches aus Oesterreichisch Schlesien*, ii. 259.

[3] *Arctic Papers for the Expedition* of 1875 (R. Geogr. Soc.), p. 274.

[4] Azara, *Voyages dans l'Amérique Méridionale*, ii. 137.

[5] Charlevoix, *Histoire du Paraguay*, i. 74.

雨師

After many prayers and rituals, the Lord of the Rain responds.

Australian aborigines.

rush from their houses armed with sword and lance. The Raja placed himself at their head, and with shouts and yells they hewed and hacked at the invisible foe. An old woman was observed to be especially active in defending her house, slashing the air right and left with a long sabre.[1]

In the light of these examples a story told by Herodotus, which his modern critics have treated as a fable, is perfectly credible. He says, without however vouching for the truth of the tale, that once in the land of the Psylli, the modern Tripoli, the wind blowing from the Sahara had dried up all the water-tanks. So the people took counsel and marched in a body to make war on the south wind. But when they entered the desert, the simoom swept down on them and buried them to a man.[2] The story may well have been told by one who watched them disappearing, in battle array, with drums and cymbals beating, into the red cloud of whirling sand. It is still said of the Bedouins of Eastern Africa that "no whirlwind ever sweeps across the path without being pursued by a dozen savages with drawn creeses, who stab into the centre of the dusty column in order to drive away the evil spirit that is believed to be riding on the blast."[3] So in Australia the huge columns of red sand that move rapidly across a desert tract are thought by the blackfellows to be spirits passing along. Once an athletic young black ran after one of these moving columns to kill it with boomerangs. He was away two or three hours and came back very weary, saying he had killed Koochee (the demon), but that Koochee

---

[1] W. A. Henry, "Bijdrage tot de Kennis der Bataklanden," in *Tijdschrift voor Indische Taal-Land-en Volkenkunde*, xvii. 23 *sq.*

[2] Herodotus, iv. 173; Aulus Gellius, xvi. 11.

[3] Harris, *Highlands of Ethiopia*, i. 352.

had growled at him and he must die.[1]   Even where
these dust columns are not attacked they are still
regarded with awe.   In some parts of India they are
supposed to be *bhuts* going to bathe in the Ganges.[2]
Californian Indians think that they are happy souls
ascending to the heavenly land.[3]

When a gust lifts the hay in the meadow, the
Breton peasant throws a knife or a fork at it to prevent
the devil from carrying off the hay.[4]   German peasants
throw a knife or a hat at a whirlwind because there is
a witch or a wizard in it.[5]

§ 3.—*Incarnate gods*

These examples, drawn from the beliefs and
practices of rude peoples all over the world, may
suffice to prove that the savage, whether European or
otherwise, fails to recognise those limitations to his
power over nature which seem so obvious to us.   In a
society where every man is supposed to be endowed
more or less with powers which we should call supernatural, it is plain that the distinction between gods
and men is somewhat blurred, or rather has scarcely
emerged.   The conception of gods as supernatural
beings entirely distinct from and superior to man,
and wielding powers to which he possesses nothing
comparable in degree and hardly even in kind, has
been slowly evolved in the course of history.   At first
the supernatural agents are not regarded as greatly, if

---

[1] Brough Smyth, *Aborigines of Victoria*, i. 457 *sq.* ; cp. *id.* ii. 270 ; *Journ. Anthrop. Inst.* xiii. p. 194 *note.*

[2] Denzil C. J. Ibbetson, *Settlement Report of the Panipat Tahsil and Karnal Parganah of the Karnal District*, p. 154.

[3] Stephen Powers, *Tribes of California*, p. 328.

[4] Sébillot, *Coutumes populaires de la Haute-Bretagne*, p. 302 *sq.*

[5] Mannhardt, *A.W.F.* p. 85.

at all, superior to man ; for they may be frightened
and coerced by him into doing his will.   At this stage
of thought the world is viewed as a great democracy ;
all beings in it, whether natural or supernatural, are
supposed to stand on a footing of tolerable equality.
But with the growth of his knowledge man learns to
realise more clearly the vastness of nature and his
own littleness and feebleness in presence of it.   The
recognition of his own helplessness does not, however,
carry with it a corresponding belief in the impotence
of those supernatural beings with which his imagination
peoples the universe.   On the contrary it enhances his
conception of their power.   For the idea of the world
as a system of impersonal forces acting in accordance
with fixed and invariable laws has not yet fully dawned
or darkened upon him.   The germ of the idea he
certainly has, and he acts upon it, not only in magic
art, but in much of the business of daily life.   But the
idea remains undeveloped, and so far as he attempts
consciously to explain the world he lives in, he pictures
it as the manifestation of conscious will and personal
agency.   If then he feels himself to be so frail and
slight, how vast and powerful must he deem the beings
who control the gigantic machinery of nature !   Thus
as his old sense of equality with the gods slowly
vanishes, he resigns at the same time the hope of
directing the course of nature by his own unaided
resources, that is, by magic, and looks more and more
to the gods as the sole repositories of those supernatural
powers which he once claimed to share with them.
With the first advance of knowledge, therefore, prayer
and sacrifice assume the leading place in religious
ritual ; and magic, which once ranked with them as a
legitimate equal, is gradually relegated to the back-

ground and sinks to the level of a black art.   It is now regarded as an encroachment, at once vain and impious, on the domain of the gods, and as such encounters the steady opposition of the priests, whose reputation and influence gain or lose with those of their gods.   Hence, when at a late period the distinction between religion and superstition has emerged, we find that sacrifice and prayer are the resource of the pious and enlightened portion of the community, while magic is the refuge of the superstitious and ignorant.   But when, still later, the conception of the elemental forces as personal agents is giving way to the recognition of natural law ; then magic, based as it implicitly is on the idea of a necessary and invariable sequence of cause and effect, independent of personal will, reappears from the obscurity and discredit into which it had fallen, and by investigating the causal sequences in nature, directly prepares the way for science.   Alchemy leads up to chemistry.

The notion of a man-god or of a human being endowed with divine or supernatural powers, belongs essentially to that earlier period of religious history in which gods and men are still viewed as beings of much the same order, and before they are divided by the impassable gulf which, to later thought, opens out between them.   Strange, therefore, as may seem to us the idea of a god incarnate in human form, it has nothing very startling for early man, who sees in a man-god or a god-man only a higher degree of the same supernatural powers which he arrogates in perfect good faith to himself.   Such incarnate gods are common in rude society.   The incarnation may be temporary or permanent.   In the former case, the incarnation—commonly known as inspiration or possession—reveals itself in supernatural knowledge rather than in supernatural power. In other words, its usual manifestations are divination and prophesy rather than miracles. On the other hand, when the incarnation is not merely temporary, when the divine spirit has permanently taken up its abode in a human body, the god-man is usually expected to vindicate his character by working miracles. Only we have to remember that by men at this stage of thought miracles are not considered as breaches of natural law. Not conceiving the existence of natural law, primitive man cannot conceive a breach of it. A miracle is to him merely an unusually striking manifestation of a common power.

The belief in temporary incarnation or inspiration is world-wide. Certain persons are supposed to be possessed from time to time by a spirit or deity; while the possession lasts, their own personality lies in abeyance, the presence of the spirit is revealed by convulsive shiverings and shakings of the man's whole body, by wild gestures and excited looks, all of which are referred, not to the man himself, but to the spirit which has entered into him ; and in this abnormal state all his utterances are accepted as the voice of the god or spirit dwelling in him and speaking through him. In Mangaia the priests in whom the gods took up their abode from time to time were called "god-boxes" or, for shortness, "gods." Before giving oracles as gods, they drank an intoxicating liquor, and in the frenzy thus produced their wild words were received as the voice of the god.[1] But examples of such temporary inspiration are so common in every part of the world

---

[1] Gill, *Myths and Songs of the South Pacific*, p. 35.

and are now so familiar through books on ethnology, that it is needless to cite illustrations of the general principle.[1] It may be well, however, to refer to two particular modes of producing temporary inspiration, because they are perhaps less known than some others, and because we shall have occasion to refer to them later on. One of these modes of producing inspiration is by sucking the fresh blood of a sacrificed victim. In the temple of Apollo Diradiotes at Argos, a lamb was sacrificed by night once a month; a woman, who had to observe a rule of chastity, tasted the blood of the lamb, and thus being inspired by the god she prophesied or divined.[2] At Aegira in Achaea the priestess of Earth drank the fresh blood of a bull before she descended into the cave to prophesy.[3] In Southern India a devil-dancer "drinks the blood of the sacrifice, putting the throat of the decapitated goat to his mouth. Then, as if he had acquired new life, he begins to brandish his staff of bells, and to dance with a quick but wild unsteady step. Suddenly the afflatus descends. There is no mistaking that glare, or those frantic leaps. He snorts, he stares, he gyrates. The demon has now taken bodily possession of him; and, though he retains the power of utterance and of motion, both are under the demon's control, and his separate consciousness is in abeyance. . . . The devil-dancer is now worshipped as a present deity, and every bystander consults him respecting his disease, his wants, the welfare of his absent relatives, the offerings to be made for the accomplishment of his

---

[1] See for examples E. B. Tylor, *Primitive Culture*,[2] ii. 131 *sqq.*

[2] Pausanias, ii. 24, 1. κάτοχος ἐκ τοῦ θεοῦ γίνεται is the expression.

[3] Pliny, *Nat. Hist.* xxviii. 147.

Pausanias (vii. 25, 13) mentions the draught of bull's blood as an ordeal to test the chastity of the priestess. Doubtless it was thought to serve both purposes.

wishes, and, in short, respecting everything for which superhuman knowledge is supposed to be available."[1] At a festival of the Minahassa in northern Celebes, after a pig has been killed, the priest rushes furiously at it, thrusts his head into the carcass and drinks of the blood. Then he is dragged away from it by force and set on a chair, whereupon he begins to prophesy how the rice crop will turn out that year. A second time he runs at the carcass and drinks of the blood; a second time he is forced into the chair and continues his predictions. It is thought there is a spirit in him which possesses the power of prophecy.[2] At Rhetra, a great religious capital of the Western Slavs, the priest tasted the blood of the sacrificed oxen and sheep in order the better to prophesy.[3] The true test of a Dainyal or diviner among some of the Hindoo Koosh tribes is to suck the blood from the neck of a decapitated goat.[4] The other mode of producing temporary inspiration, to which I shall here refer, is by means of a branch or leaves of a sacred tree. Thus in the Hindoo Koosh a fire is kindled with twigs of the sacred cedar; and the Dainyal or sibyl, with a cloth over her head, inhales the thick pungent smoke till she is seized with convulsions and falls senseless to the ground. Soon she rises and raises a shrill chant, which is caught up

---

[1] Caldwell, "On demonolatry in Southern India," *Journal of the Anthropological Society of Bombay*, i. 101 *sq.*

[2] J. G. F. Riedel, "De Minahasa in 1825," *Tijdschrift v. Indische Taal-Land-en Volkenkunde*, xviii. 517 *sq.* Cp. N. Graafland, *De Minahassa*, i. 122; Dumont D'Urville, *Voyage autour du Monde et à la recherche de La Perouse*, v. 443.

[3] F. J. Mone, *Geschichte des Heidenthums im nördlichen Europa*, i. 188.

[4] Biddulph, *Tribes of the Hindoo Koosh*, p. 96. For other instances of priests or representatives of the deity drinking the warm blood of the victim, cp. *Tijdschrift v. Nederlandsch Indië*, 1849, p. 395; Oldfield, *Sketches from Nipal*, ii. 296 *sq.*; *Asiatic Researches*, iv. 40, 41, 50, 52 (8vo. ed.); Paul Soleillet, *L'Afrique Occidentale*, p. 123 *sq.* To snuff up the savour of the sacrifice was similarly supposed to produce inspiration. Tertullian, *Apologet.* 23.

and loudly repeated by her audience.[1] So Apollo's prophetess ate the sacred laurel before she prophesied.[2] It is worth observing that many peoples expect the victim as well as the priest or prophet to give signs of inspiration by convulsive movements of the body; and if the animal remains obstinately steady, they esteem it unfit for sacrifice.   Thus when the Yakuts sacrifice to an evil spirit, the beast must bellow and roll about, which is considered a token that the evil spirit has entered into it.[3] Apollo's prophetess could give no oracles unless the victim to be sacrificed trembled in every limb when the wine was poured on its head. But for ordinary Greek sacrifices it was enough that the victim should shake its head; to make it do so, water was poured on it.[4] Many other peoples (Tonquinese, Hindoos, Chuwash, etc.) have adopted the same test of a suitable victim; they pour water or wine on its head; if the animal shakes its head it is accepted for sacrifice; if it does not, it is rejected.[5]

The person temporarily inspired is believed to acquire, not merely divine knowledge, but also, at least occasionally, divine power.   In Cambodia, when an epidemic breaks out, the inhabitants of several villages unite and go with a band of music at their head to look for the man whom the local god is

[1] Biddulph, *Tribes of the Hindoo Koosh*, p. 97.
[2] Lucian, *Bis accus.*, 1 ; Tzetzes, *Schol. ad Lycophr.*, 6.
[3] Vambery, *Das Türkenvolk*, p. 158.
[4] Plutarch, *De defect. oracul.* 46, 49.
[5] D. Chwolsohn, *Die Ssabier und der Ssabismus*, ii. 37 ; *Lettres édifiantes et curieuses*, xvi. 230 *sq.* ; *Panjab Notes and Queries*, iii. No. 721 ; *Journal of the Anthropological Society of Bombay*, i. 103 ; S. Mateer, *The Land of Charity*, 216 ; *id.*, *Native Life in Travancore*, p. 94 ; A. C. Lyall, *Asiatic Studies*, p. 14 ; Biddulph, *Tribes of the Hindoo Koosh*, p. 131 ; Pallas, *Reisen in verschiedenen Provinzen des russischen Reiches*, i. 91 ; Vambery, *Das Türkenvolk*, p. 485 ; Erman, *Archiv für wissenschaftliche Kunde von Russland*, i. 377.   When the Rao of Kachh sacrifices a buffalo, water is sprinkled between its horns; if it shakes its head, it is unsuitable; if it nods its head, it is sacrificed. *Panjab Notes and Queries*, i. No. 911. This is probably a modern misinterpretation of the old custom.

believed to have chosen for his temporary incarnation.
When found, the man is taken to the altar of the god,
where the mystery of incarnation takes place.   Then
the man becomes an object of veneration to his
fellows, who implore him to protect the village against
the plague.[1]   The image of Apollo at Hylæ in Phocis
was believed to impart superhuman strength.   Sacred
men, inspired by it, leaped down precipices, tore up
huge trees by the roots, and carried them on their
backs along the narrowest defiles.[2]   The feats performed by inspired dervishes belong to the same class.

Thus far we have seen that the savage, failing to
discern the limits of his ability to control nature,
ascribes to himself and to all men certain powers which
we should now call supernatural.   Further, we have
seen that over and above this general supernaturalism,
some persons are supposed to be inspired for short
periods by a divine spirit, and thus temporarily to enjoy
the knowledge and power of the indwelling deity.
From beliefs like these it is an easy step to the conviction that certain men are permanently possessed by
a deity, or in some other undefined way are endued
with so high a degree of supernatural powers as to be
ranked as gods and to receive the homage of prayer
and sacrifice.   Sometimes these human gods are restricted to purely supernatural or spiritual functions.
Sometimes they exercise supreme political power in
addition.   In the latter case they are kings as well as
gods, and the government is a theocracy.   I shall give
examples of both.

In the Marquesas Islands there was a class of men
who were deified in their life-time.   They were sup-

---

[1] Moura, *Le Royaume du Cambodge*, i. 177 *sq.*   [2] Pausanias, x. 32, 6.

posed to wield a supernatural power over the elements ;
they could give abundant harvests or smite the ground
with barrenness ; and they could inflict disease or
death. Human sacrifices were offered to them to avert
their wrath. There were not many of them, at the
most one or two in each island. They lived in mystic
seclusion. Their powers were sometimes, but not
always, hereditary. A missionary has described one of
these human gods from personal observation. The
god was a very old man who lived in a large house
within an enclosure. In the house was a kind of altar,
and on the beams of the house and on the trees round
it were hung human skeletons, head down. No one
entered the enclosure, except the persons dedicated to
the service of the god ; only on days when human
victims were sacrificed might ordinary people penetrate
into the precinct. This human god received more
sacrifices than all the other gods ; often he would sit on
a sort of scaffold in front of his house and call for two
or three human victims at a time. They were always
brought, for the terror he inspired was extreme. He
was invoked all over the island, and offerings were sent
to him from every side.[1] Again, of the South Sea
Islands in general we are told that each island had a
man who represented or personified the divinity. Such
men were called gods, and their substance was confounded with that of the deity. The man-god was
sometimes the king himself ; oftener he was a priest
or subordinate chief.[2] Tanatoa, King of Raiatea, was
deified by a certain ceremony performed at the chief
temple. "As one of the divinities of his subjects,

[1] Vincendon-Dumoulin et Desgraz, *Iles Marquises*, pp. 226, 240 *sq.*

[2] Moerenhout, *Voyages aux Iles du Grand Océan*, i. 479 ; Ellis, *Polynesian Researches*, iii. 94.

therefore, the king was worshipped, consulted as an oracle and had sacrifices and prayers offered to him."[1] This was not an exceptional case. The kings of the island regularly enjoyed divine honours, being deified at the time of their accession.[2] At his inauguration the king of Tahiti received a sacred girdle of red and yellow feathers, "which not only raised him to the highest earthly station, but identified him with their gods."[3] The gods of Samoa generally appeared in animal form, but sometimes they were permanently incarnate in men, who gave oracles, received offerings (occasionally of human flesh), healed the sick, answered prayers, and so on.[4] In regard to the old religion of the Fijians, and especially of the inhabitants of Somo-somo, it is said that "there appears to be no certain line of demarcation between departed spirits and gods, nor between gods and living men, for many of the priests and old chiefs are considered as sacred persons, and not a few of them will also claim to themselves the right of divinity. 'I am a god,' Tuikilakila would say; and he believed it too."[5] In the Pelew Islands it is believed that every god can take possession of a man and speak through him. The possession may be either temporary or permanent; in the latter case the chosen person is called a *korong*. The god is free in his choice, so the position of *korong* is not hereditary. After the death of a *korong* the god is for some time unrepresented, until he suddenly makes his appearance in a new Avatar. The person thus chosen gives signs

[1] Tyerman and Bennet, *Journal of Voyages and Travels in the South Sea Islands, China, India, etc.*, i. 524; cp. p. 529 *sq.*
[2] Tyerman and Bennet, *op. cit.* i. 529 *sq.*
[3] Ellis, *Polynesian Researches*, iii. 108.

[4] Turner, *Samoa*, pp. 37, 48, 57, 58, 59, 73.
[5] Hazlewood in Erskine's *Cruise among the Islands of the Western Pacific*, p. 246 *sq.* Cp. Wilkes's *Narrative of the U. S. Exploring Expedition*, iii. 87.

of the divine presence by behaving in a strange way ;
he gapes, runs about, and performs a number of senseless acts. At first people laugh at him, but his sacred
mission is in time recognised, and he is invited to
assume his proper position in the state. Generally
this position is a distinguished one and confers on him
a powerful influence over the whole community. In
some of the islands the god is political sovereign of
the land ; and hence his new incarnation, however
humble his origin, is raised to the same high rank, and
rules, as god and king, over all the other chiefs.[1] In
time of public calamity, as during war or pestilence,
some of the Molucca Islanders used to celebrate a festival of heaven. If no good result followed, they bought
a slave, took him at the next festival to the place of
sacrifice, and set him on a raised place under a certain
bamboo-tree. This tree represented heaven and had
been honoured as its image at previous festivals. The
portion of the sacrifice which had previously been
offered to heaven was now given to the slave, who ate
and drank it in the name and stead of heaven. Henceforth the slave was well treated, kept for the festivals
of heaven, and employed to represent heaven and
receive the offerings in its name.[2] In Tonquin every
village chooses its guardian spirit, often in the form of
an animal, as a dog, tiger, cat, or serpent. Sometimes
a living person is selected as patron-divinity. Thus a
beggar persuaded the people of a village that he was
their guardian spirit ; so they loaded him with honours
and entertained him with their best.[3] In India "every

---

[1] Kubary, "Die Religion der Pelauer," in Bastian's *Allerlei aus Volks - und Menschenkunde*, i. 30 *sqq.*

[2] F. Valentyn, *Oud en nieuw Oost-Indiën*, iii. 7 *sq.*

[3] Bastian, *Die Völker des östlichen Asien*, iv. 383.

king is regarded as little short of a present god."[1]
The Indian law-book of Manu goes farther and says
that "even an infant king must not be despised from
an idea that he is a mere mortal; for he is a great
deity in human form."[2]   There is said to be a sect in
Orissa who worship the Queen of England as their
chief divinity.   And to this day in India all living
persons remarkable for great strength or valour or for
supposed miraculous powers run the risk of being
worshipped as gods.   Thus, a sect in the Punjaub
worshipped a deity whom they called Nikkal Sen.
This Nikkal Sen was no other than the redoubted
General Nicholson, and nothing that the general could
do or say damped the enthusiasm of his adorers.   The
more he punished them, the greater grew the religious
awe with which they worshipped him.[3]   Amongst the
Todas, a pastoral people of the Neilgherry Hills of
Southern India, the dairy is a sanctuary, and the milkman (*pâlâl*) who attends to it is a god.   On being
asked whether the Todas salute the sun, one of these
divine milkmen replied, "Those poor fellows do so,
but I," tapping his chest, "I, a god! why should I
salute the sun?"   Every one, even his own father, pros-
trates himself before the milkman, and no one would
dare to refuse him anything.   No human being, except
another milkman, may touch him; and he gives oracles
to all who consult him, speaking with the voice of
a god.[4]

The King of Iddah told the English officers of the
Niger Expedition, "God made me after his own

---

[1] Monier Williams, *Religious Life and Thought in India*, p. 259.
[2] *The Laws of Manu*, vii. 8, trans. by G. Bühler.
[3] Monier Williams, *op. cit.* p. 259 *sq.*
[4] Marshall, *Travels among the Todas*, pp. 136, 137; cp. pp. 141, 142; Metz, *Tribes of the Neilgherry Hills*, p. 19 *sqq.*

image ; I am all the same as God ; and He appointed me a king."[1]

Sometimes, at the death of the human incarnation, the divine spirit transmigrates into another man. In the kingdom of Káffa, in Eastern Africa, the heathen part of the people worship a spirit called *Deòce*, to whom they offer prayer and sacrifice, and whom they invoke on all important occasions. This spirit is incarnate in the grand magician or pope, a person of great wealth and influence, ranking almost with the king, and wielding the spiritual, as the king wields the temporal, power. It happened that, shortly before the arrival of a Christian missionary in the kingdom, this African pope died, and the priests, fearing that the missionary would assume the position vacated by the deceased pope, declared that the *Deòce* had passed into the king, who henceforth, uniting the spiritual with the temporal power, reigned as god and king.[2] Before beginning to work at the salt-pans in a Laosian village, the workmen offer sacrifice to a local divinity. This divinity is incarnate in a woman and transmigrates at her death into another woman.[3] In Bhotan the spiritual head of the government is a person called the Dhurma Raja, who is supposed to be a perpetual incarnation of the deity. At his death the new incarnate god shows himself in an infant by the refusal of his mother's milk and a preference for that of a cow.[4] The Buddhist Tartars believe in a great number of living Buddhas, who officiate as Grand Lamas at the head of the most

---

[1] Allen and Thomson, *Narrative of the Expedition to the River Niger in* 1841, i. 288.

[2] G. Massaja, *I miei trentacinque anni di missione nell' alta Etiopia* (Rome and Milan, 1888), v. 53 *sq.*

[3] E. Aymonier, *Notes sur le Laos,* p. 141 *sq.*

[4] Robinson, *Descriptive Account of Assam,* p. 342 *sq.*; *Asiatic Researches,* xv. 146.

important monasteries.　When one of these Grand
Lamas dies his disciples do not sorrow, for they know
that he will soon reappear, being born in the form of
an infant.　Their only anxiety is to discover the place
of his birth.　If at this time they see a rainbow they
take it as a sign sent them by the departed Lama to
guide them to his cradle.　Sometimes the divine infant
himself reveals his identity.　" I am the Grand Lama,"
he says, " the living Buddha of such and such a temple.
Take me to my old monastery.　I am its immortal
head."　In whatever way the birthplace of the Buddha
is revealed, whether by the Buddha's own avowal or
by the sign in the sky, tents are struck, and the joyful
pilgrims, often headed by the king or one of the most
illustrious of the royal family, set forth to find and
bring home the infant god.　Generally he is born in
Tibet, the holy land, and to reach him the caravan has
often to traverse the most frightful deserts.　When at
last they find the child they fall down and worship him.
Before, however, he is acknowledged as the Grand
Lama whom they seek he must satisfy them of his
identity.　He is asked the name of the monastery of
which he claims to be the head, how far off it is, and
how many monks live in it ; he must also describe the
habits of the deceased Grand Lama and the manner of
his death.　Then various articles, as prayer-books,
tea-pots, and cups, are placed before him, and he has
to point out those used by himself in his previous life.
If he does so without a mistake his claims are admitted,
and he is conducted in triumph to the monastery.[1]　At
the head of all the Lamas is the Dalai Lama of Lhasa,
the Rome of Tibet.　He is regarded as a living god

---

[1] Huc, *Souvenirs d'un Voyage dans la Tartarie et le Thibet*, i. 279 *sqq.* ed.
12mo.

and at death his divine and immortal spirit is born again in a child. According to some accounts the mode of discovering the Dalai Lama is similar to the method, already described, of discovering an ordinary Grand Lama. Other accounts speak of an election by lot. Wherever he is born, the trees and plants, it is said, put forth green leaves; at his bidding flowers bloom and springs of water rise; and his presence diffuses heavenly blessings. His palace stands on a commanding height; its gilded cupolas are seen sparkling in the sunlight for miles.[1]

Issuing from the sultry valleys upon the lofty plateau of the Colombian Andes, the Spanish conquerors were astonished to find, in contrast to the savage hordes they had left in the sweltering jungles below, a people enjoying a fair degree of civilisation, practising agriculture, and living under a government which Humboldt has compared to the theocracies of Tibet and Japan. These were the Chibchas, Muyscas, or Mozcas, divided into two kingdoms, with capitals at Bogota and Tunja, but united apparently in spiritual allegiance to the high pontiff of Sogamozo or Iraca. By a long and ascetic novitiate, this ghostly ruler was reputed to have acquired such sanctity that the waters and the rain obeyed him, and the weather depended on his will.[2] Weather kings are common in Africa. Thus the

[1] Huc, *op. cit.* ii. 279, 347 *sq.*; Meiners, *Geschichte der Religionen*, i. 335 *sq.*; Georgi, *Beschreibung aller Nationen des Russischen Reichs*, p. 415; A. Erman, *Travels in Siberia*, ii. 303 *sqq.*; *Journal of the Roy. Geogr. Soc.*, xxxviii. (1868), 168, 169; *Proceedings of the Roy. Geogr. Soc.* N.S. vii. (1885) 67. In the *Journal Roy. Geogr. Soc.*, *l.c.*, the Lama in question is called the Lama Gûrû; but the context shows that he is the great Lama of Lhasa.

[2] Alex. von. Humboldt, *Researches concerning the Institutions and Monuments of the Ancient Inhabitants of America*, ii. 106 *sqq.*; Waitz, *Anthropologie der Naturvölker*, iv. 352 *sqq.*; J. G. Müller, *Geschichte der Amerikanischen Urreligionen*, p. 430 *sq.*; Martius, *Zur Ethnographie Amerikas*, p. 455; Bastian, *Die Culturländer des alten Amerika*, ii. 204 *sq.*

Waganda of Central Africa believe in a god of Lake Nyanza, who sometimes takes up his abode in a man or woman. The incarnate god is much feared by all the people, including the king and the chiefs. He is consulted as an oracle; by his word he can inflict or heal sickness, withhold rain, and cause famine. Large presents are made him when his advice is sought.[1] Often the king himself is supposed to control the weather. The king of Loango is honoured by his people "as though he were a god; and he is called Sambee and Pango, which mean god. They believe that he can let them have rain when he likes; and once a year, in December, which is the time they want rain, the people come to beg of him to grant it to them." On this occasion the king, standing on his throne, shoots an arrow into the air, which is supposed to bring on rain.[2] Much the same is said of the king of Mombaza.[3] The king of Quiteva, in Eastern Africa, ranks with the deity; "indeed, the Caffres acknowledge no other gods than their monarch, and to him they address those prayers which other nations are wont to prefer to heaven. . . . Hence these unfortunate beings, under the persuasion that their king is a deity, exhaust their utmost means and ruin themselves in gifts to obtain with more facility what they need. Thus, prostrate at his feet, they implore of him, when the weather long continues dry, to intercede with heaven that they may have rain; and when too much

---

[1] R. W. Felkin, "Notes on the Waganda Tribe of Central Africa," in *Proceedings of the Royal Society of Edinburgh*, xiii. 762; C. T. Wilson and R. W. Felkin, *Uganda and the Egyptian Soudan*, i. 206.

[2] "The Strange Adventures of Andrew Battel," in Pinkerton's *Voyages and Travels*, xvi. 330; Proyart, "History of Loango, Kakongo, and other Kingdoms in Africa," in Pinkerton, xvi. 577; Dapper, *Description de l'Afrique*, p. 335.

[3] Ogilby, *Africa*, p. 615; Dapper, *op. cit.* p. 400.

rain has fallen, that they may have fair weather ; thus, also, in case of winds, storms, and everything, they would either deprecate or implore." [1] Amongst the Barotse, a tribe on the upper Zambesi, "there is an old, but waning belief, that a chief is a demigod, and in heavy thunderstorms the Barotse flock to the chief's yard for protection from the lightning. I have been greatly distressed at seeing them fall on their knees before the chief, entreating him to open the water-pots of heaven and send rain upon their gardens. . . . The king's servants declare themselves to be invincible, because they are the servants of God (meaning *the king*)." [2] The chief of Mowat, New Guinea, is believed to have the power of affecting the growth of crops for good or ill, and of coaxing the *dugong* and turtle to come from all parts and allow themselves to be taken. [3]

Amongst the Antaymours of Madagascar the king is responsible for the growth of the crops and for every misfortune that befalls the people. [4] In many places the king is punished if rain does not fall and the crops do not turn out well. Thus, in some parts of West Africa, when prayers and offerings presented to the king have failed to procure rain, his subjects bind him with ropes and take him by force to the grave of his forefathers, that he may obtain from them the needed rain. [5] It appears that the Scythians also, when food was scarce, put their king in bonds. [6] The Banjars in

[1] Dos Santos, "History of Eastern Ethiopia," in Pinkerton, *Voyages and Travels*, xvi. 682, 687 *sq.*

[2] F. S. Arnot, *Garengauze; or, Seven Years' Pioneer Mission Work in Central Africa*, London, N.D. (preface dated March 1889), p. 78.

[3] MS. notes by E. Beardmore.

[4] Waitz, *Anthropologie der Naturvölker*, ii. 439.

[5] Labat, *Relation historique de l'Ethiopie Occidentale*, ii. 172-176.

[6] Schol. on Apollonius Rhod. ii. 1248. καὶ Ἡρόδωρος ξένως περὶ τῶν δεσμῶν τοῦ Προμηθέως ταῦτα. Εἶναι γὰρ αὐτὸν Σκυθῶν βασιλέα φησί · καὶ μὴ δυνάμενον παρέχειν τοῖς ὑπηκόοις τὰ ἐπιτήδεια, διὰ τὸν καλούμενον Ἀετὸν ποταμὸν ἐπικλύζειν τὰ πεδία, δεθῆναι ὑπὸ τῶν Σκυθῶν.

West Africa ascribe to their king the power of causing
rain or fine weather. So long as the weather is fine
they load him with presents of grain and cattle. But
if long drought or rain threatens to spoil the crops,
they insult and beat him till the weather changes.[1]
When the harvest fails or the surf on the coast is too
heavy to allow of fishing, the people of Loango accuse
their king of a " bad heart " and depose him.[2] On the
Pepper Coast the high priest or Bodio is responsible
for the health of the community, the fertility of the
earth, and the abundance of fish in the sea and rivers ;
and if the country suffers in any of these respects the
Bodio is deposed from his office.[3] So the Burgundians
of old deposed their king if the crops failed.[4] Some
peoples have gone further and killed their kings in
times of scarcity. Thus, in the time of the Swedish
king Domalde a mighty famine broke out, which lasted
several years, and could be stayed by the blood neither
of beasts nor of men. So, in a great popular assembly
held at Upsala, the chiefs decided that king Domalde
himself was the cause of the scarcity and must be
sacrificed for good seasons. So they slew him and
smeared with his blood the altars of the gods. Again,
we are told that the Swedes always attributed good or
bad crops to their kings as the cause. Now, in the
reign of King Olaf, there came dear times and famine,
and the people thought that the fault was the king's,
because he was sparing in his sacrifices. So, muster-
ing an army, they marched against him, surrounded

---

[1] H. Hecquard, *Reise an der Küste und in das Innere von West Afrika*, p. 78.

[2] Bastian, *Die Deutsche Expedition an der Loango-Küste*, i. 354, ii. 230.

[3] J. Leighton Wilson, *West Afrika*, p. 93 (German translation).

[4] Ammianus Marcellinus, xxviii. 5, 14.

his dwelling, and burned him in it, "giving him to Odin as a sacrifice for good crops."[1] In 1814, a pestilence having broken out among the reindeer of the Chukch, the Shamans declared that the beloved chief Koch must be sacrificed to the angry gods; so the chief's own son stabbed him with a dagger.[2] On the coral island of Niuē, or Savage Island, in the South Pacific, there formerly reigned a line of kings. But as the kings were also high priests, and were supposed to make the food grow, the people became angry with them in times of scarcity and killed them; till at last, as one after another was killed, no one would be king, and the monarchy came to an end.[3] As in these cases the divine kings, so in ancient Egypt the divine beasts, were responsible for the course of nature. When pestilence and other calamities had fallen on the land, in consequence of a long and severe drought, the priests took the sacred animals secretly by night, and threatened them, but if the evil did not abate they slew the beasts.[4]

From this survey of the religious position occupied by the king in rude societies we may infer that the claim to divine and supernatural powers put forward by the monarchs of great historical empires like those of Egypt, Mexico, and .Peru, was not the simple outcome of inflated vanity or the empty expression of a grovelling adulation; it was merely a survival and extension of the old savage apotheosis of living kings.

---

[1] Snorro Starleson, *Chronicle of the Kings of Norway* (trans. by S. Laing), saga i. chs. 18, 47. Cp. Liebrecht, *Zur Volkskunde*, p. 7; Scheffer, *Upsalia*, p. 137.

[2] C. Russwurm, "Aberglaube in Russland," in *Zeitschrift für Deutsche Mythologie und Sittenkunde*, iv. 162; Liebrecht, *op. cit.*, p. 15.

[3] Turner, *Samoa*, p. 304 *sq.*

[4] Plutarch, *Isis et Osiris*, 73.

Thus, for example, as children of the Sun the Incas of
Peru were revered like gods ; they could do no wrong,
and no one dreamed of offending against the person,
honour, or property of the monarch or of any of the
royal race.   Hence, too, the Incas did not, like most
people, look on sickness as an evil.   They considered
it a messenger sent from their father the Sun to call his
son to come and rest with him in heaven.   Therefore the
usual words in which an Inca announced his approaching end were these : " My father calls me to come and
rest with him."   They would not oppose their father's
will by offering sacrifice for recovery, but openly
declared that he had called them to his rest.[1] The
Mexican kings at their accession took an oath that they
would make the sun to shine, the clouds to give rain,
the rivers to flow, and the earth to bring forth fruits
in abundance.[2]   By Chinese custom the emperor is
deemed responsible if the drought be at all severe, and
many are the self-condemnatory edicts on this subject
published in the pages of the *Peking Gazette*.   However it is rather as a high priest than as a god that the
Chinese emperor bears the blame ; for in extreme cases
he seeks to remedy the evil by personally offering
prayers and sacrifices to heaven.[3]   The Parthian
monarchs of the Arsacid house styled themselves
brothers of the sun and moon and were worshipped as
deities.   It was esteemed sacrilege to strike even a
private member of the Arsacid family in a brawl.[4]
The kings of Egypt were deified in their lifetime, and
their worship was celebrated in special temples and by

---

[1] Garcilasso de la Vega, *First Part
of the Royal Commentaries of the Yncas*,
bk. ii. chs. 8 and 15 (vol. i. pp. 131,
155, Markham's Trans.)

[2] Bancroft, *Native Races of the
Pacific States*, ii. 146.
[3] Dennys, *Folk-lore of China*, p. 125.
[4] Ammianus Marcellinus, xxiii. 6,
§ 5 and 6.

special priests.　Indeed the worship of the kings
sometimes cast that of the gods into the shade.　Thus
in the reign of Merenra a high official declared that
he had built many holy places in order that the spirits
of the king, the ever-living Merenra, might be invoked "more than all the gods."[1]　The King of
Egypt seems to have shared with the sacred animals
the blame of any failure of the crops.[2]　He was
addressed as "Lord of heaven, lord of earth, sun, life
of the whole world, lord of time, measurer of the sun's
course, Tum for men, lord of well-being, creator of the
harvest, maker and fashioner of mortals, bestower of
breath upon all men, giver of life to all the host of
gods, pillar of heaven, threshold of the earth, weigher
of the equipoise of both worlds, lord of rich gifts, in-
creaser of the corn" etc.[3]　Yet, as we should expect,
the exalted powers thus ascribed to the king differed
in degree rather than in kind from those which every
Egyptian claimed for himself.　Tiele observes that
"as every good man at his death became Osiris, as
every one in danger or need could by the use of magic
sentences assume the form of a deity, it is quite comprehensible how the king, not only after death, but
already during his life, was placed on a level with the
deity."[4]

Thus it appears that the same union of sacred

[1] C. P. Tiele, *History of the Egyptian Religion*, p. 103 *sq.*　On the worship of the kings see also E. Meyer, *Geschichte des Altertums*, i. § 52 ; A. Erman, *Aegypten und aegyptisches Leben im Altertum*, p. 91 *sqq.*; V. von Strauss und Carnen, *Die altägyptischen Götter und Göttersagen*, p. 467 *sqq.*

[2] Ammianus Marcellinus, xxviii. 5, 14 ; Plutarch, *Isis et Osiris*, 73.

[3] V. von Strauss und Carnen, *op. cit.* p. 470.

[4] Tiele, *History of the Egyptian Religion*, p. 105.　The Babylonian and Assyrian kings seem also to have been regarded as gods ; at least the oldest names of the kings on the monuments are preceded by a star, the mark for "god."　But there is no trace in Babylon and Assyria of temples and priests for the worship of the kings.　See Tiele, *Babylonisch - Assyrische Geschichte*, p. 492 *sq.*

Thunder-Fighters fighting off a storm cloud.
Illustration by Frederic Remington.

Osiris, a chief god of Egyptian mythology.

functions with a royal title which meets us in the King of the Wood at Nemi, the Sacrificial King at Rome and the King Archon at Athens, occurs frequently outside the limits of classical antiquity and is a common feature of societies at all stages from barbarism to civilisation. Further, it appears that the royal priest is often a king in fact as well as in name, swaying the sceptre as well as the crosier. All this confirms the tradition of the origin of the titular and priestly kings in the republics of ancient Greece and Italy. At least by showing that the combination of spiritual and temporal power, of which Graeco - Italian tradition preserved the memory, has actually existed in many places, we have obviated any suspicion of improbability that might have attached to the tradition. Therefore we may now fairly ask, May not the King of the Wood have had an origin like that which a probable tradition assigns to the Sacrificial King of Rome and the King Archon of Athens? In other words, may not his predecessors in office have been a line of kings whom a republican revolution stripped of their political power, leaving them only their religious functions and the shadow of a crown? There are at least two reasons for answering this question in the negative. One reason is drawn from the abode of the priest of Nemi; the other from his title, the King of the Wood. If his predecessors had been kings in the ordinary sense, he would surely have been found residing, like the fallen kings of Rome and Athens, in the city of which the sceptre had passed from him. This city must have been Aricia, for there was none nearer. But Aricia, as we have seen, was three miles off from his forest sanctuary by the lake shore. If he reigned, it was not in the city, but in the greenwood. Again his title, King of the Wood, hardly allows us to suppose that he had ever been a king in the common sense of the word. More likely he was a king of nature, and of a special side of nature, namely, the woods from which he took his title. If we could find instances of what we may call departmental kings of nature, that is of persons supposed to rule over particular elements or aspects of nature, they would probably present a closer analogy to the King of the Wood than the divine kings we have been hitherto considering, whose control of nature is general rather than special. Instances of such departmental kings are not wanting.

On a hill at Bomma (the mouth of the Congo) dwells Namvulu Vumu, King of the Rain and Storm.[1] Of some of the tribes on the Upper Nile we are told that they have no kings in the common sense; the only persons whom they acknowledge as such are the Kings of the Rain, *Mata Kodou*, who are credited with the power of giving rain at the proper time, that is in the rainy season. Before the rains begin to fall at the end of March the country is a parched and arid desert; and the cattle, which form the people's chief wealth, perish for lack of grass. So, when the end of March draws on, each householder betakes himself to the King of the Rain and offers him a cow that he may make the rain to fall soon. If no shower falls, the people assemble and demand that the king shall give them rain; and if the sky still continues cloudless, they rip up his belly in which he is believed to keep the storms. Amongst the Bari tribe one of these Rain Kings made rain

---

[1] Bastian, *Die Deutsche Expedition an der Loango-Küste*, ii. 230.

by sprinkling water on the ground out of a hand-bell.[1]

Among tribes on the outskirts of Abyssinia a similar office exists and has been thus described by an observer. "The priesthood of the Alfai, as he is called by the Barea and Kunáma, is a remarkable one; he is believed to be able to make rain. This office formerly existed among the Algeds and appears to be still common to the Nuba negroes. The Alfai of the Bareas, who is also consulted by the northern Kunáma, lives near Tembádere on a mountain alone with his family. The people bring him tribute in the form of clothes and fruits, and cultivate for him a large field of his own. He is a kind of king, and his office passes by inheritance to his brother or sister's son. He is supposed to conjure down rain and to drive away the locusts. But if he disappoints the people's expectation and a great drought arises in the land, the Alfai is stoned to death, and his nearest relations are obliged to cast the first stone at him. When we passed through the country, the office of Alfai was still held by an old man; but I heard that rain-making had proved too dangerous for him and that he had renounced his office."[2]

In the backwoods of Cambodia live two mysterious sovereigns known as the King of the Fire and the King of the Water. Their fame is spread all over the south of the great Indo-Chinese peninsula; but only a faint echo of it has reached the West. No European, so far as is known, has ever seen them; and their very existence might have passed for a fable, were it not

[1] "Excursion de M. Brun-Rollet dans la région supérieure du Nil," *Bulletin de la Société de Géographie*, Paris, 1852, pt. ii. p. 421 *sqq.*

[2] W. Munzinger, *Ostafrikanische Studien*, p. 474 (Schaffhausen, 1864).

that till a few years ago communications were regularly maintained between them and the King of Cambodia, who year by year exchanged presents with them. The Cambodian gifts were passed from tribe to tribe till they reached their destination; for no Cambodian would essay the long and perilous journey. The tribe amongst whom the Kings of Fire and Water reside is the Chréais or Jaray, a race with European features but a sallow complexion, inhabiting the forest-clad mountains and high plateaux which separate Cambodia from Annam. Their royal functions are of a purely mystic or spiritual order; they have no political authority; they are simple peasants, living by the sweat of their brow and the offerings of the faithful. According to one account they live in absolute solitude, never meeting each other and never seeing a human face. They inhabit successively seven towers perched upon seven mountains, and every year they pass from one tower to another. People come furtively and cast within their reach what is needful for their subsistence. The kingship lasts seven years, the time necessary to inhabit all the towers successively; but many die before their time is out. The offices are hereditary in one or (according to others) two royal families, who enjoy high consideration, have revenues assigned to them, and are exempt from the necessity of tilling the ground. But naturally the dignity is not coveted, and when a vacancy occurs, all eligible men (they must be strong and have children) flee and hide themselves. Another account, admitting the reluctance of the hereditary candidates to accept the crown, does not countenance the report of their hermit-like seclusion in the seven towers. For it represents the people as prostrating themselves before the mystic kings whenever they appear in public, it being thought that a terrible hurricane would burst over the country if this mark of homage were omitted.

The same report says that the Fire King, the more important of the two, and whose supernatural powers have never been questioned, officiates at marriages, festivals, and sacrifices in honour of the Yan. On these occasions a special place is set apart for him ; and the path by which he approaches is spread with white cotton cloths. A reason for confining the royal dignity to the same family is that this family is in possession of certain famous talismans which would lose their virtue or disappear if they passed out of the family. These talismans are three : the fruit of a creeper called *Cui*, gathered ages ago but still fresh and green ; a rattan, also very old and still not dry ; lastly a sword containing a Yan or spirit, who guards it constantly and works miracles with it. To this wondrous brand sacrifices of buffaloes, pigs, fowls, and ducks are offered for rain. It is kept swathed in cotton and silk ; and amongst the annual presents sent by the King of Cambodia were rich stuffs to wrap the sacred sword.

In return the Kings of Fire and Water sent him a huge wax candle and two calabashes, one full of rice and the other of sesame. The candle bore the impress of the Fire King's middle finger. Probably the candle was thought to contain the seed of fire, which the Cambodian monarch thus received once a year fresh from the Fire King himself. The holy candle was kept for sacred uses. On reaching the capital of Cambodia it was entrusted to the Brahmans, who laid it up beside the regalia, and with the wax made tapers which were burned on the altars on solemn days. As the candle was the special gift of the Fire King, we may conjecture that the rice and sesame were the special gift of the Water King. The latter was doubtless king of rain as well as of water, and the fruits of the earth were boons conferred by him on men. In times of calamity, as during plague, floods, and war, a little of this sacred rice and sesame was scattered on the ground "to appease the wrath of the maleficent spirits." [1]

These, then, are examples of what I have called departmental kings of nature. But it is a far cry to Italy from the forests of Cambodia and the sources of the Nile. And though Kings of Rain, Water and Fire have been found, we have still to discover a King of the Wood to match the Arician priest who bore that title. Perhaps we shall find him nearer home.

§ 4.—*Tree-worship*

In the religious history of the Aryan race in Europe the worship of trees has played an important part. Nothing could be more natural. For at the dawn of history Europe was covered with immense primeval forests, in which the scattered clearings must have appeared like islets in an ocean of green. Down to the first century before our era the Hercynian forest stretched eastward from

---

[1] J. Moura, *Le Royaume du Cambodge*, i. 432-436; Aymonier, "Notes sur les coutumes et croyances superstitieuses des Cambodgiens," in *Cochin-* *chine Française, Excursions et Reconnaissances*, No. 16, p. 172 *sq.*; *id.*, *Notes sur le Laos*, p. 60.

the Rhine for a distance at once vast and unknown ;
Germans whom Caesar questioned had travelled for
two months through it without reaching the end.[1]
In our own country the wealds of Kent, Surrey, and
Sussex are remnants of the great forest of Anderida,
which once clothed the whole of the south eastern
portion of the island. Westward it seems to have
stretched till it joined another forest that extended
from Hampshire to Devon. In the reign of Henry
II the citizens of London still hunted the wild bull
and the boar in the forest of Hampstead. Even
under the later Plantagenets the royal forests were
sixty-eight in number. In the forest of Arden it
was said that down to modern times a squirrel
might leap from tree to tree for nearly the whole
length of Warwickshire.[2] The excavation of prehistoric pile-villages in the valley of the Po has
shown that long before the rise and probably the
foundation of Rome the north of Italy was covered
with dense forests of elms, chestnuts, and especially
of oaks.[3] Archaeology is here confirmed by history ;
for classical writers contain many references to
Italian forests which have now disappeared.[4] In
Greece the woods of the present day are a mere
fraction of those which clothed great tracts in antiquity,
and which at a more remote epoch may have spanned
the Greek peninsula from sea to sea.[5]

From an examination of the Teutonic words for
"temple" Grimm has made it probable that amongst

---

[1] Caesar, *Bell. Gall.* vi. 25.

[2] Elton, *Origins of English History*,
pp. 3, 106 *sq.*, 224.

[3] W. Helbig, *Die Italiker in der
Poebene*, p. 25 *sq.*

[4] H. Nissen, *Italische Landeskunde*,
p. 431 *sqq.*

[5] Neumann und Partsch, *Physika-
lische Geographie von Griechenland*,
p. 357 *sqq.*

the Germans the oldest sanctuaries were natural woods.[1]
However this may be, tree-worship is well attested
for all the great European families of the Aryan stock.
Amongst the Celts the oak-worship of the Druids is
familiar to every one.[2]　Sacred groves were common
among the ancient Germans, and tree-worship is hardly
extinct amongst their descendants at the present day.[3]
At Upsala, the old religious capital of Sweden, there
was a sacred grove in which every tree was regarded
as divine.[4]　Amongst the ancient Prussians (a Slavonian people) the central feature of religion was the
reverence for the sacred oaks, of which the chief stood
at Romove, tended by a hierarchy of priests who kept
up a perpetual fire of oak-wood in the holy grove.[5]
The Lithuanians were not converted to Christianity
till towards the close of the fourteenth century, and
amongst them at the date of their conversion the worship of trees was prominent.[6]　Proofs of the prevalence
of tree-worship in ancient Greece and Italy are abundant.[7]　Nowhere, perhaps, in the ancient world was
this antique form of religion better preserved than in
the heart of the great metropolis itself.　In the Forum,
the busy centre of Roman life, the sacred fig-tree of
Romulus was worshipped down to the days of the
empire, and the withering of its trunk was enough to
spread consternation through the city.[8]　Again, on the

---

[1] Grimm, *Deutsche Mythologie*,[4] i.
53 *sqq.*

[2] The *locus classicus* is Pliny, *Nat.
Hist.* xvi. § 249 *sqq.*

[3] Grimm, *D. M.* i. 56 *sqq.*

[4] Adam of Bremen, *Descriptio Insul.
Aquil.* p. 27.

[5] " Prisca antiquorum Prutenorum
religio," in *Respublica sive Status Regni
Poloniae, Lituaniae, Prussiae, Livoniae,*
etc. (Elzevir, 1627), p. 321 *sq.* ; Dusburg,
Chronicon Prussiae, ed. Hartknoch,

p. 79 ; Hartknoch, *Alt - und Neues
Preussen*, p. 116 *sqq.*

[6] Mathias Michov, " De Sarmatia
Asiana atque Europea," in *Novus Orbis
regionum ac insularum veteribus incognitarum* (Paris, 1532), pp. 455 *sq.* 456
[wrongly numbered 445, 446] ; Martin
Cromer, *De origine et rebus gestis Polo-
norum* (Basel, 1568), p. 241.

[7] See Bötticher, *Der Baumkultus der
Hellenen.*

[8] Pliny, *Nat. Hist.* xv. § 77 ; Taci-
tus, *Ann.* xiii. 58.

The Sacrificial King of Rome, who combined sacred functions with a royal title.

Ancient Druids.

slope of the Palatine Hill grew a cornel-tree which was esteemed one of the most sacred objects in Rome. Whenever the tree appeared to a passer-by to be drooping, he set up a hue and cry which was echoed by the people in the street, and soon a crowd might be seen running from all sides with buckets of water, as if (says Plutarch) they were hastening to put out a fire.[1]

But it is necessary to examine in some detail the notions on which tree-worship is based. To the savage the world in general is animate, and trees are no exception to the rule. He thinks that they have souls like his own and he treats them accordingly. Thus the Wanika in Eastern Africa fancy that every tree and especially every cocoa-nut tree has its spirit; "the destruction of a cocoa-nut tree is regarded as equivalent to matricide, because that tree gives them life and nourishment, as a mother does her child."[2] Siamese monks, believing that there are souls everywhere and that to destroy anything whatever is forcibly to dispossess a soul, will not break a branch of a tree "as they will not break the arm of an innocent person."[3] These monks, of course, are Buddhists. But Buddhist animism is not a philosophical theory. It is simply a common savage dogma incorporated in the system of an historical religion. To suppose with Benfey and others that the theories of animism and transmigration current among rude peoples of Asia are derived from Buddhism is to reverse the facts. Buddhism in this respect borrowed from savagery, not savagery from Buddhism. Again, the Dyaks ascribe souls to trees and do not dare to cut down an old tree. In some

---

[1] Plutarch, *Romulus*, 20.

[2] J. L. Krapf, *Travels, Researches, and Missionary Labours during an Eigh-* teen *Years' Residence in Eastern Africa*, p. 198.

[3] Loubere, *Historical Relation of the Kingdom of Siam*, p. 126.

places, when an old tree has been blown down, they set it up, smear it with blood, and deck it with flags "to appease the soul of the tree."[1] People in Congo place calabashes of palm-wine at the foot of certain trees for the trees to drink when they are thirsty.[2] In India shrubs and trees are formally married to each other or to idols.[3] In the North West Provinces of India a marriage ceremony is performed in honour of a newly-planted orchard; a man holding the Salagram represents the bride-groom, and another holding the sacred Tulsí (*Ocymum sanctum*) represents the bride.[4] On Christmas Eve German·peasants used to tie fruit-trees together with straw ropes to make them bear fruit, saying that the trees were thus married.[5]

In the Moluccas when the clove-trees are in blossom they are treated like pregnant women. No noise must be made near them; no light or fire must be carried past them at night; no one must approach them with his hat on, but must uncover his head. These precautions are observed lest the tree should be frightened and bear no fruit, or should drop its fruit too soon, like the untimely delivery of a woman who has been frightened in her pregnancy.[6] So when the paddy (rìce) is in bloom the Javanese say it is pregnant and make no noises (fire no guns, etc.) near

---

[1] Hupe " Over de godsdienst, zeden, enz. der Dajakker's" in *Tijdschrift voor Neêrland's Indië*, 1846, dl. iii. 158.

[2] Merolla, " Voyage to Congo," in Pinkerton's *Voyages and Travels*, xvi. 236.

[3] Monier Williams, *Religious Life and Thought in India*, p. 334 *sq.*

[4] Sir Henry M. Elliot and J. Beames, *Memoirs on the History etc. of the*

Races of the North Western Provinces of India, i. 233.

[5] *Die gestriegelte Rockenphilosophie* (Chemnitz, 1759), p. 239 *sq.* ; U. Jahn, *Die deutsche Opfergebräuche bei Ackerbau und Viehzucht*, p. 214 *sqq.*

[6] Van Schmid, " Aanteekeningen, nopens de zeden, gewoonten en gebruiken, etc., der bevolking van de eilanden Saparoea, etc." in *Tijdschrift v. Neêrland's Indië*, 1843, dl. ii. 605; Bastian, *Indonesien*, i. 156.

the field, fearing that if they did so the crop would be all straw and no grain.[1]   In Orissa, also, growing rice is "considered as a pregnant woman, and the same ceremonies are observed with regard to it as in the case of human females."[2]

Conceived as animate, trees are necessarily supposed to feel injuries done to them.   When an oak is being felled " it gives a kind of shriekes or groanes, that may be heard a mile off, as if it were the genius of the oake lamenting.   E. Wyld, Esq., hath heard it severall times."[3]   The Ojebways "very seldom cut down green or living trees, from the idea that it puts them to pain, and some of their medicine-men profess to have heard the wailing of the trees under the axe."[4] Old peasants in some parts of Austria still believe that forest-trees are animate, and will not allow an incision to be made in the bark without special cause; they have heard from their fathers that the tree feels the cut not less than a wounded man his hurt.   In felling a tree they beg its pardon.[5]   So in Jarkino the woodman craves pardon of the tree he cuts down.[6]   Again, when a tree is cut it is thought to bleed.   Some Indians dare not cut a certain plant, because there comes out a red juice which they take for the blood of the plant.[7]   In Samoa there was a grove of trees which no one dared cut.   Once some strangers tried to do so, but blood flowed from the tree, and the sacrilegious strangers fell ill and died.[8]   Till 1855 there was a sacred larch-tree at Nauders, in the Tyrol,

[1] Van Hoëvell, *Ambon en meer bepaaldelijk de Oeliasers*, p. 62.
[2] *The Indian Antiquary*, i. 170.
[3] J. Aubrey, *Remaines of Gentilisme*, p. 247.
[4] Peter Jones's *History of the Ojebway Indians*, p. 104.

[5] A. Peter, *Volksthümliches aus Österreichisch-Schlesien*, ii. 30.
[6] Bastian, *Indonesien*, i. 154; cp. *id.*, *Die Völker des östlichen Asien*, ii. 457 *sq.*, iii. 251 *sq.*, iv. 42 *sq.*
[7] Loubere, *Siam*, p. 126.
[8] Turner, *Samoa*, p. 63.

which was thought to bleed whenever it was cut; moreover the steel was supposed to penetrate the woodman's body to the same depth that it penetrated the tree, and the wound on the tree and on the man's body healed together.[1]

Sometimes it is the souls of the dead which are believed to animate the trees. The Dieyerie tribe of South Australia regard as very sacred certain trees, which are supposed to be their fathers transformed; hence they will not cut the trees down, and protest against the settlers doing so.[2] Some of the Philippine Islanders believe that the souls of their forefathers are in certain trees, which they therefore spare. If obliged to fell one of these trees they excuse themselves to it by saying that it was the priest who made them fell it.[3] In an Annamite story an old fisherman makes an incision in the trunk of a tree which has drifted ashore; but blood flows from the cut, and it appears that an empress with her three daughters, who had been cast into the sea, are embodied in the tree.[4] The story of Polydorus will occur to readers of Virgil.

In these cases the spirit is viewed as incorporate in the tree; it animates the tree and must suffer and die with it. But, according to another and no doubt later view, the tree is not the body, but merely the abode of the tree-spirit, which can quit the injured tree as men quit a dilapidated house. Thus when the Pelew Islanders are felling a tree, they conjure the spirit of

---

[1] Mannhardt, *Baumkultus*, p. 35 *sq.*

[2] *Native Tribes of South Australia*, p. 280.

[3] Blumentritt, "Der Ahnencultus und die religiösen Anschauungen der Malaien des Philippinen-Archipels," in *Mittheilungen der Wiener Geogr. Gesellschaft*, 1882, p. 165 *sq.*

[4] Landes, "Contes et légendes annamites," No. 9, in *Cochinchine Française, Excursions et Reconnaissances*, No. 20, p. 310.

the tree to leave it and settle on another.[1] The Pádams of Assam think that when a child is lost it has been stolen by the spirits of the wood. So they retaliate on the spirits by cutting down trees till they find the child. The spirits, fearing to be left without a tree in which to lodge, give up the child, and it is found in the fork of a tree.[2] Before the Katodis fell a forest-tree, they choose a tree of the same kind and worship it by presenting a cocoa-nut, burning incense, applying a red pigment, and begging it to bless the undertaking.[3] The intention, perhaps, is to induce the spirit of the former tree to shift its quarters to the latter. In clearing a wood, a Galeleze must not cut down the last tree till the spirit in it has been induced to go away.[4] The Mundaris have sacred groves which were left standing when the land was cleared, lest the sylvan gods, disquieted at the felling of the trees, should abandon the place.[5] The Miris in Assam are unwilling to break up new land for cultivation so long as there is fallow land available; for they fear to offend the spirits of the woods by cutting down trees unnecessarily.[6]

In Sumatra, so soon as a tree is felled, a young tree is planted on the stump; and some betel and a few small coins are also placed on it.[7] Here the purpose is unmistakable. The spirit of the tree is offered a new home in the young tree planted on the stump of the old one, and the offering of betel and money is meant

---

[1] Kubary in Bastian's *Allerlei aus Mensch-und Volkenkunde,* i. 52.

[2] Dalton, *Ethnology of Bengal,* p. 25; Bastian, *Völkerstämme am Brahmaputra,* p. 37.

[3] *Journal R. Asiatic Society,* vii. (1843) 29.

[4] Bastian, *Indonesien,* i. 17.

[5] Dalton, *Ethnology of Bengal,* pp. 186, 188; cp. Bastian, *Völkerstämme am Brahmaputra,* p. 9.

[6] Dalton, *op. cit.* p. 33; Bastian, *op. cit.* p. 16. Cp. W. Robertson Smith, *The Religion of the Semites,* i. 125.

[7] Van Hasselt, *Volksbeschrijving van Midden-Sumatra,* p. 156.

to compensate him for the disturbance he has suffered.
So in the island of Chedooba, on felling a large tree,
one of the woodmen was always ready with a green
sprig, which he ran and placed on the middle of the
stump the instant the tree fell.[1]　For the same
purpose German woodmen make a cross upon the
stump while the tree is falling, in the belief that this
enables the spirit of the tree to live upon the
stump.[2]

Thus the tree is regarded, sometimes as the body,
sometimes as merely the house of the tree-spirit; and
when we read of sacred trees which may not be cut
down because they are the seat of spirits, it is not
always possible to say with certainty in which way the
presence of the spirit in the tree is conceived.　In the
following cases, perhaps, the trees are conceived as the
dwelling-place of the spirits rather than as their bodies.
The old Prussians, it is said, believed that gods inhabited high trees, such as oaks, from which they gave
audible answers to inquirers; hence these trees were
not felled, but worshipped as the homes of divinities.[3]
The great oak at Romove was the especial dwelling-
place of the god; it was veiled with a cloth, which
was, however, removed to allow worshippers to see the
sacred tree.[4]　The Battas of Sumatra have been known
to refuse to cut down certain trees because they were

[1] *Handbook of Folk-lore*, p. 19 (proof).

[2] Mannhardt, *Baumkultus*, p. 83.

[3] Erasmus Stella, "De Borussiae antiquitatibus," in *Novus Orbis regionum ac insularum veteribus incognitarum*, p. 510; Lasiczki (Lasicius), "De diis Samagitarum caeterorumque Sarmatarum," in *Respublica sive Status Regni Poloniae, Lituaniae, Prussiae, Livoniae*, etc. (Elzevir, 1627), p. 299

sq. There is a good and cheap reprint of Lasiczki's work by W. Mannhardt in *Magazin herausgegeben von der Lettisch-Literärischen Gesellschaft*, xiv. 82 *sqq.* (Mitau, 1868).

[4] Simon Grünau, *Preussische Chronik*, ed. Perlbach (Leipzig 1876), p. 89; "Prisca antiquorum Prutenorum religio," in *Respublica sive Status Regni Poloniae* etc., p. 321.

the abode of mighty spirits which would resent the injury.[1] The Curka Coles of India believe that the tops of trees are inhabited by spirits which are disturbed by the cutting down of the trees and will take vengeance.[2] The Samogitians thought that if any one ventured to injure certain groves, or the birds or beasts in them, the spirits would make his hands or feet crooked.[3]

Even where no mention is made of wood-spirits, we may generally assume that when a grove is sacred and inviolable, it is so because it is believed to be either inhabited or animated by sylvan deities. In Livonia there is a sacred grove in which, if any man fells a tree or breaks a branch, he will die within the year.[4] The Wotjaks have sacred groves. A Russian who ventured to hew a tree in one of them fell sick and died next day.[5] Sacrifices offered at cutting down trees are doubtless meant to appease the wood-spirits. In Gilgit it is usual to sprinkle goat's blood on a tree of any kind before cutting it down.[6] Before thinning a grove a Roman farmer had to sacrifice a pig to the god or goddess of the grove.[7] The priestly college of the Arval Brothers at Rome had to make expiation when a rotten bough fell to the ground in the sacred grove, or when an old tree was blown down by a storm or dragged down by a weight of snow on its branches.[8]

When a tree comes to be viewed, no longer as the body of the tree-spirit, but simply as its dwelling-place which it can quit at pleasure, an important advance

---

[1] B. Hagen, "Beiträge zur Kenntniss der Battareligion," in *Tijdschrift voor Indische Taal-Land-en Volkenkunde*, xxviii. 530 *note*.

[2] Bastian, *Die Völker des östlichen Asien*, i. 134.

[3] Matthias Michov, in *Novus Orbis regionum ac insularum veteribus incognitarum*, p. 457.

[4] Grimm, *Deutsche Mythologie*,[4] i. 497 ; cp. ii. 540, 541.

[5] Max Buch, *Die Wotjäken*, p. 124.

[6] Biddulph, *Tribes of the Hindoo Koosh*, p. 116.

[7] Cato, *De agri cultura*, 139.

[8] Henzen, *Acta fratrum arvalium* (Berlin, 1874), p. 138.

has been made in religious thought. Animism is passing into polytheism. In other words, instead of regarding each tree as a living and conscious being, man now sees in it merely a lifeless, inert mass, tenanted for a longer or shorter time by a supernatural being who, as he can pass freely from tree to tree, thereby enjoys a certain right of possession or lordship over the trees, and, ceasing to be a tree-soul, becomes a forest god. As soon as the tree-spirit is thus in a measure disengaged from each particular tree, he begins to change his shape and assume the body of a man, in virtue of a general tendency of early thought to clothe all abstract spiritual beings in concrete human form. Hence in classical art the sylvan deities are depicted in human shape, their woodland character being denoted by a branch or some equally obvious symbol.[1] But this change of shape does not affect the essential character of the tree-spirit. The powers which he exercised as a tree-soul incorporate in a tree, he still continues to wield as a god of trees. This I shall now prove in detail. I shall show, first, that trees considered as animate beings are credited with the power of making the rain to fall, the sun to shine, flocks and herds to multiply, and women to bring forth easily; and, second, that the very same powers are attributed to tree-gods conceived as anthropomorphic beings or as actually incarnate in living men.

First, then, trees or tree-spirits are believed to give rain and sunshine. When the missionary Jerome of Prague was persuading the heathen Lithuanians to fell their sacred groves, a multitude

---

[1] On the representations of Silvanus, the Roman wood-god, see Jordan in Preller's *Römische Mythologie*,[3] i. 393 note; Baumeister, *Denkmäler des clas-sischen Altertums*, iii. 1665 *sq.* A good representation of Silvanus bearing a pine branch is given in the Sale Catalogue of H. Hoffmann, Paris, 1888, pt. ii.

A ceremony in honor of the tree deity in New Guinea.

A tribe in Liberia, Africa, offering a sacrifice to the tree-spirit.

of women besought the Prince of Lithuania to stop him, saying that with the woods he was destroying the house of god from which they had been wont to get rain and sunshine.[1] The Mundaris in Assam think if a tree in the sacred grove is felled, the sylvan gods evince their displeasure by withholding rain.[2] In Cambodia each village or province has its sacred tree, the abode of a spirit. If the rains are late, the people sacrifice to the tree.[3] To extort rain from the tree-spirit a branch is sometimes dipped in water, as we have seen above.[4] In such cases the spirit is doubtless supposed to be immanent in the branch, and the water thus applied to the spirit produces rain by a sort of sympathetic magic, exactly as we saw that in New Caledonia the rain-makers pour water on a skeleton, believing that the soul of the deceased will convert the water into rain.[5] There is hardly room to doubt that Mannhardt is right in explaining as a rain-charm the European custom of drenching with water the trees which are cut at certain popular festivals, as midsummer, Whitsuntide, and harvest.[6]

Again, tree-spirits make the crops to grow. Amongst the Mundaris every village has its sacred grove, and "the grove deities are held responsible for the crops, and are especially honoured at all the great agricultural festivals."[7] The negroes of the Gold Coast are in the habit of sacrificing at the foot of certain tall trees, and they think that if one of these

[1] Aeneas Sylvius, *Opera* (Bâle, 1571), p. 418 [wrongly numbered 420]; cp. Erasmus Stella, "De Borussiae antiquitatibus," in *Novus Orbis regionum ac insularum veteribus incognitarum*, p. 510.

[2] Dalton, *Ethnology of Bengal*, p. 186.

[3] Aymonier in *Excursions et Reconnaissances*, No. 16. p. 175 *sq.*

[4] See above, pp. 13, 21.

[5] Above, p. 16.

[6] Mannhardt, *B. K.* pp. 158, 159, 170, 197, 214, 351, 514.

[7] Dalton, *Ethnology of Bengal*, p. 188.

trees were felled, all the fruits of the earth would perish.[1] Swedish peasants stick a leafy branch in each furrow of their corn-fields, believing that this will ensure an abundant crop.[2] The same idea comes out in the German and French custom of the Harvest-May. This is a large branch or a whole tree, which is decked with ears of corn, brought home on the last waggon from the harvest-field, and fastened on the roof of the farmhouse or of the barn, where it remains for a year. Mannhardt has proved that this branch or tree embodies the tree-spirit conceived as the spirit of vegetation in general, whose vivifying and fructifying influence is thus brought to bear upon the corn in particular. Hence in Swabia the Harvest-May is fastened amongst the last stalks of corn left standing on the field; in other places it is planted on the corn-field and the last sheaf cut is fastened to its trunk.[3] The Harvest-May of Germany has its counterpart in the *eiresione* of ancient Greece.[4] The *eiresione* was a branch of olive or laurel, bound about with ribbons and hung with a variety of fruits. This branch was carried in procession at a harvest festival and was fastened over the door of the house, where it remained for a year. The object of preserving the Harvest-May or the *eiresione* for a year is that the life-giving virtue of the bough may foster the growth of the crops throughout the year. By the end of the year the virtue of the bough is supposed to be exhausted and it is replaced by a new one. Following a similar train of thought some of the Dyaks of Sarawak are

---

[1] Labat, *Voyage du Chevalier des Marchais en Guinée, Isles voisines, et à Cayenne* (Paris, 1730), i. 338.

[2] L. Lloyd, *Peasant Life in Sweden,* p. 266.

[3] Mannhardt, *B. K.* p. 190 *sqq.*

[4] Mannhardt, *A. W. F.* p. 212 *sqq.*

careful at the rice harvest to take up the roots of a
certain bulbous plant, which bears a beautiful crown
of white and fragrant flowers. These roots are
preserved with the rice in the granary and are planted
again with the seed-rice in the following season; for
the Dyaks say that the rice will not grow unless a
plant of this sort be in the field.[1]

Customs like that of the Harvest-May appear to
exist in India and Africa. At a harvest festival of
the Lhoosai of S. E. India the chief goes with his
people into the forest and fells a large tree, which
is then carried into the village and set up in the
midst. Sacrifice is offered, and spirits and rice are
poured over the tree. The ceremony closes with
a feast and a dance, at which the unmarried men
and girls are the only performers.[2] Among the
Bechuanas the hack-thorn is very sacred, and it would
be a serious offence to cut a bough from it and carry
it into the village during the rainy season. But when
the corn is ripe in the ear the people go with axes, and
each man brings home a branch of the sacred hack-
thorn, with which they repair the village cattle-yard.[3]
Many tribes of S. E. Africa will not cut down timber
while the corn is green, fearing that if they did so,
the crops would be destroyed by blight, hail, or early
frost.[4]

Again, the fructifying power of the tree is put
forth at seed-time as well as at harvest. Among the
Aryan tribes of Gilgit, on the north-western frontier
of India, the sacred tree is the *Chili*, a species of cedar
(*Juniperus excelsa*). At the beginning of wheat-

---

[1] H. Low, *Sarawak*, p. 274.
[2] T. H. Lewin, *Wild Races of South-eastern India*, p. 270.
[3] J. Mackenzie, *Ten years north of the Orange River*, p. 385.
[4] Rev. J. Macdonald, MS. notes.

sowing the people receive from the Raja's granary a quantity of wheat, which is placed in a skin mixed with sprigs of the sacred cedar. A large bonfire of the cedar wood is lighted, and the wheat which is to be sown is held over the smoke. The rest is ground and made into a large cake, which is baked on the same fire and given to the ploughman.[1] Here the intention of fertilising the seed by means of the sacred cedar is unmistakable. In all these cases the power of fostering the growth of crops, and, in general, of cultivated plants, is ascribed to trees. The ascription is not unnatural. For the tree is the largest and most powerful member of the vegetable kingdom, and man is familiar with it before he takes to cultivating corn. Hence he naturally places the feebler and, to him, newer plant under the dominion of the older and more powerful.

Again, the tree-spirit makes the herds to multiply and blesses women with offspring. The sacred *Chili* or cedar of Gilgit was supposed to possess this virtue in addition to that of fertilising the corn. At the commencement of wheat-sowing three chosen unmarried youths, after undergoing daily washing and purification for three days, used to start for the mountain where the cedars grew, taking with them wine, oil, bread, and fruit of every kind. Having found a suitable tree they sprinkled the wine and oil on it, while they ate the bread and fruit as a sacrificial feast. Then they cut off the branch and brought it to the village, where, amid general rejoicing, it was placed on a large stone beside running water. "A goat was then sacrificed, its blood poured over the cedar branch, and a

---

[1] Biddulph, *Tribes of the Hindoo Koosh*, p. 103 *sq.*

wild dance took place, in which weapons were brandished about, and the head of the slaughtered goat was borne aloft, after which it was set up as a mark for arrows and bullet-practice. Every good shot was rewarded with a gourd full of wine and some of the flesh of the goat. When the flesh was finished the bones were thrown into the stream and a general ablution took place, after which every man went to his house taking with him a spray of the cedar. On arrival at his house he found the door shut in his face, and on his knocking for admission, his wife asked, 'What have you brought?' To which he answered, 'If you want children, I have brought them to you; if you want food, I have brought it; if you want cattle, I have brought them; whatever you want, I have it.' The door was then opened and he entered with his cedar spray. The wife then took some of the leaves and pouring wine and water on them placed them on the fire, and the rest were sprinkled with flour and suspended from the ceiling. She then sprinkled flour on her husband's head and shoulders, and addressed him thus: 'Ai Shiri Bagerthum, son of the fairies, you have come from far!' *Shiri Bagerthum*, 'the dreadful king,' being the form of address to the cedar when praying for wants to be fulfilled. The next day the wife baked a number of cakes, and taking them with her, drove the family goats to the Chili stone. When they were collected round the stone, she began to pelt them with pebbles, invoking the Chili at the same time. According to the direction in which the goats ran off, omens were drawn as to the number and sex of the kids expected during the ensuing year. Walnuts and pomegranates were then placed on the Chili stone, the cakes were distributed and eaten, and the goats followed to pasture in whatever direction they showed a disposition to go. For five days afterwards this song was sung in all the houses :—

> ' Dread Fairy King, I sacrifice before you,
> How nobly do you stand ! you have filled up my house,
> You have brought me a wife when I had not one,
> Instead of daughters you have given me sons.
> You have shown me the ways of right,
> You have given me many children.' " [1]

Here the driving of the goats to the stone on which the cedar had been placed is clearly meant to impart to them the fertilising influence of the cedar. In Europe the May-tree (May-pole) is supposed to possess similar powers over both women and cattle. In some parts of Germany on the 1st of May the peasants set up May-trees at the doors of stables and byres, one May-tree for each horse and cow ; this is thought to make the cows yield much milk.[2] Camden says of the Irish, "They fancy a green bough of a tree, fastened on May-day against the house, will produce plenty of milk that summer." [3]

On the 2d of July some of the Wends used to set up an oak-tree in the middle of the village with an iron cock fastened to its top ; then they danced round it, and drove the cattle round it to make them thrive.[4]

Some of the Esthonians believe in a mischievous spirit called Metsik, who lives in the forest and has the weal of the cattle in his hands. Every year a new image of him is prepared. On an appointed day all the villagers assemble and make a straw man, dress

---

[1] Biddulph, *op. cit.* p. 106 *sq.*
[2] Mannhardt, *B. K.* p. 161; E. Meier, *Deutsche Sagen, Sitten und Gebräuche aus Schwaben*, p. 397; A. Peter, *Volksthümliches aus Öster-reichisch-Schlesien*, ii. 286 ; Reinsberg-Düringsfeld, *Fest-Kalendar aus Böhmen*, p. 210.

[3] Quoted by Brand, *Popular Antiquities*, i. 227, Bohn's ed.

[4] Mannhardt, *B. K.* p. 174.

According to Chinese beliefs, at the felling of a tree, the tree-spirit
could be seen to rush out in the shape of a bull.

A May-pole, shown in Elizabethan times. The May-pole was supposed to possess fertilizing powers over women and cattle.

him in clothes, and take him to the common pasture land of the village. Here the figure is fastened to a high tree, round which the people dance noisily. On almost every day of the year prayer and sacrifice are offered to him that he may protect the cattle. Sometimes the image of Metsik is made of a corn-sheaf and fastened to a tall tree in the wood. The people perform strange antics before it to induce Metsik to guard the corn and the cattle.[1]

The Circassians regard the pear-tree as the protector of cattle. So they cut down a young pear-tree in the forest, branch it, and carry it home, where it is adored as a divinity. Almost every house has one such pear-tree. In autumn, on the day of the festival, it is carried into the house with great ceremony to the sound of music and amid the joyous cries of all the inmates, who compliment it on its fortunate arrival. It is covered with candles, and a cheese is fastened to its top. Round about it they eat, drink, and sing. Then they bid it good-bye and take it back to the courtyard, where it remains for the rest of the year, set up against the wall, without receiving any mark of respect.[2]

The common European custom of placing a green bush on May Day before the house of a beloved maiden probably originated in the belief of the fertilising power of the tree-spirit.[3] Amongst the Kara-Kirgiz barren women roll themselves on the ground under a solitary apple-tree, in order to obtain offspring.[4]

[1] Holzmayer, "Osiliana," *Verhandlungen der Estnischen Gesell. zu Dorpat*, vii. 10 *sq.*; Mannhardt, *B. K.* p. 407 *sq.*

[2] Potocki, *Voyage dans les steps d'Astrakhan et du Caucase* (Paris, 1829), i. 309.

[3] Mannhardt, *B. K.* p. 163 *sqq.* To his authorities add, for Sardinia, R. Tennant, *Sardinia and its Resources* (Rome and London, 1885), p. 185 *sq.*

[4] Radloff, *Proben der Volkslitteratur der nördlichen Türkischen Stämme*, v. 2.

Lastly, the power of granting to women an easy delivery at child-birth is ascribed to trees both in Sweden
and Africa.   In some districts of Sweden there was
formerly a *bårdträd* or guardian-tree (lime, ash, or
elm) in the neighbourhood of every farm.   No one
would pluck a single leaf of the sacred tree, any injury
to which was punished by ill-luck or sickness.   Pregnant women used to clasp the tree in their arms in
order to ensure an easy delivery.[1]   In some negro
tribes of the Congo region pregnant women make
themselves garments out of the bark of a certain
sacred tree, because they believe that this tree delivers
them from the dangers that attend child-bearing.[2]
The story that Leto clasped a palm-tree and an olive-
tree or two laurel-trees when she was about to give
birth to Apollo and Artemis perhaps points to a
similar Greek belief in the efficacy of certain trees to
facilitate delivery.[3]

From this review of the beneficent qualities commonly ascribed to tree-spirits, it is easy to understand
why customs like the May-tree or May-pole have
prevailed so widely and figured so prominently in the
popular festivals of European peasants.   In spring or
early summer or even on Midsummer Day, it was and
still is in many parts of Europe the custom to go out to
the woods, cut down a tree and bring it into the village,
where it is set up amid general rejoicings.   Or the
people cut branches in the woods, and fasten them on
every house.   The intention of these customs is to
bring home to the village, and to each house, the
blessings which the tree-spirit has in its power to bestow.

---

[1] Mannhardt, *B. K.* p. 51 *sq.*
[2] Merolla, "Voyage to Congo," in
Pinkerton's *Voyages and Travels*, xvi.
236 *sq.*

[3] Bötticher, *Der Baumkultus der
Hellenen*, p. 30 *sq.*

Hence the custom in some places of planting a May-tree before every house, or of carrying the village May-tree from door to door, that every household may receive its share of the blessing. Out of the mass of evidence on this subject a few examples may be selected.

Sir Henry Piers, in his *Description of Westmeath*, writing in 1682 says: "On May-eve, every family sets up before their door a green bush, strewed over with yellow flowers, which the meadows yield plentifully. In countries where timber is plentiful, they erect tall slender trees, which stand high, and they continue almost the whole year; so as a stranger would go nigh to imagine that they were all signs of ale-sellers, and that all houses were ale-houses."[1] In Northamptonshire a young tree ten or twelve feet high used to be planted before each house on May Day so as to appear growing.[2] "An antient custom, still retained by the Cornish, is that of decking their doors and porches on the 1st of May with green boughs of sycamore and hawthorn, and of planting trees, or rather stumps of trees, before their houses."[3] In the north of England it was formerly the custom for young people to rise very early on the morning of the 1st of May, and go out with music into the woods, where they broke branches and adorned them with nosegays and crowns of flowers. This done, they returned about sunrise and fastened the flower-decked branches over the doors and windows of their houses.[4] At Abingdon in Berkshire young people formerly went about in groups on May morning, singing a carol of which the following are some of the verses—

---

[1] Quoted by Brand, *Popular Antiquities*, i. 246 (ed. Bohn).

[2] Dyer, *British Popular Customs*, p. 254.

[3] Borlase, cited by Brand, *op. cit.* i. 222.

[4] Brand, *op. cit.* i. 212 *sq.*

" We've been rambling all the night ;
And sometime of this day ;
And now returning back again,
We bring a garland gay.

"A garland gay we bring you here ;
And at your door we stand ;
It is a sprout well budded out,
The work of our Lord's hand."[1]

At the villages of Saffron Walden and Debden
in Essex on the 1st of May little girls go about
in parties from door to door singing a song almost
identical with the above and carrying garlands ; a doll
dressed in white is usually placed in the middle of each
garland.[2]   At Seven Oaks on May Day the children
carry boughs and garlands from house to house, begging
for pence.   The garlands consist of two hoops interlaced crosswise, and covered with blue and yellow
flowers from the woods and hedges.[3]   In some
villages of the Vosges Mountains on the first Sunday
of May young girls go in bands from house to
house, singing a song in praise of May, in which
mention is made of the " bread and meal that come in
May."   If money is given them, they fasten a green
bough to the door ; if it is refused, they wish the family
many children and no bread to feed them.[4]   In
Mayenne (France), boys who bore the name of
Maillotins used to go about from farm to farm on
the 1st of May singing carols, for which they received
money or a drink ; they planted a small tree or a branch
of a tree.[5]

On the Thursday before Whitsunday the Russian
villagers " go out into the woods, sing songs, weave

[1] Dyer, *Popular British Customs*, p.
233.
[2] Chambers, *Book of Days*, i. 578 ;
Dyer, *op. cit.* p. 237 *sq.*

[3] Dyer, *op. cit.* p. 243.
[4] E. Cortet, *Fêtes religieuses*, p. 167 *sqq.*
[5] *Revue des Traditions populaires*, ii.
200.

garlands, and cut down a young birch-tree, which they dress up in woman's clothes, or adorn with many-coloured shreds and ribbons. After that comes a feast, at the end of which they take the dressed-up birch-tree, carry it home to their village with joyful dance and song, and set it up in one of the houses, where it remains as an honoured guest till Whitsunday. On the two intervening days they pay visits to the house where their 'guest' is; but on the third day, Whitsunday, they take her to a stream and fling her into its waters," throwing their garlands after her. "All over Russia every village and every town is turned, a little before Whitsunday, into a sort of garden. Everywhere along the streets the young birch-trees stand in rows, every house and every room is adorned with boughs, even the engines upon the railway are for the time decked with green leaves."[1] In this Russian custom the dressing of the birch in woman's clothes shows how clearly the tree is conceived as personal; and the throwing it into a stream is most probably a rain-charm. In some village of Altmark it was formerly the custom for serving-men, grooms, and cowherds to go from farm to farm at Whitsuntide distributing crowns made of birch-branches and flowers to the farmers; these crowns were hung up in the houses and left till the following year.[2]

In the neighbourhood of Zabern in Alsace bands of people go about carrying May-trees. Amongst them is a man dressed in a white shirt, with his face blackened; in front of him is carried a large May-tree, but each member of the band also carries a smaller one. One of the company carries a huge basket in which he

---

[1] Ralston, *Songs of the Russian People*, p. 234 *sq.*

[2] A. Kuhn, *Märkische Sagen und Märchen*, p. 315.

collects eggs, bacon, etc.[1]   In some parts of Sweden on
the eve of May Day lads go about carrying each a
bunch of fresh-gathered birch twigs, wholly or partially
in leaf.   With the village fiddler at their head they go
from house to house singing May songs; the purport
of which is a prayer for fine weather, a plentiful
harvest, and worldly and spiritual blessings.   One of
them carries a basket in which he collects gifts of
eggs and the like.   If they are well received they
stick a leafy twig in the roof over the cottage door.[2]

But in Sweden midsummer is the season when
these ceremonies are chiefly observed.   On the Eve
of St. John (23d June) the houses are thoroughly
cleansed and garnished with green boughs and
flowers.   Young fir-trees are raised at the door-way
and elsewhere about the homestead; and very often
small umbrageous arbours are constructed in the
garden.   In Stockholm on this day a leaf-market is
held at which thousands of May-poles (*Maj Stänger*)
six inches to twelve feet high, decorated with leaves,
flowers, slips of coloured paper, gilt egg-shells, strung
on reeds, etc. are exposed for sale.   Bonfires are lit
on the hills and the people dance round them and
jump over them.   But the chief event of the day
is setting up the May-pole.   This consists of a straight
and tall spruce-pine tree, stripped of its branches.
"At times hoops and at others pieces of wood, placed
crosswise, are attached to it at intervals; whilst at
others it is provided with bows, representing so to
say, a man with his arms akimbo.   From top to
bottom not only the 'Maj Stäng' (May-pole) itself,
but the hoops, bows, etc. are ornamented with leaves,

---

[1] Mannhardt, *B. K.* p. 162.   [2] L. Lloyd, *Peasant Life in Sweden*,
p. 235.

flowers, slips of various cloth, gilt egg-shells, etc. ;
and on the top of it is a large vane, or it may be a
flag." The raising of the May-pole, the decoration
of which is done by the village maidens, is an affair
of much ceremony ; the people flock to it from all
quarters and dance round it in a great ring.[1] In
some parts of Bohemia also a May-pole or midsummer-
tree is erected on St. John's Eve. The lads fetch a
tall fir or pine from the wood and set it up on a
height, where the girls deck it with nosegays, garlands,
and red ribbons. Then they pile brushwood, dry
wood, and other combustible materials about the tree,
and, when darkness has fallen, set the whole on fire.
While the fire was burning the lads used to climb
up the tree and fetch down the garlands and ribbons
which the girls had fastened to it ; but as this led
to accidents, the custom has been forbidden. Sometimes the young people fling burning besoms into the
air, or run shouting down hill with them. When the
tree is consumed, the young men and their sweethearts
stand on opposite sides of the fire, and look at each
other through garlands and through the fire, to see
whether they will be true lovers and will wed. Then
they throw the garlands thrice across the smouldering
fire to each other. When the blaze has died down,
the couples join hands and leap thrice across the
glowing embers. The singed garlands are taken
home, and kept carefully in the house throughout
the year. Whenever a thunder-storm bursts, part of
the garlands are burned on the hearth ; and when
the cattle are sick or are calving, they get a portion
of the garlands to eat. The charred embers of the
bonfire are stuck in the cornfields and meadows and

---

[1] L. Lloyd, *op. cit.* p. 257 *sqq.*

on the roof of the house, to keep house and field from bad weather and injury. [1]

It is hardly necessary to illustrate the custom of setting up a village May-tree or May-pole on May Day. One point only—the renewal of the village May-tree—requires to be noticed. In England the village May-pole seems as a rule, at least in later times, to have been permanent, not renewed from year to year. [2] Sometimes, however, it was renewed annually. Thus, Borlase says of the Cornish people: " From towns they make incursions, on May-eve, into the country, cut down a tall elm, bring it into the town with rejoicings, and having fitted a straight taper pole to the end of it, and painted it, erect it in the most public part, and upon holidays and festivals dress it with garlands of flowers or ensigns and streamers." [3] An annual renewal seems also to be implied in the description by Stubbs, a Puritanical writer, of the custom of drawing home the May-pole by twenty or forty yoke of oxen. [4] In some parts of Germany and Austria the May-tree or Whitsuntide-tree is renewed annually, a fresh tree being felled and set up. [5]

We can hardly doubt that originally the practice everywhere was to set up a new May-tree every year. As the object of the custom was to bring in the fructifying spirit of vegetation, newly awakened in spring, the end would have been defeated if, instead of a living tree, green and sappy, an old withered one had been erected year after year or allowed to stand permanently. When, however, the meaning of the

---

[1] Reinsberg-Düringsfeld, *Fest-Kalendar aus Böhmen*, p. 308 *sq.*

[2] Hone, *Every-day Book*, i. 547 *sqq.* ; Chambers, *Book of Days*, i. 571.

[3] Quoted by Brand, *op. cit.* i. 237.

[4] *Id.*, *op. cit.* i. 235.

[5] Mannhardt, *B. K.* p. 169 *sq. note.*

custom had been forgotten, and the May-tree was regarded simply as a centre for holiday merrymaking,
people saw no reason for felling a fresh tree every
year, and preferred to let the same tree stand permanently, only decking it with fresh flowers on May
Day. But even when the May-pole had thus become a
fixture, the need of giving it the appearance of being a
green tree, not a dead pole, was sometimes felt. Thus
at Weverham in Cheshire "are two May-poles, which
are decorated on this day (May Day) with all due
attention to the ancient solemnity ; the sides are
hung with garlands, and the top terminated by a birch
or other tall slender tree with its leaves on ; the bark
being peeled, and the stem spliced to the pole, so as
to give the appearance of one tree from the summit." [1]
Thus the renewal of the May-tree is like the renewal
of the Harvest-May ; each is intended to secure a
fresh portion of the fertilising spirit of vegetation,
and to preserve it throughout the year. But whereas
the efficacy of the Harvest-May is restricted to
promoting the growth of the crops, that of the May-
tree or May-branch extends also, as we have seen,
to women and cattle. Lastly, it is worth noting that
the old May-tree is sometimes burned at the end
of the year. Thus in the district of Prague young
people break pieces off the public May-tree and
place them behind the holy pictures in their rooms,
where they remain till next May Day, and are then
burned on the hearth.[2] In Würtemberg the bushes
which are set up on the houses on Palm Sunday are
sometimes left there for a year and then burnt.[3] The

---

[1] Hone, *Every-day Book*, ii. 597 *sq.*
[2] Reinsberg-Düringsfeld, *Fest-Kalendar aus Böhmen*, p. 217 ; Mannhardt,
B. K. p. 566.

[3] Birlinger, *Völksthümliches aus
Schwaben*, ii. 74 *sq.*; Mannhardt, *B.
K.* p. 566.

eiresione (the Harvest-May of Greece) was perhaps burned at the end of the year.[1]

So much for the tree-spirit conceived as incorporate or immanent in the tree. We have now to show that the tree-spirit is often conceived and represented as detached from the tree and clothed in human form, and even as embodied in living men or women. The evidence for this anthropomorphic representation of the tree-spirit is largely to be found in the popular customs of European peasantry.

There is an instructive class of cases in which the tree-spirit is represented simultaneously in vegetable form and in human form, which are set side by side as if for the express purpose of explaining each other. In these cases the human representative of the tree-spirit is sometimes a doll or puppet, sometimes a living person ; but whether a puppet or a person, it is placed beside a tree or bough ; so that together the person or puppet, and the tree or bough, form a sort of bilingual inscription, the one being, so to speak, a translation of the other. Here, therefore, there is no room left for doubt that the spirit of the tree is actually represented in human form. Thus in Bohemia, on the fourth Sunday in Lent, young people throw a puppet called Death into the water ; then the girls go into the wood, cut down a young tree, and fasten to it a puppet dressed in white clothes to look like a woman ; with this tree and puppet they go from house to house collecting gratuities and singing songs with the refrain—

> " We carry Death out of the village,
> We bring Summer into the village." [2]

---

[1] Aristophanes, *Plutus*, 1054 ; Mannhardt, *A. W. F.* p. 222 *sq.*

[2] Reinsberg-Düringsfeld, *Fest-Kalendar aus Böhmen*, p. 86 *sqq.* ; Mannhardt, *B. K.* p. 156.

Here, as we shall see later on, the "Summer" is the spirit of vegetation returning or reviving in spring. In some places in this country children go about asking for pence with some small imitations of May-poles, and with a finely dressed doll which they call the Lady of the May.[1] In these cases the tree and the puppet are obviously regarded as equivalent.

At Thann, in Alsace, a girl called the Little May Rose, dressed in white, carries a small May-tree, which is gay with garlands and ribbons. Her companions collect gifts from door to door, singing a song—

> " Little May Rose turn round three times,
>   Let us look at you round and round !
>   Rose of the May, come to the greenwood away,
>   We will be merry all.
>   So we go from the May to the roses."

In the course of the song a wish is expressed that those who give nothing may lose their fowls by the marten, that their vine may bear no clusters, their tree no nuts, their field no corn ; the produce of the year is supposed to depend on the gifts offered to these May singers.[2] Here and in the cases mentioned above, where children go about with green boughs on May Day singing and collecting money, the meaning is that with the spirit of vegetation they bring plenty and good luck to the house, and they expect to be paid for the service. In Russian Lithuania, on the 1st of May, they used to set up a green tree before the village. Then the rustic swains chose the prettiest girl, crowned her, swathed her in birch branches and set her beside the May-tree, where they danced, sang, and shouted

---

[1] Chambers, *Book of Days*, i. 573.   [2] Mannhardt, *B. K.* p. 312.

"O May! O May!"[1] In Brie (Isle de France) a
May-tree is set up in the midst of the village ; its top
is crowned with flowers ; lower down it is twined with
leaves and twigs, still lower with huge green branches.
The girls dance round it, and at the same time a lad
wrapt in leaves and called Father May is led about.[2]
In Bavaria, on the 2d of May, a *Walber* (?) tree is
erected before a tavern, and a man dances round it,
enveloped in straw from head to foot in such a way
that the ears of corn unite above his head to form a
crown. He is called the *Walber*, and used to be led
in solemn procession through the streets, which were
adorned with sprigs of birch.[3] In Carinthia, on St.
George's Day (24th April), the young people deck
with flowers and garlands a tree which has been felled
on the eve of the festival. The tree is then carried in
procession, accompanied with music and joyful acclamations, the chief figure in the procession being the Green
George, a young fellow clad from head to foot in green
birch branches. At the close of the ceremonies the
Green George, that is an effigy of him, is thrown into
the water. It is the aim of the lad who acts Green
George to step out of his leafy envelope and substitute
the effigy so adroitly that no one shall perceive the
change. In many places, however, the lad himself
who plays the part of Green George is ducked in a
river or pond, with the express intention of thus ensuring rain to make the fields and meadows green in
summer. In some places the cattle are crowned and
driven from their stalls to the accompaniment of a
song—

---

[1] Mannhardt, *B. K.* p. 313.

[2] *Ib.* p. 314.

[3] *Bavaria, Landes-und Volkskunde des Königreichs Bayern*, iii. 357 ; Mann-hardt, *B. K.* p. 312 *sq.*

" Green George we bring,
Green George we accompany,
May he feed our herds well,
If not, to the water with him." [1]

Here we see that the same powers of making rain and
fostering the cattle, which are ascribed to the tree-
spirit regarded as incorporate in the tree, are also attributed to the tree-spirit represented by a living man.

An example of the double representation of the
spirit of vegetation by a tree and a living man is reported from Bengal. The Oraons have a festival in
spring while the sál trees are in blossom, because
they think that at this time the marriage of earth is
celebrated and the sál flowers are necessary for the
ceremony.   On an appointed day the villagers go with
their priest to the Sarna, the sacred grove, a remnant
of the old sál forest in which a goddess Sarna Burhi,
or woman of the grove, is supposed to dwell.   She is
thought to have great influence on the rain ; and the
priest arriving with his party at the grove sacrifices to
her five fowls, of which a morsel is given to each person present.   Then they gather the sál flowers and
return laden with them to the village.   Next day the
priest visits every house, carrying the flowers in a wide
open basket.   The women of each house bring out
water to wash his feet as he approaches, and kneeling
make him an obeisance.   Then he dances with them
and places some of the sál flowers over the door of the
house and in the women's hair.   No sooner is this done
than the women empty their water-jugs over him, drenching him to the skin.   A feast follows, and the young
people, with sál flowers in their hair, dance all night on
the village green.[2]   Here, the equivalence of the flower-

---

[1] Mannhardt, *B. K.* p. 313 *sq.*   [2] Dalton, *Ethnology of Bengal*, p. 261.

bearing priest to the goddess of the flowering-tree
comes out plainly.   For she is supposed to influence
the rain, and the drenching of the priest with water is,
doubtless, like the ducking of the Green George in
Bavaria, a rain-charm.   Thus the priest, as if he were
the tree goddess herself, goes from door to door dis-
pensing rain and bestowing fruitfulness on each house,
but especially on the women.

Without citing more examples to the same effect,
we may sum up the result of the preceding paragraphs
in the words of Mannhardt.   " The customs quoted
suffice to establish with certainty the conclusion that
in these spring processions the spirit of vegetation is
often represented both by the May-tree and in addition by a man dressed in green leaves or flowers or by
a girl similarly adorned.   It is the same spirit which
animates the tree and is active in the inferior plants
and which we have recognised in the May-tree and
the Harvest-May.   Quite consistently the spirit is also
supposed to manifest his presence in the first flower
of spring and reveals himself both in a girl representing a May-rose, and also, as giver of harvest, in the
person of the *Walber*.   The procession with this
representative of the divinity was supposed to produce
the same beneficial effects on the fowls, the fruit-trees,
and the crops as the presence of the deity himself.   In
other words, the mummer was regarded not as an
image but as an actual representative of the spirit of
vegetation ; hence the wish expressed by the attendants
on the May-rose and the May-tree that those who
refuse them gifts of eggs, bacon, etc. may have no share
in the blessings which it is in the power of the itinerant
spirit to bestow.   We may conclude that these begging
processions with May-trees or May-boughs from door

to door ("bringing the May or the summer") had everywhere originally a serious and, so to speak, sacramental
significance; people really believed that the god of
growth was present unseen in the bough; by the procession he was brought to each house to bestow his
blessing. The names May, Father May, May Lady,
Queen of the May, by which the anthropomorphic spirit
of vegetation is often denoted, show that the conception of the spirit of vegetation is blent with a personification of the season at which his powers are most
strikingly manifested."[1]

Thus far we have seen that the tree-spirit or the
spirit of vegetation in general is represented either in
vegetable form alone, as by a tree, bough, or flower; or
in vegetable and human form simultaneously, as by a
tree, bough, or flower in combination with a puppet or
a living person. It remains to show that the representation of him by a tree, bough, or flower is sometimes
entirely dropped, while the representation of him by a
living person remains. In this case the representative
character of the person is generally marked by dressing him or her in leaves or flowers; sometimes too it
is indicated by the name he or she bears.

We saw that in Russia at Whitsuntide a birch-tree
is dressed in woman's clothes and set up in the house.
Clearly equivalent to this is the custom observed on
Whit-Monday by Russian girls in the district of Pinsk.
They choose the prettiest of their number, envelop
her in a mass of foliage taken from the birch-trees and
maples, and carry her about through the village. In a
district of Little Russia they take round a "poplar,"
represented by a girl wearing bright flowers in her hair.[2]

---

[1] Mannhardt, *B. K.* p. 315 *sq.*   [2] Ralston, *Songs of the Russian People*, p. 234.

In the Département de l'Ain (France) on the 1st of
May eight or ten boys unite, clothe one of their number
in leaves, and go from house to house begging.[1]
At Whitsuntide in Holland poor women used to go
about begging with a little girl called Whitsuntide
Flower (*Pinxterbloem*, perhaps a kind of iris); she was
decked with flowers and sat in a waggon. In North
Brabant she wears the flowers from which she takes
her name and a song is sung—

> " Whitsuntide Flower
> Turn yourself once round." [2]

In Ruhla (Thüringen) as soon as the trees begin
to grow green in spring, the children assemble on a
Sunday and go out into the woods, where they choose
one of their playmates to be the Little Leaf Man.
They break branches from the trees and twine them
about the child till only his shoes peep out from the
leafy mantle.   Holes are made in it for him to see
through, and two of the children lead the Little Leaf
Man that he may not stumble or fall. Singing and
dancing they take him from house to house, asking
for gifts of food (eggs, cream, sausage, cakes). Lastly
they sprinkle the Leaf Man with water and feast on
the food they have collected.[3]   In England the best-
known example of these leaf-clad mummers is the
Jack-in-the-Green, a chimney-sweeper who walks
encased in a pyramidal-shaped framework of wicker-
work, which is covered with holly and ivy, and
surmounted by a crown of flowers and ribbons. Thus
arrayed he dances on May Day at the head of a troop

---

[1] Mannhardt, *B. K.* p. 318.
[2] Mannhardt, *B. K.* p. 318; Grimm,
Deutsche Mythologie,[4] ii. 657.

[3] Mannhardt, *B. K.* p. 320; Witzschel, *Sagen, Sitten und Gebräuche aus
Thüringen*, p. 211.

of chimney-sweeps, who collect pence.[1] In some
parts also of France a young fellow is encased in a
wicker framework covered with leaves and is led
about.[2] In Frickthal (Aargau) a similar frame of
basketwork is called the Whitsuntide Basket. As
soon as the trees begin to bud, a spot is chosen in the
wood, and here the village lads make the frame with
all secrecy, lest others should forestall them. Leafy
branches are twined round two hoops, one of which
rests on the shoulders of the wearer, the other
encircles his calves; holes are made for his eyes and
mouth; and a large nosegay crowns the whole. In
this guise he appears suddenly in the village at the
hour of vespers, preceded by three boys blowing on
horns made of willow bark. The great object of his
supporters is to set up the Whitsuntide Basket beside
the village well, and to keep it and him there, despite
the efforts of the lads from neighbouring villages, who
seek to carry off the Whitsuntide Basket and set it
up at their own well.[3] In the neighbourhood of
Ertingen (Würtemberg) a masker of the same sort,
known as the Lazy Man (*Latzmann*), goes about the
village on Midsummer Day; he is hidden under a
great pyramidal or conical frame of wicker-work, ten
or twelve feet high, which is completely covered with
sprigs of fir. He has a bell which he rings as he
goes, and he is attended by a suite of persons dressed
up in character—a footman, a colonel, a butcher, an
angel, the devil, the doctor, etc. They march in
Indian file and halt before every house, where each
of them speaks in character, except the Lazy Man,

[1] Mannhardt, *B. K.* p. 322; Hone,
Every-day Book, i. 583 *sqq.*; Dyer,
British Popular Customs, p. 230 *sq.*

[2] Mannhardt, *B. K.* p. 323.

[3] *Ib.*

who says nothing. With what they get by begging from door to door they hold a feast.[1]

In the class of cases of which the above are specimens it is obvious that the leaf-clad person who is led about is equivalent to the May-tree, May-bough, or May-doll, which is carried from house to house by children begging. Both are representatives of the beneficent spirit of vegetation, whose visit to the house is recompensed by a present of money or food.

Often the leaf-clad person who represents the spirit of vegetation is known as the king or the queen; thus, for example, he or she is called the May King, Whitsuntide King, Queen of May, and so on. These titles, as Mannhardt observes, imply that the spirit incorporate in vegetation is a ruler, whose creative power extends far and wide.[2]

In a village near Salzwedel a May-tree is set up at Whitsuntide and the boys race to it; he who reaches it first is king; a garland of flowers is put round his neck and in his hand he carries a May-bush, with which, as the procession moves along, he sweeps away the dew. At each house they sing a song, wishing the inmates good luck, referring to the " black cow in the stall milking white milk, black hen on the nest laying white eggs," and begging a gift of eggs, bacon, etc.[3] In some villages of Brunswick at Whitsuntide a May King is completely enveloped in a May-bush. In some parts of Thüringen also they have a May King at Whitsuntide, but he is got up rather differently. A frame of wood is made in which

---

[1] Birlinger, *Volksthümliches aus Schwaben*, ii. 114 *sq.*; Mannhardt, *B. K.* p. 325.

[2] Mannhardt, *B. K.* p. 341 *sq.*

[3] Kuhn und Schwartz, *Norddeutsche Sagen, Märchen und Gebräuche*, p. 380.

a man can stand; it is completely covered with birch boughs and is surmounted by a crown of birch and flowers, in which a bell is fastened. This frame is placed in the wood and the May King gets into it. The rest go out and look for him, and when they have found him they lead him back into the village to the magistrate, the clergyman, and others, who have to guess who is in the verdurous frame. If they guess wrong, the May King rings his bell by shaking his head, and a forfeit of beer or the like must be paid by the unsuccessful guesser.[1] In some parts of Bohemia on Whit-Monday the young fellows disguise themselves in tall caps of birch bark adorned with flowers. One of them is dressed as a king and dragged on a sledge to the village green, and if on the way they pass a pool the sledge is always overturned into it. Arrived at the green they gather round the king; the crier jumps on a stone or climbs up a tree and recites lampoons about each house and its inmates. Afterwards the disguises of bark are stripped off and they go about the village in holiday attire, carrying a May-tree and begging. Cakes, eggs, and corn are sometimes given them.[2] At Grossvargula, near Langensalza, in last century a Grass King used to be led about in procession at Whitsuntide. He was encased in a pyramid of poplar branches, the top of which was adorned with a royal crown of branches and flowers. He rode on horseback with the leafy pyramid over him, so that its lower end touched the ground, and an opening was left in it only for his face. Surrounded by a cavalcade of

---

[1] Kuhn und Schwartz, *op. cit.* p. 384; Mannhardt, *B. K.* p. 342.

[2] Reinsberg-Düringsfeld, *Fest-Kalendar aus Böhmen*, p. 260 *sq.*; Mannhardt, *B. K.* p. 342 *sq.*

young fellows, he rode in procession to the town hall, the parsonage, etc., where they all got a drink of beer. Then under the seven lindens of the neighbouring Sommerberg, the Grass King was stripped of his green casing; the crown was handed to the Mayor, and the branches were stuck in the flax fields in order to make the flax grow tall.[1] In this last trait the fertilising influence ascribed to the representative of the tree-spirit comes out clearly. In the neighbourhood of Pilsen (Bohemia) a conical hut of green branches, without any door, is erected at Whitsuntide in the midst of the village. To this hut rides a troop of village lads with a king at their head. He wears a sword at his side and a sugar-loaf hat of rushes on his head. In his train are a judge, a crier, and a personage called the Frog-flayer or Hangman. This last is a sort of ragged merryandrew, wearing a rusty old sword and bestriding a sorry hack. On reaching the hut the crier dismounts and goes round it looking for a door. Finding none, he says, "Ah, this is perhaps an enchanted castle; the witches creep through the leaves and need no door." At last he draws his sword and hews his way into the hut, where there is a chair, on which he seats himself and proceeds to criticise in rhyme the girls, farmers, and farm-servants of the neighbourhood. When this is over, the Frog-flayer steps forward and, after exhibiting a cage with frogs in it, sets up a gallows on which he hangs the frogs in a row.[2] In the neighbourhood of Plas the ceremony differs in some points. The king and his soldiers are completely clad in bark, adorned

---

[1] Mannhardt, *B. K.* p. 347 *sq.*; Witzschel, *Sagen, Sitten und Gebräuche aus Thüringen*, p. 203.

[2] Reinsberg-Düringsfeld, *Fest-Kalendar aus Böhmen*, p. 253 *sqq.*

with flowers and ribbons; they all carry swords and
ride horses, which are gay with green branches and
flowers.   While the village dames and girls are being
criticised at the arbour, a frog is secretly pinched and
poked by the crier till it quacks.   Sentence of death
is passed on the frog by the king; the hangman
beheads it and flings the bleeding body among the
spectators.   Lastly, the king is driven from the hut
and pursued by the soldiers.[1]   The pinching and
beheading of the frog are doubtless, as Mannhardt
observes,[2] a rain-charm.   We have seen[3] that some
Indians of the Orinoco beat frogs for the express
purpose of producing rain, and that killing a frog is
a German rain-charm.

Often the spirit of vegetation in spring is represented by a queen instead of a king.   In the
neighbourhood of Libchowic (Bohemia), on the fourth
Sunday in Lent, girls dressed in white and wearing
the first spring flowers, as violets and daisies, in their
hair, lead about the village a girl who is called the
Queen and is crowned with flowers.   During the
procession, which is conducted with great solemnity,
none of the girls may stand still, but must keep whirling
round continually and singing.   In every house the
Queen announces the arrival of spring and wishes the
inmates good luck and blessings, for which she
receives presents.[4]   In German Hungary the girls
choose the prettiest girl to be their Whitsuntide Queen,
fasten a towering wreath on her brow, and carry her
singing through the streets.   At every house they
stop, sing old ballads, and receive presents.[5]   In the

---

[1] Reinsberg-Düringsfeld, *Fest-Kalendar aus Böhmen*, p. 262; Mannhardt,
B. K. p. 353 *sq.*
[2] *B. K.* p. 355.   [3] Above, p. 18.

[4] Reinsberg-Düringsfeld, *Fest-Kalendar aus Böhmen*, p. 93; Mannhardt,
B. K. p. 344.
[5] Mannhardt, *B. K.* p. 343 *sq.*

south-east of Ireland on May Day the prettiest girl
used to be chosen Queen of the district for twelve
months. She was crowned with wild flowers ; feasting,
dancing, and rustic sports followed, and were closed by
a grand procession in the evening. During her year
of office she presided over rural gatherings of young
people at dances and merrymakings. If she married
before next May Day her authority was at an end,
but her successor was not elected till that day came
round.[1] The May Queen is common in France [2] and
familiar in England.

Again the spirit of vegetation is sometimes
represented by a king and queen, a lord and lady, or
a bridegroom and bride. Here again the parallelism
holds between the anthropomorphic and the vegetable
representation of the tree-spirit, for we have seen
above that trees are sometimes married to each other.[3]
In a village near Königgrätz (Bohemia) on Whit-
Monday the children play the king's game, at which a
king and a queen march about under a canopy, the
queen wearing a garland, and the youngest girl
carrying two wreaths on a plate behind them. They
are attended by boys and girls called groom's men and
bridesmaids, and they go from house to house
collecting gifts.[4] Near Grenoble, in France, a king
and queen are chosen on the 1st of May and are set on
a throne for all to see.[5] At Headington, near Oxford,
children used to carry garlands from door to door on

---

[1] Dyer, *British Popular Customs*,
p. 270 *sq.*

[2] Mannhardt, *B. K.* p. 344 *sq.* ;
Cortet, *Fêtes religieuses*, p. 160 *sqq.* ;
Monnier, *Traditions populaires com-
parées*, p. 282 *sqq.* ; Bérenger-Féraud,
Réminiscences populaires de la Provence,
p. 1 *sqq.*

[3] Above, p. 60.

[4] Reinsberg-Düringsfeld, *Fest-Kalendar aus Böhmen*, p. 265 *sq.* ; Mannhardt,
B. K. p. 422.

[5] Monnier, *Traditions populaires comparées*, p. 304 ; Mannhardt, *B. K.* p.
423.

May Day.   Each garland was carried by two girls,
and they were followed by a lord and lady—a boy and
girl linked together by a white handkerchief, of which
each held an end, and dressed with ribbons, sashes,
and flowers.   At each door they sang a verse—

> " Gentlemen and ladies,
>   We wish you happy May ;
>   We come to show you a garland,
>   Because it is May-day."

On receiving money the lord put his arm about his
lady's waist and kissed her.[1]   In some Saxon villages
at Whitsuntide a lad and a lass disguise themselves
and hide in the bushes or high grass outside the
village.   Then the whole village goes out with music
" to seek the bridal pair."   When they find the couple
they all gather round them, the music strikes up, and
the bridal pair is led merrily to the village.   In the
evening they dance.   In some places the bridal pair
is called the prince and the princess.[2]

In the neighbourhood of Briançon (Dauphiné) on
May Day the lads wrap up in green leaves a young
fellow whose sweetheart has deserted him or married
another.   He lies down on the ground and feigns to be
asleep.   Then a girl who likes him, and would marry
him, comes and wakes him, and raising him up offers
him her arm and a flag.   So they go to the alehouse,
where the pair lead off the dancing.   But they must
marry within the year, or they are treated as old
bachelor and old maid, and are debarred the company
of the young folk.   The lad is called the bridegroom
of the month of May (*le fiancé du mois de May*).   In
the alehouse he puts off his garment of leaves, out of

---

[1] Brand, *Popular Antiquities*, i.
233 *sq.* Bohn's ed. ; Mannhardt, *B. K.*
p. 424.

[2] E. Sommer, *Sagen, Märchen und
Gebräuche aus Sachsen und Thüringen*,
p. 151 *sq.* ; Mannhardt, *B. K.* p. 431 *sq.*

which, mixed with flowers, his partner in the dance
makes a nosegay, and wears it at her breast next day,
when he leads her again to the alehouse.[1] Like this
is a Russian custom observed in the district of
Nerechta on the Thursday before Whitsunday. The
girls go out into a birch-wood, wind a girdle or band
round a stately birch, twist its lower branches into a
wreath, and kiss each other in pairs through the
wreath. The girls who kiss through the wreath call
each other gossips. Then one of the girls steps
forward, and mimicking a drunken man, flings herself
on the ground, rolls on the grass, and feigns to go
fast asleep. Another girl wakens the pretended sleeper
and kisses him ; then the whole bevy trips singing
through the wood to twine garlands, which they throw
into the water. In the fate of the garlands floating on
the stream they read their own.[2] In this custom the rôle
of the sleeper was probably at one time sustained by a
lad. In these French and Russian customs we have a
forsaken bridegroom, in the following a forsaken bride.
On Shrove Tuesday the Slovenes of Oberkrain drag
a straw puppet with joyous cries up and down the
village ; then they throw it into the water or burn it,
and from the height of the flames they judge of the
abundance of the next harvest. The noisy crew is
followed by a female masker, who drags a great board
by a string and gives out that she is a forsaken bride.[3]

Viewed in the light of what has gone before, the
awakening of the forsaken sleeper in these ceremonies
probably represents the revival of vegetation in
spring. But it is not easy to assign their respective

---

[1] This custom was told to Mannhardt by a French prisoner in the war of 1870-71, *B. K.* p. 434.

[2] Mannhardt, *B. K.* p. 434 *sq.*

[3] *Ib.* p. 435.

Planting the village May-pole on May Day, a custom to invoke the fruitful spirit of vegetation, newly awakened in the spring.

A CEREMONY VPON CANDELMAS EVE

DOWN with ye Rosemary, & so
Down with ye Baies, & Mistletoe:
Down with ye Holly, Ivie, all,
Wherewith ye Drest ye Xmas Hall:
Ye so ye Svperstitiovs finde,
No One Leaft Branch there left Behind:
For Look, how many leaves There Be
Neglected there, Mayds, trvst to Me,
So Many Goblins Yov Shall See,

R: Herrick

On Candlemas night, the mistress and servants prepare a "Brud's bed" just before retiring, in hopes of obtaining a good crop.

rôles to the forsaken bridegroom and to the girl
who wakes him from his slumber.   Is the sleeper
the leafless forest or the bare earth of winter ?   Is
the girl who wakens him the fresh verdure or the
genial sunshine of spring ?   It is hardly possible, on
the evidence before us, to answer these questions.
The Oraons of Bengal, it may be remembered,
celebrate the marriage of earth in the springtime,
when the sál-tree is in blossom.   But from this we
can hardly argue that in the European ceremonies
the sleeping bridegroom is "the dreaming earth"
and the girl the spring blossoms.

In the Highlands of Scotland the revival of
vegetation in spring used to be graphically represented as follows.   On Candlemas day (2d February) in the Hebrides "the mistress and servants of
each family take a sheaf of oats, and dress it up in
women's apparel, put it in a large basket, and lay
a wooden club by it, and this they call Brüd's bed ;
and then the mistress and servants cry three times,
Brüd is come, Brüd is welcome.   This they do just
before going to bed, and when they rise in the
morning they look among the ashes, expecting to
see the impression of Brüd's club there ; which if
they do they reckon it a true presage of a good crop
and prosperous year, and the contrary they take as
an ill omen."[1]   The same custom is described by
another witness thus :   "Upon the night before
Candlemas it is usual to make a bed with corn and
hay, over which some blankets are laid, in a part of
the house near the door.   When it is ready, a person
goes out and repeats three times, . . . 'Bridget,

---

[1] Martin, "Description of the Western Islands of Scotland," in Pinkerton's
Voyages and Travels, iii. 613 ; Mannhardt, *B. K.* p. 436.

Bridget, come in ; thy bed is ready.' One or more candles are left burning near it all night." [1]

Often the marriage of the spirit of vegetation in spring, though not directly represented, is implied by naming the human representative of the spirit "the Bride," and dressing her in wedding attire. Thus in some villages of Altmark at Whitsuntide, while the boys go about carrying a May-tree or leading a boy enveloped in leaves and flowers, the girls lead about the May Bride, a girl dressed as a bride with a great nosegay in her hair. They go from house to house, the May Bride singing a song in which she asks for a present, and tells the inmates of each house that if they give her something they will themselves have something the whole year through ; but if they give her nothing they will themselves have nothing. [2] In some parts of Westphalia two girls lead a flower-crowned girl called "the Whitsuntide Bride" from door to door, singing a song in which they ask for eggs. [3] In Bresse in the month of May a girl called *la Mariée* is tricked out with ribbons and nosegays and is led about by a gallant. She is preceded by a lad carrying a green May-tree, and appropriate verses are sung. [4]

§ 5.—*Tree-worship in antiquity*

Such then are some of the ways in which the tree-spirit or the spirit of vegetation is represented

---

[1] *Scotland and Scotsmen in the Eighteenth Century*, from the MSS. of John Ramsay of Ochtertyre. Edited by Alex. Allardyce (Edinburgh, 1888), ii. 447.

[2] Kuhn, *Märkische Sagen und Märchen*, p. 318 *sqq.* ; Mannhardt, *B. K.* p. 437.

[3] Mannhardt, *B. K.* p. 438.

[4] Monnier, *Traditions populaires comparées*, p. 283 *sq.* ; Cortet, *Fêtes religieuses*, p. 162 *sq.* ; Mannhardt, *B. K.* p. 439 *sq.*

in the customs of our European peasantry. From
the remarkable persistence and similarity of such
customs all over Europe we are justified in concluding that tree-worship was once an important
element in the religion of the Aryan race in
Europe, and that the rites and ceremonies of the
worship were marked by great uniformity everywhere, and did not substantially differ from those
which are still or were till lately observed by our
peasants at their spring and midsummer festivals.
For these rites bear internal marks of great
antiquity, and this internal evidence is confirmed by
the resemblance which the rites bear to those of rude
peoples elsewhere.[1] Therefore it is hardly rash to
infer, from this consensus of popular customs, that
the Greeks and Romans, like the other Aryan
peoples of Europe, once practised forms of tree-
worship similar to those which are still kept up by
our peasantry. In the palmy days of ancient
civilisation, no doubt, the worship had sunk to the
level of vulgar superstition and rustic merrymaking,
as it has done among ourselves. We need not
therefore be surprised that the traces of such
popular rites are few and slight in ancient literature.
They are not less so in the polite literature of
modern Europe ; and the negative argument cannot
be allowed to go for more in the one case than in
the other. Enough, however, of positive evidence
remains to confirm the presumption drawn from
analogy. Much of this evidence has been collected
and analysed with his usual learning and judgment
by W. Mannhardt.[2] Here I shall content myself
with citing certain Greek festivals which seem to be

---

[1] Above, pp. 69 *sqq.*, 85.   [2] See especially his *Antike Wald-und Feldkulte.*

the classical equivalents of an English May Day in the olden time.

Every few years the Boeotians of Plataea held a festival which they called the Little Daedala. On the day of the festival they went out into an ancient oak forest, the trees of which were of gigantic girth. Here they set some boiled meat on the ground, and watched the birds that gathered round it. When a raven was observed to carry off a piece of the meat and settle on an oak, the people followed it and cut down the tree. With the wood of the tree they made an image, dressed it as a bride, and placed it on a bullock-cart with a bridesmaid beside it. It seems then to have been drawn to the banks of the river Asopus and back to the town, attended by a piping and dancing crowd. After the festival the image was put away and kept till the celebration of the Great Daedala, which fell only once in sixty years. On this great occasion all the images that had accumulated from the celebrations of the Little Daedala were dragged on carts in solemn procession to the river Asopus, and then to the top of Mount Cithaeron. Here an altar had been constructed of square blocks of wood fitted together and surmounted by a heap of brushwood. Animals were sacrificed by being burned on the altar, and the altar itself, together with the images, were consumed by the flames. The blaze, we are told, rose to a prodigious height and was seen for many miles. To explain the origin of the festival it was said that once upon a time Hera had quarrelled with Zeus and left him in high dudgeon. To lure her back Zeus gave out that he was about to marry the nymph Plataea, daughter of the river Asopus. He caused a wooden image to be made, dressed and veiled as a bride, and conveyed on a bullock-cart. Transported with rage and jealousy, Hera flew to the cart, and tearing off the veil of the pretended bride, discovered the deceit that had been practised on her. Her rage was now changed to laughter, and she became reconciled to her husband Zeus.[1]

The resemblance of this festival to some of the European spring and midsummer festivals is tolerably close. We have seen that in Russia at Whitsuntide the villagers go out into the wood, fell a birch-tree, dress it in woman's clothes, and bring it back to the village with dance and song. On the third day it is thrown into the water.[2] Again, we have seen that in Bohemia on Midsummer Eve the village lads fell a tall fir or pine-tree in the wood and set it up on a height, where it is adorned with garlands, nosegays, and ribbons, and afterwards burnt.[3] The reason for burning the tree will appear afterwards; the custom itself is not uncommon in modern Europe. In some parts of the Pyrenees a tall and slender tree is cut down on May Day and kept till Midsummer Eve. It is then rolled to the top of a hill, set up, and burned.[4] In Angoulême on St. Peter's Day, 29th June, a tall leafy poplar is set up in the market-place and burned.[5] In Cornwall "there was formerly a great bonfire on midsummer-eve; a large summer pole was fixed in the centre, round which the fuel was heaped up. It had a large bush on the top of it."[6] In Dublin on May-morning boys used to go out and cut a May-bush, bring it back to town, and then burn it.[7]

[1] Pausanias, ix. 3; Plutarch, *ap.* Eusebius, *Praepar. Evang.* iii. 1 *sq.*
[2] Above, p. 76 *sq.*
[3] Above, p. 79.
[4] *B. K.* p. 177.
[5] *B. K.* p. 177 *sq.*
[6] Brand, *Popular Antiquities*, i. 318, Bohn's ed. ; *B. K.* p. 178.
[7] Hone, *Every-day Book*, ii. 595 *sq.*; *B. K.* p. 178.

Probably the Boeotian festival belonged to the same class of rites. It represented the marriage of the powers of vegetation in spring or midsummer, just as the same event is represented in modern Europe by a King and Queen or a Lord and Lady of the May. In the Boeotian, as in the Russian, ceremony the tree dressed as a woman represents the English May-pole and May-queen in one. All such ceremonies, it must be remembered, are not, or at least were not originally, mere spectacular or dramatic exhibitions. They are magical charms designed to produce the effect which they dramatically represent. If the revival of vegetation in spring is represented by the awakening of a sleeper, the representation is intended actually to quicken the growth of leaves and blossoms ; if the marriage of the powers of vegetation is represented by a King and Queen of May, the idea is that the powers so represented will really be rendered more productive by the ceremony. In short, all these spring and midsummer festivals fall under the head of sympathetic magic. The event which it is desired to bring about is represented dramatically, and the very representation is believed to effect, or at least to contribute to, the production of the desired event. In the case of the Daedala the story of Hera's quarrel with Zeus and her sullen retirement may perhaps without straining be interpreted as a mythical expression for a bad season and the failure of the crops. The same disastrous effects were attributed to the anger and seclusion of Demeter after the loss of her daughter Proserpine.[1] Now the institution of a festival is often explained by a mythical story of the occurrence upon a particular occasion of those very calamities which it is the real

---

[1] Pausanias, viii. 42.

object of the festival to avert; so that if we know the myth told to account for the historical origin of the festival, we can often infer from it the real intention with which the festival was celebrated. If, therefore, the origin of the Daedala was explained by a story of a failure of crops and consequent famine, we may infer that the real object of the festival was to prevent the occurrence of such disasters; and, if I am right in my interpretation of the festival, the object was supposed to be effected by a dramatic representation of the marriage of the divinities most concerned with the production of vegetation.[1] The marriage of Zeus and Hera was dramatically represented at annual festivals in various parts of Greece,[2] and it is at least a fair conjecture that the nature and intention of these ceremonies were such as I have assigned to the Plataean festival of the Daedala; in other words, that Zeus and Hera at these festivals were the Greek equivalents of the Lord and Lady of the May. Homer's glowing picture of Zeus and Hera couched on fresh hyacinths and crocuses,[3] like Milton's description of the dalliance of Zephyr and Aurora, "as he met her once a-Maying," was perhaps painted from the life.

Still more confidently may the same character be vindicated for the annual marriage at Athens of the

---

[1] Once upon a time the Wotjaks of Russia, being distressed by a series of bad harvests, ascribed the calamity to the wrath of one of their gods, *Keremet*, at being unmarried. So they went in procession to the sacred grove, riding on gaily-decked waggons, as they do when they are fetching home a bride. At the sacred grove they feasted all night, and next morning they cut in the grove a square piece of turf which they took home with them. "What they meant by this marriage ceremony," says the writer who reports it, "it is not easy to imagine. Perhaps, as Bechterew thinks, they meant to marry *Keremet* to the kindly and fruitful *mukylč in*, the earth-wife, in order that she might influence him for good."—Max Buch, *Die Wotjäken, eine ethnologische Studie* (Stuttgart, 1882), p. 137.

[2] At Cnossus in Crete, Diodorus, v. 72; at Samos, Lactantius, *Instit.* i. 17; at Athens, Photius, *sv.* ἱερὸν γάμον; *Etymolog. Magn. sv.* ἱερομνήμονες, p. 468. 52.

[3] *Iliad*, xiv. 347 *sqq.*

Queen to Dionysus in the Flowery Month (*Anthes-terion*) of spring.[1]   For Dionysus, as we shall see later on, was essentially a god of vegetation, and the Queen at Athens was a purely religious or priestly functionary.[2] Therefore at their annual marriage in spring he can hardly have been anything but a King, and she a Queen, of May.   The women who attended the Queen at the marriage ceremony would correspond to the bridesmaids who wait on the May-queen.[3]   Again, the story, dear to poets and artists, of the forsaken and sleeping Ariadne waked and wedded by Dionysus, resembles so closely the little drama acted by French peasants of the Alps on May Day[4] that, considering the character of Dionysus as a god of vegetation, we can hardly help regarding it as the description of a spring ceremony corresponding to the French one.   In point of fact the marriage of Dionysus and Ariadne is believed by Preller to have been acted every spring in Crete.[5] His evidence, indeed, is inconclusive, but the view itself is probable.   If I am right in instituting the comparison, the chief difference between the French and the Greek ceremonies must have been that in the former the sleeper was the forsaken bridegroom, in the latter the forsaken bride; and the group of stars in the sky, in which fancy saw Ariadne's wedding-crown,[6] could only have been a translation to heaven of the garland worn by the Greek girl who played the Queen of May.

On the whole, alike from the analogy of modern

---

[1] Demosthenes, *Neaer.* § 73 *sqq.* p. 1369 *sq.*; Hesychius, *svv.* Διονύσου γάμος and γεραραί; *Etymol. Magn. sv.* γεραίραι; Pollux, viii. 108; Aug. Mommsen, *Heortologie*, p. 357 *sqq.*; Hermann, *Gottesdienstliche Alter-thümer*,[2] § 32. 15, § 58. 11 *sqq.*

[2] Above, p. 7.

[3] Above, p. 94.

[4] Above, p. 95 *sq.*

[5] Preller, *Griech. Mythol.*[3] i. 559.

[6] Hyginus, *Astronomica*, i. 5.

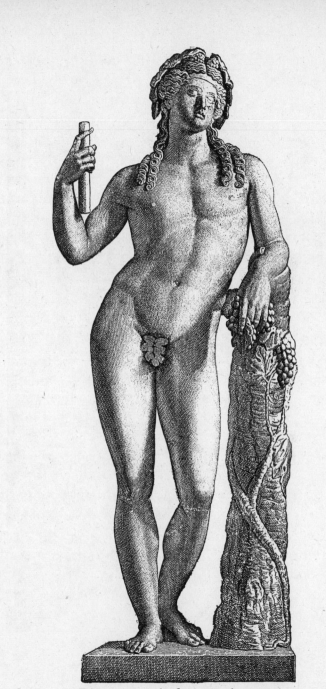

Dionysus, god of wine and vegetation.

The sleeping Ariadne, who in the legend was wakened and wed by Dionysus.

folk-custom and from the facts of ancient ritual and
mythology, we are justified in concluding that the
archaic forms of tree-worship disclosed by the spring
and midsummer festivals of our peasants were practised
by the Greeks and Romans in prehistoric times. Do
then these forms of tree-worship help to explain the
priesthood of Aricia, the subject of our inquiry? I
believe they do. In the first place the attributes of
Diana, the goddess of the Arician grove, are those of
a tree-spirit or sylvan deity. Her sanctuaries were in
groves, indeed every grove was her sanctuary,[1] and she
is often associated with the wood-god Silvanus in
inscriptions.[2] Like a tree-spirit, she helped women in
travail, and in this respect her reputation appears to
have stood high at the Arician grove, if we may judge
from the votive offerings found on the spot.[3] Again,
she was the patroness of wild animals;[4] just as in
Finland the wood-god Tapio was believed to care for
the wild creatures that roamed the wood, they being
considered his cattle.[5] So, too, the Samogitians
deemed the birds and beasts of the woods sacred,
doubtless because they were under the protection of
the god of the wood.[6] Again, there are indications
that domestic cattle were protected by Diana,[7] as they
certainly were supposed to be by Silvanus.[8] But
we have seen that special influence over cattle is
ascribed to wood-spirits; in Finland the herds enjoyed
the protection of the wood-gods both while they were

[1] Servius on Virgil, *Georg.* iii.
332, *nam, ut diximus, et omnis quercus Jovi est consecrata, et omnis lucus
Dianae.*

[2] Roscher's *Lexikon d. Griech u.
Röm. Mythologie,* c. 1005.

[3] See above, p. 4. For Diana in this
character, see Roscher, *op. cit.* c. 1007.

[4] Roscher, c. 1006 *sq.*

[5] Castren, *Finnische Mythologie,* p. 97.

[6] Mathias Michov, "De Sarmatia
Asiana atque Europea," in *Novus Orbis
regionum ac insularum veteribus incognitarum,* p. 457.

[7] Livy, i. 45; Plutarch, *Quaest.
Rom.* 4.

[8] Virgil, *Aen.* viii. 600 *sq.,* with
Servius's note.

in their stalls and while they strayed in the forest.[1]
Lastly, in the sacred spring which bubbled, and the
perpetual fire which seems to have burned in the
Arician grove,[2] we may perhaps detect traces of other
attributes of forest gods, the power, namely, to make
the rain to fall and the sun to shine.[3]   This last attribute perhaps explains why Virbius, the companion
deity of Diana at Nemi, was by some believed to be
the sun.[4]

Thus the cult of the Arician grove was essentially
that of a tree-spirit or wood deity.   But our examination of European folk-custom demonstrated that a tree-
spirit is frequently represented by a living person, who
is regarded as an embodiment of the tree-spirit and
possessed of its fertilising powers ; and our previous
survey of primitive belief proved that this conception of a god incarnate in a living man is common
among rude races.   Further we have seen that the
living person who is believed to embody in himself the tree-spirit is often called a king, in which
respect, again, he strictly represents the tree-spirit.
For the sacred cedar of the Gilgit tribes is called,
as we have seen, "the Dreadful King";[5] and
the chief forest god of the Finns, by name Tapio,
represented as an old man with a brown beard, a high
hat of fir-cones and a coat of tree-moss, was styled the
Wood King, Lord of the Woodland, Golden King of
the Wood.[6]   May not then the King of the Wood in
the Arician grove have been, like the King of May,
the Grass King, and the like, an incarnation of the
tree-spirit or spirit of vegetation ?   His title, his sacred

---

[1] Castren, *op. cit.* p. 97 *sq.*
[2] Above, p. 4 *sq.*
[3] Above, p. 66 *sq.*   [4] Above, p. 6.
[5] Above, p. 71.
[6] Castren, *Finnische Mythologie*, pp. 92, 95.

office, and his residence in the grove all point to this
conclusion, which is confirmed by his relation to the
Golden Bough. For since the King of the Wood
could only be assailed by him who had plucked the
Golden Bough, his life was safe from assault so long
as the bough or the tree on which it grew remained
uninjured. In a sense, therefore, his life was bound
up with that of the tree; and thus to some extent he
stood to the tree in the same relation in which the
incorporate or immanent tree-spirit stands to it. The
representation of the tree-spirit both by the King of
the Wood and by the Golden Bough (for it will hardly
be disputed that the Golden Bough was looked upon
as a very special manifestation of the divine life of the
grove) need not surprise us, since we have found that
the tree-spirit is not unfrequently thus represented in
double, first by a tree or a bough, and second by a
living person.

On the whole then, if we consider his double character as king and priest, his relation to the Golden
Bough, and the strictly woodland character of the
divinity of the grove, we may provisionally assume
that the King of the Wood, like the May King and
his congeners of Northern Europe, was deemed a
living incarnation of the tree-spirit. As such he would
be credited with those miraculous powers of sending
rain and sunshine, making the crops to grow, women
to bring forth, and flocks and herds to multiply, which
are popularly ascribed to the tree-spirit itself. The
reputed possessor of powers so exalted must have been
a very important personage, and in point of fact his
influence appears to have extended far and wide. For[1]
in the days when the champaign country around was

---

[1] *Historic. Roman. Fragm.* ed. Peter, p. 52 (first ed.)

still parcelled out among the petty tribes who composed the Latin League, the sacred grove on the
Alban Mountain is known to have been an object
of their common reverence and care.   And just as
the kings of Cambodia used to send offerings to the
mystic Kings of Fire and Water far in the dim depths
of the tropical forest, so, we may well believe, from all
sides of the broad Latian plain the eyes and steps of
Italian pilgrims turned to the quarter where, standing
sharply out against the faint blue line of the Apen-
nines or the deeper blue of the distant sea, the Alban
Mountain rose before them, the home of the mysterious priest of Nemi, the King of the Wood.

CHAPTER II

THE PERILS OF THE SOUL

"O liebe flüchtige Seele
Dir ist so bang und weh!"
HEINE.

§ 1.—*Royal and priestly taboos*

IN the preceding chapter we saw that in early
society the king or priest is often thought to be
endowed with supernatural powers or to be an incarnation of a deity; in consequence of which the course
of nature is supposed to be more or less under his
control, and he is held responsible for bad weather,
failure of the crops, and similar calamities. Thus far
it appears to be assumed that the king's power over
nature, like that over his subjects and slaves, is
exerted through definite acts of will; and therefore
if drought, famine, pestilence, or storms arise, the
people attribute the misfortune to the negligence or
guilt of their king, and punish him accordingly with
stripes and bonds, or, if he remains obdurate, with
deposition and death. Sometimes, however, the course
of nature, while regarded as dependent on the king,
is supposed to be partly independent of his will. His
person is considered, if we may express it so, as the

dynamical centre of the universe, from which lines of force radiate to all quarters of the heaven ; so that any motion of his—the turning of his head, the lifting of his hand — instantaneously affects and may seriously disturb some part of nature.   He is the point of support on which hangs the balance of the world ; and the slightest irregularity on his part may over-throw the delicate equipoise.   The greatest care must, therefore, be taken both by and of him ; and his whole life, down to its minutest details, must be so regulated that no act of his, voluntary or involuntary, may dis-arrange or upset the established order of nature.   Of this class of monarchs the Mikado or Dairi, the spiritual emperor of Japan, is a typical example.   He is an incarnation of the sun goddess, the deity who rules the universe, gods and men included ; once a year all the gods wait upon him and spend a month at his court.   During that month, the name of which means " without gods," no one frequents the temples, for they are believed to be deserted.[1]

The following description of the Mikado's mode of life was written about two hundred years ago :[2]—

" Even to this day the princes descended of this family, more particularly those who sit on the throne, are looked upon as persons most holy in themselves, and as Popes by birth.   And, in order to preserve these advantageous notions in the minds of their sub-jects, they are obliged to take an uncommon care of their sacred persons, and to do such things, which, examined according to the customs of other nations,

[1] *Manners and Customs of the Japan-ese in the Nineteenth Century.   From recent Dutch Visitors to Japan, and the German of Dr. Ph. Fr. von Siebold* (London, 1841), p. 141 *sqq.*

[2] Kaempfer, " History of Japan," in Pinkerton's *Voyages and Travels,* vii. 716 *sq.*

would be thought ridiculous and impertinent. It will not be improper to give a few instances of it. He thinks that it would be very prejudicial to his dignity and holiness to touch the ground with his feet; for this reason, when he intends to go anywhere, he must be carried thither on men's shoulders. Much less will they suffer that he should expose his sacred person to the open air, and the sun is not thought worthy to shine on his head. There is such a holiness ascribed to all the parts of his body, that he dares to cut off neither his hair, nor his beard, nor his nails. However, lest he should grow too dirty, they may clean him in the night when he is asleep ; because, they say, that which is taken from his body at that time hath been stolen from him, and that such a theft doth not prejudice his holiness or dignity. In ancient times, he was obliged to sit on the throne for some hours every morning, with the imperial crown on his head, but to sit altogether like a statue, without stirring either hands or feet, head or eyes, nor indeed any part of his body, because, by this means, it was thought that he could preserve peace and tranquillity in his empire ; for if, unfortunately, he turned himself on one side or the other, or if he looked a good while towards any part of his dominions, it was apprehended that war, famine, fire, or some great misfortune was near at hand to desolate the country. But it having been afterwards discovered that the imperial crown was the palladium which by its mobility could preserve peace in the empire, it was thought expedient to deliver his imperial person, consecrated only to idleness and pleasures, from this burthensome duty, and therefore the crown is at present placed on the throne for some hours every morning. His victuals must be dressed every time in new pots, and served at table in new dishes : both are very clean and neat, but made only of common clay ; that without any considerable expense they may be laid aside, or broken, after they have served once. They are generally broke, for fear they should come into the hands of laymen, for they believe religiously that if any layman should presume to eat his food out of these sacred dishes, it would swell and inflame his mouth and throat. The like ill effect is dreaded from the Dairi's sacred habits ; for they believe that if a layman should wear them, without the Emperor's express leave or command, they would occasion swellings and pains in all parts of his body." To the same effect an earlier account of the Mikado says : "It was considered as a shameful degradation for him even to touch the ground with his foot. The sun and moon were not even permitted to shine upon his head. None of the superfluities of the body were ever taken from him, neither his hair, his beard, nor his nails were cut. Whatever he eat was dressed in new vessels."[1]

Similar priestly or rather divine kings are found, at a lower level of barbarism, on the west coast of Africa. At Shark Point near Cape Padron, in Lower Guinea, lives the priestly king Kukulu, alone in a wood. He may not touch a woman nor leave his house ; indeed he may not even quit his chair, in which he is obliged to sleep sitting, for if he lay down no wind would arise and navigation would be stopped. He regulates storms, and in general maintains a wholesome and

---

[1] Caron, "Account of Japan," in Pinkerton's *Voyages and Travels*, vii. 613. Compare Varenius, *Descriptio regni Japoniae*, p. 11, Nunquam *attingebant (quemadmodum et hodie id observat) pedes ipsius terram : radiis Solis caput nunquam illustrabatur : in apertum aërem non procedebat*, etc.

equable state of the atmosphere.[1]   In the kingdom of
Congo (West Africa) there was a supreme pontiff
called Chitomé or Chitombé, whom the negroes regarded as a god on earth and all powerful in heaven.
Hence before they would taste the new crops they
offered him the first-fruits, fearing that manifold misfortunes would befall them if they broke this rule.
When he left his residence to visit other places within
his jurisdiction, all married people had to observe strict
continence the whole time he was out; for it was supposed that any act of incontinence would prove fatal
to him.   And if he were to die a natural death, they
thought that the world would perish, and the earth,
which he alone sustained by his power and merit, would
immediately be annihilated.[2]   Amongst the semi-
barbarous nations of the New World, at the date of
the Spanish conquest, there were found hierarchies
or theocracies like those of Japan.   Some of these
we have already noticed.[3]   But the high pontiff of
the Zapotecs in Southern Mexico appears to have
presented a still closer parallel to the Mikado.   A
powerful rival to the king himself, this spiritual lord
governed Yopaa, one of the chief cities of the kingdom, with absolute dominion.   It is impossible, we
are told, to over-rate the reverence in which he was
held.   He was looked on as a god whom the earth
was not worthy to hold nor the sun to shine upon.
He profaned his sanctity if he even touched the
ground with his foot.   The officers who bore his
palanquin on their shoulders were members of the
highest families; he hardly deigned to look on any-

---

[1] A. Bastian, *Die deutsche Expedition an der Loango-Küste*, i. 287 *sq.* ;
cp. *id.*, p. 353 *sq.*

[2] Labat, *Relation historique de
l'Ethiopie Occidentale*, i. 254 *sqq.*

[3] Above, pp. 44, 49.

thing around him ; and all who met him fell with their
faces to the earth, fearing that death would overtake
them if they saw even his shadow. A rule of continence
was regularly imposed on the Zapotec priests, especially
upon the high pontiff; but "on certain days in each
year, which were generally celebrated with feasts and
dances, it was customary for the high priest to become
drunk. While in this state, seeming to belong neither
to heaven nor to earth, one of the most beautiful of the
virgins consecrated to the service of the gods was
brought to him." If the child she bore him was a
son, he was brought up as a prince of the blood,
and the eldest son succeeded his father on the pon-
tifical throne. [1] The supernatural powers attributed
to this pontiff are not specified, but probably they
resembled those of the Mikado and Chitomé.

Wherever, as in Japan and West Africa, it is
supposed that the order of nature, and even the existence of the world, is bound up with the life of the
king or priest, it is clear that he must be regarded by
his subjects as a source both of infinite blessing and
of infinite danger. On the one hand, the people have
to thank him for the rain and sunshine which foster
the fruits of the earth, for the wind which brings ships
to their coasts, and even for the existence of the earth
beneath their feet. But what he gives he can
refuse ; and so close is the dependence of nature on
his person, so delicate the balance of the system of
forces whereof he is the centre, that the slightest
irregularity on his part may set up a tremor which
shall shake the earth to its foundations. And

---

[1] Brasseur de Bourbourg, *Hist. des nations civilisées du Mexique et de
l'Amérique-centrale*, iii. 29 *sq.* ; Bancroft, *Native Races of the Pacific States*, ii.
142 *sq.*

if nature may be disturbed by the slightest involuntary act of the king, it is easy to conceive the
convulsion which his death might occasion. The
death of the Chitomé, as we have seen, was thought
to entail the destruction of the world. Clearly, therefore, out of a regard for their own safety, which might
be imperilled by any rash act of the king, and still
more by his death, the people will exact of their king
or priest a strict conformity to those rules, the
observance of which is necessary for his own preservation, and consequently for the preservation of
his people and the world. The idea that early
kingdoms are despotisms in which the people exist
only for the sovereign, is wholly inapplicable to the
monarchies we are considering. On the contrary,
the sovereign in them exists only for his subjects;
his life is only valuable so long as he discharges the
duties of his position by ordering the course of nature
for his people's benefit. So soon as he fails to do so
the care, the devotion, the religious homage which
they had hitherto lavished on him, cease and are
changed into hatred and contempt; he is dismissed
ignominiously, and may be thankful if he escapes with
his life. Worshipped as a god by them one day, he
is killed by them as a criminal the next. But in this
changed behaviour of the people there is nothing capri-
cious or inconsistent. On the contrary, their conduct
is entirely of a piece. If their king is their god, he is
or should be also their preserver; and if he will not
preserve them, he must make room for another who
will. So long, however, as he answers their expecta-
tions, there is no limit to the care which they take of
him, and which they compel him to take of himself.
A king of this sort lives hedged in by a ceremonious

etiquette, a network of prohibitions and observances, of which the intention is not to contribute to his dignity, much less to his comfort, but to restrain him from conduct which, by disturbing the harmony of nature, might involve himself, his people, and the universe in one common catastrophe. Far from adding to his comfort, these observances, by trammelling his every act, annihilate his freedom and often render the very life, which it is their object to preserve, a burden and sorrow to him.

Of the supernaturally endowed kings of Loango it is said that the more powerful a king is, the more taboos is he bound to observe; they regulate all his actions, his walking and his standing, his eating and drinking, his sleeping and waking.[1] To these restraints the heir to the throne is subject from infancy; but as he advances in life the number of abstinences and ceremonies which he must observe increases, "until at the moment that he ascends the throne he is lost in the ocean of rites and taboos."[2] The kings of Egypt, as we have seen,[3] were worshipped as gods, and the routine of their daily life was regulated in every detail by precise and unvarying rules. "The life of the kings of Egypt," says Diodorus,[4] "was not like that of other monarchs who are irresponsible and may do just what they choose; on the contrary, everything was fixed for them by law, not only their official duties, but even the details of their daily life. . . . The hours both of day and night were arranged at which the king had to do, not what he pleased, but what was prescribed for him. . . . For not only were the times

---

[1] Bastian, *Die deutsche Expedition an der Loango-Küste*, i. 355.

[2] Dapper, *Description de l'Afrique*, p. 336.

[3] P. 49 *sq.*

[4] *Bibl. Hist.* i. 70.

appointed at which he should transact public business or sit in judgment ; but the very hours for his walking and bathing and sleeping with his wife, and, in short, performing every act of life, were all settled. Custom enjoined a simple diet ; the only flesh he might eat was veal and goose, and he might only drink a prescribed quantity of wine." Of the taboos imposed on priests, the rules of life observed by the Flamen Dialis at Rome furnish a striking example. As the worship of Virbius at Nemi was conducted, as we have seen,[1] by a Flamen, who may possibly have been the King of the Wood himself, and whose mode of life may have resembled that of the Roman Flamen, these rules have a special interest for us. They were such as the following : The Flamen Dialis might not ride or even touch a horse, nor see an army under arms, nor wear a ring which was not broken, nor have a knot on any part of his garments ; no fire except a sacred fire might be taken out of his house ; he might not touch wheaten flour or leavened bread ; he might not touch or even name a goat, a dog, raw meat, beans, and ivy ; he might not walk under a vine ; the feet of his bed had to be daubed with mud ; his hair could be cut only by a free man and with a bronze knife, and his hair and nails when cut had to be buried under a lucky tree ; he might not touch a dead body nor enter a place where one was burned ; he might not see work being done on holy days ; he might not be uncovered in the open air ; if a man in bonds were taken into his house, he had to be unbound and the cords had to be drawn up through a hole in the roof and so let down into the street. His wife, the Flaminica, had to observe nearly the same rules, and others of her own

---

[1] P. 6.

besides. She might not ascend more than three steps of the kind of staircase called Greek; at a certain festival she might not comb her hair; the leather of her shoes might not be made from a beast that had died a natural death, but only from one that had been slain or sacrificed; if she heard thunder she was tabooed till she had offered an expiatory sacrifice.[1]

The burdensome observances attached to the royal or priestly office produced their natural effect. Either men refused to accept the office, which hence tended to fall into abeyance; or accepting it, they sank under its weight into spiritless creatures, cloistered recluses, from whose nerveless fingers the reigns of government slipped into the firmer grasp of men who were often content to wield the reality of sovereignty without its name. In some countries this rift in the supreme power deepened into a total and permanent separation of the spiritual and temporal powers, the old royal house retaining their purely religious functions, while the civil government passed into the hands of a younger and more vigorous race.

To take examples. We saw[2] that in Cambodia it is often necessary to force the kingships of Fire and Water upon the reluctant successors, and that in Savage Island the monarchy actually came to an end because at last no one could be induced to accept the dangerous distinction.[3] In some parts of West Africa, when the king dies, a family council is secretly held to determine his successor. He on whom the choice falls is suddenly seized, bound, and

---

[1] Aulus Gellius, x. 15; Plutarch, *Quaest. Rom.* 109-112; Pliny, *Nat. Hist.* xxviii. 146; Servius on Virgil, *Aen.* i. *vv.* 179, 448, iv. 518; Macrobius, *Saturn.* i. 16, 8 *sq.*; Festus, p. 161 A, ed. Müller. For more details see Marquardt, *Römische Staatsverwaltung*, iii.[2] 326 *sqq.*

[2] P. 54.

[3] P. 48.

thrown into the fetish-house, where he is kept in durance till he consents to accept the crown. Sometimes the heir finds means of evading the honour which it is sought to thrust upon him; a ferocious chief has been known to go about constantly armed, resolute to resist by force any attempt to set him on the throne.[1] The Mikados of Japan seem early to have resorted to the expedient of transferring the honours and burdens of supreme power to their infant children; and the rise of the Tycoons, long the temporal sovereigns of the country, is traced to the abdication of a certain Mikado in favour of his three-year-old son. The sovereignty having been wrested by a usurper from the infant prince, the cause of the Mikado was championed by Yoritomo, a man of spirit and conduct, who overthrew the usurper and restored to the Mikado the shadow, while he retained for himself the substance, of power. He bequeathed to his descendants the dignity he had won, and thus became the founder of the line of Tycoons. Down to the latter half of the sixteenth century the Tycoons were active and efficient rulers; but the same fate overtook them which had befallen the Mikados; entangled in the same inextricable web of custom and law, they degenerated into mere puppets, hardly stirring from their palaces and occupied in a perpetual round of empty ceremonies, while the real business of government was managed by the council of state.[2] In Tonquin the monarchy ran a similar course. Living like his predecessors in effeminacy and sloth, the king was driven from the throne by an ambitious adventurer named Mack, who from a fisherman had risen to be

---

[1] Bastian, *Die deutsche Expedition an der Loango-Küste*, i. 354 *sq.*; ii. 9, 11.

[2] *Manners and Customs of the Japanese*, pp. 199 *sqq.* 355 *sqq.*

Grand Mandarin. But the king's brother Tring put down the usurper and restored the king, retaining, however, for himself and his descendants the dignity of general of all the forces. Thenceforward the kings or *dovas*, though vested with the title and pomp of sovereignty, ceased to govern. While they lived secluded in their palaces, all real political power was wielded by the hereditary generals or *chovas*.[1] The custom regularly observed by the Tahitian kings of abdicating on the birth of a son, who was immediately proclaimed sovereign and received his father's homage, may perhaps have originated, like the similar custom occasionally practised by the Mikados, in a wish to shift to other shoulders the irksome burden of royalty; for in Tahiti as elsewhere the sovereign was subjected to a system of vexatious restrictions.[2] In Mangaia, another Polynesian island, religious and civil authority were lodged in separate hands, spiritual functions being discharged by a line of hereditary kings, while the temporal government was entrusted from time to time to a victorious war-chief, whose investiture, however, had to be completed by the king. To the latter were assigned the best lands, and he received daily offerings of the choicest food.[3] American examples of the partition of authority between an emperor and a pope have already been cited from the early history of Mexico and Colombia.[4]

---

[1] Richard, "History of Tonquin," in Pinkerton's *Voyages and Travels*, ix. 744 *sqq.*

[2] Ellis, *Polynesian Researches*, iii. 99 *sqq.* ed. 1836.

[3] Gill, *Myths and Songs of the South Pacific*, p. 293 *sqq.*   [4] Pp. 44, 113.

§ 2.—*The nature of the soul*

But if the object of the taboos observed by a divine king or priest is to preserve his life, the question arises, How is their observance supposed to effect this end ?   To understand this we must know the nature of the danger which threatens the king's life, and which it is the intention of the taboos to guard against.   We must, therefore, ask : What does early man understand by death ?   To what causes does he attribute it ? And how does he think it may be guarded against ?

As the savage commonly explains the processes of inanimate nature by supposing that they are produced by living beings working in or behind the phenomena, so he explains the phenomena of life itself.   If an animal lives and moves, it can only be, he thinks, because there is a little animal inside which moves it. If a man lives and moves, it can only be because he has a little man inside who moves him.   The animal inside the animal, the man inside the man, is the soul.   And as the activity of an animal or man is explained by the presence of the soul, so the repose of sleep or death is explained by its absence ; sleep or trance being the temporary, death being the permanent absence of the soul.   Hence if death be the permanent absence of the soul, the way to guard against it is either to prevent the soul from leaving the body, or, if it does depart, to secure that it shall return.   The precautions adopted by savages to secure one or other of these ends take the form of prohibitions or taboos, which are nothing but rules intended to ensure either the continued presence or the return of the soul.   In short, they are life-preservers or life-

guards.   These general statements will now be illustrated by examples.

Addressing some Australian blacks, a European
missionary said, "I am not one, as you think, but two."
Upon this they laughed.   "You may laugh as much
as you like," continued the missionary, " I tell you that
I am two in one; this great body that you see is one;
within that there is another little one which is not
visible.   The great body dies, and is buried, but the
little body flies away when the great one dies."   To
this some of the blacks replied, "Yes, yes.   We also
are two, we also have a little body within the breast."
On being asked where the little body went after death,
some said it went behind the bush, others said it went
into the sea, and some said they did not know.[1]   The
Hurons thought that the soul had a head and body,
arms and legs; in short, that it was a complete little
model of the man himself.[2]   The Eskimos believe that
"the soul exhibits the same shape as the body it
belongs to, but is of a more subtle and ethereal nature."[3]
So exact is the resemblance of the mannikin to the
man, in other words, of the soul to the body, that, as
there are fat bodies and thin bodies, so there are fat
souls and thin souls;[4] as there are heavy bodies and
light bodies, long bodies and short bodies, so there are
heavy souls and light souls, long souls and short souls.
The people of Nias (an island to the west of Sumatra)
think that every man, before he is born, is asked how
long or how heavy a soul he would like, and a soul of
the desired weight or length is measured out to him.

---

[1] *Journal of the Anthropological Institute*, vii. 282.

[2] *Relations des Jesuites*, 1634, p. 17;
id., 1636, p. 104; *id.*, 1639, p. 43
(Canadian reprint).

[3] H. Rink, *Tales and Traditions of
the Eskimo*, p. 36.

[4] Gill, *Myths and Songs of the South
Pacific*, p. 171.

The heaviest soul ever given out weighs about ten grammes. The length of a man's life is proportioned to the length of his soul; children who die young had short souls.[1] Sometimes, however, as we shall see, the human soul is conceived not in human but in animal form.

The soul is commonly supposed to escape by the natural openings of the body, especially the mouth and nostrils. Hence in Celebes they sometimes fasten fish-hooks to a sick man's nose, navel, and feet, so that if his soul should try to escape it may be hooked and held fast.[2] One of the "properties" of a Haida medicine-man is a hollow bone, in which he bottles up departing souls, and so restores them to their owners.[3] The Marquesans used to hold the mouth and nose of a dying man, in order to keep him in life, by preventing his soul from escaping.[4] When any one yawns in their presence the Hindus always snap their thumbs, believing that this will hinder the soul from issuing through the open mouth.[5] The Itonamas in South America seal up the eyes, nose, and mouth of a dying person, in case his ghost should get out and carry off other people.[6] In Southern Celebes, to prevent the escape of a woman's soul at childbirth, the nurse ties a band as tightly as possible round the body of the expectant mother.[7] And lest the soul of the babe should

---

[1] H. Sundermann, "Die Insel Nias und die Mission daselbst," in *Allgemeine Missions - Zeitschrift*, bd. xi. October 1884, p. 453.

[2] B. F. Matthes, *Over de Bissoes of heidensche priesters en priesteressen der Boeginezen*, p. 24.

[3] G. M. Dawson, "On the Haida Indians of the Queen Charlotte Islands," in *Geological Survey of Canada, Report of Progress for* 1878-1879, pp. 123 B, 139 B.

[4] Waitz, *Anthropologie der Naturvölker*, vi. 397 *sq.*

[5] *Panjab Notes and Queries*, ii. No. 665.

[6] D'Orbigny, *L'Homme Américain*, ii. 241; *Transact. Ethnol. Soc. of London*, iii. 322 *sq.*; Bastian, *Culturländer des alten Amerika*, i. 476.

[7] B. F. Matthes, *Bijdragen tot de Ethnologie van Zuid - Celebes*, p. 54.

escape and be lost as soon as it is born, the Alfoers
of Celebes, when a birth is about to take place, are
careful to close every opening in the house, even the
keyhole; and they stop up every chink and cranny in
the walls. Also they tie up the mouths of all animals
inside and outside the house, for fear one of them
might swallow the child's soul. For a similar reason
all persons present in the house, even the mother
herself, are obliged to keep their mouths shut the
whole time the birth is taking place. When the
question was put, Why they did not hold their noses
also, lest the child's soul should get into one of them?
the answer was that breath being exhaled as well as
inhaled through the nostrils, the soul would be expelled before it could have time to settle down.[1]

Often the soul is conceived as a bird ready to take
flight. This conception has probably left traces in
most languages,[2] and it lingers as a metaphor in poetry.
But what is metaphor to a modern European poet
was sober earnest to his savage ancestor, and is still
so to many people. The Malays carry out the
conception in question to its practical conclusion. If
the soul is a bird on the wing, it may be attracted by
rice, and so prevented from taking its perilous flight.
Thus in Java when a child is placed on the ground for
the first time (a moment which uncultured people seem
to regard as especially dangerous), it is put in a hen-
coop and the mother makes a clucking sound, as if she
were calling hens.[3] Amongst the Battas of Sumatra,
when a man returns from a dangerous enterprise, grains
of rice are placed on his head, and these grains are

[1] Zimmermann, *Die Inseln des Indischen und Stillen Meeres*, ii. 386 *sq.*

[2] Cp. the Greek ποτάομαι, ἀνα-
πτερόω, etc.

[3] G. A. Wilken, "Het animisme
bij de volken van den Indischen
Archipel," in *De Indische Gids*, June
1884, p. 944.

called *padiruma tondi*, that is, " means to make the soul
(*tondi*) stay at home." In Java also rice is placed on
the head of persons who have escaped a great danger
or have returned home unexpectedly after it had been
supposed that they were lost.[1] In Celebes they
think that a bridegroom's soul is apt to fly away at
marriage, so coloured rice is scattered over him to
induce it to stay. And, in general, at festivals in
South Celebes rice is strewed on the head of the
person in whose honour the festival is held, with the
object of detaining his soul, which at such times is
in especial danger of being lured away by envious
demons.[2]

The soul of a sleeper is supposed to wander away
from his body and actually to visit the very places of
which he dreams. But this absence of the soul has its
dangers, for if from any cause it should be permanently
detained away from the body, the person, deprived of
his soul, must die.[3] Many causes may detain the
sleeper's soul. Thus, his soul may meet the soul of
another sleeper and the two souls may fight ; if a
Guinea negro wakens with sore bones in the morning,
he thinks that his soul has been thrashed by another
soul in sleep.[4] Or it may meet the soul of a person
just deceased and be carried off by it ; hence in the
Aru Islands the inmates of a house will not sleep the
night after a death has taken place in it, because the
soul of the deceased is supposed to be still in the house

---

[1] Wilken, *l.c.*

[2] B. F. Matthes, *Bijdragen tot de
Ethnologie van Zuid-Celebes*, p. 33 ; *id.,
Over de Bissoes of heidensche priesters
en priesteressen der Boeginezen*, p. 9 *sq.*;
*id., Makassaarsch-Hollandsch Woor-
denboek*, *svv.* Kôerrôe and soemâñgá, pp.
41, 569. Of these two words, the

former means the sound made in calling
fowls, and the latter means the soul. The
expression for the ceremonies described
in the text is *ápakôerrôe soemâñgá.*

[3] Shway Yoe, *The Burman, his Life
and Notions*, ii. 100.

[4] J. L. Wilson, *West Afrika*, p. 162
sq. (German translation).

and they fear to meet it in a dream.[1]   Again, the soul
may be prevented by physical force from returning.
The Santals tell how a man fell asleep, and growing
very thirsty, his soul, in the form of a lizard, left his
body and entered a pitcher of water to drink.   Just
then the owner of the pitcher happened to cover it;
so the soul could not return to the body and the man
died.   While his friends were preparing to burn the
body some one uncovered the pitcher to get water.
The lizard thus escaped and returned to the body,
which immediately revived; so the man rose up and
asked his friends why they were weeping.   They told
him they thought he was dead and were about to burn
his body.   He said he had been down a well to get
water but had found it hard to get out and had just
returned.   So they saw it all.[2]   A similar story is
reported from Transylvania as follows.   In the account
of a witch's trial at Mühlbach last century it is said
that a woman had engaged two men to work in her
vineyard.   After noon they all lay down to rest as
usual.   An hour later the men got up and tried to
waken the woman, but could not.   She lay motionless
with her mouth wide open.   They came back at sunset and still she lay like a corpse.   Just at that moment
a big fly came buzzing past, which one of the men
caught and shut up in his leathern pouch.   Then
they tried again to waken the woman but could not.
Afterwards they let out the fly; it flew straight into
the woman's mouth and she awoke.   On seeing

---

[1] J. G. F. Riedel, *De sluik-en
kroesharige rassen tusschen Selebes en
Papua*, p. 267.   For detention of
sleeper's soul by spirits and consequent
illness, see also Mason, quoted in
Bastian's *Die Völker des östlichen Asien*,
ii. 387 *note*.

[2] *Indian Antiquary*, 1878, vii.
273; Bastian, *Völkerstämme am
Brahmaputra*, p. 127. Similar story
(lizard form of soul not mentioned) told
by Hindus, *Panjab Notes and Queries*,
iii. No. 679.

this the men had no further doubt that she was a witch.[1]

It is a common rule with primitive people not to waken a sleeper, because his soul is away and might not have time to get back; so if the man wakened without his soul, he would fall sick. If it is absolutely necessary to waken a sleeper, it must be done very gradually, to allow the soul time to return.[2] In Bombay it is thought equivalent to murder to change the appearance of a sleeper, as by painting his face in fantastic colours or giving moustaches to a sleeping woman. For when the soul returns, it will not be able to recognise its body and the person will die.[3] The Servians believe that the soul of a sleeping witch often leaves her body in the form of a butterfly. If during its absence her body be turned round, so that her feet are placed where her head was before, the butterfly soul will not find its way back into her body through the mouth, and the witch will die.[4]

But in order that a man's soul should quit his body, it is not necessary that he should be asleep.

---

[1] E. Gerard, *The Land beyond the Forest*, ii. 27 *sq.* A similar story is told in Holland, J. W. Wolf, *Nederlandsche Sagen*, No. 251, p. 344 *sq.* The stories of Hermotimus and King Gunthram belong to the same class. In the latter the king's soul comes out of his mouth as a small reptile. The soul of Aristeas issued from his mouth in the form of a raven. Pliny, *Nat. Hist.* vii. § 174; Lucian, *Musc. Encom.* 7; Paulus, *Hist. Langobardorum*, iii. 34. In an East Indian story of the same type the sleeper's soul issues from his nose in the form of a cricket. Wilken in *De Indische Gids*, June 1884, p. 940. In a Swabian story a girl's soul creeps out of her mouth in the form of a white mouse. Birlinger, *Volksthümliches aus Schwaben*, i. 303.

[2] Shway Yoe, *The Burman*, ii. 103; Bastian, *Die Völker des östlichen Asien*, ii. 389; Blumentritt, "Der Ahnencultus und die religiösen Anschauungen der Malaien des Philippinen-Archipels," in *Mittheilungen d. Wiener Geogr. Gesellschaft*, 1882, p. 209; Riedel, *De sluik-en kroesharige rassen tusschen Selebes en Papua*, p. 440; *id.*, "Die Landschaft Dawan oder West-Timor," in *Deutsche Geographische Blätter*, x. 280.

[3] *Panjab Notes and Queries*, iii. No. 530.

[4] Ralston, *Songs of the Russian People*, p. 117 *sq.*

It may quit him in his waking hours, and then sickness or (if the absence is prolonged) death will be the result. Thus the Mongols sometimes explain sickness by supposing that the patient's soul is absent, and either does not care to return to its body or cannot find the way back. To secure the return of the soul it is therefore necessary on the one hand to make its body as attractive as possible, and on the other hand to show it the way home. To make the body attractive all the sick man's best clothes and most valued possessions are placed beside him ; he is washed, incensed, and made as comfortable as possible ; and all his friends march thrice round the hut calling out the sick man's name and coaxing his soul to return. To help the soul to find its way back a coloured cord is stretched from the patient's head to the door of the hut. The priest in his robes reads a list of the horrors of hell and the dangers incurred by souls which wilfully absent themselves from their bodies. Then turning to the assembled friends and the patient he asks, " Is it come ? " All answer Yes, and bowing to the returning soul throw seed over the sick man. The cord which guided the soul back is then rolled up and placed round the patient's neck, who must wear it for seven days without taking it off. No one may frighten or hurt him, lest his soul, not yet familiar with its body, should again take flight.[1] In an Indian story a king conveys his soul into the dead body of a Brahman, and a hunchback conveys his soul into the deserted body of the king. The hunchback is now king and the king is a Brahman. However,

---

[1] Bastian, *Die Seele und ihre Erscheinungwesen in der Ethnographie*, p. 36.

the hunchback is induced to show his skill by transferring his soul to the dead body of a parrot, and the
king seizes the opportunity to regain possession of
his own body.[1]   In another Indian story a Brahman
reanimates the dead body of a king by conveying
his own soul into it.   Meantime the Brahman's
body has been burnt, and his soul is obliged to remain
in the body of the king.[2]

The departure of the soul is not always voluntary.   It may be extracted from the body against its
will by ghosts, demons, or sorcerers.   Hence, when
a funeral is passing the house, the Karens of Burma
tie their children with a special kind of string to a
particular part of the house, in case the souls of
the children should leave their bodies and go into
the corpse which is passing.   The children are
kept tied in this way until the corpse is out of sight.[3]
And after the corpse has been laid in the grave, but
before the earth has been filled in, the mourners and
friends range themselves round the grave, each
with a bamboo split lengthwise in one hand and a
little stick in the other ; each man thrusts his bamboo
into the grave, and drawing the stick along the
groove of the bamboo points out to his soul that
in this way it may easily climb up out of the grave.
While the earth is being filled in, the bamboos are
kept out of the way, lest the souls should be in
them, and so should be inadvertently buried with
the earth as it is being thrown into the grave ; and
when the people leave the spot they carry away
the bamboos, begging their souls to come with

---

[1] *Pantschatantra*, Benfey, p. 124 *sqq.*
[2] *Katha Sarit Ságara*, trans. Taw-
ney, i. 21 *sq.*

[3] E. B. Cross, "On the Karens,"
in *Journal of the American Oriental
Society*, iv. 311.

them.[1]   Further, on returning from the grave each
Karen provides himself with three little hooks made
of branches of trees, and calling his spirit to follow
him, at short intervals, as he returns, he makes a
motion as if hooking it, and then thrusts the hook
into the ground. This is done to prevent the soul
of the living from staying behind with the soul of
the dead.[2]   When a mother dies leaving a young
baby, the Burmese think that the "butterfly" or
soul of the baby follows that of the mother, and that
if it is not recovered the child must die. So a wise
woman is called in to get back the baby's soul. She
places a mirror near the corpse, and on the mirror a
piece of feathery cotton down. Holding a cloth in
her open hands at the foot of the mirror, she with wild
words entreats the mother not to take with her the
"butterfly" or soul of her child, but to send it back.
As the gossamer down slips from the face of the
mirror she catches it in the cloth and tenderly places
it on the baby's breast. The same ceremony is sometimes observed when one of two children that have
played together dies, and is thought to be luring away
the soul of its playmate to the spirit-land. It is sometimes performed also for a bereaved husband or wife.[3]
In the Island of Keisar (East Indies) it is thought im-
prudent to go near a grave at night, lest the ghosts
should catch and keep the soul of the passer-by.[4] The
Key Islanders believe that the souls of their forefathers, angry at not receiving food, make people sick
by detaining their souls. So they lay offerings of food

---

[1] A. R. M'Mahon, *The Karens of
the Golden Chersonese*, p. 318.
[2] F. Mason, "Physical Character of
the Karens," in *Journal of the Asiatic
Society of Bengal*, 1866, pt. ii. p. 28 *sq.*
[3] C. J. S. F. Forbes, *British*

Burma, p. 99 *sq.* ; Shway Yoe, *The
Burman*, ii. 102 ; Bastian, *Die
Völker des östlichen Asien*, ii. 389.
[4] Riedel, *De sluik-en kroesharige
rassen tusschen Selebes en Papua*,
p. 414.

on the grave and beg their ancestors to allow the soul of the sick to return or to drive it home speedily if it should be lingering by the way.[1]

In Bolang Mongondo, a district in the west of Celebes, all sickness is ascribed to the ancestral spirits who have carried off the patient's soul. The object therefore is to bring back the patient's soul and restore it to the sufferer. An eye-witness has thus described the attempted cure of a sick boy. The priestesses, who acted as physicians, made a doll of cloth and fastened it to the point of a spear, which an old woman held upright. Round this doll the priestesses danced, uttering charms, and chirruping as when one calls a dog. Then the old woman lowered the point of the spear a little, so that the priestesses could reach the doll. By this time the soul of the sick boy was supposed to be in the doll, having been brought into it by the incantations. So the priestesses approached it cautiously on tiptoe and caught the soul in the many-coloured cloths which they had been waving in the air. Then they laid the soul on the boy's head, that is, they wrapped his head in the cloth in which the soul was supposed to be, and stood still for some moments with great gravity, holding their hands on the patient's head. Suddenly there was a jerk, the priestesses whispered and shook their heads, and the cloth was taken off—the soul had escaped. The priestesses gave chase to it, running round and round the house, clucking and gesticulating as if they were driving hens into a poultry-yard. At last they recaptured the soul at the foot of the stair and restored it to its owner as before.[2] Much in the same way an Australian

---

[1] Riedel, *op. cit.* p. **221** *sq*

[2] N. Ph. Wilken en J. A. Schwarz, "Het heidendom en de Islam in Bolaang Mongondou," in *Mededeelingen van wege het Nederlandsche Zendeling-genootschap*, 1867, xi. 263 *sq*.

medicine-man will sometimes bring the lost soul of a sick man into a puppet and restore it to the patient by pressing the puppet to his breast.[1] In Uea, one of the Loyalty Islands, the souls of the dead seem to have been credited with the power of stealing the souls of the living. For when a man was sick the soul-doctor would go with a large troop of men and women to the graveyard. Here the men played on flutes and the women whistled softly to lure the soul home. After this had gone on for some time they formed in procession and moved homewards, the flutes playing and the women whistling all the way, leading back the wandering soul and driving it gently along with open palms. On entering the patient's dwelling they commanded the soul in a loud voice to enter his body.[2] In Madagascar, when a sick man had lost his soul, his friends went to the family tomb, and making a hole in it, begged the soul of the patient's father to give them a soul for his son, who had none. So saying they clapped a bonnet on the hole, and folding up the soul in the bonnet, brought it to the patient, who put the bonnet on his head, and thus received a new soul or got back his old one.[3]

Often the abduction of a man's soul is set down to demons. The Annamites believe that when a man meets a demon and speaks to him, the demon inhales the man's breath and soul.[4] When a Dyak is about to leave a forest through which he has been walking alone, he never forgets to ask the demons to give him back his soul, for it may be that some forest-devil has

[1] James Dawson, *Australian Aborigines*, p. 57 *sq.*

[2] W. W. Gill, *Myths and Songs of the South Pacific*, p. 171 *sq.*

[3] G. A. Wilken, "Het animisme," in *De Indische Gids*, June 1884, p. 937.

[4] Landes, "Contes et légendes annamites," No. 76 in *Cochinchine Française, Excursions et Reconnaissances*, No. 23, p. 80.

carried it off. For the abduction of a soul may take place without its owner being aware of his loss, and it may happen either while he is awake or asleep.[1] In the Moluccas when a man is unwell it is thought that some devil has carried away his soul to the tree, mountain, or hill where he (the devil) dwells. A sorcerer having pointed out the devil's abode, the friends of the patient carry thither cooked rice, fruit, fish, raw eggs, a hen, a chicken, a silken robe, gold, armlets, etc. Having set out the food in order they pray, saying : "We come to offer to you, O devil, this offering of food, clothes, gold, etc. ; take it and release the soul of the patient for whom we pray. Let it return to his body and he who now is sick shall be made whole." Then they eat a little and let the hen loose as a ransom for the soul of the patient ; also they put down the raw eggs ; but the silken robe, the gold, and the armlets they take home with them. As soon as they are come to the house they place a flat bowl containing the offerings which have been brought back at the sick man's head, and say to him : "Now is your soul released, and you shall fare well and live to gray hairs on the earth."[2] A more modern account from the same region describes how the friend of the patient, after depositing his offerings on the spot where the missing soul is supposed to be, calls out thrice the name of the sick person, adding, "Come with me, come with me." Then he returns, making a motion with a cloth as if he had caught the soul in it. He must not look to right or left or speak a word to any one he meets, but must go straight to the patient's house. At the door he stands, and calling out the sick

---

[1] Perelaer, *Ethnographische Be-schrijving der Dajaks*, p. 26 *sq.*

[2] Fr. Valentyn, *Oud en nieuw Oost-Indiën*, iii. 13 *sq.*

person's name, asks whether he is returned. Being answered from within that he is returned, he enters and lays the cloth in which he has caught the soul on the patient's throat, saying, " Now you are returned to the house." Sometimes a substitute is provided ; a doll, dressed up in gay clothing and tinsel, is offered to the demon in exchange for the patient's soul with these words, " Give us back the ugly one which you have taken away and receive this pretty one instead." [1] Similarly the Mongols make up a horse of birch-bark and a doll, and invite the demon to take the doll instead of the patient and to ride away on the horse. [2]

Demons are especially feared by persons who have just entered on a new house. Hence at a house-warming among the Alfoers of Celebes the priest performs a ceremony for the purpose of restoring their souls to the inmates. He hangs up a bag at the place of sacrifice and then goes through a list of the gods. There are so many of them that this takes him the whole night through without stopping. In the morning he offers the gods an egg and some rice. By this time the souls of the household are supposed to be gathered in the bag. So the priest takes the bag, and holding it on the head of the master of the house says, " Here you have your soul—go (soul) to-morrow away again." He then does the same, saying the same words, to the housewife and all the other members of the family. [3] Amongst the same Alfoers one way of

---

[1] Van Schmidt, " Aanteekeningen, nopens de zeden, gewoonten en gebrui-ken, benevens de vooroordeelen en bij-gelovigheden der bevolking van de eilanden Saparoea, Haroekoe, Noessa Laut, en van een gedeelte van de zuid-kust van Ceram," in *Tijdschrift voor Neêrland's Indië*, 1843, dl. ii. 511 *sqq.*

[2] Bastian, *Die Seele*, p. 36 *sq.* ; J. G.

Gmelin, *Reise durch Sibirien*, ii. 359 *sq.*

[3] P. N. Wilken, " Bijdragen tot de kennis van de zeden en gewoonten der Alfoeren in de Minahassa," in *Mede-deelingen van wege het Nederlandsche Zendelinggenootschap*, 1863, vii. 146 *sq.* Why the priest, after restoring the soul, tells it to go away again, is not clear.

recovering a sick man's soul is to let down a bowl
by a belt out of a window and fish for the soul till
it is caught in the bowl and hauled up.[1]   Among
the same people, when a priest is bringing back a
sick man's soul which he has caught in a cloth,
he is preceded by a girl holding the large leaf of a
certain palm over his head as an umbrella to keep
him and the soul from getting wet, in case it should
rain ; and he is followed by a man brandishing a
sword to deter other souls from any attempt at
rescuing the captured soul.[2]

The Samoans tell how two young wizards, passing a house where a chief lay very sick, saw a
company of gods from the mountain sitting in the
doorway. They were handing from one to another
the soul of the dying chief. It was wrapped in
a leaf, and had been passed from the gods inside
the house to those sitting in the doorway. One of
the gods handed the soul to one of the wizards,
taking him for a god in the dark, for it was night.
Then all the gods rose up and went away ; but the
wizard kept the chief's soul. In the morning some
women went with a present of fine mats to fetch a
famous physician. The wizards were sitting on the
shore as the women passed, and they said to the
women, "Give us the mats and we will heal him."
So they went to the chief's house. He was very ill,
his jaw hung down, and his end seemed near. But
the wizards undid the leaf and let the soul into him
again, and forthwith he brightened up and lived.[3]

The Battas of Sumatra believe that the soul of a

---

[1] Riedel, "De Minahasa in 1825,"
in *Tijdschrift voor Indische Taal-Land-
en Volkenkunde*, xviii. 523.

[2] N. Graafland, *De Minahassa*, i.
327 *sq.*

[3] G. Turner, *Samoa*, p. 142 *sq.*

living man may transmigrate into the body of an
animal.   Hence, for example, the doctor is sometimes
desired to extract the patient's soul from the body
of a fowl, in which it has been hidden away by an evil
spirit.[1]

Sometimes the lost soul is brought back in a
visible shape.   In Melanesia a woman knowing that
a neighbour was at the point of death heard a rustling in her house, as of a moth fluttering, just at
the moment when a noise of weeping and lamentation told her that the soul was flown.   She caught
the fluttering thing between her hands and ran
with it, crying out that she had caught the soul.
But though she opened her hands above the
mouth of the corpse, it did not revive.[2]   The
Salish or Flathead Indians of Oregon believe that
a man's soul may be separated for a time from his
body without causing death and without the man
being aware of his loss.   It is necessary, however,
that the lost soul should be soon found and restored
to the man or he will die.   The name of the man who
has lost his soul is revealed in a dream to the
medicine-man, who hastens to inform the sufferer of
his loss.   Generally a number of men have sustained
a like loss at the same time ; all their names are
revealed to the medicine-man, and all employ him to
recover their souls.   The whole night long these
soulless men go about the village from lodge to lodge,
dancing and singing.   Towards daybreak they go
into a separate lodge, which is closed up so as to be

---

[1] J. B. Neumann, "Het Pane en
Bila - stroomgebied op het eiland
Sumatra," in *Tijdschrift van het
Nederlandsch Aardrijkskundig Genoot-
schap*, ii. de Serie, dl. iii., Afdeeling :

meer uitgebreide artikelen, No. 2
(1886), p. 302.
[2] Codrington, "Religious Beliefs and
Practices in Melanesia," in *Journal of
the Anthropological Institute*, x. 281.

totally dark. A small hole is then made in the roof, through which the medicine-man, with a bunch of feathers, brushes in the souls, in the shape of bits of bone and the like, which he receives on a piece of matting. A fire is next kindled, by the light of which the medicine-man sorts out the souls. First he puts aside the souls of dead people, of which there are usually several; for if he were to give the soul of a dead person to a living man, the man would die instantly. Next he picks out the souls of all the persons present, and making them all to sit down before him, he takes the soul of each, in the shape of a splinter of bone, wood, or shell, and placing it on the owner's head, pats it with many prayers and contortions till it descends into the heart and so resumes its proper place.[1] In Amboina the sorcerer, to recover a soul detained by demons, plucks a branch from a tree, and waving it to and fro as if to catch something, calls out the sick man's name. Returning he strikes the patient over the head and body with the branch, into which the lost soul is supposed to have passed, and from which it returns to the patient.[2] In the Babar Islands offerings for evil spirits are laid at the root of a great tree (*wokiorai*), from which a leaf is plucked and pressed on the patient's forehead and breast; the lost soul, which is in the leaf, is thus restored to its owner.[3] In some other islands of the same seas, when a man returns ill and speechless from the forest, it is inferred that the evil spirits which dwell in the great trees have caught and kept his

---

[1] Horatio Hale, *U. S. Exploring Expedition, Ethnography and Philology*, p. 208 *sq.* Cp. Wilkes, *Narrative of the U.S. Exploring Expedition* (London, 1845), iv. 448 *sq.*

[2] Riedel, *De sluik - en kroesharige rassen tusschen Selebes en Papua*, p. 77 *sq.*

[3] *Ib.* p. 356 *sq.*

soul.   Offerings of food are therefore left under a tree and the soul is brought home in a piece of wax.[1] Amongst the Dyaks of Sarawak the priest conjures the lost soul into a cup, where it is seen by the uninitiated as a lock of hair, but by the initiated as a miniature human being.   This is supposed to be thrust by the priest into a hole in the top of the patient's head.[2]   In Nias the sick man's soul is restored to him in the shape of a firefly, visible only to the sorcerer, who catches it in a cloth and places it on the forehead of the patient.[3]

Again, souls may be extracted from their bodies or detained on their wanderings not only by ghosts and demons but also by men, especially by sorcerers.   In Fiji if a criminal refused to confess, the chief sent for a scarf with which "to catch away the soul of the rogue."   At the sight, or even at the mention of the scarf the culprit generally made a clean breast.   For if he did not, the scarf would be waved over his head till his soul was caught in it, when it would be carefully folded up and nailed to the end of a chief's canoe ; and for want of his soul the criminal would pine and die.[4] The sorcerers of Danger Island used to set snares for souls.   The snares were made of stout cinet, about fifteen to thirty feet long, with loops on either side of different sizes, to suit the different sizes of souls ; for fat souls there were large loops, for thin souls there were small ones.   When a man was sick against whom the sorcerers had a grudge, they set up these soul-

---

[1] Riedel, *op. cit.* p. 376.

[2] Spenser St. John, *Life in the Forests of the Far East,* i. 189.   Sometimes the souls resemble cotton seeds (*ib.*) Cp. *id.* i. 183.

[3] Nieuwenhuisen en Rosenberg, "Ver-

slag omtrent het Eiland Nias," in *Verhandel. van het Batav. Genootsch. van Kunsten en Wetenschappen,* xxx. 116 ; Rosenberg, *Der Malayische Archipel,* p. 174.

[4] Williams, *Fiji and the Fijians,* i. 250.

Diana, returning from the hunt, with her attendant huntresses.

A Congolese village.

snares near his house and watched for the flight of his
soul. If in the shape of a bird or an insect it was
caught in the snare the man would infallibly die.[1]
Among the Sereres of Senegambia, when a man wishes
to revenge himself on his enemy he goes to the *Fitaure*
(chief and priest in one), and prevails on him by presents to conjure the soul of his enemy into a large jar
of red earthenware, which is then deposited under a
consecrated tree. The man whose soul is shut up in
the jar soon dies.[2] Some of the Congo negroes think
that enchanters can get possession of human souls, and
enclosing them in tusks of ivory, sell them to the white
man, who makes them work for him in his country
under the sea. It is believed that very many of the
coast labourers are men thus obtained ; so when these
people go to trade they often look anxiously about for
their dead relations. The man whose soul is thus sold
into slavery will die "in due course, if not at the time."[3]

In Hawaii there were sorcerers who caught souls
of living people, shut them up in calabashes, and gave
them to people to eat. By squeezing a captured soul
in their hands they discovered the place where people
had been secretly buried.[4] Amongst the Canadian
Indians, when a wizard wished to kill a man, he sent
out his familiar spirits, who brought him the victim's
soul in the shape of a stone or the like. The wizard
struck the soul with a sword or an axe till it bled profusely, and as it bled the man to whom it belonged
languished and died.[5] In Amboina if a doctor is con-

---

[1] Gill, *Myths and Songs of the South
Pacific*, p. 171; *id.*, *Life in the Southern
Isles*, p. 181 *sqq.*
[2] L. J. B. Bérenger-Féraud, *Les
Peuplades de la Sénégambie* (Paris, 1879),
p. 277.

[3] W. H. Bentley, *Life on the Congo*
(London, 1887), p. 71.
[4] Bastian, *Allerlei aus Volks-und
Menschenkunde* (Berlin, 1888), i. 119.
[5] *Relations des Jésuites*, 1637, p.
50.

vinced that a patient's soul has been carried away by a
demon beyond recovery, he seeks to supply its place
with a soul abstracted from another man.   For this
purpose he goes by night to a house and asks, "Who's
there?"   If an inmate is incautious enough to answer,
the doctor takes up from before the door a clod of
earth, into which the soul of the person who replied is
believed to have passed.   This clod the doctor lays
under the sick man's pillow, and performs certain ceremonies by which the stolen soul is conveyed into the
patient's body.   Then as he goes home the doctor
fires two shots to frighten the soul from returning to
its proper owner.[1]   A Karen wizard will catch the
wandering soul of a sleeper and transfer it to the
body of a dead man.   The latter, therefore, comes to
life as the former dies.   But the friends of the sleeper
in turn engage a wizard to steal the soul of another
sleeper, who dies as the first sleeper comes to life.   In
this way an indefinite succession of deaths and resurrections is supposed to take place.[2]

The Indians of the Nass River, British Columbia,
think that a doctor may swallow his patient's soul by
mistake.   A doctor who is believed to have done so
is made by the other doctors to stand over the patient,
while one of them thrusts his fingers down the doctor's
throat, another kneads him in the stomach with his
knuckles, and a third slaps him on the back.   If the
soul is not in him after all, and if the same process has
been repeated upon all the doctors without success, it
is concluded that the soul must be in the head-doctor's
box.   A party of doctors, therefore, waits upon him at

[1] Riedel, *De sluik-en kroesharige
rassen tusschen Selebes en Papua*, p.
.78 *sq.*

[2] E. B. Cross, "On the Karens," in
*Journal of the American Oriental
Society*, iv. 307.

his house and requests him to produce his box. When he has done so and arranged its contents on a new mat, they take him and hold him up by the heels with his head in a hole in the floor. In this position they wash his head, and "any water remaining from the ablution is taken and poured upon the sick man's head."[1]

Other examples of the recall and recovery of souls will be found referred to beneath.[2]

But the spiritual dangers I have enumerated are not the only ones which beset the savage. Often he regards his shadow or reflection as his soul, or at all

---

[1] J. B. McCullagh in *The Church Missionary Gleaner*, xiv. No. 164 (August 1887), p. 91. The same account is copied from the "North Star" (Sitka, Alaska, December 1888), in *Journal of American Folk-lore*, ii. 74 *sq.* Mr. McCullagh's account (which is closely followed in the text) of the latter part of the custom is not quite clear. It would seem that failing to find the soul in the head-doctor's box it occurs to them that he may have swallowed it, as the other doctors were at first supposed to have done. With a view of testing this hypothesis they hold him up by the heels to empty out the soul ; and as the water with which his head is washed may possibly contain the missing soul, it is poured on the patient's head to restore the soul to him. We have already seen that the recovered soul is often conveyed into the sick person's head.

[2] Riedel, *De Topantunuasu of oorspronkelijke volksstammen van Central Selebes* (overgedrukt uit de *Bijdragen tot de Taal-Land-en Volkenkunde van Nederlandsch-Indië*, 5e volgr. i.), p. 17 ; Neumann, "Het Pane en Bila-stroomgebied," in *Tijdschrift van het Nederlandsch Aardrijkskundig Genootschap*, ii. de Serie, dl. iii., Afdeeling : meer uitgebreide artikelen, No. 2 (1886), p. 300 *sq.* ; Priklonski, "Die Jakuten," in Bastian's *Allerlei aus Volks-und Menschenkunde*, ii. 218 *sq.* ; Bastian, *Die Völker des östlichen Asien*, ii. 388, iii. 236 ; *id.*, *Völkerstämme am Brahmaputra*, p. 23 ; *id.*, "Hügelstämme Assam's," in *Verhandlungen d. Berlin. Gesell. f. Anthropol. Ethnol. und Urgeschichte*, 1881, p. 156 ; Shway Yoe, *The Burman*, i. 283 *sq.*, ii. 101 *sq.*; Sproat, *Scenes and Studies of Savage Life*, p. 214 ; Doolittle, *Social Life of the Chinese*, p. 110 *sq.* (ed. Paxton Hood) ; T. Williams, *Fiji and the Fijians*, i. 242 ; E. B. Cross, "On the Karens," in *Journal of the American Oriental Society*, iv. 309 *sq.* ; A. W. Howitt, "On some Australian Beliefs," in *Journ. Anthrop. Instit.* xiii. 187 *sq.* ; *id.*, "On Australian Medicine Men," in *Journ. Anthrop. Inst.* xvi. 41 ; E. P. Houghton, "On the Land Dayaks of Upper Sarawak," in *Memoirs of the Anthropological Society of London*, iii. 196 *sq.* ; L. Dahle, "Sikidy and Vintana," in *Antananarivo Annual and Madagascar Annual*, xi. (1887) p. 320 *sq.* ; C. Leemius, *De Lapponibus Finmarchiae eorumque lingua, vitâ et religione pristina commentatio* (Copenhagen, 1767), p. 416 *sq.* Some time ago my friend Professor W. Robertson Smith suggested to me that the practice of hunting souls, which is denounced in Ezekiel xiii. 17 *sqq.* must have been akin to those described in the text.

events as a vital part of himself, and as such it is
necessarily a source of danger to him. For if it is
trampled upon, struck, or stabbed, he will feel the
injury as if it were done to his person; and if it is
detached from him entirely (as he believes that it may
be) he will die. In the island of Wetar there are
magicians who can make a man ill by stabbing his
shadow with a pike or hacking it with a sword.[1]
After Sankara had destroyed the Buddhists in India,
it is said that he journeyed to Nepaul, where he had
some difference of opinion with the Grand Lama. To
prove his supernatural powers, he soared into the air.
But as he mounted up, the Grand Lama, perceiving
his shadow swaying and wavering on the ground,
struck his knife into it and down fell Sankara and
broke his neck.[2] In the Babar Islands the demons get
power over a man's soul by holding fast his shadow, or
by striking and wounding it.[3] There are stones in
Melanesia on which, if a man's shadow falls, the demon
of the stone can draw out his soul.[4] In Amboina and
Uliase, two islands near the equator, and where,
therefore, there is little or no shadow cast at noon, it
is a rule not to go out of the house at mid-day, because
it is supposed that by doing so a man may lose the
shadow of his soul.[5] The Mangaians tell of a mighty
warrior, Tukaitawa, whose strength waxed and waned
with the length of his shadow. In the morning, when
his shadow fell longest, his strength was greatest; but
as the shadow shortened towards noon his strength
ebbed with it, till exactly at noon it reached its lowest

---

[1] Riedel, *De sluik-en kroesharige
rassen tusschen Selebes en Papua*, p.
440.
[2] Bastian, *Die Völker des östlichen
Asien*, v. 455.

[3] Riedel, *op. cit.* p. 340.
[4] Codrington, "Religious Beliefs and
Practices in Melanesia," in *Journ.
Anthrop. Instit.* x. 281.
[5] Riedel, *op. cit.* p. 61.

point; then, as the shadow stretched out in the afternoon, his strength returned. A certain hero discovered the secret of Tukaitawa's strength and slew
him at noon.[1]   It is possible that even in lands outside
the tropics the fact of the diminished shadow at noon
may have contributed, even if it did not give rise, to
the superstitious dread with which that hour has been
viewed by various peoples, as by the Greeks, ancient
and modern, and by the Roumanians of Transylvania.[2]
In this fact, too, we may perhaps detect the reason
why noon was chosen by the Greeks as the hour for
sacrificing to the shadowless dead.[3]   The ancients
believed that in Arabia if a hyaena trod on a man's
shadow it deprived him of the power of speech and
motion; and that if a dog, standing on a roof in the
moonlight, cast a shadow on the ground and a hyaena
trod on it, the dog would fall down as if dragged with
a rope.[4]   Clearly in these cases the shadow, if not
equivalent to the soul, is at least regarded as a living
part of the man or the animal, so that injury done to
the shadow is felt by the person or animal as if it were
done to his body.   Whoever entered the sanctuary of
Zeus on Mount Lycaeus in Arcadia was believed to
lose his shadow and to die within the year.[5]   Nowhere,
perhaps, does the equivalence of the shadow to the
life or soul come out more clearly than in some

---

[1] Gill, *Myths and Songs of the South
Pacific*, p. 284 *sqq.*
[2] Bernard Schmidt, *Das Volksleben
der Neugriechen*, pp. 94 *sqq.*, 119 *sq.* ;
Grimm, *Deutsche Mythologie*,[4] ii. 972 ;
Rochholz, *Deutscher Glaube und
Brauch*, i. 62 *sqq.* ; E Gerard, *The
Land beyond the Forest*, i. 331.
[3] Schol. on Aristophanes, *Ran.* 293.
[4] [Aristotle] *Mirab. Auscult.* 145
(157) ; *Geoponica*, xv. 1.   In the latter
passage, for κατάγει ἑαυτήν we must

read κ. αὐτόν, an emendation neces-
sitated by the context, and confirmed
by the passage of Damīrī quoted and
translated by Bochart, *Hierozoicon*,
i. c. 833, "*cum ad lunam calcat um-
bram canis, qui supra tectura est, canis
ad eam* [scil. hyaenam] *decidit, et ea
illum devorat.*"   Cp. W. Robertson
Smith, *The Religion of the Semites*, i.
122.
[5] Pausanias, viii. 38, 6 ; Polybius,
xvi. 12, 7 ; Plutarch, *Quaest. Graec.* 39.

customs practised to this day in South-Eastern Europe.
In modern Greece, when the foundation of a new
building is being laid, it is the custom to kill a cock, a
ram, or a lamb, and to let its blood flow on the foundation stone, under which the animal is afterwards
buried. The object of the sacrifice is to give strength
and stability to the building. But sometimes, instead
of killing an animal, the builder entices a man to the
foundation stone, secretly measures his body, or a part
of it, or his shadow, and buries the measure under the
foundation stone ; or he lays the foundation stone upon
the man's shadow. It is believed that the man will
die within the year.[1] The Bulgarians still observe a
similar custom. If they cannot get a human shadow
they measure the shadow of the first animal that comes
that way.[2] The Roumanians of Transylvania think
that he whose shadow is thus immured will die within
forty days ; so persons passing by a building which is
in course of erection may hear a warning cry, " Beware
lest they take thy shadow!" Not long ago there were
still shadow-traders whose business it was to provide
architects with the shadows necessary for securing
their walls.[3] In these cases the measure of the shadow
is looked on as equivalent to the shadow itself, and to
bury it is to bury the life or soul of the man, who,
deprived of it, must die. Thus the custom is a substitute for the old custom of immuring a living person
in the walls, or crushing him under the foundation
stone of a new building, in order to give strength and
durability to the structure.

As some peoples believe a man's soul to be in his

[1] B. Schmidt, *Das Volksleben der
Neugriechen*, p. 196 *sq.*

[2] Ralston, *Songs of the Russian
People*, p. 127.

[3] W. Schmidt, *Das Jahr und seine
Tage in Meinung und Brauch der Ro-
mänen Siebenbürgens*, p. 27 ; E. Gerard,
The Land beyond the Forest, ii. 17 *sq.*

shadow, so other (or the same) peoples believe it to be in his reflection in water or a mirror. Thus "the Andamanese do not regard their shadows but their reflections (in any mirror) as their souls."[1] Some of the Fijians thought that man has two souls, a light one and a dark one; the dark one goes to Hades, the light one is his reflection in water or a mirror.[2] When the Motumotu of New Guinea first saw their likenesses in a looking-glass they thought that their reflections were their souls.[3] The reflection-soul, being external to the man, is exposed to much the same dangers as the shadow-soul. As the shadow may be stabbed, so may the reflection. Hence an Aztec mode of keeping sorcerers from the house was to leave a vessel of water with a knife in it behind the door. When a sorcerer entered he was so much alarmed at seeing his reflection in the water transfixed by a knife that he turned and fled.[4] The Zulus will not look into a dark pool because they think there is a beast in it which will take away their reflections, so that they die.[5] The Basutos say that crocodiles have the power of thus killing a man by dragging his reflection under water.[6] In Saddle Island (Melanesia) there is a pool "into which if any one looks he dies; the malignant spirit takes hold upon his life by means of his reflection on the water."[7]

---

[1] E. H. Mann, *Aboriginal Inhabitants of the Andaman Islands*, p. 94.

[2] Williams, *Fiji*, i. 241.

[3] James Chalmers, *Pioneering in New Guinea* (London, 1887), p. 170.

[4] Sahagun, *Histoire générale des choses de la Nouvelle-Espagne* (Paris, 1880), p. 314. The Chinese hang brass mirrors over the idols in their houses, because it is thought that evil spirits entering the house and seeing themselves in the mirrors will be scared away (*China Review*, ii. 164).

[5] Callaway, *Nursery Tales, Traditions, and Histories of the Zulus*, p. 342.

[6] Arbousset et Daumas, *Voyage d'exploration au Nord-est de la Colonie du Cap de Bonne-Espérance*, p. 12.

[7] Codrington, "Religious Beliefs and Practices in Melanesia," in *Journ. Anthrop. Instit.* x. 313.

We can now understand why it was a maxim both in ancient India and ancient Greece not to look at one's reflection in water, and why the Greeks regarded it as an omen of death if a man dreamed of seeing himself so reflected.[1] They feared that the water-spirits would drag the person's reflection (soul) under water, leaving him soulless to die. This was probably the origin of the classical story of the beautiful Narcissus, who pined and died in consequence of seeing his reflection in the water.. The explanation that he died for love of his own fair image was probably devised later, after the old meaning of the story was forgotten. The same ancient belief lingers, in a faded form, in the English superstition that whoever sees a water-fairy must pine and die.

> "Alas, the moon should ever beam
> To show what man should never see !—
> I saw a maiden on a stream,
> And fair was she !
>
> "I staid to watch, a little space,
> Her parted lips if she would sing ;
> The waters closed above her face
> With many a ring.
>
> "I know my life will fade away,
> I know that I must vainly pine,
> For I am made of mortal clay,
> But she's divine !"

Further, we can now explain the widespread custom of covering up mirrors or turning them to the wall after a death has taken place in the house. It is feared that the soul, projected out of the person in the shape of his reflection in the mirror, may be carried off by the ghost of the departed, which is commonly supposed to linger about the house till the burial. The custom

---

[1] *Fragmenta Philosoph. Graec.* ed. Mullach, i. 510; Artemidorus, *Onirocr.* ii. 7 ; *Laws of Manu,* iv. 38.

is thus exactly parallel to the Aru custom of not sleeping in a house after a death for fear that the soul, projected out of the body in a dream, may meet the ghost
and be carried off by it.[1]   In Oldenburg it is thought
that if a person sees his image in a mirror after a
death he will die himself.   So all the mirrors in the
house are covered up with white cloth.[2]   In some
parts of Germany after a death not only the mirrors
but everything that shines or glitters (windows, clocks,
etc.) is covered up,[3] doubtless because they might
reflect a person's image.   The same custom of covering up mirrors or turning them to the wall after a
death prevails in England, Scotland, and Madagascar.[4]
The Suni Mohammedans of Bombay cover with a
cloth the mirror in the room of a dying man and do
not remove it until the corpse is carried out for burial.
They also cover the looking-glasses in their bedrooms
before retiring to rest at night.[5]   The reason why sick
people should not see themselves in a mirror, and
why the mirror in a sick-room is therefore covered up,[6]
is also plain ; in time of sickness, when the soul
might take flight so easily, it is particularly dangerous
to project the soul out of the body by means of the
reflection in a mirror.   The rule is therefore precisely
parallel to the rule observed by some peoples of not
allowing sick people to sleep ;[7] for in sleep the soul
is projected out of the body, and there is always a
risk that it may not return.   " In the opinion of the
Raskolniks a mirror is an accursed thing, invented by

---

[1] See above, p. 125 *sq.*

[2] Wattke, *Der deutsche Volksaberglaube,*[2] § 726.

[3] *Ib.*

[4] *Folk-lore Journal,* iii. 281 ; Dyer,
English Folk-lore, p. 109 ; J. Napier,
Folk-lore, or Superstitious Beliefs in the
West of Scotland, p. 60 ; Ellis, *History
of Madagascar,* i. 238 ; *Revue d'Ethno-
graphie,* v. 215.

[5] *Panjab Notes and Queries,* ii. 906.

[6] *Folk-lore Journal,* vi. 145 *sq.* ;
Panjab Notes and Queries, ii., No. 378.

[7] *Journ. Anthrop. Inst.* xv. 82 *sqq.*

the devil," [1] perhaps on account of the mirror's supposed power of drawing out the soul in the reflection and so facilitating its capture.

As with shadows and reflections, so with portraits ; they are often believed to contain the soul of the person portrayed. People who hold this belief are naturally loth to have their likenesses taken ; for if the portrait is the soul, or at least a vital part of the person portrayed, whoever possesses the portrait will be able to exercise a fatal influence over the original of it. Thus the Canelos Indians of South America think that their soul is carried away in their picture. Two of them having been photographed were so alarmed that they came back next day on purpose to ask if it were really true that their souls had been taken away. [2] When Mr. Joseph Thomson tried to photograph some of the Wa-teita in Eastern Africa, they imagined that he was a magician trying to get possession of their souls, and that if he got their likenesses they themselves would be entirely at his mercy. [3] An Indian, whose portrait the Prince of Wied wished to get, refused to let himself be drawn, because he believed it would cause his death. [4] The Mandans also thought that they would soon die if their portrait was in the hands of another ; they wished at least to have the artist's picture as a kind of antidote or guarantee. [5] The same belief still lingers in various parts of Europe. Some old women in the Greek island of Carpathus were very angry a few years ago at having their likenesses drawn,

---

[1] Ralston, *Songs of the Russian People*, p. 117. The objection, however, may be merely Puritanical. Professor W. Robertson Smith informs me that the peculiarities of the Raskolniks are largely due to exaggerated Puritanism.

[2] A. Simson, " Notes on the Jívaros and Canelos Indians," in *Journ. Anthrop. Inst.* ix. 392.

[3] J. Thomson, *Through Masai Land*, p. 86.

[4] Maximilian Prinz zu Wied, *Reise in das Innere Nord-Amerika*, i. 417.

[5] *Ib.* ii. 166.

thinking that in consequence they would pine and die.[1] Some people in Russia object to having their silhouettes taken, fearing that if this is done they will die before the year is out.[2]   There are persons in the West of Scotland " who refuse to have their likeness taken lest it prove unlucky ; and give as instances the cases of several of their friends who never had a day's health after being photographed."[3]

§ 3.—*Royal and priestly taboos (continued)*

So much for the primitive conceptions of the soul and the dangers to which it is exposed.   These conceptions are not limited to one people or country ; with variations of detail they are found all over the world, and survive, as we have seen, in modern Europe. Beliefs so deep-seated and so widespread must necessarily have contributed to shape the mould in which the early kingship was cast.   For if every individual was at such pains to save his own soul from the perils which threatened it from so many sides, how much more carefully must *he* have been guarded upon whose life hung the welfare and even the existence of the whole people, and whom therefore it was the common interest of all to preserve ?   Therefore we should expect to find the king's life protected by a system of precautions or safeguards still more numerous and minute than those which in primitive society every man adopts

---

[1] " A far-off Greek Island," *Blackwood's Magazine*, February 1886, p. 235.

[2] Ralston, *Songs of the Russian People*, p. 117.

[3] James Napier, *Folk-lore: or, Superstitious Beliefs in the West of Scotland*, p. 142. For more examples of the same sort, see R. Andree, *Ethnographische Parallelen und Vergleiche*, Neue Folge (Leipzig, 1889), p. 18 *sqq.*

for the safety of his own soul. Now in point of fact the life of the early kings is regulated, as we have séen and shall see more fully presently, by a very exact code of rules. May we not then conjecture that these rules are the very safeguards which on *à priori* grounds we expect to find adopted for the protection of the king's life? An examination of the rules themselves confirms this conjecture. For from this it appears that some of the rules observed by the kings are identical with those observed by private persons out of regard for the safety of their souls; and even of those which seem peculiar to the king, many, if not all, are most readily explained on the hypothesis that they are nothing but safeguards or lifeguards of the king. I will now enumerate some of these royal rules or taboos, offering on each of them such comments and explanations as may serve to set the original intention of the rule in its proper light.

As the object of the royal taboos is to isolate the king from all sources of danger, their general effect is to compel him to live in a state of seclusion, more or less complete, according to the number and stringency of the taboos he observes. Now of all sources of danger none are more dreaded by the savage than magic and witchcraft, and he suspects all strangers of practising these black arts. To guard against the baneful influence exerted voluntarily or involuntarily by strangers is therefore an elementary dictate of savage prudence. Hence before strangers are allowed to enter a district, or at least before they are permitted to mingle freely with the people of the district, certain ceremonies are often performed by the natives of the country for the purpose of disarming the strangers of their magical powers, of counteracting the

baneful influence which is believed to emanate from
them, or of disinfecting, so to speak, the tainted
atmosphere by which they are supposed to be
surrounded.   Thus in the island of Nanumea (South
Pacific) strangers from ships or from other islands
were not allowed to communicate with the people until
they all, or a few as representatives of the rest, had
been taken to each of the four temples in the island,
and prayers offered that the god would avert any
disease or treachery which these strangers might have
brought with them.   Meat offerings were also laid
upon the altars, accompanied by songs and dances in
honour of the god.   While these ceremonies were
going on, all the people except the priests and their
attendants kept out of sight.[1]   On returning from an
attempted ascent of the great African mountain
Kilimanjaro, which is believed by the neighbouring
tribes to be tenanted by dangerous demons, Mr.
New and his party, as soon as they reached the border
of the inhabited country, were disenchanted by the
inhabitants, being sprinkled with "a professionally
prepared liquor, supposed to possess the potency of
neutralising evil influences, and removing the spell
of wicked spirits."[2]   In the interior of Yoruba (West
Africa) the sentinels at the gates of towns often oblige
European travellers to wait till nightfall before they
admit them, the fear being that if the strangers were
admitted by day the devils would enter behind them.[3]
Amongst the Ot Danoms of Borneo it is the custom
that strangers entering the territory should pay to

[1] Turner, *Samoa*, p. 291 *sq.*
[2] Charles New, *Life, Wanderings, and Labours in Eastern Africa*, p. 432.
Cp. *ib.* pp. 400, 402.   For the demons
on Mt. Kilimanjaro, see also Krapf,
Travels, Researches etc. *in Eastern Africa*, p. 192.
[3] Pierre Bouche, *La Côte des Esclaves et le Dahomey*, p. 133.

the natives a certain sum, which is spent in the sacrifice of animals (buffaloes or pigs) to the spirits of
the land and water, in order to reconcile them to the
presence of the strangers, and to induce them not to
withdraw their favour from the people of the land,
but to bless the rice-harvest, etc.[1]　The men of a
certain district in Borneo, fearing to look upon a
European traveller lest he should make them ill,
warned their wives and children not to go near him.
These who could not restrain their curiosity killed
fowls to appease the evil spirits and smeared themselves with the blood.[2]　In Laos before a stranger
can be accorded hospitality the master of the house
must offer sacrifice to the ancestral spirits; otherwise
the spirits would be offended and would send disease
on the inmates.[3]　In the Mentawej Islands when a
stranger enters a house where there are children, the
father or other member of the family takes the ornament which the children wear in their hair and hands
it to the stranger, who holds it in his hands for a
while and then gives it back to him.　This is thought
to protect the children from the evil effect which the
sight of a stranger might have upon them.[4]　At
Shepherd's Isle Captain Moresby had to be disenchanted
before he was allowed to land his boat's crew.　When
he leaped ashore a devil-man seized his right hand
and waved a bunch of palm leaves over the captain's
head.　Then "he placed the leaves in my left hand,
putting a small green twig into his mouth, still holding me fast, and then, as if with great effort, drew
the twig from his mouth—this was extracting the evil

[1] C. A. L. M. Schwaner, *Borneo*, ii.
77.
[2] *Ib.* ii. 167.

[3] E. Aymonier, *Notes sur le Laos*,
p. 196.
[4] Rosenberg, *Der Malayische Archipel*, p. 198.

spirit—after which he blew violently, as if to speed
it away. I now held a twig between my teeth, and
he went through the same process." Then the two
raced round a couple of sticks fixed in the ground
and bent to an angle at the top, which had leaves tied
to it. After some more ceremonies the devil-man
concluded by leaping to the level of Captain Moresby's
shoulders (his hands resting on the captain's shoulders)
several times, " as if to show that he had conquered
the devil, and was now trampling him into the earth." [1]
North American Indians "have an idea that strangers,
particularly white strangers, are ofttimes accompanied
by evil spirits. Of these they have great dread, as
creating and delighting in mischief. One of the duties
of the medicine chief is to exorcise these spirits.
I have sometimes ridden into or through a camp
where I was unknown or unexpected, to be confronted
by a tall, half-naked savage, standing in the middle
of the circle of lodges, and yelling in a sing-song,
nasal tone, a string of unintelligible words." [2] When
Crevaux was travelling in South America he entered
a village of the Apalai Indians. A few moments after
his arrival some of the Indians brought him a number
of large black ants, of a species whose bite is painful, fastened on palm leaves. Then all the people
of the village, without distinction of age or sex,
presented themselves to him, and he had to sting
them all with the ants on their faces, thighs, etc.
Sometimes when he applied the ants too tenderly they
called out " More! more!" and were not satisfied till
their skin was thickly studded with tiny swellings like
what might have been produced by whipping them

---

[1] Capt. John Moresby, *Discoveries
and Surveys in New Guinea*, p. 102 *sq.*

[2] R. I. Dodge, *Our Wild Indians*
(Hartford, Conn. ; 1886), p. 119.

with nettles.[1] The object of this ceremony is made plain by the custom observed in Amboina and Uliase of sprinkling sick people with pungent spices, such as ginger and cloves, chewed fine, in order by the prickling sensation to drive away the demon of disease which may be clinging to their persons.[2] With a similar intention some of the natives of Borneo and Celebes sprinkle rice upon the head or body of a person supposed to be infested by dangerous spirits ; a fowl is then brought, which, by picking up the rice from the person's head or body, removes along with it the spirit or ghost which is clinging like a burr to his skin. This is done, for example, to persons who have attended a funeral, and who may therefore be supposed to be infested by the ghost of the deceased.[3] Similarly Basutos, who have carried a corpse to the grave, have their hands scratched with a knife from the tip of the thumb to the tip of the forefinger, and magic stuff is rubbed into the wound,[4] for the purpose, no doubt. of removing the ghost which may be adhering to their skin. The people of Nias carefully scrub and scour the weapons and clothes which they buy, in order to efface all connection between the things and the persons from whom they bought them.[5] It is probable that the same dread of strangers, rather than any desire to do them honour, is the motive of certain ceremonies which are sometimes observed at their reception, but of which the intention is not directly

---

[1] J. Crevaux, *Voyages dans l'Amérique du Sud*, p. 300.

[2] Riedel, *De sluik-en kroesharige rassen tusschen Selebes en Papua*, p. 78.

[3] Perelaer, *Ethnographische Beschrijving der Dajaks*, pp. 44, 54, 252 ; Matthes, *Bijdragen tot de Ethnologie van Zuid-Celebes*, p. 49.

[4] H. Grützner, "Ueber die Gebräuche der Basutho," in *Verhandl. d. Berlin. Gesell. f. Anthropologie*, etc. 1877, p. 84 *sq.*

[5] Nieuwenhuisen en Rosenberg, "Verslag omtrent het eiland Nias," in *Verhandel. v. h. Batav. Genootsch. v. Kunsten en Wetenschappen*, xxx. 26.

stated.   In Afghanistan and in some parts of Persia
the traveller, before he enters a village, is frequently
received with a sacrifice of animal life or food, or of
fire and incense.   The recent Afghan Boundary Mission,
in passing by villages in Afghanistan, was often met
with fire and incense.[1]   Sometimes a tray of lighted
embers is thrown under the hoofs of the traveller's horse,
with the words, "You are welcome."[2]   On entering a
village in Central Africa Emin Pasha was received
with the sacrifice of two goats;   their blood was
sprinkled on the path and the chief stepped over the
blood to greet Emin.[3]   Amongst the Eskimos of
Cumberland Inlet, when a stranger arrives at an
encampment, the sorcerer goes out to meet him.   The
stranger folds his arms and inclines his head to one
side, so as to expose his cheek, upon which the
sorcerer deals a terrible blow, sometimes felling him to
the ground.   Next the sorcerer in his turn presents
his cheek and receives a buffet from the stranger.
Then they kiss each other, the ceremony is over, and
the stranger is hospitably received by all.[4]   Sometimes
the dread of strangers and their magic is too great to
allow of their reception on any terms.   Thus when
Speke arrived at a certain village the natives shut
their doors against him, " because they had never
before seen a white man nor the tin boxes that the
men were carrying : ' Who knows,' they said, ' but that
these very boxes are the plundering Watuta transformed
and come to kill us ?   You cannot be admitted.'   No

---

[1] *Journal of the Anthropological Society of Bombay*, i. 35.

[2] E. O'Donovan, *The Merv Oasis* (London, 1882), ii. 58.

[3] *Emin Pasha in Central Africa*, being a Collection of his Letters and Journals (London, 1888), p. 107.

[4] *Narrative of the Second Arctic Expedition made by Charles F. Hall.* Edited by Prof. J. G. Nourse, U.S.N. (Washington, 1879), p. 269 *note*.

persuasion could avail with them, and the party had to proceed to the next village."[1]

The fear thus entertained of alien visiters is often mutual. Entering a strange land, the savage feels that he is treading enchanted ground, and he takes steps to guard against the demons that haunt it and the magical arts of its inhabitants. Thus on going to a strange land the Maoris performed certain ceremonies to make it *noa* (common), lest it might have been previously *tapu* (sacred).[2] When Baron Miklucho-Maclay was approaching a village on the Maclay Coast of New Guinea, one of the natives who accompanied him broke a branch from a tree and going aside whispered to it for a while; then going up to each member of the party, one after another, he spat something upon his back and gave him some blows with the branch. Lastly, he went into the forest and buried the branch under withered leaves in the thickest part of the jungle. This ceremony was believed to protect the party against all treachery and danger in the village they were approaching.[3] The idea probably was that the malignant influences were drawn off from the persons into the branch and buried with it in the depths of the forest. In Australia, when a strange tribe has been invited into a district and is approaching the encampment of the tribe which owns the land, "the strangers carry lighted bark or burning sticks in their hands, for the purpose, they say, of clearing and purifying the air."[4] So when two Greek armies were

---

[1] J. A. Grant, *A Walk across Africa*, p. 104 *sq.*

[2] E. Shortland, *Traditions and Superstitions of the New Zealanders*, p. 103.

[3] N. von Miklucho-Maclay, "Eth-nologische Bemerkungen über die Papuas der Maclay-Küste in Neu-Guinea," in *Natuurkundig Tijdschrift voor Nederlandsch Indie*, xxxvi. 317 *sq.*

[4] Brough Smyth, *Aborigines of Victoria*, i. 134.

advancing to the onset, sacred men used to march in front of each, bearing lighted torches, which they flung into the space between the hosts and then retired unmolested.[1]

Again, it is thought that a man who has been on a journey may have contracted some magic evil from the strangers with whom he has been brought into contact. Hence on returning home, before he is readmitted to the society of his tribe and friends, he has to undergo certain purificatory ceremonies. Thus the Bechuanas "cleanse or purify themselves after journeys by shaving their heads, etc., lest they should have contracted from strangers some evil by witchcraft or sorcery."[2] In some parts of Western Africa when a man returns home after a long absence, before he is allowed to visit his wife, he must wash his person with a particular fluid, and receive from the sorcerer a certain mark on his forehead, in order to counteract any magic spell which a stranger woman may have cast on him in his absence, and which might be communicated through him to the women of his village.[3] Two Hindoo ambassadors, who had been sent to England by a native prince and had returned to India, were considered to have so polluted themselves by contact with strangers that nothing but being born again could restore them to purity. "For the purpose of regeneration it is directed to make an image of pure gold of the female power of nature, in the shape either of a woman or of a cow. In this statue the person to be regenerated is enclosed, and dragged through the

---

[1] Scholiast on Euripides, *Phoeniss.* 1377. These men were sacred to the war-god (Ares), and were always spared in battle.

[2] John Campbell, *Travels in South Africa, being a Narrative of a Second Journey in the Interior of that Country*, ii. 205.

[3] Ladislaus Magyar, *Reisen in Süd-Afrika*, p. 203.

usual channel. As a statue of pure gold and of proper dimensions would be too expensive, it is sufficient to make an image of the sacred *Yoni*, through which the person to be regenerated is to pass." Such an image of pure gold was made at the prince's command, and his ambassadors were born again by being dragged through it.[1] When Damaras return home after a long absence, they are given a small portion of the fat of particular animals which is supposed to possess certain virtues.[2] In some of the Moluccas, when a brother or young blood-relation returns from a long journey, a young girl awaits him at the door with a *caladi* leaf in her hand and water in the leaf. She throws the water over his face and bids him welcome.[3] The natives of Savage Island (South Pacific) invariably killed, not only all strangers in distress who were drifted to their shores, but also any of their own people who had gone away in a ship and returned home. This was done out of dread of disease. Long after they began to venture out to ships they would not immediately use the things they obtained from them, but hung them up in quarantine for weeks in the bush.[4]

When precautions like these are taken on behalf of the people in general against the malignant influence supposed to be exercised by strangers, we shall not be surprised to find that special measures are adopted to protect the king from the same insidious danger. In the middle ages the envoys who visited a Tartar Khan were obliged to pass between two fires before they were admitted to his presence, and the gifts they brought were also carried between the fires. The

---

[1] *Asiatick Researches*, vi. 535 *sq.* ed. 4to (p. 537 *sq.* ed. 8vo).
[2] C. J. Andersson, *Lake Ngami*, p. 223.
[3] François Valentyn, *Oud en nieuw Oost-Indiën*, iii. 16.
[4] Turner, *Samoa*, p. 305 *sq.*

reason assigned for the custom was that the fire purged away any magic influence which the strangers might mean to exercise over the Khan.[1]   When subject chiefs come with their retinues to visit Kalamba (the most powerful chief of the Bashilange in the Congo Basin) for the first time or after being rebellious, they have to bathe, men and women together, in two brooks on two successive days, passing the nights in the open air in the market-place. After the second bath they proceed, entirely naked, to the house of Kalamba, who makes a long white mark on the breast and forehead of each of them.   Then they return to the market-place and dress, after which they undergo the pepper ordeal.   Pepper is dropped into the eyes of each of them, and while this is being done the sufferer has to make a confession of all his sins, to answer all questions that may be put to him, and to take certain vows.   This ends the ceremony, and the strangers are now free to take up their quarters in the town for as long as they choose to remain.[2]   At Kilema, in Eastern Africa, when a stranger arrives, a medicine is made out of a certain plant or a tree fetched from a distance, mixed with the blood of a sheep or goat.   With this mixture the stranger is besmeared or besprinkled before he is admitted to the presence of the king.[3]   The King of Monomotapa (South-East Africa) might not wear any foreign stuffs for fear of their being poisoned.[4]   The

---

[1] De Plano Carpini, *Historia Mongolorum quos nos Tartaros appellamus*, ed. D'Avezac (Paris, 1838), cap. iii. § iii. p. 627, cap. ult. § i. x. p. 744, and Appendix, p. 775; "Travels of William de Rubriquis into Tartary and China," in Pinkerton's *Voyages and Travels*, vii. 82 *sq.*

[2] Paul Pogge, "Bericht über die Station Mukenge," in *Mittheilungen der Afrikanischen Gesellschaft in Deutschland*, iv. (1883-1885) 182 *sq.*

[3] J. L. Krapf, *Travels, Researches, and Missionary Labours during an Eighteen Years' Residence in Eastern Africa*, p. 252 *sq.*

[4] Dapper, *Description de l'Afrique*, p. 391.

King of Kakongo (West Africa) might not possess or even touch European goods, except metals, arms, and articles made of wood and ivory. Persons wearing foreign stuffs were very careful to keep at a distance from his person, lest they should touch him.[1] The King of Loango might not look upon the house of a white man.[2]

In the opinion of savages the acts of eating and drinking are attended with special danger; for at these times the soul may escape from the mouth, or be extracted by the magic arts of an enemy present. Precautions are therefore taken to guard against these dangers. Thus of the Battas of Sumatra it is said that "since the soul can leave the body, they always take care to prevent their soul from straying on occasions when they have most need of it. But it is only possible to prevent the soul from straying when one is in the house. At feasts one may find the whole house shut up, in order that the soul (*tondi*) may stay and enjoy the good things set before it."[3] In Fiji persons who suspected others of plotting against them avoided eating in their presence, or were careful to leave no fragment of food behind.[4] The Zafimanelo in Madagascar lock their doors when they eat, and hardly any one ever sees them eating.[5] The Warua will not allow any one to see them eating and drinking, being doubly particular that no person of the opposite

[1] Proyart, "History of Loango, Kakongo," etc., in Pinkerton's *Voyages and Travels*, xvi. 583; Dapper, *op. cit.* p. 340; J. Ogilby, *Africa* (London, 1670), p. 521. Cp. Bastian, *Die deutsche Expedition an der Loango-Küste*, i. 288.

[2] Bastian, *op. cit.* i. 268 *sq.*

[3] J. B. Neumann, "Het Pane-en Bila-Stroomgebied op het eiland Sumatra," in *Tijdschrift van het Nederlandsch Aardrijkskundig Genootschap*, ii. de Serie, dl. iii., Afdeeling : meer uitgebreide artikelen, No. 2, p. 300.

[4] Th. Williams, *Fiji and the Fijians*, i. 249.

[5] J. Richardson, "Tanala Customs, Superstitions and Beliefs," in *The Antananarivo Annual and Madagascar Magazine*, No. ii. p. 219.

sex shall see them doing so. "I had to pay a man to let me see him drink; I could not make a man let a woman see him drink." When offered a drink of *pombe* they often ask that a cloth may be held up to hide them whilst drinking. Further, each man and woman must cook for themselves; each person must have his own fire.[1] If these are the ordinary precautions taken by common people, the precautions taken by kings are extraordinary. The King of Loango may not be seen eating or drinking by man or beast under pain of death. A favourite dog having broken into the room where the king was dining, the king ordered it to be killed on the spot. Once the king's own son, a boy of twelve years old, inadvertently saw the king drink. Immediately the king ordered him to be finely apparelled and feasted, after which he commanded him to be cut in quarters, and carried about the city with a proclamation that he had seen the king drink. "When the king has a mind to drink, he has a cup of wine brought; he that brings it has a bell in his hand, and as soon as he has delivered the cup to the king he turns his face from him and rings the bell, on which all present fall down with their faces to the ground, and continue so till the king has drank. . . . His eating is much in the same style, for which he has a house on purpose, where his victuals are set upon a bensa or table : which he goes to and shuts the door; when he has done, he knocks and comes out. So that none ever see the king eat or drink. For it is believed that if any one should, the king shall immediately die."[2] The rules

[1] Lieut. Cameron, *Across Africa*, ii. 71 (ed. 1877); *id.*, in *Journ. Anthrop. Inst.* vi. 173.

[2] "Adventures of Andrew Battel," in Pinkerton's *Voyages and Travels*, xvi. 330; Dapper, *Description de l'Afrique*, p. 330; Bastian, *Die deutsche Expedition an der Loango-Küste*, i. 262 *sq.*; R. F. Burton, *Abeokuta and the Cameroons Mountains*, i. 147.

observed by the neighbouring King of Kakongo were similar ; it was thought that the king would die if any of his subjects were to see him drink.[1]   It is a capital offence to see the King of Dahomey at his meals. When he drinks in public, as he does on extraordinary occasions, he hides himself behind a curtain, or hand-kerchiefs are held up round his head, and all the people throw themselves with their faces to the earth.[2]   Any one who saw the Muato Jamwo (a great potentate in the Congo Basin) eating or drinking would certainly be put to death.[3]   When the King of Tonga ate all the people turned their backs to him.[4]   In the palace of the Persian kings there were two dining-rooms opposite each other ; in one of them the king dined, in the other his guests.   He could see them through a curtain on the door, but they could not see him.   Generally the king took his meals alone ; but sometimes his wife or some of his sons dined with him.[5]

In these cases, however, the intention may perhaps be to hinder evil influences from entering the body rather than to prevent the escape of the soul.   To the former rather than to the latter motive is to be ascribed the custom observed by some African sultans of veiling their faces.   The Sultan of Darfur wraps up his face with a piece of white muslin, which goes round his head several times, covering his mouth and nose first, and then his forehead, so that only his eyes are visible.   The same custom of veiling the face as a mark of sovereignty is said to be observed in other

[1] Proyart's "History of Loango, Kakongo," etc., in Pinkerton's *Voyages and Travels*, xvi. 584.

[2] J. L. Wilson, *West Afrika*, p. 148 (German trans.) ; John Duncan, *Travels in Western Africa*, i. 222.   Cp. W. W. Reade, *Savage Africa*, p. 543.

[3] Paul Pogge, *Im Reiche des Muato Jamwo* (Berlin, 1880), p. 231.

[4] Capt. James Cook, *Voyages*, v. 374 (ed. 1809).

[5] Heraclides Cumanus in Athenaeus, iv. 145 B-D.

The beautiful Narcissus, who pined and died in consequence of seeing his reflection in the water.

Timor couple, in the Malay Archipelago

parts of Central Africa.[1] The Sultan of Wadai always speaks from behind a curtain; no one sees his face except his intimates and a few favoured persons.[2] Amongst the Touaregs of the Sahara all the men (but not the women) keep the lower part of their face, especially the mouth, veiled constantly; the veil is never put off, not even in eating or sleeping.[3] In Samoa a man whose family god was the turtle might not eat a turtle, and if he helped a neighbour to cut up and cook one he had to wear a bandage tied over his mouth, lest an embryo turtle should slip down his throat, grow up, and be his death.[4] In West Timor a speaker holds his right hand before his mouth in speaking lest a demon should enter his body, and lest the person with whom he converses should harm the speaker's soul by magic.[5] In New South Wales for some time after his initiation into the tribal mysteries, a young blackfellow (whose soul at this time is in a critical state) must always cover his mouth with a rug when a woman is present.[6] Popular expressions in the language of civilised peoples, such as to have one's heart in one's mouth, show how natural is the idea that the life or soul may escape by the mouth or nostrils.[7]

[1] Mohammed Ibn-Omar el Tounsy, *Voyage au Darfour* (Paris, 1845), p. 203; *Travels of an Arab Merchant* [Mohammed Ibn-Omar el Tounsy] *in Soudan*, abridged from the French (of Perron) by Bayle St. John, p. 91 *sq.*

[2] Mohammed Ibn-Omar el Tounsy, *Voyage au Ouadây* (Paris, 1851), p. 375.

[3] H. Duveyrier, *Exploration du Sahara. Les Touareg du Nord*, p. 391 *sq.*; Reclus, *Nouvelle Géographie Universelle*, xi. 838 *sq.*; James Richardson, *Travels in the Great Desert of Sahara*, ii. 208. Amongst the Arabs men sometimes veiled their faces. Wellhausen, *Reste Arabischen Heidentumes*, p. 146.

[4] Turner, *Samoa*, p. 67 *sq.*

[5] Riedel, "Die Landschaft Dawan oder West-Timor," in *Deutsche Geographische Blätter*, x. 230.

[6] A. W. Howitt, "On some Australian Ceremonies of Initiation," in *Journ. Anthrop. Inst.* xiii. 456.

[7] Compare μόνον οὐκ ἐπὶ τοῖς χείλεσι τὰς ψυχὰς ἔχοντας Dio Chrysostomus, *Orat.* xxxii. i. 417, ed. Dindorf; *mihi anima in naso esse, stabam tanquam mortuus*, Petronius, *Sat.* 62; *in primis labris animam habere*, Seneca, *Natur Quaest.* iii. praef. 16.

By an extension of the like precaution kings are sometimes forbidden ever to leave their palaces ; or, if they are allowed to do so, their subjects are forbidden to see them abroad. We have seen that the priestly king at Shark Point, West Africa, may never quit his house or even his chair, in which he is obliged to sleep sitting.[1] After his coronation the King of Loango is confined to his palace, which he may not leave.[2] The King of Ibo (West Africa) "does not step out of his house into the town unless a human sacrifice is made to propitiate the gods : on this account he never goes out beyond the precincts of his premises."[3] The kings of Aethiopia were worshipped as gods, but were mostly kept shut up in their palaces.[4] The kings of Sabaea (Sheba), the spice country of Arabia, were not allowed to go out of their palaces ; if they did so, the mob stoned them to death.[5] But at the top of the palace there was a window with a chain attached to it. If any man deemed he had suffered wrong, he pulled the chain, and the king perceived him and called him in and gave judgment.[6] So to this day the kings of Corea, whose persons are sacred and receive "honours almost divine," are shut up in their palace from the age of twelve or fifteen ; and if a suitor wishes to obtain justice of the king he sometimes lights a great bonfire on a mountain facing the palace; the king sees the fire and informs himself of the case.[7] The

---

[1] See above, p. 112.

[2] Bastian, *Die Loango-Küste*, i. 263. However, a case is recorded in which he marched out to war (*ib.* i. 268 *sq.*)

[3] S. Crowther and J. C. Taylor, *The Gospel on the Banks of the Niger*, p. 433. On p. 379 mention is made of the king's "annual appearance to the public," but this may have taken place within "the precincts of his premises."

[4] Strabo, xvii. 2, 2, σέβονται δ' ὡς θεοὺς τοὺς βασιλέας, κατακλείστους ὄντας καὶ οἰκουροὺς τὸ πλέον.

[5] Strabo, xvi. 4, 19; Diodorus Siculus, iii. 47.

[6] Heraclides Cumanus in Athenaeus, 517 B.C.

[7] Ch. Dallet, *Histoire de l'Église de Corée* (Paris, 1874), i. xxiv - xxvi. The king sometimes, though rarely,

King of Tonquin was permitted to appear abroad twice
or thrice a year for the performance of certain religious
ceremonies ; but the people were not allowed to look
at him.   The day before he came forth notice was
given to all the inhabitants of the city and country to
keep from the way the king was to go ; the women
were obliged to remain in their houses and durst not
show themselves under pain of death, a penalty which
was carried out on the spot if any one disobeyed the
order, even through ignorance.   Thus the king was
invisible to all but his troops and the officers of his
suite.[1]   In Mandalay a stout lattice-paling, six feet
high and carefully kept in repair, lined every street in
the walled city and all those in the suburbs through
which the king was likely at any time to pass.   Behind
this paling, which stood two feet or so from the houses,
all the people had to stay when the king or any of the
queens went out.   Any one who was caught outside
it by the beadles after the procession had started was
severely handled, and might think himself lucky if he
got off with a beating.   No one was supposed to look
through the holes in the lattice-work, which were
besides partly stopped up with flowering shrubs.[2]

Again, magic mischief may be wrought upon a
man through the remains of the food he has partaken
of, or the dishes out of which he has eaten.   Thus
the Narrinyeri in South Australia think that if a man
eats of the sacred animal (totem) of his tribe, and an
enemy gets hold of a portion of the flesh, the latter

leaves his palace.   When he does so,
notice is given beforehand to the people.
All doors must be shut and each householder must kneel before his threshold
with a broom and a dust-pan in his
hand.   All windows, especially the
upper ones, must be sealed with slips of
paper, lest some one should look down
upon the king.   W. E. Griffis, *Corea,
the Hermit Nation,* p. 222.

[1] Richard, "History of Tonquin,"
in Pinkerton's *Voyages and Travels,* ix.
746.

[2] Shway Yoe, *The Burman,* i. 308 *sq.*

can make it grow in the inside of the eater, and so cause his death. Therefore when a man eats of his totem he is careful to eat it all or else to conceal or destroy the remains.[1] In Tana, one of the New Hebrides, people bury or throw into the sea the leavings of their food, lest these should fall into the hands of the disease - makers. For if a disease-maker finds the remnants of a meal, say the skin of a banana, he picks it up and burns it slowly in the fire. As it burns the person who ate the banana falls ill and sends to the disease-maker, offering him presents if he will stop burning the banana skin.[2] Hence no one may touch the food which the King of Loango leaves upon his plate; it is buried in a hole in the ground. And no one may drink out of the king's vessel.[3] Similarly no man may drink out of the same cup or glass with the King of Fida (in Guinea); "he hath always one kept particularly for himself; and that which hath but once touched another's lips he never uses more, though it be made of metal that may be cleansed by fire."[4] Amongst the Alfoers of Celebes there is a priest called the *Leleen*, whose duty appears to be to make the rice grow. His functions begin about a month before the rice is sown, and end after the crop is housed. During this time he has to observe certain taboos; amongst others he may not eat or drink with any one else, and he may drink out of no vessel but his own.[5]

We have seen that the Mikado's food was cooked

[1] *Native Tribes of South Australia*, p. 63; Taplin, "Notes on the mixed races of Australia," in *Journ. Anthrop. Inst.* iv. 53.

[2] Turner, *Samoa*, p. 320 *sq.*

[3] Dapper, *Description de l'Afrique*, p. 330.

[4] Bosman's "Guinea," in Pinkerton's *Voyages and Travels*, xvi. 487.

[5] P. N. Wilken, "Bijdragen tot de kennis van de zeden en gewoonten der Alfoeren in de Minahassa," in *Mededeelingen van wege het Nederlandsche Zendelinggenootschap*, xi. (1863) 126.

every day in new pots and served up in new dishes;
both pots and dishes were of common clay, in order
that they might be broken or laid aside after they had
been once used. They were generally broken, for it
was believed that if any one else ate his food out of
these sacred dishes his mouth and throat would become swollen and inflamed. The same ill effect was
thought to be experienced by any one who should
wear the Mikado's clothes without his leave; he would
have swellings and pains all over his body.[1] In the
evil effects thus supposed to follow upon the use of
the Mikado's vessels or clothes we see that other side
of the divine king's or god-man's character to which
attention has been already called. The divine person
is a source of danger as well as of blessing; he must
not only be guarded, he must also be guarded against.
His sacred organism, so delicate that a touch may
disorder it, is also electrically charged with a powerful
spiritual force which may discharge itself with fatal
effect on whatever comes in contact with it. Hence
the isolation of the man-god is quite as necessary for
the safety of others as for his own. His divinity is a
fire, which, under proper restraints, confers endless
blessings, but, if rashly touched or allowed to break
bounds, burns and destroys what it touches.
Hence the disastrous effects supposed to attend a
breach of taboo; the offender has thrust his hand into
the divine fire, which shrivels up and consumes him
on the spot. To take an example from the taboo we
are considering. It happened that a New Zealand
chief of high rank and great sanctity had left the
remains of his dinner by the wayside. A slave, a

---

[1] Kaempfer's "History of Japan," in Pinkerton's *Voyages and Travels*, vii. 717.

stout, hungry fellow, coming up after the chief had gone, saw the unfinished dinner, and ate it up without asking questions. Hardly had he finished when he was informed by a horror-stricken spectator that the food of which he had eaten was the chief's. "I knew the unfortunate delinquent well. He was remarkable for courage, and had signalised himself in the wars of the tribe. . . . No sooner did he hear the fatal news than he was seized by the most extraordinary convulsions and cramp in the stomach, which never ceased till he died, about sundown the same day. He was a strong man, in the prime of life, and if any pakeha [European] freethinker should have said he was not killed by the *tapu* [taboo] of the chief, which had been communicated to the food by contact, he would have been listened to with feelings of contempt for his ignorance and inability to understand plain and direct evidence."[1] This is not a solitary case. A Maori woman having eaten of some fruit, and being afterwards told that the fruit had being taken from a tabooed place, exclaimed that the spirit of the chief whose sanctity had been thus profaned would kill her. This was in the afternoon, and next day by twelve o'clock she was dead.[2] An observer who knows the Maoris well, says, "Tapu [taboo] is an awful weapon. I have seen a strong young man die the same day he was tapued; the victims die under it as though their strength ran out as water."[3] A Maori chief's tinder-box was once the means of killing several persons; for having been lost by him, and found by some men who used it to

---

[1] *Old New Zealand*, by a Pakeha Maori (London, 1884), p. 96 *sq.*

[2] W. Brown, *New Zealand and its Aborigines* (London, 1845), p. 76.

For more examples of the same kind see *ib.* p. 77 *sq.*

[3] E. Tregear, "The Maoris of New Zealand," in *Journ. Anthrop. Inst.* xix. 100.

light their pipes, they died of fright on learning to whom it had belonged. So too the garments of a high New Zealand chief will kill any one else who wears them. A chief was observed by a missionary to throw down a precipice a blanket which he found too heavy to carry. Being asked by the missionary why he did not leave it on a tree for the use of a future traveller, the chief replied that "it was the fear of its being taken by another which caused him to throw it where he did, for if it were worn, his tapu" (*i.e.* his spiritual power communicated by contact to the blanket and through the blanket to the man) "would kill the person."[1]

No wonder therefore that the savage should rank these human divinities amongst what he regards as the dangerous classes, and should impose exactly the same restraints upon the one as upon the other. For instance, those who have defiled themselves by touching a dead body are regarded by the Maoris as in a very dangerous state, and are sedulously shunned and isolated. But the taboos observed by and towards these defiled persons (*e.g.* they may not touch food with their hands, and the vessels used by them may not be used by other people) are identical with those observed by and towards sacred chiefs.[2] And, in general, the prohibition to use the dress, vessels, etc., of certain persons and the effects supposed to follow an infraction of the rule are exactly the same whether the persons to whom the things belong are sacred or what we might call unclean and polluted. As the garments which have been touched by a sacred chief

---

[1] R. Taylor, *Te Ika a Maui: or, New Zealand and its Inhabitants,*[2] p. 164.

[2] A. S. Thomson, *The Story of New Zealand,* i. 101 *sqq.*; *Old New Zealand,* by a Pakeha Maori, pp. 94, 104 *sqq.*

kill those who handle them, so do the things which have been touched by a menstruous woman. An Australian blackfellow, who discovered that his wife had lain on his blanket at her menstrual period, killed her and died of terror himself within a fortnight.[1] Hence Australian women at these times are forbidden under pain of death to touch anything that men use. They are also secluded at child-birth, and all vessels used by them during their seclusion are burned.[2] Amongst some of the Indians of North America also women at menstruation are forbidden to touch men's utensils, which would be so defiled by their touch that their subsequent use would be attended by certain mischief or misfortune.[3] Amongst the Eskimo of Alaska no one will willingly drink out of the same cup or eat out of the same dish that has been used by a woman at her confinement until it has been purified by certain incantations.[4] Amongst some of the Tinneh Indians of North America the dishes out of which girls eat during their seclusion at puberty "are used by no other person, and wholly devoted to their own use."[5] Again amongst some Indian tribes of North America men who have slain enemies are considered to be in a state of uncleanness, and will not eat or drink out of any dish or smoke out of any pipe but their own for a considerable time after the slaughter, and no one will willingly use their dishes or pipes. They live in a kind of seclusion during this time, at the end of which all

[1] *Journ. Anthrop. Inst.* ix. 458.

[2] W. Ridley, "Report on Australian Languages and Traditions," in *Journ. Anthrop. Inst.* ii. 268.

[3] Alexander Mackenzie, *Voyages from Montreal through the Continent of North America*, cxxiii.

[4] *Report of the International Polar Expedition to Point Barrow, Alaska* (Washington, 1885), p. 46.

[5] "Customs of the New Caledonian Women," in *Journ. Anthrop. Inst.* vii. 206.

the dishes and pipes used by them during their seclusion are burned.[1] Amongst the Kafirs, boys at circumcision live secluded in a special hut, and when they are healed all the vessels which they had used during their seclusion and the boyish mantles which they had hitherto worn are burned together with the hut.[2] When a young Indian brave is out on the war-path for the first time the vessels he eats and drinks out of must be touched by no one else.[3]

Thus the rules of ceremonial purity observed by divine kings, chiefs, and priests, by homicides, women at child-birth, and so on, are in some respects alike. To us these different classes of persons appear to differ totally in character and condition; some of them we should call holy, others we might pronounce unclean and polluted. But the savage makes no such moral distinction between them; the conceptions of holiness and pollution are not yet differentiated in his mind. To him the common feature of all these persons is that they are dangerous and in danger, and the danger in which they stand and to which they expose others is what we should call spiritual or supernatural, that is, imaginary. The danger, however, is not less real because it is imaginary; imagination acts upon man as really as does gravitation, and may kill him as certainly as a dose of prussic acid. To seclude these persons from the rest of the world so that the dreaded spiritual danger shall neither reach them, nor spread from them, is the object of the taboos which they have to observe.

---

[1] S. Hearne, *A Journey from Prince of Wales's Fort in Hudson's Bay to the Northern Ocean*, p. 204 *sqq.*

[2] L. Alberti, *De Kaffers* (Amsterdam, 1810), p. 76 *sq.*; H. Lichtenstein, *Reisen im südlichen Afrika*, i. 427.

[3] *Narrative of the Captivity and Adventures of John Tanner* (London, 1830), p. 122.

These taboos act, so to say, as electrical insulators to preserve the spiritual force with which these persons are charged from suffering or inflicting harm by contact with the outer world.[1]

No one was allowed to touch the body of the King or Queen of Tahiti;[2] and no one may touch the King of Cambodia, for any purpose whatever, without his express command. In July 1874 the king was thrown from his carriage and lay insensible on the ground, but not one of his suite dared to touch him; a European coming to the spot carried the injured monarch to his palace.[3] No one may touch the King of Corea; and if he deigns to touch a subject, the spot touched becomes sacred, and the person thus honoured must wear a visible mark (generally a cord of red silk) for the rest of his life. Above all, no iron may touch the king's body. In 1800 King Tieng-tsong-tai-oang died of a tumour in the back, no one dreaming of employing the lancet, which would probably have saved his life. It is said that one king suffered terribly from an abscess in the lip, till his physician called in a jester, whose antics made the king laugh heartily, and so the abscess burst.[4] Roman and Sabine priests might not be shaved with iron but only with bronze razors or shears;[5] and whenever an iron graving-tool was brought into the sacred grove of the Arval Brothers at Rome for the purpose of cutting an inscription in stone, an expiatory sacrifice of a lamb and a pig was offered, which was repeated when the graving-tool was removed from the

---

[1] On the nature of taboo, see especially W. Robertson Smith, *Religion of the Semites*, i. 142 *sqq.* 427 *sqq.*

[2] Ellis, *Polynesian Researches*, iii. 102.

[3] J. Moura, *Le Royaume du Cambodge*, i. 226.

[4] Ch. Dallet, *Histoire de l'Église de Corée*, i. xxiv. *sq.*; Griffis, *Corea, the Hermit Nation*, p. 219.

[5] Macrobius, *Sat.* v. 19, 13; Servius on Virgil, *Aen.* i. 448; Joannes Lydus, *De mens.* i. 31.

Kafir youth

Worship of an African King.

grove.[1] In Crete sacrifices were offered to Menedemus without the use of iron, because, it was said,
Menedemus had been killed by an iron weapon in the
Trojan war.[2] The Archon of Plataeae might not touch
iron ; but once a year, at the annual commemoration
of the men who fell at the battle of Plataeae, he was
allowed to carry a sword wherewith to sacrifice a bull.[3]
To this day a Hottentot priest never uses an iron
knife, but always a sharp splint of quartz in sacrificing
an animal or circumcising a lad.[4] Amongst the Moquis
of Arizona stone knives, hatchets, etc., have passed
out of common use, but are retained in religious ceremonies.[5] Negroes of the Gold Coast remove all iron
or steel from their person when they consult their
fetish.[6] The men who made the need-fire in Scotland
had to divest themselves of all metal.[7] In making the
clavie (a kind of Yule-tide fire-wheel) at Burghead, no
hammer may be used ; the hammering must be done
with a stone.[8] Amongst the Jews no iron tool was
used in building the temple at Jerusalem or in making
an altar.[9] The old wooden bridge (*Pons Sublicius*) at
Rome, which was considered sacred, was made and
had to be kept in repair without the use of iron or
bronze.[10] It was expressly provided by law that the
temple of Jupiter Liber at Furfo might be repaired

---

[1] *Acta Fratrum Arvalium*, ed. Henzen, pp. 128-135; Marquardt, *Römische
Staatsverwaltung*,iii.[2](*Das Sacralwesen*),
p. 459 *sq.*
[2] Callimachus, referred to by the Old
Scholiast on Ovid, *Ibis*. See Callimachus, ed. Blomfield, p. 216; Lobeck,
Aglaophamus, p. 686.
[3] Plutarch, *Aristides*, 21.   This
passage I owe to Mr. W. Wyse.
[4] Theophilus Hahn, *Tsuni - Goam,
the Supreme Being of the Khoi-Khoi*,
p. 22.

[5] J. G. Bourke, *The Snake Dance of
the Moquis of Arizona*, p. 178 *sq.*
[6] C. F. Gordon Cumming, *In the
Hebrides* (ed. 1883), p. 195.
[7] James Logan, *The Scottish Gael*
(ed. Alex. Stewart), ii. 68 *sq.*
[8] C. F. Gordon Cumming, *In the
Hebrides*, p. 226; E. J. Guthrie, *Old
Scottish Customs*, p. 223.
[9] 1 Kings vi. 7 ; Exodus xx. 25.
[10] Dionysius Halicarn. *Antiquit.
Roman.* iii. 45, v. 24; Plutarch, *Numa*,
9 ; Pliny, *Nat. Hist.* xxxvi. § 100.

with iron tools.[1]   The council chamber at Cyzicus was constructed of wood without any iron nails, the beams being so arranged that they could be taken out and replaced.[2]   The late Raja Vijyanagram, a member of the Viceroy's Council, and described as one of the most enlightened and estimable of Hindu princes, would not allow iron to be used in the construction of buildings within his territory, believing that its use would inevitably be followed by small-pox and other epidemics.[3]

This superstitious objection to iron perhaps dates from that early time in the history of society when iron was still a novelty, and as such was viewed by many with suspicion and dislike.   For everything new is apt to excite the awe and dread of the savage. "It is a curious superstition," says a recent pioneer in Borneo, "this of the Dusuns, to attribute anything —whether good or bad, lucky or unlucky—that happens to them to something novel which has arrived in their country.   For instance, my living in Kindram has caused the intensely hot weather we have experienced of late."[4]   The first introduction of iron ploughshares into Poland having been followed by a succession of bad harvests, the farmers attributed the badness of the crops to the iron ploughshares, and discarded them for the old wooden ones.[5]   The general dislike of innovation, which always makes itself strongly felt in the sphere of religion, is sufficient by itself to

---

[1] *Acta Fratrum Arvalium*, ed. Henzen, p. 132; *Corpus Inscriptionum Latinarum*, i. No. 603.

[2] Pliny, *l.c.*

[3] *Indian Antiquary*, x. (1881) 364.

[4] Frank Hatton, *North Borneo* (1886), p. 233.

[5] Alexand. Guagninus, "De ducatu Samogitiae," in *Respublica sive Status Regni Poloniae, Lituaniae, Prussiae, Livoniae* etc. (Elzevir, 1627), p. 276; Johan. Lasicius, "De diis Samogitarum caeterorumque Sarmatum," in *Respublica*, etc. (*ut supra*), p. 294 (p. 84 ed. Mannhardt, in *Magazin herausgeg. von der Lettisch - Literär. Gesellsch.* bd. xiv.)

account for the superstitious aversion to iron entertained by kings and priests and attributed by them
to the gods; possibly this aversion may have been
intensified in places by some such accidental cause as
the series of bad seasons which cast discredit on iron
ploughshares in Poland.   But the disfavour in which
iron is held by the gods and their ministers has another
side.   The very fact that iron is deemed obnoxious to
spirits furnishes men with a weapon which may be
turned against the spirits when occasion serves.   As
their dislike of iron is supposed to be so great that
they will not approach persons and things protected
by the obnoxious metal, iron may obviously be employed
as a charm for banning ghosts and other dangerous
spirits.   And it often is so used.   Thus when Scotch
fishermen were at sea, and one of them happened
to take the name of God in vain, the first man who
heard him called out "Cauld airn," at which every
man of the crew grasped the nearest bit of iron and
held it between his hands for a while.[1]   In Morocco
iron is considered a great protection against demons;
hence it is usual to place a knife or dagger under
a sick man's pillow.[2]   In India "the mourner who
performs the ceremony of putting fire into the dead
person's mouth carries with him a piece of iron: it
may be a key or a knife, or a simple piece of iron, and
during the whole time of his separation (for he is
unclean for a certain time, and no one will either touch
him or eat or drink with him, neither can he change
his clothes[3]) he carries the piece of iron about with

[1] E. J. Guthrie, *Old Scottish Customs*,
p. 149; Ch. Rogers, *Social Life in Scotland* (London, 1886), iii. 218.
   [2] A. Leared, *Morocco and the Moors*,
p. 273.

[3] The reader may observe how closely
the taboos laid upon mourners resemble
those laid upon kings.   From what has
gone before the reason of the resemblance is obvious.

him to keep off the evil spirit. In Calcutta the Bengali clerks in the Government Offices used to wear a small key on one of their fingers when they had been chief mourners."[1] In the north-east of Scotland immediately after a death had taken place, a piece of iron, such as a nail or a knitting-wire, used to be stuck into all the meal, butter, cheese, flesh, and whisky in the house, "to prevent death from entering them." The neglect of this precaution is said to have been closely followed by the corruption of the food and drink; the whisky has been known to become as white as milk.[2] When iron is used as a protective charm after a death, as in these Hindu and Scotch customs, the spirit against which it is directed is the ghost of the deceased.[3]

There is a priestly king to the north of Zengwih in Burma, revered by the Sotih as the highest spiritual and temporal authority, into whose house no weapon or cutting instrument may be brought.[4] This rule may perhaps be explained by a custom observed by various peoples after a death; they refrain from the use of sharp instruments so long as the ghost of the deceased is supposed to be near, lest they should wound it. Thus after a death the Roumanians of Transylvania are careful not to leave a knife lying with the sharp edge uppermost as long as the corpse remains in the house, "or else the soul will be forced to ride on the blade."[5] For seven days

---

[1] *Panjab Notes and Queries*, iii. No. 282.

[2] Walter Gregor, *The Folk-lore of the North-East of Scotland*, p. 206.

[3] This is expressly said in *Panjab Notes and Queries*, iii. No. 846. On iron as a protective charm see also Liebrecht, *Gervasius von Tilbury*, p. 99 *sqq.*; *id.*, *Zur Volkskunde*, p. 311; L. Strackerjan, *Aberglaube und Sagen aus dem Herzogthum Oldenburg*, § 233; Wuttke, *Der deutsche Volksaberglaube*[2], § 414 *sq.*; Tylor, *Primitive Culture*, i. 140; Mannhardt, *Der Baumkultus*, 132 *note*.

[4] Bastian, *Die Völker des östlichen Asien*, i. 136.

[5] E. Gerard, *The Land beyond the Forest*, i. 312; W. Schmidt, *Das Jahr und seine Tage in Meinung und Brauch der Romänen Siebenbürgens*, p. 40.

after a death, the corpse being still in the house, the Chinese abstain from the use of knives and needles, and even of chopsticks, eating their food with their fingers.[1]   Amongst the Innuit (Eskimos) of Alaska for four days after a death the women in the village do no sewing, and for five days the men do not cut wood with an axe.[2]   On the third, sixth, ninth, and fortieth days after the funeral the old Prussians and Lithuanians used to prepare a meal, to which, standing at the door, they invited the soul of the deceased.   At these meals they sat silent round the table and used no knives, and the women who served up the food were also without knives.   If any morsels fell from the table they were left lying there for the lonely souls that had no living relations or friends to feed them.   When the meal was over the priest took a broom and swept the souls out of the house, saying, "Dear souls, ye have eaten and drunk.   Go forth, go forth."[3]   In cutting the nails and combing the hair of a dead prince in South Celebes only the back of the knife and of the comb may be used.[4]   The Germans say that a knife should not be left edge upwards, because God and the spirits dwell there, or because it will cut the face of God and the angels.[5]   We can now understand why no cutting instrument may be taken into the house of the Burmese pontiff.   Like so many priestly kings, he is probably regarded as divine,

---

[1] J. H. Gray, *China*, i. 288.

[2] W. H. Dall, *Alaska and its Resources*, p. 146; *id.* in *American Naturalist*, xii. 7.

[3] Jo. Meletius, "De religione et sacrificiis veterum Borussorum," in *De Russorum Muscovitarum et Tartarorum religione, sacrificiis, nuptiarum, funerum ritu* (Spires, 1582), p. 263; Hartknoch, *Alt und neues Preussen* (Frankfort and Leipzig, 1684), p. 187 *sq.*

[4] B. F. Matthes, *Bijdragen tot de Ethnologie van Zuid-Celebes*, p. 136.

[5] Tettau und Temme, *Die Volkssagen Ostpreussens, Litthauens und Westpreussens*, p. 285; Grimm, *Deutsche Mythologie*,[4] iii. 454; cp. *id.* pp. 441, 469; Grohmann, *Aberglauben und Gebräuche aus Böhmen und Mähren*, p. 198.

and it is therefore right that his sacred spirit should not be exposed to the risk of being cut or wounded whenever it quits his body to hover invisible in the air or to fly on some distant mission.

We have seen that the Flamen Dialis was forbidden to touch or even name raw flesh.[1] In the Pelew Islands when a raid has been made on a village and a head carried off, the relations of the slain man are tabooed and have to submit to certain observances in order to escape the wrath of his ghost. They are shut up in the house, touch no raw flesh, and chew beetel over which an incantation has been uttered by the exorcist. After this the ghost of the slaughtered man goes away to the enemy's country in pursuit of his murderer.[2] The taboo is probably based on the common belief that the soul or spirit of the animal is in the blood. As tabooed persons are believed to be in a perilous state—for example, the relations of the slain man are liable to the attacks of his indignant ghost—it is especially necessary to isolate them from contact with spirits; hence the prohibition to touch raw meat. But as usual the taboo is only the special enforcement in particular circumstances of a general rule; in other words, its observance is particularly enjoined in circumstances which are supposed especially to call for its application, but apart from such special circumstances the prohibition is also observed, though less strictly, as an ordinary rule of life. Thus some of the Esthonians will not taste blood because they believe that it contains the animal's soul, which would enter the body of the person who

[1] Plutarch, *Quaest. Rom.* 110; Aulus Gellius, x. 15, 12.

[2] J. Kubary, *Die socialen Einrichtungen der Pelauer* (Berlin, 1885), p. 126 *sq.*

tasted the blood.[1]   Some Indian tribes of North
America, "through a strong principle of religion,
abstain in the strictest manner from eating the blood
of any animal, as it contains the life and spirit of the
beast."   These Indians "commonly pull their new-
killed venison (before they dress it) several times
through the smoke and flame of the fire, both by the
way of a sacrifice and to consume the blood, life, or
animal spirits of the beast, which with them would be
a most horrid abomination to eat."[2]   Many of the
Slave, Hare, and Dogrib Indians scruple to taste the
blood of game; hunters of the former tribes collect the
blood in the animal's paunch and bury it in the snow.[3]
Jewish hunters poured out the blood of the game
they had killed and covered it up with dust.   They
would not taste the blood, believing that the soul or
life of the animal was in the blood, or actually was the
blood.[4]   The same belief was held by the Romans,[5]
and is shared by the Arabs,[6] and by some of the
Papuan tribes of New Guinea.[7]

It is a common rule that royal blood must not be
shed upon the ground.   Hence when a king or one of
his family is to be put to death a mode of execution is
devised by which the royal blood shall not be spilt
upon the earth.   About the year 1688 the generalis-
simo of the army rebelled against the King of Siam
and put him to death "after the manner of royal
criminals, or as princes of the blood are treated when

---

[1] F. J. Wiedemann, *Aus dem inneren und äussern Leben der Ehsten* (St. Petersburg, 1876), pp. 448, 478.

[2] James Adair, *History of the American Indians*, pp. 134, 117.

[3] E. Petitot, *Monographie des Dènè-Dindjié*, p. 76.

[4] Leviticus xvii. 10-14. The Hebrew word translated "life" in the English version of verse 11 means also "soul" (marginal note in the Revised Version). Cp. Deuteronomy xii. 23-25.

[5] Servius on Virgil, *Aen.* v. 79 ; cp. *id.* on *Aen.* iii. 67.

[6] J. Wellhausen, *Reste Arabischen Heidentumes*, p. 217.

[7] A. Goudswaard, *De Papoewa's van de Geelvinksbaai* (Schiedam, 1863), p. 77.

convicted of capital crimes, which is by putting them into a large iron caldron, and pounding them to pieces with wooden pestles, because none of their royal blood must be spilt on the ground, it being, by their religion, thought great impiety to contaminate the divine blood by mixing it with earth."[1]   Other Siamese modes of executing a royal person are starvation, suffocation, stretching him on a scarlet cloth and thrusting a billet of odoriferous "saunders wood" into his stomach,[2] or lastly, sewing him up in a leather sack with a large stone and throwing him into the river; sometimes the sufferer's neck is broken with sandal-wood clubs before he is thrown into the water.[3]   When Kublai Khan defeated and took his uncle Nayan, who had rebelled against him, he caused Nayan to be put to death by being wrapt in a carpet and tossed to and fro till he died, "because he would not have the blood of his Line Imperial spilt upon the ground or exposed in the eye of Heaven and before the Sun."[4]   "Friar Ricold mentions the Tartar maxim: 'One Khan will put another to death to get possession of the throne, but he takes great care that the blood be not spilt. For they say that it is highly improper that the blood of the Great Khan should be spilt upon the ground; so they cause the victim to be smothered somehow or other.' The like feeling prevails at the court of Burma, where a peculiar mode of execution without bloodshed is reserved for princes of the blood."[5]   In Tonquin the ordinary mode of execution is beheading, but persons of

---

[1] Hamilton's "Account of the East Indies," in Pinkerton's *Voyages and Travels*, viii. 469.   Cp. W. Robertson Smith, *Religion of the Semites*, i. 349, *note* 2.

[2] De la Loubere, *A New Historical Account of the Kingdom of Siam* (London, 1693), p. 104 *sq.*

[3] Pallegoix, *Description du Royaume Thai ou Siam*, i. 271, 365 *sq.*

[4] Marco Polo, trans. by Col. H. Yule (2d ed. 1875), i. 335.

[5] Col. H. Yule on Marco Polo, *l.c.*

the blood royal are strangled.[1]   In Ashantee the blood
of none of the royal family may be shed; if one of
them is guilty of a great crime he is drowned in the
river Dah.[2]   In Madagascar the blood of nobles might
not be shed; hence when four Christians of that class
were to be executed they were burned alive.[3]   When
a young king of Uganda comes of age all his brothers
are burnt except two or three, who are preserved to
keep up the succession.[4]   The reluctance to shed royal
blood seems to be only a particular case of a general
reluctance to shed blood or at least to allow it to fall
on the ground.   Marco Polo tells us that in his day
persons found on the streets of Cambaluc (Pekin) at
unseasonable hours were arrested, and if found guilty
of a misdemeanour were beaten with a stick.   " Under
this punishment people sometimes die, but they adopt
it in order to eschew bloodshed, for their *Bacsis* say
that it is an evil thing to shed man's blood."[5]   When
Captain Christian was shot by the Manx Government
at the Restoration in 1660, the spot on which he stood
was covered with white blankets, that his blood might
not fall on the ground.[6]   Amongst some primitive
peoples, when the blood of a tribesman has to be shed
it is not suffered to fall upon the ground, but is
received upon the bodies of his fellow tribesmen.
Thus in some Australian tribes boys who are being
circumcised are laid on a platform, formed by the
living bodies of the tribesmen;[7] and when a boy's tooth

[1] Baron's " Description of the Kingdom of Tonqueen," in Pinkerton's *Voyages and Travels*, ix. 691.

[2] T. E. Bowdich, *Mission from Cape
Coast Castle to Ashantee* (London, 1873),
p. 207.

[3] Sibree, *Madagascar and its People*,
p. 430.

[4] C. T. Wilson and R. W. Felkin,
Uganda and the Egyptian Soudan, i.
200.

[5] Marco Polo, i. 399, Yule's translation, 2d ed.

[6] Sir Walter Scott, note 2 to *Peveril
of the Peak*, ch. v.

[7] *Native Tribes of South Australia*,

is knocked out as an initiatory ceremony, he is seated on the shoulders of a man, on whose breast the blood flows and may not be wiped away.[1]   When Australian blacks bleed each other as a cure for headache, and so on, they are very careful not to spill any of the blood on the ground, but sprinkle it on each other.[2]   We have already seen that in the Australian ceremony for making rain the blood which is supposed to imitate the rain is received upon the bodies of the tribesmen.[3] In South Celebes at child-birth a female slave stands under the house (the houses being raised on posts above the ground) and receives in a basin on her head the blood which trickles through the bamboo floor.[4] The unwillingness to shed blood is extended by some peoples to the blood of animals.   When the Wanika in Eastern Africa kill their cattle for food, "they either stone or beat the animal to death, so as not to shed the blood."[5]   Amongst the Damaras cattle killed for food are suffocated, but when sacrificed they are speared to death.[6]   But like most pastoral tribes in Africa, both the Wanika and Damaras very seldom kill their cattle, which are indeed commonly invested with a kind of sanctity.[7]   In killing an animal for food the Easter Islanders do not shed its blood, but stun it

---

p. 230; E. J. Eyre, *Journals of Expeditions of Discovery into Central Australia,* ii. 335; Brough Smyth, *Aborigines of Victoria,* i. 75 *note.*

[1] Collins, *Account of the English Colony of New South Wales* (London, 1798), p. 580.

[2] *Native Tribes of South Australia,* p. 224 *sq.*; Angas, *Savage Life and Scenes in Australia and New Zealand,* i. 110 *sq.*

[3] Above, p. 20.

[4] B. F. Matthes, *Bijdragen tot de Ethnologie van Zuid-Celebes,* p. 53.

[5] Lieut. Emery, in *Journal of the R. Geogr. Soc.* iii. 282.

[6] Ch. Andersson, *Lake Ngami,* p. 224.

[7] Ch. New, *Life, Wanderings, and Labours in Eastern Africa,* p. 124; Francis Galton, "Domestication of Animals," in *Transactions of the Ethnolog. Soc. of London,* iii. 135. On the original sanctity of domestic animals, see above all W. Robertson Smith, *The Religion of the Semites,* i. 263 *sqq.,* 277 *sqq.*

or suffocate it in smoke.[1]   The explanation of the
reluctance to shed blood on the ground is probably to
be found in the belief that the soul is in the blood, and
that therefore any ground on which it may fall necessarily becomes taboo or sacred.   In New Zealand
anything upon which even a drop of a high chief's
blood chances to fall becomes taboo or sacred to him.
For instance, a party of natives having come to visit
a chief in a fine new canoe, the chief got into it, but in
doing so a splinter entered his foot, and the blood
trickled on the canoe, which at once became sacred to
him.   The owner jumped out, dragged the canoe
ashore opposite the chief's house, and left it there.
Again, a chief in entering a missionary's house knocked
his head against a beam, and the blood flowed.   The
natives said that in former times the house would have
belonged to the chief.[2]   As usually happens with
taboos of universal application, the prohibition to spill
the blood of a tribesman on the ground applies
with peculiar stringency to chiefs and kings, and
is observed in their case long after it has ceased to
be observed in the case of others.

We have seen that the Flamen Dialis was not
allowed to walk under a trellised vine.[3]   The reason
for this prohibition was perhaps as follows.   It has been
shown that plants are considered as animate beings
which bleed when cut, the red juice which exudes from
some plants being regarded as the blood of the plant.[4]
The juice of the grape is therefore naturally conceived
as the blood of the vine.[5]   And since, as we have just

---

[1] L. Linton Palmer, "A Visit to
Easter Island," in *Journ. R. Geogr.
Soc.* xl. (1870) 171.

[2] R. Taylor, *Te Ika a Maui; or, New
Zealand and its Inhabitants,*[2] p. 164 *sq.*

[3] Plutarch, *Quaest. Rom.* 112;
Aulus Gellius, x. 15, 13.

[4] Above, p. 61 *sq.*

[5] Cp. W. Robertson Smith, *op. cit.*
p. 213 *sq.*

seen, the soul is often believed to be in the blood, the juice of the grape is regarded as the soul, or as containing the soul, of the vine. This belief is strengthened by the intoxicating effects of wine. For, according to primitive notions, all abnormal mental states, such as intoxication or madness, are caused by the entrance of a spirit into the person ; such mental states, in other words, are regarded as forms of possession or inspiration. Wine, therefore, is considered on two distinct grounds as a spirit or containing a spirit ; first because, as a red juice, it is identified with the blood of the plant, and second because it intoxicates or inspires. Therefore if the Flamen Dialis had walked under a trellised vine, the spirit of the vine, embodied in the clusters of grapes, would have been immediately over his head and might have touched it, which for a person like him in a state of permanent taboo [1] would have been highly danger-ous. This interpretation of the prohibition will be made probable if we can show, first, that wine has been actually viewed by some peoples as blood and intoxication as inspiration produced by drinking the blood ; and, second, that it is often considered dangerous, especially for tabooed persons, to have either blood or a living person over their heads.

With regard to the first point, we are informed by Plutarch that of old the Egyptian kings neither drank wine nor offered it in libations to the gods, because they held it to be the blood of beings who had once fought against the gods, the vine having sprung from their rotting bodies ; and the frenzy of intoxication was explained by the supposition that the drunken man was

---

[1] *Dialis cotidie feriatus est*, Aulus Gellius, x. 15, 16.

filled with the blood of the enemies of the gods.[1]   The
Aztecs regarded *pulque* or the wine of the country as
bad, on account of the wild deeds which men did under
its influence.   But these wild deeds were believed to
be the acts, not of the drunken man, but of the wine-
god by whom he was possessed and inspired ; and so
seriously was this theory of inspiration held that if any
one spoke ill of or insulted a tipsy man, he was liable
to be punished for disrespect to the wine-god incarnate
in his votary.   Hence, says Sahagun, it was believed,
not without ground, that the Indians intoxicated themselves on purpose to commit with impunity crimes
for which they would certainly have been punished if
they had committed them sober.[2]   Thus it appears
that on the primitive view intoxication or the inspiration produced by wine is exactly parallel to the inspiration produced by drinking the blood of animals.[3]
The soul or life is in the blood, and wine is the blood
of the vine.   Hence whoever drinks the blood of an
animal is inspired with the soul of the animal or of the
god, who, as we have seen,[4] is often supposed to enter
into the animal before it is slain ; and whoever drinks
wine drinks the blood, and so receives into himself
the soul or spirit, of the god of the vine.

With regard to the second point, the fear of passing
under blood or under a living person, we are told that
some of the Australian blacks have a dread of passing
under a leaning tree or even under the rails of a
fence.   The reason they give is that a woman may

---

[1] Plutarch, *Isis et Osiris*, c. 6.
A myth apparently akin to this has
been preserved in some native Egyptian
writings.   See Ad.. Erman, *Aegypten
und aegyptisches Leben im Altertum*, p.
364.

[2] Bernardino de Sahagun, *Histoire
générale des choses de la Nouvelle-
Espagne*, traduite par Jourdanet et
Siméon (Paris, 1880), p. 46 *sq*.
[3] See above, p. 34 *sq*.
[4] P. 35.

have been upon the tree or fence, and some blood from her may have fallen on it and might fall from it on them.[1] In Ugi, one of the Solomon Islands, a man will never, if he can help it, pass under a tree which has fallen across the path, for the reason that a woman may have stepped over it before him.[2] Amongst the Karens of Burma "going under a house, especially if there are females within, is avoided; as is also the passing under trees of which the branches extend downwards in a particular direction, and the but-end of fallen trees, etc."[3] The Siamese think it unlucky to pass under a rope on which women's clothes are hung, and to avert evil consequences the person who has done so must build a chapel to the earth-spirit.[4]

Probably in all such cases the rule is based on a fear of being brought into contact with blood, especially the blood of women. From a like fear a Maori will never lean his back against the wall of a native house.[5] For the blood of women is believed to have disastrous effects upon males. In the Encounter Bay tribe of South Australia boys are warned that if they see the blood of women they will early become gray-headed and their strength will fail prematurely.[6] Men of the Booandik tribe think that if they see the blood of their women they will not be able to fight against their enemies and will be killed; if the sun dazzles their eyes at a fight, the first woman they afterwards meet is sure to get a blow from their club.[7] In the

[1] E. M. Curr, *The Australian Race* (Melbourne and London, 1887), iii. 179.

[2] H. B. Guppy, *The Solomon Islands and their Natives* (London, 1887), p. 41.

[3] E. B. Cross, "On the Karens," in *Journal of the American Oriental Society*, iv. (1854) 312.

[4] Bastian, *Die Völker des östlichen Asien*, iii. 230.

[5] For the reason see Shortland, *Traditions and Superstitions of the New Zealanders*, pp. 112 sq., 292.

[6] *Native Tribes of South Australia*, p. 186.

[7] Mrs. James Smith, *The Booandik Tribe*, p. 5.

island of Wetar it is thought that if a man or a lad comes upon a woman's blood he will be unfortunate in war and other undertakings, and that any precautions he may take to avoid the misfortune will be vain.[1] The people of Ceram also believe that men who see women's blood will be wounded in battle.[2]   Similarly the Ovahereró (Damaras) of South Africa think that if they see a lying-in woman shortly after child-birth they will become weaklings and will be shot when they go to war.[3]   It is an Esthonian belief that men who see women's blood will suffer from an eruption on the skin.[4]

Again, the reason for not passing under dangerous objects, like a vine or women's blood, is a fear that they may come in contact with the head ; for among primitive people the head is peculiarly sacred.   The special sanctity attributed to it is sometimes explained by a belief that it is the seat of a spirit which is very sensitive to injury or disrespect.   Thus the Karens suppose that a being called the *tso* resides in the upper part of the head, and while it retains its seat no harm can befall the person from the efforts of the seven *Kelahs*, or personified passions.   " But if the *tso* becomes heedless or weak certain evil to the person is the result.   Hence the head is carefully attended to, and all possible pains are taken to provide such dress and attire as will be pleasing to the *tso*." [5] The Siamese think that a spirit called *Khuan*, or *Chom Kuan*, dwells in the human head, of which it is the

---

[1] Riedel, *De sluik-en kroesharige rassen tusschen Selebes en Papua*, p. 450.

[2] Riedel, *op. cit.* p. 139 ; cp. *id.* p. 209.

[3] E. Dannert, " Customs of the Ovaherero at the Birth of a Child," in (South African) *Folk-lore Journal*, ii. 63.

[4] F. J. Wiedemann, *Aus dem innern und äussern Leben der Ehsten*, p. 475.

[5] E. B. Cross, " On the Karens," in *Journal of the American Oriental Society*, iv. 311 *sq.*

guardian spirit. The spirit must be carefully protected from injury of every kind; hence the act of shaving or cutting the hair is accompanied with many ceremonies. The *Khuan* is very sensitive on points of honour, and would feel mortally insulted if the head in which he resides were touched by the hand of a stranger. When Dr. Bastian, in conversation with a brother of the king of Siam, raised his hand to touch the prince's skull in order to illustrate some medical remarks he was making, a sullen and threatening murmur bursting from the lips of the crouching courtiers warned him of the breach of etiquette he had committed, for in Siam there is no greater insult to a man of rank than to touch his head. If a Siamese touch the head of another with his foot, both of them must build chapels to the earth-spirit to avert the omen. Nor does the guardian spirit of the head like to have the hair washed too often; it might injure or incommode him. It was a grand solemnity when the king of Burmah's head was washed with water taken from the middle of the river. Whenever the native professor, from whom Dr. Bastian took lessons in Burmese at Mandalay, had his head washed, which took place as a rule once a month, he was generally absent for three days together, that time being consumed in preparing for, and recovering from, the operation of head-washing. Dr. Bastian's custom of washing his head daily gave rise to much remark.[1]

Again, the Burmese think it an indignity to have any one, especially a woman, over their heads, and for this reason Burmese houses have never more than one story. The houses are raised on posts above the ground, and whenever anything fell through the floor

---

[1] Bastian, *Die Völker des östlichen Asien*, ii. 256, iii. 71, 230, 235 *sq.*

Dr. Bastian had always difficulty in persuading a servant to fetch it from under the house. In Rangoon a priest, summoned to the bedside of a sick man, climbed up a ladder and got in at the window rather than ascend the staircase, to reach which he must have passed under a gallery. A pious Burman of Rangoon, finding some images of Buddha in a ship's cabin, offered a high price for them, that they might not be degraded by sailors walking over them on the deck.[1] Similarily the Cambodians esteem it a grave offence to touch a man's head; some of them will not enter a place where anything whatever is suspended over their heads; and the meanest Cambodian would never consent to live under an inhabited room. Hence the houses are built of one story only; and even the Government respects the prejudice by never placing a prisoner in the stocks under the floor of a house, though the houses are raised high above the ground.[2] The same superstition exists amongst the Malays; for an early traveller reports that in Java people "wear nothing on their heads, and say that nothing must be on their heads . . . and if any person were to put his hand upon their head they would kill him; and they do not build houses with storeys, in order that they may not walk over each other's heads."[3] It is also found in full force throughout Polynesia. Thus of Gattanewa, a Marquesan chief, it is said that "to touch the top of his head, or any thing which had been on his head was sacrilege. To pass over his head

---

[1] Bastian, *op. cit.* ii. 150; Sangermano, *Description of the Burmese Empire* (Rangoon, 1885), p. 131; C. F. S. Forbes, *British Burma*, p. 334; Shway Yoe, *The Burman*, i. 91.

[2] J. Moura, *Le Royaume du Cambodge*, i. 178, 388.

[3] Duarte Barbosa, *Description of the Coasts of East Africa and Malabar in the beginning of the Sixteenth Century* (Hakluyt Society, 1866), p. 197.

was an indignity never to be forgotten. Gattanewa, nay, all his family, scorned to pass a gateway which is ever closed, or a house with a door; all must be as open and free as their unrestrained manners. He would pass under nothing that had been raised by the hand of man, if there was a possibility of getting round or over it. Often have I seen him walk the whole length of our barrier, in preference to passing between our water-casks; and at the risk of his life scramble over the loose stones of a wall, rather than go through the gateway."[1] Marquesan women have been known to refuse to go on the decks of ships for fear of passing over the heads of chiefs who might be below.[2] But it was not the Marquesan chiefs only whose heads were sacred; the head of every Marquesan was taboo, and might neither be touched nor stepped over by another; even a father might not step over the head of his sleeping child.[3] No one was allowed to be over the head of the king of Tonga.[4] In Hawaii (the Sandwich Islands) if a man climbed upon a chief's house or upon the wall of his yard, he was put to death; if his shadow fell on a chief, he was put to death; if he walked in the shadow of a chief's house with his head painted white or decked with a garland or wetted with water, he was put to death.[5] In Tahiti any one who stood over the king or queen, or passed his hand over their heads, might be put to death.[6] Until certain rites were performed over it, a Tahitian infant was

[1] David Porter, *Journal of a Cruise made to the Pacific Ocean in the U.S. Frigate Essex* (New York, 1822), ii. 65.

[2] Vincendon-Dumoulin et Desgraz, *Iles Marquises*, p. 262.

[3] Langsdorff, *Reise um die Welt*, i. 115 *sq.*

[4] Capt. James Cook, *Voyages*, v. 427 (ed. 1809).

[5] Jules Remy, *Ka Mooolelo Hawaii, Histoire de l'Archipel Havaiien* (Paris and Leipzig, 1862), p. 159.

[6] Ellis, *Polynesian Researches*, iii. 102.

especially taboo ; whatever touched the child's head, while it was in this state, became sacred and was deposited in a consecrated place railed in for the purpose at the child's house. If a branch of a tree touched the child's head, the tree was cut down ; and if in its fall it injured another tree so as to penetrate the bark, that tree also was cut down as unclean and unfit for use. After the rites were performed, these special taboos ceased ; but the head of a Tahitian was always sacred, he never carried anything on it, and to touch it was an offence.[1] The head of a Maori chief was so sacred that "if he only touched it with his fingers, he was obliged immediately to apply them to his nose, and snuff up the sanctity which they had acquired by the touch, and thus restore it to the part from whence it was taken."[2] In some circumstances the tabooed person is forbidden to touch his head at all. Thus in North America, Tinneh girls at puberty, Creek lads during the year of their initiation into manhood, and young braves on their first war-path, are forbidden to scratch their heads with their fingers, and are provided with a stick for the purpose.[3] But to return to the Maoris. On account of the sacredness of his head "a chief could not blow the fire with his mouth, for the breath being sacred, communicated his sanctity to it, and a brand might be taken by a slave, or a man of another tribe, or the fire might be used for other purposes,

---

[1] James Wilson, *A Missionary Voyage to the Southern Pacific Ocean* (London, 1799), p. 354 *sq.*

[2] R. Taylor, *Te Ika a Maui : or, New Zealand and its Inhabitants*, p. 165.

[3] "Customs of the New Caledonian Women," in *Journ. Anthrop. Inst.* vii. 206 ; B. Hawkins, "Sketch of the Creek Country," in *Collections of the Georgia Historical Society*, iii. pt. i. (Savannah, 1848), p. 78 ; A. S. Gatschet, *Migration Legend of the Creek Indians*, i. 185 ; *Narrative of the Captivity and Adventures of John Tanner* (London, 1830), p. 122 ; Kohl, *Kitschi-Gami*, ii. 168.

such as cooking, and so cause his death."[1]   It is a crime for a sacred person in New Zealand to leave his comb, or anything else which has touched his head, in a place where food has been cooked, or to suffer another person to drink out of any vessel which has touched his lips.   Hence when a chief wishes to drink he never puts his lips to the vessel, but holds his hands close to his mouth so as to form a hollow, into which water is poured by another person, and thence is allowed to flow into his mouth. If a light is needed for his pipe, the burning ember taken from the fire must be thrown away as soon as it is used ; for the pipe becomes sacred because it has touched his mouth ; the coal becomes sacred because it has touched the pipe ; and if a particle of the sacred cinder were replaced on the common fire, the fire would also become sacred and could no longer be used for cooking.[2]   Some Maori chiefs, like other Polynesians, object to go down into a ship's cabin from fear of people passing over their heads.[3]   Dire misfortune was thought by the Maoris to await those who entered a house where any article of animal food was suspended over their heads. " A dead pigeon, or a piece of pork hung from the roof was a better protection from molestation than a sentinel."[4]   If I am right, the reason for the special objection to having animal food over the head is the fear of bringing the sacred head into contact with the spirit

[1] R. Taylor, *l.c.*

[2] E. Shortland, *The Southern Districts of New Zealand*, p. 293; *id.*, *Traditions and Superstitions of the New Zealanders*, p. 107, *sq.*

[3] J. Dumont D'Urville, *Voyage autour du Monde et à la recherche de La Pérouse, exécuté sous son commandement*

sur la corvette Astrolabe. Histoire du Voyage, ii. 534.

[4] R. A. Cruise, *Journal of a Ten Months' Residence in New Zealand* (London, 1823), p. 187 ; Dumont D'Urville, *op. cit.* ii. 533 ; E. Shortland, *The Southern Districts of New Zealand* (London, 1851), p. 30.

"No one may touch the King of Corea"

New Zealanders.

of the animal ; just as the reason why the Flamen Dialis might not walk under a vine was the fear of bringing his sacred head into contact with the spirit of the vine.

When the head was considered so sacred that it might not even be touched without grave offence, it is obvious that the cutting of the hair must have been a delicate and difficult operation. The difficulties and dangers which, on the primitive view, beset the operation are of two kinds. There is first the danger of disturbing the spirit of the head, which may be injured in the process and may revenge itself upon the person who molests him. Secondly, there is the difficulty of disposing of the shorn locks. For the savage believes that the sympathetic connection which exists between himself and every part of his body continues to exist even after the physical connection has been severed, and that therefore he will suffer from any harm that may befall the severed parts of his body, such as the clippings of his hair or the parings of his nails. Accordingly he takes care that these severed portions of himself shall not be left in places where they might either be exposed to accidental injury or fall into the hands of malicious persons who might work magic on them to his detriment or death. Such dangers are common to all, but sacred persons have more to fear from them than ordinary people, so the precautions taken by them are proportionately stringent. The simplest way of evading the danger is of course not to cut the hair at all ; and this is the expedient adopted where the danger is thought to be more than usually great. The Frankish kings were not allowed to cut their hair.[1] A Haida medicine-man may neither cut

---

[1] Agathias i. 3 ; Grimm, *Deutsche Rechtsalterthümer*, p. 239 *sqq.*

nor comb his hair, so it is always long and tangled.[1] Amongst the Alfoers of Celebes the *Leleen* or priest who looks after the rice-fields may not cut his hair during the time that he exercises his special functions, that is, from a month before the rice is sown until it is housed.[2] In Ceram men do not cut their hair : if married men did so, they would lose their wives ; if young men did so, they would grow weak and enervated.[3] In Timorlaut, married men may not cut their hair for the same reason as in Ceram, but widowers and men on a journey may do so after offering a fowl or a pig in sacrifice.[4] Here men on a journey are specially permitted to cut their hair ; but elsewhere men travelling abroad have been in the habit of leaving their hair uncut until their return. The reason for the latter custom is probably the danger to which, as we have seen, a traveller is believed to be exposed from the magic arts of the strangers amongst whom he sojourns ; if they got possession of his shorn hair, they might work his destruction through it. The Egyptians on a journey kept their hair uncut till they returned home.[5] "At Tâif when a man returned from a journey his first duty was to visit the Rabba and poll his hair."[6] The custom of keeping the hair unshorn during a dangerous expedition seems to have been observed, at least occasionally, by the Romans.[7] Achilles kept unshorn his yellow hair,

[1] G. M. Dawson "On the Haida Indians of the Queen Charlotte Islands," in *Geological Survey of Canada, Report of Progress for* 1878-79, p. 123 B.

[2] P. N. Wilken, "Bijdragen tot de kennis van de zeden en gewoonten der Alfoeren in de Minahassa," in *Mededeelingen van wege het Nederlandsche Zendelingᵍenootschap*, vii. (1863) p. 126.

[3] Riedel, *De sluik-en kroesharige*

rassen tusschen Selebes en Papua, p. 137.   [4] Riedel, *op. cit.* p. 292 *sq.*

[5] Diodorus Siculus, i. 18.

[6] W. Robertson Smith, *Kinship and Marriage in Early Arabia*, p. 152 *sq.*

[7] Valerius Flaccus, *Argonaut.* i. 378 *sq.* :—

"*Tectus et Eurytion servato colla capillo,
Quem pater Aonias reducem tondebit ad aras.*"

because his father had vowed to offer it to the river
Sperchius if ever his son came home from the wars
beyond the sea.[1]   Again, men who have taken a vow
of vengeance sometimes keep their hair unshorn till
they have fulfilled their vow.   Thus of the Marquesans
we are told that "occasionally they have their head
entirely shaved, except one lock on the crown, which
is worn loose or put up in a knot.   But the latter
mode of wearing the hair is only adopted by them
when they have a solemn vow, as to revenge the death
of some near relation, etc.   In such case the lock is
never cut off until they have fulfilled their promise."[2]
Six thousand Saxons once swore that they would not
cut their hair nor shave their beards until they had
taken vengeance on their enemies.[3]   On one occasion
a Hawaiian taboo is said to have lasted thirty years
"during which the men were not allowed to trim
their beards, etc."[4]   While his vow lasted, a Nazarite
might not have his hair cut: "All the days of the
vow of his separation there shall no razor come upon
his head."[5]   Possibly in this case there was a special
objection to touching the tabooed man's head with
iron.   The Roman priests, as we have seen, were
shorn with bronze knives.   The same feeling probably gave rise to the European rule that a child's
nails should not be cut during the first year, but
that if it is absolutely necessary to shorten them they
should be bitten off by the mother or nurse.[6]   For

[1] Homer, *Iliad*, xxiii. 141 *sqq.*

[2] D. Porter, *Journal of a Cruise
made to the Pacific Ocean*, ii. 120.

[3] Paulus Diaconus, *Hist. Langobard.*
iii. 7.

[4] Ellis, *Polynesian Researches*, iv.
387.

[5] Numbers vi. 5.

[6] J. A. E. Köhler, *Volksbrauch*, etc.

im Voigtlande, p. 424 ; W. Henderson,
Folk-lore of the Northern Counties, p. 16
sq.; F. Panzer, *Beitrag zur deutschen
Mythologie*, i. 258 ; Zingerle, *Sitten,
Bräuche und Meinungen des Tiroler
Volkes*,[2] Nos. 46, 72 ; J. W. Wolf,
Beiträge zur deutschen Mythologie, i.
208 (No. 45), 209 (No. 53) ; Knoop,
Volkssagen, Erzählungen, etc. *aus dem*

in all parts of the world a young child is believed to be especially exposed to supernatural dangers, and particular precautions are taken to guard it against them; in other words, the child is under a number of taboos, of which the rule just mentioned is one. "Among Hindus the usual custom seems to be that the nails of a first-born child are cut at the age of six months. With other children a year or two is allowed to elapse."[1] The Slave, Hare, and Dogrib Indians of North America do not cut the nails of female children till they are four years of age.[2] In some parts of Germany it is thought that if a child's hair is combed in its first year the child will be unlucky;[3] or that if a boy's hair is cut before his seventh year he will have no courage.[4]

But when it is necessary to cut the hair, precautions are taken to lessen the dangers which are supposed to attend the operation. Amongst the Maoris many spells were uttered at hair-cutting; one, for example, was spoken to consecrate the obsidian knife with which the hair was cut; another was pronounced to avert the thunder and lightning which hair-cutting was believed to cause.[5] "He who has had his hair cut is in the immediate charge of the Atua (spirit); he is removed from the contact and society of

östlichen Hinterpommern, p. 157 (No. 23); E. Veckenstedt, *Wendische Sagen, Märchen und abergläubische Gebräuche*, p. 445; J. Haltrich, *Zur Volkskunde der Siebenbürger Sachsen*, p. 313; E. Krause, "Abergläubische Kuren u. sonstiger Aberglaube in Berlin," *Zeitschrift für Ethnologie*, xv. 84.

[1] *Panjab Notes and Queries*, ii. No. 1092.

[2] G. Gibbs, "Notes on the Tinneh or Chepewyan Indians of British and Russian America," in *Annual Report of the Smithsonian Institution*, 1866, p. 305; W. Dall, *Alaska and its Resources*, p. 202. The reason alleged by the Indians (that if the girls' nails were cut sooner the girls would be lazy and unable to embroider in porcupine quill-work) is probably a late invention, like the reasons assigned in Europe for the similar custom (the commonest being that the child would become a thief).

[3] Knoop, *l.c.*

[4] Wolf, *Beiträge zur deutschen Mythologie*, i. 209 (No. 57).

[5] R. Taylor, *New Zealand and its Inhabitants*, p. 206 *sqq.*

his family and his tribe; he dare not touch his food himself; it is put into his mouth by another person; nor can he for some days resume his accustomed occupations or associate with his fellow men."[1]   The person who cuts the hair is also tabooed; his hands having been in contact with a sacred head, he may not touch food with them or engage in any other employment; he is fed by another person with food cooked over a sacred fire.   He cannot be released from the taboo before the following day, when he rubs his hands with potato or fern root which has been cooked on a sacred fire; and this food having been taken to the head of the family in the female line and eaten by her, his hands are freed from the taboo.   In some parts of New Zealand the most sacred day of the year was that appointed for hair-cutting; the people assembled in large numbers on that day from all the neighbour-hood.[2]   It is an affair of state when the king of Cambodia's hair is cut.   The priests place on the barber's fingers certain old rings set with large stones, which are supposed to contain spirits favourable to the kings, and during the operation the Brahmans keep up a noisy music to drive away the evil spirits.[3]   The hair and nails of the Mikado could only be cut while he was asleep,[4] perhaps because his soul being then absent from his body, there was less chance of injuring it with the shears.

But even when the hair and nails have been safely cut, there remains the difficulty of disposing of them,

---

[1] Richard A. Cruise, *Journal of a Ten Months' Residence in New Zealand*, p. 283 *sq.* Cp. Dumont D'Urville, *Voyage autour du Monde et à la recherche de La Pérouse. Histoire du Voyage* (Paris, 1832), ii. 533.

[2] E. Shortland, *Traditions and Superstitions of the New Zealanders*, p. 108 *sqq.*; Taylor, *l.c.*

[3] J. Moura, *Le Royaume du Cambodge*, i. 226 *sq.*

[4] See above, p. 111.

for their owner believes himself liable to suffer from any harm that may befall them. Thus, an Australian girl, sick of a fever, attributed her illness to the fact that some months before a young man had come behind her and cut off a lock of her hair; she was sure he had buried it and that it was rotting. "Her hair," she said, "was rotting somewhere, and her *Marm-bu-la* (kidney fat) was wasting away, and when her hair had completely rotted, she would die."[1] A Marquesan chief told Lieutenant Gamble that he was extremely ill, the Happah tribe having stolen a lock of his hair and buried it in a plantain leaf for the purpose of taking his life. Lieut. Gamble argued with him, but in vain; die he must unless the hair and the plantain leaf were brought back to him; and to obtain them he had offered the Happahs the greater part of his property. He complained of excessive pain in the head, breast and sides.[2] When an Australian blackfellow wishes to get rid of his wife, he cuts off a lock of her hair in her sleep, ties it to his spear-thrower, and goes with it to a neighbouring tribe, where he gives it to a friend. His friend sticks the spear-thrower up every night before the camp fire, and when it falls down it is a sign that his wife is dead.[3] The way in which the charm operates was explained to Mr. Howitt by a Mirajuri man. "You see," he said, "when a blackfellow doctor gets hold of something belonging to a man and roasts it with things, and sings over it, the fire catches hold of the smell of the man, and that settles the poor fellow."[4] In Germany it is a common

---

[1] Brough Smyth, *Aborigines of Victoria*, i. 468 *sq.*

[2] D. Porter, *Journal of a Cruise made to the Pacific Ocean*, ii. 188.

[3] J. Dawson, *Australian Aborigines*, p. 36.

[4] A. W. Howitt, "On Australian Medicine-men," in *Journ. Anthrop. Inst.*

notion that if birds find a person's cut hair, and build
their nests with it, the person will suffer from headache ;[1] sometimes it is thought that he will have an
eruption on the head.[2] Again it is thought that cut
or combed out hair may disturb the weather by
producing rain and hail, thunder and lightning.
We have seen that in New Zealand a spell was
uttered at hair-cutting to avert thunder and lightning. In the Tirol, witches are supposed to use
cut or combed out hair to make hail-stones or
thunder-storms with.[3] Thlinket Indians have been
known to attribute stormy weather to the fact that
a girl had combed her hair outside of the house.[4]
The Romans seem to have held similar views, for
it was a maxim with them that no one on ship-
board should cut his hair or nails except in a storm,[5]
that is, when the mischief was already done. In
West Africa, when the Mani of Chitombe or Jumba
died, the people used to run in crowds to the corpse
and tear out his hair, teeth, and nails, which they kept
as a rain-charm, believing that otherwise no rain
would fall. The Makoko of Anzikos begged the
missionaries to give him half their beards as a rain-

---

xvi. 27. Cp. E. Palmer, "Notes on
some Australian Tribes," in *Journ.
Anthrop. Inst.* xiii. 293 ; James
Bonwick, *Daily Life of the Tasmanians*,
p. 178 ; James Chalmers, *Pioneering in
New Guinea*, p. 187 ; J. S. Polack,
*Manners and Customs of the New
Zealanders*, i. 282 ; Bastian, *Die
Völker des östlichen Asien*, iii. 270 ;
Langsdorff, *Reise um die Welt*, i. 134 *sq.*
A. S. Thomson, *The Story of New
Zealand*, i. 79, 116 *sq.* ; Ellis, *Poly-
nesian Researches*, i. 364 ; Zingerle,
*Sitten, Bräuche und Meinungen des
Tiroler Volkes*,[2] No. 178.

[1] Meier, *Deutsche Sagen, Sitten und
Gebräuche aus Schwaben*, p. 509; Panzer,
Beitrag zur deutschen Mythologie, i.
258; J. A. E. Köhler, *Volksbrauch
etc. im Voigtlande*, p. 425 ; A. Witzschel,
*Sagen, Sitten und Gebräuche aus Thür-
ingen*, p. 282; Zingerle, *op. cit.* No. 180;
Wolf, *Beiträge zur deutschen Mythologie*,
i. 224 (No. 273).

[2] Zingerle, *op. cit.* No. 181.

[3] Zingerle, *op. cit.* Nos. 176, 179.

[4] A. Krause, *Die Tlinkit-Indianer*.
(Jena, 1885), p. 300.

[5] Petronius, *Sat.* 104.

charm.[1] In some Victorian tribes the sorcerer used to burn human hair in time of drought; it was never burned at other times for fear of causing a deluge of rain. Also when the river was low, the sorcerer would place human hair in the stream to increase the supply of water.[2]

To preserve the cut hair and nails from injury and from the dangerous uses to which they may be put by sorcerers, it is necessary to deposit them in some safe place. Hence the natives of the Maldives carefully keep the cuttings of their hair and nails and bury them, with a little water, in the cemeteries; "for they would not for the world tread upon them nor cast them in the fire, for they say that they are part of their body and demand burial as it does; and, indeed, they fold them neatly in cotton; and most of them like to be shaved at the gates of temples and mosques."[3] In New Zealand the severed hair was deposited on some sacred spot of ground "to protect it from being touched accidentally or designedly by any one."[4] The shorn locks of a chief were gathered with much care and placed in an adjoining cemetery.[5] The Tahitians buried the cuttings of their hair at the temples.[6] The cut hair and nails of the Flamen Dialis were buried under a lucky tree.[7] The hair of the Vestal virgins was hung upon an ancient lotus-tree.[8] In Germany

[1] Bastian, *Die deutsche Expedition an der Loango-Küste*, i. 231 *sq.*; *id.*, *Ein Besuch in San Salvador*, p. 117.

[2] W. Stanbridge, "On the Aborigines of Victoria," in *Transact. Ethnolog. Soc. of London*, i. 300.

[3] François Pyrard, *Voyages to the East Indies, the Maldives, the Moluccas, and Brazil*. Translated by Albert Gray (Hakluyt Society, 1887), i. 110 *sq.*

[4] Shortland, *Traditions and Superstitions of the New Zealanders*, p. 110.

[5] Polack, *Manners and Customs of the New Zealanders*, i. 38 *sq.*

[6] James Wilson, *A Missionary Voyage to the Southern Pacific Ocean*, p. 355.

[7] Aulus Gellius, x. 15, 15.

[8] Pliny, *Nat. Hist.* xvi. 235; Festus, *s.v. capillatam vel capillarem arborem.*

the clippings of hair used often to be buried under an elder-bush.[1]   In Oldenburg cut hair and nails are wrapt in a cloth which is deposited in a hole in an elder-tree three days before the new moon ; the hole is then plugged up.[2]   In the West of Northumberland it is thought that if the first parings of a child's nails are buried under an ash-tree, the child will turn out a fine singer.[3]   In Amboina before a child may taste sago-pap for the first time, the father cuts off a lock of the child's hair which he buries under a sago palm.[4]   In the Aru Islands, when a child is able to run alone, a female relation cuts off a lock of its hair and deposits it on a banana-tree.[5]   In the island of Roti it is thought that the first hair which a child gets is not his own and that, if it is not cut off, it will make him weak and ill.   Hence, when the child is about a month old, his hair is cut off with much ceremony.   As each of the friends who are invited to the ceremony enters the house he goes up to the child, cuts off a little of its hair and drops it into a cocoa-nut shell full of water.   Afterwards the father or another relation takes the hair and packs it into a little bag made of leaves, which he fastens to the top of a palm-tree.   Then he gives the leaves of the palm a good shaking, climbs down, and goes home without speaking to any one.[6]   Indians of the Yukon territory, Alaska, do not throw away their cut hair and nails, but tie them up in little bundles and place them in the crotches of trees or anywhere where they will

---

[1] Wuttke, *Der deutsche Volksaberglaube*,[2] § 464.

[2] W. Mannhardt, *Germanische Mythen*, p. 630.

[3] W. Henderson, *Folk-lore of the Northern Counties*, p. 17.

[4] Riedel, *De sluik-en kroesharige rassen tusschen Selebes en Papua*, p. 74.

[5] Riedel, *op. cit.* p. 265.

[6] G. Heijmering "Zeden en gewoonten op het eiland Rottie," in *Tijdschrift voor Neêrland's Indië* (1843), dl. ii. 634-637.

not be disturbed by animals. For "they have a superstition that disease will follow the disturbance of such remains by animals."[1] The clipped hair and nails are often buried in any secret place, not necessarily in a temple or cemetery or under a tree, as in the cases already mentioned. In Swabia it is said that cut hair should be buried in a place where neither sun nor moon shines, therefore in the ground, under a stone, etc.[2] In Danzig it is buried in a bag under the threshold.[3] In Ugi, one of the Solomon Islands, men bury their hair lest it should fall into the hands of an enemy who would make magic with it and so bring sickness or calamity on them.[4] The Zend Avesta directs that the clippings of hair and the parings of nails shall be placed in separate holes, and that three, six, or nine furrows shall be drawn round each hole with a metal knife.[5] In the Grihya-Sûtras it is provided that the hair cut from a child's head at the end of the first, third, fifth, or seventh year shall be buried in the earth at a place covered with grass or in the neighbourhood of water.[6] The Madi or Moru tribe of Central Africa bury the parings of their nails in the ground.[7] The Kafirs carry still further this dread of allowing any portion of themselves to fall into the hands of an enemy ; for not only do they bury their cut hair and nails in a sacred place, but when one of them cleans the head of another he preserves the insects which he

[1] W. Dall, *Alaska and its Resources*, p. 54; F. Whymper, "The Natives of the Youkon River," in *Transact. Ethnolog. Soc. of London*, vii. 174.

[2] E. Meier, *Deutsche Sagen, Sitten und Gebräuche aus Schwaben*, p. 509.

[3] W. Mannhardt, *Germanische Mythen*, p. 630.

[4] H. B. Guppy, *The Solomon Islands and their Natives*, p. 54.

[5] Fargaard, xvii.

[6] *Grihya-Sûtras*, translated by H. Oldenberg (Oxford, 1886), vol. i. p. 57.

[7] R. W. Felkin, "Notes on the Madi or Moru tribe of Central Africa," in *Proceedings of the Royal Society of Edinburgh*, xii. (1882-84) p. 332.

finds, "carefully delivering them to the person to whom they originally appertained, supposing, according to their theory, that as they derived their support from the blood of the man from whom they were taken, should they be killed by another the blood of his neighbour would be in his possession, thus placing in his hands the power of some superhuman influence."[1] Amongst the Wanyoro of Central Africa all cuttings of the hair and nails are carefully stored under the bed and afterwards strewed about among the tall grass.[2] In North Guinea they are carefully hidden (it is not said where) "in order that they may not be used as a fetish for the destruction of him to whom they belong.[3] In Bolang Mongondo (Celebes) the first hair cut from a child's head is kept in a young cocoa-nut, which is commonly hung on the front of the house, under the roof.[4]

Sometimes the severed hair and nails are preserved, not to prevent them from falling into the hands of a magician, but that the owner may have them at the resurrection of the body, to which some races look forward. Thus the Incas of Peru "took extreme care to preserve the nail-parings and the hairs that were shorn off or torn out with a comb; placing them in holes or niches in the walls, and if they fell out, any other Indian that saw them picked them up and put them in their places again. I very often asked different Indians, at various times, why

[1] A. Steedman, *Wanderings and Adventures in the Interior of Southern Africa* (London, 1835), i. 266.

[2] *Emin Pasha in Central Africa, being a Collection of his Letters and Journals* (London, 1888), p. 74.

[3] J. L. Wilson, *West Afrika*, p. 159 (German trans.)

[4] N. P. Wilken en J. A. Schwarz, "Allerlei over het land en volk van Bolaang Mongondou," in *Mededeelingen van wege het Nederlandsche Zendeling-genootschap*, xi. (1867) p. 322.

they did this, in order to see what they would say, and they all replied in the same words, saying, 'Know that all persons who are born must return to life' (they have no word to express resuscitation), 'and the souls must rise out of their tombs with all that belonged to their bodies. We, therefore, in order that we may not have to search for our hair and nails at a time when there will be much hurry and confusion, place them in one place, that they may be brought together more conveniently, and, whenever it is possible, we are also careful to spit in one place.'"[1] In Chile this custom of stuffing the shorn hair into holes in the wall is still observed, it being thought the height of imprudence to throw the hair away.[2] Similarly the Turks never throw away the parings of their nails, but carefully keep them in cracks of the walls or of the boards, in the belief that they will be needed at the resurrection.[3] Some of the Esthonians keep the parings of their finger and toe nails in their bosom, in order to have them at hand when they are asked for them at the day of judgment.[4] The Fors of Central Africa object to cut any one else's nails, for should the part cut off be lost and not delivered into its owner's hands, it will have to be made up to him somehow or other after death. The parings are buried in the ground.[5] To spit upon the hair before throwing it away is thought in some parts of Europe sufficient to prevent

---

[1] Garcilasso de la Vega, *First part of the Royal Commentaries of the Yncas*, bk. ii. ch. 7 (vol. i. p. 127, Markham's translation).

[2] *Mélusine*, 1878, c. 583 *sq.*

[3] *The People of Turkey*, by a Consul's daughter and wife, ii. 250.

[4] Boecler-Kreutzwald, *Der Ehsten* *abergläubische Gebräuche, Weisen und Gewohnheiten*, p. 139 ; F. J. Wiedemann, *Aus dem innern und äussern Leben der Ehsten*, p. 491.

[5] R. W. Felkin, "Notes on the For tribe of Central Africa," in *Proceedings of the Royal Society of Edinburgh*, xiii. (1884-86) p. 230.

Madi tribesmen.

Kafir village.

its being used by witches.[1]   Spitting as a protective
charm is well known.

Some people burn their loose hair to save it from
falling into the power of sorcerers.   This is done by
the Patagonians and some of the Victorian tribes.[2]
The Makololo of South Africa either burn it or bury
it secretly,[3] and the same alternative is sometimes
adopted by the Tirolese.[4]   Cut and combed out hair is
burned in Pomerania and sometimes at Liége.[5]   In
Norway the parings of nails are either burned or buried,
lest the elves or the Finns should find them and make
them into bullets wherewith to shoot the cattle.[6]
This destruction of the hair or nails plainly involves
an inconsistency of thought.   The object of the destruction is avowedly to prevent these severed portions
of the body from being used by sorcerers.   But the
possibility of their being so used depends upon the
supposed sympathetic connection between them and
the man from whom they were severed.   And if this
sympathetic connection still exists, clearly these severed
portions cannot be destroyed without injury to the
man.

Before leaving this subject, on which I have perhaps dwelt too long, it may be well to call attention to
the motive assigned for cutting a young child's hair in
Roti.[7]   In that island the first hair is regarded as a
danger to the child, and its removal is intended to avert
the danger.   The reason of this may be that as a

---

[1] Zingerle, *Sitten, Bräuche und Meinungen des Tiroler Volkes*,[2] Nos. 176,
580 ; *Mélusine*, 1878, c. 79.

[2] Musters, "On the Races of Pata-
gonia," in *Journ. Anthrop. Inst.* i.
197 ; J. Dawson, *Australian Aborigines*,
p. 36.

[3] David Livingstone, *Narrative of
Expedition to the Zambesi*, p. 46 *sq.*

[4] Zingerle, *op. cit.* Nos. 177, 179,
180.

[5] M. Jahn, *Hexenwesen und Zauberei
in Pommern*, p. 15 ; *Mélusine*, 1878, c.
79.

[6] E. H. Meyer, *Indogermanische
Mythen*, ii. *Achilleis* (Berlin, 1887), p.
523.

[7] Above, p. 201.

young child is almost universally supposed to be in a
tabooed or dangerous state, it is necessary, in removing
the taboo, to destroy the separable parts of the child's
body on the ground that they are infected, so to say,
by the virus of the taboo and as such are dangerous.
The cutting of the child's hair would thus be exactly
parallel to the destruction of the vessels which have
been used by a tabooed person.[1] This view is borne
out by a practice, observed by some Australians, of
burning off part of a woman's hair after childbirth as
well as burning every vessel which has been used by
her during her seclusion.[2] Here the burning of the
woman's hair seems plainly intended to serve the same
purpose as the burning of the vessels used by her ; and
as the vessels are burned because they are believed to be
tainted with a dangerous infection, so, we must suppose,
is also the hair. We can, therefore, understand the
importance attached by many peoples to the first cutting of a child's hair and the elaborate ceremonies by
which the operation is accompanied.[3] Again, we can
understand why a man should poll his head after a
journey.[4] For we have seen that a traveller is often
believed to contract a dangerous infection from
strangers and that, therefore, on his return home he is
obliged to submit to various purificatory ceremonies
before he is allowed to mingle freely with his own
people.[5] On my hypothesis the polling of the hair is
simply one of these purificatory or disinfectant ceremonies. The cutting of the hair after a vow may
have the same meaning. It is a way of ridding the

---

[1] Above, pp. 167, 169 *sqq.*

[2] W. Ridley, "Report on Australian Languages and Traditions," in *Journ. Anthrop. Inst.* ii. 268.

[3] See G. A. Wilken, *Ueber das Haar-opfer und einige andere Trauerge-bräuche bei den Völkern Indonesiens*, p. 94 *sqq.* ; H. Ploss, *Das Kind in Brauch und Sitte der Völker,*[2] i. 289 *sqq.*

[4] Above, p. 194. [5] Above, p. 157 *sq.*

man of what has been infected by the dangerous state
of taboo, sanctity, or uncleanness (for all these are
only different expressions for the same primitive conception) under which he laboured during the continuance of the vow.   Similarly at some Hindu places
of pilgrimage on the banks of rivers men who have
committed great crimes or are troubled by uneasy
consciences have every hair shaved off by professional
barbers before they plunge into the sacred stream,
from which "they emerge new creatures, with all the
accumulated guilt of a long life effaced."[1]

As might have been expected, the superstitions of
the savage cluster thick about the subject of food ; and
he abstains from eating many animals and plants,
wholesome enough in themselves, but which for one
reason or another he considers would prove dangerous
or fatal to the eater.   Examples of such abstinence
are too familiar and far too numerous to quote.   But
if the ordinary man is thus deterred by superstitious
fear from partaking of various foods, the restraints of
this kind which are laid upon sacred or tabooed persons, such as kings and priests, are still more numerous
and stringent.   We have already seen that the Flamen
Dialis was forbidden to eat or even name several plants
and animals, and that the flesh diet of the Egyptian
kings was restricted to veal and goose.[2]   The *Gangas*
or fetish priests of the Loango Coast are forbidden to
eat or even see a variety of animals and fish, in consequence of which their flesh diet is extremely limited ;
often they live only on herbs and roots, though they
may drink fresh blood.[3]   The heir to the throne of

[1] Monier Williams, *Religious Thought and Life in India*, p. 375.
[2] Above, p. 117.
[3] Bastian, *Die deutsche Expedition an der Loango-Küste*, ii. 170. The blood may be drunk by them as a medium of inspiration. See above, p. 34 *sq.*

Loango is forbidden from infancy to eat pork; from early childhood he is interdicted the use of the *cola* fruit in company; at puberty he is taught by a priest not to partake of fowls except such as he has himself killed and cooked; and so the number of taboos goes on increasing with his years.[1] In Fernando Po the king after installation is forbidden to eat *cocco* (*arum acaule*), deer, and porcupine, which are the ordinary foods of the people.[2] Amongst the Murrams of Manipur (a district of Eastern India, on the border of Burma), "there are many prohibitions in regard to the food, both animal and vegetable, which the chief should eat, and the Murrams say the chief's post must be a very uncomfortable one."[3] To explain the ultimate reason why any particular food is prohibited to a whole tribe or to certain of its members would commonly require a far more intimate knowledge of the history and beliefs of the tribe than we possess. The general motive of such prohibitions is doubtless the same which underlies the whole taboo system, namely, the conservation of the tribe and the individual.

It would be easy to extend the list of royal and priestly taboos, but the above may suffice as specimens. To conclude this part of our subject it only remains to state summarily the general conclusions to which our inquiries have thus far conducted us. We have seen that in savage or barbarous society there are often found men to whom the superstition of their fellows ascribes a controlling influence over the general course of nature. Such men are accordingly adored and treated as gods. Whether these human divinities

---

[1] Dapper, *Description de l'Afrique,* p. 336.

[2] T. J. Hutchinson, *Impressions of Western Africa* (London, 1858), p. 198.

[3] G. Watt (quoting Col. W. J. M'Culloch), "The Aboriginal Tribes of Manipur," in *Journ. Anthrop. Inst.* xvi. 360.

also hold temporal sway over the lives and fortunes
of their fellows, or whether their functions are purely
spiritual and supernatural, in other words, whether they
are kings as well as gods or only the latter, is a distinction which hardly concerns us here.   Their supposed divinity is the essential fact with which we have
to deal.   In virtue of it they are a pledge and guarantee to their worshippers of the continuance and
orderly succession of those physical phenomena upon
which mankind depends for subsistence.   Naturally,
therefore, the life and health of such a god-man are
matters of anxious concern to the people whose welfare
and even existence are bound up with his ; naturally
he is constrained by them to conform to such rules as
the wit of early man has devised for averting the ills
to which flesh is heir, including the last ill, death.
These rules, as an examination of them has shown, are
nothing but the maxims with which, on the primitive
view, every man of common prudence must comply
if he would live long in the land.   But while in the
case of ordinary men the observance of the rules is
left to the choice of the individual, in the case of the
god-man it is enforced under penalty of dismissal from
his high station, or even of death.   For his worshippers have far too great a stake in his life to allow him
to play fast and loose with it.   Therefore all the
quaint superstitions, the old-world maxims, the vener-
able saws which the ingenuity of savage philosophers
elaborated long ago, and which old women at chimney
corners still impart as treasures of great price to their
descendants gathered round the cottage fire on winter
evenings—all these antique fancies clustered, all these
cobwebs of the brain were spun about the path of the
old king, the human god, who, immeshed in them like

a fly in the toils of a spider, could hardly stir a limb for the threads of custom, "light as air but strong as links of iron," that crossing and recrossing each other in an endless maze bound him fast within a network of observances from which death or deposition alone could release him.

To students of the past the life of the old kings and priests thus teems with instruction. In it was summed up all that passed for wisdom when the world was young. It was the perfect pattern after which every man strove to shape his life; a faultless model constructed with rigorous accuracy upon the lines laid down by a barbarous philosophy. Crude and false as that philosophy may seem to us, it would be unjust to deny it the merit of logical consistency. Starting from a conception of the vital principle as a tiny being or soul existing in, but distinct and separable from, the living being, it deduces for the practical guidance of life a system of rules which in general hangs well together and forms a fairly complete and harmonious whole. The flaw—and it is a fatal one— of the system lies not in its reasoning, but in its premises; in its conception of the nature of life, not in any irrelevancy of the conclusions which it draws from that conception. But to stigmatise these premises as ridiculous because we can easily detect their falseness, would be ungrateful as well as unphilosophical. We stand upon the foundation reared by the generations that have gone before, and we can but dimly realise the painful and prolonged efforts which it has cost humanity to struggle up to the point, no very exalted one after all, which we have reached. Our gratitude is due to the nameless and forgotten toilers, whose patient thought and active exertions have largely made us what we are. The amount of new knowledge which one age, certainly which one man, can add to the common store is small, and it argues stupidity or dishonesty, besides ingratitude, to ignore the heap while vaunting the few grains which it may have been our privilege to add to it. There is indeed little danger at present of undervaluing the contributions which modern times and even classical antiquity have made to the general advancement of our race. But when we pass these limits, the case is different. Contempt and ridicule or abhorrence and denunciation are too often the only recognition vouchsafed to the savage and his ways. Yet of the benefactors whom we are bound thankfully to commemorate, many, perhaps most, were savages. For when all is said and done our resemblances to the savage are still far more numerous than our differences from him ; and what we have in common with him, and deliberately retain as true and useful, we owe to our savage forefathers who slowly acquired by experience and transmitted to us by inheritance those seemingly fundamental ideas which we are apt to regard as original and intuitive. We are like heirs to a fortune which has been handed down for so many ages that the memory of those who built it up is lost, and its possessors for the time being regard it as having been an original and unalterable possession of their race since the beginning of the world. But reflection and inquiry should satisfy us that to our predecessors we are indebted for much of what we thought most our own, and that their errors were not wilful extravagances or the ravings of insanity, but simply hypotheses, justifiable as such at the time when they were propounded, but which a fuller experience has proved to be inadequate. It is only by the

successive testing of hypotheses and rejection of the
false that truth is at last elicited. After all, what we
call truth is only the hypothesis which is found to
work best. Therefore in reviewing the opinions and
practices of ruder ages and races we shall do well to
look with leniency upon their errors as inevitable slips
made in the search for truth, and to give them the
benefit of that indulgence which we may one day stand
in need of ourselves : *cum excusatione itaque veteres
audiendi sunt.*

CHAPTER III

KILLING THE GOD

"Sed adhuc supersunt aliae superstitiones, quarum secreta pandenda sunt, . . . ut et in istis profanis religionibus sciatis mortes esse hominum consecratas."—FIRMICUS MATERNUS, *De errore profanarum religionum*, c. 6.

§ 1.—*Killing the divine king*

LACKING the idea of eternal duration primitive man naturally supposes the gods to be mortal like himself. The Greenlanders believed that a wind could kill their most powerful god, and that he would certainly die if he touched a dog. When they heard of the Christian God, they kept asking if he *never* died, and being informed that he did not, they were much surprised and said that he must be a very great god indeed.[1] In answer to the inquiries of Colonel Dodge, a North American Indian stated that the world was made by the Great Spirit. Being asked which Great Spirit he meant, the good one or the bad one, "Oh, neither of *them*," replied he, "the Great Spirit that made the world is dead long ago. He could not possibly have lived as long as this."[2] A tribe in the Philippine Islands told the Spanish conquerors that the grave of

---

[1] Meiners, *Geschichte der Religionen*, i. 48.

[2] R. I. Dodge, *Our Wild Indians*, p. 112.

the Creator was upon the top of Mount Cabunian.[1] Heitsi-eibib, a god or divine hero of the Hottentots, died several times and came to life again. His graves are generally to be met with in narrow passes between mountains.[2] The grave of Zeus, the great god of Greece, was shown to visiters in Crete as late as about the beginning of our era.[3] The body of Dionysus was buried at Delphi beside the golden statue of Apollo, and his tomb bore the inscription, "Here lies Dionysus dead, the son of Semele."[4] According to one account, Apollo himself was buried at Delphi; for Pythagoras is said to have carved an inscription on his tomb, setting forth how the god had been killed by the python and buried under the tripod.[5] Cronus was buried in Sicily,[6] and the graves of Hermes, Aphrodite, and Ares were shown in Hermopolis, Cyprus, and Thrace.[7]

If the great invisible gods are thus supposed to die, it is not to be expected that a god who dwells in the flesh and blood of a man should escape the same fate. Now primitive peoples, as we have seen, sometimes believe that their safety and even that of the world is bound up with the life of one of these god-men or human incarnations of the divinity. Naturally, therefore, they take the utmost care of his life, out of a regard for their own. But no amount of care and precaution will prevent the man-god from growing old and feeble and at last dying. His worshippers have

[1] Blumentritt, "Der Ahnencultus und die relig. Anschauungen der Malaien des Philippinen-Archipels," in *Mittheilungen d. Wiener Geogr. Gesellschaft*, 1882, p. 198.

[2] Theophilus Hahn, *Tsuni-Goam, the Supreme Being of the Khoi-Khoi*, pp. 56, 69.

[3] Diodorus, iii. 61; Pomponius Mela, ii. 7, 112; Minucius Felix, *Octavius*, 21.

[4] Plutarch, *Isis et Osiris*, 35; Philochorus, *Fragm.* 22, in Müller's *Fragm. Hist. Graec.* i. p. 387.

[5] Porphyry, *Vit. Pythag.* 16.

[6] Philochorus, *Fr.* 184, in *Fragm. Hist. Graec.* ii. p. 414.

[7] Lobeck, *Aglaophamus*, p. 574 *sq.*

to lay their account with this sad necessity and to
meet it as best they can.　The danger is a formidable
one ; for if the course of nature is dependent on the
man-god's life, what catastrophes may not be expected
from the gradual enfeeblement of his powers and their
final extinction in death ?　There is only one way
of averting these dangers.　The man-god must be
killed as soon as he shows symptoms that his powers
are beginning to fail, and his soul must be transferred
to a vigorous successor before it has been seriously
impaired by the threatened decay.　The advantages
of thus putting the man-god to death instead of allowing him to die of old age and disease are, to the
savage, obvious enough.　For if the man-god dies
what we call a natural death, it means, according
to the savage, that his soul has either voluntarily
departed from his body and refuses to return, or more
commonly that it has been extracted or at least detained
in its wanderings by a demon or sorcerer.[1]　In any of
these cases the soul of the man-god is lost to his
worshippers ; and with it their prosperity is gone and
their very existence endangered.　Even if they could
arrange to catch the soul of the dying god as it left his
lips or his nostrils and so transfer it to a successor, this
would not effect their purpose ; for, thus dying of
disease, his soul would necessarily leave his body in
the last stage of weakness and exhaustion, and as such
it would continue to drag out a feeble existence in the
body to which it might be transferred.　Whereas by
killing him his worshippers could, in the first place,
make sure of catching his soul as it escaped and
transferring it to a suitable successor ; and, in the
second place, by killing him before his natural force

---

[1] See above, p. 121 *sqq.*

was abated, they would secure that the world should not fall into decay with the decay of the man-god. Every purpose, therefore, was answered, and all dangers averted by thus killing the man-god and transferring his soul, while yet at its prime, to a vigorous successor.

Some of the reasons for preferring a violent death to the slow death of old age or disease are obviously as applicable to common men as to the man-god. Thus the Mangaians think that "the spirits of those who die a natural death are excessively feeble and weak, as their bodies were at dissolution ; whereas the spirits of those who are slain in battle are strong and vigorous, their bodies not having been reduced by disease."[1] Hence, men sometimes prefer to kill themselves or to be killed before they grow feeble, in order that in the future life their souls may start fresh and vigorous as they left their bodies, instead of decrepit and worn out with age and disease. Thus in Fiji, "self-immolation is by no means rare, and they believe that as they leave this life, so they will remain ever after. This forms a powerful motive to escape from decrepitude, or from a crippled condition, by a voluntary death."[2] Or, as another observer of the Fijians puts it more fully, "the custom of voluntary suicide on the part of the old men, which is among their most extraordinary usages, is also connected with their superstitions respecting a future life. They believe that persons enter upon the delights of their elysium with the same faculties, mental and physical, that they possess at the hour of death, in short, that the spiritual life commences where the corporeal existence terminates.

---

[1] Gill, *Myths and Songs of the South Pacific*, p. 163.

[2] Ch. Wilkes, *Narrative of the U.S. Exploring Expedition* (London, 1845), iii. 96.

With these views, it is natural that they should desire to pass through this change before their mental and bodily powers are so enfeebled by age as to deprive them of their capacity for enjoyment.   To this motive must be added the contempt which attaches to physical weakness among a nation of warriors, and the wrongs and insults which await those who are no longer able to protect themselves.   When therefore a man finds his strength declining with the advance of age, and feels that he will soon be unequal to discharge the duties of this life, and to partake in the pleasures of that which is to come, he calls together his relations, and tells them that he is now worn out and useless, that he sees they are all ashamed of him, and that he has determined to be buried."   So on a day appointed they meet and bury him alive.[1]   In Vaté (New Hebrides) the aged were buried alive at their own request.   It was considered a disgrace to the family of an old chief if he was not buried alive.[2]   Of the Kamants, a Jewish tribe in Abyssinia, it is reported that "they never let a person die a natural death, but if any of their relatives is nearly expiring, the priest of the village is called to cut his throat ; if this be omitted, they believe that the departed soul has not entered the mansions of the blessed."[3]

But it is with the death of the god-man—the divine king or priest—that we are here especially concerned. The people of Congo believed, as we have seen, that if their pontiff the Chitomé were to die a natural death,

[1] *U.S. Exploring Expedition, Ethnology and Philology*, by H. Hale (Philadelphia, 1846), p. 65.   Cp. Th. Williams, *Fiji and the Fijians*, i. 183 ; J. E. Erskine, *Journal of a Cruise among the Islands of the Western Pacific*, p. 248.

[2] Turner, *Samoa*, p. 335.
[3] Martin Flad, *A Short Description of the Falasha and Kamants in Abyssinia*, p. 19.

the world would perish, and the earth, which he alone sustained by his power and merit, would immediately be annihilated. Accordingly when he fell ill and seemed likely to die, the man who was destined to be his successor entered the pontiff's house with a rope or a club and strangled or clubbed him to death.[1] The Ethiopian kings of Meroe were worshipped as gods ; but whenever the priests chose, they sent a messenger to the king, ordering him to die, and alleging an oracle of the gods as their authority for the command. This command the kings always obeyed down to the reign of Ergamenes, a contemporary of Ptolemy II, King of Egypt. Having received a Greek education which emancipated him from the superstitions of his countrymen, Ergamenes ventured to disregard the command of the priests, and, entering the Golden Temple with a body of soldiers, put the priests to the sword.[2] In the kingdom of Unyoro in Central Africa, custom still requires that as soon as the king falls seriously ill or begins to break up from age, he shall be killed by his own wives ; for, according to an old prophecy, the throne will pass away from the dynasty in the event of the king dying a natural death.[3] When the king of Kibanga, on the Upper Congo, seems near his end, the sorcerers put a rope round his neck, which they draw gradually tighter till he dies.[4] It seems to have been a Zulu custom to put the king to death as soon as he began to have wrinkles or gray hairs. At least this seems implied in the following

---

[1] J. B. Labat, *Relation historique de l'Ethiopie Occidentale*, i. 260 *sq.* ; W. Winwood Reade, *Savage Africa*, p. 362.

[2] Diodorus Siculus, iii. 6 ; Strabo, xvii. 2, 3.

[3] *Emin Pasha in Central Africa*, being a Collection of his Letters and Journals (London, 1888), p. 91.

[4] P. Guillemé, " Credenze religiose dei Negri di Kibanga nell' Alto Congo," in *Archivio per lo studio delle tradizioni popolari*, vii. (1888) p. 231.

passage, written by one who resided for some time at the court of the notorious Zulu tyrant Chaka, in the early part of this century : " The extraordinary violence of the king's rage with me was mainly occasioned by that absurd nostrum, the hair oil, with the notion of which Mr. Farewell had impressed him as being a specific for removing all indications of age. From the first moment of his having heard that such a preparation was attainable, he evinced a solicitude to procure it, and on every occasion never forgot to remind us of his anxiety respecting it; more especially on our departure on the mission his injunctions were particularly directed to this object. It will be seen that it is one of the barbarous customs of the Zoolas in their choice or election of their kings that he must neither have wrinkles nor gray hairs, as they are both distinguishing marks of disqualification for becoming a monarch of a warlike people. It is also equally indispensable that their king should never exhibit those proofs of having become unfit and incompetent to reign ; it is therefore important that they should conceal these indications so long as they possibly can. Chaka had become greatly apprehensive of the approach of gray hairs; which would at once be the signal for him to prepare to make his exit from this sublunary world, it being always followed by the death of the monarch."[1]

The custom of putting kings to death as soon as they suffered from any personal defect prevailed two centuries ago in the Kafir kingdoms of Sofala, to the north of the present Zululand. These kings of Sofala, as we have seen,[2] were regarded as gods by their people, being entreated to give rain or sunshine, according as each might

---

[1] Nathaniel Isaacs, *Travels and Adventures in Eastern Africa*, i. p. 295 *sq.*; cp. pp. 232, 290 *sq.*
[2] Above, p. 45 *sq.*

be wanted.   Nevertheless a slight bodily blemish, such as the loss of a tooth, was considered a sufficient cause for putting one of these god-men to death, as we learn from the following passage of an old historian.   " Contiguous to the domains of the Quiteva [the king of the country bordering on the river Sofala], are those of another prince called Sedanda.   This prince becoming afflicted with leprosy, resolved on following implicitly the laws of the country, and poisoning himself, conceiving his malady to be incurable, or at least that it would render him so loathsome in the eyes of his people that they would with difficulty recognise him. In consequence he nominated his successor, holding as his opinion that sovereigns who should serve in all things as an example to their people ought to have no defect whatever, even in their persons ; that when any defects may chance to befall them they cease to be worthy of life and of governing their dominions ; and preferring death in compliance with this law to life, with the reproach of having been its violator.   But this law was not observed with equal scrupulosity by one of the Quitevas, who, having lost a tooth and feeling no disposition to follow the practice of his predecessors, published to the people that he had lost a front tooth, in order that when they might behold, they yet might be able to recognise him ; declaring at the same time that he was resolved on living and reigning as long as he could, esteeming his existence requisite for the welfare of his subjects.   He at the same time loudly condemned the practice of his predecessors, whom he taxed with imprudence, nay, even with madness, for having condemned themselves to death for casual accidents to their persons, confessing plainly that it would be with much regret, even when the course of nature should bring him to his end, that he should submit to die. He observed, moreover, that no reasonable being, much less a monarch, ought to anticipate the scythe of time ; and, abrogating this mortal law, he ordained that all his successors, if sane, should follow the precedent he gave, and the new law established by him." [1]

This King of Sofala was, therefore, a bold reformer like Ergamenes, King of Ethiopia. We may conjecture that the ground for putting the Ethiopian kings to death was, as in the case of the Zulu and Sofala kings, the appearance on their person of any bodily defect or sign of decay ; and that the oracle which the priests alleged as the authority for the royal execution was to the effect that great calamities would result from the reign of a king who had any blemish on his body ; just as an oracle warned Sparta against a "lame reign," that is, the reign of a lame king.[2] This conjecture is confirmed by the fact that the kings of Ethiopia were chosen for their size, strength, and beauty long before the custom of killing them was abolished.[3] To this day the Sultan of Wadâi must have no obvious bodily defect, and a king of Angoy cannot be crowned if he has a single blemish, such as a broken or filed tooth or the scar of an old wound.[4] It is only natural, therefore, to suppose, especially

---

[1] Dos Santos, " History of Eastern Ethiopia " (published at Paris in 1684), in Pinkerton's *Voyages and Travels*, xvi. 684.

[2] Plutarch, *Agesilaus*, 3.

[3] Herodotus, iii. 20 ; Aristotle, *Politics*, iv. 4, 4 ; Athenaeus, xiii. p. 566. According to Nicolaus Damascenus (*Fr.* 142, in *Fragm. Historic. Graecor.* ed. C. Müller, iii. p. 463), the handsomest and bravest man was only raised to the throne when the king had no heirs, the heirs being the sons of his sisters. But this limitation is not mentioned by the other authorities. Among the Gordioi the fattest man was chosen king ; among the Syrakoi, the tallest, or the man with the longest head. Zenobius, v. 25.

[4] G. Nachtigal, *Saharâ und Sûdân* (Leipzig, 1889), iii. 225 ; Bastian, *Die deutsche Expedition an der Loango-Küste*, i. 220.

with the other African examples before us, that any bodily defect or symptom of old age appearing on the person of the Ethiopian monarch was the signal for his execution. At a later time it is recorded that if the King of Ethiopia became maimed in any part of his body all his courtiers had to suffer the same mutilation.[1] But this rule may perhaps have been instituted at the time when the custom of killing the king for any personal defect was abolished ; instead of compelling the king to die because, *e.g.*, he had lost a tooth, all his subjects would be obliged to lose a tooth, and thus the invidious superiority of the subjects over the king would be cancelled. A rule of this sort is still observed in the same region at the court of the Sultans of Darfur. When the Sultan coughs, every one makes the sound *ts ts* by striking the tongue against the root of the upper teeth ; when he sneezes, the whole assembly utters a sound like the cry of the jeko ; when he falls off his horse, all his followers must fall off likewise ; if any one of them remains in the saddle, no matter how high his rank, he is laid on the ground and beaten.[2] At the court of the King of Uganda in Central Africa, when the king laughs, every one laughs ; when he sneezes, every one sneezes ; when he has a cold, every one pretends to have a cold ; when he has his hair cut, so has every one.[3] At the court of Boni in Celebes it is a rule that whatever the king does all the courtiers must do. If he stands, they stand ; if he sits, they sit ;

---

[1] Strabo, xvii. 2, 3 ; Diodorus, iii. 7.

[2] Mohammed Ebn- Omar El-Tounsy, *Voyage au Darfour* (Paris, 1845), p. 162 *sq.* ; *Travels of an Arab Merchant in Soudan*, abridged from the French by Bayle St. John (London, 1854), p.

78 ; *Bulletin de la Société de Géographie* (Paris) IVme Série, iv. (1852) p. 539 *sq.*

[3] R. W. Felkin, " Notes on the Waganda Tribe of Central Africa," in *Proceedings of the Royal Society of Edinburgh*, xiii. (1884-1886) p. 711.

if he falls off his horse, they fall off their horses; if
he bathes, they bathe, and passers-by must go into the
water in the dress, good or bad, which they happen to
have on.[1]   But to return to the death of the divine
man. The old Prussians acknowledged as their supreme
lord a ruler who governed them in the name of the
gods, and was known as God's Mouth (*Kirwaido*).
When he felt himself weak and ill, if he wished to leave
a good name behind him, he had a great heap made of
thorn-bushes and straw, on which he mounted and delivered a long sermon to the people, exhorting them to
serve the gods and promising to go to the gods and
speak for the people.   Then he took some of the perpetual fire which burned in front of the holy oak-tree,
and lighting the pile with it burned himself to death.[2]

In the cases hitherto described, the divine king
or priest is suffered by his people to retain office
until some outward defect, some visible symptom of
failing health or advancing age warns them that he
is no longer equal to the discharge of his divine
duties; but not until such symptoms have made
their appearance is he put to death. Some peoples,
however, appear to have thought it unsafe to wait for
even the slightest symptom of decay and have preferred to kill the king while he was still in the full
vigour of life. Accordingly, they have fixed a term
beyond which he might not reign, and at the close of
which he must die, the term fixed upon being short
enough to exclude the probability of his degenerat-
ing physically in the interval. In some parts of
Southern India the period fixed was twelve years.

---

[1] *Narrative of events in Borneo and
Celebes, from the Journals of James
Brooke, Esq., Rajah of Sarawak.* By
Captain R. Mundy, i. 134.

[2] Simon Grunau, *Preussische Chronik*, herausgegeben von Dr. M. Perlbach (Leipzig, 1876), i. p. 97.

Thus, according to an old traveller, in the province of Quilacare " There is a Gentile house of prayer, in which there·is an idol which they hold in great account, and every twelve years they celebrate a great feast to it, whither all the Gentiles go as to a jubilee.   This temple possesses many lands and much revenue ; it is a very great affair.   This province has a king over it ; who has not more than twelve years to reign from jubilee to jubilee.   His manner of living is in this wise, that is to say, when the twelve years are completed, on the day of this feast there assemble together innumerable people, and much money is spent in giving food to Bramans.   The king has a wooden scaffolding made, spread over with silken hangings ; and on that·day he goes to bathe at a tank with great ceremonies and sound of music, after that he comes to the idol and prays to it, and mounts on to the scaffolding, and there before all the people he takes some very sharp knives and begins to cut off his nose, and then his ears and his lips and all his members and as much flesh of himself as he can ; and he throws it away very hurriedly until so much of his blood is spilled that he begins to faint, and then he cuts his throat himself.   And he performs this sacrifice to the idol ; and whoever desires to reign other twelve years, and undertake this martyrdom for love of the idol, has to be present looking on at this ; and from that place they raise him up as king." [1]

Formerly the Samorin or King of Calicut, on the Malabar coast, had also to cut his throat in public at the end of a twelve years' reign.   But towards the end of the seventeenth century the rule had been

---

[1] Barbosa, *A Description of the Coasts of East Africa and Malabar in the beginning of the Sixteenth Century* (Hakluyt Society, 1866), p. 172 *sq.*

modified as follows : " A new custom is followed by
the modern Samorins, that jubilee is proclaimed
throughout his dominions, at the end of twelve years,
and a tent is pitched for him in a spacious plain, and a
great feast is celebrated for ten or twelve days, with
mirth and jollity, guns firing night and day, so at the
end of the feast any four of the guests that have a mind
to gain a crown by a desperate action, in fighting their
way through 30 or 40,000 of his guards, and kill the
Samorin in his tent, he that kills him succeeds him in
his empire.   In anno 1695, one of those jubilees happened, and the tent pitched near Pennany, a sea-port
of his, about fifteen leagues to the southward of Calicut.   There were but three men that would venture on
that desperate action, who fell in, with sword and
target among the guard, and, after they had killed and
wounded many were themselves killed. One of the
desperados had a nephew of fifteen or sixteen years
of age, that kept close by his uncle in the attack on
the guards, and, when he saw him fall, the youth got
through the guards into the tent, and made a stroke at
his Majesty's head, and had certainly despatched him,
if a large brass lamp which was burning over his head,
had not marred the blow ; but, before he could make
another he was killed by the guards ; and, I believe,
the same Samorin reigns yet.   I chanced to come that
time along the coast and heard the guns for two or
three days and nights successively." [1]

In some places it appears that the people could not
trust the king to remain in full bodily and mental
vigour for more than a year ; hence at the end of a
year's reign he was put to death, and a new king

---

[1] Alex. Hamilton, " A new Account of the East Indies," in Pinkerton's
Voyages and Travels, viii. 374.

appointed to reign in his turn a year, and suffer death
at the end of it. At least this is the conclusion to
which the following evidence points. According to
the historian Berosus, who as a Babylonian priest
spoke with ample knowledge, there was annually celebrated in Babylon a festival called the Sacaea. It
began on the 16th day of the month Lous, and lasted
for five days. During these five days masters and
servants changed places, the servants giving orders
and the masters obeying them. A prisoner condemned
to death was dressed in the king's robes, seated on the
king's throne, allowed to issue whatever commands he
pleased, to eat, drink, and enjoy himself, and to lie
with the king's concubines. But at the end of the
five days he was stripped of his royal robes, scourged,
and crucified.[1] This custom might perhaps have been
explained as merely a grim jest perpetrated in a season
of jollity at the expense of an unhappy criminal. But
one circumstance—the leave given to the mock king
to enjoy the king's concubines—is decisive against this
interpretation. Considering the jealous seclusion of

---

[1] Athenaeus, xiv. p. 639 C; Dio
Chrysostom, *Orat.* iv. p. 69 *sq.* (vol. i.
p. 76, ed. Dindorf). Dio Chryso-
stom does not mention his authority, but
it was probably either Berosus or Ctesias.
Though the execution of the mock king
is not mentioned in the passage of
Berosus cited by Athenaeus, the
omission is probably due to the fact
that the mention of it was not germane
to Athenaeus's purpose, which was
simply to give a list of festivals at
which masters waited on their servants.
That the ζωγάνης was put to death is
further shown by Macrobius, *Sat.* iii.
7, 6, "*Animas vero sacratorum hominum quos † zanas Graeci vocant, dis
debitas aestimabant,*" where for *zanas*
we should probably read ζωγάνας with
Liebrecht, in *Philologus,* xxii. 710, and

Bachofen, *Die Sage von Tanaquil,* p.
52, *note* 16. The custom, so far as
appears from our authorities, does not
date from before the Persian domina-
tion in Babylon; but probably it was
much older. In the passage of Dio
Chrysostom ἐκρέμασαν should be translated "crucified" (or "impaled"),
not "hung." It is strange that this,
the regular, sense of κρεμάννυμι, as
applied to executions, should not
be noticed even in the latest edition
of Liddell and Scott's *Greek Lexicon.*
Hanging, though a mode of suicide,
was not a mode of execution in antiquity
either in the east or west. In one of
the passages cited by L. and S. for the
sense "to hang" (Plutarch, *Caes.* 2),
the context proves that the meaning is
"to crucify."

an oriental despot's harem we may be quite certain that permission to invade it would never have been granted by the despot, least of all to a condemned criminal, except for the very gravest cause. This cause could hardly be other than that the condemned man was about to die in the king's stead, and that to make the substitution perfect it was necessary he should enjoy the full rights of royalty during his brief reign. There is nothing surprising in this substitution. The rule that the king must be put to death either on the appearance of any symptom of bodily decay or at the end of a fixed period is certainly one which, sooner or later, the kings would seek to abolish or modify. We have seen that in Ethiopia and Sofala the rule was boldly set aside by enlightened monarchs; and that in Calicut the old custom of killing the king at the end of twelve years was changed into a permission granted to any one at the end of the twelve years' period to attack the king, and, in the event of killing him, to reign in his stead; though, as the king took care at these times to be surrounded by his guards, the permission was little more than a form. Another way of modifying the stern old rule is seen in the Babylonian custom just described. When the time drew near for the king to be put to death (in Babylon this appears to have been at the end of a single year's reign) he abdicated for a few days, during which a temporary king reigned and suffered in his stead. At first the temporary king may have been an innocent person, possibly a member of the king's own family; but with the growth of civilisation the sacrifice of an innocent person would be revolting to the public sentiment, and accordingly a condemned criminal would be invested with the brief and fatal sovereignty. In the sequel we shall find other examples of a dying criminal representing a dying god. For we must not forget that the king is slain in his character of a god, his death and resurrection, as the only means of perpetuating the divine life unimpaired, being deemed necessary for the salvation of his people and the world.

In some places this modified form of the old custom has been further softened down. The king still abdicates annually for a short time and his place is filled by a more or less nominal sovereign; but at the close of his short reign the latter is no longer killed, though sometimes a mock execution still survives as a memorial of the time when he was actually put to death. To take examples. In the month of Méac (February) the King of Cambodia annually abdicated for three days. During this time he performed no act of authority, he did not touch the seals, he did not even receive the revenues which fell due. In his stead there reigned a temporary king called Sdach Méac, that is, King February. The office of temporary king was hereditary in a family distantly connected with the royal house, the sons succeeding the fathers and the younger brothers the elder brothers, just as in the succession to the real sovereignty. On a favourable day fixed by the astrologers the temporary king was conducted by the mandarins in triumphal procession. He rode one of the royal elephants, seated in the royal palanquin, and escorted by soldiers who, dressed in appropriate costumes, represented the neighbouring peoples of Siam, Annam, Laos, and so on. Instead of the golden crown he wore a peaked white cap, and his regalia, instead of being of gold encrusted with diamonds, were of rough wood. After paying homage to the real king, from whom he received the sovereignty for three days,

together with all the revenues accruing during that
time (though this last custom has been omitted for
some time), he moved in procession round the palace
and through the streets of the capital. On the third
day, after the usual procession, the temporary king
gave orders that the elephants should trample under
foot the "mountain of rice," which was a scaffold of
bamboo surrounded by sheaves of rice. The people
gathered up the rice, each man taking home a little
with him to secure a good harvest. Some of it was also
taken to the king, who had it cooked and presented to
the monks.[1]

In Siam on the sixth day of the moon in the
sixth month (the end of April) a temporary king is
appointed, who for three days enjoys the royal prerogatives, the real king remaining shut up in his palace.
This temporary king sends his numerous satellites in
all directions to seize and confiscate whatever they can
find in the bazaar and open shops ; even the ships and
junks which arrive in harbour during the three days
are confiscated to him and must be redeemed. He
goes to a field in the middle of the city, whither is
brought a gilded plough drawn by gaily-decked oxen.
After the plough has been anointed and the oxen
rubbed with incense, the mock king traces nine furrows
with the plough, followed by aged dames of the palace
scattering the first seed of the season. As soon as the
nine furrows are drawn, the crowd of spectators rushes
in and scrambles for the seed which has just been sown,
believing that, mixed with the seed-rice, it will ensure
a plentiful crop. Then the oxen are unyoked, and

---

[1] E. Aymonier, *Notice sur le Cam-*
bodge, p. 61 ; J. Moura, *Le Royaume du*
Cambodge, i. 327 *sq.* For the connection
of the temporary king's family with the
royal house, see Aymonier, *op. cit.* p.
36 *sq.*

rice, maize, sesame, sago, bananas, sugar-cane, melons, etc. are set before them; whatever they eat first will, it is thought, be dear in the year following, though some people interpret the omen in the opposite sense. During this time the temporary king stands leaning against a tree with his right foot resting on his left knee. From standing thus on one foot he is popularly known as King Hop; but his official title is Phaya Phollathep, "Lord of the Heavenly Hosts."[1] He is a sort of Minister of Agriculture; all disputes about fields, rice, and so on, are referred to him. There is moreover another ceremony in which he personates the king. It takes place in the second month (which falls in the cold season) and lasts three days. He is conducted in procession to an open place opposite the Temple of the Brahmans, where there are a number of poles dressed like May-poles, upon which the Brahmans swing. All the while that they swing and dance, the Lord of the Heavenly Hosts has to stand on one foot upon a seat which is made of bricks plastered over, covered with a white cloth, and hung with tapestry. He is supported by a wooden frame with a gilt canopy, and two Brahmans stand one on each side of him. The dancing Brahmans carry buffalo horns with which they draw water from a large copper caldron and sprinkle it on the people; this is supposed to bring good luck, causing the people to dwell in peace and quiet, health and prosperity. The time during which the Lord of the Heavenly Hosts has to stand on one foot is about three hours. This is thought "to prove the dispositions of the Devattas and spirits." If he lets his foot down

---

[1] Pallegoix, *Description du Royaume Thai ou Siam*, i. 250; Bastian, *Die Völker des östlichen Asien*, iii. 305-309, 526-528; Turpin, *History of Siam*, in Pinkerton's *Voyages and Travels*, ix. 581 *sq.* Bowring (*Siam*, i. 158 *sq.*) copies, as usual, from Pallegoix.

"he is liable to forfeit his property and have his family enslaved by the king; as it is believed to be a bad omen, portending destruction to the state, and instability to the throne. But if he stand firm he is believed to have gained a victory over evil spirits, and he has moreover the privilege, ostensibly at least, of seizing any ship which may enter the harbour during these three days, and taking its contents, and also of entering any open shop in the town and carrying away what he chooses."[1]

In Upper Egypt on the first day of the solar year by Coptic reckoning, that is on 10th September, when the Nile has generally reached its highest point, the regular government is suspended for three days and every town chooses its own ruler. This temporary lord wears a sort of tall fool's cap and a long flaxen beard, and is enveloped in a strange mantle. With a wand of office in his hand and attended by men disguised as scribes, executioners, etc., he proceeds to the Governor's house. The latter allows himself to be deposed; and the mock king, mounting the throne, holds a tribunal, to the decisions of which even the governor and his officials must bow. After three days the mock king is condemned to death; the envelope or shell in which he was encased is committed to the flames, and from its ashes the Fellah creeps forth.[2]

Sometimes the temporary king occupies the throne, not annually, but once for all at the beginning of each reign. Thus in the kingdom of Jambi (in Sumatra) it is the custom that at the beginning of a new reign a man of the people should occupy the throne and

[1] Lieut. Col. James Low, "On the Laws of Muung Thai or Siam," in *Journal of the Indian Archipelago*, i. (Singapore, 1847) p. 339; Bastian, *Die Völker des östlichen Asien*, iii. 98, 314, 526 *sq.*

[2] C. B. Klunzinger, *Bilder aus Oberägypten, der Wüste und dem Rothen Meere*, p. 180 *sq.*

exercise the royal prerogatives for a single day. The
origin of the custom is explained by a tradition that
there were once five royal brothers, the four elder
of whom all declined the crown on the ground of
various bodily defects, leaving it to their youngest
brother. But the eldest occupied the throne for one
day, and reserved for his descendants a similar privilege
at the beginning of every reign. Thus the office of
temporary king is hereditary in a family akin to the
royal house.[1] In Bilaspur it seems to be the custom,
after the death of a Rajah, for a Brahman to eat rice
out of the dead Rajah's hand, and then to occupy the
throne for a year. At the end of the year the Brahman
receives presents and is dismissed from the territory,
being forbidden apparently to return. " The idea seems
to be that the spirit of the Rájá enters into the Bráhman
who eats the *khír* (rice and milk) out of his hand when
he is dead, as the Brahman is apparently carefully
watched during the whole year, and not allowed to go
away." The same or a similar custom is believed to
obtain among the hill states about Kángrá.[2] At the
installation of a prince of Carinthia a peasant, in whose
family the office was hereditary, ascended a marble
stone which stood surrounded by meadows in a spacious
valley ; on his right stood a black mother-cow, on his
left an ugly mare. A rustic crowd gathered about
him. Then the future prince, dressed as a peasant
and carrying a shepherd's staff, drew near, attended by
courtiers and magistrates. On perceiving him the
peasant called out, " Who is this whom I see coming
so proudly along ? " The people answered, " The

---

[1] J. W. Boers, "Oud volksgebruik in het Rijk van Jambi," in *Tijdschrift
voor Neêrland's Indië*, iii. (1840), dl. i. 372 *sqq.*

[2] *Panjab Notes and Queries*, i. 674.

prince of the land." The peasant was then prevailed on to surrender the marble seat to the prince on condition of receiving sixty pence, the cow and mare, and exemption from taxes. But before yielding his place he gave the prince a light blow on the cheek.[1]

Some points about these temporary kings deserve to be specially noticed before we pass to the next branch of the evidence. In the first place, the Cambodian and Siamese examples bring clearly out the fact that it is especially the divine or supernatural functions of the king which are transferred to his temporary substitute. This appears from the belief that by keeping up his foot the temporary king of Siam gained a victory over the evil spirits ; whereas by letting it down he imperilled the existence of the state. Again, the Cambodian ceremony of trampling down the " mountain of rice," and the Siamese ceremony of opening the ploughing and sowing, are charms to produce a plentiful harvest, as appears from the belief that those who carry home some of the trampled rice or of the seed sown will thereby secure a good crop. But the task of making the crops grow, thus deputed to the temporary kings, is one of the supernatural functions regularly supposed to be discharged by kings in primitive society. The rule that the mock king must stand on one foot upon a raised seat in the rice-field was perhaps originally meant as a charm to make the crop grow high ; at least this was the object of a similar ceremony observed by the old Prussians. The tallest girl, standing on one foot upon a seat, with her lap full of cakes, a cup of brandy in her right hand and a piece of elm-bark

---

[1] Aeneas Sylvius, *Opera* (Bâle, 1571), p. 409 *sq.* ; Grimm, *Deutsche Rechtsalterthümer*, p. 253. According to Grimm (who does not refer to Aeneas Sylvius) the cow and mare stood beside the prince, not the peasant.

or linden-bark in her left, prayed to the god Waiz-ganthos that the flax might grow as high as she was standing. Then, after draining the cup, she had it refilled, and poured the brandy on the ground as an offering to Waizganthos, and threw down the cakes for his attendant sprites. If she remained steady on one foot throughout the ceremony, it was an omen that the flax crop would be good; but if she let her foot down, it was feared that the crop might fail.[1] The gilded plough with which the Siamese mock king opens the ploughing may be compared with the bronze ploughs which the Etruscans employed at the ceremony of founding cities;[2] in both cases the use of iron was probably forbidden on superstitious grounds.[3]

Another point to notice about these temporary kings is that in two places (Cambodia and Jambi) they come of a stock which is believed to be akin to the royal family. If the view here taken of the origin of these temporary kingships is correct, the fact that the temporary king is sometimes of the same race as the real king admits of a ready explanation. When the king first succeeded in getting the life of another accepted as a sacrifice in lieu of his own, he would have to show that the death of that other would serve the purpose quite as well as his own would have done. Now it was as a god that the king had to die; there-fore the substitute who died for him had to be invested, at least for the occasion, with the divine attributes of the king. This, as we have just seen, was certainly the case with the temporary kings of Siam and Cam-

---

[1] Lasicius, "De diis Samagitarum caeterorumque Sarmatarum," in *Respublica sive Status Regni Poloniae, Lituaniae, Prussiae, Livoniae,* etc. (Elzevir, 1627), p. 306 *sq.*; *id.* edited by W. Mannhardt in *Magazin herausgegeben von der Lettisch-Literärischen Gesellschaft,* xiv. 91 *sq.*

[2] Macrobius, *Saturn.* v. 19, 13.

[3] See above, p. 172 *sqq.*

bodia; they were invested with the supernatural functions, which in an earlier stage of society were the special attributes of the king.   But no one could so well represent the king in his divine character as his son, who might be supposed to share the divine afflatus of his father.   No one, therefore, could so appropriately die for the king and, through him, for the whole people, as the king's son.   There is evidence that amongst the Semites of Western Asia (the very region where the redemption of the king's life by the sacrifice of another comes out so unmistakably in the Sacaean festival) the king, in a time of national danger, sometimes gave his own son to die as a sacrifice for the people.   Thus Philo of Byblus, in his work on the Jews, says : " It was an ancient custom in a crisis of great danger that the ruler of a city or nation should give his beloved son to die for the whole people, as a ransom offered to the avenging demons ; and the children thus offered were slain with mystic rites.   So Cronus, whom the Phoenicians call Israel, being king of the land and having an only-begotten son called Jeoud (for in the Phoenician tongue Jeoud signifies ' only-begotten '), dressed him in royal robes and sacrificed him upon an altar in a time of war, when the country was in great danger from the enemy."[1] When the King of Moab was besieged by the Israelites and hard beset, he took his eldest son, who should have reigned in his stead, and offered him for a burnt offering on the wall.[2]   But amongst the Semites the practice of sacrificing their children was not confined to kings.   In times of great calamity, such as pestilence, drought, or defeat in war, the Phoenicians

---

[1] Philo of Byblus, quoted by Eusebius, *Praepar. Evang.* i. 10, 29 *sq.*
[2] 2 Kings iii. 27.

used to sacrifice one of their dearest to Baal. " Phoenician history," says an ancient writer, " is full of such
sacrifices." [1]   When the Carthaginians were defeated
and besieged by Agathocles, they ascribed their disasters to the wrath of Baal; for whereas in former
times they had been wont to sacrifice to him their own
children, they had latterly fallen into the habit of buy-
ing children and rearing them to be victims. So, to
appease the angry god, two hundred children of the
noblest families were picked out for sacrifice, and the
tale of victims was swelled by not less than three
hundred more who volunteered to die for the father-
land. They were sacrificed by being placed, one by
one, on the sloping hands of the brazen image, from
which they rolled into a pit of fire. [2]   If an aristocracy
thus adopted the practice of sacrificing other people's
children instead of their own, kings may very well
have followed or set the example. A final mitigation
of the custom would be the substitution of condemned
criminals for innocent victims. Such a substitution
is known to have taken place in the human sacrifices
annually offered in Rhodes to Baal. [3]

The custom of sacrificing children, especially the
first born, is not peculiarly Semitic. In some tribes
of New South Wales the first-born child of every
woman was eaten by the tribe as part of a religious
ceremony. [4]   The Indians of Florida sacrificed their
first-born male children. [5]   Amongst the people of
Senjero in Eastern Africa we are told that many
families " must offer up their first-born sons as sacri-

---

[1] Porphyry, *De abstin.* ii. 56.

[2] Diodorus, xx. 14.

[3] Porphyry, *De abstin.* ii. 54.

[4] Brough Smyth, *Aborigines of Victoria*, ii. 311.

[5] Strachey, *Historie of travaille into Virginia Britannia* (Hakluyt Society), p. 84.

Cutting of the hair by the Incas.

Sacrifice of the first-born male child among Florida Indians.

fices, because once upon a time, when summer and
winter were jumbled together in a bad season, and
the fruits of the earth would not ripen, the soothsayers enjoined it.   At that time a great pillar
of iron is said to have stood at the entrance of
the capital, which by the advice of the soothsayers
was broken down by order of the king, upon which
the seasons became regular again.   To avert the
recurrence of such a confusion of the seasons, the
soothsayers are reported to have enjoined the king
to pour human blood once a year on the base of the
broken shaft of the pillar, and also upon the throne.
Since then certain families are obliged to deliver up
their first-born sons, who are sacrificed at an appointed
time." [1]   The heathen Russians often sacrificed their
first-born to the god Perun. [2]

The condemnation and pretended death by fire of
the mock king in Egypt is probably a reminiscence
of a real custom of burning him.   Evidence of a
practice of burning divine personages will be forth-
coming later on.   In Bilaspur the expulsion of the
Brahman who had occupied the king's throne for
a year is perhaps a substitute for putting him to
death.

The explanation here given of the custom of
killing divine persons assumes, or at least is readily
combined with, the idea that the soul of the slain
divinity is transmitted to his successor.   Of this trans-
mission I have no direct proof; and so far a link in

---

[1] J. L. Krapf, *Travels, Researches,
and Missionary Labours during an
Eighteen Years' Residence in Eastern
Africa*, p. 69 *sq.* Dr. Krapf, who
reports the custom at second hand,
thinks that the existence of the pillar
may be doubted, but that the rest of
the story harmonises well enough with
African superstition.

[2] .F. J. Mone, *Geschichte des Heidenthums im nördlichen Europa*, i.
119.

the chain of evidence is wanting. But if I cannot prove by actual examples this succession to the soul of the slain god, it can at least be made probable that such a succession was supposed to take place. For it has been already shown that the soul of the incarnate deity is often supposed to transmigrate at death into another incarnation;[1] and if this takes place when the death is a natural one, there seems no reason why it should not take place when the death is a violent one. Certainly the idea that the soul of a dying person may be transmitted to his successor is perfectly familiar to primitive peoples. In Nias the eldest son usually succeeds his father in the chieftainship. But if from any bodily or mental defect the eldest son is incapacitated from ruling, the father determines in his life-time which of his sons shall succeed him. In order, however, to establish his right of succession it is necessary that the son upon whom his father's choice falls shall catch in his mouth or in a bag the last breath, and with it the soul, of the dying chief. For whoever catches his last breath is chief equally with the appointed successor. Hence the other brothers, and sometimes also strangers, crowd round the dying man to catch his soul as it passes. The houses in Nias are raised above the ground on posts, and it has happened that when the dying man lay with his face on the floor, one of the candidates has bored a hole in the floor and sucked in the chief's last breath through a bamboo tube. When the chief has no son, his soul is caught in a bag, which is fastened to an image made to represent the deceased; the

---

[1] Above, p. 42 *sqq.*

soul is then believed to pass into the image.[1]
Amongst the Takilis or Carrier Indians of North-
West America, when a corpse is burned the priest
pretends to catch the soul of the deceased in his hands,
which he closes with many gesticulations. He then
communicates the captured soul to the dead man's
successor by throwing his hands towards and blowing
upon him. The person to whom the soul is thus
communicated takes the name and rank of the
deceased. On the death of a chief the priest thus
fills a responsible and influential position, for he may
transmit the soul to whom he will, though, doubtless,
he generally follows the regular line of succession.[2]
Algonkin women who wished to become mothers
flocked to the side of a dying person in the hope of
receiving and being impregnated by the passing soul.
Amongst the Seminoles of Florida when a woman
died in childbed the infant was held over her face
to receive her parting spirit.[3] The Romans caught
the breath of dying friends in their mouths, and so
received into themselves the soul of the departed.[4]
The same custom is said to be still practised in
Lancashire.[5] We may therefore fairly suppose that
when the divine king or priest is put to death his
spirit is believed to pass into his successor.

---

[1] Nieuwenhuisen en Rosenberg, "Verslag omtrent het eiland Nias," in *Verhandelingen van het Batav. Genootschap van Kunsten en Wetenschappen*, xxx. 85 ; Rosenberg, *Der Malayische Archipel*, p. 160 ; Chatelin, "Godsdienst en bijgeloof der Niassers," in *Tijdschrift voor Indische Taal-Land-en Volkenkunde*, xxvi. 142 *sq.;* Sundermann, "Die Insel Nias und die Mission daselbst," in *Allgemeine Missions-Zeitschrift*, xi. 445.

[2] Ch. Wilkes, *Narrative of the U.S. Exploring Expedition* (London, 1845), iv. 453 ; *U.S. Exploring Expedition, Ethnography and Philology*, by H. Hale, p. 203.

[3] D. G. Brinton, *Myths of the New World*, p. 270 *sq.*

[4] Servius on Virgil, *Aen.* iv. 685 ; Cicero, *In Verr.* ii. 5, 45 ; K. F. Hermann, *Griech. Privatalterthümer*, ed. Blumner, p. 362 *note* 1.

[5] Harland and Wilkinson, *Lancashire Folk-lore*, p. 7 *sq.*

§ 2.—*Killing the tree-spirit*

It remains to ask what light the custom of killing the divine king or priest sheds upon the subject of our inquiry. In the first chapter we saw reason to suppose that the King of the Wood was regarded as an incarnation of the tree-spirit or of the spirit of vegetation, and that as such he would be endowed, in the belief of his worshippers, with a supernatural power of making the trees to bear fruit, the crops to grow, and so on. His life must therefore have been held very precious by his worshippers, and was probably hedged in by a system of elaborate precautions or taboos like those by which, in so many places, the life of the god-man has been guarded against the malignant influence of demons and sorcerers. But we have seen that the very value attached to the life of the man-god necessitates his violent death as the only means of preserving it from the inevitable decay of age. The same reasoning would apply to the King of the Wood; he too had to be killed in order that the divine spirit, incarnate in him, might be transferred in unabated vigour to his successor. The rule that he held office till a stronger should slay him might be supposed to secure both the preservation of his divine life in full vigour and its transference to a suitable successor as soon as that vigour began to be impaired. For so long as he could maintain his position by the strong hand, it might be inferred that his natural force was not abated; whereas his defeat and death at the hands of another proved that his strength was beginning to fail and that it was time his divine life should be lodged in a less

dilapidated tabernacle. This explanation of the rule
that the King of the Wood had to be slain by his
successor at least renders that rule perfectly intelligible.
Moreover it is countenanced by the analogy of the
Chitombé, upon whose life the existence of the world
was supposed to hang, and who was therefore slain by
his successor as soon as he showed signs of breaking
up. Again, the terms on which in later times the
King of Calicut held office are identical with those
attached to the office of King of the Wood, except
that whereas the former might be assailed by a
candidate at any time, the King of Calicut might
only be attacked once every twelve years. But as
the leave granted to the King of Calicut to reign
so long as he could defend himself against all
comers was a mitigation of the old rule which set a
fixed term to his life, so we may conjecture that the
similar permission granted to the King of the Wood
was a mitigation of an older custom of putting him
to death at the end of a set period. In both cases the
new rule gave to the god-man at least a chance for
his life, which under the old rule was denied him ; and
people probably reconciled themselves to the change
by reflecting that so long as the god-man could
maintain himself by the sword against all assaults,
there was no reason to apprehend that the fatal
decay had set in.

The conjecture that the King of the Wood was
formerly put to death at the expiry of a set term,
without being allowed a chance for his life, will be
confirmed if evidence can be adduced of a custom
of periodically killing his counterparts, the human
representatives of the tree-spirit, in Northern Europe.
Now in point of fact such a custom has left unmis-

takable traces of itself in the rural festivals of the peasantry. To take examples.

In Lower Bavaria the Whitsuntide representative of the tree-spirit—the *Pfingstl* as he was called—was clad from top to toe in leaves and flowers. On his head he wore a high pointed cap, the ends of which rested on his shoulders, only two holes being left in it for his eyes. The cap was covered with water flowers and surmounted with a nosegay of peonies. The sleeves of his coat were also made of water-plants, and the rest of his body was enveloped in alder and hazel leaves. On each side of him marched a boy holding up one of the *Pfingstl*'s arms. These two boys carried drawn swords, and so did most of the others who formed the procession. They stopped at every house where they hoped to receive a present; and the people, in hiding, soused the leaf-clad boy with water. All rejoiced when he was well drenched. Finally he waded into the brook up to his middle; whereupon one of the boys, standing on the bridge, pretended to cut off his head.[1] At Wurmlingen in Swabia a score of young fellows dress themselves on Whit-Monday in white shirts and white trousers, with red scarves round their waists and swords hanging from the scarves. They ride on horse-back into the wood, led by two trumpeters blowing their trumpets. In the wood they cut down leafy oak branches, in which they envelop from head to foot him who was the last of their number to ride out of the village. His legs, however, are encased separately, so that he may be able to mount his horse again. Further, they give him a long artificial neck, with an

---

[1] Fr. Panzer, *Beitrag zur deutschen Mythologie*, i. 235 *sq.*; W. Mannhardt, *Baumkultus*, p. 320 *sq.*

artificial head and a false face on the top of it. Then a May-tree is cut, generally an aspen or beech about ten feet high; and being decked with coloured handkerchiefs and ribbons it is entrusted to a special "May-bearer." The cavalcade then returns with music and song to the village. Amongst the personages who figure in the procession are a Moorish king with a sooty face and a crown on his head, a Dr. Iron-Beard, a corporal, and an executioner. They halt on the village green, and each of the characters makes a speech in rhyme. The executioner announces that the leaf-clad man has been condemned to death and cuts off his false head. Then the riders race to the May-tree, which has been set up a little way off. The first man who succeeds in wrenching it from the ground as he gallops past keeps it with all its decorations. The ceremony is observed every second or third year.[1]

In Saxony and Thüringen there is a Whitsuntide ceremony called "chasing the Wild Man out of the bush," or "fetching the Wild Man out of the wood." A young fellow is enveloped in leaves or moss and called the Wild Man. He hides in the wood and the other lads of the village go out to seek him. They find him, lead him captive out of the wood, and fire at him with blank muskets. He falls like dead to the ground, but a lad dressed as a doctor bleeds him, and he comes to life again. At this they rejoice and binding him fast on a waggon take him to the village, where they tell all the people how they have caught the Wild Man. At every house they receive a gift.[2] In

---

[1] E. Meier, *Deutsche Sagen, Sitten und Gebräuche aus Schwaben*, pp. 409-419; W. Mannhardt, *Baumkultus*, p. 349 *sq.*

[2] E. Sommer, *Sagen, Märchen und Gebräuche aus Sachsen und Thüringen*, p. 154 *sq.*; W. Mannhardt, *Baumkultus*, p. 335 *sq.*

the Erzgebirge the following custom was annually observed at Shrovetide about the beginning of the seventeenth century. Two men disguised as Wild Men, the one in brushwood and moss, the other in straw, were led about the streets, and at last taken to the market-place, where they were chased up and down, shot and stabbed. Before falling they reeled about with strange gestures and spirted blood on the people from bladders which they carried. When they were down, the huntsmen placed them on boards and carried them to the alehouse, the miners marching beside them and winding blasts on their mining tools as if they had taken a noble head of game.[1] A very similar Shrovetide custom is still observed in the neighbourhood of Schluckenau (Bohemia). A man dressed up as a Wild Man is chased through several streets till he comes to a narrow lane across which a cord is stretched. He stumbles over the cord and, falling to the ground, is overtaken and caught by his pursuers. The executioner runs up and stabs with his sword a bladder filled with blood which the Wild Man wears round his body; so the Wild Man dies, while a stream of blood reddens the ground. Next day a straw-man, made up to look like the Wild Man, is placed on a litter, and, accompanied by a great crowd, is taken to a pool into which it is thrown by the executioner. The ceremony is called "burying the Carnival."[2]

In Semic (Bohemia) the custom of beheading the King is observed on Whit-Monday. A troop of young people disguise themselves; each is girt with a girdle of bark and carries a wooden sword and a

---

[1] W. Mannhardt, *Baumkultus*, p. 336.

[2] Reinsberg-Düringsfeld, *Fest-Kal-* *ender aus Böhmen*, p. 61; W. Mannhardt, *Baumkultus*, p. 336 *sq.*

trumpet of willow-bark.   The King wears a robe
of tree-bark adorned with flowers, on his head is a
crown of bark decked with flowers and branches,
his feet are wound about with ferns, a mask hides
his face, and for a sceptre he has a hawthorn switch
in his hand.   A lad leads him through the village by a rope fastened to his foot, while the rest
dance about, blow their trumpets, and whistle.   In
every farmhouse the King is chased round the room,
and one of the troop, amid much noise and outcry,
strikes with his sword a blow on the King's robe of
bark till it rings again.   Then a gratuity is demanded.[1]
The ceremony of decapitation, which is here somewhat
slurred over, is carried out with a greater semblance of
reality in other parts of Bohemia.   Thus in some villages of the Königgrätz district on Whit-Monday the
girls assemble under one lime-tree and the young men
under another, all dressed in their best and tricked out
with ribbons.   The young men twine a garland for the
Queen and the girls for the King.   When they have
chosen the King and Queen they all go in procession,
two and two, to the alehouse, from the balcony of
which the crier proclaims the names of the King and
Queen.   Both are then invested with the insignia of
their dignity and are crowned with the garlands,
while the music plays up.   Then some one gets on
a bench and accuses the King of various offences,
such as ill-treating the cattle.   The King appeals to
witnesses and a trial ensues, at the close of which the
judge, who carries a white wand as his badge of office,
pronounces a verdict of " guilty " or " not guilty."   If
the verdict is " guilty " the judge breaks his wand, the

---

[1] Reinsberg-Düringsfeld, *Fest-Kalender aus Böhmen*, p. 263; W. Mannhardt, *Baumkultus*, p. 343.

King kneels on a white cloth, all heads are bared, and a soldier sets three or four hats, one above the other, on the King's head. The judge then pronounces the word "guilty" thrice in a loud voice, and orders the crier to behead the King. The crier obeys by striking off the King's hats with his wooden sword.[1]

But perhaps, for our purpose, the most instructive of these mimic executions is the following Bohemian one, which has been in part described already.[2] In some places of the Pilsen district (Bohemia) on Whit-Monday the King is dressed in bark, ornamented with flowers and ribbons ; he wears a crown of gilt paper and rides a horse, which is also decked with flowers. Attended by a judge, an executioner and other characters, and followed by a train of soldiers, all mounted, he rides to the village square, where a hut or arbour of green boughs has been erected under the May-trees, which are firs, freshly cut, peeled to the top, and dressed with flowers and ribbons. After the dames and maidens of the village have been criticised and a frog beheaded, in the way already described, the cavalcade rides to a place previously determined upon, in a straight, broad street. Here they draw up in two lines and the King takes to flight. He is given a short start and rides off at full speed, pursued by the whole troop. If they fail to catch him he remains King for another year, and his companions must pay his score at the alehouse in the evening. But if they overtake and catch him he is scourged with hazel rods or beaten with the wooden swords and compelled to dismount. Then the executioner asks, "Shall I behead this King?" The answer is given, "Behead him;" the executioner

----

[1] Reinsberg-Düringsfeld, *Fest-Kalender aus Böhmen*, p. 269 *sq.*
[2] See above, p. 92 *sq.*

The wild man.

Midsummer bonfire.

brandishes his axe, and with the words, "One, two, three, let the King headless be!" he strikes off the King's crown. Amid the loud cries of the bystanders the King sinks to the ground ; then he is laid on a bier and carried to the nearest farmhouse.[1]

In the personages who are thus slain in mimicry it is impossible not to recognise representatives of the tree-spirit or spirit of vegetation, as he is supposed to manifest himself in spring. The bark, leaves, and flowers in which the actors are dressed, and the season of the year at which they appear, show that they belong to the same class as the Grass King, King of the May, Jack-in-the-Green, and other representatives of the vernal spirit of vegetation which we examined in the first chapter. As if to remove any possible doubt on this head, we find that in two cases[2] these slain men are brought into direct connection with May-trees, which are (as we have seen) the impersonal, as the May King, Grass King, etc., are the personal representatives of the tree-spirit. The drenching of the *Pfingstl* with water and his wading up to the middle into the brook are, therefore, no doubt rain-charms like those which have been already described.[3]

But if these personages represent, as they certainly do, the spirit of vegetation in spring, the question arises, Why kill them? What is the object of slaying the spirit of vegetation at any time and above all in spring, when his services are most wanted? The only answer to this question seems to be given in the explanation already proposed of the custom of killing the divine king or priest. The divine life, incarnate in a material and mortal body, is liable

---

[1] Reinsberg-Düringsfeld, *Fest-Kalender aus Böhmen*, p. 264 *sq.*; W. Mannhardt, *Baumkultus*, p. 353 *sq.*   [2] See pp. 243, 246.   [3] See p. 15 *sqq.*

to be tainted and corrupted by the weakness of the frail medium in which it is for a time enshrined ; and if it is to be saved from the increasing enfeeblement which it must necessarily share with its human incarnation as he advances in years, it must be detached from him before, or at least as soon as, he exhibits signs of decay, in order to be transferred to a vigorous successor. This is done by killing the old representative of the god and conveying the divine spirit from him to a new incarnation. The killing of the god, that is, of his human incarnation, is, therefore, only a necessary step to his revival or resurrection in a better form. Far from being an extinction of the divine spirit, it is only the beginning of a purer and stronger manifestation of it. If this explanation holds good of the custom of killing divine kings and priests in general, it is still more obviously applicable to the custom of annually killing the representative of the tree-spirit or spirit of vegetation in spring. For the decay of vegetation in winter is readily interpreted by primitive man as an enfeeblement of the spirit of vegetation ; the spirit has (he thinks) grown old and weak and must therefore be renovated by being slain and brought to life in a younger and fresher form. Thus the killing of the representative of the tree-spirit in spring is regarded as a means to promote and quicken the growth of vegetation. For the killing of the tree-spirit is associated always (we must suppose) implicitly, and sometimes explicitly also, with a revival or resurrection of him in a more youthful and vigorous form. Thus in the Saxon and Thüringen custom, after the Wild Man has been shot he is brought to life again by a doctor ;[1] and in the Wurmlingen ceremony there

---

[1] See p. 243.

figures a Dr. Iron-Beard, who probably once played a similar part; certainly in another spring ceremony (to be described presently) Dr. Iron-Beard pretends to restore a dead man to life. But of this revival or resurrection of the god we shall have more to say anon.

The points of similarity between these North European personages and the subject of our inquiry —the King of the Wood or priest of Nemi—are sufficiently striking. In these northern maskers we see kings, whose dress of bark and leaves, along with the hut of green boughs and the fir-trees under which they hold their court, proclaim them unmistakably as, like their Italian counterpart, Kings of the Wood. Like him they die a violent death; but like him they may escape from it for a time by their bodily strength and agility; for in several of these northern customs the flight and pursuit of the king is a prominent part of the ceremony, and in one case at least if the king can outrun his pursuers he retains his life and his office for another year. In this last case, in fact, the king holds office on condition of running for his life once a year, just as the King of Calicut in later times held office on condition of defending his life against all comers once every twelve years, and just as the priest of Nemi held office on condition of defending himself against any assault at any time. In all these cases the life of the god-man is prolonged on condition of showing, in a severe physical contest of fight or flight, that his bodily strength is not decayed, and that, therefore, the violent death, which sooner or later is inevitable, may for the present be postponed. With regard to flight it is noticeable that flight figured conspicuously both in the legend and the practice of the King of the Wood. He

had to be a runaway slave (*fugitivus*) in memory of the
flight of Orestes, the traditional founder of the worship ;
hence the Kings of the Wood are described by an
ancient writer as "both strong of hand and fleet of foot."[1]
Perhaps if we knew the ritual of the Arician grove fully
we might find that the king was allowed a chance for
his life by flight, like his Bohemian brother.   We may
conjecture that the annual flight of the priestly king at
Rome (*regifugium*)[2] was at first a flight of the same
kind ; in other words, that he was originally one of those
divine kings who are either put to death after a fixed
period or allowed to prove by the strong hand or the
fleet foot that their divinity is vigorous and unimpaired.   One more point of resemblance may be
noted between the Italian King of the Wood and his
northern counterparts.   In Saxony and Thüringen the
representative of the tree-spirit, after being killed, is
brought to life again by a doctor.   This is exactly what
legend affirmed to have happened to the first King of
the Wood at Nemi, Hippolytus or Virbius, who after
he had been killed by his horses was restored to life
by the physician Aesculapius.[3]   Such a legend tallies
well with the theory that the slaying of the King of the
Wood was only a step to his revival or resurrection in
his successor.

It has been assumed that the mock killing of the
Wild Man and of the King in North European folk-
custom is a modern substitute for an ancient custom of
killing them in earnest.   Those who best know the
tenacity of life possessed by folk-custom and its tendency, with the growth of civilisation, to dwindle from
solemn ritual into mere pageant and pastime, will be

---

[1] Above, p. 4.   [2] Marquardt, *Römische Staatsverwaltung*, iii.[2] 323 *sq.*
[3] See above, p. 6.

least likely to question the truth of this assumption. That human sacrifices were commonly offered by the ancestors of the civilised races of North Europe (Celts, Teutons, and Slavs) is certain.[1] It is not, therefore, surprising that the modern peasant should do in mimicry what his forefathers did in reality. We know as a matter of fact that in other parts of the world mock human sacrifices have been substituted for real ones. Thus Captain Bourke was informed by an old chief that the Indians of Arizona used to offer human sacrifices at the Feast of Fire when the days are shortest. The victim had his throat cut, his breast opened, and his heart taken out by one of the priests. This custom was abolished by the Mexicans, but for a long time afterwards a modified form of it was secretly observed as follows. The victim, generally a young man, had his throat cut, and blood was allowed to flow freely; but the medicine-men sprinkled "medicine" on the gash, which soon healed up, and the man recovered.[2] So in the ritual of Artemis at Halae in Attica, a man's throat was cut and the blood allowed to gush out, but he was not killed.[3] At the funeral of a chief in Nias slaves are sacrificed; a little of their hair is cut off, and then they are beheaded. The victims are generally purchased for the purpose, and their number is proportioned to the wealth and power of the deceased. But if the number required is excessively great or cannot be procured, some of the chief's own slaves undergo a sham sacrifice. They are told, and believe, that

---

[1] Caesar, *Bell. Gall.* vi. 16; Adam of Bremen, *Descript. Insul. Aquil.* c. 27; Olaus Magnus, iii. 6; Grimm, *Deutsche Mythologie*,[4] i. 35 *sqq.*; Mone, *Geschichte des nordischen Heidenthums*, i. 69, 119, 120, 149, 187 *sq.*

[2] J. G. Bourke, *Snake Dance of the Moquis of Arizona*, p. 196 *sq.*

[3] Euripides, *Iphig. in Taur.* 1458 *sqq.*

they are about to be decapitated ; their heads are placed on a log and their necks struck with the back of a sword. The fright drives some of them crazy.[1] When a Hindoo has killed or ill-treated an ape, a bird of prey of a certain kind, or a cobra capella, in the presence of the worshippers of Vishnu, he must expiate his offence by the pretended sacrifice and resurrection of a human being. An incision is made in the victim's arm, the blood flows, he grows faint, falls, and feigns to die. Afterwards he is brought to life by being sprinkled with blood drawn from the thigh of a worshipper of Vishnu. The crowd of spectators is fully convinced of the reality of this simulated death and resurrection.[2] Sometimes the mock sacrifice is carried out, not on a living person but on an image. Thus an Indian law-book, the *Calica Puran*, prescribes that when the sacrifice of lions, tigers, or human beings is required, an image of a lion, tiger, or man shall be made with butter, paste, or barley meal, and sacrificed instead.[3] Some of the Gonds of India formerly offered human sacrifices ; they now sacrifice straw-men instead.[4] Colonel Dalton was told that in some of their villages the Bhagats (Hindooised Oraons) "annually make an image of a man in wood, put clothes and ornaments on it, and present it before the altar of a Mahádeo. The person who officiates as priest on the occasion says : ' O, Mahádeo, we sacrifice this man to you according to ancient customs. Give us rain in due season, and a

---

[1] Nieuwenhuisen en Rosenberg,"Verslag omtrent het eiland Nias," in *Verhandelingen van het Batav. Genootsch. van Kunsten en Wetenschappen*, xxx. 43.

[2] J. A. Dubois, *Moeurs, Institutions et Cérémonies des Peuples de l'Inde*,i. 151 *sq.*

[3] "The Rudhirádhyáyă, or sanguinary chapter," translated from the *Calica Puran* by W. C. Blaquiere, in *Asiatick Researches*, v. 376 (8vo. ed. London, 1807).

[4] Dalton, *Ethnology of Bengal*, p. 281.

plentiful harvest.' Then with one stroke of the axe the head of the image is struck off, and the body is removed and buried." [1]

§ 3.—*Carrying out Death*

Thus far I have offered an explanation of the rule which required that the priest of Nemi should be slain by his successor. The explanation claims to be no more than probable ; our scanty knowledge of the custom and of its history forbids it to be more. But its probability will be augmented in proportion to the extent to which the motives and modes of thought which it assumes can be proved to have operated in primitive society. Hitherto the god with whose death and resurrection we have been chiefly concerned has been the tree-god. Tree-worship may perhaps be regarded (though this is a conjecture) as occupying an intermediate place in the history of religion, between the religion of the hunter and shepherd on the one side, whose gods are mostly animals, and the religion of the husbandman on the other hand, in whose worship the cultivated plants play a leading part. If then I can show that the custom of killing the god and the belief in his resurrection originated, or at least existed, in the hunting and pastoral stage of society, when the slain god was an animal, and survived into the agricultural stage, when the slain god was the corn or a human being representing the corn, the probability of my explanation will have been considerably increased. This I shall attempt to do in the remainder of this chapter, in the course of which

---

[1] Dalton, *Ethnology of Bengal*, p. 258 *sq.*

I hope to clear up some obscurities which still remain, and to answer some objections which may have suggested themselves to the reader.

We start from the point at which we left off— the spring customs of European peasantry. Besides the ceremonies already described there are two kindred sets of observances in which the simulated death of a divine or supernatural being is a leading feature. These observances are commonly known as " Burying the Carnival," and " Driving or carrying out Death." Both customs are chiefly practised, or at least best known, on German and Slavonic ground. The former custom is observed on the last day of the Carnival, namely, Shrove Tuesday (*Fastnacht*), or on the first day of Lent, namely, Ash Wednesday. The latter custom is commonly observed on the Fourth Sunday in Lent, which hence gets the name of Dead Sunday (*Todtensonntag*) ; but in some places it is observed a week earlier ; in others again, as amongst the Czechs of Bohemia, a week later. Originally the date of the celebration of the " Carrying out Death " appears not to have been fixed, but to have depended on the appearance of the first swallow or of some other natural phenomenon.[1] A Bohemian form of the custom of " Burying the Carnival " has been already described.[2] The following Swabian form is obviously similar. In the neighbourhood of Tübingen on Shrove Tuesday a straw-man, called the Shrovetide Bear, is made up ; he is dressed in a pair of old trousers, and a

[1] Grimm, *Deutsche Mythologie*,[4] ii. 645 ; K. Haupt, *Sagenbuch der Lausitz*, ii. 58 ; Reinsberg - Düringsfeld, *Fest - Kalender aus Böhmen*, p. 86 *sq.* ; id., *Das festliche Jahr*, p. 77 *sq.* The Fourth Sunday in Lent is also known as Mid-Lent, because it falls in the middle of Lent, or as *Laetare* from the first word of the liturgy for the day. In the Roman Calendar it is the Sunday of the Rose, *Domenica rosae.*

[2] See p. 244.

fresh black-pudding or two squirts filled with blood are inserted in his neck.   After a formal condemnation he is beheaded, laid in a coffin, and on Ash Wednesday is buried in the churchyard.   This is called " Burying the Carnival" ("*die Fastnacht vergraben* ").[1] Amongst some of the Saxons of Transylvania the Carnival is hung.   Thus at Braller on Ash Wednesday or Shrove Tuesday two white and two chestnut horses draw a sledge on which is placed a straw-man swathed in a white cloth ; beside him is a cart-wheel which is kept turning round.   Two lads disguised as old men follow the sledge lamenting.   The rest of the village lads, mounted on horseback and decked with ribbons, accompany the procession, which is headed by two girls crowned with evergreen and drawn in a waggon or sledge.   A trial is held under a tree, at which lads disguised as soldiers pronounce sentence of death. The two old men try to rescue the straw-man and to fly with him, but to no purpose ; he is caught by the two girls and handed over to the executioner, who hangs him on a tree.   In vain the old men try to climb up the tree and take him down ; they always tumble down, and at last in despair they throw themselves on the ground and weep and howl for the hanged man.   An official then makes a speech in which he declares that the Carnival was condemned to death because he had done them harm, by wearing out their shoes and making them tired and sleepy.[2] At the " Burial of Carnival " in Lechrain, a man dressed as a woman in black clothes is carried on a litter or bier by four men ; he is lamented over by men disguised as

---

[1] E. Meier, *Deutsche Sagen, Sitten und Gebraüche aus Schwaben*, p. 371.

[2] J. Haltrich, *Zur Volkskunde der Siebenbürger Sachsen* (Wien, 1885), p. 284 *sq.*

women in black clothes, then thrown down before the village dung-heap, drenched with water, buried in the dung-heap, and covered with straw.[1]　Similarly in Schörzingen, near Schömberg, the "Carnival (Shrovetide) Fool" was carried all about the village on a bier, preceded by a man dressed in white, and followed by a devil who was dressed in black and carried chains, which he clanked.　One of the train collected gifts. After the procession the Fool was buried under straw and dung.[2]　In Rottweil the "Carnival Fool" is made drunk on Ash Wednesday and buried under straw amid loud lamentation.[3]　In Wurmlingen the Fool is represented by a young fellow enveloped in straw, who is led about the village by a rope as a "Bear" on Shrove Tuesday and the preceding day.　He dances to the flute.　Then on Ash Wednesday a straw-man is made, placed on a trough, carried out of the village to the sound of drums and mournful music, and buried in a field.[4]　In Altdorf and Weingarten on Ash Wednesday the Fool, represented by a straw-man, is carried about and then thrown into the water to the accompaniment of melancholy music. In other villages of Swabia the part of fool is played by a live person, who is thrown into the water after being carried about in procession.[5]　At Balwe, in Westphalia, a straw-man is made on Shrove Tuesday and thrown into the river amid rejoicings.　This is called, as usual, "Burying the Carnival."[6]　On the evening of Shrove Tuesday, the Esthonians make a

[1] Leoprechting, *Aus dem Lechrain*, p. 162 *sqq.* ; Mannhardt, *Baumkultus*, p. 411.

[2] E. Meier, *Deutsche Sagen, Sitten und Gebräuche aus Schwaben* p. 374; cp. Birlinger, *Volksthümliches aus Schwaben*, ii. 55.

[3] E. Meier, *op. cit.* p. 372.

[4] E. Meier, *op. cit.* p. 373.

[5] E. Meier, *op. cit.* pp. 373, 374.

[6] A. Kuhn, *Sagen, Gebräuche und Märchen aus Westfalen*, ii. 130.

straw figure called *metsik* or "wood-spirit;" one year
it is dressed with a man's coat and hat, next year with
a hood and a petticoat.   This figure is stuck on a long
pole, carried across the boundary of the village with
loud cries of joy, and fastened to the top of a tree in
the wood.   The ceremony is believed to be a protection against all kinds of misfortune.[1] Sometimes the
resurrection of the pretended dead person is enacted.
Thus, in some parts of Swabia, on Shrove Tuesday
Dr. Iron-Beard professes to bleed a sick man, who
thereupon falls as dead to the ground; but the doctor
at last restores him to life by blowing air into him
through a tube.[2]   In the Harz mountains, when Carnival is over, a man is laid on a baking-trough and
carried with dirges to a grave; but in the grave, instead of the man, a glass of brandy is placed.   A
speech is delivered and then the people return to the
village-green or meeting-place, where they smoke the
long clay pipes which are distributed at funerals.   On
the morning of Shrove Tuesday in the following year
the brandy is dug up and the festival begins by every
one tasting the brandy which, as the phrase goes, has
come to life again.[3]

The ceremony of "Carrying out Death" presents
much the same features as "Burying the Carnival;"
except that the figure of Death is oftener drowned
or burned than buried, and that the carrying out of
Death is generally followed by a ceremony, or at least
accompanied by a profession, of bringing in Summer,
Spring, or Life.   Thus, in some villages of Thüringen
on the Fourth Sunday of Lent, the children used to
carry a puppet of birchen twigs through the village,

---

[1] F. J. Wiedemann, *Aus dem inneren
und äusseren Leben der Ehsten*, p. 353.

[2] E. Meier, *op. cit.* p. 374.
[3] H. Pröhle, *Harzbilder*, p. 54.

and then threw it into a pool, while they sang, "We
carry the old Death out behind the herdsman's old
house ; we have got Summer, and Kroden's (?) power
is destroyed."[1]   In one village of Thüringen (Dob-
schwitz near Gera), the ceremony of "Driving out
Death" is still annually observed on the 1st of March.
The young people make up a figure of straw or the
like materials, dress it in old clothes which they have
begged from the houses in the village, and carry it out
and throw it into the river.   On returning to the
village they announce the fact to the people, and
receive eggs and other victuals as a reward.   In other
villages of Thüringen, in which the population was
originally Slavonic, the carrying out of the puppet
is accompanied with the singing of a song, which
begins, "Now we carry Death out of the village and
Spring into the village." [2]   In Bohemia the children
go out with a straw-man, representing Death, to the
end of the village, where they burn it, singing—

> "Now carry we Death out of the village,
> The new Summer into the village,
> Welcome dear Summer,
> Green little corn !" [3]

At Tabor (Bohemia) the figure of Death is carried
out of the town and flung from a high rock into the
water, while they sing—

> "Death swims on the water,
> Summer will soon be here,
> We carried Death away for you,
> We brought the Summer.
> And do thou, O holy Marketa,
> Give us a good year
> For wheat and for rye." [4]

---

[1] Aug. Witzschel, *Sagen, Sitten
und Gebräuche aus Thüringen*, p.
193.
[2] Witzschel, *op. cit.* p. 199.

[3] Grimm, *Deutsche Mythologie*,[4] ii.
642.
[4] Reinsberg-Düringsfeld, *Fest - Kalender aus Böhmen*, p. 90 *sq.*

In other parts of Bohemia they carry Death to the
end of the village, singing—

> " We carry Death out of the village,
>   And the New Year into the village.
>   Dear Spring, we bid you welcome,
>   Green grass, we bid you welcome."

Behind the village they erect a pyre, on which they
burn the straw figure, reviling and scoffing at it the
while.   Then they return, singing—

> " We have carried away Death,
>   And brought Life back.
>   He has taken up his quarters in the village,
>   Therefore sing joyous songs." [1]

At Nürnberg, girls of seven to eighteen years of
age, dressed in their best, carry through the streets
a little open coffin in which is a doll, hidden under a
shroud.   Others carry a beech branch, with an apple
fastened to it for a head, in an open box.   They sing,
" We carry Death into the water, it is well," or, " We
carry Death into the water, carry him in and out
again." [2]

The effigy of Death is often regarded with fear
and treated with marks of hatred and contempt.   In
Lusatia the figure is sometimes made to look in at the
window of a house, and it is believed that some one
in the house will die within the year unless his life
is redeemed by the payment of money.[3]   Again, after
throwing the effigy away, the bearers sometimes run
home lest Death should follow them ; and if one
of them falls in running, it is believed that he will
die within the year.[4]   At Chrudim, in Bohemia, the

---

[1] Reinsberg - Düringsfeld, *op. cit.*
p. 91.
[2] Grimm, *Deutsche Mythologie*,⁴ ii.
639 *sq.* ; Mannhardt, *Baumkultus*, p. 412.

[3] Grimm, *op. cit.* ii. 644 ; K.
Haupt, *Sagenbuch der Lausitz*, ii.
55.
[4] Grimm, *op. cit.* ii. 640, 643.

figure of Death is made out of a cross, with a head and mask stuck at the top, and a shirt stretched out on it. On the Fifth Sunday in Lent the boys take this effigy to the nearest brook or pool, and standing in a line throw it into the water. Then they all plunge in after it ; but as soon as it is caught no one more may enter the water. The boy who did not enter the water or entered it last will die within the year, and he is obliged to carry the Death back to the village. The effigy is then burned.[1] On the other hand it is believed that no one will die within the year in the house out of which the figure of Death has been carried ;[2] and the village out of which Death has been driven is sometimes supposed to be protected against sickness and plague.[3] In some villages of Austrian Silesia on the Saturday before Dead Sunday an effigy is made of old clothes, hay, and straw, for the purpose of driving Death out of the village. On Sunday the people, armed with sticks and straps, assemble before the house where the figure is lodged. Four lads then draw the effigy by cords through the village amid exultant shouts, while all the others beat it with their sticks and straps. On reaching a field which belongs to a neighbouring village they lay down the figure, cudgel it soundly, and scatter the fragments over the field. The people believe that the village from which Death has been thus carried out will be safe from any infectious disease for the whole year.[4] In Slavonia the figure of Death is cudgelled and then

---

[1] Vernalecken, *Mythen und Bräuche des Volkes in Oesterreich*, p. 294 *sq.* ; Reinsberg-Düringsfeld, *Fest - Kalender aus Böhmen*, p. 90.

[2] Grimm, *Deutsche Mythologie*,[4] ii. 640.

[3] J. A. E. Köhler, *Volksbrauch, Aberglauben, Sagen und andre alte Ueberlieferungen im Voigtlande*, p. 171.

[4] Reinsberg-Düringsfeld, *Das fest-liche Jahr*, p. 80.

rent in two.[1]   In Poland the effigy, made of hemp and straw, is flung into a pool or swamp with the words, " The devil take thee." [2]

The custom of " sawing the Old Woman," which is or used to be observed in Italy and Spain on the Fourth Sunday in Lent, is doubtless, as Grimm supposes, merely another form of the custom of "carrying out Death." A great hideous figure representing the oldest woman of the village was dragged out and sawn in two, amid a prodigious noise made with cow-bells, pots and pans, etc.[3]   In Palermo the ceremony used to be still more realistic. At Mid-Lent an old woman was drawn through the streets on a cart, attended by two men dressed in the costume of the *Compagnia de' Bianchi*, a society or religious order whose function it was to attend and console prisoners condemned to death. A scaffold was erected in a public square ; the old woman mounted it, and two mock executioners proceeded, amid a storm of huzzas and hand-clapping, to saw through her neck or rather through a bladder of blood which had been previously fitted to her neck. The blood gushed out and the old woman pretended to swoon and die. The last of these mock executions took place in 1737.[4] At Florence, during the fifteenth and sixteenth centuries, the Old Woman was represented by a figure stuffed with walnuts and dried figs and fastened to the top of a ladder. At Mid-Lent this effigy was sawn through the middle under the *Loggie* of the Mercato Nuovo, and as the dried fruits tumbled out they were scrambled for by the crowd. A trace of the custom is still to be seen in the practice, observed

[1] Ralston, *Songs of the Russian People*, p. 211.   [2] *Ib.* p. 210.   [3] Grimm, *Deutsche Mythologie*,[4] ii. 652 ; H. Usener, " Italische Mythen," in *Rheinisches Museum*, N. F. xxx. (1875) p. 191 *sq.*   [4] G. Pitrè, *Spettacoli e feste popolari siciliane* (Palermo, 1881), p. 207 *sq.*

by urchins, of secretly pinning paper ladders to the shoulders of women of the lower classes who happen to show themselves in the streets on the morning of Mid-Lent.[1] A similar custom is observed by urchins in Rome; and at Naples on the 1st of April boys cut strips of cloth into the shape of saws, smear them with gypsum, and strike passers-by with their "saws" on the back, thus imprinting the figure of a saw upon their clothes.[2] At Montalto in Calabria boys go about at Mid-Lent with little saws made of cane and jeer at old people, who therefore generally stay indoors on that day. The Calabrian women meet together at this time and feast on figs, chestnuts, honey, etc.; this they call "sawing the Old Woman"—a reminiscence probably of a custom like the old Florentine one.[3]

In Barcelona on the day in question boys run about the streets, some with saws, others with billets of wood, others again with cloths in which they collect gratuities. They sing a song in which it is said that they are looking for the oldest woman of the city for the purpose of sawing her in two in honour of Mid-Lent; at last, pretending to have found her, they saw something in two and burn it. A like custom is found amongst the South Slavs. In Lent the Croats tell their children that at noon an old woman is being sawn in two outside the gates; and in Carniola also the saying is current that at Mid-Lent an old woman is taken out of the village and sawn in two. The North Slavonian expression for keeping Mid-Lent is *bábu rezati*, that is, " sawing the Old Wife."[4]

[1] *Archivio per lo studio delle tradizioni popolari*, iv. (1885) p. 294 *sq.*

[2] H. Usener, *op. cit.* p. 193.

[3] Vincenzo Dorsa, *La tradizione greco-latina negli usi e nelle credenze* popolari della Calabria citeriore (Cosenza, 1884), p. 43 *sq.*

[4] Grimm, *Deutsche Mythologie*,[4] ii. 652; H. Usener, "Italische Mythen," in *Rheinisches Museum*, N. F. xxx. 1875) p. 191 *sq.*

In the preceding ceremonies the return of Spring, Summer, or Life, as a sequel to the expulsion of Death, is only implied or at most announced. In the following ceremonies it is plainly enacted. In some parts of Bohemia the effigy of Death is buried at sunset; then the girls go out into the wood and cut down a young tree with a green crown, hang a doll dressed as a woman on it, deck the whole with green, red, and white ribbons, and march in procession with their *Líto* (Summer) into the village, collecting gifts and singing—

"We carried Death out of the village,
We are carrying Summer into the village."[1]

In many Silesian villages the figure of Death, after being treated with respect, is stripped of its clothes and flung with curses into the water, or torn in pieces in a field. Then a fir-tree adorned with ribbons, coloured egg-shells, and motley bits of cloth, is carried through the streets by boys who collect pennies and sing—

"We have carried Death out,
We are bringing the dear Summer back,
The Summer and the May
And all the flowers gay."[2]

At Eisenach on the Fourth Sunday in Lent young people used to fasten a straw-man, representing Death, to a wheel, which they trundled to the top of a hill. Then setting fire to the figure they allowed it and the wheel to roll downhill. Next they cut a tall fir-tree, tricked it out with ribbons, and set it up in the plain. The men then climbed the tree to fetch down the

[1] Reinsberg-Düringsfeld, *Fest-Kalender aus Böhmen*, p. 89 *sq.* ; W. Mannhardt, *Baumkultus*, p. 156. This custom has been already referred to. See p. 82.

[2] Reinsberg-Düringsfeld, *Das festliche Jahr*, p. 82 ; Philo vom Walde, *Schlesien in Sage und Brauch.* (N.D. preface dated 1883), p. 122.

ribbons.[1] In Upper Lusatia the figure of Death, made of straw and rags, is dressed in a veil furnished by the last bride and a shirt furnished by the house in which the last death occurred. Thus arrayed the figure is stuck on the end of a long pole and carried at full speed by the tallest and strongest girl, while the rest pelt the effigy with sticks and stones. Whoever hits it will be sure to live through the year. In this way Death is carried out of the village and thrown into the water or over the boundary of the next village. On their way home each one breaks a green branch and carries it gaily with him till he reaches the village, when he throws it away. Sometimes the young people of the next village, upon whose land the figure has been thrown, run after them and hurl it back, not wishing to have Death among them. Hence the two parties occasionally come to blows.[2]

In these cases Death is represented by the puppet which is thrown away, Summer or Life by the branches or trees which are brought back. But sometimes a new potency of life seems to be attributed to the image of Death itself, and by a kind of resurrection it becomes the instrument of the general revival. Thus in some parts of Lusatia women alone are concerned in carrying out Death, and suffer no male to meddle with it. Attired in mourning, which they wear the whole day, they make a puppet of straw, clothe it in a white shirt, and give it a broom in one hand and a scythe in the other. Singing songs and pursued by urchins throwing stones, they carry the puppet to the village boundary, where they tear it in pieces. Then they cut down

---

[1] Witzschel, *Sagen, Sitten und Gebräuche aus Thüringen*, p. 192 *sq.*

[2] Grimm, *Deutsche Mythologie*,[4] ii. 643 *sq.* ; K. Haupt, *Sagenbuch der Lausitz*, ii. 54 *sq.* ; Mannhardt, *Baumkultus*, p. 412 *sq.* ; Ralston, *Songs of the Russian People*, p. 211.

a fine tree, hang the shirt on it, and carry it home
singing.[1]   On the Feast of Ascension the Saxons of a
village near Hermanstadt (Transylvania) observe the
ceremony of "carrying out Death" in the following
manner.   After forenoon church all the school-girls
repair to the house of one of their number, and
there dress up the Death.   This is done by tying a
threshed-out corn-sheaf into the rough semblance of a
head and body, while the arms are simulated by a
broomstick stuck horizontally.   The figure is dressed
in the Sunday clothes of a village matron.   It is then
displayed at the window that all people may see it on
their way to afternoon church.   As soon as vespers
are over the girls seize the effigy and, singing a hymn,
carry it in procession round the village.   Boys are
excluded from the procession.   After the procession
has traversed the village from end to end, the figure is
taken to another house and stripped of its attire ; the
naked straw bundle is then thrown out of the window
to the boys, who carry it off and fling it into the
nearest stream.   This is the first act of the drama.
In the second, one of the girls is solemnly invested
with the clothes and ornaments previously worn by
the figure of Death, and, like it, is led in procession
round the village to the singing of the same hymns
as before.   The ceremony ends with a feast at
the house of the girl who acted the chief part ; as
before, the boys are excluded.   "According to popular
belief, it is allowed to eat fruit only after this day, as
now the 'Death,' that is, the unwholesomeness—has
been expelled from them.   Also the river in which the
Death has been drowned may now be considered fit for
public bathing.   If this ceremony be neglected in the

---

[1] Grimm, *op. cit.* ii. 644 ; K. Haupt, *op. cit.* ii. 55.

village where it is customary, such neglect is supposed to entail death to one of the young people, or loss of virtue to a girl."[1]

In the first of these two ceremonies the tree which is brought home after the destruction of the figure of Death is plainly equivalent to the trees or branches which, in the preceding customs, were brought back as representatives of Summer or Life, after Death had been thrown away or destroyed. But the transference of the shirt worn by the effigy of Death to the tree clearly indicates that the tree is a kind of revivification, in a new form, of the destroyed effigy.[2] This comes out also in the Transylvanian custom; the dressing of a girl in the clothes worn by the Death, and the leading her about the village to the same songs which had been sung when the Death was being carried about, show that she is intended to be a kind of resuscitation of the being whose effigy has just been destroyed. These examples therefore suggest that the Death whose demolition is represented in these ceremonies cannot be regarded as the purely destructive agent which we understand by Death. If the tree which is brought back as an embodiment of the reviving vegetation of spring is clothed in the shirt worn by the Death which has been just destroyed, the object certainly cannot be to check and counteract the revival of vegetation; it can only be to foster and promote it. Therefore the being which has just been destroyed— the so-called Death—must be supposed to be endowed with a vivifying and quickening influence, which it can communicate to the vegetable and even the animal world. This ascription of a life-giving virtue to the

---

[1] E. Gerard, *The Land beyond the Forest*, ii. 47-49.

[2] This is also the view taken of the custom by Mannhardt, *Baumkultus*, p. 419.

figure of Death is put beyond a doubt by the custom, observed in some places, of taking pieces of the straw effigy of Death and placing them in the fields to make the crops grow, or in the manger to make the cattle thrive. Thus in Spachendorf (Austrian Silesia) the figure of Death made of straw, brushwood, and rags, is carried out with wild songs to an open place outside the village and there burned, and while it is burning a general struggle takes place for the pieces, which are pulled out of the flames with bare hands. Each one who secures a fragment of the effigy ties it to a branch of the largest tree in his garden, or buries it in his field, in the belief that this causes the crops to grow better.[1] In the Troppau district (Austrian Silesia) the straw figure which the boys make on the Fourth Sunday in Lent is dressed by the girls in woman's clothes and hung with ribbons, necklace, and garlands. Attached to a long pole it is carried out of the village, followed by a troop of young people of both sexes, who alternately frolic, lament, and sing songs. Arrived at its destination—a field outside the village—the figure is stripped of its clothes and ornaments; then the crowd rushes on it and tears it to bits, scuffling for the fragments. Every one tries to get a wisp of the straw of which the effigy was made, because such a wisp, placed in the manger, is believed to make the cattle thrive.[2] Or the straw is put in the hens' nest, it being supposed that this prevents the hens from carrying away their eggs, and makes them brood much better.[3] The same attribution of a fertilising power to the figure of Death appears in the belief that

---

[1] Vernalecken, *Mythen und Bräuche des Volkes in Oesterreich*, p. 293 *sq.*

[2] Reinsberg - Düringsfeld, *Das fest-liche Jahr*, p. 82.

[3] Philo vom Walde, *Schlesien in Sage und Brauch*, p. 122.

if the bearers of the figure, after throwing it away, meet cattle and strike them with their sticks, this will render the cattle prolific.[1] Perhaps the sticks had been previously used to beat the Death,[2] and so had acquired the fertilising power ascribed to the effigy. In Leipzig at Mid-Lent men and women of the lowest class used to carry through all the streets a straw effigy of Death, which they exhibited to young wives, and finally threw into the river, alleging that this made young wives fruitful, cleansed the city, and averted the plague and other sickness from the inhabitants for that year.[3]

It seems hardly possible to separate from the May-trees the trees or branches which are brought into the village after the destruction of the Death. The bearers who bring them in profess to be bringing in the Summer;[4] therefore the trees obviously represent the Summer; and the doll which is sometimes attached to the Summer-tree is a duplicate representative of the Summer, just as the May is sometimes represented at the same time by a May-tree and a May Lady.[5] Further, the Summer-trees are adorned like May-trees with ribbons, etc.; like May-trees, when large, they are planted in the ground and climbed up; and like May-trees, when small, they are carried from door to door by boys or girls singing songs and collecting money.[6] And as if to demonstrate the identity of the two sets of customs the bearers of the Summer-tree sometimes announce that they are bringing in the Summer

[1] Grimm, *Deutsche Mythologie*,[4] ii. 640 *sq.*   [2] See above, p. 260.
[3] K. Schwenk, *Die Mythologie der Slawen*, p. 217 *sq.*
[4] Above, p. 263.

[5] See above, pp. 83, 263.
[6] Above, p. 263, and Grimm, *Deutsche Mythologie*,[4] ii. 644; Reinsberg-Düringsfeld, *Fest-Kalender aus Böhmen*, p. 87 *sq.*

and the May.[1] The customs, therefore, of bringing
in the May and bringing in the Summer are essentially
the same; and the Summer-tree is merely another
form of the May-tree, the only distinction (besides
that of name) being in the time at which they are
respectively brought in; for while the May-tree is
usually fetched in on the 1st of May or at Whitsuntide, the Summer-tree is fetched in on the Fourth
Sunday in Lent. Therefore, if the explanation here
adopted of the May-tree (namely, that it is an embodiment of the tree-spirit or spirit of vegetation) is
correct, the Summer-tree must likewise be an embodiment of the tree-spirit or spirit of vegetation. But
we have seen that the Summer-tree is in some cases
a revivification of the effigy of Death. It follows,
therefore, that in these cases the effigy called Death
must be an embodiment of the tree-spirit or spirit of
vegetation. This inference is confirmed, first, by
the vivifying and fertilising influence which the fragments of the effigy of Death are believed to exercise
both on vegetable and on animal life;[2] for this influence, as we saw in the first chapter, is supposed
to be a special attribute of the tree-spirit. It is
confirmed, secondly, by observing that the effigy of
Death is sometimes composed of birchen twigs, of
the branch of a beech-tree, of a threshed-out corn-
sheaf, or of hemp;[3] and that sometimes it is hung
on a little tree and so carried about by girls collecting money,[4] just as is done with the May-tree and
the May Lady, and with the Summer-tree and the

---

[1] Above, p. 263.

[2] See above, p. 266 *sqq.*

[3] Above, pp. 257, 259, 265; and
Grimm, *D. M.*[4] ii. 643.

[4] Reinsberg-Düringsfeld, *Fest-Kalender aus Böhmen*, p. 88. Sometimes the
effigy of Death (without a tree) is
carried round by boys who collect
gratuities. Grimm, *D. M.*[4] ii. 644.

doll attached to it. In short we are driven to regard
the expulsion of Death and the bringing in of Summer
as, in some cases at least, merely another form of that
death and resuscitation of the spirit of vegetation
in spring which we saw enacted in the killing and
resurrection of the Wild Man.[1] The burial and
resurrection of the Carnival is probably another way
of expressing the same idea. The burying of the
representative of the Carnival under a dung-heap
is natural, if he is supposed to possess a quickening
and fertilising influence like that ascribed to the
effigy of Death. By the Esthonians, indeed, the straw
figure which is carried out of the village in the usual
way on Shrove Tuesday is not called the Carnival,
but the Wood-spirit (*Metsik*), and the identity of it
with the wood-spirit is further shown by fixing it
to the top of a tree in the wood, where it remains
for a year, and is besought almost daily with prayers
and offerings to protect the herds ; for like a true
wood-spirit the *Metsik* is a patron of cattle. Sometimes the *Metsik* is made of sheafs of corn.[2] Therefore, we may fairly conjecture that the names Carnival,
Death, and Summer, are comparatively late and inadequate expressions for the beings personified or
embodied in the customs described. The very
abstractness of the names bespeaks a modern origin ;
the personification of times and seasons like the
Carnival and Summer, or of an abstract notion like
death, is hardly primitive. But the ceremonies themselves bear the stamp of a dateless antiquity ; therefore
we can hardly help supposing that in their origin the

---

[1] Above, p. 243.

[2] Wiedemann, *Aus dem inneren und
äusseren Leben der Ehsten*, p. 353 ; Holzmayer, " Osiliana," in *Verhandlungen
der gelehrten Estnischen Gesellschaft
zu Dorpat*, vii. Heft 2, p. 10 *sq.* ;
W. Mannhardt, *Baumkultus*, p. 407 *sq.*

ideas which they embodied were of a more simple and concrete order. The conception of a tree, perhaps of a particular kind of tree (for some savages have no word for tree in general), or even of an individual tree, is sufficiently concrete to supply a basis from which by a gradual process of generalisation the wider conception of a spirit of vegetation might be reached. But this general conception of vegetation would readily be confounded with the season in which it manifests itself; hence the substitution of Spring, Summer, or May for the tree-spirit or spirit of vegetation would be easy and natural. Again the concrete notion of the dying tree or dying vegetation would by a similar process of generalisation glide into a notion of death in general; so that instead of the carrying out of the dying or dead vegetation in spring (as a preliminary to its revival) we should in time get a carrying out of Death itself. The view that in these spring cere-monies Death meant originally the dying or dead vegetation of winter has the high support of W. Mannhardt; and he confirms it by the analogy of the name Death as applied to the spirit of the ripe corn. Commonly the spirit of the ripe corn is con-ceived, not as dead, but as old, and hence it goes by the name of the Old Man or the Old Woman. But in some places the last sheaf cut at harvest, which is generally believed to be the seat of the corn spirit, is called "the Dead One;" children are warned against entering the corn-fields because Death sits in the corn; and, in a game played by Saxon children in Transylvania at the maize harvest, Death is repre-sented by a child completely covered with maize leaves.[1]

---

[1] W. Mannhardt, *Baumkultus*, pp. 417-421.

The supposition that behind the conceptions of Death, Carnival, Summer, etc., as embodied in these spring ceremonies, there lurk older and more concrete notions is to a certain extent countenanced by the fact that in Russia funeral ceremonies like those of "Burying the Carnival" and "Carrying out Death" are celebrated under the names, not of Death or the Carnival, but of certain mythic figures, Kostrubonko, Kostroma, Kupalo, Lada, and Yarilo. These Russian ceremonies are observed both in spring and at midsummer. Thus "in Little Russia it used to be the custom at Eastertide to celebrate the funeral of a being called Kostrubonko, the deity of the spring. A circle was formed of singers who moved slowly around a girl who lay on the ground as if dead, and as they went they sang—

> ' Dead, dead is our Kostrubonko !
> Dead, dead is our dear one ! '

until the girl suddenly sprang up, on which the chorus joyfully exclaimed—

> ' Come to life, come to life has our Kostrubonko !
> Come to life, come to life has our dear one ! ' " [1]

On the Eve of St. John (Midsummer Eve) a figure of Kupalo is made of straw and "is dressed in woman's clothes, with a necklace and a floral crown. Then a tree is felled, and, after being decked with ribbons, is set up on some chosen spot. Near this tree, to which they give the name of Marena [Winter or Death], the straw figure is placed, together with a table, on which stand spirits and viands. Afterwards a bonfire is lit, and the young men and maidens jump over it in couples, carrying the figure with them. On

---

[1] Ralston, *Songs of the Russian People*, p. 221.

the next day they strip the tree and the figure of their ornaments, and throw them both into a stream."[1]   On St. Peter's Day (29th June) or on the following Sunday, "the Funeral of Kostroma" or of Lada or of Yarilo is celebrated in Russia.   In the Governments of Penza and Simbirsk the "funeral" used to be represented as follows.   A bonfire was kindled on the 28th of June, and on the next day the maidens chose one of their number to play the part of Kostroma.   Her companions saluted her with deep obeisances, placed her on a board, and carried her to the bank of a stream. There they bathed her in the water, while the oldest girl made a basket of lime-tree bark and beat it like a drum.   Then they returned to the village and ended the day with processions, games, and dances.[2]   In the Murom district, Kostroma was represented by a straw figure dressed in woman's clothes and flowers.   This was laid in a trough and carried with songs to the bank of a lake or river.   Here the crowd divided into two sides, of which the one attacked and the other defended the figure.   At last the assailants gained the day, stripped the figure of its dress and ornaments, tore it in pieces, trod the straw of which it was made under foot, and flung it into the stream; while the defenders of the figure hid their faces in their hands and pretended to bewail the death of Kostroma.[3]   In the district of Kostroma the burial of Yarilo was celebrated on the 29th or 30th of June.   The people chose an old man and gave him a small coffin containing a Priapus-like figure representing Yarilo.   This he carried out of the town, followed by women chanting

---

[1] Ralston, *op. cit.* p. 241.
[2] Ralston, *op. cit.* p. 243 *sq.*; W. Mannhardt, *Baumkultus*, p. 414.

[3] W. Mannhardt, *Baumkultus*, p. 414 *sq.*; Ralston, *op. cit.* p. 244.

dirges and expressing by their gestures grief and
despair. In the open fields a grave was dug, and
into it the figure was lowered amid weeping and
wailing, after which games and dances were begun,
"calling to mind the funeral games celebrated in old
times by the pagan Slavonians."[1] In Little Russia
the figure of Yarilo was laid in a coffin and carried
through the streets after sunset surrounded by drunken
women, who kept repeating mournfully, "He is dead!
he is dead!" The men lifted and shook the figure as
if they were trying to recall the dead man to life.
Then they said to the women, "Women, weep not.
I know what is sweeter than honey." But the women
continued to lament and chant, as they do at funerals.
"Of what was he guilty? He was so good. He will
arise no more. O how shall we part from thee? What
is life without thee? Arise, if only for a brief hour.
But he rises not, he rises not." At last the Yarilo
was buried in a grave.[2]

These Russian customs are plainly of the same
nature as those which in Austria and Germany are
known as "Burying the Carnival" and "Carrying out
Death." Therefore if my interpretation of the latter
is right, the Russian Kostroma, Yarilo, etc. must also
have been originally embodiments of the spirit of
vegetation, and their death must have been regarded
as a necessary preliminary to their revival. The
revival as a sequel to the death is enacted in the
first of the ceremonies described, the death and
resurrection of Kostrubonko. The reason why in
some of these Russian ceremonies the death of the
spirit of vegetation is celebrated at midsummer may

---

[1] Ralston, *op. cit.* p. 245; W. Mannhardt, *Baumkultus*, p. 416.
[2] W. Mannhardt, *l.c.*; Ralston, *l.c.*

be that the decline of summer is dated from Midsummer Day, after which the days begin to shorten,
and the sun sets out on his downward journey—

> " To the darksome hollows
> Where the frosts of winter lie."

Such a turning-point of the year, when vegetation
might be thought to share the incipient though still
almost imperceptible decay of summer, might very
well be chosen by primitive man as a fit moment for
resorting to those magic ceremonies by which he
hopes to stay the decline, or at least to ensure the
revival, of plant life.

But while the death of vegetation appears to have
been represented in all, and its revival in some, of these
spring and midsummer ceremonies, there are features
in some of them which can hardly be explained on
this hypothesis alone. The solemn funeral, the lamentations, and the mourning attire, which often characterise
these ceremonies, are indeed appropriate at the death
of the beneficent spirit of vegetation. But what shall
we say of the glee with which the effigy is often carried
out, of the sticks and stones with which it is assailed,
and the taunts and curses which are hurled at
it ? What shall we say of the dread of the effigy
evinced by the haste with which the bearers scamper
home as soon as they have thrown it away, and by
the belief that some one must soon die in any house
into which it has looked ? This dread might perhaps be explained by a belief that there is a certain
infectiousness in the dead spirit of vegetation which
renders its approach dangerous. But this explanation,
besides being rather strained, does not cover the rejoicings which often attend the carrying out of Death.

We must therefore recognise two distinct and seemingly opposite features in these ceremonies; on the
one hand, sorrow for the death, and affection and respect
for the dead; on the other hand, fear and hatred of the
dead, and rejoicings at his death. How the former of
these features is to be explained I have attempted
to show; how the latter came to be so closely associated
with the former is a question which I shall try to answer
in the sequel.

Before we quit these European customs to go
farther afield, it will be well to notice that occasionally
the expulsion of Death or of a mythic being is conducted without any visible representative of the personage expelled. Thus at Königshain, near Görlitz
(Silesia), all the villagers, young and old, used to go
out with straw torches to the top of a neighbouring
hill, called *Todtenstein* (Death-stone), where they lit
their torches, and so returned home singing, "We
have driven out Death, we are bringing back
Summer."[1] In Albania young people light torches of
resinous wood on Easter Eve, and march in procession through the village brandishing them. At last
they throw the torches into the river, saying, "Ha,
Kore, we fling you into the river, like these torches,
that you may return no more." Some say that the
intention of the ceremony is to drive out winter; but
Kore is conceived as a malignant being who devours
children.[2]

In the Kânagrâ district, India, there is a custom
observed by young girls in spring which closely
resembles some of the European spring ceremonies
just described. It is called the *Ralî Ka melâ*, or

---

[1] Grimm, *Deutsche Mythologie*,[4] ii.   [2] J. G. von Hahn, *Albanesische*
644.   *Studien*, i. 160.

fair of Ralî, the *Ralî* being a small painted earthen
image of Siva or Pârvatî. It lasts through most
of Chet (March-April) up to the Sankrânt of Baisâkh (April), and is in vogue all over the Kânagrâ
district. Its celebration is entirely confined to young
girls. On a morning in March all the young girls
of the village take small baskets of *dûb* grass and
flowers to a certain fixed spot, where they throw them
in a heap. Round this heap they stand in a circle and
sing. This goes on every day for ten days, till the
heap of grass and flowers has reached a fair height.
Then they cut in the jungle two branches having three
prongs at one end, and place them, prongs downwards,
over the heap of flowers, so as to make two tripods or
pyramids. On the single uppermost points of these
branches they get an image-maker to construct two
clay images, one to represent Siva, and the other
Pârvatî. The girls then divide themselves into two
parties, one for Siva and one for Pârvatî, and marry
the images in the usual way, leaving out no part of the
ceremony. After the marriage they have a feast, the
cost of which is defrayed by contributions solicited
from their parents. Then at the next Sankrânt
(Baisâkh) they all go together to the riverside, throw
the images into a deep pool, and weep over the place,
as though they were performing funeral obsequies.
The boys of the neighbourhood often annoy them by
diving after the images, bringing them up, and waving
them about while the girls are crying over them. The
object of the fair is said to be to secure a good
husband.[1]

That in this Indian ceremony the deities Siva and
Pârvatî are conceived as spirits of vegetation seems to

---

[1] Captain R. C. Temple, in *Indian Antiquary*, xi. (1882) p. 297 *sq.*

be proved by the fact that their images are placed on branches over a heap of grass and flowers. Here, as often in European folk-custom, the divinities of vegetation are represented in duplicate, by plants and by puppets. The marriage of these Indian deities in spring corresponds to the European ceremonies in which the marriage of the vernal spirits of vegetation is represented by the King and Queen of May, the May Bride, Bridegroom of the May, etc.[1] The throwing of the images into the water, and the mourning for them, are the equivalents of the European customs of throwing the dead spirit of vegetation (under the name of Death, Yarilo, Kostroma, etc.) into the water and lamenting over it. Again, in India, as often in Europe, the rite is performed exclusively by females. The notion that the ceremony was effective for procuring husbands to the girls can be explained by the quickening and fertilising influence which the spirit of vegetation is believed to exert upon human and animal, as well as upon vegetable life.[2]

§ 4.—*Adonis*

But it is in Egypt and Western Asia that the death and resurrection of vegetation appear to have been most widely celebrated with ceremonies like those of modern Europe. Under the names of Osiris, Adonis, Thammuz, Attis, and Dionysus, the Egyptians, Syrians, Babylonians, Phrygians, and Greeks represented the decay and revival of vegetation with rites which, as the ancients themselves recognised,

---

[1] See above, p. 94 *sqq.*   [2] Above, p. 70 *sqq.*

were substantially the same, and which find their
parallels in the spring and midsummer customs of our
European peasantry. The nature and worship of these
deities have been discussed at length by many learned
writers ; all that I propose to do is to sketch those
salient features in their ritual and legends which seem
to establish the view here taken of their nature. We
begin with Adonis or Thammuz.

The worship of Adonis was practised by the
Semitic peoples of Syria, from whom it was borrowed
by the Greeks as early at least as the fifth century
before Christ. The name Adonis is the Phoenician
Adon, "lord."[1] He was said to have been a fair
youth, beloved by Aphrodite (the Semitic Astarte),
but slain by a boar in his youthful prime. His death
was annually lamented with a bitter wailing, chiefly
by women ; images of him, dressed to resemble
corpses, were carried out as to burial and then thrown
into the sea or into springs ;[2] and in some places his
revival was celebrated on the following day.[3] But
the ceremonies varied somewhat both in the manner
and the season of their celebration in different places.
At Alexandria images of Adonis and Aphrodite were
displayed on two couches ; beside them were set ripe
fruits of all kinds, cakes, plants growing in flower pots,
and green bowers twined with anise. The marriage
of the lovers was celebrated one day, and on the next
the image of Adonis was borne by women attired as
mourners, with streaming hair and bared breasts, to

---

[1] Baudissin, *Studien zur semitischen
Religionsgeschichte*, i. 299 ; W. Mannhardt, *Antike Wald-und Feldkulte*, p.
274.

[2] Plutarch, *Alcibiades*, 18 ; Zenobius,
Centur. i. 49 ; Theocritus, xv. 132 *sq.* ;
Eustathius on Homer, *Od*. xi. 590.

[3] Besides Lucian (cited below) see
Jerome, *Comment. in Ezechiel.* viii.
14, *in qua (solemnitate) plangitur
quasi mortuus, et postea reviviscens,
canitur atque laudatur . . . interfectionem et resurrectionem Adonidis
planctu et gaudio prosequens.*

the sea-shore and committed to the waves.[1] The
date at which this Alexandrian ceremony was observed
is not expressly stated; but from the mention of the
ripe fruits it has been inferred that it took place in
late summer.[2] At Byblus the death of Adonis was
annually mourned with weeping, wailing, and beating
of the breast; but next day he was believed to come
to life again and ascend up to heaven in the presence
of his worshippers.[3] This celebration appears to have
taken place in spring; for its date was determined by
the discoloration of the river Adonis, and this has
been observed by modern travellers to occur in spring.
At that season the red earth washed down from the
mountains by the rain tinges the water of the river
and even the sea for a great way with a blood-red
hue, and the crimson stain was believed to be the
blood of Adonis, annually wounded to death by the
boar on Mount Lebanon.[4] Again, the red anemone[5]
was said to have sprung from the blood of Adonis;
and as the anemone blooms in Syria about Easter, this
is a fresh proof that the festival of Adonis, or at least
one of his festivals, was celebrated in spring. The
name of the flower is probably derived from Naaman
("darling"), which seems to have been an epithet of
Adonis. The Arabs still call the anemone "wounds
of the Naaman."[6]

---

[1] Theocritus, xv.

[2] W. Mannhardt, op. cit. p. 277.

[3] Lucian, De dea Syria, 6. The
words ἐς τὸν ἠέρα πέμπουσι imply that
the ascension was supposed to take place
in the presence, if not before the eyes,
of the worshipping crowds.

[4] Lucian, op. cit. 8. The discoloration of the river and the sea was
observed by Maundrell on 17th March
1697. See his "Journey from Aleppo
to Jerusalem," in Bohn's Early Travels
in Palestine, edited by Thomas Wright,

p. 411. Renan observed the discolora-
tion at the beginning of February;
Baudissin, Studien, i. 298 (referring to
Renan, Mission de Phénicie, p. 283).
Milton's lines will occur to most readers.

[5] Ovid, Metam. x. 735, compared
with Bion i. 66. The latter, however,
makes the anemone spring from the tears,
as the rose from the blood of Adonis.

[6] W. Robertson Smith, "Ctesias and
the Semiramis legend," in English
Historical Review, April 1887, following Lagarde.

An allegorical representation of Death

Aphrodite, goddess of beauty
and love, was the lover
of Adonis.

The resemblance of these ceremonies to the Indian and European ceremonies previously described is obvious. In particular, apart from the somewhat doubtful date of its celebration, the Alexandrian ceremony is almost identical with the Indian. In both of them the marriage of two divinities, whose connection with vegetation seems indicated by the fresh plants with which they are surrounded, is celebrated in effigy, and the effigies are afterwards mourned over and thrown into the water.[1] From the similarity of these customs to each other and to the spring and midsummer customs of modern Europe we should naturally expect that they all admit of a common explanation. Hence, if the explanation here adopted of the latter is correct, the ceremony of the death and resurrection of Adonis must also have been a representation of the decay and revival of vegetation. The inference thus based on the similarity of the customs is confirmed by the following features in the legend and ritual of Adonis. His connection with vegetation comes out at once in the common story of his birth. He was said to have been born from a myrrh-tree, the bark of which bursting, after a ten months' gestation, allowed the lovely infant to come forth. According to some, a boar rent the bark with his tusk and so opened a passage for the babe. A faint rationalistic colour was given to the legend by saying that his mother was a woman named Myrrh, who had been turned into a myrrh-tree soon after she had conceived the child.[2] Again the story that Adonis

---

[1] In the Alexandrian ceremony, however, it appears to have been the image of Adonis only which was thrown into the sea.

[2] Apollodorus, *Biblioth.* iii. 14, 4 ;

Schol. on Theocritus, i. 109; Antoninus Liberalis, 34 ; Tzetzes on Lycophron, 829 ; Ovid, *Metam.* x. 489 *sqq.* ; Servius on Virgil, *Aen.* v. 72, and on *Bucol.* x. 18 ; Hyginus, *Fab.* 58, 164 ;

spent half, or according to others a third, of the
year in the lower world and the rest of it in the
upper world,[1] is explained most simply and naturally by supposing that he represented vegetation,
especially the corn, which lies buried in the earth
half the year and reappears above ground the
other half. Certainly of the annual phenomena of
nature there is none which suggests so obviously
the idea of a yearly death and resurrection as the
disappearance and reappearance of vegetation in
autumn and spring. Adonis has been taken for the
sun; but there is nothing in the sun's annual course
within the temperate and tropical zones to suggest
that he is dead for half or a third of the year and
alive for the other half or two-thirds. He might,
indeed, be conceived as weakened in winter,[2] but
dead he could not be thought to be; his daily reappearance contradicts the supposition. Within the
arctic circle, where the sun annually disappears for a
continuous period of from twenty-four hours to six
months, according to the latitude, his annual death
and resurrection would certainly be an obvious idea;
but no one has suggested that the Adonis worship
came from those regions. On the other hand the
annual death and revival of vegetation is a conception
which readily presents itself to men in every stage of
savagery and civilisation; and the vastness of the
scale on which this yearly decay and regeneration

Fulgentius, iii. 8. The word Myrrha
or Smyrna is borrowed from the
Phoenician (Liddell and Scott, Greek
Lexicon, s.v. σμύρνα). Hence the
mother's name, as well as the son's,
was taken directly from the Semites.

[1] Schol. on Theocritus, iii. 48;
Hyginus, Astronom. ii. 7; Lucian,
Dialog. deor. xi. 1; Cornutus, De

natura deorum, 28, p. 163 sq. ed.
Osannus; Apollodorus, iii. 14, 4.

[2] Thus, after the autumnal equinox
the Egyptians celebrated the "nativity
of the sun's walking-sticks," because, as
the sun declined daily in the sky, and his
heat and light diminished, he was supposed to need a staff with which to support his steps. Plutarch, Isis et Osiris, 52.

takes place, together with man's intimate dependence on it for subsistence, combine to render it the most striking annual phenomenon in nature, at least within the temperate zones. It is no wonder that a phenomenon so important, so striking, and so universal should, by suggesting similar ideas, have given rise to similar rites in many lands. We may, therefore, accept as probable an explanation of the Adonis worship which accords so well with the facts of nature and with the analogy of similar rites in other lands, and which besides is countenanced by a considerable body of opinion amongst the ancients themselves.[1]

The character of Thammuz or Adonis as a cornspirit comes out plainly in an account of his festival given by an Arabic writer of the tenth century. In describing the rites and sacrifices observed at the different seasons of the year by the heathen Syrians of Harran, he says :—" Thammuz (July). In the middle of this month is the festival of el-Bûgât, that is, of the weeping women, and this is the Tâ-uz festival, which is celebrated in honour of the god Tâ-uz. The women bewail him, because his lord slew him so cruelly, ground his bones in a mill, and then scattered them to

---

[1] Schol. on Theocritus, iii. 48, ὁ Ἄδωνις, ἤγουν ὁ σῖτος ὁ σπειρόμενος, ἐξ μῆνας ἐν τῇ γῇ ποιεῖ ἀπὸ τῆς σπορᾶς, καὶ ἐξ μῆνας ἔχει αὐτὸν ἡ Ἀφροδίτη, τουτέστιν ἡ εὐκρασία τοῦ ἀέρος. καὶ ἐκτότε λαμβάνουσιν αὐτὸν οἱ ἄνθρωποι. Jerome on Ezech. c. viii. 14. *Eadem gentilitas hujuscemodi fabulas poetarum, quae habent turpitudinem, interpretatur subtiliter interfectionem et resurrectionem Adonidis planctu et gaudio prosequens: quorum alterum in seminibus, quae moriuntur in terra, alterum in segetibus, quibus mortua semina renascuntur, ostendi putat.* Ammianus Marcellinus, xix. 1, 11, *in sollemnibus Adonidis sacris, quod simulacrum aliquod esse frugum adultarum religiones mysticae docent.* Id. xxii. 9, 15, *amato Veneris, ut fabulae fingunt, apri dente ferali deleto, quod in adulto flore sectarum est indicium frugum.* Clemens Alexandr. *Hom.* 6, 11 (quoted by W. Mannhardt, *Antike Wald-und Feldkulte*, p. 281), λάμβανουσι δὲ καὶ Ἄδωνιν εἰς ὡραίους καρπούς. Etymolog. Magn. Ἄδωνις κύριον · δύναται καὶ ὁ καρπὸς εἶναι ἀδωνις · οἷον ἀδώνειος καρπός, ἀρέσκων. Eusebius, *Praepar. Evang.* iii. 11, 9, Ἄδωνις τῆς τῶν τελείων καρπῶν ἐκτομῆς σύμβολον.

the wind. The women (during this festival) eat nothing which has been ground in a mill, but limit their diet to steeped wheat, sweet vetches, dates, raisins, and the like."[1]   Thammuz (of which Tâ-uz is only another form of pronunciation) is here like Burns's John Barleycorn—

> " They wasted, o'er a scorching flame,
>   The marrow of his bones ;
> But a miller us'd him worst of all,
>   For he crush'd him between two stones." [2]

But perhaps the best proof that Adonis was a deity of vegetation is furnished by the gardens of Adonis, as they were called.   These were baskets or pots filled with earth, in which wheat, barley, lettuces, fennel, and various kinds of flowers were sown and tended for eight days, chiefly or exclusively by women. Fostered by the sun's heat, the plants shot up rapidly, but having no root withered as rapidly away, and at the end of eight days were carried out with the images of the dead Adonis, and flung with them into the sea or into springs.[3]   At Athens these ceremonies were observed at midsummer.   For we know that the fleet which Athens fitted out against Syracuse, and by the destruction of which her power was permanently crippled, sailed at midsummer, and by an ominous coincidence the sombre rites of Adonis were being celebrated at the very time.   As the troops marched down to the harbour to embark, the streets through which they

---

[1] D. Chwolsohn, *Die Ssabier und der Ssabismus*, ii. 27 ; *id.*, *Ueber Tammûz und die Menschenverehrung bei den alten Babyloniern*, p. 38.

[2] The comparison is due to Felix Liebrecht (*Zur Volkskunde*, p. 259).

[3] For the authorities see W. Mannhardt, *Antike Wald-und Feldkulte*, p. 279, *note* 2, and p. 280, *note* 2 ; to which add Diogenianus, i. 14 ; Plutarch, *De sera num. vind.* 17.   Women only are mentioned as planting the gardens of Adonis by Plutarch, *l.c.*; Julian, *Convivium*, p. 329 ed. Spanheim (p. 423 ed. Hertlein) ; Eustathius on Homer, *Od.* xi. 590.   On the other hand Diogenianus, *l.c.* says φυτεύοντες ἢ φυτεύουσαι.

passed were lined with coffins and corpse-like effigies, and the air was rent with the noise of women wailing, for the dead Adonis. The circumstance cast a gloom over the sailing of the most splendid armament that Athens ever sent to sea.[1]

These gardens of Adonis are most naturally interpreted as representatives of Adonis or manifestations of his power; they represented him, true to his original nature, in vegetable form, while the images of him, with which they were carried out and cast into the water, represented him in his later anthropomorphic form. All these Adonis ceremonies, if I am right, were originally intended as charms to promote the growth and revival of vegetation; and the principle by which they were supposed to produce this effect was sympathetic magic. As was explained in the first chapter, primitive people suppose that by representing or mimicking the effect which they desire to produce they actually help to produce it; thus by sprinkling water they make rain, by lighting a fire they make sunshine, and so on. Similarly by mimicking the growth of crops, they hope to insure a good harvest. The rapid growth of the wheat and barley in the gardens of Adonis was intended to make the corn shoot up; and the throwing of the gardens and of the images into the water was a charm to secure a due supply of fertilising rain.[2] The same, I take it, was the object of throwing the

---

[1] Plutarch, *Alcibiades*, 18; *id.*, *Nicias*, 13. The date of the sailing of the fleet is given by Thucydides, vi. 30, θέρους μεσοῦντος ἤδη.

[2] In hot southern countries like Egypt and the Semitic regions of Western Asia, where vegetation depends chiefly or entirely upon irrigation, the purpose of the charm is doubtless to secure a plentiful flow of water in the streams. But as the ultimate object and the charms for securing it are the same in both cases, it has not been thought necessary always to point out the distinction.

effigies of Death and the Carnival into water in the corresponding ceremonies of modern Europe. We have seen that the custom of drenching a leaf-clad person (who undoubtedly personifies vegetation) with water is still resorted to in Europe for the express purpose of producing rain.[1] Similarly the custom of throwing water on the last corn cut at harvest, or on the person who brings it home (a custom observed in Germany and France, and till quite lately in England and Scotland), is in some places practised with the avowed intent to procure rain for the next year's crops. Thus in Wallachia and amongst the Roumanians of Transylvania, when a girl is bringing home a crown made of the last ears of corn cut at harvest, all who meet her hasten to throw water on her, and two farm-servants are placed at the door for the purpose ; for they believe that if this were not done, the crops next year would perish from drought.[2] So amongst the Saxons of Transylvania, the person who wears the wreath made of the last corn cut (sometimes the reaper who cut the last corn also wears the wreath) is drenched with water to the skin ; for the wetter he is the better will be next year's harvest, and the more grain there will be threshed out.[3] At the spring ploughing in Prussia, when the ploughmen and sowers returned in the evening from their work in the fields, the farmer's wife and the servants used to splash water over them. The ploughmen and sowers retorted by seizing every one, throwing them into the pond, and ducking them under the water. The

---

[1] See above, p. 16.

[2] W. Mannhardt, *Baumkultus*, p. 214 ; W. Schmidt, *Das Jahr und seine Tage in Meinung und Brauch der Romänen Siebenbürgens*, p. 18 *sq.*

[3] G. A. Heinrich, *Agrarische Sitten und Gebräuche unter den Sachsen Siebenbürgens* (Hermanstadt, 1880), p. 24 ; Wsissocki, *Sitten und Brauch der Siebenbürger Sachsen* (Hamburg, 1888), p. 32.

farmer's wife might claim exemption on payment of
a forfeit; but every one else had to be ducked. By
observing this custom they hoped to ensure a due
supply of rain for the seed.[1] Also after harvest in
Prussia, the person who wore a wreath made of the
last corn cut was drenched with water, while a prayer
was uttered that "as the corn had sprung up and
multiplied through the water, so it might spring up and
multiply in the barn and granary."[2] In a Babylonian
legend, the goddess Istar (Astarte, Aphrodite) descends to Hades to fetch the water of life with which
to restore to life the dead Thammuz, and it appears
that the water was thrown over him at a great mourning ceremony, at which men and women stood round
the funeral pyre of Thammuz lamenting.[3] This
legend, as Mannhardt points out, is probably a mythical explanation of a Babylonian festival resembling
the Syrian festival of Adonis. At this festival, which
doubtless took place in the month Thammuz (June-
July)[4] and therefore about midsummer, the dead Thammuz was probably represented in effigy, water was
poured over him, and he came to life again. This
Babylonian legend is, therefore, of importance, since
it confirms the view that the purpose for which
the images and gardens of Adonis were thrown into
the water was to effect the resurrection of the god, that

---

[1] Matthäus Praetorius, *Deliciae Prussicae,* 55; W. Mannhardt, *Baumkultus,*
p. 214 *sq. note.*

[2] Praetorius, *op. cit.,* 60; W. Mannhardt, *Baumkultus,* p. 215, *note.*

[3] A. H. Sayce, *Religion of the
ancient Babylonians* (Hibbert Lectures,
1887), p. 221 *sqq.*; W. Mannhardt, *Antike
Wald-und Feldkulte,* p. 275.

[4] According to Jerome (on Ezechiel,
viii. 14), Thammuz was June; but

according to modern scholars the month
corresponded rather to July, or to part of
June and part of July. Movers, *Die
Phoenizier,* i. 210; Mannhardt, *A. W.F.*
p. 275. My friend, Prof. W. Robertson
Smith, informs me that owing to the
variations of the local Syrian calendars
the month Thammuz fell in different
places at different times, from midsummer to autumn, or from June to
September.

is, to secure the revival of vegetation. The connection
of Thammuz with vegetation is proved by a fragment
of a Babylonian hymn, in which Thammuz is described
as dwelling in the midst of a great tree at the centre of
the earth.[1]

The opinion that the gardens of Adonis are
essentially charms to promote the growth of vegetation, especially of the crops, and that they belong
to the same class of customs as those spring and
midsummer folk-customs of modern Europe which
have been described, does not rest for its evidence
merely on the intrinsic probability of the case.
Fortunately, we are able to show that gardens of
Adonis (if we may use the expression in a general
sense) are still planted, first, by a primitive race at
their sowing season, and, second, by European
peasants at midsummer. Amongst the Oraons and
Mundas of Bengal, when the time comes for planting
out the rice which has been grown in seed-beds, a
party of young people of both sexes go to the forest
and cut a young Karma tree, or the branch of one.
Bearing it in triumph they return dancing, singing,
and beating drums, and plant it in the middle of the
village dancing-ground. A sacrifice is offered to the
tree; and next morning the youth of both sexes,
linked arm-in-arm, dance in a great circle round the
Karma tree, which is decked with strips of coloured
cloth and sham bracelets and necklets of plaited straw.
As a preparation for the festival, the daughters of the
head-man of the village cultivate blades of barley in a
peculiar way. The seed is sown in moist, sandy soil,
mixed with turmeric, and the blades sprout and unfold
of a pale yellow or primrose colour. On the day of

---

[1] A. H. Sayce, *op. cit.* p. 238.

the festival the girls take up these blades and carry
them in baskets to the dancing-ground, where, prostrating themselves reverentially, they place some of
the plants before the Karma tree. Finally, the Karma
tree is taken away and thrown into a stream or
tank.[1] The meaning of planting these barley blades
and then presenting them to the Karma tree is hardly
open to question. We have seen that trees are
supposed to exercise a quickening influence upon the
growth of crops, and that amongst the very people in
question—the Mundas or Mundaris—"the grove
deities are held responsible for the crops."[2] Therefore,
when at the season for planting out the rice the
Mundas bring in a tree and treat it with so much
respect, their object can only be to foster thereby the
growth of the rice which is about to be planted out;
and the custom of causing barley blades to sprout
rapidly and then presenting them to the tree must
be intended to subserve the same purpose, perhaps
by reminding the tree-spirit of his duty towards the
crops, and stimulating his activity by this visible
example of rapid vegetable growth. The throwing of
the Karma tree into the water is to be interpreted
as a rain-charm. Whether the barley blades are
also thrown into the water is not said; but, if my
interpretation of the custom is right, probably they
are so. A distinction between this Bengal custom
and the Greek rites of Adonis is that in the former the
tree-spirit appears in his original form as a tree;
whereas in the Adonis worship he appears in anthropomorphic form, represented as a dead man, though
his vegetable nature is indicated by the gardens of

---

[1] Dalton, *Ethnology of Bengal*, p. 259.   [2] Above, p. 67.

Adonis, which are, so to say, a secondary manifestation of his original power as a tree-spirit.

In Sardinia the gardens of Adonis are still planted in connection with the great midsummer festival which bears the name of St. John. At the end of March or on the 1st of April a young man of the village presents himself to a girl and asks her to be his *comare* (gossip or sweetheart), offering to be her *compare*. The invitation is considered as an honour by the girl's family, and is gladly accepted. At the end of May the girl makes a pot of the bark of the cork-tree, fills it with earth, and sows a handful of wheat and barley in it. The pot being placed in the sun and often watered, the corn sprouts rapidly and has a good head by Midsummer Eve (St. John's Eve, 23d June). The pot is then called *Erme* or *Nenneri*. On St. John's Day the young man and the girl, dressed in their best, accompanied by a long retinue and preceded by children gambolling and frolicking, move in procession to a church outside the village. Here they break the pot by throwing it against the door of the church. Then they sit down in a ring on the grass and eat eggs and herbs to the music of flutes. Wine is mixed in a cup and passed round, each one drinking as it passes. Then they join hands and sing "Sweethearts of St. John" (*Compare e comare di San Giovanni*) over and over again, the flutes playing the while. When they tire of singing, they stand up and dance gaily in a ring till evening. This is the general Sardinian custom. As practised at Ozieri it has some special features. In May the pots are made of cork-bark and planted with corn, as already described. Then on the Eve of St. John the window-sills are draped with rich cloths, on which the pots are placed, adorned with crimson and blue silk and ribbons of various colours. On each of the pots they used formerly to place a statuette or cloth doll dressed as a woman, or a Priapus-like figure made of paste ; but this custom, rigorously forbidden by the Church, has fallen into disuse. The village swains go about in a troop to look at the pots and their decorations and to wait for the girls, who assemble on the public square to celebrate the festival. Here a great bonfire is kindled, round which they dance and make merry. Those who wish to be " Sweethearts of St. John " act as follows. The young man stands on one side of the bonfire and the girl on the other, and they, in a manner, join hands by each grasping one end of a long stick, which they pass three times backwards and forwards across the fire, thus thrusting their hands thrice rapidly into the flames. This seals their relationship to each other. Dancing and music go on till late at night.[1] The correspondence of these Sardinian pots of grain to the gardens of Adonis seems complete, and the images formerly placed in them answer to the images of Adonis which accompanied his gardens.

This Sardinian custom is one of those midsummer customs, once celebrated in many parts of Europe, a chief feature of which is the great bonfire round which people dance and over which they leap. Examples of these customs have already been cited from Sweden and Bohemia.[2] These examples suffici-

---

[1] Antonio Bresciani, *Dei costumi dell' isola di Sardegna comparati cogli antichissimi popoli orientali* (Rome and Turin, 1866), p. 427 *sq.* ; R. Tennant, *Sardinia and its Resources* (Rome and London, 1885), p. 187 ; S. Gabriele, "Usi dei contadini della Sardegna," *Archivio per lo studio delle tradizioni popolari,* vii. (1888) p. 469 *sq.* Tennant says that the pots are kept in a dark warm place, and that the children leap across the fire. [2] See ch. i. p. 78 *sq.*

ently prove the connection of the midsummer bonfire with vegetation ; for both in Sweden and Bohemia an essential part of the festival is the raising of a May-pole or Midsummer-tree, which in Bohemia is burned in the bonfire. Again, in the Russian midsummer ceremony cited above,[1] the straw figure of Kupalo, the representative of vegetation, is placed beside a May - pole or Midsummer - tree and then carried to and fro across a bonfire. Kupalo is here represented in duplicate, in tree - form by the Midsummer - tree, and in anthropomorphic form by the straw effigy, just as Adonis was represented both by an image and a garden of Adonis ; and the duplicate representatives of Kupalo, like those of Adonis, are finally cast into water. In the Sardinian custom the Gossips or Sweethearts of St. John probably correspond to the Lord and Lady or King and Queen of May. In the province of Blekinge (Sweden), part of the midsummer festival is the election of a Midsummer Bride, who chooses her bridegroom ; a collection is made for the pair, who for the time being are looked upon as man and wife.[2] Such Midsummer pairs are probably, like the May pairs, representatives of the spirit of vegetation in its reproductive capacity ; they represent in flesh and blood what the images of Siva and Pârvatî in the Indian ceremony, and the images of Adonis and Aphrodite in the Alexandrian ceremony, represented in effigy. The reason why ceremonies whose aim is to foster the growth of vegetation should thus be associated with bonfires ; why in particular the representative of vegetation should be burned in tree-form or passed across the fire in effigy or in the form of a living couple, will be explained later on. Here

---

[1] P. 272.　　　[2] L. Lloyd, *Peasant Life in Sweden*, p. 257.

it is enough to have proved the fact of such association and therefore to have obviated the objection which might have been raised to my interpretation of the Sardinian custom, on the ground that the bonfires have nothing to do with vegetation. One more piece of evidence may here be given to prove the contrary. In some parts of Germany young men and girls leap over midsummer bonfires for the express purpose of making the hemp or flax grow tall.[1] We may, there-fore, assume that in the Sardinian custom the blades of wheat and barley which are forced on in pots for the midsummer festival, and which correspond so closely to the gardens of Adonis, form one of those widely-spread midsummer ceremonies, the original object of which was to promote the growth of vegetation, and especially of the crops. But as, by an easy extension of ideas, the spirit of vegetation was believed to exercise a beneficent influence over human as well as animal life, the gardens of Adonis would be supposed, like the May-trees or May-boughs, to bring good luck to the family or to the individual who planted them ; and even after the idea had been abandoned that they operated actively to bring good luck, omens might still be drawn from them as to the good or bad fortune of families or individuals. It is thus that magic dwindles into divination. Accordingly we find modes of divination practised at midsummer which resemble more or less closely the gardens of Adonis. Thus an anonymous Italian writer of the sixteenth century has recorded that it was customary to sow barley and wheat a few days before the festival of St. John (Midsummer Day) and also before that of St. Vitus ; and it was believed that the person for whom they were

---

[1] W. Mannhardt, *Baumkultus*, p. 464 ; Leoprechting, *Aus dem Lechrain*, p. 183.

sown would be fortunate and get a good husband or a
good wife, if the grain sprouted well; but if they
sprouted ill, he or she would be unlucky.[1]   In various
parts of Italy and all over Sicily it is still customary to
put plants in water or in earth on the Eve of St. John,
and from the manner in which they are found to be
blooming or fading on St. John's Day omens are
drawn, especially as to fortune in love.   Amongst
the plants used for this purpose are *Ciuri di S.
Giuvanni* (St. John's wort?) and nettles.[2]   In Prussia
two hundred years ago the farmers used to send
out their servants, especially their maids, to gather
St. John's wort on Midsummer Eve or Midsummer
Day (St. John's Day).   When they had fetched
it, the farmer took as many plants as there were
persons and stuck them in the wall or between the
beams; and it was thought that the person whose
plant did not bloom would soon fall sick or die.   The
rest of the plants were tied in a bundle, fastened to the
end of a pole, and set up at the gate or wherever the
corn would be brought in at the next harvest.   This
bundle was called *Kupole;* the ceremony was known
as Kupole's festival; and at it the farmer prayed for
a good crop of hay, etc.[3]   This Prussian custom is
particularly notable, inasmuch as it strongly confirms
the opinion expressed above that Kupalo (doubtless
identical with Kupole) was originally a deity of vegetation.[4]   For here Kupalo is represented by a bundle

---

[1] G. Pitrè, *Spettacoli e feste popolari
siciliane*, p. 296 *sq.*
[2] G. Pitrè, *op. cit.* p. 302 *sq.*; Antonio
de Nino, *Usi Abruzzesi*, i. 55 *sq.*; Gubernatis, *Usi Nuziali*, p. 39 *sq.* Cp. *Archivio per lo studio delle tradizioni popolari*,
i. 135.   At Smyrna a blossom of the
agnus castus is used on St. John's Day

for a similar purpose, but the mode in
which the omens are drawn is somewhat different, *Archivio per lo studio delle
tradizioni popolari*, vii. (1888) p. 128 *sq.*
[3] Matthäus Praetorius, *Deliciae Prussicae*, herausgegeben von Dr. W. Pier-
son (Berlin, 1871), p. 56.
[4] See p. 274 *sq.*

of plants specially associated with midsummer in
folk-custom ; and her influence over vegetation is
plainly signified by placing her plant-formed representative over the place where the harvest is brought
in, as well as by the prayers for a good crop which
are uttered on the occasion.   A fresh argument is
thus supplied in support of the conclusion that the
Death, whose analogy to Kupalo, Yarilo, etc., has
been shown, was originally a personification of vegetation, more especially of vegetation as dying or dead in
winter.   Further, my interpretation of the gardens of
Adonis is confirmed by finding that in this Prussian
custom the very same kind of plants are used to form
the gardens of Adonis (as we may call them) and
the image of the deity.   Nothing could set in a
stronger light the truth of the view that the gardens
of Adonis are merely another manifestation of the
god himself.

The last example of the gardens of Adonis which
I shall cite is the following.   At the approach
of Easter, Sicilian women sow wheat, lentils, and
canary-seed in plates, which are kept in the dark and
watered every two days.   The plants soon shoot up ;
the stalks are tied together with red ribbons, and the
plates containing them are placed on the sepulchres
which, with effigies of the dead Christ, are made up
in Roman Catholic and Greek churches on Good
Friday,[1] just as the gardens of Adonis were placed on
the grave of the dead Adonis.[2]   The whole custom—
sepulchres as well as plates of sprouting grain — is

[1] G. Pitrè, *Spettacoli e feste popolari
siciliane*, p. 211.   A similar custom
is observed at Cosenza in Calabria.
Vincenzo Dorsa, *La tradizione greco-
latina*, etc., p. 50.   For the Easter
ceremonies in the Greek Church, see
R. A. Arnold, *From the Levant* (London,
1868), i. 251 *sqq.*
[2] κήπους ὡσίουν ἐπιταφίους ᾿Αδώνιδι,
Eustathius on Homer, *Od.* xi. 590.

probably nothing but a continuation, under a different name, of the Adonis worship.

§ 5.—*Attis*

The next of those gods, whose supposed death and resurrection struck such deep roots into the religious faith and ritual of Western Asia, is Attis.   He was to Phrygia what Adonis was to Syria.   Like Adonis, he appears to have been a god of vegetation, and his death and resurrection were annually mourned and rejoiced over at a festival in spring.   The legends and rites of the two gods were so much alike that the ancients themselves sometimes identified them.[1]   Attis was said to have been a fair youth who was beloved by the great Phrygian goddess Cybele.   Two different accounts of his death were current.   According to the one, he was killed by a boar, like Adonis.   According to the other, he mutilated himself under a pine-tree, and died from the effusion of blood.   The latter is said to have been the local story told by the people of Pessinus, a great centre of Cybele worship, and the whole legend of which it forms a part is stamped with a character of rudeness and savagery that speaks strongly for its antiquity.[2]   But the genuineness of the other story seems also vouched for by the fact that his worshippers, especially the people of Pes-

---

[1] Hippolytus, *Refut. omn. haeres.* v. 9, p. 168, ed. Duncker and Schneidewin ; Socrates, *Hist. Eccles.* iii. 23, §§ 51 *sqq.* p. 204.

[2] That Attis was killed by a boar was stated by Hermesianax, an elegiac poet of the fourth century B.C. (Pausanias, vii. 17) ; cp. Schol. on Nicander, *Alex.*

8.   The other story is told by Arnobius (*Adversus nationes*, v. 5 *sqq.*) on the authority of Timotheus, an otherwise unknown writer, who professed to derive it *ex reconditis antiquitatum libris et ex intimis mysteriis.*   It is obviously identical with the account which Pausanias mentions (*l.c.*) as the story current in Pessinus.

sinus, abstained from eating swine.[1]   After his death
Attis is said to have been changed into a pine-
tree.[2]   The ceremonies observed at his festival are
not very fully known, but their general order appears
to have been as follows.[3]   At the spring equinox
(22d March) a pine-tree was cut in the woods and
brought into the sanctuary of Cybele, where it was
treated as a divinity.   It was adorned with woollen
bands and wreaths of violets, for violets were said to
have sprung from the blood of Attis, as anemones
from the blood of Adonis ; and the effigy of a young
man was attached to the middle of the tree.[4]   On
the second day (23d March) the chief ceremony
seems to have been a blowing of trumpets.[5]   The
third day (24th March) was known as the Day of
Blood : the high priest drew blood from his arms
and presented it as an offering.[6]   It was perhaps
on this day or night that the mourning for Attis took
place over an effigy, which was afterwards solemnly
buried.[7]   The fourth day (25th March) was the
Festival of Joy (*Hilaria*), at which the resurrection of
Attis was probably celebrated—at least the celebration
of his resurrection seems to have followed closely upon

[1] Pausanias, vii. 17 ; Julian, *Orat.*
v. 177 B.

[2] Ovid, *Metam.* x. 103 *sqq.*

[3] On the festival see especially Mar-
quardt, *Römische Staatsverwaltung*, iii.[2]
370 *sqq.* ; Daremberg et Saglio,
*Dictionnaire des Antiquités grecques
et romaines*, i. p. 1685 *sq.* (article
" Cybèle ") ; W. Mannhardt, *Antike
Wald-und Feldkulte*, p. 291 *sqq.*; *id.*,
Baumkultus, p. 572 *sqq.*

[4] Julian, *Orat.* v. 168 C ; Joannes
Lydus, *De mensibus*, iv. 41 ; Arnobius,
Advers. nationes, v. cc. 7, 16 *sq.*; Firmicus Maternus, *De errore profan.
relig.* 27.   [5] Julian, *l.c.* and 169 C.

[6] Trebellius Pollio, *Claudius*, 4 ;
Tertullian, *Apologet.* 25.   For other
references, see Marquardt, *l.c.*

[7] Diodorus, iii. 59 ; Firmicus
Maternus, *De err. profan. relig.* 3 ;
Arnobius, *Advers. nat.* v. 16 ; Schol.
on Nicander, *Alex.* 8 ; Servius on
Virgil, *Aen.* ix. 116 ; Arrian, *Tactica*,
33.   The ceremony described in Firmicus Maternus, c. 22 (*nocte quadam
simulacrum in lectica supinum ponitur
et per numeros digestis fletibus plangitur. . . . Idolum sepelis.   Idolum
plangis*, etc.), may very well be the
mourning and funeral rites of Attis, to
which he had more briefly referred in
c. 3.

that of his death.[1] The Roman festival closed on
27th March with a procession to the brook Almo, in
which the bullock-cart of the goddess, her image, and
other sacred objects were bathed. But this bath of the
goddess is known to have also formed part of her
festival in her Asiatic home. On returning from the
water the cart and oxen were strewn with fresh spring
flowers.[2]

The original character of Attis as a tree-spirit is
brought out plainly by the part which the pine-tree
plays in his legend and ritual. The story that he was
a human being transformed into a pine-tree is only one
of those transparent attempts at rationalising the old
beliefs which meet us so frequently in mythology.
His tree origin is further attested by the story that he
was born of a virgin, who conceived by putting in her
bosom a ripe almond or pomegranate.[3] The bringing in
of the pine-tree from the wood, decked with violets
and woollen bands, corresponds to bringing in the
May-tree or Summer-tree in modern folk-custom ;
and the effigy which was attached to the pine-tree was
only a duplicate representative of the tree-spirit or

---

[1] On the *Hilaria* see Macrobius,
Saturn. i. 21, 10 ; Julian, *Orat.* v.
168 D, 169 D ; Damascius, *Vita
Isidori*, in Photius, p. 345 A 5 *sqq.* ed.
Bekker. On the resurrection, see
Firmicus Maternus, 3, *reginae suae
amorem* [*Phryges*] *cum luctibus annuis
consecrarunt, et ut satis iratae mulieri
facerent aut ut paenitenti solacium
quaererent, quem paulo ante sepelierant
revixisse jactarunt. . . . Mortem ipsius*
[*i.e.* of Attis] *dicunt, quod semina
collecta conduntur, vitam rursus quod
jacta semina annuis vicibus † recon-
duntur* [*renascuntur*, C. Halm]. Again
cp. id. 22, *Idolum sepelis. Idolum
plangis, idolum de sepultura proferis, et
miser cum haec feceris gaudes ;* and

Damascius, *l.c.* τὴν τῶν ἱλαρίων καλου-
μένην ἑορτήν · ὅπερ ἐδήλου τὴν ἐξ ᾅδου
γεγονυῖαν ἡμῶν σωτηρίαν. This last
passage, compared with the formula in
Firmicus Maternus, c. 22

θαρρεῖτε μύσται τοῦ θεοῦ σεσωμένου ·
ἔσται γὰρ ἡμῖν ἐκ πόνων σωτηρία,

makes it probable that the ceremony
described by Firmicus, c. 22, is the
resurrection of Attis.

[2] Ovid, *Fast.* iv. 337 *sqq.* ; Ammianus Marcellinus, xxiii. 3. For other
references see Marquardt and Mannhardt, *ll.cc.*

[3] Pausanias, vii. 17 ; Arnobius, *Adv.
nationes*, v. 6. ; cp. Hippolytus, *Refut.
omn. haeres.* v. 9, pp. 166, 168.

Attis.   At what point of the ceremonies the violets
and the effigy were attached to the tree is not said,
but we should assume this to be done after the
mimic death and burial of Attis.   The fastening of his
effigy to the tree would then be a representation of
his coming to life again in tree-form, just as the
placing of the shirt of the effigy of Death upon a
tree represents the revival of the spirit of vegetation in
a new form.[1]   After being attached to the tree, the
effigy was kept for a year and then burned.[2]   We have
seen that this was apparently sometimes done with the
May-pole;[3] and we shall see presently that the effigy
of the corn-spirit, made at harvest, is often preserved
till it is replaced by a new effigy at next year's harvest.
The original intention of thus preserving the effigy for
a year and then replacing it by a new one was
doubtless to maintain the spirit of vegetation in fresh
and vigorous life.   The bathing of the image of
Cybele was probably a rain-charm, like the throwing
of the effigies of Death and of Adonis into the
water.   Like tree-spirits in general, Attis appears to
have been conceived as exercising power over the
growth of corn, or even to have been identified with the
corn.   One of his epithets was "very fruitful;" he was
addressed as the "reaped green (or yellow) ear of corn,"
and the story of his sufferings, death, and resurrection
was interpreted as the ripe grain wounded by the
reaper, buried in the granary, and coming to life again
when sown in the ground.[4]   His worshippers abstained
from eating seeds and the roots of vegetables,[5] just
as at the Adonis ceremonies women abstained from

---

[1] See above, p. 264 *sq.*

[2] Firmicus Maternus, 27.

[3] Above, p. 81.

[4] Hippolytus, *Ref. omn. haeres.* v. cc. 8, 9, pp. 162, 168; Firmicus Maternus, *De errore prof. relig.* 3.

[5] Julian, *Orat.* v. 174 A B.

eating corn ground in a mill. Such acts would probably have been esteemed a sacrilegious partaking of the life or of the bruised and broken body of the god.

From inscriptions it appears that both at Pessinus and Rome the high priest of Cybele was regularly called Attis.[1] It is therefore a reasonable conjecture that the high priest played the part of the legendary Attis at the annual festival.[2] We have seen that on the Day of Blood he drew blood from his arms, and this may have been an imitation of the self-inflicted death of Attis under the pine-tree. It is not inconsistent with this supposition that Attis was also represented at these ceremonies by an effigy; for we have already had cases in which the divine being is first represented by a living person and afterwards by an effigy, which is then burned or otherwise destroyed.[3] Perhaps we may go a step farther and conjecture that this mimic killing of the priest (if it was such), accompanied by a real effusion of his blood, was in Phrygia, as it has been elsewhere, a substitute for a human sacrifice which in earlier times was actually offered. Professor W. M. Ramsay, whose authority on all questions relating to Phrygia no one will dispute, is of opinion that at these Phrygian ceremonies "the representative of the god was probably slain each year by a cruel death, just as the god himself died."[4] We know from Strabo[5] that the priests of Pessinus were at one time potentates as well as priests; they may, there-

---

[1] Duncker, *Geschichte des Alterthums*,[5] i. 456, *note* 4; Roscher, *Ausführliches Lexikon d. griech. u. röm. Mythologie*, i. c. 724. Cp. Polybius, xxii. 20 (18).

[2] The conjecture is that of Henzen in *Annal. d. Inst.* 1856, p. 110, referred to in Roscher, *l.c.*

[3] See pp. 84, 231.

[4] Article "Phrygia," in *Encyclopaedia Britannica*, ninth ed. xviii. 853.

[5] xii. 5, 3.

fore, have belonged to that class of divine kings or popes whose duty it was to die each year for their people and the world. As a god of vegetation, annually slain, the representative of Attis would be parallel to the Wild Man, the King, etc., of north European folk-custom, and to the Italian priest of Nemi.

§ 6.—*Osiris*

There seem to be some grounds for believing that Osiris, the great god of ancient Egypt, was one of those personifications of vegetation, whose annual death and resurrection have been celebrated in so many lands. But as the chief of the gods he appears to have absorbed the attributes of other deities, so that his character and rites present a complex of heterogeneous elements which, with the scanty evidence at our disposal, it is hardly possible to sort out. It may be worth while, however, to put together some of the facts which lend support to the view that Osiris or at least one of the deities out of whom he was compounded was a god of vegetation, analogous to Adonis and Attis.

The outline of his myth is as follows.[1] Osiris was the son of the earth-god Qeb (or Seb, as the name is sometimes transliterated).[2] Reigning as a king on earth, he reclaimed the Egyptians from savagery, gave them

---

[1] The myth, in a connected form, is only known from Plutarch, *Isis et Osiris*, cc. 13-19. Some additional details, recovered from Egyptian sources, will be found in the work of Adolf Erman, *Aegypten und aegyptisches Leben im Altertum*, p. 365 *sqq.*

[2] Le Page Renouf, *Hibbert Lectures*, 1879, p. 110; Brugsch, *Religion und Mythologie der alten Aegypter*, p. 614; Ad. Erman, *l.c.*; Ed. Meyer, *Geschichte des Altertums*, i. § 56 *sq.*

laws, and taught them to worship the gods.   Before his
time the Egyptians had been cannibals.   But Isis, the
sister and wife of Osiris, discovered wheat and barley
growing wild, and Osiris introduced the cultivation of
these grains amongst his people, who forthwith abandoned cannibalism and took kindly to a corn diet.[1]
Afterwards Osiris travelled over the world diffusing
the blessings of civilisation wherever he went.   But on
his return his brother Set (whom the Greeks called
Typhon), with seventy-two others, plotted against him,
and having inveigled him into a beautifully decorated
coffer, they nailed it down on him, soldered it fast
with molten lead, and flung it into the Nile.   It floated
down to the sea.   This happened on the 17th day of
the month Athyr.   Isis put on mourning, and wandered
disconsolately up and down seeking the body, till at last
she found it at Byblus, on the Syrian coast, whither it
had drifted with the waves.   An *erica* tree had shot up
and enfolded the coffer within its stem, and the King
of Byblus, admiring the fine growth of the tree, had
caused it to be cut down and converted into a pillar of
his palace.   From him Isis obtained leave to open the
trunk of the tree, and having taken out the coffer, she
carried it away with her.   But she left it to visit her
son Horus at Butus in the Delta, and Typhon found
the coffer as he was hunting a boar by the light of a
full moon.[2]   He recognised the body of Osiris, rent it
into fourteen pieces, and scattered them abroad.   Isis
sailed up and down the marshes in a papyrus boat
seeking the fragments, and as she found each she
buried it.   Hence many graves of Osiris were shown
in Egypt.   Others said that Isis left an effigy of Osiris

[1] Plutarch, *Isis et Osiris*, 13 ; Diodorus, i. 14 ; Tibullus, i. 7, 29 *sqq.*
[2] Plutarch, *Isis et Osiris*, 8.

Osiris, the great god of ancient Egypt, was one of the
personifications of vegetation.

Horus, a hawk-headed god, was son of Osiris, with whom he is
shown here.

in every city, pretending it was his body, in order that
Osiris might be worshipped in many places, and to
prevent Typhon from discovering the real corpse.
Afterwards her son Horus fought against Typhon,
conquered him, and bound him fast. But Isis, to
whom he had been delivered, loosed his bonds and let
him go. This angered Horus, and he pulled the
crown from his mother's head; but Hermes replaced
it with a helmet made in the shape of a cow's head.
Typhon was subsequently defeated in two other battles.
The rest of the myth included the dismemberment of
Horus and the beheading of Isis.

So much for the myth of Osiris. Of the annual
rites with which his death and burial were celebrated
we unfortunately know very little. The mourning
lasted five days,[1] from the 8th to the 12th of the
month Athyr.[2] The ceremonies began with the
"earth-ploughing," that is, with the opening of the
field labours, when the waters of the Nile are sinking. The other rites included the search for the
mangled body of Osiris, the rejoicings at its discovery, and its solemn burial. The burial took place
on the 11th of November, and was accompanied
by the recitation of lamentations from the liturgical
books. These lamentations, of which several copies
have been discovered in modern times, were put in the

---

[1] So Brugsch, *op. cit.* p. 617. Plutarch, *op. cit.* 39, says four days, beginning with the 17th of the month Athyr.

[2] In the Alexandrian year the month
Athyr corresponded to November.
But as the old Egyptian year was
vague, that is, made no use of intercala-
tion, the astronomical date of each
festival varied from year to year, till it
had passed through the whole cycle of
the astronomical year. From the fact,

therefore, that, when the calendar became fixed, Athyr fell in November,
no inference can be drawn as to the
date at which the death of Osiris was
originally celebrated. It is thus perfectly possible that it may have been
originally a harvest festival, though the
Egyptian harvest falls, not in November,
but in April; cp. Selden, *De diis Syris*,
p. 335 *sq.*; Parthey on Plutarch, *Isis et
Osiris*, c. 39.

mouth of Isis and Nephthys, sisters of Osiris. " In form and substance," says Brugsch, " they vividly recall the dirges chanted at the Adonis' rites over the dead god."[1] Next day was the joyous festival of Sokari, that being the name under which the hawk-headed Osiris of Memphis was invoked. The solemn processions of priests which on this day wound round the temples with all the pomp of banners, images, and sacred emblems, were amongst the most stately pageants that ancient Egypt could show. The whole festival ended on the 16th of November with a special rite called the erection of the *Tatu*, *Tat*, or *Ded* pillar.[2] This pillar appears from the monuments to have been a column with cross bars at the top, like the yards of a mast, or more exactly like the superposed capitals of a pillar.[3] On a Theban tomb the king himself, assisted by his relations and a priest, is represented hauling at the ropes by which the pillar is being raised. The pillar was interpreted, at least in later Egyptian theology, as the backbone of Osiris. It might very well be a conventional representation of a tree stripped of its leaves ; and if Osiris was a tree-spirit, the bare trunk and branches of a tree might naturally be described as his backbone. The erection of the column would then be, as Erman interprets it, a representation of the resurrection of Osiris, which, as we learn from Plutarch, appears to have been celebrated at his mysteries.[4] Perhaps the ceremony which

---

[1] Brugsch, *l.c.* For a specimen of these lamentations see Brugsch, *op. cit.* p. 631 *sq.*; *Records of the Past*, ii. 119 *sqq.* For the annual ceremonies of finding and burying Osiris, see also Firmicus Maternus, *De errore profanarum religionum*, 2 § 3 ; Servius on Virgil, *Aen.* iv. 609.

[2] Brugsch, *op. cit.* p. 617 *sq.*; Erman, *Aegypten und aegyptisches Leben im Altertum*, p. 377 *sq.*

[3] Erman, *l.c.*; Wilkinson, *Manners and Customs of the Ancient Egyptians* (London, 1878), iii. 68, 82 ; Tiele, *History of the Egyptian Religion*, p. 46.

[4] Plutarch, *Isis et Osiris*, 35. ὁμο-

Plutarch describes as taking place on the third day of the festival (the 19th day of the month Athyr) may also have referred to the resurrection. He says that on that day the priests carried the sacred ark down to the sea. Within the ark was a golden casket, into which drinking-water was poured. A shout then went up that Osiris was found. Then some mould was mixed with water, and out of the paste thus formed a crescent-shaped image was fashioned, which was then dressed in robes and adorned.[1]

The general similarity of the myth and ritual of Osiris to those of Adonis and Attis is obvious. In all three cases we see a god whose untimely and violent death is mourned by a loving goddess and annually celebrated by their worshippers. The character of Osiris as a deity of vegetation is brought out by the legend that he was the first to teach men the use of corn, and by the fact that his annual festival began with ploughing the earth. He is said also to have introduced the cultivation of the vine.[2] In one of the chambers dedicated to Osiris in the great temple of Isis at Philae the dead body of Osiris is represented with stalks of corn springing from it, and a priest is watering the stalks from a pitcher which he holds in his hand. The accompanying inscription sets forth that " This is the form of him whom one may not name, Osiris of the mysteries, who springs from the returning waters."[3] It would seem impossible to devise a more graphic way of representing Osiris as a personification of the corn ; while the inscription proves that this personification was the kernel of the

---

λογεῖ δὲ καὶ τὰ τιτανικὰ καὶ νὺξ τελεία
τοῖς λεγομένοις 'Οσίριδος διασπασμοῖς καὶ
ταῖς ἀναβιώσεσι καὶ παλιγγενεσίαις,
ὁμοίως δὲ καὶ τὰ περὶ τὰς ταφάς.

[1] Plutarch, *Isis et Osiris*, 39.

[2] Tibullus, i. 7, 33 *sqq.*

[3] Brugsch, *op. cit.* p. 621.

mysteries of the god, the innermost secret that was
only revealed to the initiated. In estimating the
mythical character of Osiris very great weight must
be given to this monument. The legend that his
mangled remains were scattered up and down the
land may be a mythical way of expressing either the
sowing or the winnowing of the grain. The latter
interpretation is supported by the story that Isis placed
the severed limbs of Osiris on a corn-sieve.[1] Or the
legend may be a reminiscence of the custom of slaying
a human victim (probably considered as a representative of the corn-spirit) and distributing his flesh or
scattering his ashes over the fields to fertilise them.
We have already seen that in modern Europe the
figure of " Death " is sometimes torn in pieces, and that
the fragments are then buried in the fields to make
the crops grow well.[2] Later on we shall meet with
examples of human victims being treated in the same
way. With regard to the ancient Egyptians, we have
it on the authority of Manetho that they used to burn
red-haired men and scatter their ashes with winnowing-
fans.[3] That this custom was not, as might perhaps
have been supposed, a mere way of wreaking their
spite on foreigners, amongst whom rather than
amongst the native Egyptians red-haired people
would generally be found, appears from the fact that
the oxen which were sacrificed had also to be red ; a
single black or white hair found on a beast would have
disqualified it for the sacrifice.[4] The red hair of the
human victims was thus probably essential ; the fact
that they were generally foreigners was only accidental.

---

[1] Servius on Virgil, *Georg.* i. 166.

[2] Above, p. 267.

[3] Plutarch, *Isis et Osiris*, 73, cp. 33 ;
Diodorus, i. 88.

[4] Plutarch, *op. cit.* 31 ; Herodotus,
ii. 38.

If, as I conjecture, these human sacrifices were intended to promote the growth of the crops—and the *winnowing* of their ashes seems to support this view—red-haired victims were perhaps selected as best fitted to represent the spirit of the golden grain. For when a god is represented by a living person, it is natural that the human representative should be chosen on the ground of his supposed resemblance to the god. Hence the ancient Mexicans, conceiving the maize as a personal being who went through the whole course of life between seed-time and harvest, sacrificed new-born babes when the maize was sown, older children when it had sprouted, and so on till it was fully ripe, when they sacrificed old men.[1] A name for Osiris was the "crop" or "harvest";[2] and the ancients sometimes explained him as a personification of the corn.[3]

But Osiris was not only a corn-spirit; he was also a tree-spirit, and this was probably his original character; for, as we have already observed, the corn-spirit seems to be only an extension of the older tree-spirit. His character as a tree-spirit was represented very graphically in a ceremony described by Firmicus Maternus.[4] A pine-tree was cut down, the centre was hollowed out, and with the wood thus excavated an image of Osiris was made, which was then "buried"

---

[1] Herrera, quoted by Bastian, *Culturländer des alten Amerika*, ii. 639.

[2] Lefébure, *Le mythe Osirien* (Paris, 1874-75), p. 188.

[3] Firmicus Maternus, *De errore profanarum religionum*, 2, § 6, *defensores eorum volunt addere physicam rationem, frugum semina Osirim dicentes esse ; Isim terram, Tyfonem calorem : et quia maturatae fruges calore ad vitam hominum colliguntur et divisae a terrae consortio separantur et rursus adpro-pinquante hieme seminantur, hanc volunt esse mortem Osiridis, cum fruges recondunt, inventionem vero, cum fruges genitali terrae fomento conceptae annua rursus coeperint procreatione generari ;* Eusebius, *Praepar. Evang.* iii. 11, 31, ὁ δὲ Ὄσιρις παρ᾽ Αἰγυπτίοις τὴν κάρπιμον παρίστησι δύναμιν, ἣν θρήνοις ἀπομειλίσσονται εἰς γῆν ἀφανιζομένην ἐν τῷ σπόρῳ, καὶ ὑφ᾽ ἡμῶν καταναλισκομένην εἰς τὰς τροφάς.

[4] *Op. cit.* 27, § 1.

in the hollow of the tree. Here, again, it is hard to imagine how the conception of a tree as tenanted by a personal being could be more plainly expressed. The image of Osiris thus made was kept for a year and then burned, exactly as was done with the image of Attis which was attached to the pine-tree. The ceremony of cutting the tree, as described by Firmicus Maternus, appears to be alluded to by Plutarch.[1] It was probably the ritual counterpart of the mythical discovery of the body of Osiris enclosed in the *erica* tree. We may conjecture that the erection of the *Tatu* pillar at the close of the annual festival of Osiris[2] was identical with the ceremony described by Firmicus; it is to be noted that in the myth the *erica* tree formed a pillar in the King's house. Like the similar custom of cutting a pine-tree and fastening an image to it in the rites of Attis, the ceremony perhaps belonged to that class of customs of which the bringing in the May-pole is among the most familiar. As to the pine-tree in particular, at Denderah the tree of Osiris is a conifer, and the coffer containing the body of Osiris is here represented as enclosed within the tree.[3] A pine-cone is often represented on the monuments as offered to Osiris, and a MS. of the Louvre speaks of the cedar as sprung from Osiris.[4] The sycamore and the tamarisk are also his trees. In inscriptions he is spoken of as residing in them;[5] and his mother Nut is frequently represented in a sycamore.[6] In a sepulchre

---

[1] *Isis et Osiris*, 21, αἰνῶ δὲ τομὴν ξύλου καὶ σχίσιν λίνου καὶ χοὰς χεομένας, διὰ τὸ πολλὰ τῶν μυστικῶν ἀναμεμῖχθαι τούτοις. Again, c. 42, τὸ δὲ ξύλον ἐν ταῖς λεγομέναις Ὀσίριδος ταφαῖς τέμνοντες κατασκευάζουσι λάρνακα μηνοειδῆ.

[2] See above, p. 304.

[3] Lefébure, *Le mythe Osirien*, pp.

[4] Lefébure, *op. cit.* pp. 195, 197.

[5] Birch, in Wilkinson's *Manners and Customs of the Ancient Egyptians* (London, 1878), iii. 84.

[6] Wilkinson, *op. cit.* iii. 63 *sq.*; Ed. Meyer, *Geschichte des Alterthums*, i. §§ 56, 60.

194, 198, referring to Mariette, *Denderah*, iv. 66 and 72.

An Egyptian sacrificial parade.

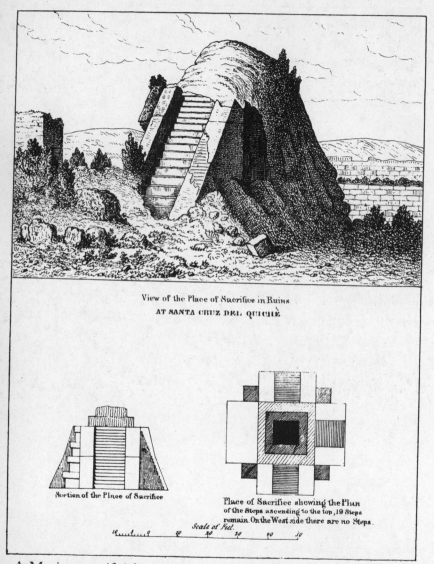

View of the Place of Sacrifice in Ruins
AT SANTA CRUZ DEL QUICHÈ

Section of the Place of Sacrifice

Place of Sacrifice showing the Plan
of the Steps ascending to the top, 19 Steps
remain. On the West side there are no Steps.

Scale of Feet.

A Mexican sacrificial temple: a view of the ruins and the plans of the
original place of sacrifice.

at How (Diospolis Parva) a tamarisk is represented
overshadowing the coffer of Osiris; and in the series
of sculptures which represent the mystic history of
Osiris in the great temple of Isis at Philae, a tamarisk
is depicted with two men pouring water on it. The
inscription on this last monument leaves no doubt,
says Brugsch, that the verdure of the earth is believed
to be connected with the verdure of the tree, and that
the sculpture refers to the grave of Osiris at Philae, of
which Plutarch says that it was overshadowed by a
methide plant, taller than any olive-tree. This sculpture, it may be observed, occurs in the same chamber
in which Osiris is represented as a corpse with ears of
corn sprouting from him.[1] In inscriptions Osiris is
referred to as "the one in the tree," "the solitary one
in the acacia," etc.[2] On the monuments he sometimes
appears as a mummy covered with a tree or with
plants.[3] It accords with the character of Osiris as a
tree-spirit that his worshippers were forbidden to injure
fruit-trees, and with his character as a god of vegetation in general that they were not allowed to stop up
wells of water, which are so important for purposes of
irrigation in hot southern lands.[4]

The original meaning of the goddess Isis is still
more difficult to determine than that of her brother
and husband Osiris. Her attributes and epithets were
so numerous that in the hieroglyphics she is called

---

[1] Wilkinson, *op. cit.* iii. 349 *sq.*;
Brugsch, *Religion und Mythologie der
alten Aegypter*, p. 621; Plutarch, *Isis et
Osiris*, 20. In Plutarch *l.c.* Parthey
proposes to read μυρίκης for μηθίδης,
and this conjecture appears to be
accepted by Wilkinson, *l.c.*

[2] Lefébure, *Le mythe Osirien*, p. 191.

[3] Lefébure, *op. cit.* p. 188.

[4] Plutarch, *Isis et Osiris*, 35. One
of the points in which the myths of

Isis and Demeter agree, is that both
goddesses in their search for the loved
and lost one are said to have sat down,
sad at heart and weary, on the edge of
a well. Hence those who had been
initiated at Eleusis were forbidden to
sit on a well. Plutarch, *Isis et Osiris*,
15; Homer, *Hymn to Demeter*,
98 *sq.*; Pausanias, i. 39, 1; Apollodorus, i. 5, 1; Nicander, *Theriaca*,
486; Clemens Alex., *Protrept.* ii. 20.

"the many-named," "the thousand-named," and in Greek inscriptions "the myriad-named."[1] Tiele confesses candidly that "it is now impossible to tell precisely to what natural phenomena the character of Isis at first referred."[2] Mr. Renouf states that Isis was the Dawn,[3] but without assigning any reason whatever for the identification. There are at least some grounds for seeing in her a goddess of corn. According to Diodorus, whose authority appears to have been the Egyptian historian Manetho, the discovery of wheat and barley was attributed to Isis, and at her festivals stalks of these grains were carried in procession to commemorate the boon she had conferred on men. Further, at harvest-time, when the Egyptian reapers had cut the first stalks, they laid them down and beat their breasts, lamenting and calling upon Isis.[4] Amongst the epithets by which she is designated on the inscriptions are "creatress of the green crop," "the green one, whose greenness is like the greenness of the earth," and "mistress of bread."[5] According to Brugsch she is "not only the creatress of the fresh verdure of vegetation which covers the earth, but is actually the green corn-field itself, which is personified as a goddess."[6] This is confirmed by her epithet *Sochit* or *Sochet,* meaning "a corn-field," a sense which the word still retains in Coptic.[7] It is in this character of a corn-goddess that the Greeks conceived Isis, for they

---

[1] Brugsch, *Religion und Mythologie der alten Aegypter,* p. 645.

[2] C. P. Tiele, *History of Egyptian Religion,* p. 57.

[3] *Hibbert Lectures,* 1879, p. 111.

[4] Diodorus, i. 14. Eusebius (*Praeparat. Evang.* iii. 3) quotes from Diodorus (i. 11-13) a long passage on the early religion of Egypt, prefacing

the quotation (c. 2) with the remark γράφει δὲ καὶ τὰ περὶ τούτων πλατύτερον μὲν ὁ Μανέθως, ἐπετετμημένως δὲ ὁ Διόδωρος, which seems to imply that Diodorus epitomised Manetho.

[5] Brugsch, *op. cit.* p. 647.

[6] Brugsch, *op. cit.* p. 649.

[7] Brugsch, *l.c.*

identified her with Demeter.[1] In a Greek epigram she is described as "she who has given birth to the fruits of the earth," and "the mother of the ears of corn,"[2] and in a hymn composed in her honour she speaks of herself as "queen of the wheat-field," and is described as "charged with the care of the fruitful furrow's wheat-rich path."[3]

Osiris has been sometimes interpreted as the sun-god; and this view has been held by so many distinguished writers in modern times that a few words of reply seem called for. If we inquire on what evidence Osiris has been identified with the sun or the sun-god, it will be found on examination that the evidence is minute in quantity and dubious, where it is not absolutely worthless, in quality. The diligent Jablonski, the first modern scholar to collect and examine the testimony of classical writers on Egyptian religion, says that it can be shown in many ways that Osiris is the sun, and that he could produce a cloud of witnesses to prove it, but that it is needless to do so, since no learned man is ignorant of the fact.[4] Of the writers whom he condescends to quote, the only two who expressly identify Osiris with the sun are Diodorus and Macrobius. The passage in Diodorus runs thus:[5] "It is said that the aboriginal inhabitants of Egypt, looking up to the sky, and smitten with awe and wonder at the nature of the universe, supposed that there were two gods, eternal and primeval, the sun and the moon, of whom they named the sun Osiris and the moon Isis." Even if Diodorus's authority for this statement is Manetho, as there is some ground for believing,[6]

---

[1] Herodotus, ii. 59, 156; Diodorus, i. 13, 25, 96; Apollodorus, ii. 1, 3; Tzetzes, *Schol. in Lycophron.* 212.
[2] *Antholog. Planud.* 264, 1.
[3] *Orphica*, ed. Abel, p. 295 *sqq.*
[4] Jablonski, *Pantheon Ageyptiorum* (Frankfurt, 1750), i. 125 *sq.*
[5] i. 11.
[6] See p. 310, *note.*

little or no weight can be attached to it. For it is plainly a philosophical, and therefore a late, explanation of the first beginnings of Egyptian religion, reminding us of Kant's familiar saying about the starry heavens and the moral law rather than of the rude traditions of a primitive people. Jablonski's second authority, Macrobius, is no better but rather worse. For Macrobius was the father of that large family of mythologists who resolve all or most gods into the sun. According to him Mercury was the sun, Mars was the sun, Janus was the sun, Saturn was the sun, so was Jupiter, also Nemesis, likewise Pan, etc.[1] It was, therefore, nearly a matter of course that he should identify Osiris with the sun.[2] But apart from the general principle, so frankly enunciated by Professor Maspero, that all the gods are the sun ("*Comme tous les dieux, Osiris est le soleil*"),[3] Macrobius has not much cause to show for identifying Osiris in particular with the sun. He argues that Osiris must be the sun because an eye was one of his symbols. The premise is correct,[4] but what exactly it has to do with the conclusion is not clear. The opinion that Osiris was the sun is also mentioned, but not accepted, by Plutarch,[5] and it is referred to by Firmicus Maternus.[6]

Amongst modern Egyptologists, Lepsius, in identifying Osiris with the sun, appears to rely mainly on the passage of Diodorus already quoted. But the monuments, he adds, also show "that down to a late time Osiris was sometimes conceived as *Ra*. In this quality he is named *Osiris-Ra* even in the 'Book of the Dead,'

---

[1] See the *Saturnalia*, bk. i.
[2] *Saturn.* i. 21, 11.
[3] Maspero, *Histoire ancienne des peuples de l'Orient*[4] (Paris, 1886), p. 35.

[4] Wilkinson, *Manners and Customs of the Ancient Egyptians* (London, 1878), iii. 353.
[5] *Isis et Osiris*, 52.
[6] *De errore profan. religionum*, 8.

and Isis is often called 'the royal consort of Ra.'"[1]
That Ra was both the physical sun and the sun-god is
of course undisputed; but with every deference for the
authority of so great a scholar as Lepsius, it may be
doubted whether such identification can be taken as
evidence of the original character of Osiris.   For the
religion of ancient Egypt[2] may be described as a con-
federacy of local cults which, while maintaining against
each other a certain measure of jealous and even hostile
independence, were yet constantly subjected to the
fusing and amalgamating action of political centralisa-
tion and philosophical reflection.   The history of the
religion appears to have largely consisted of a struggle
between these opposite forces or tendencies.   On the
one side there was the conservative tendency to preserve the local cults with all their distinctive features,
fresh, sharp, and crisp, as they had been handed down
from an immemorial past.   On the other side there
was the progressive tendency, favoured by the gradual
fusion of the people under a powerful central government, first to dull the edge of these provincial distinc-
tions, and finally to break them down completely and
merge them in a single national religion.   The conservative party probably mustered in its ranks the
great bulk of the people, their prejudices and affections
being warmly enlisted in favour of the local deity,
with whose temple and rites they had been familiar
from childhood; and the popular aversion to change,
based on the endearing effect of old association, must

---

[1] Lepsius, "Ueber den ersten aegyptischen Götterkreis und seine geschichtlich-mythologische Entstehung," in *Abhandlungen der königlichen Akademie der Wissenschaften zu Berlin*, 1851, p. 194 *sq.*

[2] The view here taken of the history of Egyptian religion is based on the sketch in Erman's *Aegypten und aegyptisches Leben im Altertum*, p. 351 *sqq.*

have been strongly reinforced by the less disinterested opposition of the local clergy, whose material interests would necessarily suffer with any decay of their shrines. On the other hand· the kings, whose power and glory rose with the political and ecclesiastical consolidation of the nation, were the natural champions of religious unity; and their efforts would be seconded by the cultured and reflecting minority, who could hardly fail to be shocked by the many barbarous and revolting elements in the local rites. As usual in such cases, the process of religious unification appears to have been largely effected by discovering points of similarity, real or imaginary, between various local gods, which were thereupon declared to be only different names or manifestations of the same god.

Of the deities who thus acted as centres of attraction, absorbing in themselves a multitude of minor divinities, by far the most important was the sun-god Ra. There appear to have been few gods in Egypt who were not at one time or other identified with him. Ammon of Thebes, Horus of the East, Horus of Edfu, Chnum of Elephantine, Atum of Heliopolis, all were regarded as one god, the sun. Even the water-god Sobk, in spite of his crocodile shape, did not escape the same fate. Indeed one king, Amenhôtep IV, undertook to sweep away all the old gods at a stroke and replace them by a single god, the "great living disc of the sun."[1] In the hymns composed in his honour, this deity is referred to as "the living disc of the sun, besides whom there is none other." He is said to have made "the far heaven" and "men, beasts, and birds; he strengtheneth

---

[1] On this attempted revolution in religion see Lepsius in *Verhandl. d. königl. Akad. d. Wissensch. zu Berlin,* 1851, pp. 196-201; Erman, *op. cit.* p. 355 *sqq.*

Isis, goddess of corn, was revered for increasing fruitfulness of
the earth in many ways.

Horus, son of Isis and Osiris.

the eyes with his beams, and when he showeth himself, all flowers live and grow, the meadows flourish at his upgoing and are drunken at his sight, all cattle skip on their feet, and the birds that are in the marsh flutter for joy." It is he "who bringeth the years, createth the months, maketh the days, calculateth the hours, the lord of time, by whom men reckon." In his zeal for the unity of god, the king commanded to erase the names of all other gods from the monuments, and to destroy their images. His rage was particularly directed against the god Ammon, whose name and likeness were effaced wherever they were found; even the sanctity of the tomb was violated in order to destroy the memorials of the hated god. In some of the halls of the great temples at Carnac, Luxor, and other places, all the names of the gods, with a few chance exceptions, were scratched out. In no inscription cut in this king's reign was any god mentioned save the sun. He even changed his own name, Amenhôtep, because it was compounded of Ammon, and took instead the name of Chuen-'eten, "gleam of the sun's disc." His death was followed by a violent reaction. The old gods were reinstated in their rank and privileges; their names and images were restored; and new temples were built. But all the shrines and palaces reared by the late king were thrown down; even the sculptures that referred to him and to his god in rock-tombs and on the sides of hills were erased or filled up with stucco; his name appears on no later monument, and was carefully omitted from all official lists.

This attempt of King Amenhôtep IV is only an extreme example of a tendency which appears to have been at work on the religion of Egypt as far back as we can trace it.   Therefore, to come back to our point, in attempting to discover the original character of any Egyptian god, no weight can be given to the identification of him with other gods, least of all with the sun-god Ra.   Far from helping to follow up the trail, these identifications only cross and confuse it. The best evidence for the original character of the Egyptian gods is to be found in their ritual and myths, so far as these are known (which unfortunately is little enough), and in the figured representations of them on the monuments.   It is on evidence drawn from these sources that I rely mainly for the interpretation of Osiris as a deity of vegetation.

Amongst a younger generation of scholars, Tiele is of opinion that Osiris is the sun, because "in the hymns, his accession to the throne of his father is compared to the rising of the sun, and it is even said of him in so many words: 'He glitters on the horizon, he sends out rays of light from his double feather and inundates the world with it, as the sun from out the highest heaven.'"[1]   By the same token Marie Antoinette must have been a goddess of the morning star, because Burke saw her at Versailles "just above the horizon, decorating and cheering the elevated sphere she just began to move in,—glittering like the morning star, full of life, and splendour, and joy." If such comparisons prove anything, they prove that Osiris was *not* the sun.   There are always two terms to a comparison ; a thing cannot be compared to itself.   But Tiele also appeals to the monuments.   What is his evidence ?   Osiris is sometimes represented by a figure surmounted by "the so-called Tat pillar, entirely made up of a kind of superimposed capitals, one of which has a rude face scratched

---

[1] Tiele, *History of the Egyptian Religion*, p. 44.

upon it." Tiele is of opinion that this rude face is "intended, no doubt, to represent the shining sun."[1] If every "rude face scratched" is to be taken as a symbol of the shining sun, sun-worship will be discovered in some unexpected places. But, on the whole, Tiele, like Jablonski, prudently keeps to the high ground of vague generalities, and the result of his occasional descents to the level of facts is not such as to encourage him to prolong his stay. "Were we to come down to details," he says, "and to attend to slight variations, we should be lost in an ocean of symbolism and mysticism."[2] This is like De Quincey's attitude towards murder. "General principles I will suggest. But as to any particular case, once for all I will have nothing to do with it." There is no having a man who takes such lofty ground.

Mr. Le Page Renouf also considers that Osiris is the sun,[3] and his position is still stronger than Tiele's. For whereas Tiele produces bad arguments for his view, Mr. Renouf produces none at all, and therefore cannot possibly be confuted.

The ground upon which some recent writers seem chiefly to rely for the identification of Osiris with the sun is that the story of his death fits better with the solar phenomena than with any other in nature. It may readily be admitted that the daily appearance and disappearance of the sun might very naturally be expressed by a myth of his death and resurrection ; and writers who regard Osiris as the sun are careful to emphasise the fact that it is the diurnal, and not the annual, course of the sun to which they understand the myth to apply. Mr. Renouf expressly admits that the

---

[1] Tiele, *op. cit.* p. 46.
[2] *Ib.* p. 45.
[3] Le Page Renouf, *Hibbert Lectures,* 1879, p. 111 *sqq.*

Egyptian sun cannot with any show of reason be described as dead in winter.[1]   But if his *daily* death was the theme of the legend, why was it celebrated by an *annual* ceremony?   This fact alone seems fatal to the interpretation of the myth as descriptive of sunset and sunrise.   Again, though the sun may be said to die daily, in what sense can he be said to be torn in pieces?[2]

In the course of our inquiry, it has, I trust, been made clear that there is another natural phenomenon

---

[1] *Hibbert Lectures*, 1879, p. 113. Cp. Maspero, *Histoire ancienne*,[4] p. 35; Ed. Meyer, *Geschichte des Alterthums*, i. §§ 55, 57.

[2] There are far more plausible grounds for identifying Osiris with the moon than with the sun—1. He was said to have lived or reigned twenty-eight years; Plutarch, *Isis et Osiris*, cc. 13, 42. This might be taken as a mythical expression for a lunar month. 2. His body was rent into fourteen pieces (*ib.* cc. 18, 42). This might be interpreted of the moon on the wane, losing a piece of itself on each of the fourteen days which make up the second half of a lunation. It is expressly mentioned that Typhon found the body of Osiris at the full moon (*ib.* 8); thus the dismemberment of the god would begin with the waning of the moon. 3. In a hymn supposed to be addressed by Isis to Osiris, it is said that Thoth

" Placeth thy soul in the bark Ma-at,
In that name which is thine, of GOD
    MOON."
And again,
"Thou *who comest to us as a child each
    month*,
We do not cease to contemplate thee,
Thine emanation heightens the brilliancy
Of the stars of Orion in the firmament,"
    etc.

Records of the Past, i. 121 *sq.*; Brugsch, *Religion und Mythologie der alten Aegypter*, p. 629 *sq.* Here then Osiris is identified with the moon in set terms. If in the same hymn he is said to "illuminate us like Ra" (the sun), this, as we have already seen, is no reason for identifying him with the sun, but quite the contrary. 4. At the new moon of the month Phanemoth, being the beginning of spring, the Egyptians celebrated what they called "the entry of Osiris into the moon." Plutarch, *Is. et Os.* 43. 5. The bull Apis, which was regarded as an image of the soul of Osiris (*Is. et Os.* cc. 20, 29), was born of a cow which was believed to have been impregnated by the moon (*ib.* 43). 6. Once a year, at the full moon, pigs were sacrificed simultaneously to the moon and Osiris. Herodotus, ii. 47; Plutarch, *Is. et Os.* 8. The relation of the pig to Osiris will be examined later on.

Without attempting to explain in detail why a god of vegetation, as I take Osiris to have been, should have been brought into such close connection with the moon, I may refer to the intimate relation which is vulgarly believed to subsist between the growth of vegetation and the phases of the moon. See *e.g.* Pliny, *Nat. Hist.* ii. 221, xvi. 190, xvii. 108, 215, xviii. 200, 228, 308, 314; Plutarch, *Quaest. Conviv.* iii. 10, 3; Aulus Gellius, xx. 8, 7; Macrobius, *Saturn.* vii. 16, 29 *sq.* Many examples are furnished by the ancient writers on agriculture, *e.g.* Cato, 37, 4; Varro, i. 37; *Geoponica*, i. 6.

to which the conception of death and resurrection is as applicable as to sunset and sunrise, and which, as a matter of fact has been so conceived and represented in folk-custom.   This phenomenon is the annual growth and decay of vegetation.   A strong reason for interpreting the death of Osiris as the decay of vegetation rather than as the sunset is to be found in the general (though not unanimous) voice of antiquity, which classed together the worship and myths of Osiris, Adonis, Attis, Dionysus, and Demeter, as religions of essentially the same type.[1]   The consensus of ancient opinion on this subject seems too great to be rejected as a mere fancy.   So closely did the rites of Osiris resemble those of Adonis at Byblus that some of the people of Byblus themselves maintained that it was Osiris and not Adonis whose death was mourned by them.[2]   Such a view could certainly not have been held if the rituals of the two gods had not been so alike as to be almost indistinguishable.   Again, Herodotus found the similarity between the rites of Osiris and Dionysus so great, that he thought it impossible the latter could have arisen independently; they must, he thought, have been recently borrowed, with slight alterations, by the Greeks from the Egyptians.[3] Again, Plutarch, a very intelligent student of comparative religion, insists upon the detailed resemblance of the rites of Osiris to those of Dionysus.[4]   We cannot

---

[1] Herodotus, ii. 42, 49, 59, 144, 156 ; Plutarch, *Isis et Osiris*, 13, 35 ; *id.*, *Quaest. Conviv.* iv. 5, 3 ; Diodorus, i. 13, 25, 96, iv. 1 ; *Orphica*, Hymn 42 ; Eusebius, *Praepar. Evang.* iii. 11, 31 ; Servius on Virgil, *Aen.* xi. 287 ; *id.*, on *Georg.* i. 166 ; Hippolytus, *Refut. omn. haeres.* v. 9, p. 168 ; Socrates, *Eccles. Hist.* iii. 23, p. 204 ; Tzetzes, *Schol. in Lycophron*, 212 ; Διηγήματα, xxii. 2, in *Mythographi Graeci*, ed. Westermann, p. 368 ; Nonnus, *Dionys.* iv. 269 *sq.*; Cornutus, *De natura deorum*, c. 28 ; Clemens Alexandr. *Protrept.* ii. 19 ; Firmicus Maternus, *De errore profan. relig.* 7.

[2] Lucian, *De dea Syria*, 7.

[3] Herodotus, ii. 49.

[4] Plutarch, *Isis et Osiris*, 35.

reject the evidence of such intelligent and trustworthy witnesses on plain matters of fact which fell under their own cognisance. Their explanations of the worships it is indeed possible to reject, for the meaning of religious cults is often open to question ; but resemblances of ritual are matters of observation. Therefore, those who explain Osiris as the sun are driven to the alternative of either dismissing as mistaken the testimony of antiquity to the similarity of the rites of Osiris, Adonis, Attis, Dionysus, and Demeter, or of interpreting all these rites as sun-worship. No modern scholar has fairly faced and accepted either side of this alternative. To accept the former would be to affirm that we know the rites of these deities better than the men who practised, or at least who witnessed them. To accept the latter would involve a wrenching, clipping, mangling, and distorting of myth and ritual from which even Macrobius shrank.[1] On the other hand, the view that the essence of all these rites was the mimic death and revival of vegetation, explains them separately and collectively in an easy and natural way, and harmonises with the general testimony borne by antiquity to their substantial similarity. The evidence for thus explaining Adonis, Attis, and Osiris has now been presented to the reader ; it remains to do the same for Dionysus and Demeter.

§ 7.—*Dionysus*

The Greek god Dionysus or Bacchus[2] is best known as the god of the vine, but he was also a god

---

[1] Osiris, Attis, Adonis, and Dionysus were all explained by him as the sun ; but he stopped short at Demeter (Ceres), whom, however, he interpreted as the moon. See the *Saturnalia*, bk. i.

[2] On Dionysus in general see Preller,

of trees in general.   Thus we are told that almost all
the Greeks sacrificed to " Dionysus of the tree."[1]   In
Boeotia one of his titles was " Dionysus in the tree."[2]
His image was often merely an upright post, without
arms, but draped in a mantle, with a bearded mask
to represent the head, and with leafy boughs projecting from the head or body to show the nature
of the deity.[3]   On a vase his rude effigy is depicted
appearing out of a low tree or bush.[4]   He was the
patron of cultivated trees;[5] prayers were offered to
him that he would make the trees grow;[6] and he was
especially honoured by husbandmen, chiefly fruit-
growers, who set up an image of him, in the shape
of a natural tree-stump, in their orchards.[7]   He was
said to have discovered all tree-fruits, amongst which
apples and figs are particularly mentioned;[8] and he
was himself spoken of as doing a husbandman's work.[9]
He was referred to as " well-fruited," " he of the green
fruit," and "making the fruit to grow."[10] One of his titles
was " teeming " or " bursting " (as of sap or blossoms);[11]
and there was a Flowery Dionysus in Attica and at
Patrae in Achaea.[12]   Amongst the trees particularly
sacred to him, in addition to the vine, was the pine-tree.[13]

Griechische Mythologie,[3] i. 544 *sqq.*;
Fr. Lenormant, article " Bacchus " in
Daremberg et Saglio, *Dictionnaire
des Antiquités grecques et romaines,*
i. 591 *sqq.*; Voigt and Thraemer's
article " Dionysus," in Roscher's *Ausführliches Lexikon der griech. und röm.
Mythologie,* i. c. 1029 *sqq.*

[1] Plutarch, *Quaest. Conviv.* v. 3,
Διονύσῳ δὲ δενδρίτῃ πάντες, ὡς ἔπος
εἰπεῖν, Ἕλληνες θύουσιν.

[2] Hesychius, *s.v.* Ἔνδενδρος.

[3] See the pictures of his images,
taken from ancient vases, in Bötticher,
Baumkultus der Hellenen, plates 42,
43, 43 A, 43 B, 44 ; Daremberg et
Saglio, *op. cit.* i. 361, 626.

[4] Daremberg et Saglio, *op. cit.* i. 626.

[5] Cornutus, *De natura deorum,* 30.

[6] Pindar, quoted by Plutarch, *Isis
et Osiris,* 35.

[7] Maximus Tyrius, *Dissertat.* viii.
i.

[8] Athenaeus, iii. pp. 78 C, 82 D.

[9] Himerius, *Orat.* i. 10, Διόνυσος
γεωργεῖ.

[10] *Orphica,* Hymn l. 4, liii. 8.

[11] Aelian, *Var. Hist.* iii. 41 ;
Hesychius, *s.v.* Φλέω[s]. Cp. Plutarch,
Quaest. Conviv. v. 8, 3.

[12] Pausanias, i. 31, 4 ; *id.* vii. 21,
6 (2).

[13] Plutarch, *Quaest. Conviv.* v. 3.

The Delphic oracle commanded the Corinthians to worship a particular pine-tree "equally with the god," so they made two images of Dionysus out of it, with red faces and gilt bodies.[1]   In art a wand, tipped with a pine-cone, is commonly carried by the god or his worshippers.[2]   Again, the ivy and the fig-tree were especially associated with him.   In the Attic township of Acharnae there was a Dionysus Ivy;[3] at Lacedaemon there was a Fig Dionysus; and in Naxos, where figs were called *meilicha*, there was a Dionysus Meilichios, the face of whose image was made of fig-wood.[4]

Like the other gods of vegetation whom we have been considering, Dionysus was believed to have died a violent death, but to have been brought to life again; and his sufferings, death, and resurrection were enacted in his sacred rites.   The Cretan myth, as related by Firmicus, ran thus.   He was said to have been the bastard son of Jupiter (Zeus), a Cretan king.   Going abroad, Jupiter transferred the throne and sceptre to the child Dionysus, but, knowing that his wife Juno (Hera) cherished a jealous dislike of the child, he entrusted Dionysus to the care of guards upon whose fidelity he believed he could rely.   Juno, however, bribed the guards, and amusing the child with toys and a cunningly-wrought looking-glass lured him into an ambush, where her satellites, the Titans, rushed upon him, cut him limb from limb, boiled his body

---

[1] Pausanias, ii. 2, 6 (5) *sq.* Pausanias does not mention the kind of tree ; but from Euripides, *Bacchae*, 1064 *sqq.*, and Philostratus, *Imag.* i. 17 (18), we may infer that it was a pine ; though Theocritus (xxvi. 11) speaks of it as a mastich-tree.

[2] Müller-Wieseler, *Denkmäler der*

alten *Kunst*, ii. pl. xxxii. *sqq.* ; Baumeister, *Denkmäler des klassischen Altertums*, i. figures 489, 491, 492, 495. Cp. Lenormant in Daremberg et Saglio, i. 623 ; Lobeck, *Aglaophamus*, p. 700.

[3] Pausanias, i. 31, 6 (3).

[4] Athenaeus, iii. p. 78 C.

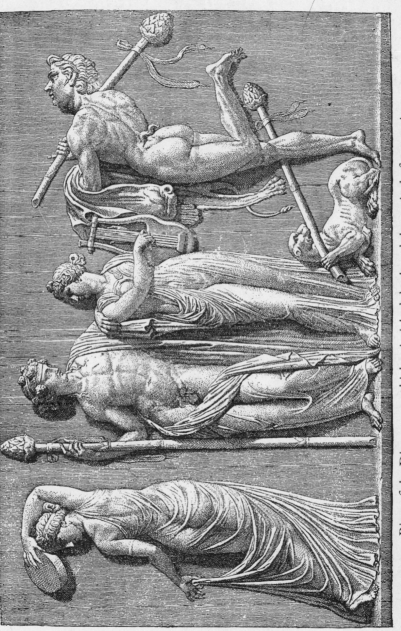

Rites of the Dionyseans which mimicked death and the revival of vegetation.

Juno, wife of Jupiter who destroyed
Dionysus, Jupiter's son by another
woman.

with various herbs and ate it.   But his sister Minerva,
who had shared in the deed, kept his heart and gave it
to Jupiter on his return, revealing to him the whole
history of the crime.   In his rage, Jupiter put the
Titans to death by torture, and, to soothe his grief for
the loss of his son, made an image in which he enclosed
the child's heart, and then built a temple in his honour.[1]
In this version a Euhemeristic turn has been given to
the myth by representing Jupiter and Juno (Zeus and
Hera) as a king and queen of Crete.   The guards
referred to are the mythical Curetes who danced a
war-dance round the infant Dionysus as they are said
to have done round the infant Zeus.[2]   Pomegranates
were supposed to have sprung from the blood of
Dionysus,[3] as anemones from the blood of Adonis
and violets from the blood of Attis.   According to
some, the severed limbs of Dionysus were pieced
together, at the command of Zeus, by Apollo, who
buried them on Parnassus.[4]   The grave of Dionysus
was shown in the Delphic temple beside a golden
statue of Apollo.[5]   Thus far the resurrection of the
slain god is not mentioned, but in other versions
of the myth it is variously related.   One version,
which represented Dionysus as a son of Demeter,
averred that his mother pieced together his mangled
limbs and made him young again.[6]   In others it is
simply said that shortly after his burial he rose from

[1] Firmicus Maternus, *De errore profanarum religionum*, 6.
[2] Clemens Alexandr., *Protrept*. ii. 17.
Cp. Lobeck, *Aglaophamus*, p. 1111 *sqq.*
[3] Clemens Alexandr., *Protrept*. ii. 19.
[4] Clemens Alexandr., *Protrept*. ii. 18;
Proclus on Plato's Timaeus, iii. 200 D,
quoted by Lobeck, *Aglaophamus*, p. 562,
and by Abel, *Orphica*, p. 234.   Others
said that the mangled body was pieced

together, not by Apollo but by Rhea.
Cornutus, *De natura deorum*, 30.
[5] Lobeck, *Aglaophamus*, p. 572 *sqq.*
For a conjectural restoration of the
temple, based on ancient authorities
and an examination of the scanty
remains, see an article by Professor
J. H. Middleton, in *Journal of Hellenic
Studies*, vol. ix. p. 282 *sqq.*
[6] Diodorus, iii. 62.

the dead and ascended up to heaven;[1] or that Zeus raised him up as he lay mortally wounded;[2] or that Zeus swallowed the heart of Dionysus and then begat him afresh by Semele,[3] who in the common legend figures as mother of Dionysus. Or, again, the heart was pounded up and given in a potion to Semele, who thereby conceived him.[4]

Turning from the myth to the ritual, we find that the Cretans celebrated a biennial[5] festival at which the sufferings and death of Dionysus were represented in every detail.[6] Where the resurrection formed part of the myth, it also was enacted at the rites,[7] and it even appears that a general doctrine of resurrection, or at least of immortality, was inculcated on the worshippers; for Plutarch, writing to console his wife on the death of their infant daughter, comforts her with the thought of the immortality of the soul as taught by tradition and revealed in the mysteries of Dionysus.[8] A different form of the myth of the death and resurrection of Dionysus is that he descended into Hades to bring up his mother Semele from the dead.[9] The local Argive tradition was that he descended

[1] Macrobius, *Comment. in Somn. Scip.* i. 12, 12 ; *Scriptores rerum mythicarum Latini tres Romae nuper reperti* (commonly referred to as *Mythographi Vaticani*), ed. G. H. Bode (Cellis, 1834), iii. 12, 5, p. 246; Origen, *c. Cels.* iv. 171, quoted by Lobeck, *Aglaophamus*, p. 713.

[2] Himerius, *Orat.* ix. 4.

[3] Proclus, *Hymn to Minerva*, in Lobeck, *Aglaophamus*, p. 561 ; *Orphica*, ed. Abel, p. 235.

[4] Hyginus, *Fab.* 167.

[5] The festivals of Dionysus were biennial in many places. See Schömann, *Griechische Alterthümer*,[3] ii. 500 *sqq.* (The terms for the festival were τριετηρίς, τριετηρικός, both terms of

the series being included in the numeration, in accordance with the ancient mode of reckoning.) Probably the festivals were formerly annual and the period was afterwards lengthened, as has happened with other festivals. See W. Mannhardt, *Baumkultus*, pp. 172, 175, 491, 533 *sq.*, 598. Some of the festivals of Dionysus, however, were annual.

[6] Firmicus Maternus, *De err. prof. relig.* 6.

[7] *Mythogr. Vatic.* ed. Bode, *l.c.*

[8] Plutarch, *Consol. ad uxor.* 10. Cp. *id.*, *Isis et Osiris*, 35 ; *id.*, *De ei Delphico*, 9 ; *id.*, *De esu carnium*, i. 7.

[9] Pausanias, ii. 31, 2, and 37, 5 ; Apollodorus, iii. 5, 3.

through the Alcyonian lake ; and his return from the
lower world, in other words his resurrection, was
annually celebrated on the spot by the Argives, who
summoned him from the water by trumpet blasts,
while they threw a lamb into the lake as an offering
to the warder of the dead.[1]   Whether this was a spring
festival does not appear, but the Lydians certainly
celebrated the advent of Dionysus in spring ; the god
was supposed to bring the season with him.[2]   Deities
of vegetation, who are supposed to pass a certain
portion of each year underground, naturally come to be
regarded as gods of the lower world or of the dead.
Both Dionysus and Osiris were so conceived.[3]

A feature in the mythical character of Dionysus,
which at first sight appears inconsistent with his nature
as a deity of vegetation, is that he was often conceived
and represented in animal shape, especially in the
form, or at least with the horns, of a bull.   Thus he
is spoken of as "cow-born," "bull," "bull-shaped,"
"bull-faced," "bull-browed," "bull-horned," "horn-
bearing," "two-horned," "horned."[4]   He was believed
to appear, at least occasionally, as a bull.[5]   His images
were often, as at Cyzicus, made in bull shape,[6] or with
bull horns;[7] and he was painted with horns.[8]   Types
of the horned Dionysus are found amongst the sur-

---

[1] Pausanias, ii. 37, 5 *sq.* ; Plutarch, *Isis et Osiris*, 35 ; *id.*, *Quaest Conviv.* iv. 6, 2.

[2] Himerius, *Orat.* iii. 6, xiv. 7.

[3] For Dionysus, see Lenormant in Daremberg et Saglio, i. 632.   For Osiris, see Wilkinson, *Manners and Customs of the Ancient Egyptians* (London, 1878), iii. 65.

[4] Plutarch, *Isis et Osiris*, 35 ; *id.*, *Quaest. Graec.* 36 ; Athenaeus, xi. 476 A ; Clemens Alexandr., *Protrept.* ii. 16 ; *Orphica*, Hymn xxx. *vv.* 3, 4,

xlv. 1, lii. 2, liii. 8 ; Euripides, *Bacchae*, 99 ; Schol. on Aristophanes, *Frogs*, 357 ; Nicander, *Alexipharmaca*, 31 ; Lucian, *Bacchus*, 2.

[5] Euripides, *Bacchae*, 920 *sqq.*, 1017.

[6] Plutarch, *Isis et Osiris*, 35 ; Athenaeus, *l.c.*

[7] Diodorus, iii. 64, 2, iv. 4, 2 ; Cornutus, *De natura deorum*, 30.

[8] Diodorus, *l.c.* ; Tzetzes, *Schol. in Lycophr.* 209 ; Philostratus, *Imagines*, i. 14 (15).

viving monuments of antiquity.[1] On one statuette he appears clad in a bull's hide, the head, horns, and hoofs hanging down behind.[2] At his festivals Dionysus was believed to appear in bull form. The women of Elis hailed him as a bull, and prayed him to come with his bull's-foot. They sang, "Come here, Dionysus, to thy holy temple by the sea; come with the Graces to thy temple, rushing with thy bull's-foot, O goodly bull, O goodly bull!"[3] According to the myth, it was in the shape of a bull that he was torn to pieces by the Titans;[4] and the Cretans, in representing the sufferings and death of Dionysus, tore a live bull to pieces with their teeth.[5] Indeed, the rending and devouring of live bulls and calves appear to have been a regular feature of the Dionysiac rites.[6] The practice of representing the god in bull form or with some of the features of a bull, the belief that he appeared in bull form to his worshippers at the sacred rites, and the legend that it was in bull form that he had been torn in pieces—all these facts taken together leave no room to doubt that in rending and devouring a live bull at his festival his worshippers believed that they were killing the god, eating his flesh, and drinking his blood.

Another animal whose form Dionysus assumed was the goat. One of his names was "Kid."[7] To save him from the wrath of Hera, his father Zeus changed

---

[1] Müller-Wieseler, *Denkmäler der alten Kunst*, ii. pl. xxxiii.; Daremberg et Saglio, i. 619 *sq.*, 631; Roscher, *Ausführl. Lexikon*, i. c. 1149 *sqq.*

[2] Welcker, *Alte Denkmäler*, v. taf. 2.

[3] Plutarch, *Quaest. Graec.* 36; *id.*, *Isis et Osiris*, 35.

[4] Nonnus, *Dionys.* vi. 205.

[5] Firmicus Maternus, *De errore profan. religionum*, 6.

[6] Euripides, *Bacchae*, 735 *sqq.*; Schol. on Aristophanes, *Frogs*, 357.

[7] Hesychius, *s.v.* Ἔριφος ὁ Διόνυσος, on which there is a marginal gloss ὁ μικρὸς αἴξ, ὁ ἐν τῷ ἔαρι φαινόμενος, ἤγουν ὁ πρώϊμος; Stephanus Byzant. *s.v.* Ἀκρώρεια. The title Εἰραφιώτης is probably to be explained in the same way. [Homer], *Hymn* xxxiv. 2; Porphyry, *De abstin.* iii. 17; Dionysius, *Perieg.* 576; *Etymolog. Magnum*, p. 371, 57.

Minerva, sister of Dionysus, who revealed his murder to Jupiter.

Sacrifice of the bull, a feature of Dionysiac rites.

him into a kid ;¹ and when the gods fled to Egypt to
escape the fury of Typhon, Dionysus was turned into
a goat.² Hence when his worshippers rent in pieces
a live goat and devoured it raw,³ they must have
believed that they were eating the body and blood of
the god.

This custom of killing a god in animal form, which
we shall examine more fully presently, belongs to a
very early stage in human culture, and is apt in later
times to be misunderstood. The advance of thought
tends to strip the old animal and plant gods of their
bestial and vegetable husk, and to leave their human
attributes (which are always the kernel of the conception) as the final and sole residuum. In other words,
animal and plant gods tend to become purely anthropomorphic. When they have become wholly or nearly
so, the animals and plants which were at first the
deities themselves, still retain a vague and ill-under-
stood connection with the anthropomorphic gods which
have been developed out of them. The origin of the
relationship between the deity and the animal or plant
having been forgotten, various stories are invented to
explain it. These explanations may follow one of two
lines according as they are based on the habitual or on
the exceptional treatment of the sacred animal or plant.
The sacred animal was habitually spared, and only
exceptionally slain ; and accordingly the myth might
be devised to explain either why it was spared or why

---

¹ Apollodorus, iii. 4, 3.

² Ovid, *Metam.* v. 329 ; Antoninus
Liberalis, 28 ; *Mythogr. Vatic.* ed.
Bode, i. 86, p. 29.

³ Arnobius, *Adv. nationes*, v. 19.
Cp. Suidas, *s. v.* αἰγίξειν. As fawns
appear to have been also torn in pieces
at the rites of Dionysus (Photius, *s.v.*

νεβρίξειν ; Harpocration, *s.v.* νεβρίξων),
it is probable that the fawn was another
of the god's embodiments. But of
this there seems no direct evidence.
Fawn-skins were worn both by the god
and his worshippers (Cornutus, *De
natura deorum*, c. 30). Similarly the
female Bacchanals wore goat-skins
(Hesychius, *s.v.* τραγηφόροι).

it was killed.   Devised for the former purpose, the myth would tell of some service rendered to the deity by the animal ; devised for the latter purpose, the myth would tell of some injury inflicted by the animal on the god.   The reason given for sacrificing goats to Dionysus is an example of a myth of the latter sort. They were sacrificed to him, it was said, because they injured the vine.[1]   Now the goat, as we have seen, was originally an embodiment of the god himself.   But when the god had divested himself of his animal character and had become essentially anthropomorphic, the killing of the goat in his worship came to be regarded no longer as a slaying of the god himself, but as a sacrifice to him ; and since some reason had to be assigned why the goat in particular should be sacrificed, it was alleged that this was a punishment inflicted on the goat for injuring the vine, the object of the god's especial care.   Thus we have the strange spectacle of a god sacrificed to himself on the ground that he is his own enemy.   And as the god is supposed to partake of the victim offered to him, it follows that, when the victim is the god's old self, the god eats of his own flesh.   Hence the goat-god Dionysus is represented as eating raw goat's blood ;[2] and the bull-god Dionysus is called "eater of bulls."[3]   On the analogy of these instances we may conjecture that wherever a god is described as the eater of a particular animal, the animal in question was originally nothing but the god himself.[4]

---

[1] Varro, *De re rustica* i. 2, 19 ; Virgil, *Georg.* ii. 380, and Servius, *ad l.*, and on *Aen.* iii. 118 ; Ovid, *Fasti*, i. 353 *sqq.*; *id.*, *Metam.* xv. 114 *sq.*; Cornutus, *De natura deorum*, 30.

[2] Euripides, *Bacchae*, 138 *sq.* ἀγρεύ-ων αἷμα τραγοκτόνον, ὠμοφάγον χάριν.

[3] Schol. on Aristophanes, *Frogs*, 357.

[4] Hera αἰγοφάγος at Sparta, Pausanias, iii. 15, 9 (cp. the representation of Hera clad in a goat's skin, with the animal's head and horns over her head, Müller-Wieseler, *Denkmäler der alten*

All this, however, does not explain why a deity of vegetation should appear in animal form. But the consideration of this point had better be deferred till we have discussed the character and attributes of Demeter. Meantime it remains to point out that in some places, instead of an animal, a human being was torn in pieces at the rites of Dionysus. This was the custom in Chios and Tenedos;[1] and at Potniae in Boeotia the tradition ran that it had been formerly the custom to sacrifice to the goat-smiting Dionysus a child, for whom a goat was afterwards substituted.[2] At Orchomenus the human victim was taken from the women of a certain family, called the Oleiae. At the annual festival the priest of Dionysus pursued these women with a drawn sword, and if he overtook one of them he had a right to slay her. This right was exercised as late as Plutarch's time.[3] As the slain bull or goat represented the slain god, so, we may suppose, the human victim also represented him. It is possible, however, that a tradition of human sacrifice may sometimes have been a mere misinterpretation of a sacrificial ritual in which an animal victim was treated as a human being. For example, at Tenedos the new-born calf sacrificed to Dionysus was shod in buskins, and the mother cow was tended like a woman in child-bed.[4]

Kunst, i. No. 299 B); Apollo ὀψοφάγος at Elis, Athenaeus, 346 B ; Artemis καπροφάγος in Samos, Hesychius, *s.v.* καπροφάγος ; cp. *id.*, *s.v.* κριοφάγος. Divine titles derived from *killing* animals are probably to be similarly explained, as Dionysus αἰγόβολος, Pausanias ix. 8, 2 ; Rhea or Hecate κυνοσφαγής, Tzetzes, *Schol. in Lycophr.*

77 ; Apollo λυκοκτόνος, Sophocles, *Electra*, 6 ; Apollo σαυροκτόνος, Pliny, *Nat. Hist.* xxxiv. 70.

[1] Porphyry, *De abstin.* ii. 55.
[2] Pausanias, ix. 8, 2.
[3] Plutarch, *Quaest. Graec.* 38.
[4] Aelian, *Nat. An.* xii. 34. Cp. W. Robertson Smith, *Religion of the Semites*, i. 286 *sqq.*

§ 8.—*Demeter and Proserpine*

The Greek myth of Demeter and Proserpine is substantially identical with the Syrian myth of Aphrodite (Astarte) and Adonis, the Phrygian myth of Cybele and Attis, and the Egyptian myth of Isis and Osiris. In the Greek myth, as in its Asiatic and Egyptian counterparts, a goddess—Demeter—mourns the loss of a loved one—Proserpine—who personifies the vegetation, more especially the corn, which dies in summer [1] to revive in spring. But in the Greek myth the loved and lost one is the daughter instead of the husband or lover of the goddess ; and the mother as well as the daughter is a goddess of the corn. [2] Thus, as modern scholars have recognised, [3] Demeter and Proserpine are merely a mythical reduplication of the same natural phenomenon. Proserpine, so ran the Greek myth, [4] was gathering flowers when the earth gaped, and Pluto, lord of the Dead, issuing from the abyss, carried her off on his golden car to be his bride in the gloomy subterranean world. Her sorrowing mother Demeter sought her over land and sea, and learning from the

---

[1] It is to be remembered that on the Mediterranean coasts the harvest never falls so late as autumn.

[2] On Demeter as a corn- goddess see Mannhardt, *Mythologische Forschungen*, p. 224 *sqq.* ; on Proserpine in the same character see Cornutus, *De nat. deor.* c. 28 ; Varro in Augustine, *Civ. Dei*, vii. 20 ; Hesychius, *s.v.* Φερσεφόνεια ; Firmicus Maternus, *De errore prof. relig.* 17. In his careful account of Demeter as a corn-goddess Mannhardt appears to have overlooked the very important statement of Hippolytus (*Refut. omn. haeres.* v. 8, p. 162, ed.

Duncker and Schneidewin) that at the initiation into the Eleusinian mysteries (the most famous of all the rites of Demeter) the central mystery revealed to the initiated was a reaped ear of corn.

[3] Welcker, *Griechische Götterlehre*, ii. 532 ; Preller, in Pauly's *Real-Encyclopädie für class. Alterthumswiss.* vi. 107 ; Lenormant, in Daremberg et Saglio, *Dictionnaire des Antiquités grecques et romaines*, i. pt. ii. 1047 *sqq.*

[4] Homer, *Hymn to Demeter* ; Apollodorus, i. 5 ; Ovid, *Fasti*, iv. 425 *sqq.* ; *id.*, *Metam.* v. 385 *sqq.*

Sun her daughter's fate, she suffered not the seed to grow, but kept it hidden in the ground, so that the whole race of men would have died of hunger if Zeus had not sent and fetched Proserpine from the nether world. Finally it was agreed that Proserpine should spend a third, or according to others a half,[1] of each year with Pluto underground, but should come forth in spring to dwell with her mother and the gods in the upper world. Her annual death and resurrection, that is, her annual descent into the under world and her ascension from it, appear to have been represented in her rites.[2]

With regard to the name Demeter, it has been plausibly argued by Mannhardt[3] that the first part of the word is derived from *dēai*, a Cretan word for "barley";[4] and that thus Demeter means the Barley-mother or the Corn-mother; for the root of the word appears to have been applied to different kinds of grain by different branches of the Aryans, and even of the Greeks themselves.[5] As Crete appears to have been one of the most ancient seats of the worship of Demeter,[6] it is not surprising that her name should be of Cretan origin. This explanation of the name Demeter is supported by a host of analogies which the diligence of Mannhardt has collected

---

[1] A third, according to Homer, *H. to Demeter*, 399, and Apollodorus, i. 5, 3; a half, according to Ovid, *Fasti*, iv. 614; *id.*, *Metam.* v. 567; Hyginus, *Fab.* 146.

[2] Schömann, *Griech. Alterthümer*,[3] ii. 393; Preller, *Griech. Mythologie*,[3] i. 628 *sq.*, 644 *sq.*, 650 *sq.* The evidence of the ancients on this head, though not full and definite, seems sufficient. See Diodorus, v. 4; Firmicus Maternus, cc. 7, 27; Plutarch, *Isis et Osiris*, 69; Apuleius, *Met.* vi. 2; Clemens Alex., *Protrept.* ii. §§ 12, 17.

[3] *Mythol. Forschungen*, p. 292 *sqq.*

[4] *Etymol. Magnum.* p. 264, 12 *sq.*

[5] O. Schrader, *Sprachvergleichung und Urgeschichte*[2] (Jena, 1890), pp. 409, 422; V. Hehn, *Kulturpflanzen und Hausthiere in ihrem Uebergang aus Asien*,[4] p. 54. Δηαί is doubtless equivalent etymologically to ζειαί, which is often taken to be spelt, but this seems uncertain.

[6] Hesiod, *Theog.* 971; Lenormant, in Daremberg et Saglio, i. pt. ii. p. 1029.

from modern European folk-lore, and of which the following are specimens. In Germany the corn is very commonly personified under the name of the Corn-mother. Thus in spring, when the wind sets the corn in wave-like motion, the peasants say, " There comes the Corn-mother," or " The Corn-mother is running over the field," or " The Corn-mother is going through the corn."[1] When children wish to go into the fields to pull the blue corn-flowers or the red poppies, they are told not to do so, because the Corn-mother is sitting in the corn and will catch them.[2] Or again she is called, according to the crop, the Rye-mother or the Pea-mother, and children are warned against straying in the rye or among the peas by threats of the Rye-mother or the Pea-mother. In Norway also the Pea-mother is said to sit among the peas.[3] Similar expressions are current among the Slavs. The Poles and Czechs warn children against the Corn-mother who sits in the corn. Or they call her the Old Corn-woman, and say that she sits in the corn and strangles the children who tread it down.[4] The Lithuanians say, " The Old Rye-woman sits in the corn."[5] Again the Corn-mother is believed to make the crop grow. Thus in the neighbourhood of Magdeburg it is sometimes said, " It will be a good year for flax ; the Flax-mother has been seen." At Dinkelsbühl (Bavaria) down to fifteen or twenty years ago, people believed that when the crops on a particular farm compared unfavourably with those of the neighbourhood, the reason was that the Corn-mother had punished the farmer for his sins.[6] In a village of Styria it is said that the Corn-mother, in the shape of a female

---

[1] W. Mannhardt, *Mythol. Forsch.* p. 296.   [2] *Ib.* p. 297.
[3] *Ib.* p. 297 *sq.*   [4] *Ib.* p. 299.   [5] *Ib.* p. 300.   [6] *Ib.* p. 310.

Demeter, the Corn Mother, according
to Greek myth.

Harvest attributes of Demeter.

puppet made out of the last sheaf of corn and dressed in white, may be seen at midnight in the corn-fields, which she fertilises by passing through them; but if she is angry with a farmer, she withers up all his corn.[1]

Further, the Corn-mother plays an important part in harvest customs. She is believed to be present in the handful of corn which is left standing last on the field; and with the cutting of this last handful she is caught, or driven away, or killed. In the first of these cases, the last sheaf is carried joyfully home and honoured as a divine being. It is placed in the barn, and at threshing the corn-spirit appears again.[2] In the district of Hadeln (Hanover) the reapers stand round the last sheaf and beat it with sticks in order to drive the Corn-mother out of it. They call to each other, "There she is! hit her! Take care she doesn't catch you!" The beating goes on till the grain is completely threshed out; then the Corn-mother is believed to be driven away.[3] In the neighbourhood of Danzig the person who cuts the last ears of corn makes them into a doll, which is called the Corn-mother or the Old Woman, and is brought home on the last waggon.[4] In some parts of Holstein the last sheaf is dressed in woman's clothes and called the Corn-mother. It is carried home on the last waggon, and then thoroughly drenched with water. The drenching with water is doubtless a rain-charm.[5] In the district of Bruck in Styria the last sheaf, called the Corn-mother, is made up into the shape of a woman by the oldest married woman in the village, of an age from fifty to fifty-five years. The finest ears are plucked out of it

---

[1] W. Mannhardt, *Mythol. Forsch.* p. 310 *sq.*   [2] *Ib.* p. 316.
[3] *Ib.* p. 316.   [4] *Ib.* p. 316 *sq.*   [5] See above, pp. 16 *sq.*, 286 *sq.*

and made into a wreath, which, twined with flowers, is
carried on her head by the prettiest girl of the village
to the farmer or squire, while the Corn-mother is laid
down in the barn to keep off the mice.[1] In other
villages of the same district the Corn-mother, at the
close of harvest, is carried by two lads at the top of a
pole. They march behind the girl who wears the
wreath to the squire's house, and while he receives
the wreath and hangs it up in the hall, the Corn-
mother is placed on the top of a pile of wood, where
she is the centre of the harvest supper and dance.
Afterwards she is hung up in the barn and remains
there till the threshing is over. The man who gives
the last stroke at threshing is called the son of the
Corn-mother; he is tied up in the Corn-mother, beaten,
and carried through the village. The wreath is
dedicated in church on the following Sunday ; and on
Easter Eve the grain is rubbed out of it by a seven
years' old girl and scattered amongst the young corn.
At Christmas the straw of the wreath is placed in the
manger to make the cattle thrive.[2] Here the fertilising power of the Corn-mother is plainly brought out
by scattering the seed taken from her body (for the
wreath is made out of the Corn-mother) among the
new corn ; and her influence over animal life is
indicated by placing the straw in the manger. At
Westerhüsen in Saxony the last corn cut is made in
the shape of a woman decked with ribbons and cloth.
It is fastened on a pole and brought home on the last
waggon. One of the people on the waggon keeps
waving the pole, so that the figure moves as if alive.
It is placed on the threshing-floor, and stays there till
the threshing is done.[3] Amongst the Slavs also the

---

[1] W. Mannhardt, *op. cit.* p. 317.　　[2] *Ib.* p. 317 *sq.*　　[3] *Ib.* p. 318.

last sheaf is known as the Rye-mother, the Wheat-mother, the Oats-mother, the Barley-mother, etc., according to the crop. In the district of Tarnow, Galicia, the wreath made out of the last stalks is called the Wheat-mother, Rye-mother, or Pea-mother. It is placed on a girl's head and kept till spring, when some of the grain is mixed with the seed-corn.[1] Here again the fertilising power of the Corn-mother is indicated. In France, also, in the neighbourhood of Auxerre, the last sheaf goes by the name of the Mother of the Wheat, Mother of the Barley, Mother of the Rye, or Mother of the Oats. It is left standing in the field till the last waggon is about to wend homewards. Then a puppet is made out of it, dressed with clothes belonging to the farmer, and adorned with a crown and a blue or white scarf. A branch of a tree is stuck in the breast of the puppet, which is now called the Ceres. At the dance in the evening the Ceres is placed in the middle of the floor, and the reaper who reaped fastest dances round it with the prettiest girl for his partner. After the dance a pyre is made. All the girls, each wearing a wreath, strip the puppet, pull it to pieces, and place it on the pyre, along with the flowers with which it was adorned. Then the girl who was the first to finish reaping sets fire to the pile, and all pray that Ceres may give a fruitful year. Here, as Mannhardt observes, the old custom has remained intact, though the name Ceres is a bit of schoolmaster's learning.[2] In Upper Britanny the last sheaf is always made into human shape; but if the farmer is a married man, it is made double and consists of a little corn-puppet placed inside of a large one. This is called the Mother-sheaf. It is delivered to the

---

[1] W. Mannhardt, *Mythol. Forsch.* p. 318.   [2] *Ib.* p. 318 *sq.*

farmer's wife, who unties it and gives drink-money in return.[1]

Sometimes the last sheaf is called, not the Corn-mother, but the Harvest-mother or the Great Mother. In the province of Osnabrück (Hanover) it is called the Harvest-mother; it is made up in female form, and then the reapers dance about with it. In some parts of Westphalia the last sheaf at the rye harvest is made especially heavy by fastening stones in it. It is brought home on the last waggon and is called the Great Mother, though no special shape is given it. In the district of Erfurt a very heavy sheaf (not necessarily the last) is called the Great Mother, and is carried on the last waggon to the barn, where it is lifted down by all hands amid a fire of jokes.[2]

Sometimes again the last sheaf is called the Grandmother, and is adorned with flowers, ribbons, and a woman's apron. In East Prussia, at the rye or wheat harvest, the reapers call out to the woman who binds the last sheaf, "You are getting the Old Grandmother." In the neighbourhood of Magdeburg the men and women servants strive who shall get the last sheaf, called the Grandmother. Whoever gets it will be married in the next year, but his or her spouse will be old; if a girl gets it, she will marry a widower; if a man gets it, he will marry an old crone. In Silesia the Grandmother—a huge bundle made up of three or four sheaves by the person who tied the last sheaf—was formerly fashioned into a rude likeness of the human form.[3] In the neighbourhood of Belfast the last sheaf is sometimes called Granny. It is not cut in the usual way, but all the reapers throw

---

[1] Sébillot, *Coutumes populaires de la Haute-Bretagne*, p. 306.

[2] W. Mannhardt, *M. F.* p. 319.
[3] *Ib.* p. 320.

their sickles at it and try to bring it down. It is plaited and kept till the (next?) autumn. Whoever gets it will marry in the course of the year.[1]

Oftener the last sheaf is called the Old Woman or the Old Man. In Germany it is often shaped and dressed as a woman, and the person who cuts it or binds it is said to "get the Old Woman.[2] At Altisheim in Swabia when all the corn of a farm has been cut except a single strip, all the reapers stand in a row before the strip; each cuts his share rapidly, and he who gives the last cut " has the Old Woman."[3] When the sheaves are being set up in heaps, the person who gets hold of the Old Woman, which is the largest and thickest of all the sheaves, is jeered at by the rest, who sing out to him, " He has the Old Woman and must keep her." [4] The woman who binds the last sheaf is sometimes herself called the Old Woman, and it is said that she will be married in the next year.[5] In Neusaass, West Prussia, both the last sheaf—which is dressed up in jacket, hat and ribbons—and the woman who binds it are called the Old Woman. Together they are brought home on the last waggon and are drenched with water.[6] At Hornkampe, near Tiegenhof (West Prussia), when a man or woman lags behind the rest in binding the corn, the other reapers dress up the last sheaf in the form of a man or woman, and this figure goes by the laggard's name, as "the old Michael," " the idle Trine." It is brought home on the last waggon, and, as it nears the house, the bystanders call out to the laggard, " You have got the Old Woman and must keep her." [7]

---

[1] Mannhardt, *Mythol. Forsch.* p. 321.
[2] *Ib.* pp. 321, 323, 325 *sq.*
[3] *Ib.* p. 323; Panzer, *Beitrag zur deutschen Mythologie,* ii. p. 219, No. 403.
[4] W. Mannhardt, *op. cit.* p. 325.
[5] *Ib.* p. 323.   [6] *Ib.*   [7] *Ib.* p. 323 *sq.*

In these customs, as Mannhardt has remarked, the person who is called by the same name as the last sheaf and sits beside it on the last waggon is obviously identified with it ; he or she represents the corn-spirit which has been caught in the last sheaf ; in other words, the corn-spirit is represented in duplicate, by a human being and by a sheaf.[1] The identification of the person with the sheaf is made still clearer by the custom of wrapping up in the last sheaf the person who cuts or binds it. Thus at Hermsdorf in Silesia it used to be the regular custom to tie up in the last sheaf the woman who had bound it.[2] At Weiden in Bavaria it is the cutter, not the binder, of the last sheaf who is tied up in it.[3] Here the person wrapt up in the corn represents the corn-spirit, exactly as a person wrapt in branches or leaves represents the tree-spirit.[4]

The last sheaf, designated as the Old Woman, is often distinguished from the other sheaves by its size and weight. Thus in some villages of West Prussia the Old Woman is made twice as long and thick as a common sheaf, and a stone is fastened in the middle of it. Sometimes it is made so heavy that a man can barely lift it.[5] Sometimes eight or nine sheaves are tied together to make the Old Woman, and the man who sets it up complains of its weight.[6] At Itzgrund, in Saxe-Coburg, the last sheaf, called the Old Woman, is made large with the express intention of thereby securing a good crop next year.[7] Thus the custom of making the last sheaf unusually large or heavy is a charm, working by sympathetic magic, to secure a large and heavy crop in the following year.

---

[1] W. Mannhardt, *op. cit.* p. 324.
[2] *Ib.* p. 320.
[3] *Ib.* p. 325.
[4] See above, p. 83 *sqq.*
[5] W. Mannhardt, *op. cit.* p. 324.
[6] *Ib.* p. 324 *sq.*   [7] *Ib.* p. 325.

In Denmark also the last sheaf is made larger than the others, and is called the Old Rye-woman or the Old Barley-woman. No one likes to bind it, because whoever does so will, it is believed, marry an old man or an old woman. Sometimes the last wheat-sheaf, called the Old Wheat-woman, is made up in human shape, with head, arms, and legs, is dressed in clothes and carried home on the last waggon, the harvesters sitting beside it, drinking and huzzaing.[1] Of the person who binds the last sheaf it is said, " She (or he) is the Old Rye-woman."[2]

In Scotland, when the last corn was cut after Hallowmas, the female figure made out of it was sometimes called the Carlin or Carline, *i.e.* the Old Woman. But if cut before Hallowmas, it was called the Maiden; if cut after sunset, it was called the Witch, being supposed to bring bad luck.[3] We shall return to the Maiden presently. In County Antrim, down to a few years ago, when the sickle was finally expelled by the reaping machine, the few stalks of corn left standing last on the field were plaited together; then the reapers, blindfolded, threw their sickles at the plaited corn, and whoever happened to cut it through took it home with him and put it over his door. This bunch of corn was called the Carley[4]—probably the same word as Carlin.

Similar customs are observed by Slavonic peoples. Thus in Poland the last sheaf is commonly called the Baba, that is, the Old Woman. " In the last sheaf," it is said, " sits the Baba." The sheaf itself is also called the Baba, and is sometimes composed of twelve

[1] W. Mannhardt, *op. cit.* p. 327.
[2] *Ib.* p. 328.
[3] Jamieson, *Dictionary of the Scottish Language, s.v.* " Maiden "; W. Mann-hardt, *Mythol. Forschungen*, p. 326.
[4] Communicated by my friend Prof. W. Ridgeway, of Queen's College, Cork.

smaller sheaves lashed together.[1] In some parts of Bohemia the Baba, made out of the last sheaf, has the figure of a woman with a great straw hat. It is carried home on the last harvest-waggon and delivered, along with a garland, to the farmer by two girls. In binding the sheaves the women strive not to be last, for she who binds the last sheaf will have a child next year.[2] The last sheaf is tied up with others into a large bundle, and a green branch is stuck on the top of it.[3] Sometimes the harvesters call out to the woman who binds the last sheaf, " She has the Baba," or " She is the Baba." She has then to make a puppet, some-times in female, sometimes in male form, out of the corn ; the puppet is occasionally dressed with clothes, often with flowers and ribbons only. The cutter of the last stalks, as well as the binder of the last sheaf, was also called Baba ; and a doll, called the Harvest-woman, was made out of the last sheaf and adorned with ribbons. The oldest reaper had to dance, first with this doll, and then with the farmer's wife.[4] In the district of Cracow, when a man binds the last sheaf, they say, " The Grandfather is sitting in it ;" when a woman binds it, they say, " The Baba is sitting in it," and the woman herself is wrapt up in the sheaf, so that only her head projects out of it. Thus encased in the sheaf, she is carried on the last harvest-waggon to the house, where she is drenched with water by the whole family. She remains in the sheaf till the dance is over, and for a year she retains the name of Baba.[5]

In Lithuania the name for the last sheaf is Boba (Old Woman), answering to the Polish name Baba. The Boba is said to sit in the corn which is left

---

[1] W. Mannhardt, *op. cit.* p. 328.   [2] *Ib.*   [3] *Ib.* p. 328 *sq.*
[4] *Ib.* p. 329.   [5] *Ib.* p. 330.

standing last.[1] The person who binds the last sheaf
or digs the last potato is the subject of much banter,
and receives and long retains the name of the Old
Rye-woman or the Old Potato-woman.[2] The last
sheaf—the Boba—is made into the form of a woman,
carried solemnly through the village on the last harvest-
waggon, and drenched with water at the farmer's house;
then every one dances with it.[3]

In Russia also the last sheaf is often shaped and
dressed as a woman, and carried with dance and song
to the farmhouse. Out of the last sheaf the Bulgarians
make a doll which they call the Corn-queen or Corn-
mother; it is dressed in a woman's shirt, carried round
the village, and then thrown into the river in order to
secure plenty of rain and dew for the next year's crop.
Or it is burned and the ashes strewn on the fields,
doubtless to fertilise them.[4] The name Queen, as
applied to the last sheaf, has its analogies in Northern
Europe. Thus Brand quotes from Hutchinson's *History
of Northumberland* the following: " I have seen, in
some places, an image apparelled in great finery,
crowned with flowers, a sheaf of corn placed under
her arm, and a scycle in her hand, carried out of the
village in the morning of the conclusive reaping day,
with music and much clamour of the reapers, into the
field, where it stands fixed on a pole all day, and when
the reaping is done, is brought home in like manner.
This they call the Harvest Queen, and it represents
the Roman Ceres."[5] From Cambridge also Dr. E.
D. Clarke reported that " at the Hawkie [harvest-
home], as it is called, I have seen a clown dressed in

[1] W. Mannhardt, *op. cit.* p. 330.
[2] *Ib* p. 331.   [3] *Ib.* p. 331.
[4] *Ib.* p. 332.

[5] Hutchinson, *History of Northum-
berland*, ii. *ad finem*, 17, quoted by
Brand, *Popular Antiquities*, ii. 20,
Bohn's ed.

woman's clothes, having his face painted, his head decorated with ears of corn, and bearing about him other symbols of Ceres, carried in a waggon, with great pomp and loud shouts, through the streets, the horses being covered with white sheets ; and when I inquired the meaning of the ceremony, was answered by the people, that they were drawing the Harvest Queen." [1]

Often the customs we have been examining are practised, not on the harvest field, but on the threshing-floor. The spirit of the corn, fleeing before the reapers as they cut down the corn, quits the cut corn and takes refuge in the barn, where it appears in the last sheaf threshed, either to perish under the blows of the flail or to flee thence to the still unthreshed corn of a neighbouring farm. [2] Thus the last corn to be threshed is called the Mother-corn or the Old Woman. Sometimes the person who gives the last stroke with the flail is called the Old Woman, and is wrapt in the straw of the last sheaf, or has a bundle of straw fastened on his back. Whether wrapt in the straw or carrying it on his back, he is carted through the village amid general laughter. In some districts of Bavaria, Thüringen, etc., the man who threshes the last sheaf is said to have the Old Woman or the Old Corn-woman ; he is tied up in straw, carried or carted about the village, and set down at last on the dunghill, or taken to the threshing-floor of a neighbouring farmer who has not finished his threshing. [3] In Poland the man who gives the last stroke at threshing is called Baba (Old Woman) ; he is wrapt in corn and wheeled through the village. [4] Sometimes in Lithuania the last sheaf is not threshed, but is fashioned into female

---

[1] Quoted by Brand, *op. cit.* ii. 22.
[2] W. Mannhardt, *Mythol. Forsch.* p. 333 *sq.*   [3] *Ib.* p. 334.   [4] *Ib.* p. 334.

shape and carried to the barn of a neighbour who has
not finished his threshing.[1]   In some parts of Sweden,
when a stranger woman appears on the threshing-
floor, a flail is put round her body, stalks of corn are
wound round her neck, a crown of ears is placed on
her head, and the threshers call out, "Behold the
Corn-woman."   Here the stranger woman, thus
suddenly appearing, is taken to be the corn-spirit who
has just been expelled by the flails from the corn-
stalks.[2]   In other cases the farmer's wife represents
the corn-spirit.   Thus in the Commune of Saligné,
Canton de Poiret (Vendée), the farmer's wife, along
with the last sheaf, is tied up in a sheet, placed on a
litter, and carried to the threshing machine, under
which she is shoved.   Then the woman is drawn out
and the sheaf is threshed by itself, but the woman is
tossed in the sheet (in imitation of winnowing).[3]   It
would be impossible to express more clearly the identification of the woman with the corn than by this
graphic imitation of threshing and winnowing her.

In these customs the spirit of the ripe corn is
regarded as old, or at least as of mature age.   Hence
the names of Mother, Grandmother, Old Woman, etc.
But in other cases the corn-spirit is conceived as young,
sometimes as a child who is separated from its mother
by the stroke of the sickle.   This last view appears in
the Polish custom of calling out to the man who cuts
the last handful of corn, "You have cut the navel-
string."[4]   In some districts of West Prussia the figure
made out of the last sheaf is called the Bastard, and a boy
is wrapt up in it.   The woman who binds the last sheaf

---

[1] W. Mannhardt, *op. cit.* p. 336.
[2] *Ib.* p. 336.
[3] *Ib.* p. 336 ; *Baumkultus*, p. 612.

[4] W. Mannhardt, *Die Korndämonen*,
p. 28.

and represents the Corn-mother, is told that she is about
to be brought to bed ; she cries like a woman in travail,
and an old woman in the character of grandmother
acts as midwife.   At last a cry is raised that the child
is born ; whereupon the boy who is tied up in the
sheaf whimpers and squalls like an infant.   The grandmother wraps a sack, in imitation of swaddling bands,
round the pretended baby, and it is carried joyfully to
the barn, lest it catch cold in the open air.[1]   In other
parts of North Germany, the last sheaf, or the puppet
made out of it, is called the Child, the Harvest Child,
etc.   In the North of England the last handful of
corn was cut by the prettiest girl and dressed up as
the Corn Baby or Kern Baby ; it was brought home
to music, set up in a conspicuous place at the harvest
supper, and generally kept in the parlour for the rest of
the year.   The girl who cut it was the Harvest Queen.[2]
In Kent the Ivy Girl is (or was) "a figure composed of
some of the best corn the field produces, and made as
well as they can into a human shape ; this is afterwards
curiously dressed by the women, and adorned with
paper trimmings, cut to resemble a cap, ruffles, handkerchief, etc., of the finest lace.   It is brought home
with the last load of corn from the field upon the waggon, and they suppose entitles them to a supper at the
expense of the employer."[3]   In the neighbourhood of
Balquhidder, Perthshire, the last handful of corn is cut
by the youngest girl on the field, and is made into the
rude form of a female doll, clad in a paper dress, and
decked with ribbons.   It is called the Maiden, and is
kept in the farmhouse, generally above the chimney,

---

[1] W. Mannhardt, *l.c.*

[2] *Ib.* ; Henderson, *Folk-lore of the Northern Counties*, p. 87 ; Brand, *Popular Antiquities*, ii. 20, Bohn's ed. ; Chambers's *Book of Days*, ii. 377 *sq.* Cp. *Folk-lore Journal*, vii. 50.

[3] Brand, *op. cit.* ii. 21 *sq.*

for a good while, sometimes till the Maiden of the next year is brought in. The writer of this book witnessed the ceremony of cutting the Maiden at Balquhidder in September 1888.[1] On some farms on the Gareloch, Dumbartonshire, about sixty years ago the last handful of standing corn was called the Maiden. It was divided in two, plaited, and then cut with the sickle by a girl, who, it was thought, would be lucky and would soon be married. When it was cut the reapers gathered together and threw their sickles in the air. The Maiden was dressed with ribbons and hung in the kitchen near the roof, where it was kept for several years with the date attached. Sometimes five or six Maidens might be seen hanging at once on hooks. The harvest supper was called the Kirn.[2] In other farms on the Gareloch the last handful of corn was called the Maidenhead or the Head; it was neatly plaited, sometimes decked with ribbons, and hung in the kitchen for a year, when the grain was given to the poultry.[3] In the North of Scotland, the Maiden is kept till Christmas morning, and then divided among the cattle "to make them thrive all the year round."[4] In Aberdeenshire also the last sheaf (called the clyack sheaf) was formerly cut, as it is still cut at Balquhidder, by the youngest girl on the field; then it was dressed in woman's clothes, carried home in triumph, and kept till Christmas or New Year's morning, when it was given to a mare in foal, or, failing such, to the oldest cow.[5] Lastly, a somewhat maturer, but still youthful age is assigned to the corn-spirit by

[1] *Folk-lore Journal*, vi. 268 *sq.*

[2] From information supplied by Archie Leitch, gardener, Rowmore, Garelochhead.

[3] Communicated by Mr. Macfarlane of Faslane, Gareloch.

[4] Jamieson, *Dictionary of the Scottish Language, s.v.* "Maiden."

[5] W. Gregor, in *Revue des Traditions populaires*, iii. 533 (485 B); *id., Folk-lore of the North-East of Scotland*, p. 182. An old Scottish name for the

the appellations of Bride, Oats-bride, and Wheat-bride, which in Germany and Scotland are sometimes bestowed both on the last sheaf and on the woman who binds it.[1]   Sometimes the idea implied in these names is worked out more fully by representing the productive powers of vegetation as bride and bridegroom, Thus in some parts of Germany a man and woman dressed in straw and called the Oats-wife and the Oats-man, or the Oats-bride and the Oats-bridegroom dance at the harvest festival ; then the corn-stalks are plucked from their bodies till they stand as bare as a stubble field.   In Silesia, the woman who binds the last sheaf is called the Wheat-bride or the Oats-bride. With the harvest crown on her head, a bridegroom by her side, and attended by bridesmaids, she is brought to the farmhouse with all the solemnity of a wedding procession.[2]

The harvest customs just described are strikingly analogous to the spring customs which we reviewed in the first chapter. (1.) As in the spring customs the tree-spirit is represented both by a tree and by a person,[3] so in the harvest customs the corn-spirit is represented both by the last sheaf and by the person who cuts or binds or threshes it.   The equivalence of the person to the sheaf is shown by giving him or her the same name as the sheaf, or *vice versâ ;* by wrapping him or her in the sheaf ; and by the rule observed in some places, that when the sheaf is called the Mother, it must be cut by the oldest married woman ; but when it is called

---

Maiden (*autumnalis nymphula*) was *Rapegyrne.* See Fordun, *Scotichron.* ii. 418, quoted in Jamieson's *Dict. of the Scottish Language, s.v.* "Rapegyrne."

[1] W. Mannhardt, *Die Korndämonen,* p. 30 ; *Folk-lore Journal,* vii. 50.

[2] W. Mannhardt, *l.c.* ; Sommer, *Sagen, Märchen und Gebräuche aus Sachsen und Thüringen,* p. 160 *sq.*

[3] See above, p. 83 *sqq.*

the Maiden, it must be cut by the youngest girl.[1]
Here the age of the personal representative of the
corn-spirit corresponds with that of the supposed age
of the corn-spirit, just as the human victims offered by
the Mexicans to promote the growth of the maize
varied with the age of the maize.[2]   For in the Mexican,
as in the European, custom the human beings were
probably representatives of the corn-spirit rather than
victims offered to him.   (2.) Again, the same fertilising
influence which the tree-spirit is supposed to exert over
vegetation, cattle, and even women [3] is ascribed to the
corn-spirit.   Thus, its supposed influence on vegetation is shown by the practice of taking some of the
grain of the last sheaf (in which the corn-spirit is regularly supposed to be present), and scattering it among
the young corn in spring.[4]   Its influence on cattle is
shown by giving the straw of the last sheaf to the
cattle at Christmas with the express intention of making them thrive.[5]   Lastly, its influence on women is
indicated by the custom of delivering the Mother-sheaf,
made into the likeness of a pregnant woman, to the
farmer's wife ;[6] by the belief that the woman who binds
the last sheaf will have a child next year ;[7] perhaps,
too, by the idea that the person who gets it will marry
next year.[8]

Plainly, therefore, these spring and harvest customs
are based on the same ancient modes of thought, and
form parts of the same primitive heathendom, which
was doubtless practised by our forefathers long before
the dawn of history, as it is practised to this day by

[1] Above, pp. 333, 344.
[2] Above, p. 307.
[3] Above, p. 67 *sqq.*
[4] Above, pp. 334, 335.
[5] Above, pp. 334, 345.

[6] See above, p. 335 *sq.*
[7] Above, p. 340 ; cp. Kuhn, *Westfälische Sagen, Gebräuche und Märchen*,
ii. No. 516.
[8] Above, pp. 336, 337, 345.

many of their descendants. Amongst the marks of a primitive religion, we may note the following :—

(1.) No special class of persons is set apart for the performance of the rites ; in other words, there are no priests. The rites may be performed by any one, as occasion demands.

(2.) No special places are set apart for the performance of the rites ; in other words, there are no temples. The rites may be performed anywhere, as occasion demands.

(3.) Spirits, not gods, are recognised. (*a*.) As distinguished from gods, spirits are restricted in their operations to definite departments of nature. Their names are general, not proper. Their attributes are generic, rather than individual ; in other words, there is an indefinite number of spirits of each class, and the individuals of a class are all much alike ; they have no definitely marked individuality ; no accepted traditions are current as to their origin, life, adventures, and character. (*b*.) On the other hand gods, as distinguished from spirits, are not exclusively restricted in their operations to definite departments of nature. It is true that there is generally some one department over which they preside as their special province ; but they are not rigorously confined to it ; they can exert their power for good or evil in many other spheres of nature and life. Again, they bear individual or proper names, such as Ceres, Proserpine, Bacchus ; and their individual characters and histories are fixed by current myths and the representations of art.

(4.) The rites are magical rather than propitiatory. In other words, the desired objects are attained, not by propitiating the favour of divine beings through sacrifice, prayer, and praise, but by ceremonies which, as has

been explained,[1] are believed to influence the course of
nature directly through a physical sympathy or resemblance between the rite and the effect which it is the
intention of the rite to produce.

Judged by these tests, the spring and harvest customs
of our European peasantry deserve to rank as primitive.
For no special class of persons and no special places
are set exclusively apart for their performance ; they
may be performed by any one, master or man, mistress
or maid, boy or girl ; they are practised, not in temples
or churches, but in the woods and meadows, beside
brooks, in barns, on harvest fields and cottage floors.
The supernatural beings whose existence is taken for
granted in them are spirits rather than deities ; their
functions are limited to certain well-defined departments
of nature ; their names are general, like the Barley-
mother, the Old Woman, the Maiden, not proper names
like Ceres, Proserpine, Bacchus. Their generic attributes are known, but their individual histories and
characters are not the subject of myths. For they
exist in classes rather than as individuals, and the
members of each class are indistinguishable. For
example, every farm has its Corn-mother, or its Old
Woman, or its Maiden ; but every Corn-mother is much
like every other Corn-mother, and so with the Old
Women and Maidens. Lastly, in these harvest, as in
the spring, customs, the ritual is magical rather than
propitiatory. This is shown by throwing the Corn-
mother into the river in order to secure rain and dew
for the crops ;[2] by making the Old Woman heavy in
order to get a heavy crop next year ;[3] by strewing
grain from the last sheaf amongst the young crops in

---

[1] See above, p. 9 *sqq.*   [2] Above, p. 341.   [3] Above, p. 338.

spring ;[1] and giving the last sheaf to the cattle to make them thrive.[2]

Further, the custom of keeping the puppet—the representative of the corn-spirit—till next harvest, is a charm to maintain the corn-spirit in life and activity throughout the year.[3] This is proved by a similar custom observed by the ancient Peruvians, and thus described by the historian Acosta. " They take a certain portion of the most fruitefull of the Mays [*i.e.* maize] that growes in their farmes, the which they put in a certaine granary which they doe call *Pirua*, with certaine ceremonies, watching three nightes ; they put this Mays in the richest garments they have, and beeing thus wrapped and dressed, they worship this *Pirua*, and hold it in great veneration, saying it is the mother of the mays of their inheritances, and that by this means the mays augments and is preserved. In this moneth [the sixth month, answering to May] they make a particular sacrifice, and the witches demaund of this *Pirua*, if it hath strength sufficient to continue untill the next yeare; and if it answers no, then they carry this Mays to the farme to burne, whence they brought it, according to every man's power ; then they make another *Pirua*, with the same ceremonies, saying that they renue it, to the end the seede of Mays may not perish, and if it answers that it hath force sufficient to last longer, they leave it untill the next yeare. This foolish vanity continueth to this day, and it is very common amongest the Indians to have these *Piruas*." [4] There seems to

---

[1] Above, p. 334, cp. 335.

[2] Above, pp. 334, 345.

[3] Above, p. 344 *sq.* ; W. Mannhardt, *Korndämonen*, pp. 7, 26. Amongst the Wends the last sheaf, made into a puppet and called the Old Man, is hung in the hall till next year's Old Man is brought in. Schulenburg, *Wendisches Volksthum*, p. 147. In Inverness and Sutherland the Maiden is kept till the next harvest. *Folklore Journal*, vii. 50, 53 *sq.* Cp. Kuhn, *Westfälische Sagen, Gebräuche und Märchen*, ii. Nos. 501, 517.

[4] Acosta, *Hist. of the Indies*, v. c. 28, vol. ii. p. 374 (Hakluyt Society, 1880).

be some error in this description of the custom.   Probably it was the dressed-up bunch of maize, not the
granary (*Pirua*), which was worshipped by the Peruvians and regarded as the Mother of the Maize.   This
is confirmed by what we know of the Peruvian custom
from another source.   The Peruvians, we are told,
believed all useful plants to be animated by a divine
being who causes their growth.   According to the
particular plant, these divine beings were called the
Maize-mother (*Zara-mama*), the Quinoa-mother
(*Quinoa-mama*), the Cocoa-mother (*Coca-mama*), and
the Potato-mother (*Axo-mama*).   Figures of these
divine mothers were made respectively of ears of
maize and leaves of the quinoa and cocoa plants ; they
were dressed in women's clothes and worshipped.
Thus the Maize-mother was represented by a puppet
made of stalks of maize, dressed in full female attire ;
and the Indians believed that "as mother, it had the
power of producing and giving birth to much maize."[1]
Probably, therefore, Acosta misunderstood his informant, and the Mother of the Maize which he describes
was not the granary (*Pirua*) but the bunch of maize
dressed in rich vestments.   The Peruvian Mother of
the Maize, like the harvest Maiden at Balquhidder,
was kept for a year in order that by her means the
corn might grow and multiply.   But lest her strength
might not suffice to last out the year, she was asked in
the course of the year how she felt, and if she answered
that she felt weak, she was burned and a fresh Mother
of the Maize made, "to the end the seede of Mays

[1] W. Mannhardt, *Mythol. Forsch.*
p. 342 *sq.*   Mannhardt's authority is a
Spanish tract (*Carta pastoral de exorta-
cion e instruccion contra las idolatrias de
los Indios del arçobispado de Lima*) by
Pedro de Villagomez, Archbishop of
Lima, published at Lima in 1649, and
communicated to Mannhardt by J. J.
v. Tschudi.

may not perish." Here, it may be observed, we have
a strong confirmation of the explanation already given
of the custom of killing the god, both periodically and
occasionally. The Mother of the Maize was allowed,
as a rule, to live through a year, that being the period
during which her strength might reasonably be supposed to last unimpaired ; but on any symptom of her
strength failing she was put to death and a fresh and
vigorous Mother of the Maize took her place, lest
the maize which depended on her for its existence
should languish and decay.

Hardly less clearly does the same train of thought
come out in the harvest customs formerly observed
by the Zapotecs of Mexico. At harvest the priests,
attended by the nobles and people, went in procession
to the maize fields, where they picked out the largest
and finest sheaf. This they took with great ceremony
to the town or village, and placed it in the temple upon
an altar adorned with wild flowers. After sacrificing
to the harvest god, the priests carefully wrapt up the
sheaf in fine linen and kept it till seed-time. Then the
priests and nobles met again at the temple, one of them
bringing the skin of a wild beast, elaborately ornamented, in which the linen cloth containing the sheaf
was enveloped. The sheaf was then carried once
more in procession to the field from which it had been
taken. Here a small cavity or subterranean chamber
had been prepared, in which the precious sheaf was
deposited, wrapt in its various envelopes. After
sacrifice had been offered to the gods of the fields for
an abundant crop, the chamber was closed and covered
over with earth. Immediately thereafter the sowing
began. Finally, when the time of harvest drew near,
the buried sheaf was solemnly disinterred by the

priests, who distributed the grain to all who asked for it. The packets of grain so distributed were carefully preserved as talismans till the harvest.[1] In these ceremonies, which continued to be annually celebrated long after the Spanish conquest, the intention of keeping the finest sheaf buried in the maize field from seed-time to harvest was undoubtedly to quicken the growth of the maize.

In the Punjaub, to the east of the Jumna, when the cotton boles begin to burst, it is usual "to select the largest plant in the field, and having sprinkled it with butter-milk and rice-water, it is bound all over with pieces of cotton, taken from the other plants of the field. This selected plant is called Sirdar, or Bhogaldaí, *i.e.* mother-cotton, from bhogla, a name sometimes given to a large cotton-pod, and daí (for daiya) a mother, and after salutations are made to it, prayers are offered that the other plants may resemble it in the richness of their produce." [2]

If the reader still feels any doubts as to the original meaning of the harvest customs practised by our peasantry, these doubts may be dispelled by comparing the harvest customs of the Dyaks of Borneo. At harvest the Dyaks of Northern Borneo have a special feast, the object of which is "to secure the soul of the rice, which if not so detained, the produce of their farms would speedily rot and decay." The mode of securing the soul of the rice varies in different tribes. Sometimes the priest catches it, in the form of a few grains of rice, in a white cloth. Sometimes a large shed is erected outside the village, and near it

---

[1] Brasseur de Bourbourg, *Histoire des Nations civilisées du Mexique*, iii. 40 *sqq.*

[2] H. M. Elliot, *Supplemental Glossary of Terms used in the North Western Provinces*, edited by J. Beames, i. 254.

is reared a high and spacious altar.   The corner-
posts of the altar are lofty bamboos with leafy tops,
from one of which there hangs a long narrow streamer
of white cloth.   Here gaily-dressed men and women
dance with slow and solemn steps.   Suddenly the
elders and priests rush at the white streamer, seize
the end of it, and begin dancing and swaying to and
fro, amid a burst of wild music and the yells of the
spectators.   An elder leaps on the altar and shakes
the bamboos violently, whereupon small stones, bunches
of hair and grains of rice fall at the feet of the dancers
and are carefully picked up by attendants.   These
grains of rice are the soul of the rice.   At sowing-
time some of this soul of the rice is planted with the
other seeds, "and is thus propagated and communicated."[1]   The same need of securing the soul of the
rice, if the crop is to thrive, is keenly felt by the
Karens of Burma.   When a rice-field does not
flourish, they suppose that the soul (*kelah*) of the
rice is in some way detained from the rice.   If the
soul cannot be called back, the crop will fail.   The
following formula is used in recalling the *kelah* (soul)
of the rice: "O come, rice-*kelah*, come!   Come
to the field.   Come to the rice.   With seed of each
gender, come.   Come from the river Kho, come from
the river Kaw; from the place where they meet, come.
Come from the West, come from the East.   From the
throat of the bird, from the maw of the ape, from the
throat of the elephant.   Come from the sources of rivers
and their mouths.   Come from the country of the
Shan and Burman.   From the distant kingdoms come.
From all granaries come.   O rice-*kelah*, come to the

---

[1] Spenser St. John, *Life in the Forests of the Far East*,[2] i. 187, 192 *sqq.*

rice."[1] Again, the European custom of representing the
corn-spirit in the double form of bride and bridegroom[2]
is paralleled by a custom observed at the rice-harvest
in Java.   Before the reapers begin to cut the rice, the
priest or sorcerer picks out a number of ears of rice,
which are tied together, smeared with ointment, and
adorned with flowers.   Thus decked out, the ears are
called the *padi-pĕngantèn*, that is, the Rice-bride and
the Rice-bridegroom; their wedding feast is celebrated,
and the cutting of the rice begins immediately afterwards.   Later on, when the rice is being got in, a
bridal chamber is partitioned off in the barn, and
furnished with a new mat, a lamp, and all kinds of
toilet articles.   Sheaves of rice, to represent the
wedding guests, are placed beside the Rice-bride
and the Rice-bridegroom.   Not till this has been
done may the whole harvest be housed in the barn.
And for the first forty days after the rice has been
housed, no one may enter the barn, for fear of disturbing the newly-wedded pair.[3]

Compared with the Corn-mother of Germany and
the harvest Maiden of Balquhidder, the Demeter and
Proserpine of Greece are late products of religious
growth.   But, as Aryans, the Greeks must at one time
or another have observed harvest customs like those
which are still practised by Celts, Teutons, and Slavs,
and which, far beyond the limits of the Aryan world,
have been practised by the Incas of Peru, the Dyaks
of Borneo, and the Malays of Java—a sufficient proof
that the ideas on which these customs rest are not confined to any one race, but naturally suggest themselves

---

[1] E. B. Cross, " On the Karens,"
in *Journal of the American Oriental
Society*, iv. 309.

[2] See above, p. 346.
[3] Veth, *Java*, i. 524-526.

to all untutored peoples engaged in agriculture. It is
probable, therefore, that Demeter and Proserpine,
those stately and beautiful figures of Greek mythology,
grew out of the same simple beliefs and practices
which still prevail among our modern peasantry, and
that they were represented by rude dolls made out
of the yellow sheaves on many a harvest-field long
before their breathing images were wrought in bronze
and marble by the master hands of Phidias and Praxi-
teles. A reminiscence of that olden time—a scent, so
to say, of the harvest-field—lingered to the last in the
title of the Maiden (*Kore*) by which Proserpine was
commonly known. Thus if the prototype of Demeter
is the Corn-mother of Germany, the prototype of
Proserpine is the harvest Maiden, which, autumn after
autumn, is still made from the last sheaf on the Braes
of Balquhidder. Indeed if we knew more about the
peasant-farmers of ancient Greece we should probably find that even in classical times they continued
annually to fashion their Corn-mothers (Demeters)
and Maidens (Proserpines) out of the ripe corn on
the harvest fields. But unfortunately the Demeter
and Proserpine whom we know are the denizens of
towns, the majestic inhabitants of lordly temples;
it was for such divinities alone that the refined
writers of antiquity had eyes; the rude rites performed by rustics amongst the corn were beneath
their notice. Even if they noticed them, they probably never dreamed of any connection between the
puppet of corn-stalks on the sunny stubble-field and
the marble divinity in the shady coolness of the temple.
Still the writings even of these town-bred and cultured
persons afford us an occasional glimpse of a Demeter
as rude as the rudest that a remote German village

can show.   Thus the story that Iasion begat a child
Plutus ("wealth," "abundance") by Demeter on a
thrice-ploughed field,[1] may be compared with the West
Prussian custom of the mock birth of a child on the
harvest field.[2]   In this Prussian custom the pretended
mother represents the Corn-mother (*Žytniamatka*);
the pretended child represents the Corn-baby, and
the whole ceremony is a charm to ensure a crop
next year.[3]   There are other folk-customs, observed both in spring and at harvest, with which
the legend of the begetting of the child Plutus
is probably still more intimately connected.   Their
general purport is to impart fertility to the fields by
performing, or at least mimicking, upon them the process of procreation.[4]   Another glimpse of the savage
under the civilised Demeter will be afforded farther
on, when we come to deal with another aspect of these
agricultural divinities.

The reader may have observed that in modern
folk-customs the corn-spirit is generally represented
either by a Corn-mother (Old Woman, etc.) or by a
Maiden (Corn-baby, etc.), not both by a Corn-mother

---

[1] Homer, *Od.* v. 125 *sqq.*; Hesiod,
Theog. 969 *sqq.*

[2] See above, p. 343 *sq.*

[3] It is possible that a ceremony performed in a Cyprian worship of Ariadne
may have been of this nature.   Plutarch, *Theseus*, 20, ἐν δὴ τῇ θυσίᾳ τοῦ
Γορπιαίου μηνὸς ἱσταμένου δευτέρα κατα-
κλινόμενόν τινα τῶν νεανίσκων φθέγγεσθαι
καὶ ποιεῖν ἅπερ ὠδινοῦσαι γυναῖκες.   We
have already seen grounds for regarding
Ariadne as a goddess or spirit of vegetation (above, p. 104).   If, however, the
reference is to the Syro-Macedonian
calendar, in which Gorpiaeus corresponds to September (Daremberg et
Saglio, i. 831), the ceremony could

not have been a harvest celebration, but
may have been a vintage one.   Amongst
the Minnitarees in North America, the
Prince of Neuwied saw a tall strong
woman pretend to bring up a stalk of
maize out of her stomach; the object
of the ceremony was to secure a good
crop of maize in the following year.
Maximilian, Prinz zu Wied, *Reise in
das innere Nord-Amerika*, ii. 269.

[4] W. Mannhardt, *Baumkultus*, pp.
468 *sq.*, 480 *sqq.*; *id., Antike Wald-
und Feldkulte*, p. 288 *sq.*; *id., Mythologische Forschungen*, pp. 146 *sqq.*, 340
sqq.; Van Hoëvell, *Ambon en de Oeliasers*, p. 62 *sq.*; Wilken, in *Indische
Gids*, June 1884, pp. 958, 963 *sq.* Cp.
Marco Polo, trans. Yule,[2] i. 212 *sq.*

and by a Maiden. Why then did the Greeks represent the corn both as a mother and a daughter? In the Breton custom the mother-sheaf—a large figure made out of the last sheaf with a small corn-doll inside of it—clearly represents both the Corn-mother and the Corn-daughter, the latter still unborn.[1] Again, in the Prussian custom just described, the woman who plays the part of Corn-mother represents the ripe corn; the child appears to represent next year's corn, which may be regarded, naturally enough, as the child of this year's corn, since it is from the seed of this year's harvest that next year's corn will spring. Demeter would thus be the ripe corn of this year; Proserpine the seed-corn taken from it and sown in autumn, to reappear in spring. The descent of Proserpine into the lower world[2] would thus be a mythical expression for the sowing of the seed; her reappearance in spring[3] would express the sprouting of the young corn. Thus the Proserpine of this year becomes the Demeter of the next, and this may very well have been the original form of the myth. But when with the advance of religious thought the corn came to be personified, no longer as a being that went through the whole cycle of birth, growth, reproduction, and death within a year, but as an immortal goddess, consistency requires that one of the two personifications, the mother or the daughter, should be sacrificed. But the double conception of the corn as mother and daughter was too old and too

---

[1] See above, p. 335 *sq.*

[2] Cp. Preller, *Griech. Mythol.*[3] i. 628, *note* 3. In Greece the annual descent of Proserpine appears to have taken place at the Great Eleusinian Mysteries and at the Thesmophoria, that is, about the time of the autumn sowing. But in Sicily her descent seems to have been celebrated when the corn was fully ripe (Diodorus, v. 4), that is, in summer.

[3] Homer, *Hymn to Demeter*, 401 *sqq.*; Preller, *l.c.*

deeply rooted in the popular mind to be eradicated by
logic, and so room had to be found in the reformed
myth both for mother and daughter. This was done
by assigning to Proserpine the rôle of the corn sown in
autumn and sprouting in spring, while Demeter was
left to play the somewhat vague and ill-defined part of
mother of the corn, who laments its annual disappearance underground, and rejoices over its reappearance
in spring. Thus instead of a regular succession of
divine beings, each living a year and then giving birth
to her successor, the reformed myth exhibits the conception of two divine and immortal beings, one of
whom annually disappears into and reappears from the
ground, while the other has little to do but to weep
and rejoice at the appropriate times.

This explanation of the double personification of
the corn in Greek myth assumes that both personifications (Demeter and Proserpine) are original.
But if we assume that the Greek myth started with a
single personification, the after-growth of a second
personification may perhaps be explained as follows.
On looking over the peasant harvest customs which
have been passed under review, it may be noticed that
they involve two distinct conceptions of the corn-
spirit. For whereas in some of the customs the corn-
spirit is treated as immanent in the corn, in others it is
regarded as external to it. Thus when a particular
sheaf is called by the name of the corn-spirit, and
is dressed in clothes and treated with reverence,[1]
the corn-spirit is clearly regarded as immanent in
the corn. But when the corn-spirit is said to make

---

[1] In some places it was customary
to kneel down before the last sheaf, in
others to kiss it. W. Mannhardt, *Korn-*
dämonen, 26; *id.*, *Mytholog. For-*
schungen, p. 339; *Folk-lore Journal*, vi.
270.

the corn grow by passing through it, or to blight the corn of those against whom she has a grudge,[1] she is clearly conceived as quite separate from, though exercising power over, the corn. Conceived in the latter way the corn-spirit is in a fair way to become a deity of the corn, if she has not become so already. Of these two conceptions, that of the corn-spirit as immanent in the corn is doubtless the older, since the view of nature as animated by indwelling spirits appears to have generally preceded the view of it as controlled by deities external to it ; to put it shortly, animism precedes deism. In the harvest customs of our European peasantry the conception of the corn-spirit as immanent appears to be the prevalent one ; the conception of it as external occurs rather as an exception. In Greek mythology, on the other hand, Demeter is distinctly conceived in the latter way ; she is the deity of the corn rather than the spirit immanent in it.[2] The process of thought which seems to be chiefly instrumental in producing the transition from the one mode of conception to the other is anthropomorphism, or the gradual investment of the immanent spirits with more and more of the attributes of humanity. As men emerge from savagery the tendency to anthropomorphise or humanise their divinities gains strength ; and the more anthropomorphic these become, the wider is the breach which severs them from those natural objects of which they were at first merely the animating spirits or souls. But in the progress upwards from savagery, men of the same generation do not march abreast ; and though the anthropomorphic gods may satisfy the religious wants

---

[1] Above, p. 332 *sq.*

[2] In the Homeric Hymn to Demeter, she is represented as controlling the growth of the corn. See above, p. 331.

of more advanced individuals, the more backward
members of the community will cling by preference to
the older animistic notions. Now when the spirit of
any natural object (as the corn) has been invested with
human qualities, detached from the object, and converted into a deity controlling it, the object itself is, by
the withdrawal of its spirit, left inanimate, it becomes,
so to say, a spiritual vacuum. But the popular fancy,
intolerant of such a vacuum, in other words, unable to
conceive anything as inanimate, immediately creates a
fresh mythical being, with which it peoples the vacant
object. Thus the same natural object is now represented in mythology by two separate beings ; first, by
the old spirit now separated from it and raised to the
rank of a deity ; second, by the new spirit, freshly
created by the popular fancy to supply the place
vacated by the old spirit on its elevation to a higher
sphere. The problem for mythology now is, having
got two separate personifications of the same object,
what to do with them ? How are their relations to
each other to be adjusted, and room found for both in
the mythological system ? When the old spirit or new
deity is conceived as creating or producing the object
in question, the problem is easily solved. Since the
object is believed to be produced by the old spirit, and
animated by the new one, the latter, as the soul of the
object, must also owe its existence to the former ; thus
the old spirit will stand to the new one as producer to
produced, that is (in mythology), as parent to child,
and if both spirits are conceived as female, their relation
will be that of mother and daughter. In this way, starting from a single personification of the corn as female,
mythology might in time reach a double personification
of it as mother and daughter. It would be very rash

to affirm that this was the way in which the myth of
Demeter and Proserpine actually took shape ; but it
seems a legitimate conjecture that the reduplication of
deities, of which Demeter and Proserpine furnish an
example, may sometimes have arisen in the way indicated.   For example, among the pairs of deities whom
we have been considering, it has been shown that
there are grounds for regarding both Isis and her
companion god Osiris as personifications of the corn.[1]
On the hypothesis just suggested, Isis would be the
old corn-spirit, and Osiris would be the newer one,
whose relationship to the old spirit was variously
explained as that of brother, husband, and son ;[2] for
of course mythology would always be free to account
for the coexistence of the two divinities in more ways
than one.   Further, this hypothesis offers at least a
possible explanation of the relation of Virbius to
the Arician Diana.   The latter, as we have seen,[3]
was a tree-goddess ; and if, as I have conjectured,
the Flamen Virbialis was no other than the priest
of Nemi himself, that is, the King of the Wood,
Virbius must also have been a tree-spirit.   On the
present hypothesis he was the newer tree-spirit,
whose relation to the old tree-spirit (Diana) was explained by representing him as her favourite or
lover.   It must not, however, be forgotten that this
proposed explanation of such pairs of deities as
Demeter and Proserpine, Isis and Osiris, Diana and
Virbius, is purely conjectural, and is only given for
what it is worth.

---

[1] See above, pp. 305 *sqq.*, 309 *sqq.*
[2] Pauly, *Real-Encyclopädie der class. Alterthumswiss.* v. 1011.
[3] Above, p. 105 *sq.*

§ 9.—*Lityerses*

In the preceding pages an attempt has been made to show that in the Corn-mother and harvest Maiden of Northern Europe we have the prototypes of Demeter and Proserpine. But an essential feature is still wanting to complete the resemblance. A leading incident in the Greek myth is the death and resurrection of Proserpine ; it is this incident which, coupled with the nature of the goddess as a deity of vegetation, links the myth with the cults of Adonis, Attis, Osiris, and Dionysus ; and it is in virtue of this incident that the myth is considered in this chapter. It remains, therefore, to see whether the conception of the annual death and resurrection of a god, which figures so prominently in these great Greek and Oriental worships, has not also its origin in the rustic rites observed by reapers and vine-dressers amongst the corn-shocks and the vines.

Our general ignorance of the popular superstitions and customs of the ancients has already been confessed. But the obscurity which thus hangs over the first beginnings of ancient religion is fortunately dissipated to some extent in the present case. The worships of Osiris, Adonis, and Attis had their respective seats, as we have seen, in Egypt, Syria, and Phrygia ; and in each of these countries certain harvest and vintage customs are known to have been observed, the resemblance of which to each other and to the national rites struck the ancients themselves, and, compared with the harvest customs of modern peasants and barbarians, seem to throw some light on the origin of the rites in question.

It has been already mentioned, on the authority of Diodorus, that in ancient Egypt the reapers were wont to lament over the first sheaf cut, invoking Isis as the goddess to whom they owed the discovery of corn.[1] To the plaintive song or cry sung or uttered by Egyptian reapers the Greeks gave the name of Maneros, and explained the name by a story that Maneros, the only son of the first Egyptian king, invented agriculture, and, dying an untimely death, was thus lamented by the people.[2] It appears, however, that the name Maneros is due to a misunderstanding of the formula *mââ-ne-hra*, " come thou back," which has been discovered in various Egyptian writings, for example in the dirge of Isis in the Book of the Dead.[3] Hence we may suppose that the cry *mââ-ne-hra* was chanted by the reapers over the cut corn as a dirge for the death of the corn-spirit (Isis or Osiris) and a prayer for its return. As the cry was raised over the first ears reaped, it would seem that the corn-spirit was believed by the Egyptians to be present in the first corn cut and to die under the sickle. We have seen that in Java the first ears of rice are taken to represent the Corn-bride and the Corn-bridegroom.[4] In parts of Russia the first sheaf is treated much in the same way that the last sheaf is treated elsewhere. It is reaped by the mistress herself, taken home and set in the place of honour near the holy pictures ; afterwards it is threshed separately, and some of its grain is mixed with the next year's seed-corn.[5]

---

[1] Diodorus, i. 14, ἔτι γὰρ καὶ νῦν κατὰ τὸν θερισμὸν τοὺς πρώτους ἀμηθέντας στάχυς θέντας τοὺς ἀνθρώπους κόπτεσθαι πλησίον τοῦ δράγματος κ.τ.λ. For θέντας we should perhaps read σύνθεντας, which is supported by the following δράγματος.

[2] Herodotus, ii. 79 ; Pollux, iv. 54 ; Pausanias, ix. 29 ; Athenaeus, 620 A.

[3] Brugsch, *Adonisklage und Linoslied*, p. 24.

[4] Above, p. 355.

[5] Ralston, *Songs of the Russian People*, p. 249 *sq.*

In Phoenicia and Western Asia a plaintive song, like that chanted by the Egyptian corn-reapers, was sung at the vintage and probably (to judge by analogy) also at harvest. This Phoenician song was called by the Greeks Linus or Ailinus and explained, like Maneros, as a lament for the death of a youth named Linus.[1] According to one story Linus was brought up by a shepherd, but torn to pieces by his dogs.[2] But, like Maneros, the name Linus or Ailinus appears to have originated in a verbal misunderstanding, and to be nothing more than the cry *ai lanu*, that is " woe to us," which the Phoenicians probably uttered in mourning for Adonis;[3] at least Sappho seems to have regarded Adonis and Linus as equivalent.[4]

In Bithynia a like mournful ditty, called Bormus or Borimus, was chanted by Mariandynian reapers. Bormus was said to have been a handsome youth, the son of King Upias or of a wealthy and distinguished man. One summer day, watching the reapers at work in his fields, he went to fetch them a drink of water and was never heard of more. So the reapers sought for him, calling him in plaintive strains, which they continued to use ever afterwards.[5]

In Phrygia the corresponding song, sung by harvesters both at reaping and at threshing, was called Lityerses. According to one story, Lityerses was a bastard son of Midas, King of Phrygia. He used to reap the corn, and had an enormous appetite. When a stranger happened to enter the corn-field or to pass

---

[1] Homer, *Il.* xviii. 570; Herodotus, ii. 79; Pausanias, ix. 29; Conon, *Narrat.* 19. For the form Ailinus see Suidas, *s.v.*; Euripides, *Orestes*, 1395; Sophocles, *Ajax*, 627. Cp. Moschus, *Idyl.* iii. 1; Callimachus, *Hymn to Apollo*, 20.

[2] Conon, *l.c.*

[3] W. Mannhardt, *A. W. F.* p. 281.

[4] Pausanias, *l.c.*

[5] Pollux, iv. 54; Athenaeus, 619 F, 620 A; Hesychius, *svv.* Βῶρμον and Μαριανδυνὸς θρῆνος.

by it, Lityerses gave him plenty to eat and drink, then took him to the corn-fields on the banks of the Maeander and compelled him to reap along with him. Lastly, he used to wrap the stranger in a sheaf, cut off his head with a sickle, and carry away his body, wrapt in the corn stalks. But at last he was himself slain by Hercules, who threw his body into the river.[1] As Hercules was probably reported to have slain Lityerses in the same way that Lityerses slew others (as Theseus treated Sinis and Sciron), we may infer that Lityerses used to throw the bodies of his victims into the river. According to another version of the story, Lityerses, a son of Midas, used to challenge people to a reaping match with him, and if he vanquished them he used to thrash them ; but one day he met with a stronger reaper, who slew him.[2]

There are some grounds for supposing that in these stories of Lityerses we have the description of a Phrygian harvest custom in accordance with which certain persons, especially strangers passing the harvest field, were regularly regarded as embodiments of the corn-spirit and as such were seized by the reapers, wrapt in sheaves, and beheaded, their bodies, bound up in the corn-stalks, being afterwards thrown into water as a rain-charm. The grounds for this supposition are, first, the resemblance of the Lityerses story to the harvest customs of European peasantry, and, second, the fact that human beings have been commonly killed by savage races to promote the fertility of the fields. We

---

[1] The story was told by Sositheus in his play of *Daphnis*. His verses have been preserved in the tract of an anonymous writer. See *Scriptores rerum mirabilium*, ed. Westermann, p. 220 ; also Athenaeus, 415 B ; Schol. on Theocritus, x. 41 ; Photius, Suidas, and Hesychius, *s.v. Lityerses* ; Apostolius, x. 74. Photius mentions the sickle. Lityerses is the subject of a special study by Mannhardt (*Mythologische Forschungen*, p. 1 sqq.), whom I follow.

[2] Pollux, iv. 54.

will examine these grounds successively, beginning with the former.

In comparing the story with the harvest customs of Europe,[1] three points deserve special attention, namely: I. the reaping match and the binding of persons in the sheaves; II. the killing of the corn-spirit or his representatives; III. the treatment of visitors to the harvest-field or of strangers passing it.

I. In regard to the first head, we have seen that in modern Europe the person who cuts or binds or threshes the last sheaf is often exposed to rough treatment at the hands of his fellow-labourers. For example, he is bound up in the last sheaf, and, thus encased, is carried or carted about, beaten, drenched with water, thrown on a dunghill, etc. Or, if he is spared this horseplay, he is at least the subject of ridicule or is believed destined to suffer some misfortune in the course of the year. Hence the harvesters are naturally reluctant to give the last cut at reaping or the last stroke at threshing or to bind the last sheaf, and towards the close of the work this reluctance produces an emulation among the labourers, each striving to finish his task as fast as possible, in order that he may escape the invidious distinction of being last.[2] For example, in the neighbourhood of Danzig, when the winter corn is cut and mostly bound up in sheaves, the portion which still remains to be bound is divided amongst the women binders, each of whom

---

[1] In this comparison I closely follow Mannhardt, *Myth. Forsch.* p. 18 *sqq.*

[2] Cp. above, p. 340. On the other hand, the last sheaf is sometimes an object of desire and emulation. See p. 336. It is so at Balquhidder also, *Folk-lore Journal*, vi. 269; and it was formerly so on the Gareloch, Dumbartonshire, where there was a competition for the honour of cutting it, several handfuls of standing corn being concealed under sheaves.—(From the information of Archie Leitch. See note on p. 345).

receives a swath of equal length to bind. A crowd of reapers, children, and idlers gathers round to witness the contest, and at the word, " Seize the Old Man," the women fall to work, all binding their allotted swaths as hard as they can. The spectators watch them narrowly, and the woman who cannot keep pace with the rest and consequently binds the last sheaf has to carry the Old Man (that is, the last sheaf made up in the form of a man) to the farmhouse and deliver it to the farmer with the words, "Here I bring you the Old Man." At the supper which follows, the Old Man is placed at the table and receives an abundant portion of food which, as he cannot eat it, falls to the share of the woman who carried him. Afterwards the Old Man is placed in the yard and all the people dance round him. Or the woman who bound the last sheaf dances for a good while with the Old Man, while the rest form a ring round them ; afterwards they all, one after the other, dance a single round with him. Further, the woman who bound the last sheaf goes herself by the name of the Old Man till the next harvest, and is often mocked with the cry, " Here comes the Old Man."[1] At Aschbach, Bavaria, when the reaping is nearly finished, the reapers say, " Now we will drive out the Old Man." Each of them sets himself to reap a patch of corn and reaps as fast as he can ; he who cuts the last handful or the last stalk is greeted by the rest with an exulting cry, " You have the Old Man." Sometimes a black mask is fastened on the reaper's face and he is dressed in woman's clothes ; or if the reaper is a woman, she is dressed in man's clothes ; a dance follows. At the supper the Old Man gets twice as large a portion of food as the others. At threshing, the proceedings are the same ;

---

[1] W. Mannhardt, *Myth. Forsch.* p. 19 *sq.*

the person who gives the last stroke is said to have the Old Man.[1]

These examples illustrate the contests in reaping, threshing, and binding which take place amongst the harvesters, on account of their unwillingness to suffer the ridicule and personal inconvenience attaching to the individual who happens to finish his work last. It will be remembered that the person who is last at reaping, binding, or threshing, is regarded as the representative of the corn-spirit,[2] and this idea is more fully expressed by binding him or her in corn-stalks. The latter custom has been already illustrated, but a few more instances may be added. At Kloxin, near Stettin, the harvesters call out to the woman who binds the last sheaf, "You have the Old Man, and must keep him." The Old Man is a great bundle of corn decked with flowers and ribbons, and fashioned into a rude semblance of the human form. It is fastened on a rake or strapped on a horse, and brought with music to the village. In delivering the Old Man to the farmer, the woman says—

> "Here, dear Sir, is the Old Man.
> He can stay no longer on the field,
> He can hide himself no longer,
> He must come into the village.
> Ladies and gentlemen, pray be so kind
> As to give the Old Man a present."

Forty or fifty years ago the custom was to tie up the woman herself in pease-straw, and bring her with music to the farmhouse, where the harvesters danced with her till the pease-straw fell off.[3] In other villages round Stettin, when the last harvest-waggon is being loaded, there is a regular race amongst the women,

---

[1] W. Mannhardt, *Myth. Forsch.* p. 20; Panzer, *Beitrag zur deutschen Mythologie*, ii. 217.

[2] Above, p. 346 *sq.*

[3] W. Mannhardt, *Myth. Forsch.* p. 22.

each striving not to be last.   For she who places
the last sheaf on the waggon is called the Old Man,
and is completely swathed in corn-stalks ; she is also
decked with flowers, and flowers and a helmet of straw
are placed on her head.   In solemn procession she
carries the harvest-crown to the squire, over whose
head she holds it while she utters a string of good
wishes.   At the dance which follows, the Old Man
has the right to choose his (or rather her) partner ;
it is an honour to dance with him.[1]   At Blankenfelde,
in the district of Potsdam, the woman who binds the
last sheaf at the rye-harvest is saluted with the cry,
"You have the Old Man."   A woman is then tied
up in the last sheaf in such a way that only her
head is left free ; her hair also is covered with a
cap made of rye-stalks, adorned with ribbons and
flowers.   She is called the Harvest-man, and must keep
dancing in front of the last harvest-waggon till it reaches
the squire's house, where she receives a present, and is
released from her envelope of corn.[2]   At Gommern,
near Magdeburg, the reaper who cuts the last ears
of corn is often wrapt up in corn-stalks so completely
that it is hard to see whether there is a man in the
bundle or not.   Thus wrapt up he is taken by another
stalwart reaper on his back, and carried round the
field amid the joyous cries of the harvesters.[3]   At
Neuhausen, near Merseburg, the person who binds the
last sheaf is wrapt in ears of oats and saluted as
the Oats-man, whereupon the others dance round
him.[4]   At Brie, Isle de France, the farmer himself
is tied up in the *first* sheaf.[5]   At the harvest-home
at Udvarhely, Transylvania, a person is encased in

---

[1] W. Mannhardt, *Myth. Forsch.* p. 22.   [3] *Ib.* p. 23.   [5] *Ib.* p. 24.
[2] *Ib.* p. 22 *sq.*   [4] *Ib.* p. 23 *sq.*

corn - stalks, and wears on his head a crown made out of the last ears cut. On reaching the village he is soused with water over and over.[1] At Dingelstedt, in the district of Erfurt, about fifty years ago it was the custom to tie up a man in the last sheaf. He was called the Old Man, and was brought home on the last waggon, amid huzzas and music. On reaching the farmyard he was rolled round the barn and drenched with water.[2] At Nördlingen, Bavaria, the man who gives the last stroke at threshing is wrapt in straw and rolled on the threshing - floor.[3] In some parts of Oberpfalz, Bavaria, he is said to "get the Old Man," is wrapt in straw, and carried to a neighbour who has not yet finished his threshing.[4] In Thüringen a sausage is stuck in the last sheaf at threshing, and thrown, with the sheaf, on the threshing-floor. It is called the *Barrenwurst* or *Banzenwurst*, and is eaten by all the threshers. After they have eaten it a man is encased in pease-straw, and thus attired is led through the village.[5]

"In all these cases the idea is that the spirit of the corn—the Old Man of vegetation—is driven out of the corn last cut or last threshed, and lives in the barn during the winter. At sowing-time he goes out again to the fields to resume his activity as animating force among the sprouting corn."[6]

Much the same ideas are attached to the last corn in India; for we are told that in the Central Provinces, "when the reaping is nearly done, about a *bisvá*, say a rood of land, of corn is left standing in the culti-

---

[1] W. Mannhardt, *Myth. Forsch.* p. 24.
[2] *Ib.* p. 24.   [3] *Ib.* p. 24 *sq.*
[4] *Ib.* p. 25.

[5] Witzschel, *Sagen, Sitten und Gebräuche aus Thüringen*, p. 223.
[6] W. Mannhardt, *op. cit.* p. 25 *sq.*

vator's last field, and the reapers rest a little. Then
they rush at this *bisvá*, tear it up, and cast it into the
air, shouting victory to Omkár Maháráj or Jhámájí,
or Rámjí Dás, etc., according to their respective
possessions. A sheaf is made up of this corn, tied
to a bamboo, and stuck up in the last harvest cart, and
carried home in triumph. It is fastened up in the
threshing-floor to a tree, or to the cattle-shed, where
its services are essential in averting the evil-eye." [1]

II. Passing to the second point of comparison
between the Lityerses story and European harvest
customs, we have now to see that in the latter the corn-
spirit is often believed to be killed at reaping or threshing. In the Romsdal and other parts of Norway, when
the haymaking is over, the people say that " the Old
Hay-man has been killed." In some parts of Bavaria
the man who gives the last stroke at threshing is said
to have killed the Corn-man, the Oats-man, or the
Wheat-man, according to the crop.[2] In the Canton of
Tillot, in Lothringen, at threshing the last corn the
men keep time with their flails, calling out as they
thresh, "We are killing the Old Woman! We are
killing the Old Woman!" If there is an old woman
in the house she is warned to save herself, or she will
be struck dead.[3] In Lithuania, near Ragnit, the last
handful of corn is left standing by itself, with the
words, " The Old Woman (*Boba*) is sitting in there."
Then a young reaper whets his scythe, and, with a
strong sweep, cuts down the handful. It is now said
of him that " He has cut off the Boba's head ;" and he
receives a gratuity from the farmer and a jugful of

---

[1] C. A. Elliot, *Hoshangábád Settlement Report*, p. 178, quoted in *Panjab
Notes and Queries*, iii. Nos. 8, 168.

[2] W. Mannhardt, *Myth. Forsch.* p.
31.
[3] *Ib.* p. 334.

water over his head from the farmer's wife.[1] According to another account, every Lithuanian reaper makes haste to finish his task ; for the Old Rye-woman lives in the last stalks, and whoever cuts the last stalks kills the Old Rye-woman, and by killing her he brings trouble on himself.[2] In Wilkischken (district of Tilsit) the man who cuts the last corn goes by the name of " The killer of the Rye-woman."[3] In Lithuania, again, the corn-spirit is believed to be killed at threshing as well as at reaping. When only a single pile of corn remains to be threshed, all the threshers suddenly step back a few paces, as if at the word of command. Then they fall to work plying their flails with the utmost rapidity and vehemence, till they come to the last bundle. Upon this they fling themselves with almost frantic fury, straining every nerve, and raining blows on it till the word " Halt ! " rings out sharply from the leader. The man whose flail is the last to fall after the command to stop has been given is immediately surrounded by all the rest, crying out that " He has struck the Old Rye-woman dead." He has to expiate the deed by treating them to brandy ; and, like the man who cuts the last corn, he is known as " The killer of the Old Rye - woman." [4] Sometimes in Lithuania the slain corn-spirit was represented by a puppet. Thus a female figure was made out of corn-stalks, dressed in clothes, and placed on the threshing-floor, under the heap of corn which was to be threshed last. Whoever thereafter gave the last stroke at threshing " struck the Old Woman dead."[5] We have already had examples of burning the figure which represents the corn-spirit.[6] Some-

---

[1] W. Mannhardt, *Myth. Forsch.* p. 330.   [2] *Ib.*   [3] *Ib.* p. 331.   [4] *Ib.* p. 335.   [5] *Ib.* p. 335.   [6] Above, pp. 335, 341, 350.

times, again, the corn-spirit is represented by a man, who lies down under the last corn ; it is threshed upon his body, and the people say that "the Old Man is being beaten to death." [1] We have already seen that sometimes the farmer's wife is thrust, together with the last sheaf, under the threshing-machine, as if to thresh her, and that afterwards a pretence is made of winnowing her. [2] At Volders, in the Tyrol, husks of corn are stuck behind the neck of the man who gives the last stroke at threshing, and he is throttled with a straw garland. If he is tall, it is believed that the corn will be tall next year. Then he is tied on a bundle and flung into the river. [3] In Carinthia, the thresher who gave the last stroke, and the person who untied the last sheaf on the threshing-floor, are bound hand and foot with straw bands, and crowns of straw are placed on their heads. Then they are tied, face to face, on a sledge, dragged through the village, and flung into a brook. [4] The custom of throwing the representative of the corn-spirit into a stream, like that of drenching him with water, is, as usual, a rain-charm. [5]

III. Thus far the representatives of the corn-spirit have generally been the man or woman who cuts, binds, or threshes the last corn. We now come to the cases in which the corn-spirit is represented either by a stranger passing the harvest-field (as in the Lityerses tale), or by a visitor entering it for the first time. All over Germany it is customary for the reapers or threshers to lay hold of passing strangers and bind them with a rope made of corn-stalks, till

---

[1] W. Mannhardt, *Korndäm.*, p. 26.
[2] Above, p. 343.
[3] W. Mannhardt, *M. F.* p. 50.
[4] *Ib.* p. 50 *sq.*
[5] See above, pp. 286 *sq.*, 333, 337, 340, 341.

they pay a forfeit; and when the farmer himself or one
of his guests enters the field or the threshing-floor for
the first time, he is treated in the same way. Sometimes the rope is only tied round his arm or his feet
or his neck.[1] But sometimes he is regularly swathed
in corn. Thus at Solör in Norway, whoever enters
the field, be he the master or a stranger, is tied up
in a sheaf and must pay a ransom. In the neighbourhood of Soest, when the farmer visits the
flax-pullers for the first time, he is completely
enveloped in flax. Passers-by are also surrounded by
the women, tied up in flax, and compelled to stand
brandy.[2] At Nördlingen strangers are caught with
straw ropes and tied up in a sheaf till they pay a
forfeit. At Brie, Isle de France, when any one who
does not belong to the farm passes by the harvest-field,
the reapers give chase. If they catch him, they bind
him in a sheaf and bite him, one after the other, in the
forehead, crying "You shall carry the key of the
field."[3] "To have the key" is an expression used
by harvesters elsewhere in the sense of to cut or bind
or thresh the last sheaf;[4] hence, it is equivalent to
the phrases "You have the Old Man," "You are the

---

[1] W. Mannhardt, *op. cit.* p. 32 *sqq.*
Cp. *Revue des Traditions populaires*, iii.
598.
[2] W. Mannhardt, *Mythol. Forsch.* p.
35 *sq.*
[3] *Ib.* p. 36.
[4] For the evidence, see *ib.* p. 36,
note 2. The idea which lies at the
bottom of the phrase seems to be
explained by the following Cingalese
custom. "There is a curious custom
of the threshing-floor called 'Goigote'
—the tying of the cultivator's knot.
When a sheaf of corn has been threshed
out, before it is removed the grain is
heaped up and the threshers, generally
six in number, sit round it, and taking

a few stalks, with the ears of corn
attached, jointly tie a knot and bury it
in the heap. It is left there until all
the sheaves have been threshed and the
corn winnowed and measured. The
object of this ceremony is to prevent
the devils from diminishing the quantity
of corn in the heap." C. J. R. Le
Mesurier, "Customs and Superstitions
connected with the Cultivation of Rice
in the Southern Province of Ceylon,"
in *Journal of the Royal Asiatic Society*,
N.S., xvii. (1885) 371. The "key" in
the European custom is probably intended to serve the same purpose
as the "knot" in the Cingalese
custom.

Old Man," which are addressed to the cutter, binder, or thresher of the last sheaf. Therefore, when a stranger, as at Brie, is tied up in a sheaf and told that he will "carry the key of the field," it is as much as to say that he is the Old Man, that is, an embodiment of the corn-spirit.

Thus, like Lityerses, modern reapers lay hold of a passing stranger and tie him up in a sheaf. It is not to be expected that they should complete the parallel by cutting off his head; but if they do not take such a strong step, their language and gestures are at least indicative of a desire to do so. For instance, in Mecklenburg on the first day of reaping, if the master or mistress or a stranger enters the field, or merely passes by it, all the mowers face towards him and sharpen their scythes, clashing their whet-stones against them in unison, as if they were making ready to mow. Then the woman who leads the mowers steps up to him and ties a band round his left arm. He must ransom himself by payment of a forfeit.[1] Near Ratzeburg when the master or other person of mark enters the field or passes by it, all the harvesters stop work and march towards him in a body, the men with their scythes in front. On meeting him they form up in line, men and women. The men stick the poles of their scythes in the ground, as they do in whetting them; then they take off their caps and hang them on the scythes, while their leader stands forward and makes a speech. When he has done, they all whet their scythes in measured time very loudly, after which they put on their caps. Two of the women binders then come forward; one of them ties the master or stranger (as the case may be) with corn-ears

---

[1] W. Mannhardt, *op. cit.* p. 39.

or with a silken band ; the other delivers a rhyming address.   The following are specimens of the speeches made by the reaper on these occasions.   In some parts of Pomerania every passer-by is stopped, his way being barred with a corn-rope.   The reapers form a circle round him and sharpen their scythes, while their leader says—

> " The men are ready,
> The scythes are bent,
> The corn is great and small,
> The gentleman must be mowed."

Then the process of whetting the scythes is repeated.[1] At Ramin, in the district of Stettin, the stranger, standing encircled by the reapers, is thus addressed—

> " We'll stroke the gentleman
> With our naked sword,
> Wherewith we shear meadows and fields.
> We shear princes and lords.
> Labourers are often athirst ;
> If the gentleman will stand beer and brandy
> The joke will soon be over.
> But, if our prayer he does not like,
> The sword has a right to strike." [2]

That in these customs the whetting of the scythes is really meant as a preliminary to mowing appears from the following variation of the preceding customs. In the district of Lüneburg when any one enters the harvest-field, he is asked whether he will engage a good fellow.   If he says yes, the harvesters mow some swaths, yelling and screaming, and then ask him for drink-money.[3]

On the threshing-floor strangers are also regarded as embodiments of the corn-spirit, and are treated

---

[1] W. Mannhardt, *Myth. Forsch.* p. 39 *sq.*

[2] *Ib.* p. 40.   For the speeches made by the woman who binds the stranger or the master, see *ib.* p. 41 ; Lemke, *Volksthümliches in Ostpreussen,* i. 23 *sq.*

[3] W. Mannhardt, *Myth. Forsch.* p. 41 *sq.*

accordingly.   At Wiedingharde in Schleswig when a
stranger comes to the threshing-floor he is asked
"Shall I teach you the flail-dance?"   If he says yes,
they put the arms of the threshing-flail round his neck
(as if he were a sheaf of corn), and press them together
so tightly that he is nearly choked.[1]   In some parishes
of Wermland (Sweden) when a stranger enters the
threshing-floor where the threshers are at work, they
say that "they will teach him the threshing-song."
Then they put a flail round his neck and a straw rope
about his body.   Also, as we have seen, if a stranger
woman enters the threshing-floor, the threshers put
a flail round her body and a wreath of corn-stalks
round her neck, and call out, " See the Corn-woman !
See ! that is how the Corn-maiden looks !"[2]

In these customs, observed both on the harvest-
field and on the threshing-floor, a passing stranger is
regarded as a personification of the corn, in other
words, as the corn-spirit; and a show is made of
treating him like the corn by mowing, binding, and
threshing him.   If the reader still doubts whether
European peasants can really regard a passing stranger
in this light, the following custom should set their
doubts at rest.   During the madder-harvest in the
Dutch province of Zealand a stranger passing by a
field where the people are digging the madder-roots
will sometimes call out to them *Koortspillers* (a term
of reproach).   Upon this, two of the fleetest runners

---

[1] W. Mannhardt, *op. cit.* p. 42.

[2] *Ib.* p. 42. See above, p. 343. In
Thüringen a being called the Rush-
cutter used to be much dreaded. On
the morning of St. John's Day he was
wont to walk through the fields with
sickles tied to his ankles cutting avenues
in the corn as he walked. To detect
him, seven bundles of brushwood were
silently threshed with the flail on the
threshing-floor, and the stranger who
appeared at the door of the barn during
the threshing was the Rush-cutter.
Witzschel, *Sagen, Sitten und Gebräuche aus Thüringen*, p. 221. With
the *Binsenschneider* compare the *Bil-
schneider.* Panzer, *Beitrag zur deutschen
Mythologie*, ii. 210 *sq.*

make after him, and, if they catch him, they bring him back to the madder-field and bury him in the earth up to his middle at least, jeering at him the while; then they ease nature before his face.[1] This last act is to be explained as follows. The spirit of the corn and of other cultivated plants is sometimes conceived, not as immanent in the plant, but as its owner; hence the cutting of the corn at harvest, the digging of the roots, and the gathering of fruit from the fruit-trees are each and all of them acts of spoliation, which strip him of his property and reduce him to poverty. Hence he is often known as "the Poor Man" or "the Poor Woman." Thus in the neighbourhood of Eisenach a small sheaf is sometimes left standing on the field for "the Poor Old Woman."[2] At Marksuhl, near Eisenach, the puppet formed out of the last sheaf is itself called "the Poor Woman." At

---

[1] W. Mannhardt, *op. cit.* p. 47 *sq.*

[2] *Ib.* p. 48. To prevent a rationalistic explanation of this custom, which, like most rationalistic explanations of folk-custom, would be wrong, it may be pointed out that a little of the crop is sometimes left on the field for the spirit under other names than "the Poor Old Woman." Thus in a village of the Tilsit district, the last sheaf was left standing on the field "for the Old Rye-woman." *M. F.* p. 337. In Neftenbach (Canton of Zürich) the first three ears of corn reaped are thrown away on the field "to satisfy the Cornmother and to make the next year's crop abundant." *Ib.* In Thüringen when the after-grass (*Grummet*) is being got in, a little heap is left lying on the field; it belongs to "the Little Wood-woman" in return for the blessing she has bestowed. Witzschel, *Sagen, Sitten una Gebräuche aus Thüringen*, p. 224. At Kupferberg, Bavaria, some corn is left standing on the field when the rest has been cut. Of this corn left standing, they say

that "it belongs to the Old Woman," to whom it is dedicated in the following words—

"We give it to the Old Woman;
She shall keep it.
Next year may she be to us
As kind as this time she has been."

M. F. p. 337 *sq.* These last expressions are quite conclusive. See also Mannhardt, *Korndämonen*, p. 7 *sq.* In Russia a patch of unreaped corn is left in the field and the ears are knotted together; this is called "the plaiting of the beard of Volos." "The unreaped patch is looked upon as tabooed; and it is believed that if any one meddles with it he will shrivel up, and become twisted like the interwoven ears." Ralston, *Songs of the Russian People*, p. 251. In the Northeast of Scotland a few stalks were sometimes left unreaped for the benefit of "the aul' man." W. Gregor, *Folk-lore of the North-East of Scotland*, p. 182. Here "the aul' man" is probably the equivalent of the Old Man (*der Alte*) of Germany.

Alt Lest in Silesia the man who binds the last sheaf is called the Beggar-man.[1]   In a village near Roeskilde, in Zealand (Denmark), old-fashioned peasants sometimes make up the last sheaf into a rude puppet, which is called the Rye-beggar.[2]   In Southern Schonen the sheaf which is bound last is called the Beggar; it is made bigger than the rest and is sometimes dressed in clothes.   In the district of Olmütz the last sheaf is called the Beggar; it is given to an old woman, who must carry it home, limping on one foot.[3]   Thus when the corn-spirit is conceived as a being who is robbed of his store and impoverished by the harvesters, it is natural that his representative—the passing stranger— should upbraid them; and it is equally natural that they should seek to disable him from pursuing them and recapturing the stolen property.   Now, it is an old superstition that by easing nature on the spot where a robbery is committed, the robbers secure themselves, for a certain time, against interruption.[4]   The fact, therefore, that the madder-diggers resort to this proceeding in presence of the stranger proves that they consider themselves robbers and him as the person robbed.   Regarded as such, he must be the natural owner of the madder-roots; that is, their spirit or demon; and this conception is carried out by burying him, like the madder-roots, in the ground.[5] The Greeks, it may be observed, were quite familiar with the idea that a passing stranger may be a god. Homer says that the gods in the likeness of foreigners roam up and down cities.[6]

---

[1] *M. F.* p. 48.

[2] *Ib.* p. 48 *sq.*   [3] *Ib.* p. 49.

[4] *Ib.* p. 49 *sq.*; Wuttke, *Der deutsche Volksaberglaube,*[2] § 400; Töppen, *Aberglaube aus Masuren,*[2] p. 57.

[5] The explanation of the custom is Mannhardt's.   *M. F.* p. 49.

[6] *Odyssey,* xvii. 485 *sqq.*   Cp. Plato, *Sophist,* 216 A.

Portrait of a Dyak youth of Borneo.

Two portrayals of a Mexican human sacrifice *(bas reliefs)*.

Thus in these harvest-customs of modern Europe the person who cuts, binds, or threshes the last corn is treated as an embodiment of the corn-spirit by being wrapt up in sheaves, killed in mimicry by agricultural implements, and thrown into the water.[1] These coincidences with the Lityerses story seem to prove that the latter is a genuine description of an old Phrygian harvest-custom. But since in the modern parallels the killing of the personal representative of the corn-spirit is necessarily omitted or at most enacted only in mimicry, it is necessary to show that in rude society human beings have been commonly killed as an agricultural ceremony to promote the fertility of the fields. The following examples will make this plain.

The Indians of Guayaquil (Ecuador) used to sacrifice human blood and the hearts of men when they sowed their fields.[2] At a Mexican harvest-festival, when the first-fruits of the season were offered to the sun, a criminal was placed between two immense stones, balanced opposite each other, and was crushed by them as they fell together. His remains were buried, and a feast and dance followed. This sacrifice was known as " the meeting of the stones."[3] Another series of human sacrifices offered in Mexico to make the maize thrive has been already referred to.[4] The Pawnees annually sacrificed a human victim in spring when they sowed their fields. The sacrifice was believed to have been enjoined on them by the Morning Star, or by a certain bird which the Morning

---

[1] For throwing him into the water, see p. 374.

[2] Cieza de Leon, *Travels*, translated by Markham, p. 203 (Hakluyt Society, 1864).

[3] Brasseur de Bourbourg, *Histoire des Nations civilisées du Mexique*, i. 274 ; Bancroft, *Native Races of the Pacific States*, ii. 340.

[4] Bastian, *Die Culturländer des alten Amerika*, ii. 639 (quoting Herrara). See above, p. 307.

Star had sent to them as its messenger. The bird was stuffed and preserved as a powerful "medicine." They thought that an omission of this sacrifice would be followed by the total failure of the crops of maize, beans, and pumpkins. The victim was a captive of either sex. He was clad in the gayest and most costly attire, was fattened on the choicest food, and carefully kept in ignorance of his doom. When he was fat enough, they bound him to a cross in the presence of the multitude, danced a solemn dance, then cleft his head with a tomahawk and shot him with arrows. According to one trader, the squaws then cut pieces of flesh from the victim's body, with which they greased their hoes; but this was denied by another trader who had been present at the ceremony. Immediately after the sacrifice the people proceeded to plant their fields. A particular account has been preserved of the sacrifice of a Sioux girl by the Pawnees in April 1837 or 1838. The girl had been kept for six months and well treated. Two days before the sacrifice she was led from wigwam to wigwam, accompanied by the whole council of chiefs and warriors. At each lodge she received a small billet of wood and a little paint, which she handed to the warrior next to her. In this way she called at every wigwam, receiving at each the same present of wood and paint. On the 22d of April she was taken out to be sacrificed, attended by the warriors, each of whom carried two pieces of wood which he had received from her hands. She was burned for some time over a slow fire, and then shot to death with arrows. The chief sacrificer next tore out her heart and devoured it. While her flesh was still warm it was cut in small pieces from the bones, put in little baskets, and taken to a neighbouring corn-field. Here the head chief took a piece of the flesh from a basket and squeezed a drop of blood upon the newly-deposited grains of corn. His example was followed by the rest, till all the seed had been sprinkled with the blood; it was then covered up with earth.[1]

A West African queen used to sacrifice a man and woman in the month of March. They were killed with spades and hoes, and their bodies buried in the middle of a field which had just been tilled.[2] At Lagos in Guinea it was the custom annually to impale a young girl alive soon after the spring equinox in order to secure good crops. Along with her were sacrificed sheep and goats, which, with yams, heads of maize, and plantains, were hung on stakes on each side of her. The victims were bred up for the purpose in the king's seraglio, and their minds had been so powerfully wrought upon by the fetish men that they went cheerfully to their fate.[3] A similar sacrifice is still annually offered at Benin, Guinea.[4] The Marimos, a Bechuana tribe, sacrifice a human being for the crops. The victim chosen is generally a short, stout man. He is seized by violence or intoxicated and taken to the fields, where he is killed amongst the wheat to serve as "seed" (so they phrase it). After his blood has coagulated in the sun it is burned along with the frontal bone, the flesh attached to it, and the brain;

---

[1] E. James, *Account of an Expedition from Pittsburgh to the Rocky Mountains*, ii. 80 *sq.*; Schoolcraft, *Indian Tribes*, v. 77 *sqq.*; De Smet, *Voyages aux Montagnes Rocheuses*, nouvelle ed. 1873, p. 121 *sqq.* The accounts by Schoolcraft and De Smet of the sacrifice of the Sioux girl are independent and supplement each other.

[2] Labat, *Relation historique de l'Ethiopie occidentale*, i. 380.

[3] John Adams, *Sketches taken during Ten Voyages in Africa between the years* 1786 *and* 1800, p. 25.

[4] P. Bouche, *La Côte des Esclaves*, p. 132.

the ashes are then scattered over the ground to fertilise it.   The rest of the body is eaten.[1]

The Gonds of India, a Dravidian race, kidnapped Brahman boys, and kept them as victims to be sacrificed on various occasions.   At sowing and reaping, after a triumphal procession, one of the lads was slain by being punctured with a poisoned arrow.   His blood was then sprinkled over the ploughed field or the ripe crop, and his flesh was devoured.[2]

But the best known case of human sacrifices, systematically offered to ensure good crops, is supplied by the Khonds or Kandhs, another Dravidian race in Bengal.   Our knowledge of them is derived from the accounts written by British officers who, forty or fifty years ago, were engaged in putting them down.[3]   The sacrifices were offered to the Earth Goddess, Tari Pennu or Bera Pennu, and were believed to ensure good crops and immunity from all disease and accidents.   In particular, they were considered necessary in the cultivation of turmeric, the Khonds arguing that the turmeric could not have a deep red colour without the shedding of blood.[4]   The victim or Meriah was acceptable to the goddess only if he had been purchased, or had been born a victim—that is, the son of a victim father—or had been devoted as a child by his father or guardian.   Khonds in distress often sold their children for victims, " considering the beatification of their souls certain, and their death, for the benefit of mankind, the most honourable possible."

---

[1] Arbousset et Daumas, *Voyage d'exploration au Nord-est de la Colonie du Cap de Bonne-Esperance*, p. 117 *sq.*
[2] *Panjab Notes and Queries*, ii. No. 721.

[3] Major S. C. Macpherson, *Memorials of Service in India*, p. 113 *sq.*; Major-General John Campbell, *Wild Tribes of Khondistan*, pp. 52-58, etc.
[4] J. Campbell, *op. cit.* p. 56.

A man of the Panua tribe was once seen to load a Khond with curses, and finally to spit in his face, because the Khond had sold for a victim his own child, whom the Panua had wished to marry. A party of Khonds, who saw this, immediately pressed forward to comfort the seller of his child, saying, " Your child has died that all the world may live, and the Earth Goddess herself will wipe that spittle from your face."[1] The victims were often kept for years before they were sacrificed. Being regarded as consecrated beings, they were treated with extreme affection, mingled with deference, and were welcomed wherever they went. A Meriah youth, on attaining maturity, was generally given a wife, who was herself usually a Meriah or victim; and with her he received a portion of land and farm-stock. Their offspring were also victims. Human sacrifices were offered to the Earth Goddess by tribes, branches of tribes, or villages, both at periodical festivals and on extraordinary occasions. The periodical sacrifices were generally so arranged by tribes and divisions of tribes that each head of a family was enabled, at least once a year, to procure a shred of flesh for his fields, generally about the time when his chief crop was laid down.[2]

The mode of performing these tribal sacrifices was as follows. Ten or twelve days before the sacrifice, the victim was devoted by cutting off his hair, which, until then, was kept unshorn. Crowds of men and women assembled to witness the sacrifice; none might be excluded, since the sacrifice was declared to be "for all mankind." It was preceded by several days of wild revelry and gross

[1] S. C. Macpherson, *op. cit.* p. 115 *sq.*   [2] *Ib.* p. 113.

debauchery.[1] On the day before the sacrifice the victim, dressed in a new garment, was led forth from the village in solemn procession, with music and dancing, to the Meriah grove, which was a clump of high forest trees standing a little way from the village and untouched by the axe. In this grove the victim was tied to a post, which was sometimes placed between two plants of the sankissar shrub. He was then anointed with oil, ghee, and turmeric, and adorned with flowers; and "a species of reverence, which it is not easy to distinguish from adoration," was paid to him throughout the day.[2] A great struggle now arose to obtain the smallest relic from his person; a particle of the turmeric paste with which he was smeared, or a drop of his spittle, was esteemed of sovereign virtue, especially by the women. The crowd danced round the post to music, and, addressing the earth, said, " O God, we offer this sacrifice to you ; give us good crops, seasons, and health." [3]

On the last morning the orgies, which had been scarcely interrupted during the night, were resumed, and continued till noon, when they ceased, and the assembly proceeded to consummate the sacrifice. The victim was again anointed with oil, and each person touched the anointed part, and wiped the oil on his own head. In some places the victim was then taken in procession round the village, from door to door, where some plucked hair from his head, and others begged for a drop of his spittle, with which they anointed their heads.[4] As the victim might not be bound nor make any show of resistance, the

---

[1] S. C. Macpherson, *op. cit.* p. 117 *sq.* ; J. Campbell, p. 112.

[2] S. C. Macpherson, p. 118.
[3] J. Campbell, p. 54.
[4] *Ib.* pp. 55, 112.

bones of his arms and, if necessary, his legs were
broken ; but often this precaution was rendered
unnecessary by stupefying him with opium.[1] The
mode of putting him to death varied in different
places. One of the commonest modes seems to
have been strangulation, or squeezing to death.
The branch of a green tree was cleft several feet
down the middle ; the victim's neck (in other places,
his chest) was inserted in the cleft, which the priest,
aided by his assistants, strove with all his force to
close.[2] Then he wounded the victim slightly with
his axe, whereupon the crowd rushed at the victim
and cut the flesh from the bones, leaving the head
and bowels untouched. Sometimes he was cut up
alive.[3] In Chinna Kimedy he was dragged along
the fields, surrounded by the crowd, who, avoiding
his head and intestines, hacked the flesh from his
body with their knives till he died.[4] Another very
common mode of sacrifice in the same district was
to fasten the victim to the proboscis of a wooden
elephant, which revolved on a stout post, and, as it
whirled round, the crowd cut the flesh from the victim
while life remained. In some villages Major Campbell
found as many as fourteen of these wooden elephants,
which had been used at sacrifices.[5] In one district the
victim was put to death slowly by fire. A low stage
was formed, sloping on either side like a roof ; upon it

---

[1] S. C. Macpherson, p. 119; J. Campbell, p. 113.

[2] S. C. Macpherson, p. 127. Instead of the branch of a green tree, Campbell mentions two strong planks or bamboos (p. 57) or a slit bamboo (p. 182).

[3] J. Campbell, pp. 56, 58, 120.

[4] Dalton, *Ethnology of Bengal*, p. 288, quoting Colonel Campbell's Report.

[5] J. Campbell, p. 126. The elephant represented the Earth Goddess herself, who was here conceived in elephant-form ; Campbell, pp. 51, 126. In the hill tracts of Goomsur she was represented in peacock-form, and the post to which the victim was bound bore the effigy of a peacock, Campbell, p. 54.

the victim was placed, his limbs wound round with cords to confine his struggles. Fires were then lighted and hot brands applied, to make him roll up and down the slopes of the stage as long as possible ; for the more tears he shed the more abundant would be the supply of rain. Next day the body was cut to pieces.[1]

The flesh cut from the victim was instantly taken home by the persons who had been deputed by each village to bring it. To secure its rapid arrival, it was sometimes forwarded by relays of men, and conveyed with postal fleetness fifty or sixty miles.[2] In each village all who stayed at home fasted rigidly until the flesh arrived. The bearer deposited it in the place of public assembly, where it was received by the priest and the heads of families. The priest divided it into two portions, one of which he offered to the Earth Goddess by burying it in a hole in the ground with his back turned, and without looking. Then each man added a little earth to bury it, and the priest poured water on the spot from a hill gourd. The other portion of flesh he divided into as many shares as there were heads of houses present. Each head of a house rolled his shred of flesh in leaves, and buried it in his favourite field, placing it in the earth behind his back without looking.[3] In some places each man carried his portion of flesh to the stream which watered his fields, and there hung it on a pole.[4] For three days thereafter no house was swept ; and, in one district, strict silence was observed, no fire might be given out, no wood cut, and no strangers received.

---

[1] S. C. Macpherson, p. 130.

[2] Dalton, *Ethnology of Bengal*, p. 288, referring to Colonel Campbell's Report.

[3] S. C. Macpherson, p. 129. Cp. J. Campbell, pp. 55, 58, 113, 121, 187.

[4] J. Campbell, p. 182.

The remains of the human victim (namely, the head, bowels, and bones) were watched by strong parties the night after the sacrifice; and next morning they were burned, along with a whole sheep, on a funeral pile. The ashes were scattered over the fields, laid as paste over the houses and granaries, or mixed with the new corn to preserve it from insects.[1] Sometimes, however, the head and bones were buried, not burnt.[2] After the suppression of the human sacrifices, inferior victims were substituted in some places; for instance, in the capital of Chinna Kimedy a goat took the place of a human victim.[3]

In these Khond sacrifices the Meriahs are represented by our authorities as victims offered to propitiate the Earth Goddess. But from the treatment of the victims both before and after death it appears that the custom cannot be explained as merely a propitiatory sacrifice. A part of the flesh certainly was offered to the Earth Goddess, but the rest of the flesh was buried by each householder in his fields, and the ashes of the other parts of the body were scattered over the fields, laid as paste on the granaries, or mixed with the new corn. These latter customs imply that to the body of the Meriah there was ascribed a direct or intrinsic power of making the crops to grow, quite independent of the indirect efficacy which it might have as an offering to secure the good-will of the deity. In other words, the flesh and ashes of the victim were believed to be endowed with a magical or physical power of fertilising the land. The same intrinsic power was ascribed to the blood and tears of the Meriah, his blood causing the redness of the turmeric and his tears

---

[1] S. C. Macpherson, p. 128; Dalton, *l.c.*
[2] J. Campbell, pp. 55, 182.   [3] J. Campbell, p. 187.

producing rain ; for it can hardly be doubted that, originally at least, the tears were supposed to produce rain, not merely to prognosticate it. Similarly the custom of pouring water on the buried flesh of the Meriah was no doubt a rain-charm. Again, intrinsic supernatural power as an attribute of the Meriah appears in the sovereign virtue believed to reside in anything that came from his person, as his hair or spittle. The ascription of such power to the Meriah indicates that he was much more than a mere man sacrificed to propitiate a deity. Once more, the extreme reverence paid him points to the same conclusion. Major Campbell speaks of the Meriah as " being regarded as something more than mortal,"[1] and Major Macpherson says, " A species of reverence, which it is not easy to distinguish from adoration, is paid to him."[2] In short, the Meriah appears to have been regarded as divine. As such, he may originally have represented the Earth deity or perhaps a deity of vegetation ; though in later times he came to be regarded rather as a victim offered to a deity than as himself an incarnate deity. This later view of the Meriah as a victim rather than a god may perhaps have received undue emphasis from the European writers who have described the Khond religion. Habituated to the later idea of sacrifice as an offering made to a god for the purpose of conciliating his favour, European observers are apt to interpret all religious slaughter in this sense, and to suppose that wherever such slaughter takes place, there must necessarily be a deity to whom the slaughter is believed by the slayers to be acceptable. Thus their preconceived ideas unconsciously colour and warp their descriptions of savage rites.

---

[1] J. Campbell, p. 112.   [2] S. C. Macpherson, p. 118.

The same custom of killing the representative of a god, of which strong traces appear in the Khond sacrifices, may perhaps be detected in some of the other human sacrifices described above. Thus the ashes of the slaughtered Marimo were scattered over the fields; the blood of the Brahman lad was put on the crop and field; and the blood of the Sioux girl was allowed to trickle on the seed.[1] Again, the identification of the victim with the corn, in other words, the view that he is an embodiment or spirit of the corn, is brought out in the pains which seem to be taken to secure a physical correspondence between him and the natural object which he embodies or represents. Thus the Mexicans killed young victims for the young corn and old ones for the ripe corn; the Marimos sacrifice, as "seed," a short, fat man, the shortness of his stature corresponding to that of the young corn, his fatness to the condition which it is desired that the crops may attain; and the Pawnees fattened their victims probably with the same view. Again, the identification of the victim with the corn comes out in the African custom of killing him with spades and hoes, and the Mexican custom of grinding him, like corn, between two stones.

One more point in these savage customs deserves to be noted. The Pawnee chief devoured the heart of the Sioux girl, and the Marimos and Gonds ate the victim's flesh. If, as we suppose, the victim was regarded as divine, it follows that in eating his flesh his worshippers were partaking of the body of their god. To this point we shall return later on.

The savage rites just described offer analogies to the harvest customs of Europe. Thus the fer-

---

[1] Above, pp. 383, 384.

tilising virtue ascribed to the corn-spirit is shown
equally in the savage custom of mixing the victim's
blood or ashes with the seed-corn and the European
custom of mixing the grain from the last sheaf with
the young corn in spring.[1]   Again, the identification
of the person with the corn appears alike in the
savage custom of adapting the age and stature of
the victim to the age and stature (actual or expected)
of the crop ; in the Scotch and Styrian rules that when
the corn-spirit is conceived as the Maiden the last corn
shall be cut by a young maiden, but when it is conceived
as the Corn-mother it shall be cut by an old woman ; [2]
in the Lothringian warning given to old women to save
themselves when the Old Woman is being killed, that
is, when the last corn is being threshed ; [3] and in the
Tyrolese expectation that if the man who gives the last
stroke at threshing is tall, the next year's corn will be
tall also.[4]   Further, the same identification is implied
in the savage custom of killing the representative of
the corn-spirit with hoes or spades or by grinding him
between stones, and in the European custom of pretending to kill him with the scythe or the flail.   Once
more the Khond custom of pouring water on the buried
flesh of the victim is parallel to the European customs
of pouring water on the personal representative of the
corn-spirit or plunging him into a stream.[5]   Both the
Khond and the European customs are rain-charms.

To return now to the Lityerses story.   It has been
shown that in rude society human beings have been
commonly killed to promote the growth of the crops.
There is therefore no improbability in the supposition
that they may once have been killed for a like purpose

---

[1] Above, pp. 334, 335.   [2] Above, pp. 333, 344, 345.   [3] Above, p. 372.
[4] Above, p. 374.   [5] Above, pp. 286 *sq.*, 337, 340, 374.

in Phrygia and Europe ; and when Phrygian legend and European folk-custom, closely agreeing with each other, point to the conclusion that men were so slain, we are bound, provisionally at least, to accept the conclusion. Further, both the Lityerses story and European harvest customs agree in indicating that the person slain was slain as a representative of the corn-spirit, and this indication is in harmony with the view which savages appear to take of the victim slain to make the crops flourish. On the whole, then, we may fairly suppose that both in Phrygia and in Europe the representative of the corn-spirit was annually killed upon the harvest-field. Grounds have been already shown for believing that similarly in Europe the representative of the tree-spirit was annually slain. The proofs of these two remarkable and closely analogous customs are entirely independent of each other. Their coincidence seems to furnish fresh presumption in favour of both.

To the question, how was the representative of the corn-spirit chosen? one answer has been already given. Both the Lityerses story and European folk-custom show that passing strangers were regarded as manifestations of the corn-spirit escaping from the cut or threshed corn, and as such were seized and slain. But this is not the only answer which the evidence suggests. According to one version of the Phrygian legend the victims of Lityerses were not passing strangers but persons whom he had vanquished in a reaping contest ; and though it is not said that he killed, but only that he thrashed them, we can hardly avoid supposing that in one version of the story the vanquished reapers, like the strangers in the other version, were said to have been wrapt up by Lityerses in corn-sheaves and so beheaded. The supposition is countenanced by European harvest-customs. We have seen that in Europe there is sometimes a contest amongst the reapers to avoid being last, and that the person who is vanquished in this competition, that is, who cuts the last corn, is often roughly handled. It is true we have not found that a pretence is made of killing him ; but on the other hand we have found that a pretence is made of killing the man who gives the last stroke at threshing, that is, who is vanquished in the threshing contest.[1] Now, since it is in the character of representative of the corn-spirit that the thresher of the last corn is slain in mimicry, and since the same representative character attaches (as we have seen) to the cutter and binder as well as to the thresher of the last corn, and since the same repugnance is evinced by harvesters to be last in any one of these labours, we may conjecture that a pretence has been commonly made of killing the reaper and binder as well as the thresher of the last corn, and that in ancient times this killing was actually carried out. This conjecture is corroborated by the common superstition that whoever cuts the last corn must die soon.[2] Sometimes it is thought that the person who binds the last sheaf on the field will die in the course of next year.[3] The reason for fixing on the reaper, binder, or thresher of the last corn as the representative of the corn-spirit may be this. The corn-spirit is supposed to lurk as long as he can in the corn, retreating before the reapers, the binders, and the threshers at their work. But when he is forcibly expelled from his ultimate refuge in the last corn cut or the last sheaf bound or the last grain threshed, he necessarily assumes some other form than

---

[1] Above, p. 374. [2] W. Mannhardt, *Korndämonen*, p. 5.
[3] Pfannenschmid, *Germanische Erntefeste*, p. 98.

that of the corn-stalks which had hitherto been his garments or body.   And what form can the expelled corn-spirit assume more naturally than that of the person who stands nearest to the corn from which he (the corn-spirit) has just been expelled ?   But the person in question is necessarily the reaper, binder, or thresher of the last corn.   He or she, therefore, is seized and treated as the corn-spirit himself.

Thus the person who was killed on the harvest-field as the representative of the corn-spirit may have been either a passing stranger or the harvester who was last at reaping, binding, or threshing.   But there is a third possibility, to which ancient legend and modern folk-custom alike point.   Lityerses not only put strangers to death ; he was himself slain, and probably in the same way as he had slain others, namely, by being wrapt in a corn-sheaf, beheaded, and cast into the river; and it is implied that this happened to Lityerses on his own land.   Similarly in modern harvest-customs the pretence of killing appears to be carried out quite as often on the person of the master (farmer or squire) as on that of strangers.[1]   Now when we remember that Lityerses was said to have been the son of the King of Phrygia, and combine with this the tradition that he was put to death, apparently as a representative of the corn-spirit, we are led to conjecture that we have here another trace of the custom of annually slaying one of those divine or priestly kings who are known to have held ghostly sway in many parts of Western Asia and particularly in Phrygia. The custom appears, as we have seen,[2] to have been so far modified in places that the king's son was slain in the king's stead.   Of the custom thus

---

[1] Above, p. 376 *sq.*   [2] Above, p. 235.

modified the story of Lityerses would therefore be a reminiscence.

Turning now to the relation of the Phrygian Lityerses to the Phrygian Attis, it may be remembered that at Pessinus—the seat of a priestly kingship —the high-priest appears to have been annually slain in the character of Attis, a god of vegetation, and that Attis was described by an ancient authority as "a reaped ear of corn."[1] Thus Attis, as an embodiment of the corn-spirit, annually slain in the person of his representative, might be thought to be ultimately identical with Lityerses, the latter being simply the rustic prototype out of which the state religion of Attis was developed. It may have been so; but, on the other hand, the analogy of European folk-custom warns us that amongst the same people two distinct deities of vegetation may have their separate personal representatives, both of whom are slain in the character of gods at different times of the year. For in Europe, as we have seen, it appears that one man was commonly slain in the character of the tree-spirit in spring, and another in the character of the corn-spirit in autumn. It may have been so in Phrygia also. Attis was especially a tree-god, and his connection with corn may have been only such an extension of the power of a tree-spirit as is indicated in customs like the Harvest-May.[2] Again, the representative of Attis appears to have been slain in spring; whereas Lityerses must have been slain in summer or autumn, according to the time of the harvest in Phyrgia.[3] On the whole, then, while we are not justified in regard-

---

[1] Above, p. 299.   [2] Above, p. 68.
[3] I do not know when the corn is reaped in Phrygia; but considering the high upland character of the country, harvest is probably later there than on the coasts of the Mediterranean.

ing Lityerses as the prototype of Attis, the two may
be regarded as parallel products of the same religious
idea, and may have stood to each other as in Europe
the Old Man of harvest stands to the Wild Man, the
Leaf Man, etc., of spring. Both were spirits or deities
of vegetation, and the personal representatives of both
were annually slain. But whereas the Attis worship
became elevated into the dignity of a state religion
and spread to Italy, the rites of Lityerses seem
never to have passed the limits of their native
Phrygia, and always retained their character of rustic
ceremonies performed by peasants on the harvest-field.
At most a few villages may have clubbed together, as
amongst the Khonds, to procure a human victim to
be slain as representative of the corn-spirit for their
common benefit. Such victims may have been drawn
from the families of priestly kings or kinglets, which
would account for the legendary character of Lityerses
as the son of a Phrygian king. When villages did
not so club together, each village or farm may have
procured its own representative of the corn-spirit
by dooming to death either a passing stranger or the
harvester who cut, bound, or threshed the last sheaf.
It is hardly necessary to add that in Phrygia, as in
Europe, the old barbarous custom of killing a man on
the harvest-field or the threshing-floor had doubtless
passed into a mere pretence long before the classical
era, and was probably regarded by the reapers and
threshers themselves as no more than a rough jest
which the license of a harvest-home permitted them
to play off on a passing stranger, a comrade, or even
on their master himself.

I have dwelt on the Lityerses song at length
because it affords so many points of comparison with

European and savage folk-custom. The other harvest songs of Western Asia and Egypt, to which attention has been called above,[1] may now be dismissed much more briefly. The similarity of the Bithynian Bormus[2] to the Phrygian Lityerses helps to bear out the interpretation which has been given of the latter. Bormus, whose death or rather disappearance was annually mourned by the reapers in a plaintive song, was, like Lityerses, a king's son or at least the son of a wealthy and distinguished man. The reapers whom he watched were at work on his own fields, and he disappeared in going to fetch water for them; according to one version of the story he was carried off by the (water) nymphs.[3] Viewed in the light of the Lityerses story and of European folk-custom, this disappearance of Bormus is probably a reminiscence of the custom of binding the farmer himself in a corn-sheaf and throwing him into the water. The mournful strain which the reapers sang was probably a lamentation over the death of the corn-spirit, slain either in the cut corn or in the person of a human representative; and the call which they addressed to him may have been a prayer that the corn-spirit might return in fresh vigour next year.

The Phoenician Linus song was sung at the vintage, at least in the west of Asia Minor, as we learn from Homer; and this, combined with the legend of Syleus, suggests that in ancient times passing strangers were handled by vintagers and vine-diggers in much the same way as they are said to have been handled by the reaper Lityerses. The Lydian Syleus, so ran the legend, compelled passers-by to dig for him in his vineyard, till Hercules came and killed him and dug

---

[1] Above, p. 364 *sq.*   [2] Above, p. 365.   [3] Hesychius, *s.v.* Βῶρμον.

up his vines by the roots.[1]   This seems to be the outline of a legend like that of Lityerses; but neither
ancient writers nor modern folk-custom enable us to
fill in the details.[2]   But, further, the Linus song was
probably sung also by Phoenician reapers, for Herodotus compares it to the Maneros song, which, as we
have seen, was a lament raised by Egyptian reapers
over the cut corn.   Further, Linus was identified with
Adonis, and Adonis has some claims to be regarded
as especially a corn-deity.[3]   Thus the Linus lament,
as sung at harvest, would be identical with the Adonis
lament; each would be the lamentation raised by
reapers over the dead corn-spirit.   But whereas
Adonis, like Attis, grew into a stately figure of mythology, adored and mourned in splendid cities far beyond
the limits of his Phoenician home, Linus appears to
have remained a simple ditty sung by reapers and
vintagers among the corn-sheaves and the vines.   The
analogy of Lityerses and of folk-custom, both European
and savage, suggests that in Phoenicia the slain corn-
spirit—the dead Adonis—may formerly have been
represented by a human victim; and this suggestion
is possibly supported by the Harrân legend that
Thammuz (Adonis) was slain by his cruel lord, who
ground his bones in a mill and scattered them to the
wind.[4]   For in Mexico, as we have seen, the human
victim at harvest was crushed between two stones;
and both in India and Africa the ashes of the victim
were scattered over the fields.[5]   But the Harrân
legend may be only a mythical way of expressing the

---

[1] Apollodorus, ii. 6, 3.
[2] The scurrilities exchanged in both
ancient and modern times between
vine-dressers, vintagers, and passers-by
seem to belong to a different category.

See W. Mannhardt, *Myth. Forsch.* p.
53 *sq.*
[3] Above, p. 282 *sqq.*
[4] Above, p. 283 *sq.*
[5] Above, pp. 381, 384, 389.

grinding of corn in the mill and the scattering of the seed. It seems worth suggesting that the mock king who was annually killed at the Babylonian festival of the Sacaea on the 16th of the month Lous may have represented Thammuz himself. For the historian Berosus, who records the festival and its date, probably used the Macedonian calendar, since he dedicated his history to Antiochus Soter; and in his day the Macedonian month Lous appears to have corresponded to the Babylonian month Thammuz.[1] If this conjecture is right, the view that the mock king at the Sacaea was slain in the character of a god would be established.

There is a good deal more evidence that in Egypt the slain corn-spirit—the dead Osiris—was represented by a human victim, whom the reapers slew on the harvest-field, mourning his death in a dirge, to which the Greeks, through a verbal misunderstanding, gave the name of Maneros.[2] For the legend of Busiris seems to preserve a reminiscence of human sacrifices once offered by the Egyptians in connection with the worship of Osiris. Busiris was said to have been an Egyptian king who sacrificed all strangers on the altar of Zeus. The origin of the custom was traced to a barrenness which afflicted the land of Egypt for nine years. A Cyprian seer informed Busiris that the barrenness would cease if a man were annually sacri-

---

[1] For this fact of the probable correspondence of the months, which supplies so welcome a confirmation of the conjecture in the text, I am indebted to my friend Professor W. Robertson Smith, who furnishes me with the following note: "In the Syro-Macedonian calendar Lous represents Ab, not Tammuz. Was it different in Babylon? I think it was, and one month different, at least in the early times of the Greek monarchy in Asia. For we know from a Babylonian observation in the Almagest (*Ideler*, i. 396) that in 229 B.C. Xanthicus began on February 26. It was therefore the month before the equinoctial moon, not Nisan but Adar, and consequently Lous answered to the lunar month Tammuz."　　　[2] Above, p. 364.

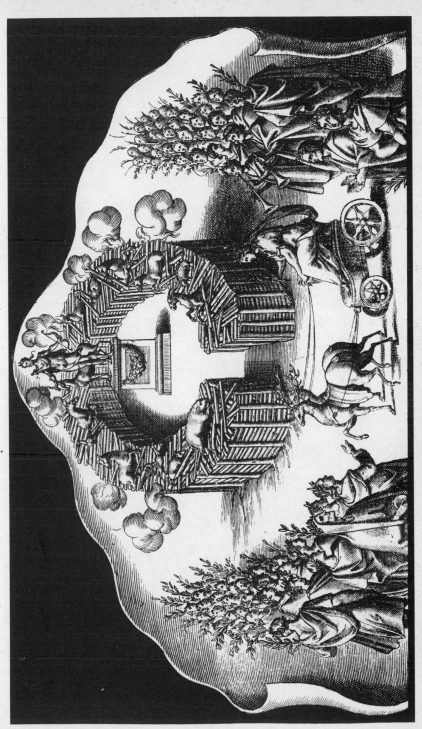

Homage to Diana.

A sacrifice in Rome.

ficed to Zeus.   So Busiris instituted the sacrifice.   But
when Hercules came to Egypt, and was being dragged
to the altar to be sacrificed, he burst his bonds and
slew Busiris and his son.[1]   Here then is a legend
that in Egypt a human victim was annually sacrificed
to prevent the failure of the crops, and a belief is
implied that an omission of the sacrifice would have
entailed a recurrence of that infertility which it was the
object of the sacrifice to prevent.   So the Pawnees, as
we have seen, believed that an omission of the human
sacrifice at planting would have been followed by a
total failure of their crops.   The name Busiris was
in reality the name of a city, *pe-Asar*, " the house
of Osiris "[2] the city being so called because it contained the grave of Osiris.   The human sacrifices
were said to have been offered at his grave, and the
victims were red-haired men, whose ashes were scattered abroad by means of winnowing-fans.[3]   In the
light of the foregoing discussion, this Egyptian tradition admits of a consistent and fairly probable explanation.   Osiris, the corn-spirit, was annually represented
at harvest by a stranger, whose red hair made him a
suitable representative of the ripe corn.   This man,
in his representative character, was slain on the harvest-
field, and mourned by the reapers, who prayed at the
same time that the corn-spirit might revive and return
(*mââ-ne-rha*, Maneros) with renewed vigour in the
following year.   Finally, the victim, or some part of
him, was burned, and the ashes scattered by winnow-

---

[1] Apollodorus, ii. 5, 11 ; Schol. on
Apollonius Rhodius, iv. 1396 ; Plutarch, *Parall.* 38.   Herodotus (ii. 45)
discredits the idea that the Egyptians
ever offered human sacrifices.   But his
authority is not to be weighed against

that of Manetho (Plutarch, *Is. et Os.*
73), who affirms that they did.
[2] E. Meyer, *Geschichte des Alterthums*, i. § 57.
[3] Diodorus, i. 88 ; Plutarch, *Is. et
Os.* 73; cp. *id.*, 30, 33.

ing-fans over the fields to fertilise them.   Here the
choice of the representative on the ground of his
resemblance to the corn which he was to represent
agrees with the Mexican and African customs already
described.[1]   Similarly the Romans sacrificed red-haired
puppies in spring, in the belief that the crops would
thus grow ripe and ruddy;[2] and to this day in sowing
wheat a Bavarian sower will sometimes wear a golden
ring, that the corn may grow yellow.[3]   Again, the
scattering of the Egyptian victim's ashes is identical
with the Marimo and Khond custom.[4]   His identification with the corn comes out again in the fact that
his ashes were winnowed ; just as in Vendée a pretence is made of threshing and winnowing the farmer's
wife, regarded as an embodiment of the corn-spirit ; or
as in Mexico the victim was ground between stones ;
or as in Africa he was slain with spades and hoes.[5]
The story that the fragments of Osiris's body were
scattered up and down the land, and buried by Isis
on the spots where they lay,[6] may very well be a
reminiscence of a custom, like that observed by the
Khonds, of dividing the human victim in pieces and
burying the pieces, often at intervals of many miles
from each other, in the fields.   However, it is possible
that the story of the dismemberment of Osiris, like
the similar story told of Thammuz, may have been
simply a mythical expression for the scattering of the
seed.   Once more, the story that the body of Osiris
enclosed in a coffer was thrown by Typhon into the

[1] Above, pp. 307, 383, 391.
[2] Festus, *s.v. Catularia.* Cp. *id.,*
s.v. rutilae canes ; Columella, x. 343 ;
Ovid, *Fasti,* iv. 905 *sqq.*; Pliny, *N. H.*
xviii. § 14.
[3] Panzer, *Beitrag zur deutschen*

Mythologie, ii. 207, No. 362 ; *Bavaria,*
Landes-und Volkskunde des Königreichs
Bayern, iii. 343.
[4] Above, pp. 384, 389.
[5] Above, pp. 381, 383.
[6] Plutarch, *Is. et Os.* 18.

Nile perhaps points to a custom of throwing the body of the victim, or at least a portion of it, into the Nile as a rain-charm, or rather to make the Nile rise. For a similar purpose Phrygian reapers seem to have thrown the headless bodies of their victims, wrapt in corn-sheaves, into a river, and the Khonds poured water on the buried flesh of the human victim. Probably when Osiris ceased to be represented by a human victim, an effigy of him was annually thrown into the Nile, just as the effigy of his Syrian counterpart, Adonis, used to be thrown into the sea at Alexandria. Or water may have been simply poured over it, as on the monument already mentioned a priest is seen pouring water over the body of Osiris, from which corn stalks are sprouting. The accompanying inscription, " This is Osiris of the mysteries, who springs from the returning waters," bears out the view that at the mysteries of Osiris a water-charm or irrigation-charm was regularly performed by pouring water on his effigy, or by throwing it into the Nile.

It may be objected that the red-haired victims were slain as representatives not of Osiris, but of his enemy Typhon ; for the victims were called Typhonian, and red was the colour of Typhon, black the colour of Osiris.[1] The answer to this objection must be reserved for the present. Meantime it may be pointed out that if Osiris is often represented on the monuments as black, he is still more commonly depicted as green,[2] appropriately enough for a corn-god, who may be conceived as black while the seed is under ground, but as green after it has sprouted. So the Greeks recognised

---

[1] Plutarch, *Is. et Os.* 22, 30, 31, 33, 73.

[2] Wilkinson, *Manners and Customs of the Ancient Egyptians* (ed. 1878), iii. 81.

both a green and a black Demeter,[1] and sacrificed to
the green Demeter in spring with mirth and gladness.[2]

Thus, if I am right, the key to the mysteries of
Osiris is furnished by the melancholy cry of the
Egyptian reapers, which down to Roman times could
be heard year after year sounding across the fields,
announcing the death of the corn-spirit, the rustic
prototype of Osiris. Similar cries, as we have seen,
were also heard on all the harvest-fields of Western Asia. By the ancients they are spoken of as
songs; but to judge from the analysis of the names
Linus and Maneros, they probably consisted only of a
few words uttered in a prolonged musical note which
could be heard for a great distance. Such sonorous
and long-drawn cries, raised by a number of strong
voices in concert, must have had a striking effect,
and could hardly fail to arrest the attention of any
traveller who happened to be within hearing. The
sounds, repeated again and again, could probably be
distinguished with tolerable ease even at a distance;
but to a Greek traveller in Asia or Egypt the foreign
words would commonly convey no meaning, and he
might take them, not unnaturally, for the name of some
one (Maneros, Linos, Lityerses, Bormus), upon whom
the reapers were calling. And if his journey led him
through more countries than one, as Bithynia and
Phrygia, or Phoenicia and Egypt, while the corn was
being reaped, he would have an opportunity of comparing the various harvest cries of the different peoples.
Thus we can readily account for the fact that these
harvest cries were so often noted and compared with
each other by the Greeks. Whereas, if they had been

---

[1] Pausanias, i. 22, 3, viii. 5, 8, viii. 42, 1.
[2] Cornutus, *De nat. deor.* c. 28.

regular songs, they could not have been heard at such distances, and therefore could not have attracted the attention of so many travellers ; and, moreover, even if the traveller were within hearing of them, he could not so easily have picked out the words. To this day Devonshire reapers utter cries of the same sort, and perform on the field a ceremony exactly analogous to that in which, if I am not mistaken, the rites of Osiris originated. The cry and the ceremony are thus described by an observer who wrote in the first half of this century. "After the wheat is all cut, on most farms in the north of Devon, the harvest people have a custom of 'crying the neck.' I believe that this practice is seldom omitted on any large farm in that part of the country. It is done in this way. An old man, or some one else well acquainted with the ceremonies used on the occasion (when the labourers are reaping the last field of wheat), goes round to the shocks and sheaves, and picks out a little bundle of all the best ears he can find ; this bundle he ties up very neat and trim, and plats and arranges the straws very tastefully. This is called 'the neck' of wheat, or wheaten-ears. After the field is cut out, and the pitcher once more circulated, the reapers, binders, and the women, stand round in a circle. The person with 'the neck' stands in the centre, grasping it with both his hands. He first stoops and holds it near the ground, and all the men forming the ring take off their hats, stooping and holding them with both hands towards the ground. They then all begin at once in a very prolonged and harmonious tone to cry 'the neck !' at the same time slowly raising themselves upright, and elevating their arms and hats above their heads ; the person with 'the neck' also raising it on high. This is done three times.

They then change their cry to ' wee yen ! '—' way yen !'
—which they sound in the same prolonged and slow
manner as before, with singular harmony and effect,
three times. This last cry is accompanied by the same
movements of the body and arms as in crying 'the
neck.' . . . After having thus repeated 'the neck'
three times, and 'wee yen,' or 'way yen,' as often,
they all burst out into a kind of loud and joyous laugh,
flinging up their hats and caps into the air, capering
about and perhaps kissing the girls. One of them
then gets ' the neck ' and runs as hard as he can down
to the farmhouse, where the dairymaid or one of the
young female domestics stands at the door prepared
with a pail of water. If he who holds 'the neck' can
manage to get into the house, in any way unseen, ọr
openly, by any other way than the door at which the
girl stands with the pail of water, then he may lawfully
kiss her ; but, if otherwise, he is regularly soused with
the contents of the bucket. On a fine still autumn
evening, the 'crying of the neck' has a wonderful
effect at a distance, far finer than that of the Turkish
muezzin, which Lord Byron eulogises so much, and
which he says is preferable to all the bells in Christen-
dom. I have once or twice heard upwards of twenty
men cry it, and sometimes joined by an equal number
of female voices. About three years back, on some
high grounds, where our people were harvesting, I
heard six or seven 'necks' cried in one night, although
I know that ṣome of them were four miles off. They
are heard through the quiet evening air, at a considerable distance sometimes." [1] Again, Mrs. Bray tells
how, travelling in Devonshire, " she saw a party of
reapers standing in a circle on a rising ground, holding

[1] Hone, *Every-day Book*, ii. c. 1170 *sq.*

their sickles aloft.   One in the middle held up some
ears of corn tied together with flowers, and the party
shouted three times (what she writes as) 'Arnack,
arnack, arnack, we *haven*, we *haven*, we *haven*.'   They
went home, accompanied by women and children
carrying boughs of flowers, shouting and singing.   The
man-servant who attended Mrs. Bray, said, 'it was only
the people making their games, as they always did, *to
the spirit of harvest*.'"[1]   Here, as Miss Burne remarks,
"'arnack, we haven!' is obviously in the Devon dialect,
'a neck (or nack)! we have un!'"   "The neck" is
generally hung up in the farmhouse, where it sometimes remains for two or three years.[2]   A similar
custom is still observed in some parts of Cornwall, as I
am informed by my friend Professor J. H. Middleton.
"The last sheaf is decked with ribbons.   Two strong-
voiced men are chosen and placed (one with the sheaf)
on opposite sides of a valley.   One shouts, 'I've
gotten it.'   The other shouts, 'What hast gotten?'
The first answers, 'I'se gotten the neck.'"

In these Devonshire and Cornish customs a particular bunch of ears, generally the last left standing,[3]
is conceived as the neck of the corn-spirit, who is consequently beheaded when the bunch is cut down.
Similarly in Shropshire the name "neck," or "the
gander's neck," used to be commonly given to the last
handful of ears left standing in the middle of the field,
when all the rest of the corn was cut.   It was plaited
together, and the reapers, standing ten or twenty
paces off, threw their sickles at it.   Whoever cut it
through was said to have cut off the gander's neck.

---

[1] Miss C. S. Burne and Miss G. F.
Jackson, *Shropshire Folk-lore*, p. 372
sq., referring to Mrs. Bray's *Traditions
of Devon*, i. 330.

[2] Hone, *op. cit.* ii. 1172.

[3] Brand, *Popular Antiquities*, ii. 20
(Bohn's ed.); Burne and Jackson, *op.
cit.* p. 371.

The "neck" was taken to the farmer's wife, who was supposed to keep it in the house "for good luck" till the next harvest came round.[1] Near Trèves, the man who reaps the last standing corn "cuts the goat's neck off."[2] At Faslane, on the Gareloch (Dumbartonshire), the last handful of standing corn was sometimes called the "head."[3] At Aurich, in East Friesland, the man who reaps the last corn "cuts the hare's tail off."[4] In mowing down the last corner of a field French reapers sometimes call out, "We have the cat by the tail."[5] In Bresse (Bourgogne) the last sheaf represented the fox. Beside it a score of ears were left standing to form the tail, and each reaper, going back some paces, threw his sickle at it. He who succeeded in severing it "cut off the fox's tail," and a cry of "*You cou cou !*" was raised in his honour.[6] These examples leave no room to doubt the meaning of the Devonshire and Cornish expression "the neck," as applied to the last sheaf. The corn-spirit is conceived in human or animal form, and the last standing corn is part of its body—its neck, its head, or its tail. Sometimes, as we have seen, it is regarded as the navel-string.[7] Lastly, the Devonshire custom of drenching with water the person who brings in "the neck" is a rain-charm, such as we have had many examples of. Its parallel in the mysteries of Osiris was the custom of pouring water on the image of Osiris or on the person who represented him.

In Germany cries of *Waul!* or *Wol!* or *Wôld!* are sometimes raised by the reapers at cutting the last corn. Thus in some places the last patch of standing

---

[1] Burne and Jackson, *l.c.*
[2] W. Mannhardt, *Myth. Forsch.* p. 185.
[3] See above, p. 345.
[4] W. Mannhardt, *Myth. Forsch.* p. 185. [5] *Ib.*
[6] *Revue des Traditions populaires*, ii. 500. [7] Above, p. 343.

corn was called the *Waul*-rye; a stick decked with flowers was inserted in it, and the ears were fastened to the stick.   Then all the reapers took off their hats and cried thrice, *Waul! Waul! Waul!* Sometimes they accompany the cry by clashing with their whetstones on their scythes.[1]

---

[1] U. Jahn, *Die deutschen Opfergebräuche bei Ackerbau und Viehzucht,* pp. 166-169 ; Pfannenschmid, *Germanische Erntefeste,* p. 104 *sq.* ; Kuhn, *Westfälische Sagen, Gebräuche und Märchen,* ii. Nos. 491, 492; Kuhn und Schwartz, *Norddeutsche Sagen, Märchen und Gebräuche,* p. 395, No. 97 ; Lynker, *Deutsche Sagen und Sitten in hessischen Gauen,* p. 256, No. 340.

END OF VOL. I

VOLUME II

§ 10.—*The corn-spirit as an animal*

In some of the examples cited above to establish the meaning of the term "neck" as applied to the last sheaf, the corn-spirit appears in animal form as a gander, a goat, a hare, a cat, and a fox. This introduces us to a new aspect of the corn-spirit, which we must now examine. By doing so we shall not only have fresh examples of killing the god, but may hope also to clear up some points which remain obscure in the myths and worship of Attis, Adonis, Osiris, Dionysus, Demeter, and Virbius.

Amongst the many animals whose forms the corn-spirit is supposed to take are the wolf, dog, hare, cock, goose, cat, goat, cow (ox, bull), pig, and horse. In one or other of these forms the corn-spirit is believed to be present in the corn, and to be caught or killed in the last sheaf. As the corn is being cut the animal flees before the reapers, and if a reaper is taken ill on the field, he is supposed to have stumbled unwittingly on the corn-spirit, who has thus punished the profane intruder. It is said " The Rye-wolf has got hold of him," "the Harvest-goat has given him a push." The person who cuts the last corn or binds the last sheaf gets the name of the animal, as the Rye-

wolf, the Rye-sow, the Oats-goat, etc., and retains the
name sometimes for a year. Also the animal is frequently represented by a puppet made out of the last
sheaf or of wood, flowers, etc., which is carried home
amid rejoicings on the last harvest waggon. Even
where the last sheaf is not made up in animal shape, it
is often called the Rye-wolf, the Hare, Goat, and so on.
Generally each kind of crop is supposed to have its
special animal, which is caught in the last sheaf, and
called the Rye-wolf, the Barley-wolf, the Oats-wolf,
the Pea-wolf, or the Potato-wolf, according to the
crop; but sometimes the figure of the animal is only
made up once for all at getting in the last crop of the
whole harvest. Sometimes the animal is believed to
be killed by the last stroke of the sickle or scythe.
But oftener it is thought to live so long as there is
corn still unthreshed, and to be caught in the last sheaf
threshed. Hence the man who gives the last stroke
with the flail is told that he has got the Corn-sow,
the Threshing-dog, etc. When the threshing is
finished, a puppet is made in the form of the animal,
and this is carried by the thresher of the last sheaf to
a neighbouring farm, where the threshing is still going
on. This again shows that the corn-spirit is believed
to live wherever the corn is still being threshed.
Sometimes the thresher of the last sheaf himself represents the animal; and if the people of the next farm,
who are still threshing, catch him, they treat him
like the animal he represents, by shutting him up in
the pig-sty, calling him with the cries commonly
addressed to pigs, and so forth.[1]

These general statements will now be illustrated
by examples. We begin with the corn-spirit con-

---

[1] W. Mannhardt, *Die Korndämonen*, pp. 1-6.

ceived as a wolf or a dog. This conception is common in France, Germany, and Slavonic countries. Thus, when the wind sets the corn in wave-like motion, the peasants often say, " The Wolf is going over, or through, the corn," " the Rye-wolf is rushing over the field," " the Wolf is in the corn," " the mad Dog is in the corn," " the big Dog is there." [1] When children wish to go into the corn-fields to pluck ears or gather the blue corn-flowers, they are warned not to do so, for " the big Dog sits in the corn," or " the Wolf sits in the corn, and will tear you in pieces," " the Wolf will eat you." The wolf against whom the children are warned is not a common wolf, for he is often spoken of as the Corn-wolf, Rye-wolf, etc. ; thus they say, " The Rye-wolf will come and eat you up, children," " the Rye-wolf will carry you off," and so forth.[2] Still he has all the outward appearance of a wolf. For in the neighbourhood of Feilenhof (East Prussia), when a wolf was seen running through a field, the peasants used to watch whether he carried his tail in the air or dragged it on the ground. If he dragged it on the ground, they went after him, and thanked him for bringing them a blessing, and even set tit-bits before him. But if he carried his tail high, they cursed him and tried to kill him. Here the wolf is the corn-spirit, whose fertilising power is in his tail.[3]

Both dog and wolf appear as embodiments of the corn-spirit in harvest-customs. Thus in some parts

---

[1] W. Mannhardt, *Roggenwolf und Roggenhund* (Danzig, 1865), p. 5 ; *id., Antike Wald-und Feldkulte*, p. 318 *sq.*; *id., Mythol. Forsch.* p. 103 ; Witzschel, *Sagen, Sitten und Gebräuche aus Thüringen*, p. 213.

[2] W. Mannhardt, *Roggenwolf u. Roggenhund*, p. 7 *sqq.* ; *id., A. W. F.* p. 319.

[3] W. Mannhardt, *Roggenwolf*, etc. p. 10.

of Silesia the person who binds the last sheaf is called the Wheat-dog or the Peas-pug.[1] But it is in the harvest-customs of the north-east of France that the idea of the Corn-dog comes out most clearly. Thus when a harvester, through sickness, weariness, or laziness, cannot or will not keep up with the reaper in front of him, they say, "The White Dog passed near him," "he has the White Bitch," or "the White Bitch has bitten him."[2] In the Vosges the Harvest-May is called the "Dog of the harvest."[3] About Lons-le-Saulnier, in the Jura, the last sheaf is called the Bitch. In the neighbourhood of Verdun the regular expression for finishing the reaping is, "They are going to kill the Dog;" and at Épinal they say, according to the crop, "We will kill the Wheat-dog, or the Rye-dog, or the Potato-dog."[4] In Lorraine it is said of the man who cuts the last corn, "He is killing the Dog of the harvest."[5] At Dux, in the Tyrol, the man who gives the last stroke at threshing is said to "strike down the Dog;"[6] and at Ahnebergen, near Stade, he is called, according to the crop, Corn-pug, Rye-pug, Wheat-pug.[7]

So with the wolf. In Germany it is said that "The Wolf sits in the last sheaf."[8] In some places they call out to the reaper, "Beware of the Wolf;" or they say, "He is chasing the Wolf out of the corn."[9] The last bunch of standing corn is called the Wolf, and the man who cuts it "has the Wolf." The last sheaf is also called the Wolf; and of the woman who binds it they say, "The Wolf is biting her," "she has the

---

[1] W. Mannhardt, *M. F.* p. 104.
[2] *Ib.*
[3] *Ib.* p. 104 *sq.* On the Harvest-May, see above, vol. i. p. 68.
[4] *Ib.* p. 105.
[6] *Ib.* pp. 30, 105.
[8] *A. W. F.* p. 320; *Roggenwolf*, p. 24.
[5] *Ib.* p. 30.
[7] *Ib.* p. 105 *sq.*
[9] *Roggenwolf*, p. 24.

Wolf," "she must fetch the Wolf" (out of the corn).[1]
Moreover, she is herself called Wolf and has to bear
the name for a whole year; sometimes, according to
the crop, she is called the Rye-wolf or the Potato-
wolf.[2]   In the island of Rügen they call out to the
woman who binds the last sheaf, "You're Wolf;" and
when she comes home she bites the lady of the house
and the stewardess, for which she receives a large
piece of meat.   The same woman may be Rye-wolf,
Wheat-wolf, and Oats-wolf, if she happens to bind the
last sheaf of rye, wheat, and oats.[3]   At Buir, in the
district of Cologne, it was formerly the custom to
give to the last sheaf the shape of a wolf.   It was
kept in the barn till all the corn was threshed.   Then
it was brought to the farmer, and he had to sprinkle
it with beer or brandy.[4]   In many places the sheaf
called the Wolf is made up in human form and dressed
in clothes.   This indicates a confusion between the
conceptions of the corn - spirit as theriomorphic (in
animal form) and as anthropomorphic (in human
form).[5]   Generally the Wolf is brought home
on the last waggon, with joyful cries.[6]

Again, the Wolf is supposed to hide himself
amongst the cut corn in the granary, until he is
driven out of the last bundle by the strokes of the
flail.   Hence at Wanzleben, near Magdeburg, after
the threshing the peasants go in procession, leading
by a chain a man, who is enveloped in the threshed out
straw and is called the Wolf.[7]   He represents the
corn-spirit who has been caught escaping from the
threshed corn.   In Trier it is believed that the Corn-

---

[1] *Roggenwolf*, p. 24.
[2] *Ib.* p. 25.
[3] *Ib.* p. 28; *A. W. F.* p. 320.
[4] *Roggenwolf*, p. 25.   [5] *Ib.* p. 26.
[6] *Ib.* p. 26; *A. W. F.* p. 320.
[7] *A. W. F.* p. 321.

wolf is killed at threshing. The men thresh the last
sheaf till it is reduced to chopped straw. In this way
they think that the Corn-wolf who was lurking in the
last sheaf, has been certainly killed.[1]

In France also the Corn-wolf appears at harvest.
Thus they call out to the reaper of the last corn,
"You will catch the Wolf." Near Chambéry they form
a ring round the last standing corn, and cry, "The
Wolf is in there." In Finisterre, when the reaping
draws near an end, the harvesters cry, "There is
the Wolf; we will catch him." Each takes a swath
to reap, and he who finishes first calls out, "I've
caught the Wolf."[2] In Guyenne, when the last corn
has been reaped, they lead a wether all round the
field. It is called "the Wolf of the field." Its horns
are decked with a wreath of flowers and corn-ears,
and its neck and body are also encircled with garlands and ribbons. All the reapers march, singing,
behind it. Then it is killed on the field. In this
part of France the last sheaf is called the *coujoulage*,
which, in the patois, means a wether. Hence the
killing of the wether represents the death of the corn-
spirit, considered as present in the last sheaf; but
two different conceptions of the corn-spirit—as a wolf
and as a wether—are mixed up together.[3]

Sometimes it appears to be thought that the Wolf,
caught in the last corn, lives during the winter in the
farmhouse, ready to renew his activity as corn-spirit in
the spring. Hence at midwinter, when the lengthening
days begin to herald the approach of spring, the Wolf
makes his appearance once more. In Poland a man,
with a wolf's skin thrown over his head, is led about
at Christmas; or a stuffed wolf is carried about by

---

[1] *A. W. F.* p. 321 *sq.*   [2] *A. W. F.* p. 320.   [3] *A. W. F.* p. 320 *sq.*

persons who collect money.[1]   There are facts which
point to an old custom of leading about a man
enveloped in leaves and called the Wolf, while his
conductors collected money.[2]

Another form which the corn-spirit often assumes
is that of a cock.   In Austria children are warned
against straying in the corn-fields, because the Corn-
cock sits there, and will peck their eyes out.[3]   In
North Germany they say that "the Cock sits in
the last sheaf;" and at cutting the last corn the
reapers cry, "Now we will chase out the Cock."
When it is cut they say, "We have caught the Cock."
Then a cock is made of flowers, fastened on a pole,
and carried home by the reapers, singing as they go.[4]
At Braller, in Transylvania, when the reapers come to
the last patch of corn, they cry, "Here we shall catch
the Cock."[5]   At Fürstenwalde, when the last sheaf is
about to be bound, the master lets loose a cock, which
he has brought in a basket, and lets it run over the
field.   All the harvesters chase it till they catch it.
Elsewhere the harvesters all try to seize the last
corn cut ; he who succeeds in grasping it must crow,
and is called Cock.[6]   The last sheaf is called Cock,
Cock-sheaf, Harvest-cock, Harvest-hen, Autumn-hen.
A distinction is made between a Wheat-cock, Bean-
cock, etc., according to the crop.[7]   At Wünschensuhl,
in Thüringen, the last sheaf is made into the shape of
a cock, and called Harvest-cock.[8]   A figure of a cock,

[1] *A. W. F.* p. 322.   [2] *Ib.* p. 323.
[3] *Die Korndämonen*, p. 13.
[4] *Ib.*; Schmitz, *Sitten und Sagen des
Eifler Volkes*, i. p. 95; Kuhn, *Westfälische
Sagen, Märchen und Gebräuche*, ii. p.
181 ; Kuhn und Schwartz, *Norddeutsche
Sagen, Märchen und Gebräuche*, p.
398.

[5] G. A. Heinrich, *Agrarische Sitten
und Gebräuche unter den Sachsen
Siebenbürgens*, p. 21.
[6] *Die Korndämonen*, p. 13.   Cp.
Kuhn and Schwartz, *l.c.*
[7] *Die Korndämonen*, p. 13.
[8] Witzschel, *Sagen, Sitten und Gebräuche aus Thüringen*, p. 220.

made of wood, pasteboard, or ears of corn, is borne in
front of the harvest-waggon, especially in Westphalia,
where the cock carries in his beak fruits of the earth
of all kinds. Sometimes the image of the cock is
fastened to the top of a May-tree on the last harvest-
waggon. Elsewhere a live cock, or a figure of one, is
attached to a harvest-crown and carried on a pole. In
Galicia and elsewhere this live cock is fastened to the
garland of corn-ears or flowers, which the leader of the
women-reapers carries on her head as she marches in
front of the harvest procession.[1] In Silesia a live
cock is presented to the master on a plate. The
harvest supper is called Harvest-cock, Stubble-cock,
etc., and a chief dish at it, at least in some places, is a
cock.[2] If a waggoner upsets a harvest-waggon, it is
said that "he has spilt the Harvest-cock," and he loses
the cock—that is, the harvest supper.[3] The harvest-
waggon, with the figure of the cock on it, is driven
round the farmhouse before it is taken to the barn.
Then the cock is nailed over, or at the side of the
house door, or on the gable, and remains there till
next harvest.[4] In East Friesland the person who
gives the last stroke at threshing is called the
Clucking-hen, and grain is strewed before him as if
he were a hen.[5]

Again, the corn-spirit is killed in the form of

---

[1] *Die Korndämonen*, p. 13 *sq.*;
Kuhn, *Westfälische Sagen, Märchen und
Gebräuche*, ii. p. 180 *sq.*; Pfannen-
schmid, *Germanische Erntefeste*, p. 110.

[2] *Die Korndämonen*, p. 14; Pfannenschmid, *op. cit.* pp. 111, 419 *sq.*

[3] *Die Korndämonen*, p. 15. So in
Shropshire, where the corn-spirit is
conceived in the form of a gander (see
above, vol. i. p. 407), the expression for

overthrowing a load at harvest is "to
lose the goose," and the penalty used
to be the loss of the goose at the harvest
supper (Burne and Jackson, *Shropshire
Folk-lore*, p. 375); and in some parts
of England the harvest supper was
called the Harvest Gosling, or the
Inning Goose (Brand, *Popular Antiquities*, ii. 23, 26, Bohn's ed.)

[4] *Die Korndämonen*, p. 14.

[5] *Ib.* p. 15.

a cock. In parts of Germany, Hungary, Poland, and Picardy, the reapers place a live cock in the corn which is to be cut last, and chase it over the field, or bury it up to the neck in the ground; afterwards they strike off its head with a sickle or scythe.[1] In many parts of Westphalia, when the harvesters bring the wooden cock to the farmer, he gives them a live cock, which they kill with whips or sticks, or behead with an old sword, or throw it into the barn to the girls, or give it to the mistress to cook. If the Harvest-cock has not been spilt—that is, if no waggon has been upset—the harvesters have the right of killing the farmyard cock by throwing stones at it or beheading it. Where this custom has fallen into disuse, it is still common for the farmer's wife to make cockie-leekie for the harvesters, and to show them the head of the cock which has been killed for the soup.[2] In the neighbourhood of Klausenburg, Transylvania, a cock is buried on the harvest-field in the earth, so that only its head appears. A young man then takes a scythe and cuts off the cock's head at a single stroke. If he fails to do this, he is called the Red Cock for a whole year, and people fear that next year's crop will be bad.[3] In the neighbourhood of Udvarhely, Transylvania, a live cock is bound up in the last sheaf and killed with a spit. It is then skinned. The flesh is thrown away, but the skin and feathers are kept till next year; and in spring the grain from the last sheaf is mixed with the feathers of the cock and scattered on the field which is to be tilled.[4] Nothing could set in a clearer

---

[1] *M. F.* p. 30.
[2] *Die Korndämonen*, p. 15.
[3] *Ib.* p. 15 *sq.*
[4] *Ib.* p. 15; *M. F.* p. 30.

light the identification of the cock with the spirit of
the corn.   By being tied up in the last sheaf and
killed, the cock is identified with the corn, and its
death with the cutting of the corn.   By keeping its
feathers till spring, then mixing them with the seed-
corn taken from the very sheaf in which the bird had
been bound, and scattering the feathers together with
the seed over the field, the identity of the bird with
the corn is again emphasised, and its quickening and
fertilising power, as the corn-spirit, is intimated in the
plainest manner.   Thus the corn-spirit, in the form of
a cock, is killed at harvest, but rises to fresh life and
activity in spring.   Again, the equivalence of the cock
to the corn is expressed, hardly less plainly, in the
custom of burying the bird in the ground, and cutting
off its head (like the ears of corn) with the scythe.

Another common embodiment of the corn-spirit is
the hare.[1]   In some parts of Ayrshire the cutting of
the last corn is called " cutting the Hare ; "[2] and in
Germany a name for the last sheaf is the Hare.[3]   In
East Prussia they say that the Hare sits in the last
patch of standing corn, and must be chased out by the
last reaper.   The reapers hurry with their work, each
being anxious not to have "to chase out the Hare ;"
for the man who does so, that is, who cuts the last
corn, is much laughed at.[4]   At Birk in Transylvania,
when the reapers come to the last patch, they cry out,
" We have the Hare."[5]   At Aurich, as we have seen,[6]
an expression for cutting the last corn is " to cut
off the Hare's tail."   " He is killing the Hare " is

---

[1] *Die Korndämonen*, p. 1.
[2] *Folk-lore Journal*, vii. 47.
[3] *Die Korndämonen*, p. 3.
[4] Lemke, *Volksthümliches in Ostpreussen*, i. 24.

[5] G. A. Heinrich, *Agrarische Sitten
und Gebräuche unter den Sachsen
Siebenbürgens*, p. 21.
[6] Above, vol. i. p. 408.

commonly said of the man who cuts the last corn in Germany, Sweden, Holland, France, and Italy.[1] In Norway the man who is thus said to "kill the Hare" must give "hare's blood," in the form of brandy, to his fellows to drink."[2]

Again, the corn-spirit sometimes takes the form of a cat.[3] Near Kiel children are warned not to go into the corn-fields because "the Cat sits there." In the Eisenach Oberland they are told "the Corn-cat will come and fetch you," "the Corn-cat goes in the corn." In some parts of Silesia at mowing the last corn they say, "the Cat is caught;" and at threshing, the man who gives the last stroke is called the Cat. In the neighbourhood of Lyons the last sheaf and the harvest supper are both called the Cat. About Vesoul when they cut the last corn they say, "We have the Cat by the tail." At Briançon, in Dauphiné, at the beginning of reaping, a cat is decked out with ribbons, flowers, and ears of corn. It is called the Cat of the ball-skin (*le chat de peau de balle*). If a reaper is wounded at his work, they make the cat lick the wound. At the close of the reaping the cat is again decked out with ribbons and ears of corn; then there is dancing and merriment. When the dance is over, the cat is solemnly stripped of its ornaments by the girls. At Grüneberg in Silesia the reaper who cuts the last corn is called the Tom-cat. He is enveloped in rye-stalks and green withes, and is furnished with a long plaited tail. Sometimes as a companion he has a man similarly dressed, who is called the (female) Cat. Their duty is to run after people whom they see and beat them with a long stick. Near Amiens the

---

[1] *M. F.* p. 29.   [2] *M. F.* p. 29 *sq.*; *Die Korndämonen*, p. 5.
[3] *A. W. F.* pp. 172-174; *M. F.* p. 30.

expression for finishing the harvest is, " They are
going to kill the Cat ; " and when the last corn is
cut a cat is killed in the farmyard. At threshing,
in some parts of France, a live cat is placed under the
last bundle of corn to be threshed, and is struck dead
with the flails. Then on Sunday it is roasted and
eaten as a holiday dish.

Further, the corn-spirit often appears in the form of
a goat. In the province of Prussia, when the corn
bends before the wind, they say, " The Goats are
chasing each other," " the wind is driving the Goats
through the corn," " the Goats are browsing there," and
they expect a very good harvest. Again they say,
" the Oats-goat is sitting in the oats-field," "the Corn-
goat is sitting in the rye-field." [1]   Children are warned
not to go into the corn-fields to pluck the blue corn-
flowers, or amongst the beans to pluck pods, because
the Rye-goat, the Corn-goat, the Oats-goat, or the
Bean-goat is sitting or lying there, and will carry them
away or kill them. [2]   When a harvester is taken sick or
lags behind his fellows at their work, they call out, "The
Harvest-goat has pushed him," " he has been pushed
by the Corn-goat." [3]   In the neighbourhood of Brauns-
berg (East Prussia) at binding the oats every harvester
makes haste " lest the Corn-goat push him." At
Oefoten in Norway each harvester has his allotted
patch to reap. When a harvester in the middle has
not finished reaping his piece after his neighbours have
finished theirs, they say of him, " He remains on the
island." And if the laggard is a man, they imitate the
cry with which they call a he-goat ; if a woman, the
cry with which they call a she-goat. [4]   Near Straubing

---

[1] W. Mannhardt, *A. W. F.* p.
155 *sq.*   [2] *Ib.* p. 157 *sq.*

[3] *Ib.* p. 159.
[4] *Ib.* p. 161 *sq.*

in Lower Bavaria, it is said of the man who cuts
the last corn that " he has the Corn-goat or the
Wheat-goat, or the Oats-goat," according to the crop.
Moreover, two horns are set up on the last heap of
corn, and it is called " the horned Goat." At Kreutz-
burg, East Prussia, they call out to the woman who is
binding the last sheaf, " The Goat is sitting in the
sheaf."[1] At Gablingen in Swabia, when the last field
of oats upon a farm is being reaped, the reapers carve
a goat out of wood. Ears of oats are inserted in its
nostrils and mouth, and it is adorned with garlands
of flowers. It is set upon the field and called the
Oats-goat. When the reaping approaches an end,
each reaper hastens to finish his piece first; he who
is the last to finish gets the Oats-goat.[2] Again, the
last sheaf is itself called the Goat. Thus, in the valley
of the Wiesent, Bavaria, the last sheaf bound on the
field is called the Goat, and they have a proverb, " The
field must bear a goat.[3] At Spachbrücken in Hesse,
the last handful of corn which is cut is called the Goat,
and the man who cuts it is much ridiculed.[4] Sometimes the last sheaf is made up in the form of a goat,[5]
and they say, " The Goat is sitting in it." Again,
the person who cuts or binds the last sheaf is called
the Goat. Thus, in parts of Mecklenburg they call
out to the woman who binds the last sheaf, " You
are the Harvest-goat." In the neighbourhood of Uel-
zen in Hanover, the harvest festival begins with " the
bringing of the Harvest-goat;" that is, the woman
who bound the last sheaf is wrapt in straw, crowned
with a harvest-wreath, and brought in a wheelbarrow

---

[1] W. Mannhardt, *A. W. F.* p. 162.
[2] Panzer, *Beitrag zur deutschen Mythologie,* ii. p. 232 *sq.* No. 426; *A. W. F.* p. 162.
[3] Panzer, *op. cit.* ii. p. 228 *sq.* No. 422; *A. W. F.* p. 163.
[4] *A. W. F.* p. 163.
[5] *Ib.* p. 164.

to the village, where a round dance takes place. About Lüneburg, also, the woman who binds the last corn is decked with a crown of corn-ears and is called the Corn-goat.[1]   In the Canton St. Gall, Switzerland, the person who cuts the last handful of corn on the field, or drives the last harvest-waggon to the barn, is called the Corn-goat or the Rye-goat, or simply the Goat.[2]   In the Canton Thurgau he is called Corn-goat; like a goat he has a bell hung round his neck, is led in triumph, and drenched with liquor.   In parts of Styria, also, the man who cuts the last corn is called Corn-goat, Oats-goat, etc.   As a rule, the man who thus gets the name of Corn-goat has to bear it a whole year till the next harvest.[3]

According to one view, the corn-spirit, who has been caught in the form of a goat or otherwise, lives in the farmhouse or barn over winter.   Thus, each farm has its own embodiment of the corn-spirit.   But, according to another view, the corn-spirit is the genius or deity, not of the corn of one farm only, but of all the corn.   Hence when the corn on one farm is all cut, he flees to another where there is still corn left standing.   This idea is brought out in a harvest-custom which was formerly observed in Skye.   The farmer who first finished reaping sent a man or woman with a sheaf to a neighbouring farmer who had not finished; the latter in his turn, when he had finished, sent on the sheaf to his neighbour who was still reaping; and so the sheaf made the round of the farms till all the corn was cut.   The sheaf was called the *goabbir bhacagh*, that is, the Cripple Goat.[4]   The corn-spirit was probably thus represented as lame because he had been

---

[1] *A. W. F.* p. 164.   [2] *Ib.* p. 164 *sq.*   [3] *Ib.* p. 165.
[4] Brand, *Popular Antiquities*, ii. 24, Bohn's ed. ; *A. W. F.* p. 165.

crippled by the cutting of the corn. We have seen that sometimes the old woman who brings home the last sheaf must limp on one foot.[1] In the Böhmer Wald mountains, between Bohemia and Bavaria, when two peasants are driving home their corn together, they race against each other to see who shall get home first. The village boys mark the loser in the race, and at night they come and erect on the roof of his house the Oats-goat, which is a colossal figure of a goat made of straw.[2]

But sometimes the corn-spirit, in the form of a goat, is believed to be slain on the harvest-field by the sickle or scythe. Thus, in the neighbourhood of Bernkastel, on the Moselle, the reapers determine by lot the order in which they shall follow each other. The first is called the fore-reaper, the last the tail-bearer. If a reaper overtakes the man in front he reaps past him, bending round so as to leave the slower reaper in a patch by himself. This patch is called the Goat; and the man for whom "the Goat is cut" in this way, is laughed and jeered at by his fellows for the rest of the day. When the tail-bearer cuts the last ears of corn, it is said "He is cutting the Goat's neck off."[3] In the neighbourhood of Grenoble, before the end of the reaping, a live goat is adorned with flowers and ribbons and allowed to run about the field. The reapers chase it and try to catch it. When it is caught, the farmer's wife holds it fast while the farmer cuts off its head. The goat's flesh serves to furnish the harvest supper. A piece of the flesh is pickled and kept till the next harvest, when another goat is killed. Then all the harvesters eat

---

[1] Above, vol. i. p. 380.   [2] *A. W. F.* p. 165.
[3] *A. W. F.* p. 166; *M. F.* p. 185.

of the flesh.   On the same day the skin of the goat is
made into a cloak, which the farmer, who works with
his men, must always wear at harvest-time if rain or
bad weather sets in.   But if a reaper gets pains in his
back, the farmer gives him the goat-skin to wear.[1]
The reason for this seems to be that the pains in
the back, being inflicted by the corn-spirit, can also be
healed by it.   Similarly we saw that elsewhere, when
a reaper is wounded at reaping, a cat, as the representative of the corn-spirit, is made to lick the wound.[2]
Esthonian reapers in the island of Mon think that the
man who cuts the first ears of corn at harvest will get
pains in his back,[3]—probably because the corn-spirit is
believed to resent especially the first wound; and, in
order to escape pains in the back, Saxon reapers in
Transylvania gird their loins with the first handful
of ears which they cut.[4]   Here, again, the corn-spirit
is applied to for healing or protection, but in his
original vegetable form, not in the form of a goat
or a cat.

Further, the corn-spirit under the form of a goat is
sometimes conceived as lurking among the cut corn in
the barn, till he is driven from it by the threshing-flail.
For example, in the neighbourhood of Marktl in
Upper Bavaria the sheaves are called Straw-goats or
simply Goats.   They are laid in a great heap on the
open field and threshed by two rows of men standing
opposite each other, who, as they ply their flails, sing a
song in which they say that they see the Straw-goat
amongst the corn-stalks.   The last Goat, that is, the
last sheaf, is adorned with a wreath of violets and other

---

[1] *A. W. F.* p. 166.
[2] Above, p. 11.
[3] Holzmayer, *Osiliana*, p. 107.

[4] G. A. Heinrich, *Agrarische Sitten
u. Gebräuche unter den Sachsen Siebenbürgens*, p. 19.   Cp. *B. K.* p. 482 *sqq.*

flowers and with cakes strung together. It is placed right in the middle of the heap. Some of the threshers rush at it and tear the best of it out; others lay on with their flails so recklessly that heads are sometimes broken. In threshing this last sheaf, each man casts up to the man opposite him the misdeeds of which he has been guilty throughout the year.[1] At Oberinntal in Tyrol the last thresher is called Goat.[2] At Tettnang in Würtemberg the thresher who gives the last stroke to the last bundle of corn before it is turned goes by the name of the He-goat, and it is said " he has driven the He-goat away." The person who, after the bundle has been turned, gives the last stroke of all, is called the She-goat.[3] In this custom it is implied that the corn is inhabited by a pair of corn-spirits, male and female. Further, the corn-spirit, captured in the form of a goat at threshing, is passed on to a neighbour whose threshing is not yet finished. In Franche Comté, as soon as the threshing is over, the young people set up a straw figure of a goat on the farmyard of a neighbour who is still threshing. He must give them wine or money in return. At Ellwangen in Würtemberg the effigy of a goat is made out of the last bundle of corn at threshing ; four sticks form its legs, and two its horns. The man who gives the last stroke with the flail must carry the Goat to the barn of a neighbour who is still threshing and throw it down on the floor ; if he is caught in the act, they tie the Goat on his back.[4] A similar custom is observed at Indersdorf in Upper Bavaria ; the man who throws the straw Goat into the neighbour's barn imitates the bleating of a goat ; if they

[1] Panzer, *Beitrag zur deutschen Mythologie*, ii. p. 225 *sqq.* No. 421 ; *A. W. F.* p. 167 *sq.*
[2] *A. W. F.* p. 168.

[3] E. Meier, *Deutsche Sagen, Sitten und Gebräuche aus Schwaben*, p. 445, No. 162 ; *A. W. F.* p. 168.
[4] *A. W. F.* p. 169.

catch him they blacken his face and tie the Goat on his back.[1] At Zabern in Elsass, when a farmer is a week or more behind his neighbours with his threshing, they set a real stuffed goat (or fox) before his door.[2] Sometimes the spirit of the corn in goat form is believed to be killed at threshing. In the district of Traunstein, Upper Bavaria, it is thought that the Oats-goat is in the last sheaf of oats. He is represented by an old rake set up on end, with an old pot for a head. The children are then told to kill the Oats-goat.[3] A stranger passing a harvest-field is sometimes taken for the Corn-goat escaping in human shape from the cut or threshed grain. Thus, when a stranger passes a harvest-field, all the labourers stop and shout as with one voice " He-goat! He-goat! " At rape-seed thresh-ing in Schleswig, which generally takes place on the field, the same cry is raised if the stranger does not take off his hat.[4]

At sowing their winter corn the Prussian Slavs used to kill a goat, consume its flesh with many superstitious ceremonies, and hang the skin on a high pole near an oak and a large stone. Here it remained till harvest. Then, after a prayer had been offered by a peasant who acted as priest (*Weidulut*), the young folk joined hands and danced round the oak and the pole. Afterwards they scrambled for the bunch of corn, and the priest distributed the herbs with a sparing hand. Then he placed the goat-skin on the large stone, sat down on it and preached to the people about the history of their forefathers and their old heathen customs and beliefs.[5] The goat-skin thus suspended

---

[1] Panzer, *op. cit.* ii. p. 224 *sq.* No. 420 ; *A .W. F.* p. 169.

[2] *A. W. F.* p. 169.

[3] *Ib.* p. 170.   [4] *Ib.* p. 170.

[5] Praetorius, *Deliciae Prussicae*, p. 23 *sq.* ; *B. K.* p. 394 *sq.*

on the field from sowing time to harvest represents the corn-spirit superintending the growth of the corn.

Another form which the corn-spirit often assumes is that of a bull, cow, or ox. When the wind sweeps over the corn they say at Conitz in West Prussia, " The Steer is running in the corn ; "[1] when the corn is thick and strong in one spot, they say in some parts of East Prussia, " The Bull is lying in the corn." When a harvester has overstrained and lamed himself, they say in the Graudenz district (West Prussia), " The Bull pushed him ;" in Lothringen they say, "He has the Bull." The meaning of both expressions is that he has unwittingly lighted upon the divine corn-spirit, who has punished the profane intruder with lameness.[2] So near Chambéry when a reaper wounds himself with his sickle, it is said that he has "the wound of the Ox."[3] In the district of Bunzlau the last sheaf is sometimes made into the shape of a horned ox, stuffed with tow and wrapt in corn-ears. This figure is called the Old Man (*der Alte*). In some parts of Bohemia the last sheaf is made up in human form and called the Buffalo-bull.[4] These cases show a confusion between the anthropomorphic and the theriomorphic conception of the corn-spirit. The confusion is parallel to that of killing a wether under the name of a wolf.[5] In the Canton of Thurgau, Switzerland, the last sheaf, if it is a large one, is called the Cow.[6] All over Swabia the last bundle of corn on the field is called the Cow ; the man who cuts the last ears " has the Cow," and is himself called Cow or Barley-cow or Oats-cow, according to the crop ; at the harvest supper he gets a nosegay of flowers and corn-ears and a more liberal allowance of drink than the rest.

---

[1] *M. F.* p. 58.
[2] *Ib.*
[3] *M. F.* p. 62.
[4] *M. F.* p. 59.
[5] Above, p. 6.
[6] *M. F.* p. 59.

But he is teased and laughed at ; so no one likes to be the Cow.[1] The Cow was sometimes represented by the figure of a woman made out of ears of corn and corn-flowers. It was carried to the farmhouse by the man who had cut the last handful of corn. The children ran after him and the neighbours turned out to laugh at him, till the farmer took the Cow from him.[2] Here again the confusion between the human and the animal form of the corn-spirit is apparent. In various parts of Switzerland the reaper who cuts the last ears of corn is called Wheat-cow, Corn-cow, Oats-cow, or Corn-steer, and is the butt of many a joke.[3] In some parts of East Prussia, when a few ears of corn have been left standing by inadvertence on the last swath, the foremost reaper seizes them and cries, "Bull! Bull!"[4] On the other hand, in the district of Rosenheim, in Upper Bavaria, when a farmer is later in getting in his harvest than his neighbours, they set up on his land a Straw-bull, as it is called. This is a gigantic figure of a bull made of stubble on a framework of wood and adorned with flowers and leaves. A label is attached to it containing doggerel verses in ridicule of the man on whose land the Straw-bull is placed.[5]

Again, the corn-spirit in the form of a bull or ox is killed on the harvest-field at the close of the reaping. At Pouilly near Dijon, when the last ears of corn are about to be cut, an ox adorned with ribbons, flowers, and ears of corn is led all round the field, followed by the whole troop of reapers dancing. Then a man

---

[1] E. Meier, *Deutsche Sagen, Sitten und Gebräuche aus Schwaben*, p. 440 *sq.* Nos. 151, 152, 153 ; Panzer, *Beitrag zur deutschen Mythologie*, ii. p. 234, No. 428 ; *M. F.* p. 59.

[2] Panzer, *op. cit.* ii. p. 233, No. 427 ; *M. F.* p. 59.

[3] *M. F.* p. 59 *sq.*

[4] *M. F.* p. 58.

[5] *M. F.* p. 58 *sq.*

disguised as the Devil cuts the last ears of corn and immediately kills the ox. Part of the flesh of the animal is eaten at the harvest supper ; part is pickled and kept till the first day of sowing in spring. At Pont à Mousson and elsewhere on the evening of the last day of reaping a calf adorned with flowers and ears of corn is led three times round the farmyard, being allured by a bait or driven by men with sticks, or conducted by the farmer's wife with a rope. The calf selected for this ceremony is the calf which was born first on the farm in the spring of the year. It is followed by all the reapers with their implements. Then it is allowed to run free ; the reapers chase it, and whoever catches it is called King of the Calf. Lastly, it is solemnly killed ; at Lunéville the man who acts as butcher is the Jewish merchant of the village.[1]

Sometimes again the corn-spirit hides himself amongst the cut corn in the barn to reappear in bull or cow form at threshing. Thus at Wurmlingen in Thüringen the man who gives the last stroke at threshing is called the Cow, or rather the Barley-cow, Oats-cow, Peas-cow, etc., according to the crop. He is entirely enveloped in straw ; his head is surmounted by sticks in imitation of horns, and two lads lead him by ropes to the well to drink. On the way thither he must low like a cow, and for a long time afterwards he goes by the name of the Cow.[2] At Obermedlingen in Swabia, when the threshing draws near an end, each man is careful to avoid giving the last stroke. He who does give it "gets the Cow," which is a straw figure dressed in an old ragged petticoat, hood, and

[1] *M. F.* p. 60.
[2] E. Meier, *Deutsche Sagen, Sitten*   *und Gebräuche aus Schwaben,* p. 444 *sq.* No. 162 ; *M. F.* p. 61.

stockings. It is tied on his back with a straw-rope ;
his face is blackened, he is tied with straw-ropes to a
wheelbarrow, and wheeled round the village.[1] Here,
again, we are met with that confusion between the
anthropomorphic and theriomorphic conception of the
corn-spirit, which has been already signalised. In
Canton Schaffhausen the man who threshes the last
corn is called the Cow ; in Canton Thurgau, the Corn-
bull ; in Canton Zürich, the Thresher-cow. In the
last-mentioned district he is wrapt in straw and bound
to one of the trees in the orchard.[2] At Arad in
Hungary the man who gives the last stroke at threshing is enveloped in straw and a cow's hide with the
horns attached to it.[3] At Pessnitz, in the district of
Dresden, the man who gives the last stroke with the
flail is called Bull. He must make a straw-man and
set it up before a neighbour's window.[4] Here, apparently, as in so many cases, the corn-spirit is passed on
to a neighbour who has not finished threshing. So at
Herbrechtingen in Thüringen the effigy of a ragged
old woman is flung into the barn of the farmer who is
last with his threshing. The man who throws it in
cries, "There is the Cow for you." If the threshers
catch him they detain him over night and punish him
by keeping him from the harvest supper.[5] In these
latter customs the confusion between the anthropomorphic and theriomorphic conception of the corn-
spirit meets us again. Further, the corn-spirit in bull
form is sometimes believed to be killed at threshing.
At Auxerre in threshing the last bundle of corn they
call out twelve times, "We are killing the Bull." In

---

[1] Panzer, *Beitrag zur deutschen
Mythologie*, ii. p. 233, No. 427.
[2] *M. F.* p. 61 *sq.*
[3] *M. F.* p. 62.
[4] *M. F.* p. 62.
[5] E. Meier, *op. cit.* p. 445 *sq.* No.
163.

the neighbourhood of Bordeaux, where a butcher kills
an ox on the field immediately after the close of the
reaping, it is said of the man who gives the last stroke
at threshing that "he has killed the Bull."[1]   At Chambéry the last sheaf is called the sheaf of the Young Ox
and a race takes place to it, in which all the reapers
join.   When the last stroke is given at threshing they
say that "the Ox is killed;" and immediately thereupon a real ox is slaughtered by the reaper who cut
the last corn.   The flesh of the ox is eaten by the
threshers at supper.[2]

We have seen that sometimes the young corn-
spirit, whose task it is to quicken the corn of the
coming year, is believed to be born as a Corn-baby on
the harvest-field.[3]   Similarly in Berry the young corn-
spirit is sometimes believed to be born on the field in
calf form.   For when a binder has not rope enough to
bind all the corn in sheaves, he puts aside the wheat
that remains over and imitates the lowing of a cow.
The meaning is that "the sheaf has given birth to a
calf."[4]   In Puy-de-Dôme when a binder cannot keep
up with the reaper whom he or she follows, they
say "He or she is giving birth to the Calf."[5]   In
some parts of Prussia, in similar circumstances,
they call out to the woman, "The Bull is coming,"
and imitate the bellowing of a bull.[6]   In these
cases the woman is conceived as the Corn-cow or
old corn-spirit, while the supposed calf is the Corn-
calf or young corn-spirit.   In some parts of Austria a
mythical calf (*Muhkälbchen*) is believed to be seen
amongst the sprouting corn in spring and to push the

[1] *M. F.* p. 60.   [2] *M. F.* p. 62.   *Légendes du Centre de la France*, ii.
[3] Above, vol. i. p. 343 *sq.*   135.   [5] *M. F.* p. 62, "*Il fait le veau.*"
[4] Laisnel de la Salle, *Croyances et*   [6] *M. F.* p. 62.

children; when the corn waves in the wind they say,
"The Calf is going about." Clearly, as Mannhardt
observes, this calf of the spring-time is the same animal
which is afterwards believed to be killed at reaping.[1]

Sometimes the corn-spirit appears in the shape of
a horse or mare. Between Kalw and Stuttgart, when
the corn bends before the wind, they say, "There runs
the Horse."[2] In Hertfordshire, at the end of the
reaping, there is or was a ceremony called "crying
the Mare." The last blades of corn left standing on
the field are tied together and called the Mare. The
reapers stand at a distance and throw their sickles at
it; he who cuts it through "has the prize, with
acclamations and good cheer." After it is cut the
reapers cry thrice with a loud voice, "I have her!"
Others answer thrice, "What have you?"—"A Mare!
a Mare! a Mare!"—"Whose is she?" is next asked
thrice. "A. B.'s," naming the owner thrice. "Whither
will you send her?"—"To C. D.," naming some neighbour who has not all his corn reaped.[3] In this custom
the corn-spirit in the form of a mare is passed on from
a farm where the corn is all cut to another farm where
it is still standing, and where therefore the corn-spirit
may be supposed naturally to take refuge. In Shropshire the custom is similar. "Crying, calling, or
shouting the mare is a ceremony performed by the
men of that farm which is the first in any parish or
district to finish the harvest. The object of it is to
make known their own prowess, and to taunt the
laggards by a pretended offer of the 'owd mar'' [old
mare] to help out their 'chem' [team]. All the men
assemble (the wooden harvest-bottle being of course

---

[1] *M. F.* p. 63.
[2] *M. F.* p. 167.

[3] Brand, *Popular Antiquities*, ii. 24,
Bohn's ed.

one of the company) in the stackyard, or, better, on
the highest ground on the farm, and there shout the
following dialogue, preceding it by a grand ' Hip, hip,
hip, hurrah !'

" ' I 'ave 'er, I 'ave 'er, I 'ave 'er !'

" ' Whad 'ast thee, whad 'ast thee, whad 'ast thee ?'

" ' A mar' ! a mar' ! a mar' !'

" ' Whose is 'er, whose is 'er, whose is 'er ?'

" ' Maister A.'s, Maister A.'s, Maister A.'s !'
(naming the farmer whose harvest is finished).

" ' W'eer sha't the' send 'er ? w'eer sha't the' send
'er ? w'eer sha't the' send 'er ?'

" ' To Maister B.'s, to Maister B.'s, to Maister
B.'s ' (naming one whose harvest is *not* finished)."

The farmer who finishes his harvest last, and who
therefore cannot send the Mare to any one else, is
said "to keep her all winter." The mocking offer
of the Mare was sometimes responded to by a
mocking acceptance of her help. Thus an old man
told an inquirer, "While we wun at supper, a mon
cumm'd wi' a autar [halter] to fatch her away."
But at one place (Longnor, near Leebotwood), down
to about 1850, the Mare used really to be sent.
"The head man of the farmer who had finished
harvest first was mounted on the best horse of the
team—the leader—both horse and man being adorned
with ribbons, streamers, etc. Thus arrayed, a boy
on foot led the pair in triumph to the neighbouring
farmhouses. Sometimes the man who took the
' mare ' received, as well as plenty of harvest-ale,
some rather rough, though good-humoured, treatment,
coming back minus his decorations, and so on." [1] In
the neighbourhood of Lille the idea of the corn-spirit

---

[1] Burne and Jackson, *Shropshire Folk-lore*, p. 373 *sq.*

in horse form is clearly preserved. When a harvester grows weary at his work, it is said, " He has the fatigue of the Horse." The first sheaf, called the "Cross of the Horse," is placed on a cross of box-wood in the barn, and the youngest horse on the farm must tread on it. The reapers dance round the last blades of corn, crying, " See the remains of the Horse." The sheaf made out of these last blades is given to the youngest horse of the parish (commune) to eat. This youngest horse of the parish clearly represents, as Mannhardt says, the corn-spirit of the following year, the Corn-foal, which absorbs the spirit of the old Corn-horse by eating the last corn cut ; for, as usual, the old corn-spirit takes his final refuge in the last sheaf. The thresher of the last sheaf is said to " beat the Horse." [1] Again, a trace of the horse-shaped corn-spirit is reported from Berry. The harvesters there are accustomed to take a noon-day sleep in the field. This is called " seeing the Horse." The leader or " King " of the harvesters gives the signal for going to sleep. If he delays giving the signal, one of the harvesters will begin to neigh like a horse, the rest imitate him, and then they all go " to see the Horse." [2]

The last animal embodiment of the corn-spirit which we shall notice is the pig (boar or sow). In Thüringen, when the wind sets the young corn in motion, they sometimes say, " The Boar is rushing through the corn." [3] Amongst the Esthonians of the island of Oesel the last sheaf is called the Rye-boar, and the man who gets it is saluted with a cry of,

---

[1] *M. F.* p. 167.
[2] Laisnel de la Salle, *Croyances et Légendes du Centre de la France,* ii. 133 ; *M. F.* p. 167 *sq.*

[3] Witzschel, *Sagen, Sitten und Gebräuche aus Thüringen,* p. 213, No. 4.

"You have the Rye-boar on your back!" In reply
he strikes up a song, in which he prays for plenty.[1]
At Kohlerwinkel, near Augsburg, at the close of the
harvest, the last bunch of standing corn is cut down,
stalk by stalk, by all the reapers in turn. He who
cuts the last stalk "gets the Sow," and is laughed at.[2]
In other Swabian villages also the man who cuts the
last corn "has the Sow," or "has the Rye-sow."[3] In
the Traunstein district, Upper Bavaria, the man who
cuts the last handful of rye or wheat "has the Sow,"
and is called Sow-driver.[4] At Friedingen, in Swabia,
the thresher who gives the last stroke is called Sow—
Barley-sow, Corn-sow, etc., according to the crop.
At Onstmettingen the man who gives the last stroke
at threshing "has the Sow;" he is often bound up
in a sheaf and dragged by a rope along the ground.[5]
And, generally, in Swabia the man who gives the last
stroke with the flail is called Sow. He may, however,
rid himself of this invidious distinction by passing on
to a neighbour the straw-rope, which is the badge of
his position as Sow. So he goes to a house and
throws the straw-rope into it, crying, "There, I
bring you the Sow." All the inmates give chase;
and if they catch him they beat him, shut him up for
several hours in the pig-sty, and oblige him to take
the "Sow" away again.[6] In various parts of Upper
Bavaria the man who gives the last stroke at threshing
must "carry the Pig"—that is, either a straw effigy of
a pig or merely a bundle of straw-ropes. This he

---

[1] Holzmayer, *Osiliana*, p. 107; *M.
F.* p. 187.
[2] Birlinger, *Aus Schwaben*, ii. 328.
[3] Panzer, *Beitrag zur deutschen
Mythologie*, ii. pp. 223, 224, Nos. 417,
419.
[4] *M. F.* p. 112.
[5] E. Meier, *Deutsche Sagen, Sitten
und Gebräuche aus Schwaben*, p. 445,
No. 162.
[6] Birlinger, *Volksthümliches aus
Schwaben*, ii. 425, No. 379.

carries to a neighbouring farm where the threshing is not finished, and throws it into the barn. If the threshers catch him they handle him roughly, beating him, blackening or dirtying his face, throwing him into filth, binding the Sow on his back, etc. ; if the bearer of the Sow is a woman they cut off her hair. At the harvest supper or dinner the man who " carried the Pig " gets one or more dumplings made in the form of pigs ; sometimes he gets a large dumpling and a number of small ones, all in pig form, the large one being called the sow and the small ones the sucking-pigs. Sometimes he has the right to be the first to put his hand into the dish and take out as many small dumplings ("sucking-pigs ") as he can, while the other threshers strike at his hand with spoons or sticks. When the dumplings are served up by the maid-servant, all the people at table cry, " Süz, süz, süz ! " being the cry used in calling pigs. Sometimes after dinner the man who " carried the Pig " has his face blackened, and is set on a cart and drawn round the village by his fellows, followed by a crowd crying, " Süz, süz, süz ! " as if they were calling swine. Sometimes, after being wheeled round the village, he is flung on the dunghill.[1]

Again, the corn-spirit in the form of a pig plays his part at sowing-time as well as at harvest. At Neuautz, in Courland, when barley is sown for the first time in the year, the farmer's wife boils the chine of a pig along with the tail, and brings it to the sower on the field. He eats of it, but cuts off the tail and sticks it in the field ; it is believed that the ears of corn will then grow as long as the tail.[2] Here the pig is the corn-spirit,

---

[1] Panzer, *Beitrag zur deutschen Mythologie*, ii. pp. 221-224, Nos. 409, 410, 411, 412, 413, 414, 415, 418.   [2] *M. F.* p. 186 *sq.*

Romans sacrificing a bull, a goat, and a pig: all these animals were supposed to be forms of the corn-spirit.

The corn-spirit embodied in pig form in the Scandinavian Yule
Boar.

whose fertilising power is sometimes supposed to
lie especially in his tail.[1] As a pig he is put in the
ground at sowing-time, and as a pig he reappears
amongst the ripe corn at harvest. For amongst
the neighbouring Esthonians, as we have seen,[2] the
last sheaf is called the Rye-boar. Somewhat similar
customs are observed in Germany. In the Salza
district, near Meiningen, a certain bone in the pig
is called "the Jew on the winnowing-fan" (*der Jud'*
auf der Wanne). The flesh of this bone is boiled
on Shrove Tuesday, but the bone is put amongst
the ashes, which the neighbours exchange as presents
on St. Peter's Day (22d February), and then mix
with the seed-corn.[3] In the whole of Hessen,
Meiningen, etc., people eat pea-soup with dried
pig-ribs on Ash Wednesday or Candlemas. The
ribs are then collected and hung in the room till
sowing-time, when they are inserted in the sown
field or in the seed-bag amongst the flax seed. This
is thought to be an infallible specific against earth-
fleas and moles, and to cause the flax to grow well
and tall.[4] In many parts of White Russia people
eat a roast lamb or sucking-pig at Easter, and then
throw the bones backwards upon the fields, to preserve the corn from hail.[5]

But the conception of the corn-spirit as embodied
in pig form is nowhere more clearly expressed than in
the Scandinavian custom of the Yule Boar. In Sweden
and Denmark at Yule (Christmas) it is the custom to
bake a loaf in the form of a boar-pig. This is called

[1] Above, p. 3.
[2] Above, p. 26 *sq.*
[3] *M. F.* p. 187.
[4] *M. F.* p. 187 *sq.*; Witzschel, *Sagen,*
Sitten und Gebräuche aus Thüringen,

pp. 189, 218; W. Kolbe, *Hessische*
Volks-Sitten und Gebräuche (Marburg,
1888), p. 35.
[5] *M. F.* p. 188; Ralston, *Songs of*
the Russian People, p. 220.

the Yule Boar. The corn of the last sheaf is often used to make it. All through Yule the Yule Boar stands on the table. Often it is kept till the sowing-time in spring, when part of it is mixed with the seed-corn and part given to the ploughmen and plough-horses or plough-oxen to eat, in the expectation of a good harvest.[1] In this custom the corn-spirit, immanent in the last sheaf, appears at midwinter in the form of a boar made from the corn of the last sheaf; and his quickening influence on the corn is shown by mixing part of the Yule Boar with the seed-corn, and giving part of it to the plough-man and his cattle to eat. Similarly we saw that the Corn-wolf makes his appearance at midwinter, the time when the year begins to verge towards spring.[2] We may conjecture that the Yule straw, of which Swedish peasants make various superstitious uses, comes, in part at least, from the sheaf out of which the Yule Boar is made. The Yule straw is long rye-straw, a portion of which is always set apart for this season. It is strewn over the floor at Christmas, and the peasants attribute many virtues to it. For example, they think that some of it scattered on the ground will make a barren field productive. Again, the peasant at Christmas seats himself on a log; his eldest son or daughter, or the mother herself, if the children are not old enough, places a wisp of the Yule straw on his knee. From this he draws out single straws, and throws them, one by one, up to the ceiling; and as many as lodge in the rafters, so many will be the sheaves of rye he

[1] *A. W. F.* p. 197 *sq.*; Panzer, *Beitrag zur deutschen Mythologie*, ii. p. 491 ; Jamieson, *Dictionary of the Scottish Language*, *s.v.* " Maiden"; Afzelius, *Volkssagen und Volkslieder aus Schwedens älterer und neuerer Zeit*, übersetzt von Ungewitter, i. 9.

[2] Above, p. 6 *sq.*

will have to thresh at harvest.[1] Again, it is only the Yule straw which may be used in binding the fruit-trees as a charm to fertilise them.[2] These uses of the Yule straw show that it is believed to possess fertilising virtues analogous to those ascribed to the Yule Boar; the conjecture is therefore legitimate that the Yule straw is made from the same sheaf as the Yule Boar. Formerly a real boar was sacrificed at Christmas,[3] and apparently also a man in the character of the Yule Boar. This, at least, may perhaps be inferred from a Christmas custom still observed in Sweden. A man is wrapt up in a skin, and carries a wisp of straw in his mouth, so that the projecting straws look like the bristles of a boar. A knife is brought, and an old woman, with her face blackened, pretends to sacrifice the man.[4]

So much for the animal embodiments of the corn-spirit as they are presented to us in the folk-customs of Northern Europe. These customs bring out clearly the sacramental character of the harvest supper. The corn-spirit is conceived as embodied in an animal; this divine animal is slain, and its flesh and blood are partaken of by the harvesters. Thus, the cock, the goose, the hare, the cat, the goat, and the ox are eaten sacramentally by the harvesters, and the pig is eaten sacramentally by ploughmen in spring.[5] Again, as a substitute for the real flesh of the divine being, bread or dumplings are made in his image and eaten sacramentally; thus, pig-shaped dumplings are eaten by the

---

[1] L. Lloyd, *Peasant Life in Sweden*, pp. 169 *sq.*, 182. On Christmas night children sleep on a bed of the Yule straw (*ib.* p. 177).

[2] Jahn, *Deutsche Opfergebräuche*, p. 215. Cp. above, vol. i. p. 60.

[3] Afzelius, *op. cit.* i. 31.

[4] Afzelius, *op. cit.* i. 9; Lloyd, *Peasant Life in Sweden*, pp. 181, 185.

[5] Above, pp. 8 *sq.*, 11, 12, 15 *sq.*, 21, 23, 28. In regard to the hare, the substitution of brandy for hare's blood is doubtless comparatively modern.

harvesters, and loaves made in boar-shape (the Yule Boar) are eaten in spring by the ploughman and his cattle.

The reader has probably remarked the complete parallelism between the anthropomorphic and the theriomorphic conceptions of the corn-spirit. The parallel may be here briefly resumed. When the corn waves in the wind it is said either that the Corn-mother or that the Corn-wolf, etc. is passing through the corn. Children are warned against straying in corn-fields either because the Corn-mother or because the Corn-wolf, etc. is there. In the last corn cut or the last sheaf threshed either the Corn-mother or the Corn-wolf, etc. is supposed to be present. The last sheaf is itself called either the Corn-mother or the Corn-wolf, etc., and is made up in the shape either of a woman or of a wolf, etc. The person who cuts, binds, or threshes the last sheaf is called either the Old Woman or the Wolf, etc., according to the name bestowed on the sheaf itself. As in some places a sheaf made in human form and called the Maiden, the Mother of the Maize, etc. is kept from one harvest to the next in order to secure a continuance of the corn-spirit's blessing; so in some places the Harvest-cock and in others the flesh of the goat is kept for a similar purpose from one harvest to the next. As in some places the grain taken from the Corn-mother is mixed with the seed-corn in spring to make the crop abundant; so in some places the feathers of the cock, and in Sweden the Yule Boar is kept till spring and mixed with the seed-corn for a like purpose. As part of the Corn-mother or Maiden is given to the cattle to eat in order that they may thrive, so part of the Yule Boar is given to the

ploughing horses or oxen in spring.   Lastly, the death
of the corn-spirit is represented by killing (in reality or
pretence) either his human or his animal representative;
and the worshippers partake sacramentally either of
the actual body and blood of the representative (human
or animal) of the divinity, or of bread made in his
likeness.

Other animal forms assumed by the corn-spirit are
the stag, roe, sheep, bear, ass, fox, mouse, stork, swan,
and kite.[1]   If it is asked why the corn-spirit should be
thought to appear in the form of an animal and of
so many different animals, we may reply that to
primitive man the simple appearance of an animal
or bird among the corn is probably sufficient of itself
to suggest a mysterious connection between the animal
or bird and the corn ; and when we remember that in
the old days, before fields were fenced in, all kinds
of animals must have been free to roam over them, we
need not wonder that the corn-spirit should have been
identified even with large animals like the horse and
cow, which nowadays could not, except by a rare
accident, be found straying among the corn.   This
explanation applies with peculiar force to the very
common case in which the animal embodiment of the
corn-spirit is believed to lurk in the last standing corn.
For at harvest a number of wild animals—hares,
rabbits, partridges, etc.—are commonly driven by the
progress of the reaping into the last patch of standing
corn, and make their escape from it as it is being cut
down.   So regularly does this happen that reapers
and others often stand round the last patch of corn
armed with sticks or guns, with which they kill the
animals as they dart out of their last refuge among the

---

[1] *Die Korndämonen*, p. 1.

corn.   Now, primitive man, to whom magical changes
of shape seem perfectly credible, finds it most natural
that the spirit of the corn, driven from his home
amongst the corn, should make his escape in the form
of the animal which is seen to rush out of the last
patch of corn as it falls under the scythe of the reaper.
Thus the identification of the corn-spirit with an
animal is analogous to the identification of him with
a passing stranger.   As the sudden appearance of a
stranger near the harvest-field or threshing-floor is, to
the primitive mind, sufficient to identify him as the
spirit of the corn escaping from the cut or threshed
corn, so the sudden appearance of an animal issuing
from the cut corn is enough to identify it with the
corn-spirit escaping from his ruined home.   The two
identifications are so analogous that they can hardly be
dissociated in any attempt to explain them.   Those
who look to some other principle than the one here
suggested for the explanation of the latter identification are bound to show that their explanation covers
the former identification also.

But however we may explain it, the fact remains
that in peasant folk-lore the corn-spirit is very commonly conceived and represented in animal form.
May not this fact explain the relation in which certain
animals stood to the ancient deities of vegetation,
Dionysus, Demeter, Adonis, Attis, and Osiris ?

To begin with Dionysus.   We have seen that he
was represented sometimes as a goat and sometimes
as a bull.   As a goat he can hardly be separated from
the minor divinities, the Pans, Satyrs, and Silenuses,
all of whom are closely associated with him and are
represented more or less completely in the form of
goats.   Thus, Pan was regularly represented in

sculpture and painting with the face and legs of a goat.[1] The Satyrs were depicted with pointed goat-ears, and sometimes with sprouting horns and short tails.[2] They were sometimes spoken of simply as goats ;[3] and in the drama their parts were played by men dressed in goat-skins.[4] Silenus is represented in art clad in a goat-skin.[5] Further, the Fauns, the Italian counterpart of the Greek Pans and Satyrs, are described as being half goats, with goat-feet and goat-horns.[6] Again, all these minor goat-formed divinities partake more or less clearly of the character of woodland deities. Thus, Pan was called by the Arcadians the Lord of the Wood.[7] The Silenuses associated with the tree-nymphs.[8] The Fauns are expressly designated as woodland deities ;[9] and their character as such is still further brought out by their association, or even identification, with Silvanus and the Silvanuses, who, as their name of itself indicates, are spirits of the woods.[10] Lastly, the association of the Satyrs with the Silenuses, Fauns, and Silvanuses,[11] proves that the Satyrs also were woodland deities. These goat-formed spirits of the woods have their counterparts in the folk-lore of Northern Europe. Thus, the Russian wood-spirits, called *Ljeschie* (from *ljes*, "wood,") are believed to appear partly in human shape, but with the horns, ears, and legs of goats. The *Ljeschi* can alter his stature at pleasure ; when he

---

[1] Herodotus, ii. 46.

[2] Preller, *Griechische Mythologie*,[3] i. 600 ; *A. W. F.* p. 138.

[3] *A. W. F.* p. 139.

[4] Pollux, iv. 118.

[5] *A. W. F.* p. 142 *sq.*

[6] Ovid, *Fasti*, ii. 361 ; iii. 312 ; v. 101 ; *id.*, *Heroides*, iv. 49.

[7] Macrobius, *Sat.* i. 22, 3.

[8] Homer, *Hymn to Aphrodite*, 262 *sqq.*

[9] Pliny, *N. H.* xii. 3 ; Ovid, *Metam.* vi. 392 ; *id.*, *Fasti*, iii. 303, 309 ; Gloss. Isid. Mart. Cap. ii. 167, cited by Mannhardt, *A. W. F.* p. 113.

[10] Pliny, *N. H.* xii. 3 ; Martianus Capella, ii. 167 ; Augustine, *Civ. Dei*, xv. 23 ; Aurelius Victor, *Origo gentis Romanae*, iv. 6.

[11] Servius on Virgil, *Ecl.* vi. 14 ; Ovid, *Metam.* vi. 392 *sq.* ; Martianus Capella, ii. 167.

walks in the wood he is as tall as the trees; when he walks in the meadows he is no higher than the grass. Some of the *Ljeschie* are spirits of the corn as well as of the wood; before harvest they are as tall as the corn-stalks, but after it they shrink to the height of the stubble.[1] This brings out—what we have remarked before—the close connection between tree-spirits and corn-spirits, and shows how easily the former may melt into the latter. Similarly the Fauns, though wood-spirits, were believed to foster the growth of the crops.[2] We have already seen how often the corn-spirit is represented in folk-custom as a goat.[3] On the whole, then, as Mannhardt argues,[4] the Pans, Satyrs, and Fauns appear to belong to a widely diffused class of wood-spirits conceived in goat-form. The fondness of goats for straying in woods and nibbling the bark of trees—to which it is well known that they are most destructive—is an obvious and perhaps sufficient reason why wood-spirits should so often be supposed to take the form of goats. The inconsistency of a god of vegetation subsisting upon the vegetation which he personifies is not one to strike the primitive mind. Such inconsistencies arise when the deity, ceasing to be immanent in the vegetation, comes to be regarded as its owner or lord; for the idea of owning the vegetation naturally leads to that of subsisting on it. We have already seen that the corn-spirit, originally conceived as immanent in the corn, afterwards comes to be regarded as its owner, who lives on it and is reduced to poverty and want by being deprived of it.[5]

Thus the representation of wood-spirits in goat-form appears to be both widespread and, to the primi-

---

[1] *B. K.* p. 138 *sq.*; *A. W. F.* p. 145.   [2] Servius on Virgil, *Georg.* i. 10.
[3] Above, p. 12 *sqq.*   [4] *A. W. F.* ch. iii.   [5] Above, vol. i. p. 379 *sq.*

tive mind, natural. Therefore when we find, as we have done, that Dionysus—a tree-god—is sometimes represented in goat form,[1] we can hardly avoid concluding that this representation is simply a part of his proper character as a tree-god and is not to be explained by the fusion of two distinct and independent cults, in one of which he originally appeared as a tree-god and in the other as a goat. If such a fusion took place in the case of Dionysus, it must equally have taken place in the case of the Pans and Satyrs of Greece, the Fauns of Italy, and the *Ljeschie* of Russia. That such a fusion of two wholly disconnected cults should have occurred once is possible; that it should have occurred twice independently is improbable; that it should have occurred thrice independently is so unlikely as to be practically incredible.

Dionysus was also represented, as we have seen,[2] in the form of a bull. After what has gone before we are naturally led to expect that his bull form must have been only another expression for his character as a deity of vegetation, especially as the bull is a common embodiment of the corn-spirit in Northern Europe;[3] and the close association of Dionysus with Demeter and Proserpine in the mysteries of Eleusis shows that he had at least strong agricultural affinities. The other possible explanation of the bull-shaped Dionysus would be that the conception of him as a bull was originally entirely distinct from the conception of him as a deity of vegetation, and that the fusion of the two conceptions was due to some such circumstance as the union of two tribes, one of which had previously worshipped a bull-god and the other a tree-god. This appears to be the view taken by Mr. Andrew Lang, who suggests that

---

[1] Above, vol. i. p. 326 *sq.*   [2] Above, vol. i. p. 325 *sq.*   [3] Above, p. 19 *sqq.*

the bull-formed Dionysus " had either been developed
out of, or had succeeded to the worship of a bull-totem."[1]
Of course this is possible. But it is not yet certain
that the Aryans ever had totemism. On the other
hand, it is quite certain that many Aryan peoples have
conceived deities of vegetation as embodied in animal
forms. Therefore when we find amongst an Aryan
people like the Greeks a deity of vegetation represented
as an animal, the presumption must be in favour of
explaining this by a principle which is certainly known
to have influenced the Aryan race rather than by one
which is not certainly known to have done so. In the
present state of our knowledge, therefore, it is safer to
regard the bull form of Dionysus as being, like his
goat form, an expression of his proper character as a
deity of vegetation.

The probability of this view will be somewhat
increased if it can be shown that in other rites than
those of Dionysus the ancients slew an ox as a representative of the spirit of vegetation. This they appear
to have done in the Athenian sacrifice known as " the
murder of the ox " (*bouphonia*). It took place about
the end of June or beginning of July, that is, about the
time when the threshing is nearly over in Attica.
According to tradition the sacrifice was instituted to
procure a cessation of drought and barrenness which had
afflicted the land. The ritual was as follows. Barley
mixed with wheat, or cakes made of them, were laid
upon the bronze altar of Zeus Polieus on the Acropolis.
Oxen were driven round the altar, and the ox which
went up to the altar and ate the offering on it was sacrificed. The axe and knife with which the beast was
slain had been previously wetted with water brought

---

[1] A. Lang, *Myth, Ritual, and Religion,* ii. 232.

A faun and a satyr.

The Temple of Eleusis, where the Eleusinian mysteries were celebrated.

by maidens called "water-carriers." The weapons were then sharpened and handed to the butchers, one of whom felled the ox with the axe and another cut its throat with the knife. As soon as he had felled the ox, the former threw the axe from him and fled ; and the man who cut the beast's throat apparently imitated his example. Meantime the ox was skinned and all present partook of its flesh. Then the hide was stuffed with straw and sewed up ; next the stuffed animal was set on its feet and yoked to a plough as if it were ploughing. A trial then took place in an ancient law-court presided over by the King (as he was called) to determine who had murdered the ox. The maidens who had brought the water accused the men who had sharpened the axe and knife ; the men who had sharpened the axe and knife blamed the men who had handed these implements to the butchers ; the men who had handed the implements to the butchers blamed the butchers ; and the butchers laid the blame on the axe and knife, which were accordingly found guilty, condemned, and cast into the sea.[1]

The name of this sacrifice,—"the *murder* of the ox,"[2]—the pains taken by each person who had a hand in the slaughter to lay the blame on some one else,

---

[1] Pausanias, i. 24, 4 ; *id*., i. 28, 10 ; Porphyry, *De abstinentia*, ii. 29 *sq*. ; Aelian, *Var. Hist.* viii. 3 ; Schol. on Aristophanes, *Peace*, 419 ; Hesychius, Suidas, and *Etymol. Magnum, s.v.* βούφονια. The date of the sacrifice (14th Skirophorion) is given by the Schol. on Aristophanes and the *Etym. Magn.* ; and this date corresponds, according to Mannhardt (*M. F.* p. 68), with the close of the threshing in Attica. No writer mentions the trial of both the axe and the knife. Pausanias speaks of the trial of the axe, Porphyry and Aelian of the trial of the knife. But from Porphyry's description it is clear that the slaughter was carried out by two men, one wielding an axe and the other a knife, and that the former laid the blame on the latter. Perhaps the knife alone was condemned. That the King Archon (on whom see above, vol. i. p. 7), presided at the trial of all lifeless objects, is mentioned by Pollux, viii. 90 ; cp. *id*. viii. 120.

[2] The real import of the name *bouphonia* was first perceived by Prof. W. Robertson Smith. See his *Religion of the Semites*, i. 286 *sqq*.

together with the formal trial and punishment of the axe or knife or both, prove that the ox was here regarded not merely as a victim offered to a god, but as itself a sacred creature, the slaughter of which was sacrilege or murder. This is borne out by a statement of Varro that to kill an ox was formerly a capital crime in Attica.[1] The mode of selecting the victim suggests that the ox which tasted the corn was viewed as the corn-deity taking possession of his own. This interpretation is supported by the following custom. In Beauce, in the district of Orleans, on the 24th or 25th of April they make a straw-man called "the great *mondard*." For they say that the old *mondard* is now dead and it is necessary to make a new one. The straw-man is carried in solemn procession up and down the village and at last is placed upon the oldest apple-tree. There he remains till the apples are gathered, when he is taken down and thrown into the water, or he is burned and his ashes cast into water. But the person who plucks the first fruit from the tree succeeds to the title of "the great *mondard*."[2] Here the straw figure, called "the great *mondard*" and placed on the apple-tree in spring, represents the spirit of the tree, who, dead in winter, revives when the apple-blossoms appear in spring. The fact, therefore, that the person who plucks the first fruit from the apple-tree receives the name of "the great *mondard*" proves that he is regarded as a representative of the tree-spirit. Primitive peoples are, as a rule, reluctant to taste the annual first-fruits of any crop, until some ceremony has been performed which makes it safe and

---

[1] Varro, *De re rustica*, ii. 5, 4. Cp. Columella, vi. praef. § 7. Perhaps, however, Varro's statement may be merely an inference drawn from the ritual of the *bouphonia* and the legend told to explain it.   [2] *B. K.* p. 409.

pious for them to do so.   The reason of this reluctance appears to be that the first-fruits either are the
property of, or actually contain, a divinity.   Therefore
when a man or animal is seen boldly to appropriate
the sacred first-fruits, he or it is naturally regarded as
the divinity himself in human or animal form taking
possession of his own.   The time of the Athenian
sacrifice—about the close of the threshing—suggests
that the wheat and barley laid upon the altar were
a harvest offering ; and the sacramental character of
the subsequent repast—all partaking of the flesh of the
divine animal—would make it parallel to the harvest
suppers of modern Europe, in which, as we have seen,
the flesh of the animal who represents the corn-spirit is
eaten by the harvesters.   Again, the tradition that the
sacrifice was instituted in order to put an end to drought
and famine is in favour of taking it as a harvest festival.
The resurrection of the corn-spirit, represented by
setting up the stuffed ox and yoking it to the plough,
may be compared with the resurrection of the tree-
spirit in the person of his representative, the Wild
Man.[1]

The ox appears as a representative of the corn-
spirit in other parts of the world.   At Great Bassam,
in Guinea, two oxen are slain annually to procure a
good harvest.   If the sacrifice is to be effectual, it is
necessary that the oxen should weep.   So all the
women of the village sit in front of the beasts, chanting, "The ox will weep ; yes, he will weep!" From
time to time one of the women walks round the beasts,
throwing manioc meal or palm wine upon them, especially into their eyes.   When tears roll down from the
eyes of the oxen, the people dance, singing, "The ox

---

[1] See above, vol. i. p. 243.

weeps! the ox weeps!" Then two men seize the tails
of the beasts and cut them off at one blow. It is
believed that a great misfortune will happen in the
course of the year if the tails are not severed at one
blow. The oxen are afterwards killed, and their flesh
is eaten by the chiefs.[1] Here the tears of the oxen,
like those of the human victims amongst the Khonds,
are probably a rain-charm. We have already seen
that the virtue of the corn-spirit, embodied in animal
form, is sometimes supposed to reside in the tail, and
that the last handful of corn is sometimes conceived as
the tail of the corn-spirit.[2] Still more clearly does the
ox appear as a personification of the corn-spirit in a
ceremony which is observed in all the provinces and
districts of China to welcome the approach of spring.
On the first day of spring the governor or prefect of
the city goes in procession to the east gate of the city,
and sacrifices to the Divine Husbandman, who is
represented with a bull's head on the body of a man.
A large effigy of an ox, cow, or buffalo has been prepared for the occasion, and stands outside of the east
gate, with agricultural implements beside it. It is
made of differently-coloured pieces of paper pasted on
a framework either by a blind man or according to the
directions of a necromancer. The colours of the paper
indicate the character of the coming year; if red prevails, there will be many fires; if white, there will be
floods and rain, etc. The mandarins walk slowly
round the ox, beating it severely at each step with rods
of various colours. It is filled with five kinds of grain,
which pour forth when the ox is broken by the blows
of the rods. The paper fragments are then set on fire,

---

[1] Hecquard, *Reise an die Küste und in das Innere von West-Afrika*, pp.
41-43.   [2] Above, p. 3, and vol. i. p. 408.

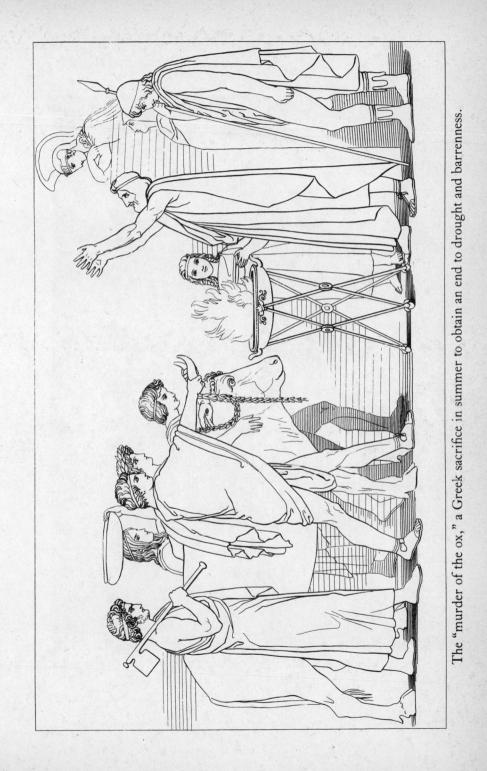

The "murder of the ox," a Greek sacrifice in summer to obtain an end to drought and barrenness.

Demeter, mother of Abundance and Fertility.

and a scramble takes place for the burning fragments, as the people believe that whoever gets one of them is sure to be fortunate throughout the year. A live buffalo is then killed, and its flesh is divided among the mandarins. According to one account, the effigy of the ox is made of clay, and, after being beaten by the governor, is stoned by the people till they break it in pieces, "from which they expect an abundant year."[1] Here the corn-spirit appears to be plainly represented by the corn-filled ox, whose fragments may therefore be supposed to bring fertility with them. We may compare the Silesian spring custom of burning the effigy of Death, scrambling for the burning fragments, and burying them in the fields to secure a good crop, and the Florentine custom of sawing the Old Woman and scrambling for the dried fruits with which she was filled.[2]

On the whole, then, we may perhaps conclude that both as a goat and as a bull Dionysus was essentially a god of vegetation. The Chinese and European customs just referred to may perhaps shed light on the custom of rending a live bull or goat at the rites of Dionysus. The animal was torn in fragments, as the Khond victim was cut in pieces, in order that the worshippers might each secure a portion of the life-giving and fertilising influence of the god. The flesh was eaten raw as a sacrament, and we may conjecture that some of it was taken home to be buried in the fields, or otherwise employed so as to convey to the fruits of the earth the quickening influence of the god of vegetation. The resurrection of Dionysus, related

---

[1] *China Review*, i. 62, 154, 162, 203 *sq.*; Doolittle, *Social Life of the Chinese*, p. 375 *sq.*, ed. Paxton Hood; Gray, *China*, ii. 115 *sq.*
[2] Above, vol. i. pp. 261, 267.

in his myth, may have been represented in his rites by stuffing and setting up the slain ox, as was done at the Athenian *bouphonia*.

Passing next to the corn-goddess Demeter, and remembering that in European folk-lore the pig is a common embodiment of the corn-spirit,[1] we may now ask, may not the pig, which was so closely associated with Demeter, be nothing but the goddess herself in animal form?   The pig was sacred to her;[2] in art she was represented carrying or accompanied by a pig;[3] and the pig was regularly sacrificed in her mysteries, the reason assigned being that the pig injures the corn and is therefore an enemy of the goddess.[4]   But after an animal has been conceived as a god or a god as an animal, it sometimes happens, as we have seen, that the god sloughs off his animal form and becomes purely anthropomorphic; and that then the animal, which at first had been slain in the character of the god, comes to be regarded as a victim offered to the god on the ground of its hostility to the deity; in short, that the god is sacrificed to himself on the ground that he is his own enemy.   This happened to Dionysus, and it may have happened to Demeter also. And in fact the rites of one of her festivals, the Thesmophoria, bear out the view that originally the pig was an embodiment of the corn-goddess herself, either Demeter or her daughter and double Proserpine.   The Thesmophoria was an autumn festival, celebrated by women alone in October,[5] and appears to have repre-

---

[1] See above, p. 26 *sqq.*

[2] Schol. on Aristophanes, *Acharn.* 747.

[3] Overbeck, *Griechische Kunst-mythologie,* ii. 493; Müller-Wieseler, *Denkmäler d. alt. Kunst,* ii. pl. viii. 94.

[4] Hyginus, *Fab.* 277; Cornutus, *De nat. deor.* c. 28; Macrobius, *Sat.* i. 12, 23; Schol. on Aristophanes, *Acharn.* 747; *id.* on *Frogs,* 338; *id.* on *Peace,* 374; Servius on Virgil, *Georg.* ii. 380; Aelian, *Nat. Anim.* x. 16.

[5] For the authorities on the Thes-

sented with mourning rites the descent of Proserpine
(or Demeter)[1] into the lower world, and with joy her
return from the dead.[2] Hence the name Descent or
Ascent variously applied to the first, and the name
Kalligeneia (fair-born) applied to the third day of the
festival. Now from a scholion on Lucian, first edited
in 1870,[3] we learn some details about the mode of
celebrating the Thesmophoria, which shed important
light on the part of the festival called the Descent or
the Ascent. The scholiast tells us that it was customary at the Thesmophoria to throw pigs, cakes of
dough, and branches of pine-trees into "the chasms of
Demeter and Proserpine," which appear to have been
sacred caverns or vaults.[4] In these caverns or vaults
there were said to be serpents, which guarded the
caverns and consumed most of the flesh of the pigs
and dough-cakes which were thrown in. Afterwards
—apparently at the next annual festival[5]—the decayed

mophoria and a discussion of some
doubtful points in the festival, I may
be permitted to refer to my article
"Thesmophoria" in the *Encyclopaedia
Britannica*, ninth ed.

[1] Photius, *s.v.* στήνια, speaks of the
ascent of *Demeter* from the lower
world; and Clement of Alexandria
speaks of both Demeter and Proserpine
as having been engulfed in the chasm
(*Protrept.* ii. § 17). The original equivalence of Demeter and Proserpine
must be borne steadily in mind.

[2] Plutarch, *Isis et Osiris*, 69; Photius,
s.v. στήνια.

[3] E. Rohde, "Unedirte Lucians-
scholien, die attischen Thesmophorien
und Haloen betreffend," in *Rheinisches
Museum*, N. F. xxv. (1870) 548
sqq. Two passages of classical writers
(Clemens Alex., *Protrept.* ii. § 17 and
Pausanias, ix. 8, 1) refer to the rites
described by the Scholiast on Lucian,
and had been rightly interpreted by
Lobeck (*Aglaophamus*, p. 827 *sqq.*)

[4] The scholiast speaks of them as
megara and *adyta*. *Megara* (from a
Phoenician word meaning "cavern,"
"subterranean chasm," Movers, *Die
Phoenizier*, i. 220) were properly subterranean vaults or chasms sacred to
the gods. See Hesychius, quoted by
Movers, *l.c.* (the passage does not
appear in M. Schmidt's minor edition
of Hesychius); Porphyry, *De antro
nymph.* 6.

[5] We infer this from Pausanias, ix.
8, 1, though the passage is incomplete
and apparently corrupt. For ἐν
Δωδώνῃ Lobeck proposes to read
ἀναδῦναι or ἀναδοθῆναι. At the spring
and autumn festivals of Isis at Tithorea
geese and goats were thrown into the
adyton and left there till the following
festival, when the remains were removed and buried at a certain spot a
little way from the temple. Pausanias,
x. 32, 14 (9). This analogy supports
the view that the pigs thrown into the
caverns at the Thesmophoria were left
there till the next festival.

remains of the pigs, the cakes, and the pine-branches were fetched by women called "drawers," who, after observing rules of ceremonial purity for three days, descended into the caverns, and, frightening away the serpents by clapping their hands, brought up the remains and placed them on the altar. Whoever got a piece of the decayed flesh and cakes, and sowed it with the seed-corn in his field, was believed to be sure of a good crop.

To explain this rude and ancient rite the following legend was told. At the moment that Pluto carried off Proserpine, a swineherd called Eubuleus was herding his swine on the spot, and his herd was engulfed in the chasm down which Pluto vanished with Proserpine. Accordingly at the Thesmophoria pigs were annually thrown into caverns in order to commemorate the disappearance of the swine of Eubuleus. It follows from this that the casting of the pigs into the vaults at the Thesmophoria formed part of the dramatic representation of Proserpine's descent into the lower world; and as no image of Proserpine appears to have been thrown in, it follows that the descent of the pigs must have been, not an accompaniment of her descent, but the descent itself; in short, the pigs were Proserpine. Afterwards when Proserpine or Demeter (for the two are equivalent) became anthropomorphic, a reason had to be found for the custom of throwing pigs into caverns at her festival; and this was done by saying that when Proserpine was carried off, there happened to be some swine browsing near, which were swallowed up along with her. The story is obviously a forced and awkward attempt to bridge over the gulf between the old conception of the corn-spirit as a pig and the new conception of her as

an anthropomorphic goddess. A trace of the older
conception survived in the legend that when Demeter
was looking for the lost Proserpine, the footprints of
the latter were obliterated by the footprints of a pig ;[1]
originally, no doubt, the footprints of the pig were the
footprints of Proserpine and of Demeter herself. A
consciousness of the intimate connection of the pig
with the corn lurks in the tradition that the swineherd
Eubuleus was a brother of Triptolemus, to whom
Demeter first imparted the secret of the corn. Indeed,
according to one version of the story, Eubuleus himself received, jointly with his brother Triptolemus, the
gift of the corn from Demeter as a reward for revealing
to her the fate of Proserpine.[2] Further, it is to be
noted that at the Thesmophoria the women appear to
have eaten swine's flesh.[3] The meal, if I am right,
must have been a solemn sacrament or communion,
the worshippers partaking of the body of the god.

As thus explained, the Thesmophoria has its analogies in the folk-customs of Northern Europe which
have been already described. As at the Thesmophoria—an autumn festival in honour of the corn-
goddess—swine's flesh was partly eaten, partly kept in
caverns till the following year, when it was taken up
to be sown with the seed-corn in the fields for the
purpose of securing a good crop ; so in the neighbourhood of Grenoble the goat killed on the harvest-field
is partly eaten at the harvest supper, partly pickled
and kept till the next harvest ;[4] so at Pouilly the ox
killed on the harvest-field is partly eaten by the harvesters, partly pickled and kept till the first day of

---

[1] Ovid, *Fasti*, iv. 461-466, upon
which Gierig remarks, "*Sues melius
poëta omisisset in hac narratione.*" Such
is the wisdom of the commentator.

[2] Pausanias, i. 14, 3.

[3] Schol. on Aristophanes, *Frogs*,
338.

[4] Above, p. 15 *sq.*

sowing in spring[1]—probably to be then mixed with
the seed, or eaten by the ploughmen, or both ; so at
Udvarhely the feathers of the cock which is killed in
the last sheaf at harvest are kept till spring, and then
sown with the seed on the field ;[2] so in Hessen and
Meiningen the flesh of pigs is eaten on Ash Wednesday
or Candlemas, and the bones are kept till sowing-time,
when they are put into the field sown or mixed with
the seed in the bag ;[3] so, lastly, the corn from the last
sheaf is kept till Christmas, made into the Yule Boar,
and afterwards broken and mixed with the seed-corn
at sowing in spring.[4] Thus, to put it generally, the
corn-spirit is killed in animal form in autumn ; part of
his flesh is eaten as a sacrament by his worshippers ;
and part of it is kept till next sowing-time or harvest as
a pledge and security for the continuance or renewal
of the corn-spirit's energies. Whether in the interval
between autumn and spring he is conceived as dead,
or whether, like the ox in the *bouphonia*, he is supposed
to come to life again immediately after being killed, is
not clear. At the Thesmophoria, according to Clement and Pausanias, as emended by Lobeck,[5] the pigs
were thrown in alive, and were supposed to reappear
at the festival of the following year. Here, therefore,
if we accept Lobeck's emendations, the corn-spirit is
conceived as alive throughout the year ; he lives and
works under ground, but is brought up each autumn to be
renewed and then replaced in his subterranean abode.[6]

---

[1] Above, p. 20 *sq.*   [2] Above, p. 9.
[3] Above, p. 29.   [4] Above, p. 29 *sq.*
[5] In Clemens Alex., *Protrept.* ii. 17,
for μεγαρίζοντες χοίρους ἐκβάλλουσι
Lobeck (*Aglaophamus*, p. 831) would
read μεγάροις ζῶντας χοίρους ἐμβάλλουσι.
For his emendation of Pausanias, see
above, p. 45.

[6] It is worth noting that in Crete,
which was an ancient seat of Demeter
worship (see above, vol. i. p. 331), the
pig was esteemed very sacred and was
not eaten, Athenaeus, 375 F-376 A.
This would not exclude the possibility
of its being eaten sacramentally, as at
the Thesmophoria.

The abduction of Proserpine by Pluto.

Poseidon and his horses. Demeter, searching for Proserpine, assumed the form of a mare to escape the addresses of Poseidon

If it is objected that the Greeks never could have conceived Demeter and Proserpine to be embodied in the form of pigs, it may be answered that in the cave of Phigalia in Arcadia the Black Demeter was represented with the head and mane of a horse on the body of a woman.[1]   Between the representation of a goddess as a pig, and the representation of her as a woman with a horse's head, there is little to choose in respect of barbarism.   The legend told of the Phigalian Demeter indicates that the horse was one of the animal forms assumed in ancient Greece, as in modern Europe,[2] by the corn-spirit.   It was said that in her search for her daughter, Demeter assumed the form of a mare to escape the addresses of Poseidon, and that, offended at his importunity, she withdrew to the cave of Phigalia.   There, robed in black, she stayed so long that the fruits of the earth were perishing, and mankind would have died of famine if Pan had not soothed the angry goddess and persuaded her to quit the cave. In memory of this event, the Phigalians set up an image of the Black Demeter in the cave ; it represented a woman dressed in a long robe, with the head and mane of a horse.[3]   The Black Demeter, in whose absence the fruits of the earth perish, is plainly a mythical expression for the state of vegetation in winter.

Passing now to Attis and Adonis, we may note a few facts which seem to show that these deities of vegetation had also, like other deities of vegetation, their animal embodiments.   The worshippers of Attis abstained from eating the flesh of swine.[4]   This fact is

---

[1] Pausanias, viii. 42.
[2] Above, p. 24 *sqq.*
[3] Pausanias, viii. 25 and 42.   On the

Phigalian Demeter, see W. Mannhardt, *M. F.* p. 244 *sqq.*
[4] Above, vol. i. p. 296 *sq.*

certainly in favour of supposing that the pig was regarded as an embodiment of Attis. And the legend that Attis was killed by a boar[1] points in the same direction. For after the examples of the goat Dionysus and the pig Demeter it may almost be laid down as a rule that an animal which is said to have injured a god was originally the god himself. Perhaps the cry of " Hyes Attes! Hyes Attes!"[2] which was raised by the worshippers of Attis, may be neither more nor less than " Pig Attis! Pig Attis!"—*hyes* being possibly a Phrygian form of the Greek *hȳs*, "a pig."

In regard to Adonis, his connection with the boar was not always explained by the story that he was killed by a boar. According to another story, a boar rent with his tusk the bark of the tree in which the infant Adonis was born.[3] According to another story, he was killed by Hephaestus on Mount Lebanon while he was hunting wild boars.[4] These variations in the legend serve to show that, while the connection of the boar with Adonis was certain, the reason of the connection was not understood, and that consequently different stories were devised to explain it. Certainly the pig was one of the sacred animals of the Syrians. At the great religious metropolis of Hierapolis pigs were neither sacrificed nor eaten, and if a man touched a pig he was unclean for the rest of the day. Some people said this was because the pigs were unclean ; others said it was because the pigs were sacred.[5] This difference of opinion points to a state of religious thought and feeling in which the ideas of sanctity and uncleanness are not yet differentiated, and which is best

---

[1] Above, vol. i. p. 296.

[2] Demosthenes, *De corona*, p. 313.

[3] Above, vol. i. p. 281.

[4] Cureton, *Spicilegium Syriacum*, p. 44.

[5] Lucian, *De dea Syria*, 54.

indicated by the word taboo.   It is quite consistent with this that the pig should have been held to be an embodiment of the divine Adonis, and the analogies of Dionysus and Demeter make it probable that the story of the hostility of the animal to the god was only a modern misunderstanding of the old view of the god as embodied in a pig.   The rule that pigs were not sacrificed or eaten by worshippers of Attis and presumably of Adonis, does not exclude the possibility that in these cults the pig was slain on solemn occasions as a representative of the god and consumed sacramentally by the worshippers.   Indeed, the sacramental killing and eating of an animal, that is the killing and eating it as a god, implies that the animal is sacred, and is, as a general rule, not killed.[1]

The attitude of the Jews to the pig was as ambiguous as that of the heathen Syrians towards the same animal.   The Greeks could not decide whether the Jews worshipped swine or abominated them.   On the one hand they might not eat swine ; but on the other hand they might not kill them.[2]   And if the former rule speaks for the uncleanness, the latter speaks still more strongly for the sanctity of the animal.   For whereas both rules may, and one rule must, be explained on the supposition that the pig was sacred ; neither rule must, and one rule cannot, be explained on the supposition that the pig was unclean.   If, therefore, we prefer the former supposition, we must conclude

---

[1] The heathen Harranians sacrificed swine once a year and ate the flesh ; En-Nedîm, in Chwolsohn's *Die Ssabier und der Ssabismus*, ii. 42. My friend Professor W. Robertson Smith has conjectured that the wild boars annually sacrificed in Cyprus on 2d April (Joannes Lydus, *De mensibus*, iv. 45) represented Adonis himself. See his *Religion of the Semites*, i. 272 *sq.*, 392.

[2] Plutarch, *Quaest. Conviv.* iv. 5.

that, originally at least, the pig was held to be sacred rather than unclean by the Israelites. This is confirmed by the fact that down to the time of Isaiah some of the Jews used to meet secretly in gardens to eat the flesh of swine and mice as a religious rite.[1] Doubtless this was a very ancient rite, dating from a time when both the pig and the mouse were venerated as divine, and when their flesh was partaken of sacramentally on rare and solemn occasions as the body and blood of gods. And in general it may be said that all so-called unclean animals were originally sacred; the reason why they were not eaten was that they were divine.

In ancient Egypt, within historical times, the pig occupied the same dubious position as in Syria and Palestine, though at first sight its uncleanness is more prominent than its sanctity. The Egyptians are generally said by Greek writers to have abhorred the pig as a foul and loathsome animal.[2] If a man so much as touched a pig in passing, he stepped into the river with all his clothes on, to wash off the taint.[3] To drink pig's milk was believed to cause leprosy to the drinker.[4] Swineherds, though natives of Egypt, were forbidden to enter any temple, and they were the only men who were thus excluded. No one would give his daughter in marriage to a swineherd, or marry a swineherd's daughter; the swineherds married among themselves.[5] Yet once a year the Egyptians sacrificed pigs to the moon and to Osiris, and not only sacrificed them, but ate of their flesh, though on any other day of the year

---

[1] Isaiah lxv. 3, 4, lxvi. 3, 17.
[2] Herodotus, ii. 47 ; Plutarch, *Isis et Osiris*, 8; Aelian, *Nat. Anim.* x. 16.
[3] Herodotus, *l.c.*
[4] Plutarch and Aelian, *ll.cc.*
[5] Herodotus, *l.c.*

they would neither sacrifice them nor taste of their flesh. Those who were too poor to offer a pig on this day baked cakes of dough, and offered them instead.[1] This can hardly be explained except by the supposition that the pig was a sacred animal which was eaten sacramentally by his worshippers once a year. The view that in Egypt the pig was a sacred animal is borne out by the very facts which, to moderns, might seem to prove the contrary. Thus the Egyptians thought, as we have seen, that to drink pig's milk produced leprosy. But exactly analogous views are held by savages about the animals and plants which they deem most sacred. Thus in the island of Wetar (between New Guinea and Celebes) people believe themselves to be variously descended from wild pigs, serpents, crocodiles, turtles, dogs, and eels ; a man may not eat an animal of the kind from which he is descended ; if he does so, he will become a leper, and go mad.[2] Amongst the Omaha Indians of North America men whose totem (sacred animal or plant) is the elk, believe that if they ate the flesh of the male elk they would break out in boils and white spots in different parts of their bodies.[3] In the same tribe men whose totem is the red maize, think that if they ate red maize they would have running sores all round their mouths.[4] The Bush negroes of Surinam, who have totemism, believe that if they ate the *capiaï*

---

[1] Herodotus, ii. 47 *sq.*; Aelian and Plutarch, *ll.cc.* Herodotus distinguishes the sacrifice to the moon from that to Osiris. According to him, at the sacrifice to the moon, the extremity of the pig's tail, together with the spleen and the caul, were covered with fat and burned ; the rest of the flesh was eaten. On the evening (not the eve, see Stein on the passage) of the festival the sacrifice to Osiris took place. Each man slew a pig before his door, then gave it to the swineherd, from whom he had bought it, to take away.

[2] Riedel, *De sluik-en kroesharige rassen tusschen Selebes en Papua*, pp. 432, 452.

[3] *Third Annual Report of the Bureau of Ethnology* (Washington), p. 225.

[4] *Ib.* p. 231.

(an animal like a pig) it would give them leprosy ;[1]
probably the *capiaï* is one of their totems.　In Samoa
each man had generally his god in the shape of some
species of animal; and if he ate one of these divine
animals, it was supposed that the god avenged himself
by taking up his abode in the eater's body, and there
generating an animal of the kind he had eaten till it
caused his death.　For example, if a man whose god
was the prickly sea-urchin, ate one of these creatures,
a prickly sea-urchin grew in his stomach and killed
him.　If his god was an eel, and he ate an eel, he
became very ill, and before he died the voice of the
god was heard from his stomach saying, " I am killing
this man ; he ate my incarnation." [2]　These examples
prove that the eating of a sacred animal is often
believed to produce skin-disease or even death ; so
far, therefore, they support the view that the pig
must have been sacred in Egypt, since the effect of
drinking its milk was believed to be leprosy.

Again, the rule that, after touching a pig, a man
had to wash himself and his clothes, also favours the
view of the sanctity of the pig.　For it is a common
belief that the effect of contact with a sacred object
must be removed, by washing or otherwise, before
a man is free to mingle with his fellows.　Thus the
Jews wash their hands after reading the sacred
scriptures.　Before coming forth from the tabernacle
after the sin-offering, the high priest had to wash
himself, and put off the garments which he had worn
in the holy place.[3]　It was a rule of Greek ritual
that, in offering an expiatory sacrifice, the sacrificer
should not touch the sacrifice, and that, after the

---

[1] J. Crevaux, *Voyages dans l'Amérique du Sud*, p. 59.

[2] Turner, *Samoa*, pp. 17 *sq.*, 50 *sq.*
[3] Leviticus xvi. 23 *sq.*

offering was made, he must wash his body and his
clothes in a river or spring before he could enter
a city or his own house.[1]   The Polynesians felt
strongly the need of ridding themselves of the sacred
contagion, if it may be so called, which they caught
by touching sacred objects.   Various ceremonies were
performed for the purpose of removing this sacred
contagion.   For example, in Tonga a man who
happened to touch a sacred chief, or anything personally belonging to him, as his clothes or his mat,
was obliged to go through the ceremony of touching
the soles of the chief's (or of any chief's) feet with
his hands, first applying the palm and then the back
of each hand ; next he had to rinse his hands in water,
or, if there was no water near, the sap of the plantain
or banana-tree might be used as a substitute.   If he
were to feed himself with his hands before he performed this ceremony, it was believed that he would
swell up and die, or at least be afflicted with scrofula
or some other disease.[2]   We have already seen what
fatal effects are supposed to follow, and do actually
follow, from contact with a sacred object in New
Zealand.[3]   In short, primitive man believes that what
is sacred is dangerous ; it is pervaded by a sort of
electrical sanctity which communicates a shock to,
even if it does not kill, whatever comes in contact
with it.   Hence the savage is unwilling to touch
or even to see that which he deems peculiarly holy.
Thus Bechuanas, of the Crocodile clan, think it
" hateful and unlucky " to meet or see a crocodile ;
the sight is thought to cause inflammation of the

---

[1] Porphyry, *De abstin.* ii. 44.   For
this and the Jewish examples I am
indebted to my friend Prof. W. Robertson Smith

[2] Mariner, *Tonga Islands*, i. 434,
note ; ii. 82, 222 *sq.*
[3] Above, vol. i. p. 167 *sqq.*

eyes. Yet the crocodile is their most sacred object ; they call it their father, swear by it, and celebrate it in their festivals.[1] The goat is the sacred animal of the Madenassana Bushmen ; yet "to look upon it would be to render the man for the time impure, as well as to cause him undefined uneasiness."[2] The Elk clan, among the Omaha Indians, believe that even to touch the male elk would be followed by an eruption of boils and white spots on the body.[3] Members of the Reptile clan in the same tribe think that if one of them touches or smells a snake, it will make his hair white.[4] In Samoa people whose god was a butterfly believed that if they caught a butterfly it would strike them dead.[5] Again, in Samoa the reddish-seared leaves of the banana-tree were commonly used as plates for handing food ; but if any member of the Wild Pigeon clan had used banana leaves for this purpose, it was believed that he would have suffered from rheumatic swellings or an eruption all over the body like chicken-pox.[6]

In the light of these parallels the beliefs and customs of the Egyptians touching the pig are probably to be explained as based upon an opinion of the extreme sanctity rather than of the extreme uncleanness of the animal ; or rather, to put it more correctly, they imply that the animal was looked on, not simply as a filthy and disgusting creature, but as a being endowed with high supernatural powers, and that as such it was regarded with that primitive

---

[1] Casalis, *The Basutos*, p. 211 ; Livingstone, *Missionary Travels and Researches in South Africa*, p. 255 ; John Mackenzie, *Ten Years north of the Orange River*, p. 135 *note*.

[2] J. Mackenzie, *l.c.*

[3] *Third Annual Report of the Bureau of Ethnology* (Washington), p. 225.

[4] *Ib.* p. 275.

[5] Turner, *Samoa*, p. 76.

[6] *Ib.* p. 70.

sentiment of religious awe and fear in which the
feelings of reverence and abhorrence are almost equally
blended.   The ancients themselves seem to have been
aware that there was another side to the horror with
which swine seemed to inspire the Egyptians.   For
the Greek astronomer and mathematician Eudoxus,
who resided fourteen months in Egypt and con-
versed with the priests,[1] was of opinion that the
Egyptians spared the pig, not out of abhorrence, but
from a regard to its utility in agriculture ; for, according to him, when the Nile had subsided, herds of swine
were turned loose over the fields to tread the seed
down into the moist earth.[2]   But when a being is thus
the object of mixed and implicitly contradictory feelings, he may be said to occupy a position of unstable
equilibrium.   In course of time one of the contradictory
feelings is likely to prevail over the other, and according as the feeling which finally predominates is that of
reverence or abhorrence, the being who is the object
of it will rise into a god or sink into a devil.   The
latter, on the whole, was the fate of the pig in Egypt.
For in historical times the fear and horror of the pig
seem certainly to have outweighed the reverence and
worship of which he must once have been the object,
and of which, even in his fallen state, he never quite
lost trace.   He came to be looked on as an embodiment of Set or Typhon, the Egyptian devil and enemy
of Osiris.   For it was in the shape of a boar that
Typhon menaced the eye of the god Horus, who
burned him and instituted the sacrifice of the pig, the
sun-god Ra having declared the pig abominable.[3]

---

[1] Diogenes Laertius, *Vitae Philos.*
viii. 8.
[2] Aelian, *Nat. Anim.* x. 16.   The
story is repeated by Pliny, *Nat. Hist.*
xviii. 168.
[3] Lefébure, *Le mythe Osirien*, i. 44.

Again, the story that Typhon was hunting a boar
when he discovered and mangled the body of Osiris,
and that this was the reason why the pig was sacrificed
once a year,[1] is a transparent modernisation of an older
story that Osiris, like Adonis and Attis, was slain or
mangled by a boar, or by Typhon in the form of a
boar. Thus, the annual sacrifice of a pig to Osiris
might naturally be interpreted as vengeance inflicted
on the hostile animal that had slain or mangled the god.
But, in the first place, when an animal is thus killed
as a solemn sacrifice once and once only in the year, it
generally or always means that the animal is divine—
that he is spared and respected the rest of the year as a
god and slain, when he is slain, also in the character of
a god.[2] In the second place, the examples of Dionysus
and Demeter, if not of Attis and Adonis, have taught
us that the animal which is sacrificed to a god on the
ground that he is the god's enemy may have been, and
probably was, originally the god himself. Therefore,
the fact that the pig was sacrificed once a year to
Osiris, and the fact that he appears to have been sacrificed on the ground that he was the god's enemy, go
to show, first, that originally the pig was a god, and,
second, that he was Osiris. At a later age the pig
was distinguished from Osiris when the latter became
anthropomorphic and his original relation to the pig
was forgotten ; later still, the pig was opposed as an
enemy to Osiris by mythologists who could think of no
reason for killing an animal in connection with the
worship of a god except that the animal was the god's

---

[1] Plutarch, *Isis et Osiris*, 8. Lefébure (*op. cit.* p. 46) recognises that in
this story the boar is Typhon himself.

[2] This important principle was first
recognised by Prof. W. Robertson
Smith. See his article "Sacrifice,"
Encycl. Britann. 9th ed. xxi. 137
sq. Cp. his *Religion of the Semites*,
pp. 353 *sq.*, 391 *sq.*

enemy ; or, as Plutarch puts it, not that which is dear to the gods, but that which is the contrary, is fit to be sacrificed.[1]   At this later stage the havoc which a wild boar notoriously makes amongst the corn would supply a plausible reason for regarding him as an enemy of the corn-spirit, though originally, if I am right, the very fact that the boar was found ranging at will through the corn was the reason for identifying him with the corn-spirit, to whom he was afterwards opposed as an enemy.   The view which identifies the pig with Osiris derives not a little support from the fact that the day on which the pigs were sacrificed to him was the day on which, according to tradition, Osiris was killed ;[2] for thus the killing of the pig was the annual representation of the killing of Osiris, just as the throwing of the pigs into the caverns at the Thesmophoria was an annual representation of the descent of Proserpine into the lower world ; and both customs are parallel to the European practice of killing a goat, cock, etc., at harvest as a representative of the corn-spirit.

Again, the view that the pig, originally Osiris himself, afterwards came to be regarded as an embodiment of his enemy Typhon, is supported by the similar relation of red-haired men and red oxen to Typhon. For in regard to the red-haired men who were burned and whose ashes were scattered with winnowing-fans, we have seen fair grounds for believing that originally, like the red-haired puppies killed at Rome in spring, they were representatives of the corn-spirit himself, that is, of Osiris, and were slain for the express purpose of making the corn turn red or golden.

---

[1] Plutarch, *Isis et Osiris*, 31.
[2] Lefébure, *Le mythe Osirien*, p. 48 *sq.*

Yet at a later time these men were explained to be representatives, not of Osiris, but of his enemy Typhon,[1] and the killing of them was regarded as an act of vengeance inflicted on the enemy of the god. Similarly, the red oxen sacrificed by the Egyptians were said to be sacrificed on the ground of their resemblance to Typhon ;[2] though it is more likely that originally they were slain on the ground of their resemblance to the corn-spirit Osiris. We have seen that the ox is a common representative of the corn-spirit and is slain as such on the harvest-field.

Osiris was regularly identified with the bull Apis of Memphis and the bull Mnevis of Heliopolis.[3] But it is hard to say whether these bulls were embodiments of him as the corn-spirit, as the red oxen appear to have been, or whether they were not rather entirely distinct deities which got fused with Osiris by syncretism. The fact that these two bulls were worshipped by *all* the Egyptians,[4] seems to put them on a different footing from the ordinary sacred animals whose cults were purely local. Hence, if the latter were evolved from totems, as they probably were, some other origin would have to be found for the worship of Apis and Mnevis. If these bulls were not originally embodiments of the corn-god Osiris, they may possibly be descendants of the sacred cattle

---

[1] Plutarch, *Isis et Osiris*, 33, 73; Diodorus, i. 88.

[2] Plutarch, *Isis et Osiris*, 31 ; Diodorus, i. 88. Cp. Herodotus, ii. 38.

[3] Plutarch, *Isis et Osiris*, 20, 29, 33, 43 ; Strabo, xvii. 1, 31 ; Diodorus, i. 21, 85 ; Duncker, *Geschichte des Alterthums*,[5] i. 55 *sqq.* On Apis and Mnevis, see also Herodotus, ii. 153, iii. 27 *sq.*; Ammianus Marcellinus, xxii. 14, 7 ;

Pliny, *Nat. Hist.* viii. 184 *sqq.* ; Solinus, xxxii. 17-21 ; Cicero, *De nat. deor.* i. 29 ; Aelian, *Nat. Anim.* xi. 10 *sq.* ; Plutarch, *Quaest. Conviv.* viii. 1, 3 ; *id.*, *Isis et Osiris*, 5, 35 ; Eusebius, *Praepar. Evang.* iii. 13, 1 *sq.* ; Pausanias, i. 18, 4, vii. 22, 3 *sq.* Both Apis and Mnevis were black bulls, but Apis had certain white spots.

[4] Diodorus, i. 21.

Osiris as a bull.

Isis as a cow.

worshipped by a pastoral people.[1] If this were so, ancient Egypt would exhibit a stratification of the three great types of religion corresponding to the three great stages of society. Totemism or (roughly speaking) the worship of wild animals—the religion of society in the hunting stage—would be represented by the worship of the local sacred animals ; the worship of cattle—the religion of society in the pastoral stage— would be represented by the cults of Apis and Mnevis; and the worship of cultivated plants, especially of corn —the religion of society in the agricultural stage— would be represented by the worship of Osiris and Isis. The Egyptian reverence for cows, which were never killed,[2] might belong either to the second or third of these stages. The fact that cows were regarded as sacred to, that is, as embodiments of Isis, who was represented with cow's horns, would indicate that they, like the red oxen, were embodiments of the corn-spirit. However, this identification of Isis with the cow, like that of Osiris with the bulls Apis and Mnevis, may be only an effect of syncretism. But whatever the original relation of Apis to Osiris may have been, there is one fact about the former which ought not to be passed over in a chapter dealing with the custom of killing the god. Although the bull Apis was worshipped as a god with much pomp and profound reverence, he was not suffered to live beyond a certain length of time which was prescribed by the sacred books, and on the expiry of which he was drowned in a holy spring.[3] The limit, according to Plutarch, was twenty-

---

[1] On the religious reverence of pastoral peoples for their cattle, and the possible derivation of the Apis and Isis-Hathor worship from the pastoral stage of society, see W. Robertson Smith, *Religion of the Semites*, i. 277 *sqq.*

[2] Herodotus, ii. 41.

[3] Pliny, *Nat. Hist.* viii. 184 ; Solinus, xxxii. 18 ; Ammianus Marcellinus, xxii. 14, 7. The spring or well in which he was drowned was perhaps the one from which his drink-

five years ;[1] but it cannot always have been enforced, for the tombs of the Apis bulls have been discovered in the present century, and from the inscriptions on them it appears that in the twenty-second dynasty two bulls lived more than twenty-six years.[2]

We are now in a position to hazard a conjecture— for it can be little more—as to the meaning of the tradition that Virbius, the first of the divine Kings of the Wood at Aricia, was killed by horses. Having found, first, that spirits of vegetation are not infrequently represented in the form of horses ;[3] and, second, that the animal which in later legends is said to have injured the god was sometimes originally the god himself, we may conjecture that the horses by which Virbius was said to have been slain were really embodiments of him as a deity of vegetation. The myth that Virbius had been killed by horses was probably invented to explain certain features in his cult, amongst others the custom of excluding horses from his sacred grove. For myth changes while custom remains constant ; men continue to do what their fathers did before them, though the reasons on which their fathers acted have been long forgotten. The history of religion is a long attempt to reconcile old custom with new reason ; to find a sound theory for an absurd practice. In the case before us we may be sure that the myth is more modern than the custom and by no means represents the original reason for excluding horses from the grove. From the fact that horses were so excluded it might be inferred that they could not be the sacred animals or embodiments of the

---

ing water was procured ; he might not drink the water of the Nile. Plutarch, *Isis et Osiris*, 5.

[1] Plutarch, *Isis et Osiris*, 56.

[2] Maspero, *Histoire ancienne*,[4] p. 31. Cp. Duncker, *Geschichte des Alterthums*,[5] i. 56.

[3] See above, p. 24 *sqq.*

god of the grove.   But the inference would be rash.
The goat was at one time a sacred animal or embodiment of Athene, as may be inferred from the practice
of representing her clad in a goat-skin (*aegis*).   Yet
the goat was neither sacrificed to her as a rule, nor
allowed to enter her great sanctuary, the Acropolis at
Athens.   The reason alleged for this was that the goat
injured the olive, the sacred tree of Athene.[1]   So far,
therefore, the relation of the goat to Athene is parallel
to the relation of the horse to Virbius, both animals
being excluded from the sanctuary on the ground of
injury done by them to the god.   But from Varro we
learn that there was an exception to the rule which
excluded the goat from the Acropolis.   Once a year,
he says, the goat was driven on to the Acropolis for a
necessary sacrifice.[2]   Now, as has been remarked
before, when an animal is sacrificed once and once
only in the year, it is probably slain, not as a victim
offered to the god, but as a representative of the god
himself.   Therefore we may infer that if a goat was
sacrificed on the Acropolis once a year, it was sacrificed
in the character of Athene herself; and it may be conjectured that the skin of the sacrificed animal was
placed on the statue of the goddess and formed the
aegis, which would thus be renewed annually.   Similarly
at Thebes in Egypt rams were sacred and were not
sacrificed.   But on one day in the year a ram was
killed, and its skin was placed on the statue of the god
Ammon.[3]   Now, if we knew the ritual of the Arician
grove better, we might find the rule of excluding
horses from it, like the rule of excluding goats from

---

[1] Athenaeus, 587 A; Pliny, *Nat.*
Hist. viii. 204.   Cp. *Encycl. Britann.*
9th ed. art. "Sacrifice," xxi. 135.

[2] Varro, *De agri cult.* i. 2, 19 *sq.*
[3] Herodotus, ii. 42.

the Acropolis at Athens, was subject to an annual exception, a horse being once a year taken into the grove and sacrificed as an embodiment of the god Virbius. By the usual misunderstanding the horse thus killed would come in time to be regarded as an enemy offered up in sacrifice to the god whom he had injured, like the pig which was sacrificed to Demeter and Osiris or the goat which was sacrificed to Athene and Dionysus. It is so easy for a writer to record a rule without noticing an exception that we need not wonder at finding the rule of the Arician grove recorded without any mention of an exception such as I suppose. If we had had only the statements of Athenaeus and Pliny, we should have known only the rule which forbade the sacrifice of goats to Athene and excluded them from the Acropolis, without being aware of the important exception which the fortunate preservation of Varro's work has revealed to us.

The conjecture that once a year a horse may have been sacrificed in the Arician grove as a representative of the deity of the grove derives some support from the fact that a horse sacrifice of a similar character took place once a year at Rome. On the 15th of October in each year a chariot-race took place on the Field of Mars. The right-hand horse of the victorious team was sacrificed to Mars by being stabbed with a spear. The object of the sacrifice was to ensure good crops. The animal's head was cut off and adorned with a string of loaves. The inhabitants of two wards—the Sacred Way and the Subura—then contended with each other who should get the head. If the people of the Sacred Way got it, they fastened it to a wall of the king's house; if the people of the Subura got it, they fastened it to the Mamilian tower. The horse's tail was cut off and carried to the king's house with such speed that the blood dripped on the hearth of the house.[1] Further, it appears that the blood of the horse was caught and preserved till the 21st of April, when it was mixed by the Vestal virgins with the blood of the unborn calves which had been sacrificed six days before. The mixture was then distributed to shepherds, and used by them for fumigating their flocks.[2]

In this ceremony the decoration of the horse's head with a string of loaves, and the alleged object of the sacrifice, namely, to procure a good harvest, clearly indicate that the horse was killed as one of those animal representatives of the corn-spirit of which we have seen so many examples. The custom of cutting off the horse's tail is like the African custom of cutting off the tails of the oxen and sacrificing them to obtain a good crop.[3] In both the Roman and the African custom the animal represents the corn-spirit, and its fructifying power is supposed to reside especially in its tail. The latter idea occurs, as we have seen, in European folk-lore.[4] Again, the custom of fumigating the cattle in spring with the blood of the horse may be compared with the custom of giving the Maiden as fodder to the cattle at Christmas, and giving the Yule Boar to the ploughing oxen or horses to eat in spring.[5] All these customs aim at ensuring the blessing of the corn-spirit on the homestead and its inmates and storing it up for another year.

The Roman sacrifice of the October horse, as it

---

[1] Festus, ed. Müller, pp. 178, 179, 220 ; Plutarch, *Quaest. Rom.* 97 ; Polybius, xii. 4 B.   The sacrifice is referred to by Julian, *Orat.* 176 D.

[2] Ovid, *Fasti*, iv. 731 *sqq.*, cp. 629 *sqq.*; Propertius, v. 1, 19 *sq.*

[3] Above, p. 41 *sq.*

[4] Above, vol. i. p. 408, vol. ii. p. 3.

[5] Above, p. 30.

was called, carries us back to the early days when the
Subura, afterwards a low and crowded quarter of the
great metropolis, was still a separate village, whose
inhabitants engaged in a friendly contest on the harvest-
field with their neighbours of Rome, then a little rural
town. The Field of Mars on which the ceremony took
place lay beside the Tiber, and formed part of the king's
domain down to the abolition of the monarchy. For
tradition ran that at the time when the last of the
kings was driven from Rome, the corn stood ripe for
the sickle on the crown lands beside the river ; but no
one would eat the accursed grain and it was flung into
the river in such heaps that, the water being low with
the summer heat, it formed the nucleus of an island.[1]
The horse sacrifice was thus an old autumn custom
observed upon the king's corn-fields at the end of the
harvest. The tail and blood of the horse, as the chief
parts of the corn-spirit's representative, were taken to
the king's house and kept there ; just as in Germany
the harvest-cock is nailed on the gable or over the
door of the farmhouse ; and as the last sheaf, in the
form of the Maiden, is carried home and kept over the
fireplace in the Highlands of Scotland. Thus the
blessing of the corn-spirit was brought to the king's
house and hearth and, through them, to the community
of which he was the head. Similarly in the spring
and autumn customs of Northern Europe the May-
pole is sometimes set up in front of the house of
the mayor or burgomaster, and the last sheaf at
harvest is brought to him as the head of the village.
But while the tail and blood fell to the king, the
neighbouring village of the Subura, which no doubt
once had a similar ceremony of its own, was gratified

---

[1] Livy, ii. 5.

Interior of the Acropolis Parthenon with the great statue of Athene.

The Acropolis, scene of Greek sacrifices.

by being allowed to compete for the prize of the horse's head. The Mamilian tower to which the Suburans nailed the horse's head when they succeeded in carrying it off, appears to have been a peel-tower or keep of the old Mamilian family, the magnates of the village.[1] The ceremony thus performed on the king's fields and at his house on behalf of the whole town and of the neighbouring village presupposes a time when each commune performed a similar ceremony on its own fields. In the rural districts of Latium the villages may have continued to observe the custom, each on its own land, long after the Roman hamlets had merged their separate harvest-homes in the common celebration on the king's lands.[2] There is no intrinsic improbability in the supposition that the sacred grove of Aricia, like the Field of Mars at Rome, may have been the scene of a common harvest celebration, at which a horse was sacrificed with the same rude rites on behalf of the neighbouring villages. The horse would represent the fructifying spirit both of the tree and of the corn, for the two ideas melt into each other, as we see in customs like the Harvest-May.

§ 11.—*Eating the god*

We have now seen that the corn-spirit is represented sometimes in human, sometimes in animal form, and that in both cases he is killed in the person of his representative and eaten sacramentally. To find examples of actually killing the human representative of the corn-spirit we had of course to go to savage

---

[1] Festus, ed. Müller, pp. 130, 131.
[2] The October horse is the subject of an essay by Mannhardt (*Mytholog. Forsch.* pp. 156-201), of which the above account is a summary.

races ; but the harvest suppers of our European peasants have furnished unmistakable examples of the sacramental eating of animals as representatives of the corn-spirit.   But further, as might have been anticipated, the new corn is itself eaten sacramentally, that is, as the body of the corn-spirit.   In Wermland, Sweden, the farmer's wife uses the grain of the last sheaf to bake a loaf in the shape of a little girl ; this loaf is divided amongst the whole household and eaten by them.[1]   Here the loaf represents the corn-spirit conceived as a maiden ; just as in Scotland the corn-spirit is similarly conceived and represented by the last sheaf made up in the form of a woman and bearing the name of the Maiden.   As usual, the corn-spirit is believed to reside in the last sheaf ; and to eat a loaf made from the last sheaf is, therefore, to eat the corn-spirit itself.   Similarly at La Palisse in France a man made of dough is hung upon the fir-tree which is carried on the last harvest-waggon.   The tree and the dough-man are taken to the mayor's house and kept there till the vintage is over.   Then the close of the harvest is celebrated by a feast at which the mayor breaks the dough-man in pieces and gives the pieces to the people to eat.[2]

In these examples the corn-spirit is represented and eaten in human shape.   In other cases, though the new corn is not baked in loaves of human shape, still the solemn ceremonies with which it is eaten suffice to indicate that it is partaken of sacramentally, that is, as the body of the corn-spirit.   For example, the following ceremonies used to be

---

[1] *M. F.* p. 179.

[2] *B. K.* p. 205.   It is not said that the dough-man is made of the new corn ; but probably this is, or once was, the case.

observed by Lithuanian peasants at eating the new
corn.   When the harvest and the sowing of the new
corn were over, each farmer held a festival called
Sabarios, that is, "the mixing or throwing together."
He took a handful of each kind of grain—wheat,
barley, oats, flax, beans, lentils, etc. ; and each handful
he divided into three parts.   The twenty-seven
portions of each grain were then thrown on a heap and
all mixed up together.   The grain used had to be the
grain which was first threshed and winnowed and
which had been set aside and kept for this purpose.
A part of the grain thus mixed was used to bake little
loaves, one for each of the household ; the rest was
mixed with more barley or oats and made into beer.
The first beer brewed from this mixture was for the
drinking of the farmer, his wife, and children ; the
second brew was for the servants.   The beer being
ready, the farmer chose an evening when no stranger
was expected.   Then he knelt down before the barrel
of beer, drew a jugful of the liquor and poured it on
the bung of the barrel, saying, "O fruitful earth, make
rye and barley and all kinds of corn to flourish."   Next
he took the jug to the parlour, where his wife and children awaited him.   On the floor of the parlour lay bound
a black or white or speckled (not a red) cock and a hen
of the same colour and of the same brood, which must
have been hatched within the year.   Then the farmer
knelt down, with the jug in his hand, and thanked
God for the harvest and prayed for a good crop next
year.   Then all lifted up their hands and said, "O
God, and thou, O earth, we give you this cock and
hen as a free-will offering."   With that the farmer
killed the fowls with the blows of a wooden spoon, for
he might not cut their heads off.   After the first prayer

and after killing each of the birds he poured out
a third of the beer. Then his wife boiled the fowls
in a new pot which had never been used before. A
bushel was then set, bottom upwards, on the floor, and
on it were placed the little loaves mentioned above
and the boiled fowls. Next the new beer was fetched,
together with a ladle and three mugs, none of which
was used except on this occasion. When the farmer
had ladled the beer into the mugs, the family knelt
down round the bushel. The father then uttered a
prayer and drank off the three mugs of beer. The
rest followed his example. Then the loaves and the
flesh of the fowls were eaten, after which the beer
went round again, till every one had emptied each of
the three mugs nine times. None of the food should
remain over; but if anything did happen to be left,
it was consumed next morning with the same ceremonies. The bones were then given to the dog to
eat; if he did not eat them all up, the remains were
buried under the dung in the cattle - stall. This
ceremony was observed at the beginning of December.
On the day on which it occurred no bad word might
be spoken.[1]

Such was the custom about two hundred years
ago. At the present day in Lithuania, when new potatoes or loaves made from the new corn are being
eaten, all the people at table pull each other's hair.[2]
The meaning of the latter custom is obscure, but a
similar custom was certainly observed by the heathen
Lithuanians at their solemn sacrifices.[3] Many of the
Esthonians of the island of Oesel will not eat bread

[1] Praetorius, *Deliciae Prussicae*, pp.
60-64 ; *A. W. F.* p. 249 *sqq.*
[2] Bezzenberger, *Litauische Forschung-*
en (Göttingen, 1882), p. 89.
[3] Simon Grunau, *Preussische Chronik*, ed. Perlbach, i. 91.

baked of the new corn till they have first taken a bite at a piece of iron.[1]   The iron is here plainly a charm, intended to render harmless the spirit that is in the corn.[2]   In Sutherlandshire at the present day, when the new potatoes are dug all the family must taste them, otherwise "the spirits in them [the potatoes] take offence, and the potatoes would not keep."[3]   In one part of Yorkshire it is still the custom for the clergyman to cut the first corn; and my informant believes that the corn so cut is used to make the communion bread.[4]   If the latter part of the custom is correctly reported (and analogy is all in its favour), it shows how the Christian communion has absorbed within itself a sacrament which is doubtless far older than Christianity.

At the close of the rice harvest in Boeroe, East Indies, each clan (*fenna*) meets at a common sacramental meal, to which every member of the clan is bound to contribute a little of the new rice.   This meal is called "eating the soul of the rice," a name which clearly indicates the sacramental character of the repast.   Some of the rice is also set apart and offered to the spirits.[5]   Amongst the Alfoers of Celebes the priest sows the first rice-seed and plucks the first ripe rice in each field.   This rice he roasts and grinds into meal, and gives some of it to each of the household.[6]   Shortly before the rice harvest in Bolang Mongondo, Celebes, an offering is made

---

[1] Holzmayer, *Osiliana*, p. 108.

[2] On iron as a charm against spirits, see above, vol. i. p. 175 *sq.*

[3] *Folk-lore Journal*, vii. 54.

[4] Communicated by the Rev. J. J. C. Yarborough, of Chislehurst, Kent. See *Folk-lore Journal*, vii. 50.

[5] G. A. Wilken, *Bijdrage tot de kennis der Alfoeren van het eiland Boeroe*, p. 26.

[6] P. N. Wilken, "Bijdragen tot de kennis van de zeden en gewoonten der Alfoeren in de Minahassa," in *Mededeelingen van wege het Nederlandsche Zendelinggenootschap*, vii. (1863) p. 127.

of a small pig or a fowl. Then the priest plucks
a little rice, first on his own field and then on those
of his neighbours. All the rice thus plucked by him
he dries along with his own, and then gives it back
to the respective owners, who have it ground and
boiled. When it is boiled the women take it back,
with an egg, to the priest, who offers the egg in
sacrifice and returns the rice to the women. Of
this rice every member of the family, down to the
youngest child, must partake. After this ceremony
every one is free to get in his rice.[1] Amongst the
Burghers, a tribe of the Neilgherry Hills in Southern
India, the first handful of seed is sown and the first
sheaf reaped by a Curumbar—a man of a different
tribe, whom the Burghers regard as sorcerers. The
grain contained in the first sheaf "is that day reduced
to meal, made into cakes, and, being offered as a
first-fruit oblation, is, together with the remainder of
the sacrificed animal, partaken of by the Burgher
and the whole of his family as the meat of a federal
offering and sacrifice."[2]

Amongst the Coorgs of Southern India the man
who is to cut the first sheaf of rice at harvest is
chosen by an astrologer. At sunset the whole household takes a hot bath and then goes to the rice-
field, where the chosen reaper cuts an armful of
rice with a new sickle, and distributes two or more
stalks to all present. Then all return to the threshing-floor. A bundle of leaves is adorned ˙ with a
stalk of rice and fastened to the post in the centre
of the threshing-floor. Enough of the new rice

---

[1] N. P. Wilken en J. A. Schwarz,
"Allerlei over het land en volk van
Bolaang Mongondou," in *Mededeel. v.
w. h. Nederl. Zendelinggen.* xi. 369 *sq.*

[2] H. Harkness, *Description of a
Singular Aboriginal Race inhabiting
the Summit of the Neilgherry Hills*, p.
56 *sq.*

is now threshed, cleaned, and ground to provide flour for the dough cakes which each member of the household is to eat. Then they go to the door of the house, where the mistress washes the feet of the sheaf-cutter, and presents to him, and after him to all the rest, a brass vessel full of milk, honey, and sugar, from which each person takes a draught. Then the man who cut the sheaf kneads a cake of rice meal, plantains, milk, honey, seven new rice corns, seven pieces of cocoa-nut, etc. Every one receives a little of this cake on an Ashvatha leaf, and eats it. The ceremony is then over and the sheaf-cutter mixes with the company. When he was engaged in cutting the rice no one might touch him.[1] Among the Hindoos of Southern India the eating of the new rice is the occasion of a family festival called Pongol. The new rice is boiled in a new pot on a fire which is kindled at noon on the day when, according to Hindoo astrologers, the sun enters the tropic of Capricorn. The boiling of the pot is watched with great anxiety by the whole family, for as the milk boils, so will the coming year be. If the milk boils rapidly, the year will be prosperous; but it will be the reverse if the milk boils slowly. Some of the new boiled rice is offered to the image of Ganesa; then every one partakes of it.[2] At Gilgit, in the Hindoo Koosh, before wheat-harvest begins, a member of every household gathers a handful of ears of corn secretly at dusk. A few of the ears are hung up over the door of the house, and the rest are roasted next morning,

---

[1] Gover, *Folk-songs of Southern India*, p. 105 *sqq.*; *Folk-lore Journal*, vii. 302 *sqq.*

[2] Gover, "The Pongol Festival in Southern India," *Journ. R. Asiatic Society*, N. S. v. (1871) p. 91 *sqq.*

and eaten steeped in milk. The day is spent in rejoicings, and next morning the harvest begins.[1]

The ceremony of eating the new yams at Onitsha, on the Quorra River, Guinea, is thus described : " Each headman brought out six yams, and cut down young branches of palm-leaves and placed them before his gate, roasted three of the yams, and got some kola-nuts and fish. After the yam is roasted, the *Libia*, or country doctor, takes the yam, scrapes it with a sort of meal, and divides it into halves ; he then takes one piece, and places it on the lips of the person who is going to eat the new yam. The eater then blows up the steam from the hot yam, and afterwards pokes the whole into his mouth, and says, 'I thank God for being permitted to eat the new yam ;' he then begins to chew it heartily, with fish likewise." [2] Amongst the Kafirs of Natal and Zululand, no one may eat of the new fruits till after a festival which marks the beginning of the Kafir year. All the people assemble at the king's kraal, where they feast and dance. Before they separate the " dedication of the people " takes place. Various fruits of the earth, as corn, mealies, and pumpkins, mixed with the flesh of a sacrificed animal and with " medicine," are boiled in great pots, and a little of this food is placed in each man's mouth by the king himself. After thus partaking of the sanctified fruits, a man is himself sanctified for the whole year, and may immediately get in his crops.[3]

[1] Biddulph, *Tribes of the Hindoo Koosh*, p. 103.

[2] Crowther and Taylor, *The Gospel on the Banks of the Niger*, p. 287 *sq.* Mr. Taylor's information is repeated in *West African Countries and Peoples*, by J. Africanus B. Horton (London, 1868), p. 180 *sq.*

[3] Speckmann, *Die Hermannsburger Mission in Afrika*, p. 150 *sq.* On the

Amongst the Creek Indians of North America, the *busk* or festival of first-fruits was the chief ceremony of the year.[1]   It was held in July or August, when the corn was ripe, and marked the end of the old year and the beginning of the new one.   Before it took place none of the Indians would eat or even handle any part of the new harvest.   Sometimes each town had its own busk; sometimes several towns united to hold one in common.   Before celebrating the busk, the people provided themselves with new clothes and new household utensils and furniture; they collected their old clothes and rubbish, together with all the remaining grain and other old provisions, cast them together in one common heap, and consumed them with fire.[2]   As a preparation for the ceremony, all the fires in the village were extinguished, and the ashes swept clean away.   In particular, the hearth or altar of the temple was dug up and the

Zulu feast of first-fruits, see also N. Isaacs, *Travels and Adventures in Eastern Africa*, ii. 291 *sq.*; Arbousset et Daumas, *Voyage d'exploration*, etc. p. 308 *sq.*; Callaway, *Religious System of the Amazulu*, p. 389 *note ; South African Folk-lore Journal*, i. 135 *sqq.*; Fritsch, *Die Eingeborenen Süd-Afrikas*, p. 143; Lewis Grout, *Zululand*, p. 160 *sqq.* From Mr. Grout's description it appears that a bull is killed and its gall drunk by the king and people. In killing it the men must use nothing but their naked hands.   The flesh of the bull is given to the boys to eat what they like and burn the rest; the men may not taste it.   As a final ceremony the king breaks a green calabash in presence of the people, "thereby signifying that he opens the new year, and grants the people leave to eat of the fruits of the season." If a man eats the new fruits before the festival, he will die or is actually put to death.

[1] The ceremony is described independently by James Adair, *History of the* *American Indians* (London, 1775), pp. 96-111; W. Bartram, *Travels through North and South Carolina, Georgia, East and West Florida* (London, 1792), p. 507 *sq.*; B. Hawkins, "Sketch of the Creek country," in *Collections of the Georgia Historical Society*, iii. (Savannah, 1848), pp. 75-78; A. A. M'Gillivray, in Schoolcraft's *Indian Tribes*, v. 267 *sq.* Adair's description is the fullest and has been chiefly followed in the text.   In *Observations on the Creek and Cherokee Indians*, by William Bartram (1789), *with prefatory and supplementary notes*, by E. G. Squier, p. 75, there is a description—extracted from an MS. of J. H. Payne (author of *Home, Sweet Home*)—of the similar ceremony observed by the Cherokees. I possess a copy of this work in pamphlet form, but it appears to be an extract from the transactions or proceedings of a society, probably an American one.   Mr. Squier's preface is dated New York, 1851.

[2] W. Bartram, *Travels*, p. 507.

ashes carried out.   Then the chief priest put some
roots of the button-snake plant, with some green tobacco
leaves and a little of the new fruits, at the bottom of
the fireplace, which he afterwards ordered to be covered
up with white clay, and wetted over with clean water.
A thick arbour of green branches of young trees was
then made over the altar.[1]   Meanwhile the women at
home were cleaning out their houses, renewing the old
hearths, and scouring all the cooking vessels that they
might be ready to receive the new fire and the new
fruits.[2]   The public or sacred square was carefully
swept of even the smallest crumbs of previous feasts,
" for fear of polluting the first-fruit offerings."   Also
every vessel that had contained or had been used about
any food during the expiring year was removed from
the temple before sunset.   Then all the men who were
not known to have violated the law of the first-fruit
offering and that of marriage during the year were
summoned by a crier to enter the holy square and
observe a solemn fast.   But the women (except six
old ones), the children, and all who had not attained
the rank of warriors were forbidden to enter the
square.   Sentinels were also posted at the corners of
the square to keep out all persons deemed impure and
all animals.   A strict fast was then observed for two
nights and a day, the devotees drinking a bitter decoction of button-snake root " in order to vomit and purge
their sinful bodies."   That the people outside the square
might also be purified, one of the old men laid down a

---

[1] So amongst the Cherokees, according to J. H. Payne, an arbour of green
boughs was made in the sacred square ;
then " a beautiful bushy-topped shade-
tree was cut down close to the roots,
and planted in the very centre of the
sacred square.   Every man then provided himself with a green bough."

[2] So Adair.   Bartram, on the other
hand, as we have seen, says that the
old vessels were burned and new ones
prepared for the festival.

quantity of green tobacco at a corner of the square ; this was carried off by an old woman and distributed to the people without, who chewed and swallowed it " in order to afflict their souls." During this general fast, the women, children, and men of weak constitution were allowed to eat after mid-day, but not before. On the morning when the fast ended, the women brought a quantity of the old year's food to the outside of the sacred square. These provisions were then brought in and set before the famished multitude, but all traces of them had to be removed before noon. When the sun was declining from the meridian, all the people were commanded by the voice of a crier to stay within doors, to do no bad act, and to be sure to extinguish and throw away every spark of the old fire. Universal silence now reigned. Then the high priest made the new fire by the friction of two pieces of wood, and placed it on the altar under the green arbour. This new fire was believed to atone for all past crimes except murder. Then a basket of new fruits was brought ; the high priest took out a little of each sort of fruit, rubbed it with bear's oil, and offered it, together with some flesh, " to the bountiful holy spirit of fire, as a first-fruit offering, and an annual oblation for sin." He also consecrated the sacred emetics (the button-snake root and the cassina or black-drink) by pouring a little of them into the fire. The persons who had remained outside now approached, without entering, the sacred square ; and the chief priest thereupon made a speech, exhorting the people to observe their old rites and customs, announcing that the new divine fire had purged away the sins of the past year, and ear-nestly warning the women that, if any of them had not extinguished the old fire, or had contracted any impurity, they must forthwith depart, " lest the divine fire should spoil both them and the people." Some of the new fire was then laid down outside the holy square ; the women carried it home joyfully, and laid it on their unpolluted hearths. When several towns had united to celebrate the festival, the new fire might thus be carried for several miles. The new fruits were then dressed on the new fires and eaten with bear's oil, which was deemed indispensable. At one point of the festival the men rubbed the new corn between their hands, then on their faces and breasts.[1] During the festival which followed, the warriors, dressed in their wild martial array, their heads covered with white down and carrying white feathers in their hands, danced round the sacred arbour, under which burned the new fire. The ceremonies lasted eight days, during which the strictest continence was practised. Towards the conclusion of the festival the warriors fought a mock battle ; then the men and women together, in three circles, danced round the sacred fire. Lastly, all the people smeared themselves with white clay and bathed in running water. They came out of the water " believing themselves out of the reach of temporal evil for their past vicious conduct." So they departed in joy and peace.

The solemn preparations thus made for eating the new corn prove that it was eaten as a sacrament. In the Boeroe and Creek customs, this sacrament is combined with a sacrifice, and in course of time the sacrifice of first-fruits tends to throw the sacrament into the shade, if not to supersede it. The mere fact of having offered the first-fruits to the gods or ancestral spirits comes now to be thought a sufficient prepara-

---

[1] B. Hawkins, " Sketch," etc., p. 76.

tion for eating the new corn ; the gods having received their share, man is free to enjoy the rest. This mode of viewing the new fruits implies that they are regarded no longer as themselves instinct with divine life, but merely as a gift bestowed by the gods upon man, who is bound to express his gratitude and homage to his divine benefactors by presenting them with a portion of the fruits of the earth. But with sacrifice, as distinct from sacrament, we are not here concerned.[1]

The custom of eating bread sacramentally as the body of a god was practised by the Aztecs before the discovery and conquest of Mexico by the Spaniards. Twice a year, in May and December, an image of the great Mexican god Huitzilopochtli or Vitzilipuztli was made of dough, then broken in pieces, and solemnly eaten by his worshippers. The May ceremony is thus described by the historian Acosta. " Two daies before this feast, the virgins whereof I have spoken (the which were shut up and secluded in the same temple and were as it were religious women) did mingle a quantitie of the seede of beetes with roasted Mays [maize], and then they did mould it with honie, making an idol of that paste in bignesse like to that of wood, putting insteede of eyes graines of greene glasse, of blue or white ; and for teeth graines of Mays set forth with all the ornament and furniture that I have said. This being finished, all the Noblemen came and brought it an exquisite and rich garment, like unto that of the idol, wherewith they did attyre it. Being thus clad and deckt, they did set it in an azured chaire and in a litter to carry it on their shoulders. The morning of this feast being come, an houre before day all the maidens came forth attired in white, with new orna-

[1] See Note on " Offerings of first-fruits " at the end of the volume.

ments, the which that day were called the Sisters of
their god Vitzilipuztli, they came crowned with garlands
of Mays rosted and parched, being like unto azahar
or the flower of orange ; and about their neckes they
had great chaines of the same, which went bauldricke-
wise under their left arme. Their cheekes were died
with vermillion, their armes from the elbow to the
wrist were covered with red parrots' feathers." Young
men, crowned like the virgins with maize, then carried
the idol in its litter to the foot of the great pyramid-
shaped temple, up the steep and narrow steps of which
it was drawn to the music of flutes, trumpets, cornets,
and drums. "While they mounted up the idoll all the
people stoode in the Court with much reverence and
feare. Being mounted to the top, and that they had
placed it in a little lodge of roses which they held
readie, presently came the yong men, which strawed
many flowers of sundrie kindes, wherewith they filled
the temple both within and without. This done, all
the virgins came out of their convent, bringing peeces
of paste compounded of beetes and rosted Mays, which
was of the same paste whereof their idol was made
and compounded, and they were of the fashion of great
bones. They delivered them to the yong men, who
carried them up and laide them at the idoll's feete,
wherewith they filled the whole place that it could
receive no more. They called these morcells of paste
the flesh and bones of Vitzilipuztli." Then the priests
came in their robes of office, "and putting themselves
in order about these morsells and peeces of paste, they
used certaine ceremonies with singing and dauncing.
By means whereof they were blessed and consecrated
for the flesh and bones of this idoll. . . . The
ceremonies, dauncing, and sacrifice ended, they went

to unclothe themselves, and the priests and superiors of the temple tooke the idoll of paste, which they spoyled of all the ornaments it had, and made many peeces, as well of the idoll itselfe as of the tronchons which were consecrated, and then they gave them to the people in maner of a communion, beginning with the greater, and continuing unto the rest, both men, women, and little children, who received it with such teares, feare, and reverence as it was an admirable thing, saying that they did eate the flesh and bones of God, wherewith they were grieved. Such as had any sicke folkes demaunded thereof for them, and carried it with great reverence and veneration."[1]

Before the festival in December, which took place at the winter solstice, an image of the god Huitzilopochtli was made of seeds of various sorts kneaded into a dough with the blood of children. The bones of the god were represented by pieces of acacia wood, This image was placed on the chief altar of the temple, and on the day of the festival the king offered incense to it. Early next day it was taken down and set on its feet in a great hall. Then a priest took a flint-tipped dart and hurled it into the breast of the dough-image, piercing it through and through. This was called "killing the god Huitzilopochtli so that his body might be eaten." One of the priests cut out the heart of the image and gave it to the king to eat. The rest of the image was divided into minute pieces, of which every man great and small, down to the male children in the cradle, received one to eat. But no woman might taste a morsel. The ceremony was called *teoqualo*, that is, " god is eaten."[2]

---

[1] Acosta, *Natural and Moral History of the Indies*, bk. v. c. 24, vol. ii.   pp. 356-360 (Hakluyt Society, 1880).
[2] Bancroft, *Native Races of the Pacific*

At another festival the Mexicans made little images in human shape to represent the cloud-capped mountains. These images were made of paste of various seeds and were dressed in paper ornaments. Some people made five, others ten, others as many as fifteen of these paste images. They were placed in the oratory of each house and worshipped. Four times in the course of the night offerings of food were made to them in tiny vessels; and people sang and played the flute before them all night. At break of day the priests stabbed the images with a weaver's instrument, cut off their heads, and tore out their hearts, which they presented to the master of the house on a green saucer. The bodies of the images were then eaten by all the family, especially by the servants, " in order that by eating them they might be preserved from certain distempers, to which those persons who were negligent of worship to those deities conceived themselves to be subject." [1]

We are now able to suggest an explanation of the proverb "there are many Manii at Aricia." [2] Certain loaves made in the shape of men were called by the Romans *maniae*, and it appears that this kind of loaf was especially made at Aricia. [3] Now, Mania, the name of one of these loaves, was also the name of the Mother or Grandmother of Ghosts, [4] to whom woollen

---

States, iii. 297-300 (after Torquemada); Clavigero, *History of Mexico*, trans. by Cullen, i. 309 *sqq.*; Sahagun, *Histoire générale des choses de la Nouvelle-Espagne*, traduite et annotée par Jourdanet et Siméon (Paris, 1880), p. 203 *sq.*; J. G. Müller, *Geschichte der amerikanischen Urreligionen*, p. 605.

[1] Clavigero, i. 311; Sahagun, pp. 74, 156 *sq.*; Müller, p. 606; Bancroft, iii. 316. This festival took place on the last day of the 16th month (which

extended from 23d December to 11th January). At another festival the Mexicans made the semblance of a bone out of paste and ate it sacramentally as the bone of the god. Sahagun, p. 33.

[2] See above, vol. i. p. 5 *sq.*

[3] Festus, ed. Müller, pp. 128, 129, 145. The reading of the last passage is, however, uncertain ("*et Ariciae genus panni fieri; quod manici † appelletur*").

[4] Varro, *De ling. lat.* ix. 61;

effigies of men and women were dedicated at the festival of the Compitalia. These effigies were hung at the doors of all the houses in Rome; one effigy was hung up for every free person in the house, and one effigy, of a different kind, for every slave. The reason was that on this day the ghosts of the dead were believed to be going about, and it was hoped that they would carry off the effigies at the door instead of the living people in the house. According to tradition, these woollen figures were substitutes for a former custom of sacrificing human beings.[1] Upon data so fragmentary and uncertain, it is of course impossible to build with certainty; but it seems worth suggesting that the loaves in human form, which appear to have been baked at Aricia, were sacramental bread, and that in the old days, when the divine King of the Wood was annually slain, loaves were made in his image, like the paste figures of the gods in Mexico, and were eaten sacramentally by his worshippers.[2]

Arnobius, *Adv. nationes*, iii. 41; Macrobius, *Saturn.* i. 7, 35; Festus, p. 128, ed. Müller. Festus speaks of the mother or grandmother of the *larvae*; the other writers speak of the mother of the *lares*.

[1] Macrobius, *l.c.*; Festus, pp. 121, 239, ed. Müller. The effigies hung up for the slaves were called *pilae*, not *maniae*. *Pilae* was also the name given to the straw-men which were thrown to the bulls to gore in the arena. Martial, *Epigr.* ii. 43, 5 *sq.*; Asconius, *In Cornel.* p. 55, ed. Kiessling and Schoell.

[2] The ancients were at least familiar with the practice of sacrificing images made of dough or other materials as substitutes for the animals themselves. It was a recognised principle that when an animal could not be easily obtained for sacrifice, it was lawful to offer an image of it made of bread or wax. Servius on Virgil, *Aen.* ii. 116.

(Similarly a North-American Indian dreamed that a sacrifice of twenty elans was necessary for the recovery of a sick girl; but the elans could not be procured, and the girl's parents were allowed to sacrifice twenty loaves instead. *Relations des Jesuites*, 1636, p. 11, ed. 1858). Poor people who could not afford to sacrifice real animals offered dough images of them. Suidas, *s.v.* βοῦς ἕβδομος; cp. Hesychius, *s. vv.* βοῦς, ἕβδομος βοῦς. Hence bakers made a regular business of baking cakes in the likeness of all the animals which were sacrificed to the gods. Proculus, quoted and emended by Lobeck, *Aglaophamus*, p. 1079. When Cyzicus was besieged by Mithridates and the people could not procure a black cow to sacrifice at the rites of Proserpine, they made a cow of dough and placed it at the altar. Plutarch, *Lucullus*, 10. In a Boeotian sacrifice to Hercules, in place of the ram which was the proper

The Mexican sacraments in honour of Huitzilopochtli were also accompanied by the sacrifice of human victims. The tradition that the founder of the sacred grove at Aricia was a man named Manius, from whom many Manii were descended, would thus be an etymological myth invented to explain the name *maniae* as applied to these sacramental loaves. A dim recollection of the original connection of these loaves with human sacrifices may perhaps be traced in the story that the effigies dedicated to Mania at the Compitalia were substitutes for human victims. The story itself, however, is probably devoid of foundation, since the practice of putting up dummies to divert the attention of demons from living people is not uncommon. For example, when an epidemic is raging, some of the Dyaks of Borneo set up wooden images at their doors in the hope that the demons of the plague will be deceived into carrying off the images instead of the people.[1] The Minahassa of Celebes will sometimes transport a sick man to another house, leaving on his bed a dummy made up of a pillow and clothes. This dummy the demon is supposed to take by mistake for the sick man, who consequently recovers.[2] Similarly in Burma it is thought that a patient will recover if an effigy be buried in a small coffin.[3]

The custom of killing the god has now been traced

---

victim, an apple was regularly substituted, four chips being stuck in it to represent legs and two to represent horns. Pollux, i. 30 *sq.* The Athenians are said to have once offered to Hercules a similar substitute for an ox. Zenobius, *Cent.* v. 22. And the Locrians, being at a loss for an ox to sacrifice, made one out of figs and sticks, and offered it instead of the animal. Zenobius, *Cent.* v. 5. At the Athenian festival of the Diasia cakes shaped like animals were sacrificed. Schol. on Thucydides, i. 126, quoted by Lobeck, *l.c.* We have seen above (p. 53) that the poorer Egyptians offered dough images of pigs and ate them sacramentally.

[1] P. J. Veth, *Borneo's Wester Afdeeling*, ii. 309.

[2] N. Graafland, *De Minahassa*, i. 326.

[3] Shway Yoe, *The Burman*, ii. 138.

amongst peoples who have reached the agricultural
stage of society. We have seen that the spirit of the
corn, or of other cultivated plants, is commonly represented either in human or in animal form, and that a
custom has prevailed of killing annually either the
human or the animal representative of the god. The
reason for thus killing the corn-spirit in the person of
his representative has been given implicitly in the
earlier part of this chapter. But, further, we have
found a widespread custom of eating the god sacramentally, either in the shape of the man or animal who
represents the god, or in the shape of bread made in
human or animal form. The reasons for thus partaking
of the body of the god are, from the primitive stand-
point, simple enough. The savage commonly believes
that by eating the flesh of an animal or man he
acquires not only the physical, but even the moral and
intellectual qualities which were characteristic of that
animal or man. To take examples. The Creeks,
Cherokees, and kindred tribes of North American
Indians "believe that nature is possessed of such a
property, as to transfuse into men and animals the
qualities, either of the food they use, or of those objects
that are presented to their senses ; he who feeds on
venison is, according to their physical system, swifter
and more sagacious than the man who lives on the
flesh of the clumsy bear, or helpless dunghill fowls, the
slow-footed tame cattle, or the heavy wallowing swine.
This is the reason that several of their old men recom-
mend, and say, that formerly their greatest chieftains
observed a constant rule in their diet, and seldom ate
of any animal of a gross quality, or heavy motion of
body, fancying it conveyed a dulness through the whole
system, and disabled them from exerting themselves

with proper vigour in their martial, civil, and religious duties."[1]   The Zaparo Indians of South America "will, unless from necessity, in most cases not eat any heavy meats, such as tapir and peccary, but confine themselves to birds, monkeys, deer, fish, etc., principally because they argue that the heavier meats make them unwieldy, like the animals who supply the flesh, impeding their agility, and unfitting them for the chase."[2] The Namaquas abstain from eating the flesh of hares, because they think it would make them faint-hearted as a hare.   But they eat the flesh of the lion, or drink the blood of the leopard or lion to get the courage and strength of these beasts.[3]   The Arabs of Eastern Africa believe that an unguent of lion's fat inspires a man with boldness, and makes the wild beasts flee in terror before him.[4]   When a serious disease has attacked a Zulu kraal, the medicine-man takes the bone of a very old dog, which has died a natural death from mere old age, or the bone of an old cow, bull, or other very old animal, and administers it to the healthy as well as to the sick people, in order that they may live to be as old as the animal of whose bone they have partaken.[5]   The Miris of Northern India prize tiger's flesh as food for men; it gives them strength and courage.   But "it is not suited for women; it would make them too strong-minded."[6]   Amongst the Dyaks of North-west Borneo young men and warriors may

---

[1] James Adair, *History of the American Indians*, p. 133.

[2] Alfred Simson, *Travels in the Wilds of Ecuador* (London, 1887), p. 168; *id.* in *Journal of the Anthrop. Institute*, vii. 503.

[3] Theophilus Hahn, *Tsuni-‖Goam, the Supreme Being of the Khoi-Khoi*, p. 106.   Compare John Buchanan, *The Shire Highlands*, p. 138; Calla-

way, *Religious System of the Amazulu*, p. 438 *note*.

[4] Jerome Becker, *La Vie en Afrique*, (Paris and Brussels, 1887), ii. 366.

[5] Callaway, *Nursery Tales, Traditions, and Histories of the Zulus*, p. 175 *note*.

[6] Dalton, *Ethnology of Bengal*, p. 33.

not eat venison, because it would make them as timid as deer ; but the women and very old men are free to eat it.[1] Men of the Buro and Aru Islands, East Indies, eat the flesh of dogs in order to be bold and nimble in war.[2] Amongst the Papuans of the Port Moresby and Motumotu districts, New Guinea, young lads eat strong pig, wallaby, and large fish, in order to acquire the strength of the animal or fish.[3] In Corea the bones of tigers fetch a higher price than those of leopards as a means of inspiring courage. A Chinaman in Soul bought and ate a whole tiger to make himself brave and fierce.[4] The special seat of courage, according to the Chinese, is the gall-bladder ; so they sometimes procure the gall-bladders of tigers and bears, and eat the bile in the belief that it will give them courage.[5] In Norse history, Ingiald, son of King Aunund, was timid in his youth, but after eating the heart of a wolf he became very bold ; and Hialto gained strength and courage by eating the heart of a bear and drinking its blood.[6] In Morocco lethargic patients are given ants to swallow ; and to eat lion's flesh will make a coward brave.[7] When a child is late in learning to speak, the Turks of Central Asia will give it the tongues of certain birds to eat.[8] A North American Indian thought that brandy must be a decoction of hearts and tongues, "Because," said he, "after drinking it I fear nothing, and I talk wonderfully."[9] The people of Darfur,

[1] St. John, *Life in the Forests of the Far East*,[2] i. 186, 206.

[2] Riedel, *De sluik-en kroesharige rassen tusschen Selebes en Papua*, pp. 10, 262.

[3] James Chalmers, *Pioneering in New Guinea*, p. 166.

[4] *Proceedings Royal Geogr. Society*, N. S. viii. (1886) p. 307.

[5] J. Henderson, "The Medicine and Medical Practice of the Chinese," *Journ.* *North China Branch R. Asiatic Society*, New Series, i. (Shanghai, 1865) p. 35 *sq.*

[6] Müller on Saxo Grammaticus, vol. ii. p. 60.

[7] Leared, *Morocco and the Moors*, p. 281.

[8] Vambery, *Das Türkenvolk*, p. 218.

[9] Charlevoix, *Histoire de la Nouvelle France*, vi. 8.

in Central Africa, think that the liver is the seat of the soul, and that a man may enlarge his soul by eating the liver of an animal. "Whenever an animal is killed its liver is taken out and eaten, but the people are most careful not to touch it with their hands, as it is considered sacred; it is cut up in small pieces and eaten raw, the bits being conveyed to the mouth on the point of a knife, or the sharp point of a stick. Any one who may accidentally touch the liver is strictly forbidden to partake of it, which prohibition is regarded as a great misfortune for him." Women are not allowed to eat liver, because they have no soul.[1]

Again, the flesh and blood of brave men are commonly eaten and drunk to inspire bravery. The Australian Kamilaroi eat the heart and liver of a brave man to get his courage.[2] It is a common practice with the Australian blacks to kill a man, cut out his caul-fat, and rub themselves with it, "the belief being that all the qualifications, both physical and mental, of the previous owner of the fat were thus communicated to him who used it."[3] The Italones of the Philippine Islands drink the blood of their slain enemies, and eat part of the back of their heads and of their entrails raw, in order to acquire their courage. For the same reason the Efugaos, another tribe of the Philippines, suck the brains of their foes.[4] Amongst the Kimbunda of Western Africa, when a new king succeeds to the throne, a brave prisoner of war is killed in order that the king and nobles may eat his flesh, and so acquire

---

[1] Felkin, "Notes on the For tribe of Central Africa," in *Proceedings of the Royal Society of Edinburgh*, xiii. (1884-1886) p. 218.

[2] W. Ridley, *Kamilaroi*, p. 160.

[3] Brough Smyth, *Aborigines of Victoria*, ii. 313.

[4] Blumentritt, "Der Ahnencultus und die religiösen Anschauungen der Malaien des Philippinen-Archipels," in *Mittheilungen d. Wiener Geogr. Gesellschaft*, 1882, p. 154.

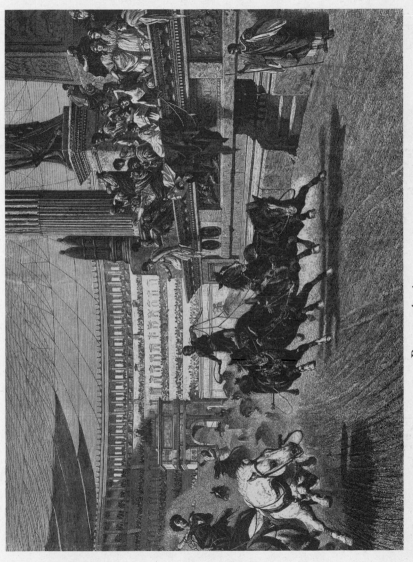

Roman chariot race.

Cannibals drink the blood of their victims.

his strength and courage.[1] The Basutos cut off pieces of their slain enemies and make them into a powder, " which is supposed to communicate to them the courage, skill, and good fortune of their adversaries."[2] The Zulus think that by eating the centre of the forehead and the eyebrow of an enemy they acquire the power of looking steadfastly at a foe.[3] In the Shire Highlands of Africa those who kill a brave man eat his heart to get his courage.[4] For the same purpose the Chinese eat the bile of notorious bandits who have been executed.[5] In New Zealand "the chief was an atua [god], but there were powerful and powerless gods ; each naturally sought to make himself one of the former ; the plan therefore adopted was to incorporate the spirits of others with their own ; thus, when a warrior slew a chief he immediately gouged out his eyes and swallowed them, the *atua tonga*, or divinity, being supposed to reside in that organ ; thus he not only killed the body, but also possessed himself of the soul of his enemy, and consequently the more chiefs he slew the greater did his divinity become."[6]

It is now easy to understand why a savage should desire to partake of the flesh of an animal or man whom he regards as divine. By eating the body of the god he shares in the god's attributes and powers. And when the god is a corn-god, the corn is his proper body ; when he is a vine-god, the juice of the grape is his blood ; and so by eating the bread and drinking

[1] Magyar, *Reisen in Süd-Afrika in den Jahren* 1849-1857, pp. 273-276.

[2] Casalis, *The Basutos*, p. 257 *sq.*

[3] Callaway, *Nursery Tales, Traditions and Histories of the Zulus*, p. 163 *note.*

[4] John Buchanan, *The Shire Highlands*, p. 138.

[5] *Journal of the North China Branch Royal Asiatic Society, l.c.*

[6] R. Taylor, *Te Ika a Maui, or New Zealand and its Inhabitants* (London, 1870), p. 352. Cp. *ib.* p. 173 ; Ellis, *Polynesian Researches*, i. 358 ; J. Dumont D'Urville, *Voyage autour du Monde sur la corvette Astrolabe*, ii. 547 ; *Journal of the Anthrop. Inst.* xix. 108.

the wine the worshipper partakes of the real body and blood of his god. Thus the drinking of wine in the rites of a vine-god like Dionysus is not an act of revelry, it is a solemn sacrament.[1]

§ 12.—*Killing the divine animal*

It remains to show that hunting and pastoral tribes, as well as agricultural peoples, have been in the habit of killing their gods. The gods whom hunters and shepherds adore and kill are animals pure and simple, not animals regarded as embodiments of other supernatural beings. Our first example is drawn from the Indians of California, who, living in a fertile country[2] under a serene and temperate sky, nevertheless rank near the bottom of the savage scale. The Acagchemen tribe of San Juan Capistrano adored the great buzzard. Once a year, at a great festival called *Panes* or birdfeast, they carried one of these birds in procession to their chief temple, which seems to have been merely an unroofed enclosure of stakes. Here they killed the bird without losing a drop of its blood. The skin was removed entire and preserved with the feathers as a relic or for the purpose of making the festal garment or *paelt*. The carcass was buried in a hole in the temple, and the old women gathered round the grave weeping and moaning bitterly, while they threw various kinds of seeds or pieces of food on it, crying out, "Why

---

[1] On the custom of eating a god, see also a paper by Felix Liebrecht, "Der aufgegessene Gott," in *Zur Volkskunde*, pp. 436-439; and especially W. R. Smith, art. "Sacrifice," *Encycl. Britann.* 9th ed. vol. xxi. p. 137 *sq*. On wine as the blood of a god, see above, vol. i. p. 183 *sqq*.

[2] This does not refer to the Californian peninsula, which is an arid and treeless wilderness of rock and sand.

did you run away ?   Would you not have been better
with us ? " and so on.   They said that the Panes was
a woman who had run off to the mountains and there
been changed into a bird by the god Chinigchinich.
They believed that though they sacrificed the bird
annually, she came to life again and returned to her
home in the mountains.   Moreover they thought that
" as often as the bird was killed, it became multiplied ;
because every year all the different Capitanes celebrated
the same feast of the Panes, and were firm in the
opinion that the birds sacrificed were but one and the
same female." [1]

The unity in multiplicity thus postulated by the
Californians is very noticeable and helps to explain
their motive for killing the divine bird.   The notion of
the life of a species as distinct from that of an individual,
easy and obvious as it seems to us, appears to be one
which the Californian savage cannot grasp.   He is
unable to conceive the life of the species otherwise
than as an individual life, and therefore as exposed to
the same dangers and calamities which menace and
finally destroy the life of the individual.   Apparently
he thinks that a species left to itself will grow old and
die like an individual, and that therefore some step
must be taken to save from extinction the particular
species which he regards as divine.   The only means
he can think of to avert the catastrophe is to kill a
member of the species in whose veins the tide of life is
still running strong and has not yet stagnated among
the fens of old age.   The life thus diverted from one
channel will flow, he fancies, more freshly and freely
in a new one ; in other words, the slain animal will

---

[1] Boscana, in Alfred Robinson's *Life in California* (New York, 1846), p. 291 *sq.* ; Bancroft, *Native Races of the Pacific States*, iii. 168.

revive and enter on a new term of life with all the spring and energy of youth.   To us this reasoning is transparently absurd, but so too is the custom.   If a better explanation, that is, one more consonant with the facts and with the principles of savage thought, can be given of the custom, I will willingly withdraw the one here proposed.   A similar confusion, it may be noted, between the individual life and the life of the species was made by the Samoans.   Each family had for its god a particular species of animal; yet the death of one of these animals, for example an owl, was not the death of the god, " he was supposed to be yet alive, and incarnate in all the owls in existence." [1]

The rude Californian rite which we have just considered has a close parallel in the religion of ancient Egypt.   The Thebans and all other Egyptians who worshipped the Theban god Ammon held rams to be sacred and would not sacrifice them.   But once a year at the festival of Ammon they killed a ram, skinned it, and clothed the image of the god in the skin.   Then they mourned over the ram and buried it in a sacred tomb.   The custom was explained by a story that Zeus had once exhibited himself to Hercules clad in the fleece and wearing the head of a ram. [2]   Of course the ram in this case was simply the beast-god of Thebes, as the wolf was the beast-god of Lycopolis, and the goat was the beast-god of Mendes.   In other words, the ram was Ammon himself.   On the monuments, it is true, Ammon appears in semi-human form with the body of a man and the head of a ram. [3]   But this only shows that he was in the usual

---

[1] Turner, *Samoa*, p. 21, cp. pp. 26, 61.
[2] Herodotus, ii. 42.   The custom has been already referred to, above, p. 63.

[3] Ed. Meyer, *Geschichte des Alterthums*, i. § 58.   Cp. Wilkinson, *Manners and Customs of the Ancient Egyptians*, iii. 1 *sqq.* (ed. 1878).

chrysalis state through which beast-gods regularly pass
before they emerge as full-fledged anthropomorphic
gods. The ram, therefore, was killed, not as a
sacrifice to Ammon, but as the god himself, whose
identity with the beast is plainly shown by the custom
of clothing his image in the skin of the slain ram.
The reason for thus killing the ram-god annually may
have been that which I have assigned for the general
custom of killing the god and for the special Californian custom of killing the divine buzzard. As
applied to Egypt, this explanation is supported by
the analogy of the bull-god Apis, who was not suffered
to outlive a certain term of years.[1] The intention of
thus putting a limit to the life of the god was, as I
have argued, to secure him from the weakness and
frailty of age. The same reasoning would explain the
custom—probably an older one—of putting the beast-
god to death annually, as was done with the ram of
Thebes.

One point in the Theban ritual — the application of the skin to the image of the god—deserves
special attention. If the god was at first the
living ram, his representation by an image must
have originated later. But how did it originate?
The answer to this question is perhaps furnished by
the practice of preserving the skin of the animal which
is slain as divine. The Californians, as we have seen,
preserved the skin of the buzzard; and the skin of the
goat, which is killed on the harvest-field as a representative of the corn-spirit, is kept for various superstitious purposes.[2] The skin in fact was kept as a
token or memorial of the god, or rather as containing
in it a part of the divine life, and it had only to be

---

[1] Above, p. 61 *sq.*   [2] Above, p. 15 *sq.*

stuffed or stretched upon a frame to become a regular image of him. At first an image of this kind would be renewed annually,[1] the new image being provided by the skin of the slain animal. But from annual images to permanent images the transition is easy. We have seen that the older custom of cutting a new May-tree every year was superseded by the practice of maintaining a permanent May-pole, which was, however, annually decked with fresh leaves and flowers and even surmounted each year by a fresh young tree.[2] Similarly when the stuffed skin, as a representative of the god, was replaced by a permanent image of him in wood, stone, or metal, the permanent image was annually clad in the fresh skin of the slain animal. When this stage had been reached, the custom of killing the ram came naturally to be interpreted as a sacrifice offered to the image, and was explained by a story like that of Ammon and Hercules.

West Africa furnishes another example of the annual killing of a sacred animal and the preservation of its skin. The negroes of Issapoo, in the island of Fernando Po, regard the cobra-capella as their guardian deity, who can do them good or ill, bestow riches or inflict disease and death. The skin of one of these reptiles is hung tail downwards from a branch of the highest tree in the public square, and the placing of it on the tree is an annual ceremony. As soon as

---

[1] The Italmens of Kamtchatka, at the close of the fishing season, used to make the figure of a wolf out of grass. This figure they carefully kept the whole year, believing that it wedded with their maidens and prevented them from giving birth to twins; for twins were esteemed a great misfortune. Steller, *Beschreibung von dem Lande Kamtschatka*, p. 327 *sq.* According to Hartknoch (*Dissertat. histor. de variis rebus Prussicis*, p. 163; *Alt-preussen*, p. 161) the image of the old Prussian god Curcho was annually renewed. But see Mannhardt, *Die Korn-dämonen*, p. 27. [2] Above, vol. i. p. 81.

the ceremony is over, all children born within the past year are carried out and their hands made to touch the tail of the serpent's skin.[1]   The latter custom is clearly a way of placing the infants under the protection of the tribal god.   Similarly in Senegambia a python is expected to visit every child of the Python clan within eight days after birth;[2] and the Psylli, a Snake clan of ancient Africa, used to expose their infants to snakes in the belief that the snakes would not harm true-born children of the clan.[3]

In the Californian, Egyptian, and Fernando Po customs the animal slain probably is, or once was, a totem.   At all events, in all three cases the worship of the animal seems to have no relation to agriculture, and may therefore be presumed to date from the hunter or pastoral stage of society.   The same may be said of the following custom, though the people who practise it—the Zuni Indians of New Mexico—are now settled in walled villages or towns of a peculiar type, and practise agriculture and the arts of pottery and weaving.   But the Zuni custom is marked by certain features which appear to place it in a somewhat different category from the preceding cases.   It may be well therefore to describe it at full length in the words of an eye-witness.

"With midsummer the heat became intense.   My brother [*i.e.* adopted Indian brother] and I sat, day after day, in the cool under-rooms of our house,—the latter [*sic*] busy with his quaint forge and crude appliances, working Mexican coins over into bangles,

---

[1] T. J. Hutchinson, *Impressions of Western Africa* (London, 1858), p. 196 *sq.*   The writer does not expressly state that a serpent is killed annually, but his statement implies it.

[2] *Revue d'Ethnographie*, iii. 397.

[3] Varro in Priscian, x. 32, vol. i. p. 524, ed. Keil ; Pliny, *Nat. Hist.* vii. § 14.   Pliny's statement is to be corrected by Varro's.

girdles, ear-rings, buttons, and what not for savage ornament. . . . One day as I sat watching him, a procession of fifty men went hastily down the hill, and off westward over the plain. They were solemnly led by a painted and shell-bedecked priest, and followed by the torch-bearing Shu-lu-wit-si, or God of Fire. After they had vanished, I asked old brother what it all meant.

"'They are going,' said he, 'to the city of the Ka-ka and the home of our others.'

"Four days after, toward sunset, costumed and masked in the beautiful paraphernalia of the Ka-k'ok-shi, or 'Good Dance,' they returned in file up the same pathway, each bearing in his arms a basket filled with living, squirming turtles, which he regarded and carried as tenderly as a mother would her infant. Some of the wretched reptiles were carefully wrapped in soft blankets, their heads and forefeet protruding,— and, mounted on the backs of the plume-bedecked pilgrims, made ludicrous but solemn caricatures of little children in the same position. While I was at supper upstairs that evening, the governor's brother-in-law came in. He was welcomed by the family as if a messenger from heaven. He bore in his tremulous fingers one of the much abused and rebellious turtles. Paint still adhered to his hands and bare feet, which led me to infer that he had formed one of the sacred embassy.

"'So you went to Ka-thlu-el-lon, did you?' I asked.

"'E'e,' replied the weary man, in a voice husky with long chanting, as he sank, almost exhausted, on a roll of skins which had been placed for him, and tenderly laid the turtle on the floor. No sooner did

Mexican priests.

A Zulu couple.

the creature find itself at liberty than it made off as fast as its lame legs would take it. Of one accord the family forsook dish, spoon, and drinking-cup, and grabbing from a sacred meal-bowl whole handfuls of the contents, hurriedly followed the turtle about the room, into dark corners, around water-jars, behind the grinding-troughs, and out into the middle of the floor again, praying and scattering meal on its back as they went. At last, strange to say, it approached the foot-sore man who had brought it.

"'Ha!' he exclaimed, with emotion; 'see, it comes to me again; ah, what great favours the fathers of all grant me this day,' and passing his hand gently over the sprawling animal, he inhaled from his palm deeply and long, at the same time invoking the favour of the gods. Then he leaned his chin upon his hand, and with large wistful eyes regarded his ugly captive as it sprawled about, blinking its meal-bedimmed eyes, and clawing the smooth floor in memory of its native element. At this juncture I ventured a question:

"'Why do you not let him go, or give him some water?'

"Slowly the man turned his eyes toward me, an odd mixture of pain, indignation, and pity on his face, while the worshipful family stared at me with holy horror.

"'Poor younger brother!' he said at last, 'know you not how precious it is? It die? It will *not* die; I tell you, it cannot die.'

"'But it will die if you don't feed it and give it water.'

"'I tell you it *cannot* die; it will only change houses to-morrow, and go back to the home of its brothers. Ah, well! How should *you* know?' he mused. Turning to the blinded turtle again : 'Ah! my poor dear lost child or parent, my sister or brother to have been! Who knows which? Maybe my own great-grandfather or mother!' And with this he fell to weeping most pathetically, and, tremulous with sobs, which were echoed by the women and children, he buried his face in his hands. Filled with sympathy for his grief, however mistaken, I raised the turtle to my lips and kissed its cold shell; then depositing it on the floor, hastily left the grief-stricken family to their sorrows. Next day, with prayers and tender beseech-ings, plumes, and offerings, the poor turtle was killed, and its flesh and bones were removed and deposited in the little river, that it might 'return once more to eternal life among its comrades in the dark waters of the lake of the dead.' The shell, carefully scraped and dried, was made into a dance-rattle, and, covered by a piece of buckskin, it still hangs from the smoke-stained rafters of my brother's house. Once a Navajo tried to buy it for a ladle ; loaded with indignant reproaches, he was turned out of the house. Were any one to venture the suggestion that the turtle no longer lived, his remark would cause a flood of tears, and he would be reminded that it had only 'changed houses and gone to live for ever in the home of "our lost others."' "[1]

In this custom we find expressed in the clearest way a belief in the transmigration of human souls into the bodies of turtles.[2] The same belief in transmigra-

---

[1] Mr. Frank H. Cushing, "My Adventures in Zuñi," in *The Century*, May 1883, p. 45 *sq.*

[2] Mr. Cushing, indeed, while he admits that the ancestors of the Zuni may have believed in transmigration, says, "Their belief, to-day, however, relative to the future life is spiritual-istic." But the expressions in the text seem to leave no room for doubting that the transmigration into turtles is a living article of Zuni faith.

tion is held by the Moqui Indians, who belong to the
same race as the Zunis.   The Moquis are divided into
totem clans—the Bear clan, Deer clan, Wolf clan,
Hare clan, etc. ; they believe that the ancestors of the
clans were bears, deer, wolves, hares, etc. ; and that at
death the members of each clan become bears, deer,
etc.[1]   The Zuni are also divided into clans, the totems
of which agree closely with those of the Moquis, and
one of their totems is the turtle.[2]   Thus their belief in
transmigration into the turtle is probably one of the
regular articles of their totem faith.   What then is the
meaning of killing a turtle in which the soul of a kins-
man is believed to be present ?   Apparently the object
is to keep up a communication with the other world in
which the souls of the departed are believed to be
assembled in the form of turtles.   It is a common
belief that the spirits of the dead return occasionally to
their old homes ; and accordingly the unseen visitors
are welcomed and feasted by the living, and then sent
upon their way.[3]   In the Zuni ceremony the dead are
fetched back in the form of turtles, and the killing of
the turtles is the way of sending back the souls to the
spirit-land.   Thus the general explanation given above
of the custom of killing a god seems inapplicable to
the Zuni custom, the true meaning of which is somewhat obscure.

Doubt also hangs over the meaning of the bear-
sacrifice offered by the Ainos, a primitive people

---

[1] Schoolcraft, *Indian Tribes*, iv. 86.
On the totem clans of the Moquis, see J.
G. Bourke, *Snake-Dance of the Moquis
of Arizona*, pp. 116 *sq.*, 334 *sqq.*
[2] For this information I am indebted
to the kindness of Captain J. G. Bourke,
3d. Cavalry, U.S. Army, author of the
work mentioned in the preceding note.

[3] The old Prussian and Japanese
customs are typical.   For the former,
see above, vol. i. p. 177.   For the
latter, Charlevoix, *Histoire et Description générale du Japon*, i. 128 *sq.* Thun-
berg, *Voyages au Japon*, etc. iv. 18 *sqq.*
A general account of such customs must
be reserved for another work.

who are found in the Japanese islands of Yesso and
Saghalien, and also in the southern of the Kurile
Islands.   It is not quite easy to make out the attitude
of the Ainos towards the bear.   On the one hand
they give it the name of *Kamui* or "god"; but
as they apply the same word to strangers,[1] it probably
means no more than a being supposed to be endowed
with superhuman powers.   Again, it is said "the bear
is their chief divinity;"[2] "in the religion of the Ainos
the bear plays a chief part;"[3] "amongst the animals
it is especially the bear which receives an idolatrous
veneration;"[4] "they worship it after their fashion.
. . . . . There is no doubt that this wild beast
inspires more of the feeling which prompts worship
than the inanimate forces of nature, and the Ainos
may be distinguished as bear-worshippers."[5]   Yet,
on the other hand, they kill the bear whenever they
can;[6] "the men spend the autumn, winter, and
spring in hunting deer and bears.   Part of their
tribute or taxes is paid in skins, and they subsist
on the dried meat;"[7] bear's flesh is indeed one of
their staple foods; they eat it both fresh and salted;[8]
and the skins of bears furnish them with clothing.[9]
In fact, the "worship" of which writers on this subject
speak appears to be paid only to the dead animal.
Thus, although they kill a bear whenever they can,
"in the process of dissecting the carcass they

[1] B. Scheube, "Der Baerencultus
und die Baerenfeste der Ainos," in
*Mittheilungen der deutschen Gesellschaft
b. S. und S. Ostasiens* (Yokama), Heft
xxii. p. 45.

[2] *Transactions of the Ethnological
Society*, iv. 36.

[3] Rein, *Japan*, i. 446.

[4] H. von Siebold, *Ethnologische Stu-*
*dien über die Ainos auf der Insel
Yesso*, p. 26.

[5] Miss Bird, *Unbeaten Tracks in
Japan* (new ed. 1885), p. 275.

[6] *Trans. Ethnol. Soc. l.c.*

[7] Miss Bird, *op. cit.* p. 269.

[8] Scheube, *Die Ainos*, p. 4.

[9] Scheube, "Baerencultus," etc. p.
45; Joest, in *Verhandlungen d. Berliner
Gesell. f. Anthropologie*, 1882, p. 188.

endeavour to conciliate the deity, whose representative they have slain, by making elaborate obeisances
and deprecatory salutations;"[1] "when a bear is
trapped or wounded by an arrow, the hunters go
through an apologetic or propitiatory ceremony."[2]
The skulls of slain bears receive a place of honour
in their huts, or are set up on sacred posts outside
the huts, and are treated with much respect; libations
of *sake*, an intoxicating liquor, are offered to them.[3]
The skulls of foxes are also fastened to the sacred
posts outside the huts; they are regarded as charms
against evil spirits, and are consulted as oracles.[4]
Yet it is expressly said, "The live fox is revered
just as little as the bear; rather they avoid it as
much as possible, considering it a wily animal."[5]
The bear cannot, therefore, be described as a sacred
animal of the Ainos, and it certainly is not a totem;
for they do not call themselves bears, they appear
to have no legend of their descent from a bear,[6]
and they kill and eat the animal freely.

But it is the bear-festival of the Ainos which concerns us here. Towards the end of winter a young
bear is caught and brought into the village. At first
he is suckled by an Aino woman; afterwards he is
fed on fish. When he grows so strong that he
threatens to break out of the wooden cage in which
he is confined, the feast is held. But "it is a peculiarly

---

[1] *Trans. Ethnol. Soc. l.c.*

[2] Miss Bird, *op. cit.* p. 277.

[3] Scheube, *Die Ainos*, p. 15; Sie-
bold, *op. cit.* p. 26; *Trans. Ethnol.
Soc. l.c.*; Rein, *Japan*, i. 447; Von
Brandt, "The Ainos and Japanese,"
in *Journ. Anthrop. Inst.* iii. 134;
Miss Bird, *op. cit.* pp. 275, 276.

[4] Scheube, *Die Ainos*, pp. 15, 16;
Journ. Anthrop. Inst. iii. 134.

[5] Scheube, *Die Ainos*, p. 16.

[6] Reclus (*Nouvelle Géographie Universelle*, vii. 755) mentions a (Japanese?)
legend which attributes the hairiness of
the Ainos to the fact of their first
ancestor having been suckled by a
bear. But in the absence of other
evidence this is no proof of totemism.

striking fact that the young bear is not kept merely to furnish a good meal; rather he is regarded and honoured as a fetish, or even as a sort of higher being."[1] The festival is generally celebrated in September or October. Before it takes place the Ainos apologise to their gods, alleging that they have treated the bear kindly as long as they could, now they can feed him no longer, and are obliged to kill him. A man who gives a bear-feast invites his relations and friends; in a small village nearly the whole community takes part in the feast. One of these festivals has been described by an eye-witness, Dr. Scheube.[2] On entering the hut he found about thirty Ainos present, men, women, and children, all dressed in their best. The master of the house first offered a libation on the fireplace to the god of the fire, and the guests followed his example. Then a libation was offered to the house-god in his sacred corner of the hut. Meanwhile the housewife, who had nursed the bear, sat by herself, silent and sad, bursting now and then into tears. Her grief was obviously unaffected, and it deepened as the festival went on. Next, the master of the house and some of the guests went out of the hut and offered libations before the bear's cage. A few drops were presented to the bear in a saucer, which he at once upset. Then the women and girls danced round the cage, their faces turned towards it, their knees slightly bent, rising and hopping on their toes. As they danced they clapped their hands and sang a monotonous song. The housewife and a few old women, who might have nursed many bears, danced tearfully, stretching out their arms to

---

[1] Rein, *Japan*, i. 447.   [2] "Der Baerencultus," etc. See above.

the bear, and addressing it in terms of endearment.
The young folks were less affected; they laughed
as well as sang. Disturbed by the noise, the bear
began to rush about his cage and howl lamentably.
Next libations were offered to the *inabos* or sacred
wands which stand outside of an Aino hut. These
wands are about a couple of feet high, and are
whittled at the top into spiral shavings.[1] Five new
wands with bamboo leaves attached to them had
been set up for the festival. This is regularly done
when a bear is killed; the leaves mean that the
bear may come to life again. Then the bear was
let out of his cage, a rope was thrown round his
neck, and he was led about in the neighbourhood
of the hut. While this was being done the men,
headed by a chief, shot at the bear with arrows
tipped with wooden buttons. Dr. Scheube had to
do so also. Then the bear was taken before the
sacred wands, a stick was put in his mouth, nine
men knelt on him and pressed his neck against a
beam. In five minutes the bear had expired without
uttering a sound. Meantime the women and girls
had taken post behind the men, where they danced,
lamenting, and beating the men who were killing
the bear. The bear's carcass was next placed on
a mat before the sacred wands; and a sword and
quiver, taken from the wands, were hung round the
beast's neck. Being a she-bear, it was also adorned
with a necklace and ear-rings. Then food and drink
were offered to it, in the shape of millet-broth, millet-
cakes, and a pot of *sake*. The men now sat down
on mats before the dead bear, offered libations to

---

[1] Scheube, "Baerencultus," etc. p. 46; *id.*, *Die Ainos*, p. 15; Miss Bird, *op. cit.* p. 273 *sq.*

it, and drank deep. Meanwhile the women and girls had laid aside all marks of sorrow, and danced merrily, none more merrily than the old women. When the mirth was at its height two young Ainos, who had let the bear out of his cage, mounted the roof of the hut and threw cakes of millet among the company, who all scrambled for them without distinction of age or sex. The bear was next skinned and disembowelled, and the trunk severed from the head, to which the skin was left hanging. The blood, caught in cups, was eagerly swallowed by the men. None of the women or children appeared to drink the blood, though custom did not forbid them to do so. The liver was cut in small pieces and eaten raw, with salt, the women and children getting their share. The flesh and the rest of the vitals were taken into the house to be kept till the next day but one, and then to be divided among the persons who had been present at the feast. Blood and liver were offered to Dr. Scheube. While the bear was being disembowelled, the women and girls danced the same dance which they had danced at the beginning—not, however, round the cage, but in front of the sacred wands. At this dance the old women, who had been merry a moment before, again shed tears freely. After the brain had been extracted from the bear's head and swallowed with salt, the skull, detached from the skin, was hung on a pole beside the sacred wands. The stick with which the bear had been gagged was also fastened to the pole, and so were the sword and quiver which had been hung on the carcass. The latter were removed in about an hour, but the rest remained standing. The whole company, men and women, danced noisily before the pole ; and another drinking-bout, in which the women joined, closed the festival.

The mode of killing the bear is described somewhat differently by Miss Bird, who, however, did not witness the ceremony. She says : "Yells and shouts are used to excite the bear ; and when he becomes much agitated a chief shoots him with an arrow, inflicting a slight wound which maddens him, on which the bars of the cage are raised, and he springs forth, very furious. At this stage the Ainos run upon him with various weapons, each one striving to inflict a wound, as it brings good luck to draw his blood. As soon as he falls down exhausted his head is cut off, and the weapons with which he has been wounded are offered to it, and he is asked to avenge himself upon them." At Usu, on Volcano Bay, when the bear is being killed, the Ainos shout, "We kill you, O bear ! come back soon into an Aino." [1] A very respectable authority, Dr. Siebold, states that the bear's own heart is frequently offered to the dead animal, in order to assure him that he is still in life. [2] This, however, is denied by Dr. Scheube, who says the heart is eaten. [3] Perhaps the custom may be observed in some places, though not in others.

The Gilyaks, a Tunguzian people of Eastern Siberia, [4] hold a bear festival of the same sort. "The bear is the object of the most refined solicitude of an entire village and plays the chief part in their religious

---

[1] Miss Bird, *op. cit.* p. 276 *sq*. Miss Bird's information must be received with caution, as there are grounds for believing that her informant deceived her.

[2] Siebold, *Ethnolog. Studien über die Ainos*, p. 26.

[3] "Baerencultus," etc. p. 50 *note*.

[4] They inhabit the banks of the lower Amoor and the north of Saghalien. E. G. Ravenstein, *The Russians on the Amur*, p. 389.

ceremonies."[1]　An old she-bear is shot and her cub is reared, but not suckled in the village.　When the bear is big enough he is taken from his cage and dragged through the village.　But first he is led to the bank of the river, for this is believed to ensure abundance of fish to each family.　He is then taken into every house in the village, where fish, brandy, etc. are offered to him.　Some people prostrate themselves before the beast.　His entrance into a house is supposed to bring a blessing ; and if he snuffs at the food offered to him, this also is a blessing.　Nevertheless they tease and worry, poke and tickle the animal continually, so that he is surly and snappish.[2]　After being thus taken to every house, he is tied to a peg and shot dead with arrows.　His head is then cut off, decked with shavings, and placed on the table where the feast is set out. Here they beg pardon of the beast and worship him. Then his flesh is roasted and eaten in special vessels of wood finely carved.　They do not eat the flesh raw nor drink the blood, as the Ainos do.　The brain and entrails are eaten last ; and the skull, still decked with shavings, is placed on a tree near the house. Then the people sing and both sexes dance in ranks, as bears.[3]

---

[1] "Notes on the River Amur and the adjacent districts," translated from the Russian, *Journal Royal Geogr. Soc.* xxviii. (1858) p. 396.

[2] Compare the custom of pinching the frog before cutting off his head, above vol. i. p. 93.　In Japan sorceresses bury a dog in the earth, tease him, then cut off his head and put it in a box to be used in magic.　Bastian, *Die Culturländer des alten Amerika*, i. 475 *note*, who adds "*wie im ostindischen Archipelago die Schutzseele gereizt wird.*" He probably refers to the Batta *Pang-hulu - balang*.　See Rosenberg, *Der*

Malayische Archipel, p. 59 *sq.*; W. Ködding, "Die Batakschen Götter," in *Allgemeine Missions-Zeitschrift*, xii. (1885) 478 *sq.*; Neumann, "Het Pane-en Bila-stroomgebied op het eiland Sumatra," in *Tijdschrift v. h. Nederl. Aardrijks Genootsch.* ii. series, dl. iii. Afdeeling : meer uitgebreide artikelen, No. 2, p. 306.

[3] W. Joest, in Scheube, *Die Ainos*, p. 17 ; *Revue d'Ethnographie*, ii. 307 *sq.* (on the authority of Mr. Seeland); *Internationales Archiv für Ethnologie*, i. 102 (on the authority of Captain Jacobsen).　What exactly is meant by

The Goldi, neighbours of the Gilyaks, treat the
bear in much the same way. They hunt and kill it ;
but sometimes they capture a live bear and keep him
in a cage, feeding him well and calling him their son
and brother. Then at a great festival he is taken
from his cage, paraded about with marked consideration, and afterwards killed and eaten. " The skull,
jaw-bones, and ears are then suspended on a tree, as
an antidote against evil spirits ; but the flesh is eaten
and much relished, for they believe that all who partake of it acquire a zest for the chase, and become
courageous." [1]

In the treatment of the captive bear by these
tribes there are features which can hardly be distinguished from worship. Such in particular is the
Gilyak custom of leading him from house to house,
that every family may receive his blessing—a custom
parallel to the European one of taking a May-tree or
a personal representative of the tree-spirit from door
to door in spring, in order that all may share the fresh
energies of reviving nature. Again the expected
resurrection of the bear is avowedly indicated by the
bamboo leaves and by the prayer addressed to him to
" come back soon into an Aino." And that the eating
of his flesh is regarded as a sacrament is made
probable by the Gilyak custom of reserving special
vessels to hold the bear's flesh on this solemn occasion.
How is the reverence thus paid to particular bears to
be reconciled with the fact that bears in general are
habitually hunted and killed by these tribes for the
sake of their flesh and skins ? On the one hand, the

"dancing as bears" (" *tanzen beide
Geschlechter Reigentänze, wie Bären,*"
Joest, *l.c.*) does not appear.

  [1] Ravenstein, *The Russians on the*
Amur, p. 379 *sq.*; T. W. Atkinson,
*Travels in the Regions of the Upper and
Lower Amoor* (London, 1860), p. 482
sq.

bear is treated as a god; on the other hand, as a creature wholly subservient to human needs. The apparent contradiction vanishes when we place our-selves at the savage point of view. The savage, we must remember, believes that animals are endowed with feelings and intelligence like those of men, and that, like men, they possess souls which survive the death of their bodies either to wander about as disembodied spirits or to be born again in animal form. To the savage, therefore, who regards all living creatures as practically on a footing of equality with man,[1] the act of killing and eating an animal must wear a very different aspect from that which the same act presents to us who regard the intelligence of animals as far inferior to our own and deny them the possession of immortal souls. Thus on the principles of his rude philosophy the savage who slays an animal believes himself exposed to the vengeance either of its disembodied spirit or of all the other animals of the same species, whom he considers as knit together, like men, by the ties of kin and the obligations of the blood feud, and therefore as bound to resent the injury done to one of their number. Accordingly the savage makes it a rule to spare the life of those animals which he has no pressing motive for killing, at least such fierce and dangerous animals as are likely to exact a bloody vengeance for the slaughter of one of their kind. Crocodiles are animals of this sort. They are only found in hot countries where, as a rule, food is

---

[1] A Bushman, questioned by the Rev. Mr. Campbell, "could not state any difference between a man and a brute—he did not know but a buffalo might shoot with bows and arrows as well as a man, if it had them." John Campbell, *Travels in South Africa, being a Narrative of a Second Journey in the Interior of that Country*, ii. 34. When the Russians first landed on one of the Alaskan islands the people took them for cuttle-fish, "on account of the buttons on their clothes." Petroff, *Alaska*, p. 145.

abundant and primitive man has therefore no reason to kill them for the sake of their tough and unpalatable flesh. Hence it is a general rule among savages to spare crocodiles, or rather only to kill them in obedience to the law of blood feud, that is, as a retaliation for the slaughter of men by crocodiles. For example, the Dyaks of Borneo will not kill a crocodile unless a crocodile has first killed a man. "For why, say they, should they commit an act of aggression, when he and his kindred can so easily repay them? But should the alligator take a human life, revenge becomes a sacred duty of the living relatives, who will trap the man-eater in the spirit of an officer of justice pursuing a criminal. Others, even then, hang back, reluctant to embroil themselves in a quarrel which does not concern them. The man-eating alligator is supposed to be pursued by a righteous Nemesis; and whenever one is caught they have a profound conviction that it must be the guilty one, or his accomplice."[1] So the natives of Madagascar never kill a crocodile "except in retaliation for one of their friends who has been destroyed by a crocodile. They believe that the wanton destruction of one of these reptiles will be followed by the loss of human life, in accordance with the principle of *lex talionis.*" The people who live near the lake Itasy in Madagascar make a yearly proclamation to the crocodiles, announcing that they will revenge the death of some of their friends by killing as many crocodiles in return and warning all

---

[1] Rev. J. Perham, "Sea Dyak Religion," *Journal of the Straits Branch of the Royal Asiatic Society*, No. 10, p. 221. Cp. C. Hupe, "Korte verhandeling over de godsdienst zeden, enz. der Dajakkers," in *Tijdschrift voor Neêrland's Indië*, 1846, dl. iii. 160; S. Müller, *Reizen en onderzoekingen in den Indischen Archipel*, i. 238; Perelaer, *Ethnographische Beschrijving der Dayaks*, p. 7.

well-disposed crocodiles to keep out of the way, as they have no quarrel with them, but only with their evil-minded relations who have taken human life.[1] The Foulahs of Senegambia respect crocodiles on similar grounds.[2] The Seminoles, Sioux, and Iowa Indians of North America spare the rattle-snake because they fear that the ghost of the dead rattle-snake would incite its kinsfolk to take vengeance.[3] No consideration will induce a Sumatran to catch or wound a tiger except in self-defence or immediately after the tiger has destroyed a friend or relation. When a European has set traps for tigers, the people of the neighbourhood have been known to go by night to the place and explain to the tiger that the traps are not set by them nor with their consent.[4]

But the savage clearly cannot afford to spare all animals. He must either eat some of them or starve, and when the question thus comes to be whether he or the animal must perish, he is forced to overcome his superstitious scruples and take the life of the beast. At the same time he does all he can to appease his victims and their kinsfolk. Even in the act of killing them he testifies his respect for them, endeavours to excuse or even conceal his share in procuring their death, and promises that their remains will be honourably treated. By thus robbing death of its terrors he hopes to reconcile his victims to their fate and to induce their fellows to come and be killed also. For example, it was a principle with the Kamtchatkans never to kill a land or sea animal without first making excuses to it and begging that the animal would not

---

[1] Sibree, *The Great African Island*, p. 269.

[2] Raffenel, *Voyage dans l'Afrique Occidentale* (Paris, 1846), p. 84 *sq.*

[3] Bastian, *Die Völker des östlichen Asien*, v. 65.

[4] Marsden, *History of Sumatra*, p. 292.

take it ill.   Also they offered it cedar-nuts, etc. to
make it think that it was not a victim but a guest at a
feast.   They believed that this prevented other animals
of the same species from growing shy.   For instance,
after they had killed a bear and feasted on its flesh, the
host would bring the bear's head before the company,
wrap it in grass, and present it with a variety of trifles.
Then he would lay the blame of the bear's death on
the Russians, and bid the beast wreak his wrath upon
them.   Also he would ask the bear to tell the other
bears how well he had been treated, that they too
might come without fear.   Seals, sea-lions, and other
animals were treated by the Kamtchatkans with the
same ceremonious respect.[1]   When the Ostiaks have
hunted and killed a bear, they cut off its head and
hang it on a tree.   Then they gather round in a circle
and pay it divine honours.   Next they run towards
the carcass uttering lamentations and saying, "Who
killed you?   It was the Russians.   Who cut off your
head?   It was a Russian axe.   Who skinned you?
It was a knife made by a Russian."   They explain,
too, that the feathers which sped the arrow on its
flight came from the wing of a strange bird, and that
they did nothing but let the arrow go.   They do all
this because they believe that the wandering ghost of
the slain bear would attack them on the first opportunity, if they did not thus appease it.[2]   Or they stuff
the skin of the slain bear with hay; and after celebrating their victory with songs of mockery and insult,
after spitting on and kicking it, they set it up on its
hind legs, "and then, for a considerable time, they

---

[1] Steller, *Beschreibung von dem Lande Kamtschatka*, pp. 280, 331.
[2] *Voyages au Nord* (Amsterdam, 1727), viii. 41, 416; Pallas, *Reise durch verschiedene Provinzen des russischen Reichs*, iii. 64; Georgi, *Beschreibung aller Nationen des russischen Reichs*, p. 83.

bestow on it all the veneration due to a guardian god."[1] When a party of Koriaks have killed a bear or a wolf, they skin the beast and dress one of themselves in the skin. Then they dance round the skin-clad man, saying that it was not they who killed the animal, but some one else, generally a Russian. When they kill a fox they skin it, wrap the body in grass, and bid him go tell his companions how hospitably he has been received, and how he has received a new cloak instead of his old one.[2] The Finns used to try to persuade a slain bear that he had not been killed by them, but had fallen from a tree, etc.[3] When the Lapps had succeeded in killing a bear with impunity, they thanked him for not hurting them and for not breaking the clubs and spears which had given him his death wounds ; and they prayed that he would not visit his death upon them by sending storms or in any other way.[4] His flesh then furnished a feast.

The reverence of hunters for the bear whom they regularly kill and eat may thus be traced all along the northern region of the Old World, from Behring's Straits to Lappland. It reappears in similar forms in North America. With the American Indians a bear hunt was an important event for which they prepared by long fasts and purgations. Before setting out they offered expiatory sacrifices to the souls of bears slain in·previous hunts, and besought them to be favourable to the hunters. When a bear was killed the hunter

---

[1] Erman, *Travels in Siberia*, ii. 43. For the veneration of the polar bear by the Samoyedes, who nevertheless kill and eat it, see *ib.* 54 *sq.*

[2] Bastian, *Der Mensch in der Geschichte*, iii. 26.

[3] Max Buch, *Die Wotjäken*, p. 139.

[4] Scheffer, *Lapponia* (Frankfort, 1673), p. 233 *sq.* The Lapps "have still an elaborate ceremony in hunting the bear. They pray and chant to his carcase, and for several days worship before eating it." E. Rae, *The White Sea Peninsula* (London, 1881), p. 276.

A bear that will be sacrificed receives a funeral oration.
Illustration by H.M. Brock.

An Aino family with their bear.

lit his pipe, and putting the mouth of it between the bear's lips, blew into the bowl, filling the beast's mouth with smoke.   Then he begged the bear not to be angry at having been killed, and not to thwart him afterwards in the chase.   The carcass was roasted whole and eaten ; not a morsel of the flesh might be left over.   The head, painted red and blue, was hung on a post and addressed by orators, who heaped praise on the dead beast.[1]   When men of the Bear clan in the Otawa tribe killed a bear, they made him a feast of his own flesh, and addressed him thus : " Cherish us no grudge because we have killed you.   You have sense ; you see that our children are hungry.   They love you and wish to take you into their bodies.   Is it not glorious to be eaten by the children of a chief ? "[2] Amongst the Nootka Indians of British Columbia, when a bear had been killed, it was brought in and seated before the head chief in an upright posture, with a chief's bonnet, wrought in figures, on its head, and its fur powdered over with white down.   A tray of provisions was then set before it, and it was invited by words and gestures to eat.   The animal was then skinned, boiled, and eaten.[3]

A like respect is testified for other dangerous animals by the hunters who regularly trap and kill them.   When Kafir hunters are in the act of showering spears on an elephant, they call out, " Don't kill us,

---

[1] Charlevoix, *Histoire de la Nouvelle France*, v. 173 *sq.* ; Chateaubriand, *Voyage en Amérique*, pp. 172 - 181 (Paris, Michel Lévy, 1870).

[2] *Lettres édifiantes et curieuses*, vi. 171.   Morgan states that the names of the Otawa totem clans had not been obtained (*Ancient Society*, p. 167). From the *Lettres édifiantes*, vi. 168-171, he might have learned the names of the Hare, Carp, and Bear clans, to which may be added the Gull clan, as I learn from an extract from *The Canadian Journal* (Toronto) for March 1858, quoted in the *Academy*, 27th September 1884, p. 203.

[3] *A Narrative of the Adventures and Sufferings of John R. Jewitt*, p. 117 (Middletown, 1820), p. 133 (Edinburgh, 1824).

great captain ; don't strike or tread upon us, mighty
chief."[1]   When he is dead they make their excuses to
him, pretending that his death was a pure accident.
As a mark of respect they bury his trunk with much
solemn ceremony ; for they say that " The elephant is
a great lord ; his trunk is his hand."[2]   Amongst some
tribes of Eastern Africa, when a lion is killed, the carcass is brought before the king, who does homage to
it by prostrating himself on the ground and rubbing
his face on the muzzle of the beast.[3]   In some parts of
Western Africa if a negro kills a leopard he is bound
fast and brought before the chiefs for having killed
one of their peers.   The man defends himself on the
plea that the leopard is chief of the forest and therefore
a stranger.   He is then set at liberty and rewarded.
But the dead leopard, adorned with a chief's bonnet,
is set up in the village, where nightly dances are held
in its honour.[4]   " Before leaving a temporary camp in
the forest, where they have killed a tapir and dried
the meat on a babracot, Indians [of Guiana] invariably
destroy this babracot, saying that should a tapir passing
that way find traces of the slaughter of one of his kind,
he would come by night on the next occasion when
Indians slept at that place, and, taking a man, would
babracot him in revenge."[5]

But it is not merely dangerous animals with whom
the savage desires to keep on good terms.   It is true
that the respect which he pays to wild beasts is in some

---

[1] Stephen Kay, *Travels and Researches in Caffraria* (London, 1833),
p. 138.

[2] Alberti, *De Kaffers aan de Zuid-
kust van Afrika* (Amsterdam, 1810),
p. 95. Alberti's information is repeated
by Lichtenstein (*Reisen im südlichen
Afrika*, i. 412), and by Rose (*Four
Years in Southern Africa*, p. 155). The

burial of the trunk is also mentioned by
Kay, *l.c.*

[3] Jerome Becker, *La Vie en Afrique*
(Paris and Brussels, 1887), ii. 298 *sq.*
305.

[4] Bastian, *Die deutsche Expedition
an der Loango-Küste*, ii. 243.

[5] Im Thurn, *Among the Indians of
Guiana*, p. 352.

measure proportioned to their strength and ferocity.
Thus the savage Stiens of Cambodia, believing that
all animals have souls which roam about after their
death, beg an animal's pardon when they kill it, lest its
soul should come and torment them.   Also they offer
it sacrifices, but these sacrifices are proportioned to
the size and strength of the animal.   The ceremonies
observed at the death of an elephant are conducted
with much pomp and last seven days.[1]   Similar dis-
tinctions are drawn by North American Indians.
" The bear, the buffalo, and the beaver are manidos
[divinities] which furnish food.   The bear is formidable,
and good to eat.   They render ceremonies to him,
begging him to allow himself to be eaten, although
they know he has no fancy for it.   We kill you, but
you are not annihilated.   His head and paws are
objects of homage. . . . Other animals are treated
similarly from similar reasons. . . . Many of the
animal manidos, not being dangerous, are often treated
with contempt—the terrapin, the weasel, polecat, etc."[2]
The distinction is instructive.   Animals which are
feared, or are good to eat, or both, are treated with
ceremonious respect; those which are neither formidable nor good to eat are despised.   We have had
examples of reverence paid to animals which are both
feared and eaten.   It remains to prove that similar
respect is shown for animals which, without being
feared, are either eaten or valued for their skins.

When Siberian sable-hunters have caught a sable,
no one is allowed to see it, and they think that if good
or evil be spoken of the captured sable, no more sables

---

[1] Mouhot, *Travels in the Central Parts of Indo-China*, i. 252 ;   Moura, *Le Royaume du Cambodge*, i. 422.

[2] Schoolcraft, *Indian Tribes*, v. 420.

will be caught. A hunter has been known to express his belief that the sables could hear what was said of them as far off as Moscow. He said that the chief reason why the sable hunt was now so unproductive was that some live sables had been sent· to Moscow. There they had been viewed with astonishment as strange animals, and the sables cannot abide that. Another, though minor, cause of the diminished take of sable was, he alleged, that the world is now much worse than it used to be, so that nowadays a hunter will sometimes hide the sable which he has got instead of putting it into the common stock. This also, said he, the sables cannot abide.[1] Alaskan hunters preserve the bones of sables and beavers out of reach of the dogs for a year and then bury them carefully, "lest the spirits who look after the beavers and sables should consider that they are regarded with contempt, and hence no more should be killed or trapped."[2] The Canadian Indians were equally particular not to let their dogs gnaw the bones, or at least certain of the bones, of beavers. They took the greatest pains to collect and preserve these bones and, when the beaver had been caught in a net, they threw them into the river. To a Jesuit who argued that the beavers could not possibly know what became of their bones, the Indians replied, "You know nothing about catching beavers and yet you will be talking about it. Before the beaver is stone dead, his soul takes a turn in the hut of the man who is killing him and makes a careful note of what is done with his bones. If the bones are given to the dogs, the other beavers would get word of it and would not let themselves be caught. Whereas,

[1] J. G. Gmelin, *Reise durch Sibirien*, ii. 278.

[2] W. Dall, *Alaska and its Resources*, p. 89.

if their bones are thrown into the fire or a river, they are quite satisfied; and it is particularly gratifying to the net which caught them."[1] Before hunting the beaver they offered a solemn prayer to the Great Beaver, and presented him with tobacco; and when the chase was over, an orator pronounced a funeral oration over the dead beavers. He praised their spirit and wisdom. "You will hear no more," said he, "the voice of the chieftains who commanded you and whom you chose from among all the warrior beavers to give you laws. Your language, which the medicine-men understand perfectly, will be heard no more at the bottom of the lake. You will fight no more battles with the otters, your cruel foes. No, beavers! But your skins shall serve to buy arms; we will carry your smoked hams to our children; we will keep the dogs from eating your bones, which are so hard."[2]

The elan, deer, and elk were treated by the North American Indians with the same punctilious respect, and for the same reason. Their bones might not be given to the dogs nor thrown into the fire, nor might their fat be dropped upon the fire, because the souls of the dead animals were believed to see what was done to their bodies and to tell it to the other beasts, living and dead. Hence, if their bodies were ill used, the animals of that species would not allow

---

[1] *Relations des Jésuites*, 1634, p. 24, ed. 1858. Nets are regarded by the Indians as living creatures who not only think and feel but also eat, speak, and marry wives. Sagard, *Le Grand Voyage du Pays des Hurons*, p. 256 (p. 178 *sq.* of the Paris reprint, Librairie Tross, 1865); S. Hearne, *Journey to the Northern Ocean*, p. 329 *sq.*; *Relations des Jésuites*, 1636, p. 109; *ib.* 1639, p. 95; Charlevoix, *Histoire de la Nouvelle France*, v. 225; Chateaubriand, *Voyage en Amérique*, p. 140 *sqq.*

[2] Chateaubriand, *Voyage en Amérique*, pp. 175, 178. They will not let the blood of beavers fall on the ground, or their luck in hunting them would be gone. *Relations des Jésuites*, 1633, p. 21. Compare the rule about not allowing the blood of kings to fall on the ground, above, vol. i. p. 179 *sqq.*

themselves to be taken, neither in this world nor in the world to come.[1]   A sick man would be asked by the medicine-man whether he had not thrown away some of the flesh of the deer or turtle, and if he answered yes, the medicine-man would say, "That is what is killing you.   The soul of the deer or turtle has entered into your body to avenge the wrong you did it."[2] The Sioux will not stick an awl or needle into a turtle, for they are sure that, if they were to do so, the turtle would punish them at some future time.[3]   The Canadian Indians would not eat the embryos of the elk, unless at the close of the hunting season ; other-wise the mother-elks would be shy and refuse to be caught.[4]   Some of the Indians believed that each sort of animal had its patron or genius who watched over and preserved it.   An Indian girl having once picked up a dead mouse, her father snatched the little creature from her and tenderly caressed and fondled it.   Being asked why he did so, he said that it was to appease the genius of mice, in order that he might not torment his daughter for eating the mouse.   With that he handed the mouse to the girl and she ate it.[5]

For like reasons, a tribe which depends for its subsistence, chiefly or in part, upon fishing is careful to treat the fish with every mark of honour and respect. The Indians of Peru "adored the fish that they caught in greatest abundance ; for they said that the first fish that was made in the world above (for so they

---

[1] Hennepin, *Nouveau voyage d'un pais plus grand que l'Europe* (Utrecht, 1698), p. 141 *sq.*; *Relations des Jésuites,* 1636, p. 109; Sagard, *Le Grand Voyage du Pays des Hurons,* p. 255 (p. 178 of the Paris reprint).   Not quite con-sistently the Canadian Indians used to kill every elan they could overtake in the chase, lest any should escape to warn their fellows (Sagard, *l.c.*)

[2] *Lettres édifiantes et curieuses,* viii. 339.

[3] Schoolcraft, *Indian Tribes,* iii. 230.

[4] *Relations des Jésuites,* 1634, p. 26.

[5] Charlevoix, *Histoire de la Nouvelle France,* v. 443.

named Heaven) gave birth to all other fish of that species, and took care to send them plenty of its children to sustain their tribe. For this reason they worshipped sardines in one region, where they killed more of them than of any other fish; in others, the skate; in others, the dogfish; in others, the golden fish for its beauty; in others, the crawfish; in others, for want of larger gods, the crabs, where they had no other fish, or where they knew not how to catch and kill them. In short, they had whatever fish was most serviceable to them as their gods."[1] The Otawa Indians of Canada, believing that the souls of dead fish passed into other bodies of fish, never burned fish bones, for fear of displeasing the souls of the fish, who would come no more to the nets.[2] The Hurons also refrained from throwing fish bones into the fire, lest the souls of the fish should go and warn the other fish not to let themselves be caught, since the Hurons would burn their bones. Moreover, they had men who preached to the fish and persuaded them to come and be caught. A good preacher was much sought after, for they thought that the exhortations of a clever man had a great effect in drawing the fish to the nets. In the Huron fishing village where the French missionary Sagard stayed, the preacher to the fish prided himself very much on his eloquence, which was of a florid order. Every evening after supper, having seen that all the people were in their places and that a strict silence was observed, he preached to the fish. His text was that the Hurons did not burn fish bones. "Then enlarging on his theme

---

[1] Garcilasso de la Vega, *Royal Commentaries of the Yncas*, First Part, bk. i. ch. 10, vol. i. p. 49 *sq*., Hakluyt Society. Cp. *id*., ii. p. 148.

[2] *Relations des Jésuites*, 1667, p. 12.

with extraordinary unction, he exhorted and conjured and invited and implored the fish to come and be caught and to be of good courage and to fear nothing, for it was all to serve their friends who honoured them and did not burn their bones."[1]   The disappearance of herring from the sea about Heligoland in 1530 was attributed by the fishermen to the fact that two lads had whipped a freshly-caught herring and then flung it back into the sea.[2]   The natives of the Duke of York Island annually decorate a canoe with flowers and ferns, lade it, or are supposed to lade it, with shell-money, and set it adrift to pay the fish for those they lose by being caught.[3]   It is especially necessary to treat the first fish caught with consideration in order to conciliate the rest of the fish, for their conduct may be supposed to be influenced by the reception given to the first of their kind which is taken.   Accordingly the Maoris always put back into the sea the first fish caught, "with a prayer that it may tempt other fish to come and be caught."[4]

Still more stringent are the precautions taken when the fish are the first of the season.   On salmon rivers, when the fish begin to run up the stream in spring, they are received with much deference by tribes who, like the Indians of the Pacific Coast of North America, subsist largely upon a fish diet.   In British Columbia the Indians used to go out to meet the first fish as they came up the river.   "They paid

---

[1] Sagard, *Le Grand Voyage du Pays des Hurons*, p. 255 *sqq.* (p. 178 *sqq.* of the Paris reprint).

[2] Schleiden, *Das Salz*, p. 47. For this reference I am indebted to my friend Prof. W. Robertson Smith.

[3] W. Powell, *Wanderings in a Wild Country*, p. 66 *sq.*

[4] R. Taylor, *Te Ika a Maui; or, New Zealand and its Inhabitants*, p. 200; A. S. Thomson, *The Story of New Zealand*, i. 202; E. Tregear, "The Maoris of New Zealand," *Journal Anthrop. Inst.* xix. 109.

court to them, and would address them thus. 'You
fish, you fish; you are all chiefs, you are; you are all
chiefs.'"[1]   Amongst the Thlinket of Alaska the first
halibut of the season is carefully handled, addressed as
a chief, and a festival is given in his honour, after
which the fishing goes on.[2]   In spring, when the
winds blow soft from the south and the salmon begin
to run up the Klamath river, the Karoks of California
dance for salmon, to ensure a good catch.   One of the
Indians, called the Kareya or God-man, retires to the
mountains and fasts for ten days.   On his return the
people flee, while he goes to the river, takes the first
salmon of the catch, eats some of it, and with the rest
kindles the sacred fire in the sweating-house. "No
Indian may take a salmon before this dance is held,
nor for ten days after it, even if his family are
starving."   The Karoks also believe that a fisherman
will take no salmon if the poles of which his spearing-
booth is made were gathered on the river-side, where
the salmon might have seen them.   The poles must
be brought from the top of the highest mountain.   The
fisherman will also labour in vain if he uses the same
poles a second year in booths or weirs, "because the
old salmon will have told the young ones about
them."[3]   Among the Indians of the Columbia River,
"when the salmon make their first appearance in the
river, they are never allowed to be cut crosswise,
nor boiled, but roasted; nor are they allowed to be
sold without the heart being first taken out, nor to
be kept over night, but must be all consumed or eaten
the day they are taken out of the water.   All these

---

[1] Lubbock, *Origin of Civilisation*,[4] p. 277, quoting *Metlahkatlah*, p. 96.

[2] W. Dall, *Alaska and its Resources*, p. 413.

[3] Stephen Powers, *Tribes of California*, p. 31 *sq.*

rules are observed for about ten days." [1]   They think
that if the heart of a fish were eaten by a stranger
at the beginning of the season, they would catch no
more fish.   Hence, they roast and eat the hearts
themselves. [2]   There is a favourite fish of the Ainos
which appears in their rivers about May and June.
They prepare for the fishing by observing rules of
ceremonial purity, and when they have gone out to
fish, the women at home must keep strict silence or the
fish would hear them and disappear.   When the first
fish is caught he is brought home and passed through a
small opening at the end of the hut, but not through
the door; for if he were passed through the door, "the
other fish would certainly see him and disappear." [3]
This explains the custom observed by other savages of
bringing game into their huts, not by the door, but by
the window, the smoke-hole, or by a special opening at
the back of the hut. [4]

With some savages a special reason for respecting
the bones of game, and generally of the animals which
they eat, is a belief that, if the bones are preserved,
they will in course of time be reclothed with flesh, and
thus the animal will come to life again.   It is, therefore, clearly for the interest of the hunter to leave
the bones intact, since to destroy them would be to
diminish the future supply of game.   Many of the Min-
netaree Indians "believe that the bones of those bisons
which they have slain and divested of flesh rise again

---

[1] Alex. Ross, *Adventures of the First
Settlers on the Oregon or Columbia
River*, p. 97.

[2] Ch. Wilkes, *Narrative of the U.S.
Exploring Expedition*, iv. 324, v. 119,
where it is said, "a dog must never be
permitted to eat the heart of a salmon;
and in order to prevent this, they cut

the heart of the fish out before they sell
it."

[3] H. C. St. John, "The Ainos," in
Journ. Anthrop. Inst. ii. 253; *id.
Notes and Sketches from the Wild Coasts
of Nipon*, p. 27 *sq.*

[4] Scheffer, *Lapponia*, p. 242 *sq.*;
Journ. Anthrop. Inst. vii. 207; *Revue
d'Ethnographie*, ii. 308 *sq.*

clothed with renewed flesh, and quickened with life, and become fat, and fit for slaughter the succeeding June."[1]   Hence on the western prairies of America, the skulls of buffalos may be seen arranged in circles and symmetrical piles, awaiting the resurrection.[2]   After feasting on a dog, the Dacotas carefully collect the bones, scrape, wash, and bury them, "partly, as it is said, to testify to the dog-species, that in feasting upon one of their number no disrespect was meant to the species itself, and partly also from a belief that the bones of the animal will rise and reproduce another."[3]   In sacrificing an animal the Lapps regularly put aside the bones, eyes, ears, heart, lungs, sexual parts (if the animal was a male), and a morsel of flesh from each limb.   Then, after eating the rest of the flesh, they laid the bones etc. in anatomical order in a coffin and buried them with the usual rites, believing that the god to whom the animal was sacrificed would reclothe the bones with flesh and restore the animal to life in Jabme-Aimo, the subterranean world of the dead. Sometimes, as after feasting on a bear, they seem to have contented themselves with thus burying the bones.[4]   Thus the Lapps expected the resurrection of the slain animal to take place in another world, resembling in this respect the Kamtchatkans, who believed that every creature, down to the smallest fly, would rise from the dead and live underground.[5]   On the

---

[1] James, *Expedition from Pittsburgh to the Rocky Mountains*, i. 257.

[2] Brinton, *Myths of the New World*, p. 278.

[3] Keating, *Expedition to the Source of St. Peter's River*, i. 452.

[4] E. J. Jessen, *De Finnorum Lapponumque Norwegicorum religione pagana tractatus singularis*, pp. 46 sq., 52 sq., 65.   The work of Jessen is bound up (paged separately) with the work of C. Leem, *De Lapponibus Finmarchiae eorumque lingua, vita, et religione pristina commentatio* (Latin and Danish), Copenhagen, 1767.   Compare Leem's work, pp. 418-420 (Latin), 428 sq., also Acerbi, *Travels through Sweden, Finnland, and Lapland*, ii. 302.

[5] Steller, *Beschreibung von dem Lande Kamtschatka*, p. 269; Kraschennikow, *Kamtschatka*, p. 246.

other hand, the North American Indians looked for
the resurrection of the animals in the present world.
The habit, observed especially by Mongolian peoples,
of stuffing the skin of a sacrificed animal, or stretching
it on a framework,[1] points rather to a belief in a resurrection of the latter sort. The objection commonly
entertained by primitive peoples to break the bones of
the animals which they have eaten or sacrificed [2] may
be based either on a belief in the resurrection of the
animals, or on a fear of intimidating the other creatures

---

[1] See Erman, referred to above, p.
111 *sq.* ; Gmelin, *Reise durch Sibirien*,
i. 274, ii. 182 *sq.*, 214 ; Vambery, *Das
Türkenvolk*, p. 118 *sq.* When a fox,
the sacred animal of the Conchucos in
Peru, had been killed, its skin was
stuffed and set up. Bastian, *Die Culturländer des alten Amerika*, i. 443.
Cp. the *bouphonia*, above, p. 38 *sq.*

[2] At the annual sacrifice of the
White Dog, the Iroquois were careful
to strangle the animal without shedding
its blood or breaking its bones. The
dog was afterwards burned. L. H.
Morgan, *League of the Iroquois*, p.
210. It is a rule with some of the
Australian blacks that in killing the
native bear they must not break his
bones. They say that the native bear
once stole all the water of the river,
and that if they were to break his bones
or take off his skin before roasting him,
he would do so again. Brough Smyth,
Aborigines of Victoria, i. 447 *sqq.* When
the Tartars whom Carpini visited killed
animals for eating, they might not break
their bones but burned them with fire.
Carpini, *Historia Mongalorum* (Paris,
1838), cap. iii. § i. 2, p. 620. North
American Indians might not break the
bones of the animals which they ate at
feasts. Charlevoix, *Histoire de la Nouvelle France*, vi. 72. In the war feast held
by Indian warriors after leaving home,
a whole animal was cooked and had to
be all eaten. No bone of it might be
broken. After being stripped of the
flesh the bones were hung on a tree.

*Narrative of the Captivity and Adven-
tures of John Tanner*, p. 287. On
St. Olaf's Day (29th July) the Karels
of Finland kill a lamb, without using a
knife, and roast it whole. None of
its bones may be broken. The lamb
has not been shorn since spring. Some
of the flesh is placed in a corner of the
room for the house - spirits, some is
deposited on the field and beside the
birch - trees which are destined to be
used as May-trees next year. W. Mannhardt, *A. W. F.* p. 160 *sq. note.* The
Innuit (Esquimaux) of Point Barrow,
Alaska, carefully preserve unbroken
the bones of the seals which they have
caught and return them to the sea,
either leaving them in an ice-crack far
out from the land or dropping them
through a hole in the ice. By doing
so they think they secure good fortune
in the pursuit of seals. *Report of the
International Expedition to Point Barrow, Alaska* (Washington, 1885), p.
40. In this last custom the idea probably is that the bones will be reclothed
with flesh and the seals come to life
again. The Mosquito Indians of Central
America carefully preserved the bones
of deer and the shells of eggs, lest the
deer or chickens should die or disappear.
Bancroft, *Native Races of the Pacific
States*, i. 741. The Yurucares of
Bolivia "carefully put by even small
fish bones, saying that unless this is
done the fish and game will disappear
from the country." Brinton, *Myths of
the New World*, p. 278.

of the same species and offending the ghosts of the slain animals. The reluctance of North American Indians to let dogs gnaw the bones of animals [1] is perhaps only a precaution to prevent the bones from being broken. There are traces in folk-tales of the same primitive belief that animals or men may come to life again, if only their bones are preserved; not uncommonly the animal or man in the story comes to life lame of a limb, because one of his bones has been eaten, broken, or lost. [2] In a Magyar tale, the hero is cut in pieces, but the serpent-king lays the bones together in their proper order, and washes them with water, whereupon the hero comes to life again. His shoulder-blade, however, had been lost, so the serpent-king supplied its place with one of gold and ivory. [3] Such stories, as Mannhardt has seen, explain why Pythagoras, who claimed to have lived many lives, one after the other, was said to have exhibited his golden leg as a proof of his supernatural pretensions. [4] Doubtless he was reported to have explained that at one of his resurrections a leg had been broken or mislaid,

[1] *Relations des Jésuites*, 1634, p. 25, ed. 1858; A. Mackenzie, *Voyages through the Continent of America*, civ; J. Dunn, *History of the Oregon Territory*, p. 99; Whymper in *Journ. Royal Geogr. Soc.* xxxviii. (1868) p. 228; *id.* in *Transact. Ethnolog. Soc.* vii. 174; A. P. Reid, "Religious Belief of the Ojibois Indians," in *Journ. Anthrop. Inst.* iii. 111. After a meal the Indians of Costa Rica gather all the bones carefully and either burn them or put them out of reach of the dogs. W. M. Gabb, *On the Indian Tribes and Languages of Costa Rica* (read before the American Philosophical Society, 20th Aug. 1875), p. 520 (Philadelphia, 1875). The fact that the bones are often burned to prevent the dogs getting them does not contradict the view suggested in the text. It may be a way of transmitting the bones to the spirit-land. The aborigines of Australia burn the bones of the animals which they eat, but for a different reason; they think that if an enemy got hold of the bones and burned them with charms, it would cause the death of the person who had eaten the animal. *Native Tribes of South Australia*, pp. 24, 196.

[2] Mannhardt, *Germanische Mythen*, pp. 57-74; *id.*, *B. K.* p. 116; Cosquin, *Contes populaires de Lorraine*, ii. 25; Hartland, "The physicians of Myddfai," *Archaeological Review*, i. 30 *sq.* In folk-tales, as in primitive custom, the blood is sometimes not allowed to fall on the ground. See Cosquin, *l.c.*

[3] W. Mannhardt, *Germ. Myth.* p. 66.

[4] Jamblichus, *Vita Pythag.* §§ 92, 135, 140; Porphyry, *Vit. Pythag.* § 28.

and that it had been replaced with one of gold. Similarly, when the murdered Pelops was restored to life, the shoulder which Demeter had eaten was replaced with one of ivory.[1] The story that one of the members of the mangled Osiris was eaten by fish, and that, when Isis collected his scattered limbs, she replaced the missing member with one of wood,[2] may perhaps belong to the same circle of beliefs.

There is a certain rule observed by savage hunters and fishers which, obscure at first sight, may be explained by this savage belief in resurrection. A traveller in America in the early part of this century was told by a half-breed Choctaw that the Indians "had an obscure story, somewhat resembling that of Jacob wrestling with an angel; and that the full-blooded Indians always separate the sinew which shrank, and that it is never seen in the venison exposed for sale ; he did not know what they did with it. His elder brother, whom I afterwards met, told me that they eat it as a rarity ; but I have also heard, though on less respectable authority, that they refrain from it, like the ancient Jews. A gentleman, who had lived on the Indian frontier, or in the nation, for ten or fifteen years, told me that he had often been surprised that the Indians always detatched the sinew ; but it had never occurred to him to inquire the reason."[3] James Adair, who knew the Indians of the South Eastern States intimately, and whose theories appear not to have distorted his view of the facts, observes that "when in the woods, the Indians cut a small piece out of the lower part of the thighs of the deer they kill, length-

---

[1] Pindar, *Olymp.* i. 37 *sqq.*, with the Scholiast.

[2] Plutarch, *Isis et Osiris*, 18. This is one of the sacred stories which the pious Herodotus (ii. 48) concealed and the pious Plutarch divulged.

[3] Adam Hodgson, *Letters from North America*, i. 244.

ways and pretty deep.   Among the great number of
venison-hams they bring to our trading houses, I do
not remember to have observed one without it. . . .
And I have been assured by a gentleman of character,
who is now an inhabitant of South Carolina, and well
acquainted with the customs of the Northern Indians,
that they also cut a piece out of the thigh of every deer
they kill, and throw it away; and reckon it such a
dangerous pollution to eat it as to occasion sickness
and other misfortunes of sundry kinds, especially by
spoiling their guns from shooting with proper force and
direction." [1]   In recent years the statement of Adair's
informant has been confirmed by the French missionary
Petitot, who has also published the "obscure story" to
which Hodgson refers.   The Loucheux and Hare-skin
Indians who roam the bleak steppes and forests that
stretch from Hudson's Bay to the Rocky Mountains,
and northward to the frozen sea, are forbidden by
custom to eat the sinew of the legs of animals.   To
explain this custom they tell the following "sacred
story."   Once upon a time a man found a burrow of
porcupines, and going down into it after the porcupines
he lost his way in the darkness, till a kind giant called
" He who sees before and behind" released him by
cleaving open the earth.   So the man, whose name
was " Fireless and Homeless," lived with the kind
giant, and the giant hunted elans and beavers for him,
and carried him about in the sheath of his flint knife.
" But know, my son," said the giant, " that he who
uses the sky as his head is angry with me, and has
sworn my destruction. · If he slays me the clouds will
be tinged with my blood ; they will be red with it, probably."   Then he gave the man an axe made of the

---

[1] Adair, *History of the American Indians*, p. 137 *sq*.

tooth of a gigantic beaver, and went forth to meet his enemy. But from under the ice the man heard a dull muffled sound. It was a whale which was making this noise because it was naked and cold. Warned by the man, the giant went toward the whale, which took human shape, and rushed upon the giant. It was the wicked giant, the kind giant's enemy. The two struggled together for a long time, till the kind giant cried, "Oh, my son! cut, cut the sinew of the leg." The man cut the sinew, and the wicked giant fell down and was slain. That is why the Indians do not eat the sinew of the leg. Afterwards, one day the sky suddenly grew red, so Fireless and Homeless knew that the kind giant was dead, and he wept.[1] This myth, it is almost needless to observe, does not really explain the custom. No people ever observed a custom because a mythical being was said to have once acted in a certain way. But, on the contrary, all peoples have invented myths to explain why they observed certain customs. Dismissing, therefore, the story of Fireless and Homeless as a myth invented to explain why the Indians abstain from eating a particular sinew, it may be suggested[2] that the original reason for observing the custom was a belief that the sinew in question was necessary to reproduction, and that deprived of it the slain animals could not come to life again and stock the steppes and prairies either of the present world or of the spirit land. We have seen that the resurrection

---

[1] Petitot, *Monographie des Dènè-Dindjie* (Paris, 1867), pp. 77, 81 *sq.*; *id., Traditions indiennes du Canada Nord-ouest* (Paris, 1886), p. 132 *sqq.*, cp. pp. 41, 76, 213, 264.

[2] The first part of this suggestion is that of my friend Prof. W. Robertson Smith. See his *Lectures on the Religion of the Semites*, first series, p. 360, *note* 2. The Faleshas, a Jewish sect of Abyssinia, after killing an animal for food, "carefully remove the vein from the thighs with its surrounding flesh." Halévy, "Travels in Abyssinia," in *Publications of the Society of Hebrew Literature*, second series, vol. ii. p. 220.

of animals is a common article of savage faith, and that when the Lapps bury the skeleton of the male bear in the hope of its resurrection they are careful to bury the genital parts along with it.[1]

Besides the animals which primitive man dreads for their strength and ferocity, and those which he reveres on account of the benefits which he expects from them, there is another class of creatures which he sometimes deems it necessary to conciliate by worship and sacrifice. These are the vermin that infest the crops. To rid himself of these deadly foes the farmer has recourse to a thousand superstitious devices, of which, though many are meant to destroy or intimidate the vermin, others aim at propitiating them and persuading them by fair means to spare the fruits of the earth. Thus Esthonian peasants, in the Island of Oesel, stand in great awe of the weevil, an insect which is exceedingly destructive to the grain. They give it a euphemistic title, and if a child is about to kill a

---

[1] It seems to be a common custom with hunters to cut out the tongues of the animals which they kill. Omaha hunters remove the tongue of a slain buffalo through an opening made in the animal's throat. The tongues thus removed are sacred and may not touch any tool or metal except when they are boiling in the kettles at the sacred tent. They are eaten as sacred food. *Third Report of the Bureau of Ethnology* (Washington), p. 289 *sq.* Indian bear-hunters cut out what they call the bear's little tongue (a fleshy mass under the real tongue) and keep it for good luck in hunting or burn it to determine from its crackling, etc., whether the soul of the slain bear is angry with them or not. Kohl, *Kitschi-Gami*, ii. 251 *sq.*; Charlevoix, *Histoire de la Nouvelle France*, v. 173; Chateaubriand, *Voyage en Amérique*, pp. 179 *sq.*, 184. In folk-tales the hero commonly cuts out the tongue of the wild beast which he has slain and preserves it as a token. The incident serves to show that the custom was a common one, since folk-tales reflect with accuracy the customs and beliefs of a primitive age. For examples of the incident, see Blade, *Contes populaires recueillis en Agenais*, pp. 12, 14; Dasent, *Tales from the Norse*, p. 133 *sq.* ('Shortshanks'); Schleicher, *Litauische Märchen*, p. 58; Sepp, *Altbayerischer Sagenschatz*, p. 114; Köhler on Gonzenbach's *Sicilianische Märchen*, ii. 230; Apollodorus, iii. 13, 3; Mannhardt, *A. W. F.* p. 53; Poestion, *Lappländische Märchen*, p. 231 *sq.* It may be suggested that the cutting out of the tongues is a precaution to prevent the slain animals from telling their fate to the live animals and thus frightening away the latter. At least this explanation harmonises with the primitive modes of thought revealed in the foregoing customs.

weevil they say, " Don't do it ; the more we hurt him, the more he hurts us." If they find a weevil they bury it in the earth instead of killing it. Some even put the weevil under a stone in the field and offer corn to it. They think that thus it is appeased and does less harm.[1] Amongst the Saxons of Transylvania, in order to keep sparrows from the corn, the sower begins by throwing the first handful of seed backwards over his head, saying, " That is for you, sparrows." To guard the corn against the attacks of leaf-flies (*Erdflöhe*) he shuts his eyes and scatters three handfuls of oats in different directions. Having made this offering to the leaf-flies he feels sure that they will spare the corn. A Transylvanian way of securing the crops against all birds, beasts, and insects, is this : After he has finished sowing, the sower goes once more from end to end of the field imitating the gesture of sowing, but with an empty hand. As he does so he says, " I sow this for the animals ; I sow it for everything that flies and creeps, that walks and stands, that sings and springs, in the name of God the Father, etc."[2] The following is a German way of freeing a garden from caterpillars. After sunset or at midnight the mistress of the house, or another female member of the family, walks all round the garden dragging a broom after her. She must not look behind her, and must keep murmuring, " Good evening, Mother Caterpillar, you shall come with your husband to church." The garden gate is left open till the following morning.[3]

Sometimes in dealing with vermin the farmer

[1] Holzmayer, *Osiliana*, p. 105 *note*.
[2] Heinrich, *Agrarische Sitten und Gebräuche unter den Sachsen Sieben-bürgens*, p. 15 *sq*.

[3] E. Krause, "Aberglaubische Kuren und sonstiger Aberglaube in Berlin," *Zeitschrift für Ethnologie*, xv. (1883) p. 93.

resorts neither to unmitigated severity nor to un-
bounded indulgence, but aims at adopting a judicious
compromise between the two; kind but firm, he
tempers severity with mercy.   An ancient Greek
treatise on farming advises the husbandman who
would rid his lands of mice to act thus : " Take a
sheet of paper and write on it as follows : ' I adjure
you, ye mice here present, that ye neither injure me
nor suffer another mouse to do so.   I give you yonder
field' (here you specify the field) ; 'but if ever I
catch you here again, by the Mother of the Gods
I will rend you in seven pieces.' Write this, and
stick the paper on an unhewn stone in the field
before sunrise, taking care to keep the written side
uppermost." [1]   Sometimes the desired object is
supposed to be attained by treating with high
distinction one or two chosen individuals of the
obnoxious species, while the rest are pursued with
relentless rigour.   In the East Indian island of
Bali, the mice which ravage the rice - fields are
caught in great numbers, and burned in the same
way that corpses are burned.   But two of the
captured mice are allowed to live, and receive a
little packet of white linen.   Then the people bow
down before them, as before gods, and let them
go.[2] In some parts of Bohemia the peasant, though
he kills field mice and gray mice without scruple,
always spares white mice.   If he finds a white mouse
he takes it up carefully, and makes a comfortable bed
for it in the window ; for if it died the luck of the
house would be gone, and the gray mice would

---

[1] *Geoponica*, xiii. 5.   According to
the commentator, the field assigned to
the mice is a neighbour's, but it may
be a patch of waste ground on the
farmer's own land.

[2] R. van Eck, " Schetsen van het
eiland Bali," in *Tijdschrift voor Nederlandsch Indië*, N.S. viii. (1879) p. 125.

multiply fearfully in the house.[1]   When caterpillars invaded a vineyard or field in Syria, the virgins were gathered, and one of the caterpillars was taken and a girl made its mother.   Then they bewailed and buried it.   Thereafter they conducted the "mother" to the place where the caterpillars were, consoling her, in order that all the caterpillars might leave the garden.[2]   On the 1st of September, Russian girls "make small coffins of turnips and other vegetables, enclose flies and other insects in them, and then bury them with a great show of mourning."[3]

In these latter examples the deference shown to a few chosen individuals of the species is apparently regarded as entitling a person to exterminate with impunity all the rest of the species upon which he can lay hands.   This principle perhaps explains the attitude, at first sight puzzling and contradictory, of the Ainos towards the bear.   The flesh and skin of the bear regularly afford them food and clothing ; but since the bear is an intelligent and powerful animal, it is necessary to offer some satisfaction or atonement to the bear species for the loss which it sustains in the death of so many of its members.   This satisfaction or atonement is made by rearing young bears, treating them, so long as they live, with respect, and killing them with extraordinary marks of sorrow and devotion.   Thus the other bears are appeased, and do not resent the slaughter of their kind by attacking the slayers or deserting the country, and thus depriving the Ainos of one of their means of subsistence.

---

[1] Grohmann, *Aberglauben und Gebräuche aus Böhmen und Mähren*, § 405.

[2] Lagarde, *Reliquiae juris ecclesiastici antiquissimae*, p. 135. For this passage I am indebted to my friend Prof. W. Robertson Smith, who kindly translated it for me from the Syriac.

[3] Ralston, *Songs of the Russian People*, p. 255.

The Hurons had men who preached to the fish and persuaded
them to come and be caught.

Kafir hunters prepare the elephants after the hunt.

Thus the primitive worship of animals assumes two forms, which are in some respects the converse of each other. On the one hand animals are respected, and are therefore neither killed nor eaten. Totemism is a form of this worship, if worship it can be called ; but it is not the only form, for we have seen that dangerous and useless animals, like the crocodile, are commonly revered and spared by men who do not regard the animal in question as their totem. On the other hand animals are worshipped because they are habitually killed and eaten. In both forms of worship the animal is revered on account of some benefit, positive or negative, which the savage hopes to receive from it. In the former worship the benefit comes either in the positive form of protection, advice, and help which the animal affords the man, or in the negative one of abstinence from injuries which it is in the power of the animal to inflict. In the latter worship the benefit takes the material form of the animal's flesh and skin. The two forms of worship are in some measure antithetical : in the one, the animal is not eaten because it is revered ; in the other, it is revered because it is eaten. But both may be practised by the same people, as we see in the case of the North American Indians, who, while they revere and spare their totem animals, also revere the animals and fish upon which they subsist. The aborigines of Australia have totemism in the most primitive form known to us, but, so far as I am aware, there is no evidence that they attempt, like the North American Indians, to conciliate the animals which they kill and eat. The means which the Australians adopt to secure a plentiful supply of game appear to be based not on conciliation, but on sympathetic magic,[1] a principle to which the North American Indians also resort for the same purpose.[2]   If this is so, it would appear that the totemistic respect for animals is older than the other, and that, before hunters think of worshipping the game as a means of ensuring an abundant supply of it, they seek to attain the same end by sympathetic magic.   This, again, would show — what there is good reason for believing — that sympathetic magic is one of the earliest means by which man endeavours to adapt the agencies of nature to his needs.

Corresponding to the two distinct types of animal worship, there are two distinct types of the custom of killing the animal god.   On the one hand, when the revered animal is habitually spared, it is nevertheless killed — and sometimes eaten — on rare and solemn occasions.   Examples of this custom have been already given and an explanation of them offered. On the other hand, when the revered animal is habitually killed, the slaughter of any one of the species involves the killing of the god, and is atoned for on the spot by apologies and sacrifices, especially when the animal is a powerful and dangerous one ; and, in addition to this ordinary and everyday atonement, there is a special annual atonement, at which a select individual of the species is slain with extraordinary marks of respect and devotion.   Clearly the two types of sacramental killing — the Egyptian and the Aino types, as we may call them for distinction — are liable to be confounded by an observer ; and,

---

[1] Compare *Native Tribes of South Australia*, p. 280, with the customs referred to in the following note.

[2] Catlin, *O-Kee-pa*, Folium reservatum ; Lewis and Clarke, *Travels to the Source of the Missouri River* (London, 1815), i. 205 *sq.*

before we can say to which type any particular
example belongs, it is necessary to ascertain whether
the animal sacramentally slain belongs to a species
which is habitually spared, or to one which is
habitually killed by the tribe. In the former case
the example belongs to the Egyptian type of sacrament, in the latter to the Aino type.

The practice of pastoral tribes appears to furnish
examples of both types of sacrament. "Pastoral
tribes," says the most learned ethnologist of the day,
"being sometimes obliged to sell their herds to
strangers who may handle the bones disrespectfully,
seek to avert the danger which such a sacrilege would
entail by consecrating one of the herd as an object of
worship, eating it sacramentally in the family circle
with closed doors, and afterwards treating the bones
with all the ceremonious respect which, strictly speaking, should be accorded to every head of cattle, but
which, being punctually paid to the representative
animal, is deemed to be paid to all. Such family
meals are found among various peoples, especially
those of the Caucasus. When amongst the Abchases
the shepherds in spring eat their common meal with
their loins girt and their staffs in their hands, this may
be looked upon both as a sacrament and as an oath of
mutual help and support. For the strongest of all
oaths is that which is accompanied with the eating of
a sacred substance, since the perjured person cannot
possibly escape the avenging god whom he has taken
into his body and assimilated."[1] This kind of sacra-

---

[1] A. Bastian, in *Verhandlungen der
Berliner Gesellschaft für Anthropologie,
Ethnologie, und Urgeschichte*, 1870-71,
p. 59. Reinegg (*Beschreibung des
Kaukasus*, ii. 12 *sq.*) describes what
seems to be a sacrament of the
Abghazses (Abchases). It takes place
in the middle of autumn. A white ox
called Ogginn appears from a holy
cave, which is also called Ogginn. It
is caught and led about amongst the
assembled men (women are excluded)

ment is of the Aino or expiatory type, since it is meant to atone to the species for the possible ill-usage of individuals.   An expiation, similar in principle but different in details, is offered by the Kalmucks to the sheep whose flesh is one of their staple foods.   Rich Kalmucks are in the habit of consecrating a white ram under the title of "the ram of heaven" or "the ram of the spirit."   The animal is never shorn and never sold; but when it grows old and its owner wishes to consecrate a new one, the old ram must be killed and eaten at a feast to which the neighbours are invited.   On a lucky day, generally in autumn when the sheep are fat, a sorcerer kills the old ram, after sprinkling it with milk.   Its flesh is eaten; the skeleton, with a portion of the fat, is burned on a turf altar; and the skin, with the head and feet, is hung up.[1]

An example of a sacrament of the Egyptian type is furnished by the Todas, a pastoral people of Southern India, who subsist largely upon the milk of their buffaloes.   Amongst them "the buffalo is to a certain degree held sacred" and "is treated with great kindness, even with a degree of adoration, by the people."[2]   They never eat the flesh of the cow buffalo, and as a rule abstain from the flesh of the male.   But

---

amid joyful cries. Then it is killed and eaten. Any man who did not get at least a scrap of the sacred flesh would deem himself most unfortunate. The bones are then carefully collected, burned in a great hole, and the ashes buried there.

[1] Bastian, *Die Völker des östlichen Asien*, vi. 632 *note*. On the Kalmucks as a people of shepherds and on their diet of mutton, see Georgi, *Beschreibung aller Nationen des russischen Reichs*, p. 406 *sq.*, cp. 207; B. Bergmann, *Nomadische Streifereien unter den Kalmücken*, ii. 80 *sqq.*, 122; Pallas, *Reise durch verschiedene Provinzen des russischen Reichs*, i. 319, 325. According to Pallas, it is only rich Kalmucks who commonly kill their sheep or cattle for eating; ordinary Kalmucks do not usually kill them except in case of necessity or at great merry-makings. It is, therefore, especially the rich who need to make expiation.

[2] W. E. Marshall, *Travels amongst the Todas*, p. 129 *sq.* On the Todas, see also above, vol. i. p. 41.

to the latter rule there is a single exception. Once a year all the adult males of the village join in the ceremony of killing and eating a very young male calf,—seemingly under a month old. They take the animal into the dark recesses of the village wood, where it is killed with a club made from the sacred tree of the Todas (the *tûde* or *Millingtonia*). A sacred fire having been made by the rubbing of sticks, the flesh of the calf is roasted on the embers of certain trees, and is eaten by the men alone, women being excluded from the assembly. This is the only occasion on which the Todas eat buffalo flesh.[1] The Madi or Moru tribe of Central Africa, whose chief wealth is their cattle, though they also practice agriculture, appear to kill a lamb sacramentally on certain solemn occasions. The custom is thus described by Dr. Felkin. "A remarkable custom is observed at stated times—once a year, I am led to believe. I have not been able to ascertain what exact meaning is attached to it. It appears, however, to relieve the people's minds, for beforehand they evince much sadness, and seem very joyful when the ceremony is duly accomplished. The following is what takes place : A large concourse of people of all ages assemble, and sit down round a circle of stones, which is erected by the side of a road (really a narrow path). A very choice lamb is then fetched by a boy, who leads it four times round the assembled people. As it passes they pluck off little bits of its fleece and place them in their hair, or on to some other part of their body. The lamb is then led up to the stones, and there killed by a man belonging to a kind of priestly order, who takes some of the blood and sprinkles it four times over the people. He

---

[1] Marshall, *op. cit.* pp. 80 *sq.* 130.

then applies it individually. On the children he makes
a small ring of blood over the lower end of the breast
bone, on women and girls he makes a mark above the
breasts, and the men he touches on each shoulder.
He then proceeds to explain the ceremony, and to
exhort the people to show kindness. . . . When this
discourse, which is at times of great length, is over,
the people rise, each places a leaf on or by the circle
of stones, and then they depart with signs of great joy.
The lamb's skull is hung on a tree near the stones,
and its flesh is eaten by the poor. This ceremony is
observed on a small scale at other times. If a family
is in any great trouble, through illness or bereavement,
their friends and neighbours come together and a lamb
is killed : this is thought to avert further evil. The
same custom prevails at the grave of departed friends,
and also on joyful occasions, such as the return of a
son home after a very prolonged absence."[1] The
sorrow thus manifested by the people at the annual
slaughter of the lamb clearly indicates that the lamb
slain is a divine animal, whose death is mourned by
his worshippers,[2] just as the death of the sacred
buzzard was mourned by the Californians and the
death of the Theban ram by the Egyptians. The
smearing each of the worshippers with the blood of
the lamb is a form of communion with the divinity ;[3]
the vehicle of the divine life is applied externally
instead of being taken internally, as when the blood is
drunk or the flesh eaten.

---

[1] R. W. Felkin, "Notes on the
Madi or Moru tribe of Central Africa,"
*Proceedings of the Royal Society of
Edinburgh*, xii. (1882-84) p. 336 *sq.*

[2] The fact that the flesh of sheep
appears to be now eaten by the tribe
as a regular article of food (Felkin, *op.
cit.* p. 307), is not inconsistent with
the original sanctity of the sheep.

[3] See W. R. Smith, *Religion of the
Semites*, i. p. 325 *sq.*

The form of communion in which the sacred animal is taken from house to house, that all may enjoy a share of its divine influence, has been exemplified by the Gilyak custom of promenading the bear through the village before it is slain. A similar form of communion with the sacred snake is observed by a Snake tribe in the Punjaub. Once a year in the month of September the snake is worshipped by all castes and religions for nine days only. At the end of August the Mirasans, especially those of the Snake tribe, make a snake of dough which they paint black and red, and place on a winnowing basket. This basket they carry round the village, and on entering any house they say—

> " God be with you all !
> May every ill be far !
> May our patron's (Gugga's) word thrive ! "

They then present the basket with the snake, saying—

> " A small cake of flour :
> A little bit of butter :
> If you obey the snake,
> You and yours shall thrive ! "

Strictly speaking, a cake and butter should be given, but it is seldom done. Every one, however, gives something, generally a handful of dough or some corn. In houses where there is a new bride or whence a bride has gone, or where a son has been born, it is usual to give a rupee and a quarter, or some cloth. Sometimes the bearers of the snake also sing—

> " Give the snake a piece of cloth,
> And he will send a lively bride."

When every house has been thus visited, the dough snake is buried and a small grave is erected over it. Hither during the nine days of September the women

come to worship. They bring a basin of curds, a
small portion of which they offer at the snake's grave,
kneeling on the ground and touching the earth with
their foreheads. Then they go home and divide the
rest of the curds among the children. Here the
dough snake is clearly a substitute for a real snake.
This is proved by the fact that in districts where
snakes abound the worship is offered, not at the
grave of the dough snake, but in the jungles where
snakes are known to be. Besides this yearly worship
performed by all the people, the members of the Snake
tribe worship in the same way every morning after a
new moon. The Snake tribe is not uncommon in the
Punjaub. Members of it will not kill a snake and
they say that its bite does not hurt them. If they
find a dead snake, they put clothes on it and give it a
regular funeral.[1]

Ceremonies closely analogous to this Indian worship
of the snake have survived in Europe into recent
times, and doubtless date from a very primitive
paganism. The best-known example is the "hunting
of the wren." By many European peoples—the
ancient Greeks and Romans, the modern Italians,
Spaniards, French, Germans, Dutch, Danes, Swedes,
English, and Welsh—the wren has been designated
the king, the little king, the king of birds, the hedge
king, etc.,[2] and has been reckoned amongst those
birds which it is extremely unlucky to kill. In
England it is thought that if any one kills a wren
or harries its nest, he will infallibly break a bone or

[1] *Panjab Notes and Queries*, ii. No.
555.

[2] See Brand, *Popular Antiquities*,
iii. 195 *sq.*, Bohn's ed.; Swainson, *Folk-
lore of British Birds*, p. 36 ; E. Rolland,
Faune populaire de la France, ii. 288
sqq. The names for it are βασιλίσκος,
regulus, *rex avium* (Pliny, *Nat. Hist.*
viii. 90 ; x. 203), *re di siepe*, *reyezuelo*,
roitelet, *roi des oiseaux*, *Zaunkönig*, etc.

Serpent worship.

A sacred serpent.

meet with some dreadful misfortune within the year;[1] sometimes it is thought that the cows will give bloody milk.[2]   In Scotland the wren is called "the Lady of Heaven's hen," and boys say—

> " Malisons, malisons, mair than ten,
> That harry the Ladye of Heaven's hen!"[3]

At Saint Donan, in Brittany, people believe that if children touch the young wrens in the nest, they will suffer from the fire of St. Lawrence, that is, from pimples on the face, legs, etc.[4]   In other parts of France it is believed that if a person kills a wren or harries its nest, his house will be struck by lightning, or that the fingers with which he did the deed will shrivel up and drop off, or at least be maimed, or that his cattle will suffer in their feet.[5]   Notwithstanding such beliefs, the custom of annually killing the wren has prevailed widely both in this country and in France.   In the Isle of Man last century the custom was observed on Christmas Eve or rather Christmas morning.   On the 24th of December, towards evening, all the servants got a holiday; they did not go to bed all night, but rambled about till the bells rang in all the churches at midnight.   When prayers were over, they went to hunt the wren, and having found one of these birds they killed it and fastened it to the top of a long pole with its wings extended.   Thus they carried it in procession to every house chanting the following rhyme—

> " We hunted the wren for Robin the Bobbin,
> We hunted the wren for Jack of the Can,
> We hunted the wren for Robin the Bobbin,
> We hunted the wren for every one."

---

[1] Brand, *Popular Antiquities*, iii. 194.

[2] Chambers, *Popular Rhymes of Scotland*, p. 188.   [3] *Ib.* p. 186.

[4] P. Sébillot, *Traditions et Superstitions de la Haute Bretagne*, ii. 214.

[5] Rolland, *op. cit.* ii. 294 *sq.*; Sébillot, *l.c.*; Swainson, *op. cit.* p. 42.

After going from house to house and collecting all the
money they could, they laid the wren on a bier " with
the utmost solemnity, singing dirges over her in the
Manks language, which they call her knell; after
which Christmas begins." After the burial the company outside the churchyard formed a circle and
danced to music. About the middle of the present
century the burial of the wren took place in the
Isle of Man on St. Stephen's Day (December 26th).
Boys went from door to door with a wren suspended
by the legs in the centre of two hoops which crossed
each other at right angles and were decorated with
evergreens and ribbons. The bearers sang certain
lines in which reference was made to boiling and
eating the bird. If at the close of the song they
received a small coin, they gave in return a feather of
the wren; so that before the end of the day the bird
often hung almost featherless. The wren was then
buried, no longer in the churchyard, but on the sea-
shore or in some waste place. The feathers distributed were preserved with religious care, it being
believed that every feather was an effectual preservative from shipwreck for a year, and a fisherman
would have been thought very foolhardy who had not
one of them.[1]

In Ireland the "hunting of the wren" still takes
place in parts of Leinster and Connaught. On
Christmas Day or St. Stephen's Day the boys hunt
and kill the wren, fasten it in the middle of a mass
of holly and ivy on the top of a broomstick, and on St.
Stephen's Day go about with it from house to house,
singing—

---

[1] G. Waldron, *Description of the Isle of Man* (reprinted for the Manx Society,
Douglas, 1865), p. 49 *sqq.*; J. Train, *Account of the Isle of Man*, ii. 124 *sqq.* 141.

" The wren, the wren, the king of all birds,
  St. Stephen's Day was caught in the furze ;
  Although he is little, his family 's great,
  I pray you, good landlady, give us a treat."

Money or food (bread, butter, eggs, etc.) were given
them, upon which they feasted in the evening.
Sometimes in Ireland, as in the Isle of Man, the bird
was hung by the leg in the centre of two hoops
crossing each other at right angles.[1] In Essex a
similar custom used to be observed at Christmas,
and the verses sung by the boys were almost identical
with those sung in Ireland.[2] In Pembrokeshire a
wren, called the King, used to be carried about on
Twelfth Day in a box with glass windows surmounted
by a wheel, from which hung various coloured ribbons.
The men and boys who carried it from house to house
sang songs, in one of which they wished "joy, health,
love, and peace" to the inmates of the house."[3]

In the first half of this century similar customs
were still observed in various parts of the south of
France. Thus at Carcassone, every year on the first
Sunday of December the young people of the street
Saint Jean used to go out of the town armed with
sticks, with which they beat the bushes, looking for
wrens. The first to strike down one of these birds
was proclaimed King. Then they returned to the
town in procession, headed by the King, who carried
the wren on a pole. On the evening of the last day
of the year the King and all who had hunted the wren
marched through the streets of the town with torches
and music. At the door of every house they stopped,

---

[1] Brand, *Popular Antiquities*, iii.
195 ; Swainson, *Folk-lore of British
Birds*, p. 36 *sq.*; Rolland, *Faune
populaire de la France*, ii. 297 ; Professor W. Ridgeway in *Academy*, 10th
May 1884, p. 332 ; Dyer, *British
Popular Customs*, p. 497.
[2] Henderson, *Folk-lore of the Northern Counties*, p. 125.
[3] Swainson, *op. cit.* p. 40 *sq.*

and one of them wrote with chalk on the door *vive le roi!* with the number of the year which was about to begin.　On the morning of Twelfth Day the King again marched in procession with great pomp, wearing a crown and a blue mantle and carrying a sceptre.　In front of him was borne the wren fastened to the top of a pole, which was adorned with a wreath of olive, oak, and mistletoe.　After hearing high mass in the church, surrounded by his officers and guards, he visited the bishop, mayor, magistrates, and the chief inhabitants, collecting money to defray the expenses of the royal banquet which took place in the evening.[1]　At Entraigues men and boys used to hunt the wren on Christmas Eve.　When they caught one alive they presented it to the priest, who, after the midnight mass, set the bird free in the church.　At Mirabeau the priest blessed the bird.　If the men failed to catch a wren and the women succeeded in doing so, the women had the right to mock and insult the men, and to blacken their faces with mud and soot, if they caught them.[2]　At La Ciotat, near Marseilles, a large body of men armed with swords and pistols used to hunt the wren every year about the end of December.　When a wren was caught it was hung on the middle of a pole which two men carried, as if it were a heavy burden.　Thus they paraded round the town; the bird was weighed in a great pair of scales; and then the company sat down to table and made merry.[3]

---

[1] Rolland, *op. cit.* ii. 295 *sq.*; J. W. Wolf, *Beiträge zur deutschen Mythologie,* ii. 437 *sq.*

[2] Rolland, *op. cit.* ii. 296 *sq.*

[3] Brand's *Popular Antiquities,* iii. 198. The "hunting of the wren" may be compared with a Swedish custom. On the 1st of May children rob the magpies' nests of both eggs and young. These they carry in a basket from house to house in the village and show them to the housewives, while one of the children sings some doggerel lines containing a threat that, if a present is not given, the hens, chickens, and eggs will fall a prey to the magpie. They receive bacon, eggs, milk, etc., upon which they afterwards feast.

The parallelism between this custom of "hunting the wren" and some of those we have considered, especially the Gilyak procession with the bear, and the Indian one with the snake, seems too close to allow us to doubt that they all belong to the same circle of ideas. The worshipful animal is killed with special solemnity once a year; and before or immediately after death, he is promenaded from door to door, that each of his worshippers may receive a portion of the divine virtues that are supposed to emanate from the dead or dying god. Religious processions of this sort must have had a great place in the ritual of European peoples in prehistoric times, if we may judge from the numerous traces of them which have survived in folk-custom. A well-preserved specimen is the following, which survived in the Highlands of Scotland and in St. Kilda down to the latter half of last century. "On the evening before New Year's Day, it is usual for the cowherd and the young people to meet together, and one of them is covered with a cow's hide. The rest of the company are provided with staves, to the end of which bits of raw hide are tied. The person covered with the hide runs thrice round the dwelling-house, *deiseil—i.e.* according to the course of the sun ; the rest pursue, beating the hide with their staves, and crying [here follows the Gaelic], ' Let us raise the noise louder and louder ; let us beat the hide.' They then come to the door of each

---

L. Lloyd, *Peasant Life in Sweden*, p. 237 *sq.* The resemblance of such customs to the "swallow song" and "crow song" of the ancient Greeks (on which see Athenaeus, pp. 359, 360) is obvious and has been remarked before now. Probably the Greek swallow-singers and crow-singers carried about dead swallows and crows or effigies of them. In modern Greece it is said to be still customary for children on 1st March to go about the streets singing spring songs and carrying a wooden swallow, which is kept turning on a cylinder. Grimm, *Deutsche Mythologie*,[4] ii. 636.

dwelling-house, and one of them repeats some verses composed for the purpose. When admission is granted, one of them pronounces within the threshold the *beannachadthurlair*, or verses by which he pretends to draw down a blessing upon the whole family [here follows the Gaelic], 'May God bless this house and all that belongs to it, cattle, stones, and timber! In plenty of meat, of bed and body-clothes, and health of men, may it ever abound!' Then each burns in the fire a little bit of hide which is tied to the end of the staff. It is applied to the nose of every person and domestic animal that belongs to the house. This, they imagine, will tend much to secure them from diseases and other misfortunes during the ensuing year. The whole of the ceremony is called *colluinn*, from the great noise which the hide makes."[1] From another authority,[2] we learn that the hide of which pieces were burned in each house and applied to the inmates was the breast part of a sheep-skin. Formerly, perhaps, pieces of the cow-hide in which the man was clad were detached for this purpose, just as in the Isle of Man a feather of the wren used to be given to each household. Similarly, as we have seen, the human victim whom the Khonds slew as a divinity was taken from house to house, and every one strove to obtain a relic of his sacred person. Such customs are only another form of that communion with the deity which is attained most completely by eating the body and drinking the blood of the god.

---

[1] John Ramsay, *Scotland and Scotsmen in the Eighteenth Century*, ii. 438 *sq.* ; cp. Chambers, *Popular Rhymes of Scotland*, p. 166 *sq.* ; Samuel Johnson, *Journey to the Western Islands of Scotland*, p. 228 *sq.* (first American edition, 1810). The custom is clearly referred to in the "Penitential of Theodore," quoted by Kemble, *Saxons in England*, i. 525 ; Elton, *Origins of English History*, p. 411 ; "*Si quis in Kal. Januar. in cervulo vel vitula vadit, id est in ferarum habitus se communicant, et vestiuntur pellibus pecudum et assumunt capita bestiarum*, etc.

[2] Chambers, *l.c.*

In the " hunting of the wren," and the procession with the man clad in a cow-skin, there is nothing to show that the customs in question have any relation to agriculture. So far as appears, they may date from the pre-agricultural era when animals were revered as divine in themselves, not merely as divine because they embodied the corn-spirit ; and the analogy of the Gilyak procession of the bear, and the Indian procession of the snake is in favour of assigning the corresponding European customs to this very early date. On the other hand, there are certain European processions of animals, or of men disguised as animals, which may possibly be purely agricultural in their origin ;[1] in other words, the animals which figure in them may have been from the first nothing but representatives of the corn-spirit conceived in animal shape. But it is at least equally possible that these processions originated in the pre-agricultural era, and have only received an agricultural tinge from the environment in which they have so long survived. But the question is an obscure and difficult one, and cannot be here discussed.

---

[1] Such are the Bohemian processions at the Carnival when a man called the Shrovetide Bear, swathed from head to foot in peas-straw and sometimes wearing a bear's mask, is led from house to house. He dances with the women of the house, and collects money and food. Then they go to the alehouse, where all the peasants assemble with their wives. For at the Carnival, especially on Shrove Tuesday, it is necessary that every one should dance, if the flax, the corn, and the vegetables are to grow well. The higher they leap the better will be the crops. Sometimes the women pull out some of the straw in which the Shrovetide Bear is swathed, and put it in the nests of the geese and fowls, believing that this will make them lay well. Reinsberg-Düringsfeld, *Fest-Kalender aus Böhmen*, pp. 49-52. On similar customs, see W. Mannhardt, *A. W. F.* pp. 183-200.

§ 13.—*Transference of evil*

The custom of killing the god has now been proved to have been practised by peoples in the hunting, pastoral, and agricultural stages of society, and the various reasons for observing the custom have been explained. One aspect of the custom still remains to be noticed. The accumulated misfortunes and sins of the whole people are sometimes laid upon the dying god, who is supposed to bear them away for ever, leaving the people innocent and happy. The notion that we can transfer our pains and griefs to some other being who will bear them in our stead is familiar to the savage mind. It arises from a very obvious confusion between the physical and the mental. Because it is possible to transfer a load of wood, stones, or what not, from our own back to the back of another, the savage fancies that it is equally possible to transfer the burden of his pains and sorrows to another, who will suffer them in his stead. Upon this idea he acts, and the result is an endless number of often very unamiable devices for putting off upon some one else the trouble which a man shrinks from bearing himself. Such devices are amongst the most familiar facts in folk-lore ; but for the benefit of readers who are not professed students of folk-lore, a few illustrations may be given.

It is not necessary that the pain or trouble should be transferred from the sufferer to a person ; it may equally well be transferred to an animal or a thing, though in the last case the thing is often only a vehicle to convey the trouble to the first person who touches it. In some of the East Indian islands

epilepsy is believed to be cured by striking the patient
on the face with the leaves of certain trees and then
throwing the leaves away.   The epilepsy is believed
to have passed into the leaves, and to have been
thrown away with them.[1]   To cure toothache some
of the Australian blacks apply a heated spear-thrower
to the cheek.   The spear-thrower is then cast away,
and the toothache goes with it, in the shape of a black
stone called *karriitch*.   Stones of this kind are found
in old mounds and sandhills.   They are carefully
collected and thrown in the direction of enemies, in
order to give them toothache.[2]   When a Moor has
a headache, he will sometimes take a lamb or a goat
and beat it till it falls down, believing that the headache will thus be transferred to the animal.[3]   After an
illness, a Bechuana king seated himself upon an ox
which lay stretched on the ground.   The native
doctor next poured water on the king's head till
it ran down over his body.   Then the head of the
ox was held in a vessel of water till the animal expired ; whereupon the doctor declared, and the people
believed, that the ox died of the king's disease, which
had been transferred to it from the king.[4]   Amongst the
Malagasy the vehicle for carrying away evils is called
a *faditra*.   "The faditra is anything selected by the
sikidy [divining-board] for the purpose of taking away
any hurtful evils or diseases that might prove injurious
to an individual's happiness, peace, or prosperity.   The
faditra may be either ashes, cut money, a sheep, a

---

[1] J. G. F. Riedel, *De sluik-en kroes-harige rassen tusschen Selebes en Papua*, pp. 266 *sq.*, 305, 357 *sq.* ; cp. *id.* pp. 141, 340.

[2] J. Dawson, *Australian Aborigines*, p. 59.

[3] Dapper, *Description de l'Afrique*, p. 117.

[4] John Campbell, *Travels in South Africa* (second journey), ii. 207 *sq.*

pumpkin, or anything else the sikidy may choose to direct.　After the particular article is appointed, the priest counts upon it all the evils that may prove injurious to the person for whom it is made, and which he then charges the faditra to take away for ever.　If the faditra be ashes, it is blown, to be carried away by the wind.　If it be cut money, it is thrown to the bottom of deep water, or where it can never be found.　If it be a sheep, it is carried away to a distance on the shoulders of a man, who runs with all his might, mumbling as he goes, as if in the greatest rage against the faditra for the evils it is bearing away.　If it be a pumpkin, it is carried on the shoulders to a little distance, and there dashed upon the ground with every appearance of fury and indignation."[1]　A Malagasy was informed by a diviner that he was doomed to a bloody death, but that possibly he might avert his fate by performing a certain rite.　Carrying a small vessel full of blood upon his head, he was to mount upon the back of a bullock ; while thus mounted, he was to spill the blood upon the bullock's head, and then send the animal away into the wilderness, whence it might never return.[2]

The Battas of Sumatra have a ceremony which they call "making the curse to fly away."　When a woman is childless, a sacrifice is offered to the gods of three grasshoppers, representing a head of cattle, a buffalo, and a horse.　Then a swallow is set free, with a prayer that the curse may fall

---

[1] Ellis, *History of Madagascar*, i. 422 *sq.*; cp. *id.* pp. 232, 435, 436 *sq.* ; Sibree, *The Great African Island*, p. 303 *sq.*

[2] Ellis, *op. cit.* i. 374 ; Sibree, *op. cit.* p. 304 ; *Antananarivo Annual and Madagascar Magazine*, iii. 263.

upon the bird and fly away with it.[1]   At the cleansing of a leper and of a house suspected of being tainted with leprosy, the Jews let a bird fly away.[2]   Amongst the Miaotse of China, when the eldest son of the house attains the age of seven years, a ceremony called "driving away the devil" takes place.   The father makes a kite of straw and lets it fly away in the desert, bearing away all evil with it.[3]   In Morocco most wealthy Moors keep a wild boar in their stables, in order that the jinn and evil spirits may be diverted from the horses and enter into the boar.[4]   The Dyaks believe that certain men possess in themselves the power of neutralising bad omens.   So, when evil omens have alarmed a farmer for the safety of his crops, he takes a small portion of his farm produce to one of these wise men, who eats it raw for a small consideration, "and thereby appropriates to himself the evil omen, which in him becomes innocuous, and thus delivers the other from the ban of the *pemali* or taboo."[5]   In Travancore, when a Rajah is dangerously ill and his life is despaired of, a holy Brahman is brought, who closely embraces the King, and says, "O King! I undertake to bear all your sins and diseases.   May your Highness live long and reign happily."   Then the sin-bearer is sent away from the country, and never allowed to return.[6]   Amongst the Burghers or Badagas of the Neilgherry Hills in Southern India, when a death has taken place, the

---

[1] Ködding, "Die Batakschen Götter," *Allgemeine Missions-Zeitschrift*, xii. (1885) 478.

[2] Leviticus xiv. 7, 53. For a similar use in Arabia see Wellhausen, *Reste arabischen Heidentumes*, p. 156; W. Robertson Smith, *Religion of the Semites*, i. 402.

[3] R. Andree, *Ethnographische Parallele und Vergleiche*, p. 29 *sq.*

[4] A. Leared, *Morocco and the Moors*, p. 301.

[5] J. Perham, "Sea Dyak Religion," in *Journ. Straits Branch Royal Asiatic Soc.* No. 10, p. 232.

[6] S. Mateer, *Native Life in Travancore*, p. 136.

sins of the deceased are laid upon a buffalo calf. A
set form of confession of sins, the same for every one,
is recited aloud, then the calf is set free, and is never
afterwards used for common purposes. " The idea
of this ceremony is that the sins of the deceased enter
the calf, or that the task of his absolution is laid on it.
They say that the calf very soon disappears, and that
it is never after heard of." [1]

Similar attempts to shift the burden of disease and
sin from one's self to another person, or to an animal
or thing, have been common in ancient and modern
Europe. Grave writers of antiquity recommended
that, if a man be stung by a scorpion, he should sit
upon an ass with his face to the tail, or whisper in
the ear of the ass, "A scorpion has stung me"; in
either case, they thought, the pain would be transferred from the man to the ass. [2] A Roman cure for
fever was to pare the patient's nails, and stick the
parings with wax upon a neighbour's door before
sunrise; the fever then passed from the sick man
to his neighbour. [3] Similar devices must have been
practised by the Greeks; for in laying down laws
for his ideal state, Plato thinks it too much to expect
that men should not be alarmed at finding certain
wax figures adhering to their doors or to the tomb-

---

[1] H. Harkness, *Singular Aboriginal
Race of the Neilgherry Hills*, p. 133;
Metz, *The Tribes Inhabiting the Neilgherry Hills*, p. 78; Jagor, "Ueber
die Badagas im Nilgiri - Gebirge,"
*Verhandl. d. Berlin. Gesell. f. An-
thropol.* (1876), p. 196 *sq.* For the
custom of letting a bullock go loose
after a death, compare also Grierson,
Bihar Peasant Life, p. 409; Ibbetson,
*Settlement Report of the Panipat, Tahsil,
and Karnal Parganah of the Karnal
district* (Allahabad, 1883) p. 137. In
the latter case it is said that the animal
is let loose "to become a pest." Perhaps the older idea was that the animal
carried away death from the survivors.
The idea of sin is not primitive.

[2] *Geoponica*, xiii. 9, xv. 1; Pliny,
Nat. Hist. xxviii. § 155. The authorities for these cures are respectively
Apuleius and Democritus. The latter
is probably not the atomic philosopher.
See *Archaeological Review*, i. 180,
note.

[3] Pliny, *Nat. Hist.* xxviii. § 86.

stones of their parents, or lying at cross-roads.[1]   In
modern Europe there is no end to such devices.
Thus the Orkney Islanders will wash a sick person
and then throw the water down at a gateway, in the
belief that the sickness will leave the patient and be
transferred to the first person who passes through the
gate.[2]   A Bavarian cure for the fever is to write
upon a piece of paper, " Fever, stay away, I am not at
home," and to put the paper in some person's pocket.
The latter then catches the fever and the patient is rid
of it.[3]   Another cure is for the patient to stick a twig
of the elder-tree in the ground without speaking. The
fever then adheres to the twig, and whoever pulls up
the twig will catch the disease.[4]   To get rid of warts,
take a string and make as many knots in it as you
have warts.   Then lay the string under a stone.
Whoever treads upon the stone will get the warts,
and you will be rid of them.[5]   Gout may be transferred
from a man to a tree thus.   Pare the nails of the
sufferer's fingers and clip some hairs from his legs.
Bore a hole in an oak, stuff the nails and hair in the
hole, stop up the hole again, and smear it with cow's
dung.   If, for three months afterwards, the patient is
free of gout, then the oak has it in his stead.[6]   A
Flemish cure for the ague is to go early in the
morning to an old willow, tie three knots in one
of its branches, say, " Good-morrow, Old One, I
give thee the cold, good-morrow, Old One," then
turn and run away without looking round.[7]   A cure

[1] Plato, *Laws*, xi. c. 12, p. 933 B.
[2] Ch. Rogers, *Social Life in Scotland*, iii. 226.
[3] G. Lammert, *Volkmedizin und medizinischer Aberglaube in Bayern*, p. 264.   [4] *Ib*. p. 263.

[5] Strackerjan, *Aberglaube und Sagen aus dem Herzogthum Oldenburg*, i. § 85.
[6] Carl Meyer, *Der Aberglaube des Mittelalters*, p. 104.
[7] Grimm, *Deutsche Mythologie*,[4] ii. 979.

current in Sunderland for a cough is to shave the patient's head and hang the hair on a bush. When the birds carry the hair to their nests, they will carry the cough with it. A Northamptonshire and Devonshire cure is to put a hair of the patient's head between two slices of buttered bread and give it to a dog. The dog will get the cough and the patient will lose it.[1] In the Greek island of Carpathus the priest ties a red thread round the neck of a sick person. Next morning the friends of the patient remove the thread and go out to the hillside, where they tie the thread to a tree, thinking that they thus transfer the sickness to the tree.[2]

The old Welsh custom known as "sin-eating" is another example of the supposed transference of evil from one person to another. According to Aubrey, "In the County of Hereford was an old Custome at funeralls to hire poor people, who were to take upon them all the sinnes of the party deceased. One of them, I remember, lived in a cottage on Rosse-high way (he was a long, leane, ugly, lamentable poor raskal). The manner was that when the Corps was brought out of the house and layd on the Biere ; a Loafe of bread was brought out, and delivered to the Sinne-eater over the corps, as also a Mazar-bowle of maple (Gossips bowle) full of beer, which he was to drinke up, and sixpence in money, in consideration whereof he took upon him (ipso facto) all the Sinnes of the Defunct, and freed him (or her) from walking after they were dead. . . . I believe this custom was heretofore used over all

---

[1] Henderson, *Folk - lore of the Northern Counties*, p. 143. Collections of cures by transference will be found in Strackerjan's work, cited above, i. § 85 *sqq.* ; W. G. Black, *Folk-medicine*, ch. ii. Cp. Grimm, *Deutsche Mythologie*,[4] ii. c. 36.

[2] *Blackwood's Magazine*, February 1886, p. 239.

Wales. . . . In North Wales the Sinne-eaters are frequently made use of; but there, instead of a Bowle
of Beere, they have a bowle of Milke."[1]   According to
a letter dated February 1, 1714-5, "within the memory
of our fathers, in Shropshire, in those villages adjoyning
to Wales, when a person dyed, there was notice given
to an old sire (for so they called him), who presently
repaired to the place where the deceased lay, and stood
before the door of the house, when some of the family
came out and furnished him with a cricket, on which
he sat down facing the door.   Then they gave him a
groat, which he put in his pocket; a crust of bread,
which he eat; and a full bowle of ale, which he drank
off at a draught.   After this he got up from the cricket
and pronounced, with a composed gesture, the ease
and rest of the soul departed for which he would pawn
his own soul.   This I had from the ingenious John
Aubrey, Esq."[2]   In recent years some doubt has been
thrown on Aubrey's account of the custom.[3]   The
practice, however, is reported to have prevailed in
a valley not far from Llandebie to a recent period.
An instance was said to have occurred about forty
years ago.[4]   Aubrey's statement is supported by the
analogy of similar customs in India.   When the Rajah

---

[1] Aubrey, *Remains of Gentilisme and
Judaisme* (Folk-lore Society, 1881), p.
35 *sq.*

[2] Bagford's letter in Leland's *Col-
lectanea*, i. 76, quoted by Brand,
Popular Antiquities, ii. 246 *sq.*, Bohn's
ed.

[3] In the *Academy*, 13th Nov. 1875, p.
505, Mr. D. Silvan Evans stated that he
knew of no such custom anywhere in
Wales; and Miss Burne knows no
example of it in Shropshire.   Burne
and Jackson, *Shropshire Folk-lore*, p.
307 *sq.*

[4] The authority for the statement is
a Mr. Moggridge, reported in *Archae-
ologia Cambrensis*, second series, iii.
330.   But Mr. Moggridge did not
speak from personal knowledge, and as
he appears to have taken it for granted
that the practice of placing bread and
salt upon the breast of a corpse was a
survival of the custom of "sin-eating,"
his evidence must be received with
caution.   He repeated his statement, in
somewhat vaguer terms, at a meeting
of the Anthropological Institute, 14th
December 1875.   See *Journ. Anthrop.
Inst.* v. 423 *sq.*

of Tanjore died in 1801, some of his bones and the bones of the two wives, who were burned with his corpse, were ground to powder and eaten, mixed with boiled rice, by twelve Brahmans. It was believed that the sins of the deceased passed into the bodies of the Brahmans, who were paid for the service.[1] A Brahman, resident in a village near Raipúr, stated that he had eaten food (rice and milk) out of the hand of the dead Rajah of Biláspúr, and that in consequence he had been placed on the throne for the space of a year. At the end of the year he had been given presents and then turned out of the territory and forbidden apparently to return. He was an outcast among his fellows for having eaten out of a dead man's hand.[2] A similar custom is believed to obtain among the hill states about Kángrá, and to have given rise to a caste of "outcaste" Brahmans. At the funeral of a Rání of Chambá rice and *ght* were eaten out of the hands of the corpse by a Brahman paid for the purpose. Afterwards a stranger, who had been caught outside the Chambá territory, was given the costly wrappings of the corpse, then told to depart and never show his face in the country again.[3] In Oude when an infant was killed it used to be buried in the room in which it had been born. On the thirteenth day afterwards the priest had to cook and eat his food in that room. By doing so he was supposed to take the whole sin upon himself and to cleanse the family from it.[4] At Utch Kurgan in Turkistan Mr. Schuyler saw an old man who was said

---

[1] Dubois, *Moeurs des Peuples de l'Inde*, ii. 32.

[2] R. ' Richardson, in *Panjab Notes and Queries*, i. No. 674.

[3] *Panjab Notes and Queries*, i. No. 674 ; ii. No. 559. Some of these customs have been already referred to in a different connection. See above, vol. i. p. 232.   [4] *Op. cit.* iii. No. 745.

to get his living by taking on himself the sins of the dead and thenceforth devoting his life to prayer for their souls.[1]

§ 14.—*Expulsion of evils*

These examples illustrate the primitive principle of the transference of ills to another person, animal, or thing. In the instances cited the principle is applied for the benefit of individuals only. But analogous proceedings are employed by barbarous peoples to rid a whole community of all their troubles at a blow. The frame of mind which prompts such whole-sale clearances of evil may be described in the language of Mr. Im Thurn, for though he wrote of the Indians of Guiana in particular, his description is capable of a much wider application. He says : " Thus the whole world of the Indian swarms with these [spiritual] beings. If by a mighty mental effort we could for a moment revert to a similar mental position we should find ourselves surrounded by a host of possibly hurtful beings, so many in number that to describe them as innumerable would fall ridiculously short of the truth. It is not therefore wonderful that the Indian fears to move beyond the light of his camp-fire after dark, or, if he is obliged to do so, carries a firebrand with him that he may at least see among what enemies he walks ; nor is it wonderful that occasionally the air round the settlement seems to the Indian to grow so full of beings that a peaiman [sorcerer], who is supposed to have the power of temporarily driving them away, is employed to effect a

---

[1] E. Schuyler, *Turkistan*, ii. 28.

general clearance of these beings, if only for a time." [1]
Such general clearances of evil influences may be
divided into two classes, according as the expelled evils
are immaterial and invisible or are embodied in a
material vehicle or scapegoat. The former may be
called the direct or immediate expulsion of evils; the
latter the indirect or mediate expulsion, or the expulsion by scapegoat. We begin with examples of the
former.

In the island of Rook, between New Guinea and
New Britain, when any misfortune has happened, all
the people run together, scream, curse, howl, and beat
the air with sticks to drive away the devil (*Marsába*),
who is supposed to be the author of the mishap.
From the spot where the mishap took place they drive
him step by step to the sea, and on reaching the shore
they redouble their shouts and blows in order to expel
him from the island. He generally retires to the sea
or to the island of Lottin. [2] The natives of New
Britain ascribe sickness, drought, the failure of crops,
and in short all misfortunes, to the influence of wicked
spirits. So at times when many people sicken and
die, as at the beginning of the rainy season, all the
inhabitants of a district, armed with branches and
clubs, go out by moonlight to the fields, where they
beat and stamp on the ground with wild howls till
morning, believing that this drives away the devils. [3]
When a village has been visited by a series of disasters
or a severe epidemic, the Minahassa of Celebes lay
the blame upon the devils who are infesting the village
and must be expelled from it. Accordingly, early one

---

[1] E. F. im Thurn, *Among the Indians of Guiana*, p. 356 *sq.*

[2] Paul Reina, "Ueber die Bewohner der Insel Rook," *Zeitschrift für allgemeine Erdkunde*, N. F. iv. 356.

[3] R. Parkinson, *Im Bismarck-Archipel*, p. 142.

morning all the people, men, women, and children, quit their homes, carrying their household goods with them, and take up their quarters in temporary huts which have been erected outside the village. Here they spend several days, offering sacrifices and preparing for the final ceremony. At last the men, some wearing masks, others with their faces blackened, and so on, but all armed with swords, guns, pikes, or brooms, steal cautiously and silently back to the deserted village. Then, at a signal from the priest, they rush furiously up and down the streets and into and under the houses (which are raised on piles above the ground), yelling and striking on walls, doors, and windows, to drive away the devils. Next, the priests and the rest of the people come with the holy fire and march nine times round each house and thrice round the ladder that leads up to it, carrying the fire with them. Then they take the fire into the kitchen, where it must burn for three days continuously. The devils are now driven away, and great and general is the joy.[1] The Alfoers of Halmahera attribute epidemics to the devil who comes from other villages to carry them off. So, in order to rid the village of the disease, the sorcerer drives away the devil. From all the villagers he receives a costly garment and places it on four vessels, which he takes to the forest and leaves at the spot where the devil is supposed to be. Then with mocking words he bids the demon abandon the place.[2]

---

[1] [P. N. Wilken], "De godsdienst en godsdienstplegtigheden der Alfoeren in de Menahassa op het eiland Celebes," *Tijdschrift voor Nederlandsch Indië*, December 1849, pp. 392-394; *id.*, "Bijdragen tot de kennis van de zeden en gewoonten der Alfoeren in de Minahassa," *Mededeelingen v. w. het Nederland. Zendelinggenootsch*. vii.

(1863) 149 *sqq.*; J. G. F. Riedel, "De Minahasa in 1825," *Tijdschrift voor Indische Taal-Land en Volkenkunde*, xviii. (1872), 521 *sq.* Wilken's first and fuller account is reprinted in Graafland's *De Minahassa*, i. 117-120.

[2] Riedel, "Galela und Tobeloresen," in *Zeitschrift f. Ethnologie*, xvii. (1885)

In the Key Islands, south of New Guinea, when sickness prevails, the people erect a stage on the shore and load it with meat and drink. Then the priest in presence of the people bans the spirits which are causing the disease, whereupon the people run back to the village at full speed, like fugitives.[1]

In the island of Nias, when a man is seriously ill and other remedies have been tried in vain, the sorcerer proceeds to exorcise the devil who is causing the illness. A pole is set up in front of the house, and from the top of the pole a rope of palm-leaves is stretched to the roof of the house. Then the sorcerer mounts the roof with a pig, which he kills and allows to roll from the roof to the ground. The devil, anxious to get the pig, lets himself down hastily from the roof by the rope of palm-leaves, and a good spirit, invoked by the sorcerer, prevents him from climbing up again. If this remedy fails, it is believed that other devils must still be lurking in the house. So a general hunt is made after them. All the doors and windows in the house are closed, except a single dormer-window in the roof. The men, shut up in the house, hew and slash with their swords right and left to the clash of gongs and the rub-a-dub of drums. Terrified at this onslaught the devils escape by the dormer-window, and sliding down the rope of palm-leaves take themselves off. As all the doors and windows, except the one in the roof, are shut, the devils cannot get into the house again. In the case of an epidemic the proceedings are similar. All the gates of the village, except one, are closed; every voice is raised, every gong and drum beaten,

---

82 ; G. A. Wilken, *Het Shamanisme bij de Volken van de Indischen Archipel*, p. 58.

[1] Riedel, *De sluik-en kroesharige rassen tusschen Selebes en Papua*, p. 239.

every sword brandished. Thus the devils are driven out and the last gate is shut behind them. For eight days thereafter the village is in a state of siege, no one being allowed to enter it.[1] When cholera has broken out in a Burmese village the able-bodied men scramble on the roofs and lay about them with bamboos and billets of wood, while all the rest of the population, old and young, stand below and thump drums, blow trumpets, yell, scream, beat floors, walls, tin-pans, everything to make a din. This uproar, repeated on three successive nights, is thought to be very effective in driving away the cholera demons.[2] When small-pox first appeared amongst the Kumis of South-Eastern India, they thought it was a devil come from Arracan. The villages were placed in a state of siege, no one being allowed to leave or enter them. A monkey was killed by being dashed on the ground, and its body was hung at the village gate. Its blood, mixed with small river pebbles, was sprinkled on the houses, the threshold of every house was swept with the monkey's tail, and the fiend was adjured to depart.[3] At Great Bassam, in Guinea, the French traveller Hecquard witnessed the exorcism of the evil spirit who was believed to make women barren. The women who wished to become mothers offered to the fetish wine-vessels or statuettes representing women suckling children. Then being assembled in the fetish hut, they were sprinkled with

---

[1] Nieuwenhuisen en Rosenberg, *Verslag omtrent het eiland Nias*, p. 116 *sq.*; Rosenberg, *Der Malayische Archipel*, p. 174 *sq.* Cp. Chatelin, " Godsdienst en Bijgeloof der Niassers," *Tijdschrift voor Indische Taal-Land-en Volkenkunde*, xxvi. 139. The Dyaks also drive the devil at the point of the sword from a house where there is sickness. See Hüpe, " Korte verhandeling over de godsdienst, zeden, enz. der Dajakkers " in *Tijdschrift voor Neêrland's Indië*, viii. (1846) dl. iii. p. 149.

[2] Forbes, *British Burma*, p. 233 ; Shway Yoe, *The Burman*, i. 282, ii. 105 *sqq.*; Bastian, *Die Völker des östlichen Asien*, ii. 98.

[3] Lewin, *Wild Tribes of South-Eastern India*, p. 226.

rum by the priest, while young men fired guns and brandished swords to drive away the demon.[1]   When sickness was prevalent in a Huron village, and all other remedies had been tried in vain, the Indians had recourse to the ceremony called *Lonouyroya*, "which is the principal invention and most proper means, so they say, to expel from the town or village the devils and evil spirits which cause, induce, and import all the maladies and infirmities which they suffer in body and mind."   Accordingly, one evening the men would begin to rush like madmen about the village, breaking and upsetting whatever they came across in the wigwams.   They threw fire and burning brands about the streets, and all night long they ran howling and singing without cessation.   Then they all dreamed of something, a knife, dog, skin, or whatever it might be, and when morning came they went from wigwam to wigwam asking for presents.   These they received silently, till the particular thing was given them which they had dreamed about.   On receiving it they uttered a cry of joy and rushed from the hut, amid the congratulations of all present.   The health of those who received what they had dreamed of was believed to be assured; whereas those who did not get what they had set their hearts upon regarded their fate as sealed.[2]

The observance of such ceremonies, from being

---

[1] Hecquard, *Reise an die Küste und in das Innere von West Afrika*, p. 43.

[2] Sagard, *Le Grand Voyage du Pays des Hurons*, p. 279 *sqq.* (195 *sq.* of the Paris reprint).   Compare *Relations des Jésuites*, 1639, pp. 88-92 (Canadian reprint), from which it appears that each man demanded the subject of his dream in the form of a riddle, which the hearers tried to solve.   The propounding of riddles is not uncommon as a superstitious observance.   Prob-

ably enigmas were originally a kind of divination.   Cp. Vambery, *Das Türkenvolk*, p. 232 *sq.*; Riedel, *De sluiken kroesharige rassen*, etc. p. 267 *sq.*   In Bolang Mongondo (Celebes) riddles may never be asked except when there is a corpse in the village.   N. P. Wilken en J. A. Schwarz, "Allerlei over het land en volk van Bolaäng Mongondou," *Mededeelingen van wege het Nederlandsch. Zendelinggenootschap*, xi. (1867) p. 357.

occasional, tends to become periodic. It comes to be thought desirable to have a general riddance of evil spirits at fixed times, usually once a year, in order that the people may make a fresh start in life, freed from all the malignant influences which have been long accumulating about them. Some of the Australian blacks annually expelled the ghosts of the dead from their territory. The ceremony was witnessed by the Rev. W. Ridley on the banks of the river Barwan. "A chorus of twenty, old and young, were singing and beating time with boomerangs. . . . Suddenly, from under a sheet of bark darted a man with his body whitened by pipeclay, his head and face coloured with lines of red and yellow, and a tuft of feathers fixed by means of a stick two feet above the crown of his head. He stood twenty minutes perfectly still, gazing upwards. An aboriginal who stood by told me he was looking for the ghosts of dead men. At last he began to move very slowly, and soon rushed to and fro at full speed, flourishing a branch as if to drive away some foes invisible to us. When I thought this pantomime must be almost over, ten more, similarly adorned, suddenly appeared from behind the trees, and the whole party joined in a brisk conflict with their mysterious assailants. . . . At last, after some rapid evolutions in which they put forth all their strength, they rested from the exciting toil which they had kept up all night and for some hours after sunrise: they seemed satisfied that the ghosts were driven away for twelve months. They were performing the same ceremony at every station along the river, and I am told it is an annual custom."[1]

---

[1] The Rev. W. Ridley, in J. D. Lang's *Queensland*, p. 441 ; cp. Ridley. *Kamilaroi*, p. 149.

Certain seasons of the year mark themselves naturally out as appropriate moments for a general expulsion
of devils.   Such a moment occurs towards the close of
an Arctic winter, when the sun reappears on the horizon
after an absence of weeks or months.   Accordingly, at
Point Barrow, the most northerly extremity of Alaska,
and nearly of America, the Eskimo choose the moment
of the sun's reappearance to hunt the mischievous spirit
Tuña from every house.   The ceremony was witnessed
a few years ago by the members of the United States
Polar Expedition, who wintered at Point Barrow.
A fire was built in front of the council-house, and an
old woman was posted at the entrance to every *iglu*
(Eskimo house).   The men gathered round the council-
fire, while the young women and girls drove the spirits
out of every *iglu* with their knives, stabbing viciously
under the bunk and deer-skins, and calling upon Tuña
to leave the *iglu*.   When they thought he had been
driven out of every hole and corner, they thrust him
down through the hole in the floor and chased him
into the open air with loud cries and frantic gestures.
Meanwhile the old woman at the entrance of the *iglu*
made passes with a long knife in the air to keep him
from returning.   Each party drove the spirit towards
the fire and invited him to go into it.   All were by
this time drawn up in a semicircle round the fire, when
several of the leading men made specific charges against
the spirit; and each after his speech brushed his clothes
violently, calling on the spirit to leave him and go into
the fire.   Two men now stepped forward with rifles
loaded with blank cartridges, while a third brought a
vessel of urine and flung it on the fire.   At the same
time one of the men fired a shot into the fire ; and as
the cloud of steam rose it received the other shot,

which was supposed to finish Tuña for the time being.[1] In autumn, when heavy gales are raging, the Eskimo of Baffin Land think that the female spirit Sedna dwells amongst them, and the most powerful enchanter is employed to drive her out. Beside a small hole in the centre of the floor a line of seal-skin is coiled up. Holding a sealing-spear in his left hand the enchanter watches the hole in the floor. Another sorcerer sits in the rear of the hut chanting songs to attract Sedna. Now she is heard approaching under the floor of the hut. When she reaches the hole the enchanter strikes her with his harpoon and pays out the line. A severe struggle ensues, but ultimately Sedna flies to her country, Adlivun. The performance is cleverly managed. When the harpoon is drawn out of the hole it is covered with blood, and the heavy breathing of Sedna can be distinctly heard under the floor.[2]

The Iroquois inaugurated the new year in January, February, or March (the time varied) with a "festival of dreams" like that which the Hurons observed on special occasions.[3] The whole ceremonies lasted several days, or even weeks, and formed a kind of Saturnalia. Men and women, variously disguised, went from wigwam to wigwam smashing and throwing down whatever they came across. It was a time of general licence; the people were supposed to be out of their senses, and therefore not to be responsible for what they did. Accordingly, many seized the opportunity of paying off old scores by belabouring obnoxious persons, drenching them with ice-cold water, and covering them with filth or hot ashes.

[1] *Report of the International Polar Expedition to Point Barrow, Alaska* (Washington, 1885), p. 42 *sq.*

[2] Franz Boas, "The Eskimo," *Proceedings and Transactions of the Royal Society of Canada for* 1887, vol. v. (Montreal, 1888), sect. ii. 36 *sq.*

[3] Above, p. 162.

Others seized burning brands or coals and flung them at the heads of the first persons they met. The only way of escaping from these persecutors was to guess what they had dreamed of. On one day of the festival the ceremony of driving away evil spirits from the village took place. Men clothed in the skins of wild beasts, their faces covered with hideous masks, and their hands with the shell of the tortoise, went from hut to hut making frightful noises; in every hut they took the fuel from the fire and scattered the embers and ashes about the floor with their hands. The general confession of sins which preceded the festival was probably a preparation for the public expulsion of evil influences; it was a way of stripping the people of their moral burdens, that these might be collected and cast out. This New Year festival is still celebrated by some of the heathen Iroquois, though it has been shorn of its former turbulence. A conspicuous feature in the ceremony is now the sacrifice of the White Dog, but this appears to have been added to the festival in comparatively modern times, and does not figure in the oldest descriptions of the ceremonies. We shall return to it later on.[1] A great annual festival of the Cherokee Indians was the Propitiation, " Cementation," or Purification festival. " It was cele-brated shortly after the first new moon of autumn, and consisted of a multiplicity of rigorous rites, fastings, ablutions, and purifications. Among the most im-portant functionaries on the occasion were seven

---

[1] Charlevoix, *Histoire de la Nouvelle France*, vi. 82 *sqq.*; Timothy Dwight, *Travels in New England and New York*, iv. 201 *sq.*; L. H. Morgan, *League of the Iroquois*, p. 207 *sqq.*; Mrs. E. A. Smith, " Myths of the Iroquois," *Second Annual Report of the Bureau of* *Ethnology* (Washington, 1883), p. 112 *sqq.*; Horatio Hale, " Iroquois sacrifice of the White Dog," *American An-tiquarian*, vii. 7 *sqq.*; W. M. Beau-champ, " Iroquois White Dog feast," *ib.* p. 235 *sqq.*

exorcisers or cleansers, whose duty it was, at a certain stage of the proceedings, to drive away evil, and purify the town. Each one bore in his hand a white rod of sycamore. ' The leader, followed by the others, walked around the national heptagon, and coming to the treasure or store-house to the west of it, they lashed the eaves of the roofs with their rods. The leader then went to another house, followed by the others, singing, and repeated the same ceremony until every house was purified.' This ceremony was repeated daily during the continuance of the festival. In performing their ablutions they went into the water and allowed their old clothes to be carried away by the stream, by which means they supposed their impurities removed." [1]

In September the Incas of Peru celebrated a festival called Situa, the object of which was to banish from the capital and its vicinity all disease and troubles. The festival fell in September because the rains begin about this time, and with the first rains there was generally much sickness. As a preparation for the festival the people fasted on the first day of the moon after the autumnal equinox. Having fasted during the day, and the night being come, they baked a coarse paste of maize. This paste was made of two sorts. One was kneaded with the blood of children aged five to ten years, the blood being obtained by bleeding the children between the eye-brows. These two kinds of paste were baked separately, because they were for different uses. Each family assembled at the house of the eldest brother to celebrate the feast; and those who had no elder brother went to

---

[1] Squier's notes upon Bartram's *Creek and Cherokee Indians*, p. 78, from the MS. of Mr. Payne. See above, p. 75 *note*.

the house of their next relation of greater age. On
the same night all who had fasted during the day
washed their bodies, and taking a little of the blood-
kneaded paste, rubbed it over their head, face, breast,
shoulders, arms, and legs.   They did this in order
that the paste might take away all their infirmities.
After this the head of the family anointed the
threshold with the same paste, and left it there as a
token that the inmates of the house had performed
their ablutions and cleansed their bodies.   Meantime
the High Priest performed the same ceremonies in the
temple of the Sun.   As soon as the Sun rose, all the
people worshipped and besought him to drive all evils
out of the city, and then they broke their fast with the
paste that had been kneaded without blood.   When
they had paid their worship and broken their fast,
which they did at a stated hour, in order that all might
adore the Sun as one man, an Inca of the blood royal
came forth from the fortress, as a messenger of the
Sun, richly dressed, with his mantle girded round his
body, and a lance in his hand.   The lance was decked
with feathers of many hues, extending from the blade
to the socket, and fastened with rings of gold.   He
ran down the hill from the fortress brandishing his
lance, till he reached the centre of the great square,
where stood the golden urn, like a fountain, that was
used for the sacrifice of *chicha.*   Here four other Incas
of the blood royal awaited him, each with a lance in
his hand, and his mantle girded up to run.   The
messenger touched their four lances with his lance,
and told them that the Sun bade them, as his messengers, drive the evils out of the city.   The four
Incas then separated and ran down the four royal
roads which led out of the city to the four quarters of

the world. While they ran, all the people, great and small, came to the doors of their houses, and with great shouts of joy and gladness shook their clothes, as if they were shaking off dust, while they cried, " Let the evils be gone. How greatly desired has this festival been by us. O Creator of all things, permit us to reach another year, that we may see another feast like this." After they had shaken their clothes, they passed their hands over their heads, faces, arms, and legs, as if in the act of washing. All this was done to drive the evils out of their houses, that the messengers of the Sun might banish them from the city. This was done not only in the streets through which the Incas ran, but generally in all quarters of the city. Moreover, they all danced, the Inca himself amongst them, and bathed in the rivers and fountains, saying that their maladies would come out of them. Then they took great torches of straw, bound round with cords. These they lighted, and passed from one to the other, striking each other with them, and saying, " Let all harm go away." Meanwhile the runners ran with their lances for a quarter of a league outside the city, where they found four other Incas ready, who received the lances from their hands and ran with them. Thus the lances were carried by relays of runners for a distance of five or six leagues, at the end of which the runners washed themselves and their weapons in rivers, and set up the lances, in sign of a boundary within which the banished evils might not return.[1]

---

[1] Garcilasso de la Vega, *Royal Commentaries of the Yncas*, pt. i. bk. vii. ch. 6, vol. ii. p. 228 *sqq.*, Markham's translation ; Molina, " Fables and Rites of the Yncas," in *Rites and Laws of the Yncas* (Hakluyt Society, 1873), p. 20 *sqq.*; Acosta, *History of the Indies*, bk. v. ch. 28, vol. ii. p. 375 *sq.* (Hakluyt Society, 1880). The accounts of Garcilasso and Molina are somewhat

The negroes of Guinea annually banish the devil from all their towns with much ceremony.   At Axim, on the Gold Coast, this annual expulsion is preceded by a feast of eight days, during which mirth and jollity reign, and "a perfect lampooning liberty is allowed, and scandal so highly exalted, that they may freely sing of all the faults, villanies, and frauds of their superiors as well as inferiors, without punishment, or so much as the least interruption."   On the eighth day they hunt out the devil with a dismal cry, running after him and pelting him with sticks, stones, and whatever comes to hand.   When they have driven him far enough out of the town, they all return.   In this way he is driven out of more than a hundred towns at the same time.   To make sure that he does not return to their houses, the women wash and scour all their wooden and earthen vessels, "to free them from all uncleanness and the devil."[1]   At Onitsha, on the Quorra River, Mr. J. C. Taylor witnessed the celebration of New Year's Day by the negroes.   It fell on 20th December 1858.   Every family brought a firebrand out into the street, threw it away, and exclaimed as they returned, "The gods of the new year!   New Year has come round again."   Mr. Taylor adds, "The meaning of the custom seems to be that the fire is to drive away the old year with its sorrows and evils, and to embrace the new year with

discrepant, but this may be explained by the statement of the latter that "in one year they added, and in another they reduced the number of ceremonies, according to circumstances."   Molina places the festival in August, Garcilasso and Acosta in September.   According to Garcilasso there were only four runners in Cuzco; according to Molina there were four hundred.   Acosta's account is very brief.   In the description given in the text features have been borrowed from all three accounts, where these seemed consistent with each other.

[1] Bosman's "Guinea," in Pinkerton's *Voyages and Travels*, xvi. 402.   Cp. Pierre Bouche, *La Côte des Esclaves*, p. 395.

hearty reception." [1]   Of all Abyssinian festivals that of
Mascal or the Cross is celebrated with the greatest
pomp.   The eve of the festival witnesses a ceremony
which doubtless belongs to the world-wide class of
customs we are dealing with.   'At sunset a discharge
of firearms takes place from all the principal houses.
" Then every one provides himself with a torch, and
during the early part of the night bonfires are kindled,
and the people parade the town, carrying their lighted
torches in their hands.   They go through their houses
too, poking a light into every dark corner in the hall,
under the couches, in the stables, kitchen, etc., as if
looking for something lost, and calling out, ' Akho,
akhoky ! turn out the spinage, and bring in the porridge ; Mascal is come ! ' . . . After this they play,
and poke fun and torches at each other." [2]

Sometimes the date of the annual expulsion of
devils is fixed with reference to the agricultural
seasons.   Among the Hos of North-Eastern India
the great festival of the year is the harvest home,
held in January, when the granaries are full of
grain, and the people, to use their own expression,
are full of devilry.   " They have a strange notion
that at this period men and women are so over-
charged with vicious propensities, that it is absolutely
necessary for the safety of the person to let off steam
by allowing for a time full vent to the passions."   The
ceremonies open with a sacrifice to the village god of
three fowls, two of which must be black.   Along with
them are offered flowers of the Palás tree, bread made
from rice-flour, and sesamum seeds.   These offerings
are presented by the village priest, who prays that

---

[1] S. Crowther and J. C. Taylor.   *The*   [2] Mansfield   Parkyns,   *Life   in*
Gospel on the Banks of the Niger, p 320.   *Abyssinia*, p. 285 *sqq.*

during the year about to begin they and their children may be preserved from all misfortune and sickness, and that they may have seasonable rain and good crops. Prayer is also made in some places for the souls of the dead. At' this time an evil spirit is supposed to infest the place, and to get rid of it men, women, and children go in procession round and through every part of the village with sticks in their hands, as if beating for game, singing a wild chant, and shouting vociferously, till they feel assured that the evil spirit must have fled. Then they give themselves up to feasting and drinking rice-beer, till they are in a fit state for the wild debauch which follows. The festival now " becomes a saturnale, during which servants forget their duty to their masters, children their reverence for parents, men their respect for women, and women all notions of modesty, delicacy, and gentleness ; they become raging bacchantes." Usually the Hos are quiet and reserved in manner, decorous and gentle to women. But during this festival " their nature appears to undergo a temporary change. Sons and daughters revile their parents in gross language, and parents their children ; men and women become almost like animals in the indulgence of their amorous propensities." The Mundaris, kinsmen and neighbours of the Hos, keep the festival in much the same manner. " The resemblance to a Saturnale is very complete, as at this festival the farm labourers are feasted by their masters, and allowed the utmost freedom of speech in addressing them. It is the festival of the harvest home ; the termination of one year's toil, and a slight respite from it before they commence again." [1]

---

[1] Dalton, *Ethnology of Bengal*, p. 196 *sq.*

III   *OF EVILS*
Amongst some of the Hindoo Koosh tribes, as among the Hos and Mundaris, the expulsion of devils takes place after harvest. When the last crop of autumn has been got in, it is thought necessary to drive away evil spirits from the granaries. A kind of porridge called *mool* is eaten, and the head of the family takes his matchlock and fires it into the floor. Then, going outside, he sets to work loading and firing till his powder horn is exhausted, while all his neighbours are similarly employed. The next day is spent in rejoicings. In Chitral this festival is called "devil-driving."[1] On the other hand the Khonds of India expel the devils at seed-time instead of at harvest. At this time they worship Pitteri Pennu, the god of increase and of gain in every shape. On the first day of the festival a rude car is made of a basket set upon a few sticks, tied upon bamboo rollers for wheels. The priest takes this car first to the house of the lineal head of the tribe, to whom precedence is given in all ceremonies connected with agriculture. Here he receives a little of each kind of seed and some feathers. He then takes the car to all the other houses in the village, each of which contributes the same things. Lastly, the car is conducted to a field without the village, attended by all the young men, who beat each other and strike the air violently with long sticks. The seed thus carried out is called the share of the "evil spirits, spoilers of the seed." "These are considered to be driven out with the car; and when it and its contents are abandoned to them, they are held to have no excuse for interfering with the rest of the seed-corn." Next day each household kills a hog over the seed for the year, and prays to Pitteri Pennu.

---

[1] Biddulph, *Tribes of the Hindoo Koosh*, p. 103.

The elders then feast upon the hogs. The young men are excluded from the repast, but enjoy the privilege of waylaying and pelting with jungle fruit their elders as they return from the feast. Upon the third day the lineal head of the tribe goes out and sows his seed, after which all the rest may do so.[1]

The people of Bali, an island to the east of Java, have periodical expulsions of devils upon a great scale. Generally the time chosen for the expulsion is the day of the "dark moon" in the ninth month. When the demons have been long unmolested the country is said to be "warm," and the priest issues orders to expel them by force, lest the whole of Bali should be rendered uninhabitable. On the day appointed the people of the village or district assemble at the principal temple. Here at a cross-road offerings are set out for the devils. After prayers have been recited by the priests, the blast of a horn summons the devils to partake of the meal which has been prepared for them. At the same time a number of men step forward and light their torches at the holy lamp which burns before the chief priest. Immediately afterwards, followed by the bystanders, they spread in all directions and march through the streets and lanes crying, "Depart! go away!" Wherever they pass, the people who have stayed at home hasten by a deafening knocking on doors, beams, rice-blocks, etc., to take their share in the expulsion of devils. Thus chased from the houses, the fiends flee to the banquet which

---

[1] W. Macpherson, *Memorials of Service in India*, p. 357 *sq*. Possibly this case belongs more strictly to the class of mediate expulsions, the devils being driven out upon the car. Perhaps, however, the car with its contents is regarded rather as a bribe to induce them to go than as a vehicle in which they are actually carted away. Anyhow it is convenient to take this case along with those other expulsions of demons which are the accompaniment of an agricultural festival.

has been set out for them ; but here the priest receives them with curses which finally drive them
from the district. When the last devil has taken his
departure, the uproar is succeeded by a dead silence,
which lasts during the next day also. The devils, it is
thought, are anxious to return to their old homes, and
in order to make them think that Bali is not Bali but
some desert island, no one may stir from his own
premises for twenty-four hours. Even ordinary
household work, including cooking, is discontinued.
Only the watchmen may show themselves in the
streets. Wreaths of thorns and leaves are hung at all
the entrances to warn strangers from entering. Not
till the third day is this state of siege raised, and even
then it is forbidden to work at the rice-fields or to buy
and sell in the market. Most people still stay at home,
striving to while away the time with cards and dice.[1]

In some parts of Fiji an annual ceremony took place
which has much the aspect of an expulsion of devils.
The time of its celebration was determined by the
appearance of a certain fish or sea-slug (*balolo*) which
swarms out in dense shoals from the coral reefs on a
single day of the year, usually in the last quarter of the
moon in November. The appearance of the sea-slugs
was the signal for a general feast at those places where
they were taken. An influential man ascended a tree
and prayed to the spirit of the sky for good crops, fair
winds, and so on. Thereupon a tremendous clatter,
with drumming and shouting, was raised by all the
people in their houses for about half an hour. This
was followed by a dead quiet for four days, during

---

[1] R. van Eck, "Schetsen van het
eiland Bali," *Tijdschrift voor Nederlandsch Indië*, N. S. viii. (1879) 58-
60. Van Eck's account is reprinted
in J. Jacobs's *Eenigen tijd onder de
Baliërs* (Batavia, 1883), p. 190 *sqq.*

which the people feasted on the sea-slug. All this time no work of any kind might be done, not even a leaf plucked nor the offal removed from the houses. If a noise was made in any house, as by a child crying, a forfeit was at once exacted by the chief. At daylight on the expiry of the fourth night the whole town was in an uproar; men and boys scampered about, knocking with clubs and sticks at the doors of the houses and crying "Sinariba." This concluded the ceremony.[1]

On the night before spring begins the Japanese throw roasted beans against the walls and floors of their houses, crying thrice loudly, "Away from here, wicked spirit!" but adding softly, "Enter, O god of riches!"[2] Amongst some of the Hindus of the Punjaub on the morning after Diwali or the festival of lamps (at which the souls of ancestors are believed to visit the house) the oldest woman of the family takes all the sweepings and rubbish of the family and throws them out, with the words, "Let all dirt and wretchedness depart from here, and all good fortune come in."[3] In Tonquin a *theckydaw* or general expulsion of malevolent spirits commonly took place once a year, especially if there was a great mortality amongst men or cattle, "the cause of which they attribute to the malicious spirits of such men as have been put to death for treason, rebellion, and conspiring the death of the king, general, or princes, and in that revenge of the punishment they have suffered, they are bent to destroy

---

[1] *U.S. Exploring Expedition, Ethnography and Philology*, by H. Hale, p. 67 *sq.*; Ch. Wilkes, *Narrative of the U.S. Exploring Expedition*, iii. 90 *sq.* According to the latter, the sea-slug was eaten by the men alone, who lived during the four days in the temple, while the women and boys remained shut up in their houses.

[2] Bastian, *Die Völker des östlichen Asien*, v. 367.

[3] *Panjab Notes and Queries*, ii. No. 792; D. C. J. Ibbetson, *Outlines of Panjab Ethnography*, p. 119.

Expulsion of devils by Fiji tribesman.

Abyssinians, one of the African tribes.

everything and commit horrible violence. To prevent which their superstition has suggested to them the institution of this theckydaw as a proper means to drive the devil away, and purge the country of evil spirits." The day appointed for the ceremony was generally the 25th of February, one month after the commencement of the new year, which began on the 25th of January. The intermediate month was a season of feasting, merry-making of all kinds, and general licence. During the whole month 'the great seal was kept shut up in a box, face downwards, and the law was, as it were, laid asleep. All courts of justice were closed; debtors could not be seized; small crimes, such as petty larceny, fighting, and assault, escaped with impunity; only treason and murder were taken account of and the malefactors detained till the great seal should come into operation again. At the close of the saturnalia the wicked spirits were driven away. Great masses of troops and artillery having been drawn up with flying colours and all the pomp of war, "the general beginneth then to offer meat offerings to the criminal devils and malevolent spirits (for it is usual and customary likewise amongst them to feast the condemned before their execution), inviting them to eat and drink, when presently he accuses them in a strange language, by characters and figures, etc., of many offences and crimes committed by them, as to their having disquieted the land, killed his elephants and horses, etc., for all which they justly deserved to be chastised and banished the country. Whereupon three great guns are fired as the last signal; upon which all the artillery and musquets are discharged, that, by their most terrible noise the devils may be driven away; and they are so blind as to, believe

for certain, that they really and effectually put them
to flight." [1]

In Cambodia the expulsion of evil spirits took place
in March. Bits of broken statues and stones, considered
as the abode of the demons, were collected and brought
to the capital. Here as many elephants were collected
as could be got together. On the evening of the full
moon volleys of musketry were fired and the elephants
charged furiously to put the devils to flight.[2] In Siam
the banishment of demons is annually carried into
effect on the last day of the old year. A signal gun
is fired from the palace; it is answered from the
next station, and so on from station to station, till the
firing has reached the outer gate of the city. Thus
the demons are driven out step by step. As soon as
this is done a consecrated rope is fastened round the
circuit of the city walls to prevent the banished demons
from returning. The rope is made of tough couch-grass
and is painted in alternate stripes of red, yellow, and
blue.[3] The Shans of Southern China annually expel the
fire-spirit. The ceremony was witnessed by the English
Mission under Colonel Sladen on the 13th of August
1868. Bullocks and cows were slaughtered in the
market-place; the meat was all sold, part of it was
cooked and eaten, while the rest was fired out of guns

[1] Baron, "Description of the Kingdom of Tonqueen," Pinkerton's *Voyages
and Travels*, ix. 673, 695 *sq.*; cp.
Richard, "History of Tonquin," *ib.* p.
746. The account of the ceremony by
Tavernier (whom Baron criticises very
unfavourably) is somewhat different.
According to him the expulsion of
wicked souls at the New Year is combined with sacrifice to the honoured dead.
See Harris, *Voyages and Travels*, i. 823.

[2] Aymonier, *Notice sur le Cambodge*,
p. 62.

[3] Bastian, *Die Völker des östlichen
Asien*, iii. 237, 298, 314, 529 *sq.*;
Pallegoix, *Royaume Thai ou Siam*, i.
252. Bastian (p. 314), with whom
Pallegoix seems to agree, distinctly
states that the expulsion takes place on
the last day of the year. Yet both
state that it occurs in the fourth month
of the year. According to Pallegoix
(i. 253) the Siamese year is composed
of twelve lunar months, and the first
month usually begins in December.
Hence the expulsion of devils would
commonly take place in March, as in
Cambodia.

at sundown. The pieces of flesh which fell on the land were supposed to become mosquitoes, those which fell in the water were believed to turn into leeches. In the evening the chief's retainers beat gongs and blew trumpets ; and when darkness had set in torches were lit and a party, preceded by the musicians, searched the central court for the fire-spirit, who is supposed to lurk about at this season with evil intent. They then searched all the rooms and the gardens, throwing the light of the torches into every nook and corner where the evil spirit might find a hiding-place.[1]

Annual expulsions of demons or of evil influences are not unknown in Europe at the present day. Amongst the heathen Wotyaks, a Finnish people of Eastern Russia, all the young girls of the village assemble on the last day of the year or on New Year's Day armed with sticks, the ends of which are split in nine places. With these they beat every corner of the house and yard, saying, "We are driving Satan out of the village." Afterwards the sticks are thrown into the river below the village, and as they float down stream Satan goes with them to the next village, from which he must be driven out in turn. In some villages the expulsion is managed otherwise. The unmarried men receive from every house in the village groats, flesh, and brandy. These they take to the field, light a fire under a fir-tree, boil the groats, and eat of the food they have brought with them, after pronouncing the words, "Go away into the wilderness, come not into the house." Then they return to the village and enter every house where there are young women. They take hold of the young women and throw them into the snow, saying, "May the spirits of

---

[1] J. Anderson, *Mandalay to Momien*, p. 308.

disease leave you." The remains of the groats and
the other food are then distributed among all the
houses in proportion to the amount that each contributed, and each family consumes its share. According to a Wotyak of the Malmyz district the young
men throw into the snow whomever they find in the
houses, and this is called "driving out Satan;" moreover some of the boiled groats are thrown into the
fire with the words, "O god, afflict us not with sickness and pestilence, give us not up as a prey to the
spirits of the wood." But the most antique form of
the ceremony is that observed by the Wotyaks of the
Kasan Government. First of all a sacrifice is offered
to the Devil at noon. Then all the men assemble on
horseback in the centre of the village, and decide with
which house they shall begin. When this question,
which often gives rise to hot disputes, is settled, they
tether their horses to the paling, and arm themselves
with whips, clubs of lime-wood, and bundles of lighted
twigs. The lighted twigs are believed to have the
greatest terrors for Satan. Thus armed, they proceed
with frightful cries to beat every corner of the house
and yard, then shut the door, and spit at the ejected
fiend. So they go from house to house, till the Devil
has been driven from every one. Then they mount
their horses and ride out of the village, yelling wildly
and brandishing their clubs in every direction. Outside of the village they fling away the clubs and spit
once more at the Devil.[1] The Cheremiss, another
Finnish people of Eastern Russia, chase Satan from
their dwellings by beating the walls with cudgels of
lime-wood. When he has fled to the wood, they pelt

---

[1] Max Buch, *Die Wotjäken*, p. 153 *sq.*

the trees with some of the cheese-cakes and eggs which furnished the feast.[1]

In Albania on Easter Eve the young people light torches of resinous wood and march in procession, swinging them, through the village. At last they throw the torches into the river, crying, "Ha, Kore! we throw you into the river, like these torches, that you may never return."[2] In some villages of Calabria the month of March is inaugurated with the expulsion of the witches. It takes place at night to the sound of the church bells, the people running about the streets and crying, "March is come." They say that the witches roam about in March, and the ceremony is repeated every Friday evening during the month.[3] In the Tyrol the expulsion of witches takes place on the first of May. On a Thursday at midnight bundles are made up of resinous splinters, black and red spotted hemlock, caper-spurge, rosemary, and twigs of the sloe. These are kept and burned on May Day by men who must first have received plenary absolution from the church. On the last three days of April all the houses are cleansed and fumigated with juniper berries and rue. On May Day, when the evening bell has rung and the twilight is falling, the ceremony of "burning out the witches," as it is called, begins. Men and boys make a racket with whips, bells, pots, and pans; the women carry censers; the dogs are unchained and run barking and yelping about. As soon as the church bells begin to ring, the bundles of twigs, fastened on poles, are set on fire and the incense

[1] Bastian, *Der Mensch in der Geschichte*, ii. 94.

[2] J. G. von Hahn, *Albanesische Studien*, i. 160. Cp. above, vol. i. p. 276.

[3] Vincenzo Dorsa, *La tradizione greco-latina negli usi e nelle credenze popolari della Calabria Citeriore*, p. 42 sq.

is ignited.   Then all the house-bells and dinner-bells
are rung, pots and pans are clashed, dogs bark, every
one must make a noise.   And amid this hubbub all
scream at the pitch of their voices,

> " Witch flee, flee from here,
> Or it will go ill with thee."

Then they run seven times round the houses, the
yards, and the village.   So the witches are smoked
out of their lurking-places and driven away.[1]   At
Brunnen in Switzerland the boys go about in
procession on Twelfth Night, carrying torches and
lanterns, and making a great noise with horns, cow-
bells, whips, etc.   This is said to frighten away the two
female spirits of the wood, Strudeli and Strätteli.[2]

§ 15.—*Scapegoats*

Thus far the examples cited have belonged to the
class of direct or immediate expulsion of ills.   It
remains to illustrate the second class of expulsions, in
which the evil influences are either embodied in a
visible form or are at least supposed to be loaded
upon a material medium, which acts as a vehicle to

---

[1] Von Alpenburg, *Mythen und Sagen Tirols*, p. 260 *sq.*   A Westphalian form of the expulsion of evil is the driving out the *Süntevögel, Sunnenvögel*, or *Sommervögel, i.e.*, the butterfly. On St. Peter's Day, 22d February, children go from house to house knocking on them with hammers and singing doggerel rhymes in which they bid the *Sommervögel* to depart.   Presents are given to them at every house.   Or the people of the house themselves go through all the rooms, knocking on all the doors, to drive away the *Sunnenvögel*.   If this ceremony is omitted, it is thought that various misfortunes will be the consequence.   The house will swarm with rats, mice, and other vermin, the cattle will be sick, the butterflies will multiply at the milk-bowls, etc.   Woeste, *Volksüberlieferungen in der Grafschaft Mark*, p. 24 ; J. W. Wolf, *Beiträge zur deutschen Mythologie*, i. 87 ; A. Kuhn, *Westfälische Sagen, Gebräuche und Märchen*, ii. §§ 366-374 ; Montanus, *Die deutschen Volksfeste, Volksbräuche*, etc., p. 21 *sq.* ; Jahn, *Die deutschen Opfergebräuche bei Ackerbau und Viehzucht*, pp. 94-96.

[2] Usener, " Italische Mythen," in *Rheinisches Museum*, N. F. xxx. 198.

draw them off from the people, village, or town. The Pomos of California celebrate an expulsion of devils every seven years, at which the devils are represented by disguised men. " Twenty or thirty men array themselves in harlequin rig and barbaric paint, and put vessels of pitch on their heads ; then they secretly go out into the surrounding mountains. These are to personify the devils. A herald goes up to the top of the assembly-house, and makes a speech to the multitude. At a signal agreed upon in the evening the masqueraders come in from the mountains, with the vessels of pitch flaming on their heads, and with all the frightful accessories of noise, motion, and costume which the savage mind can devise in representation of demons. The terrified women and children flee for life, the men huddle them inside a circle, and, on the principle of fighting the devil with fire, they swing blazing firebrands in the air, yell, whoop, and make frantic dashes at the marauding and bloodthirsty devils, so creating a terrific spectacle, and striking great fear into the hearts of the assembled hundreds of women, who are screaming and fainting and clinging to their valorous protectors. Finally the devils succeed in getting into the assembly-house, and the bravest of the men enter and hold a parley with them. As a conclusion of the whole farce, the men summon courage, the devils are expelled from the assembly-house, and with a prodigious row and racket of sham fighting are chased away into the mountains."[1] In spring, as soon as the willow leaves were full grown on the banks of the river, the Mandan Indians celebrated their great annual festival, one of the features of which was the expulsion of the devil. A man, painted black to

---

[1] S. Powers, *Tribes of California*, p. 159.

represent the devil, entered the village from the prairie, chased and frightened the women, and acted the part of a buffalo bull in the buffalo dance, the object of which was to ensure a plentiful supply of buffaloes during the ensuing year. Finally he was chased from the village, the women pursuing him with hisses and gibes, beating him with sticks, and pelting him with dirt.[1] On the last night of the year the palace of the Kings of Cambodia is purged of devils. Men painted as fiends are chased by elephants about the palace courts. When they have been expelled, a consecrated thread of cotton is stretched round the palace to keep them out.[2] The Kasyas, a hill tribe of Assam, annually expel the demons. The ceremony takes place on a fixed month in the year, and part of it consists in a struggle between two bands of men who stand on opposite sides of a stream, each side tugging at the end of a rope which is stretched across the water. In this contest, which resembles the game of "French and English," the men on one side probably represent the demons.[3] At Carmona in Andalusia,

[1] G. Catlin, *North American Indians*, i. 166 *sqq.*; *id.*, *O-kee-pa, a Religious Ceremony, and other Customs of the Mandans*.

[2] Moura, *Le Royaume du Cambodge*, i. 172. Cp. above, p. 178.

[3] A. Bastian, in *Verhandl. d. Berlin. Gesellsch. f. Anthropol.* 1881, p. 151; cp. *id.*, *Völkerstämme am Brahmaputra*, p. 6 *sq.* Amongst the Chukmas of South-east India the body of a priest is conveyed to the place of cremation on a car; ropes are attached to the car, the people divide themselves into two equal bodies and pull at the ropes in opposite directions. "One side represents the' good spirits; the other, the powers of evil. The contest is so arranged that the former are victorious. Sometimes, however, the young men representing the demons are inclined to pull too vigorously, but a stick generally quells this unseemly ardour in the cause of evil." Lewin, *Wild Tribes of South-Eastern India*, p. 185. The contest is like that between the angels and devils depicted in the frescoes of the Campo Santo at Pisa. In Burma a similar contest takes place at the funeral of a holy man; but there the original meaning of the ceremony appears to be forgotten. See Sangermano, *Description of the Burmese Empire* (ed. 1885), p. 98; Forbes, *British Burma*, p. 216 *sq.*; Shway Yoe, *The Burman*, ii. 334 *sq.*, 342. Sometimes ceremonies of this sort are instituted for a different purpose. In some East Indian islands when the people want a rainy wind from the

on one day of the year, boys are stripped naked and smeared with glue in which feathers are stuck. Thus disguised, they run from house to house, the people trying to avoid them and to bar their houses against them.[1] The ceremony is probably a relic of an annual expulsion of devils.

Oftener, however, the expelled demons are not represented at all, but are understood to be present invisibly in the material and visible vehicle which conveys them away. Here, again, it will be convenient to distinguish between occasional and periodical expulsions. We begin with the former.

The vehicle which conveys away the demons may be of various kinds. A common one is a little ship or boat. Thus, in the southern district of the island of Ceram, when a whole village suffers from sickness, a small ship is made and filled with rice, tobacco, eggs, etc., which have been contributed by all the people. A little sail is hoisted on the ship. When all is ready, a man calls out in a very loud voice, " O all ye sicknesses, ye small-poxes, agues, measles, etc., who have visited us so long and wasted us so sorely, but who now cease to plague us, we have made ready this ship for you, and we have furnished you with provender sufficient for the voyage. Ye shall have no lack of food nor of *siri* nor of *pinang* nor of tobacco. Depart, and sail away from us directly ; never come near us again, but go to a land which is far from here. Let all the tides and winds

---

west, the population of the village, men, women, and children, divide into two parties and pull against each other at the ends of a long bamboo. But the party at the eastern end must pull the harder, in order to draw the desired wind out of the west. Riedel, *De sluik-en* *kroesharige rassen tusschen Selebes en Papua*, p. 282. The Cingalese perform a ceremony like " French and English " in honour of the goddess Patiné. Forbes, *Eleven Years in Ceylon* (London, 1840), i. 358.

[1] *Folk-lore Journal*, vii. 174.

waft you speedily thither, and so convey you thither
that for the time to come we may live sound and well,
and that we may never see the sun rise on you again."
Then ten or twelve men carry the vessel to the shore,
and let it drift away with the land - breeze, feeling
convinced that they are free from sickness for ever,
or at least till the next time. If sickness attacks them
again, they are sure it is not the same sickness, but a
different one, which in due time they dismiss in the
same manner. When the demon-laden bark is lost
to sight, the bearers return to the village, whereupon
a man cries out, " The sicknesses are now gone,
vanished, expelled, and sailed away." At this all
the people come running out of their houses, passing
the word from one to the other with great joy, beating
on gongs and on tinkling instruments.[1]

Similar ceremonies are commonly resorted to in other
East Indian islands. Thus in Timorlaut, to mislead the
demons who are causing sickness, a small prao, containing the image of a man and provisioned for a long
voyage, is allowed to drift away with wind and tide. As
it is being launched, the people cry, " O sickness, go
from here ; turn back ; what do you here in this
poor land ? " Three days after this ceremony a pig is
killed, and part of the flesh is offered to Dudilaa,
who lives in the sun. One of the oldest men says,
" Old sir, I beseech you, make well the grandchildren,
children, women, and men, that we may be able to
eat pork and rice and to drink palm-wine. I will
keep my promise. Eat your share, and make all
the people in the village well." If the prao is
stranded at any inhabited spot, the sickness will break

---

[1] François Valentyn, *Oud-en nieuw Ost-Indiën*, iii. 14. Backer, *L'Archipel
Indien*, p. 377 *sq.*, copies from Valentyn.

out there. Hence a stranded prao excites much
alarm amongst the coast population, and they immediately burn it, because demons fly from fire.[1] In the
island of Buro the prao which carries away the
demons of disease is about twenty feet long, rigged
out with sails, oars, anchor, etc., and well stocked
with provisions. For a day and a night the people
beat gongs and drums, and rush about to frighten
the demons. Next morning ten stalwart young men
strike the people with branches, which have been
previously dipped in an earthen pot of water. As
soon as they have done so, they run down to the
beach, put the branches on board the prao, launch
another prao in great haste, and tow the disease-
burdened prao far out to sea. There they cast it
off, and one of them calls out, " Grandfather Small-
pox, go away—go willingly away—go visit another
land ; we have made you food ready for the voyage,
we have now nothing more to give." When they
have landed, all the people bathe together in the
sea.[2] In this ceremony the reason for striking the
people with the branches is clearly to rid them of
the disease-demons, which are then supposed to be
transferred to the branches. Hence the haste with
which the branches are deposited in the prao and
towed away to sea. So in the inland districts of
Ceram, when small-pox or other sickness is raging,
the priest strikes all the houses with consecrated
branches, which are then thrown into the river, to
be carried down to the sea ;[3] exactly as amongst
the Wotyaks of Russia the sticks which have been
used for expelling the devils from the village are

---

[1] Riedel, *De sluik-en kroesharige rassen tusschen Selebes en Papua*, p.
304 *sq.*   [2] *Ib.* p. 25 *sq.*   [3] *Ib.* p. 141.

thrown into the river, that the current may sweep the baleful burden away. In Amboina, for a similar purpose, the whole body of the patient is rubbed with a live white cock, which is then placed on a little prao and committed to the waves ;[1] and in the Babar archipelago the bark which is to carry away to sea the sickness of a whole village contains a bowl of ashes taken from every kitchen in the village, and another bowl into which all the sick people have spat.[2] The plan of putting puppets in the boat to represent sick persons, in order to lure the demons after them, is not uncommon.[3]

The practice of sending away diseases in boats is known outside the limits of the East Indian Archipelago. Thus when the people of Tikopia, a small island in the Pacific, to the north of the New Hebrides, were attacked by an epidemic cough, they made a little canoe and adorned it with flowers. Four sons of the principal chiefs carried it on their shoulders all round the island, accompanied by the whole population, some of whom beat the bushes, while others uttered loud cries. On returning to the spot from which they had set out, they launched the canoe on the sea.[4] In the Nicobar Islands, in the Bay of Bengal, when there is much sickness in a village or no fish are caught, the blame is laid upon the spirits. They

[1] Riedel, *op. cit.* p. 78.
[2] *Ib.* p. 357.
[3] *Ib.* pp. 266, 304 *sq.*, 327, 357. For other examples of sending away disease-laden boats in these islands, *ib.* pp. 181, 210; Van Eck, "Schetsen van het eiland Bali," *Tijdschrift voor Nederlandsch Indië*, N.S. viii. (1879) p. 104; Bastian, *Indonesien*, i. 147; Hupe, "Korte verhandeling over de godsdienst, zeden, enz. der Dajakkers," *Tijdschrift voor Neêrland's Indië*, 1846, dl. iii. 150; Campen, "De godsdienstbegrippen der Halmaherasche Alfoeren," *Tijdschrift voor Indische Taal-Land-en Volkenkunde*, xxvii. (1882) p. 441 ; *Journal of the Straits Branch of the Royal Asiatic Society*, No. 12, pp. 229-231 ; Van Hasselt, *Volksbeschrijving van Midden-Sumatra*, p. 98.
[4] J. Dumont D'Urville, *Voyage autour du monde et à la recherche de La Pérouse, sur la corvette Astrolabe*, v. 311.

must be propitiated with offerings. All relations and friends are invited, a huge pig is roasted, and the best of it is eaten, but some parts are offered to the shades. The heap of offerings remains in front of the house till it is carried away by the rising tide. Then the priests, their faces reddened with paint and swine's blood, pretend to catch the demon of disease, and, after a hand-to-hand struggle, force him into a model boat, made of leaves and decked with garlands, which is then towed so far to sea that neither wind nor tide is likely to drive it back to the shore.[1]

Often the vehicle which carries away the collected demons or ills of a whole community is an animal or scapegoat. In the Central Provinces of India, when cholera breaks out in a village, every one retires after sunset to his house. The priests then parade the streets, taking from the roof of each house a straw, which is burnt with an offering of rice, *ghi*, and turmeric, at some shrine to the east of the village. Chickens daubed with vermilion are driven away in the direction of the smoke, and are believed to carry the disease with them. If they fail, goats are tried, and last of all pigs.[2] When cholera is very bad among the Bhárs, Malláns, and Kurmís of India, they take a goat or a buffalo — in either case the animal must be a female, and as black as possible — then they tie some grain, cloves, and red lead in a yellow cloth on its back, and turn it out of the village. It is conducted beyond the boundary, and is not allowed to return.[3] The people of the city and cantonments of

---

[1] Roepstorff, "Ein Geisterboot der Nicobaresen," *Verhandl. der Berlin. Gesellsch. f. Anthropologie* (1881), p. 401. For Siamese applications of the same principle to the cure of individuals, see Bastian, *Die Völker des östlichen Asien*, iii. 295 *sq.*, 485 *sq.*

[2] *Panjab Notes and Queries*, i. No. 418.

[3] *Id.* iii. No. 373.

Sagar being afflicted with a violent influenza, " I had an application from the old Queen Dowager of Sagar to allow of a noisy religious procession, for the purpose of imploring deliverance from this great calamity. Men, women, and children in this procession were to do their utmost to add to the noise by 'raising their voices in psalmody,' beating upon their brass pots and pans with all their might, and discharging firearms where they could get them. Before the noisy crowd was to be driven a buffalo, which had been purchased by general subscription, in order that every family might participate in the merit. They were to follow it out eight miles, where it was to be turned loose for any man who would take it. If the animal returned the disease must return with it, and the ceremony be performed over again. . . . It was, however, subsequently determined that the animal should be a goat ; and he was driven before the crowd accordingly. I have on several occasions been requested to allow of such noisy ceremonies in cases of epidemics." [1] Once, when influenza was raging in Pithuria, a man had a small carriage made, after 'a plan of his own, for a pair of scapegoats, which were harnessed to it and driven to a wood at some distance, where they were let loose. From that hour the disease entirely ceased in the town. The goats never returned ; had they done so, " the disease must have come back with them." [2] The idea of the scapegoat is not uncommon in the hills of the Eastern Ghats. In 1886, during a severe outbreak of small-pox, the people of Jeypur made " puja " to a goat, marched it to the Ghats, and let it loose on

---

[1] *Panjab Notes and Queries*, ii. No. 1127.   [2] *Id.* ii. No. 1123.

the plains.[1]   In Southern Konkan, on the appearance
of cholera, the villagers went in procession from the
temple to the extreme boundaries of the village,
carrying a basket of cooked rice covered with red
powder, a wooden doll representing the pestilence,
and a cock.   The head of the cock was cut off at
the village boundary, and the body was thrown away.
When cholera was thus transferred from one village
to another, the second village observed the same
ceremony and passed on the scourge to its neighbours,
and so on through a number of villages.[2]   When the
Aymara Indians were suffering from a plague, they
loaded a llama with the clothes of the plague-stricken
people, and drove the animal into the mountains,
hoping that it would take the plague away with it.[3]
Sometimes the scapegoat is a man.   Some of the
aboriginal tribes of China, as a protection against
pestilence, select a man of great muscular strength to
act the part of scapegoat.   Having besmeared his face
with paint, he performs many antics with the view of
enticing all pestilential and noxious influences to attach
themselves to him only.   He is assisted by a priest.
Finally the scapegoat, hotly pursued by men and
women beating gongs and tom-toms, is driven with
great haste out of the town or village.[4]   A Hindu
cure for the murrain is to hire a man of the Chamár
caste, turn his face away from the village, brand him
with a red-hot sickle, and let him go out into the
jungle, taking the murrain with him.   He must not
look back.[5]

---

[1] F. Fawcett, "On the Saoras (or
Savaras)," *Journ. Anthrop. Soc.
Bombay*, i. 213 *note*.

[2] *Journ. Anthrop. Soc. Bombay*, i.
37.

[3] R. Andree, *Ethnographische Parallelen und Vergleiche* (first series), p. 30.

[4] J. H. Gray, *China*, ii. 306.

[5] *Panjab Notes and Queries*, i.
598.

The mediate expulsion of evils by means of a scapegoat or other material vehicle, like the immediate expulsion of them in invisible form, tends to become periodic, and for a like reason.   Thus every year, generally in March, the people of Leti, Moa, and Lakor send away all their diseases to sea.   They make a prao about six feet long, rig it with sails, oars, rudder, etc., and every family deposits in it some rice, fruit, a fowl, two eggs, insects that ravage the fields, etc.   Then they let it drift away to sea, saying, " Take away from here all kinds of sickness, take them to other islands, to other lands, distribute them in places that lie eastward, where the sun rises." [1]   The Biajas of Borneo annually send to sea a little bark laden with the sins and misfortunes of the people.   The crew of any ship that falls in with the ill-omened bark at sea will suffer all the sorrows with which it is laden.[2]   At the beginning of the dry season, every year, the Nicobar islanders carry the model of a ship through their villages.   The devils are chased out of the huts, and driven on board the little ship, which is then launched and suffered to sail away with the wind.[3]   At Sucla-Tirtha, in India, an earthen pot containing the accumulated sins of the people is (annually ?) set adrift on the river.   Legend says that the custom originated with a wicked priest who, after atoning for his guilt by a course of austerities and expiatory ceremonies, was directed to sail upon the river in a boat with white sails.   If the white sails turned black, it would be a sign that his sins were forgiven him.   They did so, and he joyfully allowed

---

[1] Riedel, *De sluik-en kroesharige rassen tusschen Selebes en Papua*, p. 393.

[2] Bastian, *Der Mensch in der Geschichte*, ii. 93.

[3] *Id.* ii. 91.

the boat to drift with his sins to sea.[1]   Amongst many
of the aboriginal tribes of China, a great festival is
celebrated in the third month of every year.   It is held
by way of a general rejoicing over what the people
believe to be a total annihilation of the ills of the past
twelve months.   This annihilation is supposed to be
effected in the following way.   A large earthenware
jar filled with gunpowder, stones, and bits of iron is
buried in the earth.   A train of gunpowder, communi-
cating with the jar, is then laid ; and a match being
applied, the jar and its contents are blown up.   The
stones and bits of iron represent the ills and disasters
of the past year, and the dispersion of them by the
explosion is believed to remove the ills and disasters
themselves.   The festival is attended with much revel-
ling and drunkenness.[2]   At Old Calabar, in Guinea,
the devils are expelled once every two years.   A
number of figures called *nabikems* are made of sticks
and bamboos, and fixed indiscriminately about the
town.   Some of them represent human beings, others
birds, crocodiles, and so on.   After three or four
weeks the devils are expected to take up their abode
in these figures.   When the night comes for their
general expulsion, the people feast and sally out in
parties, beating at empty corners, and shouting with
all their might.   Shots are fired, the *nabikems* are torn
up with violence, set in flames, and flung into the river.
The orgies last till daybreak, and the town is considered to be rid of evil influences for two years to come.[3]
Mr. George Bogle, the English envoy sent to Tibet
by Warren Hastings, witnessed the celebration of the
Tibetan New Year's Day at Teshu Lumbo the capital

---

[1] *Asiatic Researches*, ix. 96 *sq.*
[2] J. H. Gray, *China*, ii. 306 *sq.*

[3] T. J. Hutchinson, *Impressions of Western Africa*, p. 162.

of the Teshu Lama. " The figure of a man, chalked
upon paper, was laid upon the ground. Many strange
ceremonies, which to me who did not understand them
appeared whimsical, were performed about it ; and a
great fire being kindled in a corner of the court, it was
at length held over it, and being formed of combustibles,
vanished with much smoke and explosion. I was told
it was a figure of the devil." [1]

On one day of the year some of the people of the
Western Himalayas take a dog, intoxicate him with
spirits and bhang or hemp, and having fed him with
sweetmeats, lead him round the village and let him
loose. They then chase and kill him with sticks and
stones, and believe that, when they have done so, no
disease or misfortune will visit the village during the
year.[2] In some parts of Breadalbane it was formerly
the custom on New Year's Day to take a dog to the
door, give him a bit of bread, and drive him out, saying, " Get away you dog ! Whatever death of men,
or loss of cattle would happen in this house to the end
of the present year, may it all light on your head !" [3]
It appears that the white dogs annually sacrificed by
the Iroquois at their New Year Festival are, or have
been, regarded as scapegoats. According to Mr. J.
V. H. Clark, who witnessed the ceremony in January
1841, on the first day of the festival all the fires in the
village were extinguished, the ashes scattered to the
winds, and a new fire was kindled with flint and steel.
On a subsequent day, men dressed in fantastic costumes

[1] Bogle and Manning, *Tibet*, edited
by C. R. Markham, p. 106 *sq.*

[2] E. T. Atkinson, "Notes on the
History of Religion in the Himalaya of
the North-West Provinces," *Journal of*
the Asiatic Society of Bengal, liii. pt. i.
(1884), p. 62.

[3] *Scotland and Scotsmen in the Eigh-*
teenth Century, from the MSS. of John
Ramsay of Ochtertyre, edited by Alex.
Allardyce (Edinburgh, 1888), ii. 439.

Thorny bushes are placed on the threshold of cow barns, so the
witches will be caught by the thorns.

A Tibetan devil.

went round the village, gathering the sins of the people. On the morning of the last day of the festival, two white dogs, decorated with red paint, wampum, feathers, and ribbons were led out. They were soon strangled, and hung on a ladder. Firing and yelling succeeded, and half an hour later the dogs were taken into a house, "where the peoples' sins were transferred to them." The dogs were afterwards burnt on a pyre of wood.[1] According to the Rev. Mr. Kirkland, who wrote last century, the ashes of the pyre upon which one of the white dogs was burned were carried through the village and sprinkled at the door of every house.[2] Formerly, however, as we have seen,. the Iroquois expulsion of evils was immediate and not by scapegoat.[3] The Jews annually laid all the sins of the people upon the head of a goat and sent it away into the wilderness.[4]

The scapegoat upon whom the sins of the people are periodically laid, may also be a human being. At Onitsha, on the Quorra River, two human beings are annually sacrificed to take away the sins of the land. The victims are purchased by public subscription. All persons who, during the past year, have fallen into gross sins, such as incendiarism, theft, adultery, witchcraft, etc. are expected to contribute 28 *ngugas*, or a little over £2. The money thus collected is taken into the

---

[1] W. M. Beauchamp, " The Iroquois White Dog Feast," *American Antiquarian*, vii. 237.

[2] *Ib.* p. 236 ; T. Dwight, *Travels in New England and New York*, iv. 202.

[3] Above, p. 165 *sq.*

[4] Leviticus xvi. Modern Jews sacrifice a white cock on the eve of the Festival of Expiation, nine days after the beginning of their New Year. The father of the family knocks the cock thrice against his own head, saying, " Let this cock be a substitute for me, let it take my place, let death be laid upon this cock, but a happy life bestowed on me and on all Israel." Then he cuts its throat and dashes the bird violently on the ground. The intestines are thrown on the roof of the house. The flesh of the cock was formerly given to the poor. Buxtorf, *Synagoga Judaica*, c. xxv.

interior of the country and expended in the purchase of two sickly persons "to be offered as a sacrifice for all these abominable crimes—one for the land and one for the river." A man from a neighbouring town is hired to put them to death. The sacrifice of one of these victims was witnessed by the Rev. J. C. Taylor on 27th February 1858. The sufferer was a woman, about nineteen or twenty years of age. She was dragged alive along the ground, face downwards, from the king's house to the river, a distance of two miles. The crowds who accompanied her cried "Wickedness! wickedness!" The intention was "to take away the iniquities of the land. The body was dragged along in a merciless manner, as if the weight of all their wickedness was thus carried away."[1] In Siam it was formerly the custom on one day of the year to single out a woman broken down by debauchery, and carry her on a litter through all the streets to the music of drums and hautboys. The mob insulted her and pelted her with dirt; and after having carried her through the whole city, they threw her on a dunghill or a hedge of thorns outside the ramparts, forbidding her ever to enter the walls again. They believed that the woman thus drew upon herself all the malign influences of the air and of evil spirits.[2] The people of Nias offer either a red horse or a buffalo as a public sacrifice to purify the land and obtain the favour of the gods. Formerly, it is said, a man was bound to the same stake as the buffalo, and when the animal was killed, the man was driven away; no one might

---

[1] S. Crowther and J. C. Taylor, *The Gospel on the Banks of the Niger*, pp. 343-345. Cp. J. F. Schön and S. Crowther, *Journals*, p. 48 *sq.* The account of the custom by J. Africanus B. Horton (*West African Countries and Peoples* p. 185 *sq.*) is entirely from Taylor.

[2] Turpin, "History of Siam," in Pinkerton's *Voyages and Travels*, ix. 579.

receive him, converse with him, or give him food.[1]
Doubtless he was supposed to carry away the sins and
misfortunes of the people.

In Tibet the ceremony of the scapegoat is marked
by some peculiar features. The Tibetan New Year
begins with the new moon, which appears about
15th February. For twenty-three days afterwards
the government of Lhásá, the capital, is taken out
of the hands of the ordinary rulers and entrusted to
the monk of the Debang monastery who offers to
pay the highest sum for the privilege. The successful bidder is called the Jalno, and he announces
the fact in person through the streets of Lhásá,
bearing a silver stick. Monks from all the neighbouring monasteries and temples assemble to pay
him homage. The Jalno exercises his authority
in the most arbitrary manner for his own benefit, as
all the fines which he exacts are his by purchase.
The profit he makes is about ten times the amount
of the purchase money. His men go about the streets
in order to discover any conduct on the part of the
inhabitants that can be found fault with. Every
house in Lhásá is taxed at this time, and the slightest
fault is punished with unsparing rigour by fines. This
severity of the Jalno drives all working classes out
of the city till the twenty-three days are over.
Meantime, all the priests flock from the neighbourhood
to the Máchindránáth temple, where they perform
religious ceremonies. The temple is a very large one,
standing in the centre of the city, surrounded by
bazaars and shops. The idols in it are richly inlaid
with gold and precious stones. Twenty-four days

[1] Ködding, "Die Bataksche Götter," *Allgemeine Missions-Zeitschrift*, xii.
(1885) pp. 476, 478.

after the Jalno has ceased to have authority, he assumes it again, and for ten days acts in the same arbitrary manner as before. On the first of the ten days the priests assemble as before at the Máchindránáth temple, pray to the gods to prevent sickness and other evils among the people, "and, as a peace-offering, sacrifice one man. The man is not killed purposely, but the ceremony he undergoes often proves fatal.[1] Grain is thrown against his head, and his face is painted half white, half black." On the tenth day, all the troops in Lhásá march to the temple and form in line before it. The victim is brought forth from the temple and receives small donations from the assembled multitude. He then throws dice with the Jalno. If the victim wins, much evil is foreboded; but if the Jalno wins, there is great rejoicing, for it is then believed that the victim has been accepted by the gods to bear all the sins of the people of Lhásá. Thereupon his face is painted half white and half black, a leathern coat is put on him, and he is marched to the walls of the city, followed by the whole populace, hooting, shouting, and firing volleys after him. When he is driven outside the city, the people return, and the victim is carried to the Sáme monastery. Should he die shortly afterwards, the people say it is an auspicious sign; but if not, he is kept a prisoner at the monastery for a whole year, after which he is allowed to return to Lhásá.[2]

Human scapegoats, as we shall see presently, were

---

[1] The ceremony referred to is probably the one performed on the tenth day, as described in the text.

[2] "Report of a Route Survey by Pundit— from Nepal to Lhasa," etc., *Journal Royal Geogr. Soc.* xxxviii. (1868) pp. 167, 170 *sq.*; "Four Years' Journeying throught Great Tibet, by one of the Trans-Himalayan Explorers," *Proceed. Royal Geogr. Soc.* N.S. vii. (1885) p. 67 *sq.*

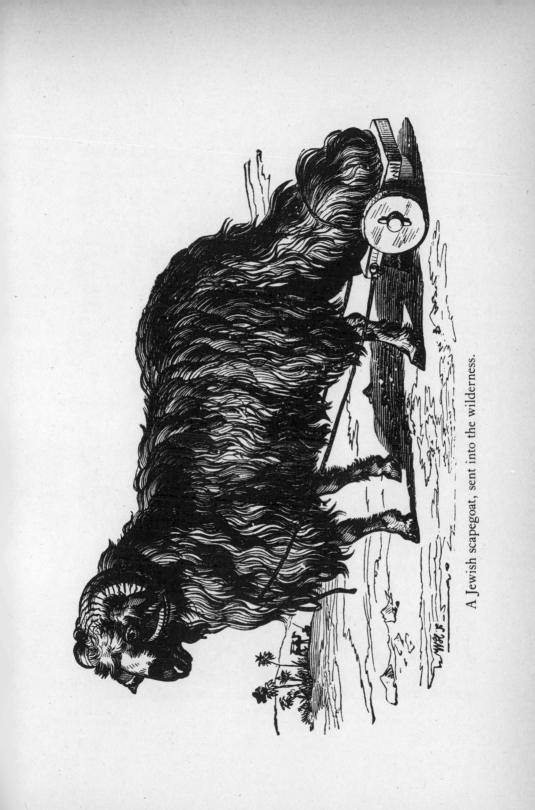

A Jewish scapegoat, sent into the wilderness.

A human sacrifice to the Nile.

well known in classical antiquity, and even in mediæval
Europe the custom seems not to have been wholly
extinct. In the town of Halberstadt in Thüringen
there was a church which was said to have been
founded by Charlemagne. In this church every year
a man was chosen, who was believed to be stained
with heinous sins. On the first day of Lent he was
brought to the church, dressed in mourning garb, with
his head muffled up. At the close of the service he
was turned out of the church. During the forty days
of Lent he perambulated the city barefoot, neither
entering the churches nor speaking to any one. The
canons took it in turn to feed him. After midnight he
was allowed to sleep on the streets. On the day
before Good Friday, after the consecration of the holy
oil, he was readmitted to the church and absolved
from his sins. The people gave him money. He
was called Adam, and was now believed to be in a
state of innocence.[1] At Entlebuch in Switzerland,
down to the close of last century, the custom of
annually expelling a scapegoat was preserved in the
ceremony of driving "Posterli" from the village into
the lands of the neighbouring village. "Posterli"
was represented by a lad disguised as an old witch or
as a goat or an ass. Amid a deafening noise of horns,
clarionets, bells, whips, etc. he was driven out. Sometimes "Posterli" was represented by a puppet, which
was drawn in a sledge and left in a corner of the
neighbouring village. The ceremony took place on
the Thursday evening of the last week but one before
Christmas.[2]

Sometimes the scapegoat is a divine animal. The

---

[1] Aeneas Sylvius, *Opera* (Bâle, 1571),   [2] Usener, "Italische Mythen,"
p. 423 *sq.*   *Rheinisches Museum*, N.F. xxx. 198.

people of Malabar share the Hindu reverence for the cow, to kill and eat which " they esteem to be a crime as heinous as homicide or wilful murder." Nevertheless " the Bramans transfer the sins of the people into one or more Cows, which are then carry'd away, both the Cows and the Sins wherewith these Beasts are charged, to what place the Braman shall appoint." [1] When the ancient Egyptians sacrificed a bull, they invoked upon its head all the evils that might otherwise befall themselves and the land of Egypt, and thereupon they either sold the bull's head to the Greeks or cast it into the river. [2] Now, it cannot be said that in the times known to us the Egyptians worshipped bulls in general, for they seem to have commonly killed and eaten them. [3] But a good many circumstances point to the conclusion that originally all cattle, bulls as well as cows, were held sacred by the Egyptians. For not only were all cows esteemed holy by them and never sacrificed, but even bulls might not be sacrificed unless they had certain natural marks ; a priest examined every bull before it was sacrificed ; if it had the proper marks, he put his seal on the animal in token that it might be sacrificed ; and if a man sacrificed a bull which had not been sealed, he was put to death. Moreover, the worship of the black bulls Apis and Mnevis, especially the former, played an important part in Egyptian religion ; all bulls that died a natural death were carefully buried in the suburbs of the cities, and their bones were afterwards collected from all parts of Egypt and buried in a single spot ; and at the sacrifice of a bull in the great

[1] J. Thomas Phillips, *Account of the Religion, Manners, and Learning of the People of Malabar*, pp. 6, 12 *sq.*

[2] Herodotus, ii. 39.

[3] Herodotus, ii. 38-41 ; Wilkinson, *Manners and Customs of the Ancient Egyptians*, iii. 403 *sqq.* (ed. 1878).

rites of Isis all the worshippers beat their breasts and mourned.[1]   On the whole, then, we are perhaps entitled to infer that bulls were originally, as cows were always, esteemed sacred by the Egyptians, and that the slain bull upon whose head they laid the misfortunes of the people was once a divine scapegoat. It seems not improbable that the lamb annually slain by the Madis of Central Africa is a divine scapegoat, and the same supposition may partly explain the Zuni sacrifice of the turtle.[2]

Lastly, the scapegoat may be a divine man. Thus, in November the Gonds of India worship Ghansyam Deo, the protector of the crops, and at the festival the god himself is said to descend on the head of one of the worshippers, who is suddenly seized with a kind of fit and, after staggering about, rushes off into the jungle, where it is believed that, if left to himself, he would die mad. As it is, he is brought back, but does not recover his senses for one or two days.   " The idea is, that one man is thus singled out as a scapegoat for the sins of the rest of the village."[3]   In the temple of the Moon the Albanians of the Eastern Caucasus kept a number of sacred slaves, of whom many were inspired and prophesied. When one of these men exhibited more than usual symptoms of inspiration and wandered solitary up and down the woods, like the Gond in the jungle, the high priest had him bound with a sacred chain and maintained him in luxury for a year. At the end of the year he was anointed with unguents and led forth to be sacrificed. A man whose business it was to slay these human victims and to whom practice had

---

[1] Herodotus, *l.c.*
[2] See above, pp. 95 *sqq.*, 137 *sq.*
[3] *Panjab Notes and Queries*, ii. No. 335.

given dexterity, advanced from the crowd and thrust a sacred spear into the victim's side, piercing his heart. From the manner in which the slain man fell, omens were drawn as to the welfare of the common-wealth. Then the body was carried to a certain spot where all the people stood upon it as a purificatory ceremony.[1] This last circumstance clearly indicates that the sins of the people were transferred to the victim, just as the Jewish priest transferred the sins of the people to the scapegoat by laying his hand on the animal's head; and since the man was believed to be possessed by the divine spirit, we have here an undoubted example of a man-god slain to take away the sins and misfortunes of the people.

The foregoing survey of the custom of publicly expelling the accumulated evils of a village or district suggests a few general observations. In the first place, it will not be disputed that what I have called the immediate and the mediate expulsions of evil are identical in intention; in other words, that whether the evils are conceived of as invisible or as embodied in a material form, is a circumstance entirely sub-ordinate to the main object of the ceremony, which is simply to effect a total clearance of all the ills that have been infesting a people. If any link were wanting to connect the two kinds of expulsion, it would be furnished by such a practice as that of sending the evils away in a boat. For here, on the one hand, the evils are invisible and intangible; and, on the other hand, there is a visible and tangible vehicle to convey them away. And a scapegoat is nothing more than such a vehicle.

---

[1] Strabo, xi. 4, 7. For the custom of standing upon a sacrificed victim, cp. Demosthenes, p. 642; Pausanias, iii. 20, 9.

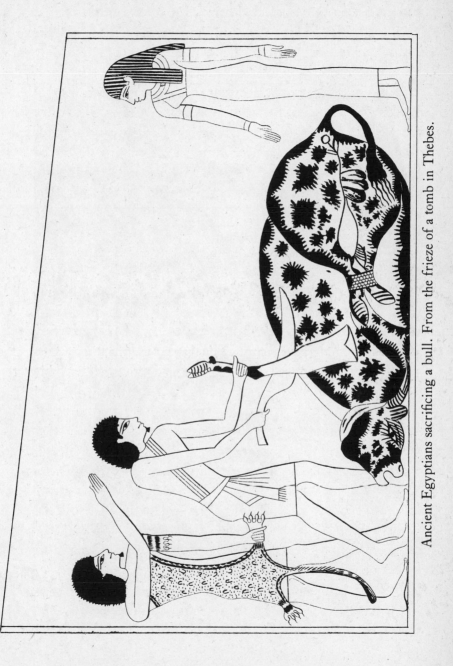

Ancient Egyptians sacrificing a bull. From the frieze of a tomb in Thebes.

People of Malibar.

In the second place, when a general clearance of evils is resorted to periodically, the interval between the celebrations of the ceremony is commonly a year, and the time of year when the ceremony takes place usually coincides with some well-marked change of season—such as the close of winter in the arctic and temperate zones, and the beginning or end of the rainy season in the tropics. The increased mortality which such climatic changes are apt to produce, especially amongst ill-fed, ill-clothed, and ill-housed savages, is set down by primitive man to the agency of demons, who must accordingly be expelled. Hence, in New Britain and Peru, the devils are or were driven out at the beginning of the rainy season. When a tribe has taken to agriculture, the time for the general expulsion of devils is naturally made to agree with one of the great epochs of the agricultural year, as sowing or harvest ; but, as these epochs themselves often coincide with changes of season, it does not follow that the transition from the hunting or pastoral to the agricultural life involves any alteration in the time of celebrating this great annual rite. Some of the agricultural communities of India and the Hindoo Koosh, as we have seen, hold their general clearance of demons at harvest, others at sowing-time. But, at whatever season of the year it is held, the general expulsion of devils commonly marks the beginning of the new year. For, before entering on a new year, people are anxious to rid themselves of the troubles that have harassed them in the past ; hence the fact that amongst so many people—Iroquois, Tonquinese, Siamese, Tibetans, etc.—the beginning of the new year is inaugurated with a solemn and public banishment of evil spirits.

In the third place, it is to be observed that this public and periodic expulsion of devils is commonly preceded or followed by a period of general licence, during which the ordinary restraints of society are thrown aside, and all offences, short of the gravest, are allowed to pass unpunished.   In Guinea and Tonquin the period of licence precedes the public expulsion of demons ; and the suspension of the ordinary government in Lhásá previous to the expulsion of the scapegoat is perhaps a relic of a similar period of universal licence.   Amongst the Hos the period of licence follows the expulsion of the devil.   Amongst the Iroquois it hardly appears whether it preceded or followed the banishment of evils.   In any case, the extraordinary relaxation of all ordinary rules of conduct on such occasions is doubtless to be explained by the general clearance of evils which precedes or follows it.   On the one hand, when a general riddance of evil and absolution from all sin is in immediate prospect, men are encouraged to give the rein to their passions, trusting that the coming ceremony will wipe out the score which they are running up so fast.   On the other hand, when the ceremony has just taken place, men's minds are freed from the oppressive sense, under which they generally labour, of an atmosphere surcharged with devils ; and in the first revulsion of joy they overleap the limits commonly imposed by custom and morality. When the ceremony takes place at harvest-time, the elation of feeling which it excites is further stimulated by the state of physical wellbeing produced by an abundant supply of food.[1]

---

[1] In the Dassera festival, as celebrated in Nepaul, we seem to have another instance of the annual expulsion of demons preceded by a time of licence.

Fourthly, the employment of a divine man or animal as a scapegoat is especially to be noted ; indeed, we are here directly concerned with the custom of banishing evils only in so far as these evils are believed to be transferred to a god who is afterwards slain. It may be suspected that the custom of employing a divine man or animal as a public scapegoat is much more widely diffused than appears from the examples cited. For, as has already been pointed out, the custom of killing a god dates from so early a period of human history that in later ages, even when the custom continues to be practised, it is liable to be misinterpreted. The divine character of the animal or man is forgotten, and he comes to be regarded merely as an ordinary victim. This is especially likely to be the case when it is a divine man who is killed. For when a nation becomes

---

The festival occurs at the beginning of October and lasts ten days. "During its continuance there is a general holiday among all classes of the people. The city of Kathmandu at this time is required to be purified, but the purification is effected rather by prayer than by water-cleansing. All the courts of law are closed, and all prisoners in jail are removed from the precincts of the city. . . . The Kalendar is cleared, or there is a jail-delivery always at the Dassera of all prisoners." This seems a trace of a period of licence. At this time "it is a general custom for masters to make an annual present, either of money, clothes, buffaloes, goats, etc., to such servants as have given satisfaction during the past year. It is in this respect, as well as in the feasting and drinking which goes on, something like our 'boxing-time' at Christmas." On the seventh day at sunset there is a parade of all the troops in the capital, including the artillery. At a given signal the regiments commence firing,

the artillery takes it up, and a general firing goes on for about twenty minutes, when it suddenly ceases. This probably represents the expulsion of the demons. "The grand cutting of the rice-crops is always postponed till the Dassera is over, and commences all over the valley the very day afterwards." See the description of the festival in Oldfield's *Sketches from Nipal*, ii. 342-351. On the Dassera in India, see Dubois, *Moeurs, Institutions et Cérémonies des Peuples de l'Inde*, ii. 329 *sqq*. Amongst the Wasuahili of East Africa New Year's Day was formerly a day of general licence, "every man did as he pleased. Old quarrels were settled, men were found dead on the following day, and no inquiry was instituted about the matter." Ch. New, *Life, Wanderings, and Labours in Eastern Africa*, p. 65. In Ashantee the annual festival of the new yams is a time of general licence. See the Note on "Offerings of first fruits" at the end of the volume.

civilised, if it does not drop human sacrifices altogether, it at least selects as victims only such criminals as would be put to death at any rate. Thus, as in the Sacaean festival at Babylon, the killing of a god may come to be confounded with the execution of a criminal.

If we ask why a dying god should be selected to take upon himself and carry away the sins and sorrows of the people, it may be suggested that in the practice of using the divinity as a scapegoat we have a combination of two customs which were at one time distinct and independent. On the one hand we have seen that it has been customary to kill the human or animal god in order to save his divine life from being weakened by the inroads of age. On the other hand we have seen that it has been customary to have a general expulsion of evils and sins once a year. Now, if it occurred to people to combine these two customs, the result would be the employment of the dying god as a scapegoat. He was killed, not originally to take away sin, but to save the divine life from the degeneracy of old age ; but, since he had to be killed at any rate, people may have thought that they might as well seize the opportunity to lay upon him the burden of their sufferings and sins, in order that he might bear it away with him to the unknown world beyond the grave.

The use of the divinity as a scapegoat clears up the ambiguity which, as we saw, appeared to hang about the European folk - custom of " carrying out Death." [1] Grounds have been shown for believing that in this ceremony the so - called Death was originally the spirit of vegetation, who was annually

---

[1] See above, vol. i. p. 275 *sq.*

slain in spring, in order that he might come to life again with all the vigour of youth. But, as we saw, there are certain features in the ceremony which are not explicable on this hypothesis alone. Such are the marks of joy with which the effigy of Death is carried out to be buried or burnt, and the fear and abhorrence of it manifested by the bearers. But these features become at once intelligible if we suppose that the Death was not merely the dying god of vegetation, but also a public scapegoat, upon whom were laid all the evils that had afflicted the people during the past year. Joy on such an occasion is natural and appropriate ; and if the dying god appears to be the object of that fear and abhorrence which are properly due not to himself, but to the sins and misfortunes with which he is laden, this arises merely from the difficulty of distinguishing or at least of marking the distinction between the bearer and the burden. When the burden is of a baleful character, the bearer of it will be feared and shunned just as much as if he were himself instinct with those dangerous properties of which, as it happens, he is only the vehicle. Similarly we have seen that disease-laden and sin-laden boats are dreaded and shunned by East Indian peoples.[1]   Again, the view that in these popular customs the Death is a scapegoat as well as a representative of the divine spirit of vegetation derives some support from the circumstance that its expulsion is always celebrated in spring and chiefly by Slavonic peoples. For the Slavonic year began in spring ;[2] and thus, in one of its aspects, the ceremony of "carrying out Death" would be an example of the widespread

---

[1] Above, pp. 186 *sq.*, 192.
[2] H. Usener, "Italische Mythen," *Rheinisches Museum*, N. F. (1875) xxx. 194.

custom of expelling the accumulated evils of the past
year before entering on a new one.

We are now prepared to notice the use of the scapegoat in classical antiquity. Every year on the 14th
of March a man clad in skins was led in procession
through the streets of Rome, beaten with long white
rods, and driven out of the city. He was called Mamurius
Veturius,[1] that is, "the old Mars," [2] and as the ceremony
took place on the day preceding the first full moon of
the old Roman year (which began on 1st March), the
skin-clad man must have represented the Mars of the
past year, who was driven out at the beginning of a
new one. Now Mars was originally not a god of war
but of vegetation. For it was to Mars that the
Roman husbandman prayed for the prosperity of his
corn and his vines, his fruit-trees and his copses ;[3] it
was to Mars that the priestly college of the Arval
Brothers, whose business it was to sacrifice for the
growth of the crops,[4] addressed their petitions almost
exclusively ;[5] and it was to Mars, as we saw,[6] that a
horse was sacrificed in October to secure an abundant
harvest. Moreover, it was to Mars, under his title of

---

[1] Joannes Lydus, *De mensibus*, iii.
29, iv. 36. Lydus places the expulsion on the Ides of March, that is 15th
March. But this seems to be a mistake. See Usener, "Italische Mythen,"
Rheinisches Museum, xxx. 209 *sqq.*
Again, Lydus does not expressly say
that Mamurius Veturius was driven
out of the city, but he implies it
by mentioning the legend that his
mythical prototype was beaten with
rods and expelled the city. Lastly,
Lydus only mentions the name Mamurius. But the full name Mamurius
Veturius is preserved by Varro, *Ling.
Lat.* vi. 45; Festus, ed. Müller, p.
131 ; Plutarch, *Numa*, 13.

[2] Usener, *op. cit.* p. 212 *sq.*; Ros-

scher, *Apollon und Mars*, p. 27 ;
Preller, *Römische Mythologie*,[3] i. 360 ;
Vaniček, *Griechisch-lateinisches etymo-
logisches Wörterbuch*, p. 715. The
three latter scholars take Veturius
as = *annuus*, because *vetus* is etymologically equivalent to ἔτος. But, as
Usener argues, it seems quite unallow-
able to take the Greek meaning of the
word instead of the Latin.

[3] Cato, *De agri cult.* 141.

[4] Varro, *De lingua latina*, v. 85.

[5] See the song of the Arval Brothers
in *Acta Fratrum Arvalium*, ed. Henzen,
p. 26 *sq.*; Wordsworth, *Fragments
and Specimens of Early Latin*, p. 158.

[6] Above, p. 64.

"Mars of the woods" (*Mars Silvanus*) that farmers offered sacrifice for the welfare of their cattle.[1] We have already seen that cattle are commonly supposed to be under the special patronage of tree-gods.[2] Once more, the fact that the vernal month of March was dedicated to Mars seems to point him out as the deity of the sprouting vegetation. Thus the Roman custom of expelling the old Mars at the beginning of the New Year in spring is identical with the Slavonic custom of "carrying out Death," if the view here taken of the latter custom is correct. The similarity of the Roman and Slavonic customs has been already remarked by scholars, who appear, however, to have taken Mamurius Veturius and the corresponding figures in the Slavonic ceremonies to be representatives of the old year rather than of the old god of vegetation.[3] It is possible that ceremonies of this kind may have come to be thus interpreted in later times even by the people who practised them. But the personification of a period of time is too abstract an idea to be primitive. However, in the Roman, as in the Slavonic, ceremony, the representative of the god appears to have been treated not only as a deity of vegetation but also as a scapegoat. His expulsion implies this ; for there is no reason why the god of vegetation, as such, should be expelled the city. But it is otherwise if he is also a scapegoat ; it then becomes necessary to drive him beyond the boundaries, that he may carry his sorrowful burden away to other lands. And, in fact, Mamurius Veturius appears to have been

---

[1] Cato, *De agri cult.* 83.
[2] Above, vol. i. p. 70 *sqq.* p. 105 *sq.*
[3] Preller, *Römische Mythologie,*[3] i. 360 ; Rosscher, *Apollon und Mars,* p. 49 ; Usener, *op. cit.* The ceremony also closely resembles the Highland New Year ceremony described above, p. 145 *sq.*

driven away to the land of the Oscans, the enemies of Rome.[1]

The ancient Greeks were also familiar with the use of a human scapegoat. At Plutarch's native town of Chaeronea in Boeotia, there was a ceremony of this kind performed by the chief magistrate at the Town Hall, and by each householder at his own home. It was called the "expulsion of hunger." A slave was beaten with

---

[1] Propertius, v. 2, 61 *sq.*; Usener, *op. cit.* p. 210. One of the functions of the Salii or dancing priests, who during March went up and down the city dancing, singing, and clashing their swords against their shields (Livy, i. 20; Plutarch, *Numa*, 13; Dionysius Halicarn. *Antiq.* ii. 70) may have been to rout out the evils or demons from all parts of the city, as a preparation for transferring them to the scapegoat Mamurius Veturius. Similarly, as we have seen (above, p. 194 *sq.*), among the Iroquois, men in fantastic costume went about collecting the sins of the people as a preliminary to transferring them to the scapegoat dogs. We have had many examples of armed men rushing about the streets and houses to drive out demons and evils of all kinds. The blows which were showered on Mamurius Veturius seem to have been administered by the Salii (Servius on Virgil, *Aen.* vii. 188; Minucius Felix, 24, 3; Preller, *Röm. Myth.*[3] i. 360, *note* 1; Rosscher, *Apollon und Mars*, p. 49). The reason for beating the scapegoat will be explained presently. As priests of Mars, the god of agriculture, the Salii probably had also certain agricultural functions. They were named from the remarkable *leaps* which they made. Now dancing and leaping high are common sympathetic charms to make the crops grow high. See Peter, *Volksthümliches aus Oesterreichisch Schlesien*, ii. 266; E. Meier, *Deutsche Sagen, Sitten und Gebräuche aus Schwaben*, p. 499, No. 333; Reinsberg-Düringsfeld, *Fest-Kalender aus Böhmen*, p. 49; O. Knoop, *Volkssagen, etc., aus dem östlichen Hinterpommern*, p. 176, No. 197; E. Sommer, *Sagen, Märchen und Gebräuche aus Sachsen und Thüringen*, p. 148; Witzschel, *Sagen, Sitten und Gebräuche aus Thüringen*, p. 190, No. 13; Woeste, *Volksüberlieferungen in der Grafschaft Mark*, p. 56; *Bavaria*, ii. 298; *id.*, iv. Abth. ii. pp. 379, 382; Heinrich, *Agrarische Sitten u. Gebräuche unter den Sachsen Siebenbürgens*, p. 11 *sq.*; Schulenberg, *Wendische Volkssagen und Gebräuche*, p. 252; Wuttke, *Der deutsche Volksaberglaube*,[2] § 657; Jahn, *Die deutsche Opfergebräuche bei Ackerbau und Viehzucht*, p. 194 *sq.*; cp. Schott, *Walachische Mährchen*, p. 301 *sq.*; Gerard, *The Land beyond the Forest*, i. 264; Cieza de Leon, *Travels* (Hakluyt Soc. 1864), p. 413. Was it one of the functions of the Salii to dance and leap on the fields at the spring or autumn sowing, or at both? The dancing processions of the Salii took place in October as well as in March (Marquardt, *Sacralwesen*,[2] p. 436 *sq.*), and the Romans sowed both in spring and autumn (Columella, ii. 9, 6 *sq*). In their song the Salii mentioned Saturnus or Saeturnus the god of sowing (Festus, p. 325, ed. Müller. *Saeturnus* is an emendation of Ritschl's. See Wordsworth, *Fragments and Specimens of Early Latin*, p. 405). The weapons borne by the Salii, while effective against demons in general, may have been especially directed against the demons who steal the seed-corn or the ripe grain. Compare the Khond and Hindoo Koosh customs described above, p. 173. In Western Africa the field labours of tilling and sowing are sometimes accompanied by dances of

rods of the *agnus castus*, and turned out of doors with the words, "Out with hunger, and in with wealth and health." When Plutarch held the office of chief magistrate of his native town he performed this ceremony at the Town Hall, and he has recorded the discussion to which the custom afterwards gave rise.[1] The ceremony closely resembles the Japanese, Hindoo, and Highland customs already described.[2]

armed men on the field. See Labat, *Voyage du Chevalier des Marchais en Guinée, Isles voisines, et à Cayenne*, ii. p. 99 of the Paris ed., p. 80 of the Amsterdam ed. ; Olivier de Sanderval, *De l'Atlantique au Niger par le Foulah-Djallon* (Paris, 1883), p. 230. In Calicut (Southern India) " they plough the land with oxen as we do, and when they sow the rice in the field they have all the instruments of the city continually sounding and making merry. They also have ten or twelve men clothed like devils, and these unite in making great rejoicing with the players on the instruments, in order that the devil may make that rice very productive." Varthema, *Travels* (Hakluyt Soc. 1863), p. 166 *sq.* The resemblance of the Salii to the sword-dancers of northern Europe has been pointed out by K. Müllenhoff, "Ueber den Schwerttanz," in *Festgaben für Gustav Homeyer* (Berlin, 1871). In England the Morris Dancers who accompanied the procession of the plough through the streets on Plough Monday (the first Monday after Twelfth Day) sometimes wore swords (Brand, *Popular Antiquities*, i. 505, Bohn's ed.), and sometimes they " wore small bunches of corn in their hats, from which the wheat was soon shaken out by the ungainly jumping which they called dancing. . . . Bessy rattled his box and danced so high that he showed his worsted stockings and corduroy breeches." Chambers, *Book of Days*, i. 94. It is to be observed that in the "Lord of Misrule," who reigned from Christmas till Twelfth Night (see Brand, *Popular Antiquities*, i. 497 *sqq.*), we have a clear trace of

one of those periods of general licence and suspension of ordinary government which so commonly occur at the end of the old year or beginning of the new one in connection with a general expulsion of evils. The fact that this period of licence immediately preceded the procession of the Morris Dancers on Plough Monday seems to indicate that the functions of these dancers were like those which I have attributed to the Salii. But the parallel cannot be drawn out here. Cp. meantime Dyer, *British Popular Customs*, pp. 31, 39. The Salii were said to have been founded by *Morrius*, King of Veii (Servius on Virgil, *Aen.* viii. 285). *Morrius* seems to be etymologically the same with *Mamurius* and *Mars* (Usener, *Italische Mythen*, p. 213). Can the English *Morris* (in *Morris* dancers) be the same? Analogy suggests that at Rome the Saturnalia, which fell in December when the Roman year began in January, may have been celebrated in February when the Roman year began in March. Thus at Rome, as in so many places, the public expulsion of evils at the New Year would be preceded by a period of general licence, such as the Saturnalia was. A trace of the former celebration of the Saturnalia in February or the beginning of March may perhaps be seen in the *Matronalia*, celebrated on 1st March, at which mistresses feasted their slaves, just as masters feasted theirs at the Saturnalia. Macrobius, *Saturn.* i. 12, 7 ; Solinus, i. 35, p. 13, ed. Mommsen ; Joannes Lydus, *De mensibus*, iii. 15.

[1] Plutarch, *Quaest. Conviv.* vi. 8.
[2] See above, pp. 176, 194.

But in civilised Greece the custom of the scapegoat took darker forms than the innocent rite over which the amiable and pious Plutarch presided. Whenever Marseilles, one of the busiest and most brilliant of Greek colonies, was ravaged by a plague, a man of the poorer classes used to offer himself as a scapegoat. For a whole year he was maintained at the public expense, being fed on choice and pure food. At the expiry of the year he was dressed in sacred garments, decked with holy branches, and led through the whole city, while prayers were uttered that all the evils of the people might fall on his head. He was then cast out of the city.[1] The Athenians regularly maintained a number of degraded and useless beings at the public expense; and when any calamity, such as plague, drought, or famine befell the city, they sacrificed two of these outcasts as scapegoats. One of the victims was sacrificed for the men and the other for the women. The former wore round his neck a string of black, the latter a string of white figs. Sometimes, it seems, the victim slain on behalf of the women was a woman. They were led about the city and then sacrificed, apparently by being stoned to death outside the city.[2] But such sacrifices were not confined to extraordinary occasions of public calamity; it appears that every year, at the festival of the Thargelia in May, two victims, one for the men and one for the women, were led out of Athens and stoned to death.[3]

---

[1] Servius on Virgil, *Aen.* iii. 57, from Petronius.

[2] Helladius, in Photius, *Bibliotheca*, p. 534 A, ed. Bekker; Schol. on Aristophanes, *Frogs*, 734, and on *Knights*, 1136; Hesychius, *s.v.* φαρμακοί; cp. Suidas, *s.vv.* κάθαρμα, φαρμακός, and φαρμακούς; Lysias, *Orat.* vi. 53.

That they were stoned is an inference from Harpocration. See next note.

[3] Harpocration, *s.v.* φαρμακός, who says δύο ἄνδρας Ἀθήνησιν ἐξῆγον καθάρσια ἐσομένους τῆς πόλεως ἐν τοῖς Θαργηλίοις, ἕνα μὲν ὑπὲρ τῶν ἀνδρῶν, ἕνα δὲ ὑπὲρ τῶν γυναικῶν. He does not expressly state that they were put to

From the Lover's Leap, a white bluff at the southern end of their island, the Leucadians used annually to hurl a criminal into the sea as a scapegoat. But to lighten his fall they fastened live birds and feathers to him, and a flotilla of small boats waited below to catch him and convey him beyond the boundary.[1] Doubtless these humane precautions were a mitigation of an earlier custom of flinging the scapegoat into the sea to drown. The custom of the scapegoat as practised by the Greeks of Asia Minor in the sixth century B.C. was as follows. When a city suffered from plague, famine, or other public calamity, an ugly or deformed person was chosen to take upon himself all the evils by which the city was afflicted. He was brought to a suitable place where dried figs, a barley loaf, and cheese were put into his hand. These he ate. Then he was beaten seven times upon his genital organs with squills and branches of the wild fig and other wild trees. Afterwards he was burned on a pyre constructed of the wood of forest trees ; and his ashes were cast into the sea.[2] A similar custom appears to have been annually celebrated by the Asiatic Greeks at the harvest festival of the Thargelia.[3]

In the ritual just described the beating of the victim with squills, branches of the wild fig, etc., cannot have been intended to aggravate his sufferings, otherwise any stick would have been good enough to

death ; but as he says that the ceremony was an imitation of the execution of a mythical Pharmacus who was stoned to death, we may infer that the victims were killed by being stoned. Suidas (*sv. φάρμακος*) copies Harpocration.

[1] Strabo, x. 2, 9. I do not know what authority Wordsworth (*Greece, Pictorial, Historical, and Descriptive,* p. 354) has for saying that the priests of Apollo, whose temple stood near

the edge of the cliff, sometimes flung themselves down in this way.

[2] Tzetzes, *Chiliades,* v. 726-761. Tzetzes's authority is the satyrical poet Hipponax.

[3] This may be inferred from the verse of Hipponax, quoted by Athenaeus, 370 B, where for φαρμάκου we should perhaps read φαρμακοῦ with Schneidewin (*Poetae lyr. Gr.*[3] ed. Bergk, ii. 763).

beat him with. The true meaning of this part of the ceremony has been explained by W. Mannhardt.[1] He points out that the ancients attributed to squills a magical power of averting evil influences, and accordingly hung them up at the doors of their houses and made use of them in purificatory rites.[2] Hence the Arcadian custom of beating the image of Pan with squills at a festival or whenever the hunters returned empty-handed,[3] must have been meant, not to punish the god, but to purify him from the harmful influences which were impeding him in the exercise of his divine functions as a god who should supply the hunter with game. Similarly the object of beating the human scapegoat on the genital organs with squills, etc., must have been to release his reproductive energies from any restraint or spell under which they might be laid by demoniacal or other malignant agency ; and as the Thargelia at which he was annually sacrificed was an early harvest festival,[4] we must recognise in him a representative of the creative and fertilising god of vegetation. The representative of the god was annually slain for the purpose I have indicated, that of maintaining the divine life in perpetual vigour, untainted by the weakness of age ; and before he was put to death it was not unnatural to stimulate his reproductive powers in order that these might be transmitted in full activity to his successor, the new god or new embodiment of the old god, who was doubtless supposed immediately to take the place of

---

[1] See his *Mytholog. Forschungen*, p. 113 *sqq.*, especially 123 *sq.* 133.

[2] Pliny, *Nat. Hist.* xx. 101 ; Dioscorides, *De mat. med.* ii. 202 ; Lucian, *Necyom.* 7 ; *id.*, *Alexander*, 47 ; Theophrastus, *Superstitious Man.*

[3] Theocritus, vii. 106 *sqq.* with the scholiast.

[4] Cp. Aug. Mommsen, *Heortologie*, 414 *sqq.*; W. Mannhardt, *A. W. F.* p. 215.

the one slain.[1] Similar reasoning would lead to a similar treatment of the scapegoat on special occasions, such as drought or famine.   If the crops did not answer to the expectation of the husbandman, this would be attributed to some failure in the generative powers of the god whose function it was to produce the fruits of the earth.   It might be thought he was under a spell or was growing old and feeble.   Accordingly he was slain in the person of his representative, with all the ceremonies already described, in order that, born young again, he might infuse his own youthful vigour into the stagnant energies of nature. On the same principle we can understand why Mamurius Veturius was beaten with rods, why the slave at the Chaeronean ceremony was beaten with the *agnus castus* (a tree to which magical properties were ascribed),[2] why the effigy of Death in north Europe is assailed with sticks and stones, and why at Babylon the criminal who played the god was scourged before he was crucified.   The purpose of the scourging was not to intensify the agony of the divine sufferer, but on the contrary to dispel any malignant influences by which at the supreme moment he might conceivably be beset.

The interpretation here given to the custom of beating the human scapegoat with certain plants is supported by many analogies. With the same intention some of the Brazilian Indians beat themselves on the genital organs with an aquatic plant, the white *aninga*, three days before or after the new

---

[1] At certain sacrifices in Yucatan blood was drawn from the genitals of a human victim and smeared on the face of the idol. De Landa, *Relation des choses de Yucatan*, ed. Brasseur de Bourbourg (Paris, 1864) p. 167. Was the original intention of this rite to transfuse into the god a fresh supply of reproductive energy?

[2] Aelian, *Nat. Anim.* ix. 26.

moon.[1] We have already had examples of the custom
of beating sick people with the leaves of certain plants
or with branches in order to rid them of the noxious
influences.[2] At the autumn festival in Peru people
used to strike each other with torches saying, " Let all
harm go away."[3] Indians of the Quixos, in South
America, before they set out on a long hunting
expedition, cause their wives to whip them with
nettles, believing that this renders them fleeter and
helps them to overtake the peccaries. They resort to
the same proceeding as a cure for sickness.[4] At Mowat
in New Guinea small boys are beaten lightly with
sticks during December "to make them grow strong
and hardy."[5] In Central Europe a similar custom is
very commonly observed in spring. On the 1st of
March the Albanians strike men and beasts with
cornel branches, believing that this is very good for
their health.[6] On Good Friday and the two previous
days people in Croatia and Slavonia take rods with
them to church, and when the service is over they beat
each other "fresh and healthy."[7] In some parts of
Russia people returning from the church on Palm
Sunday beat the children and servants who have stayed
at home with palm branches, saying, " Sickness into
the forest, health into the bones."[8] In Germany the
custom is widely known as *Schmeckostern*, being
observed at Eastertide. People beat each other,

[1] De Santa-Anna Nery, *Folk-lore Brésilien* (Paris, 1889) p. 253.

[2] Above, pp. 148 *sq.* 187. Compare Plutarch, *Parallela*, 35, where a woman is represented as going from house to house striking sick people with a hammer and bidding them be whole.

[3] Acosta, *History of the Indies*, ii. 375 (Hakluyt Soc.) See above, p. 169.

[4] Osculati, *Esplorazione delle regioni equatoriali lungo il Napo ed il fiume delle Amazzoni* (Milan, 1854), p. 118.

[5] Ed. Beardmore, *Anthropological Notes collected at Mowat, Dandai, New Guinea* (1888) (in manuscript).

[6] Hahn, *Albanesische Studien*, i. 155.

[7] F. S. Krauss, *Kroatien und Slavonien* (Vienna, 1889), p. 108.

[8] W. Mannhardt, *B. K.* p. 257.

especially with fresh green twigs of the birch. The beating is supposed to bring good luck; the person beaten will, it is believed, be free of vermin during the summer, or will have no pains in his back or his legs for a year.[1]

If the view here taken of the Greek scapegoat is correct, it obviates an objection which might otherwise be brought against the main argument of this chapter. To the theory that the priest of Nemi was slain as a representative of the spirit of the grove, it might have been objected that such a custom has no analogy in classical antiquity. But reasons have now been given for believing that the human being periodically and occasionally slain by the Asiatic Greeks was regularly treated as an embodiment of a divinity. Probably the persons whom the Athenians kept to be sacrificed were similarly treated as divine. That they were social outcasts did not matter. On the primitive view a man is not chosen to be the mouth-piece or embodiment of a god on account of his high moral qualities or social standing. The divine afflatus descends equally on the good and the bad, the lofty and the lowly. If then the civilised Greeks of Asia and Athens habitually sacrificed men whom they regarded as incarnate gods, there can be no inherent improbability in the supposition that at the dawn of history a similar custom was observed by the semi-barbarous Latins in the Arician Grove.

---

[1] W. Mannhardt, *B. K.* p. 258-263. See his whole discussion of such customs, pp. 251-303, and *Myth. Forsch.* pp. 113-153.

§ 16.—*Killing the god in Mexico*

But the religion of ancient Mexico, as it was found
and described by the Spanish conquerors in the sixteenth century, offers perhaps the closest parallels to
the rule of the Arician priesthood, as I conceive that
rule to have been originally observed. Certainly
nowhere does the custom of killing the human representative of a god appear to have been carried out
so systematically and on so extensive a scale as in
Mexico. "They tooke a captive," says Acosta,
"such as they thought good; and afore they did
sacrifice him unto their idolls, they gave him the
name of the idoll, to whom hee should be sacrificed,
and apparelled him with the same ornaments like
their idoll, saying that he did represent the same idoll.
And during the time that this representation lasted,
which was for a yeere in some feasts, in others six
moneths, and in others lesse, they reverenced and
worshipped him in the same maner as the proper
idoll; and in the meane time he did eate, drincke, and
was merry. When hee went through the streetes the
people came forth to worship him, and every one
brought him an almes, with children and sicke folkes,
that he might cure them, and bless them, suffering him
to doe all things at his pleasure, onely hee was accompanied with tenne or twelve men lest he should flie.
And he (to the end he might be reverenced as he
passed) sometimes sounded upon a small flute, that
the people might prepare to worship him. The feast
being come, and hee growne fatte, they killed him,
opened him, and eat him, making a solempne sacrifice

Sacrifice to a Mexican god.

Aztec Mexican sacrifice in the early 1800s.

of him."[1]   For example, at the annual festival of the
great god Tezcatlipoca, which fell about Easter or a
few days later, a young man was chosen to be the
living image of Tezcatlipoca for a whole year.   He
had to be of unblemished body, and he was carefully
trained to sustain his lofty role with becoming grace
and dignity.   During the year he was lapped in luxury,
and the king himself took care that the future victim
was apparelled in gorgeous attire, "for already he
esteemed him as a god."   Attended by eight pages
clad in the royal livery, the young man roamed the
streets of the capital day and night at his pleasure,
carrying flowers and playing the flute.   All who
saw him fell on their knees before him and adored
him, and he graciously acknowledged their homage.
Twenty days before the festival at which he was
to be sacrificed, four damsels, delicately nurtured,
and bearing the names of four goddesses, were given
him to be his brides.   For five days before the
sacrifice divine honours were showered on him more
abundantly than ever.   The king remained in his
palace, while the whole court went after the destined
victim.   Everywhere there were solemn banquets
and balls.   On the last day the young man, still
attended by his pages, was ferried across the lake in
a covered barge to a small and lonely temple, which,
like the Mexican temples in general, rose in the form
of a pyramid.   As he ascended the stairs of the temple
he broke at every step one of the flutes on which he
had played in the days of his glory.   On reaching
the summit he was seized and held down on a block of
stone, while a priest cut open his breast with a stone
knife, and plucking out his heart, offered it to the sun.

---

[1] Acosta, *History of the Indies*, ii. 323 (Hakluyt Soc. 1880).

His head was hung among the skulls of previous victims, and his legs and arms were cooked and prepared for the table of the lords. His place was immediately filled up by another young man, who for a year was treated with the same profound respect, and at the end of it shared the same fate.[1]

The idea that the god thus slain in the person of his representative comes to life again immediately, was graphically represented in the Mexican ritual by skinning the slain man-god and clothing in his skin a living man, who thus became the new representative of the godhead. Thus at an annual festival a woman was sacrificed who represented Toci or the Mother of the Gods. She was dressed with the ornaments, and bore the name of the goddess, whose living image she was believed to be. After being feasted and diverted with sham fights for several days, she was taken at midnight to the summit of a temple, and beheaded on the shoulders of a man. The body was immediately flayed, and one of the priests, clothing himself in the skin, became the representative of the goddess Toci. The skin of the woman's thigh was removed separately, and a young man who represented the god Cinteotl, the son of the goddess Toci, wrapt it round his face like a mask. Various ceremonies then followed, in which the two men, clad in the woman's skin, played the parts respectively of the god and goddess.[2] Again, at the annual festival of the

---

[1] Sahagun, *Histoire des choses de la Nouvelle Espagne* (Paris, 1880), pp. 61 *sq.*, 96-99, 103; Acosta, *History of the Indies*, ii. 350 *sq.*; Clavigero, *History of Mexico*, trans. by Cullen, i. 300; Bancroft, *Native Races of the Pacific States*, ii. 319 *sq.* For other Mexican instances of persons repre-senting deities and slain in that character, see Sahagun, pp. 75, 116 *sq.*, 123, 158 *sq.*, 164 *sq.*, 585 *sqq.*, 589; Acosta, ii. 384 *sqq.*; Clavigero, i. 312; Bancroft, ii. 325 *sqq.*, 337 *sq.*

[2] Sahagun, pp. 18 *sq.*, 68 *sq.*, 133-139; Bancroft, iii. 353-359.

god Totec, a number of captives having been killed and skinned, a priest clothed himself in one of their skins, and thus became the image of the god Totec. Then wearing the ornaments of the god—a crown of feathers, golden necklaces and ear-rings, scarlet shoes, etc.—he was enthroned, and received offerings of the first fruits and first flowers of the season, together with bunches of the maize which had been kept for seed.[1] Every fourth year the Quauhtitlans offered sacrifices in honour of the god of fire. On the eve of the festival they sacrificed two slaves, skinned them, and took out their thigh bones. Next day two priests clothed themselves in the skins, took the bones in their hands, and with solemn steps and dismal howlings descended the stairs of the temple. The people, who were assembled in crowds below, called out, " Behold, there come our gods."[2]

Thus it appears that human sacrifices of the sort I suppose to have prevailed at Aricia were, as a matter of fact, systematically offered on a large scale by a people whose level of culture was probably not inferior, if indeed it was not distinctly superior, to that occupied by the Italian races at the early period to which the origin of the Arician priesthood must be referred. The positive and indubitable evidence of the prevalence of such sacrifices in one part of the world may reasonably be allowed to strengthen the probability of their prevalence in places for which the evidence is less full and trustworthy. Taken all together, the evidence affords a fair presumption that the custom of killing men whom their worshippers

---

[1] Sahagun, p. 584 *sq.* For this festival see also *id.* pp. 37 *sq.* 58 *sq.* 60, 87 *sqq.* 93 ; Clavigero, i. 297 ; Bancroft, ii. 306 *sqq.*
[2] Clavigero, i. 283.

regard as divine has prevailed in many parts of the
world. Whether the general explanation which I
have offered of that custom is adequate, and whether
the rule that the priest of Aricia had to die a violent
death is, as I have tried to show, a particular instance
of the general custom, are questions which I must now
leave to the judgment of the reader.

CHAPTER IV

THE GOLDEN BOUGH

"Und grün des Lebens goldner Baum."—FAUST.

§ 1.—*Between heaven and earth*

AT the outset of this book two questions were proposed
for answer; Why had the priest of Nemi (Aricia) to
slay his predecessor? And why, before doing so,
had he to pluck the Golden Bough? Of these two
questions the first has now been answered. The
priest of Nemi, if I am right, embodied in himself
the spirit, primarily, of the woods and, secondarily, of
vegetable life in general. Hence, according as he
was well or ill, the woods, the flowers, and the fields
were believed to flourish or fade; and if he were to
die of sickness or old age, the plant world, it was
supposed, would simultaneously perish. Therefore
it was necessary that this priest of the woodlands, this
sylvan deity incarnate in a man, should be put to
death while he was still in the full bloom of his
divine manhood, in order that his sacred life, transmitted in unabated force to his successor, might renew
its youth, and thus by successive transmissions through
a perpetual line of vigorous incarnations might remain
eternally fresh and young, a pledge and security that

the buds and blossoms of spring, the verdure of summer woods, and the mellow glories of autumn would never fail.

But we have still to ask, What was the Golden Bough? and why had each candidate for the Arician priesthood to pluck it before he could slay the priest? These questions I will now try to answer.

It will be well to begin by noticing two of those rules or taboos by which, as we have seen, the life of divine kings or priests is regulated. The first of the rules to which I desire to call the reader's attention is that the divine personage may not touch the ground with his foot. This rule was observed by the Mikado of Japan and by the supreme pontiff of the Zapotecs in Mexico. The latter "profaned his sanctity if he so much as touched the ground with his foot." [1] For the Mikado to touch the ground with his foot was a shameful degradation; indeed, in the sixteenth century, it was enough to deprive him of his office. Outside his palace he was carried on men's shoulders; within it he walked on exquisitely wrought mats. [2] The king and queen of Tahiti might not touch the ground anywhere but within their hereditary domains; for the ground on which they trod became sacred. In travelling from place to place they were carried on the shoulders of sacred men. They were always accompanied by several pairs of these sacred men; and when it became necessary to change their bearers, the king and queen vaulted on to the shoulders of their new bearers without letting their feet touch the

---

[1] Bancroft, *Native Races of the Pacific States*, ii. 142.

[2] *Memorials of Japan* (Hakluyt Society, 1850), pp. 14, 141; Varenius, *Descriptio regni Japoniae*, p. 11; Caron, "Account of Japan," in Pinkerton's *Voyages and Travels*, vii. 613; Kaempfer, "History of Japan," in *id.*, vii. 716.

ground.[1]   It was an evil omen if the king of Dosuma touched the ground, and he had to perform an expiatory ceremony.[2]   The king of Persia was never seen on foot outside his palace.[3]

The second rule to be here noted is that the sun may not shine upon the divine person.   This rule was observed both by the Mikado and by the pontiff of the Zapotecs.   The latter "was looked upon as a god whom the earth was not worthy to hold, nor the sun to shine upon."[4]   The Japanese would not allow that the Mikado "should expose his sacred person to the open air, and the sun is not thought worthy to shine on his head."[5] The heir to the throne of Bogota in Colombia, South America, had to undergo a severe training from the age of sixteen; he lived in complete retirement in a temple, where he might not see the sun nor eat salt nor converse with a woman.[6]   The heir to the kingdom of Sogamoso in Colombia, before succeeding to the crown, had to fast for seven years in the temple, being shut up in the dark and not allowed to see the sun or light.[7]   The prince who was to become Inca of Peru had to fast for a month without seeing light.[8]

Now it is remarkable that these two rules—not to touch the ground and not to see the sun—are observed either separately or conjointly by girls at puberty in

---

[1] Ellis, *Polynesian Researches*, iii. 102 *sq.* ed. 1836; James Wilson, *Missionary Voyage to the Southern Pacific Ocean*, p. 329.

[2] Bastian, *Der Mensch in der Geschichte*, iii. 81.

[3] Athenaeus, 514 C.

[4] Bancroft, *l.c.*

[5] Kaempfer, "History of Japan," in Pinkerton's *Voyages and Travels*, vii. 717; Caron, "Account of Japan," *id.* vii. 613; Varenius, *Descriptio regni Japoniae*, p. 11, "*Radiis solis caput nunquam illustrabatur: in apertum aërem non procedebat.*"

[6] Waitz, *Anthropologie der Naturvölker*, iv. 359.

[7] Alonzo de Zurita, "Rapport sur les differentes classes de chefs de la Nouvelle-Espagne," p. 30, in Ternaux-Compans's *Voyages, Relations et Mémoires originaux* (Paris, 1840); Waitz, *l.c.*; Bastian, *Die Culturländer des alten Amerika*, ii. 204.

[8] Cieza de Leon, *Second Part of the Chronicle of Peru* (Hakluyt Soc. 1883), p. 18.

many parts of the world. Thus amongst the negroes of Loango girls at puberty are confined in separate huts, and they may not touch the ground with any part of their bare body.[1] Amongst the Zulus and kindred tribes of South Africa, when the first signs of puberty show themselves "while a girl is walking, gathering wood, or working in the field, she runs to the river and hides herself among the reeds for the day so as not to be seen by men. She covers her head carefully with her blanket that the sun may not shine on it and shrivel her up into a withered skeleton, assured result from exposure to the sun's beams. After dark she returns to her home and is secluded" in a hut for some time.[2]

In New Ireland girls are confined for four or five years in small cages, being kept in the dark and not allowed to set foot on the ground. The custom has been thus described by an eye-witness. "I heard from a teacher about some strange custom connected with some of the young girls here, so I asked the chief to take me to the house where they were. The house was about twenty-five feet in length, and stood in a reed and bamboo enclosure, across the entrance to which a bundle of dried grass was suspended to show that it was strictly '*tabu*.' Inside the house were three conical structures about seven or eight feet in height, and about ten or twelve feet in circumference at the bottom, and for about four feet from the ground, at which point they tapered off to a point at the top. These cages were made of the broad leaves of the pandanus-tree, sewn quite close

[1] Pechuel-Loesche, "Indiscretes aus Loango," *Zeitschrift für Ethnologie*, x. (1878) 23.

[2] Rev. James Macdonald (Reay Free Manse, Caithness), *Manners, Customs, Superstitions, and Religions of South African Tribes* (in manuscript).

together so that no light, and little or no air could
enter.   On one side of each is an opening which is
closed by a double door of plaited cocoa-nut tree and
pandanus-tree leaves.   About three feet from the
ground there is a stage of bamboos which forms the
floor.   In each of these cages we were told there was
a young woman confined, each of whom had to
remain for at least four or five years, without ever
being allowed to go outside the house.   I could
scarcely credit the story when I heard it ; the whole
thing seemed too horrible to be true.   I spoke to the
chief, and told him that I wished to see the inside of
the cages, and also to see the girls that I might make
them a present of a few beads.   He told me that it was
' _tabu_,' forbidden for any men but their own relations
to look at them ; but I suppose the promised beads
acted as an inducement, and so he sent away for some
old lady who had charge, and who alone is allowed to
open the doors. . . . She had to undo the door when
the chief told her to do so, and then the girls peeped
out at us, and, when told to do so, they held out their
hands for the beads.   I, however, purposely sat at some
distance away and merely held out the beads to them,
as I wished to draw them quite outside, that I might
inspect the inside of the cages.   This desire of mine
gave rise to another difficulty, as these girls were not
allowed to put their feet to the ground all the time
they were confined in these places.   However, they
wished to get the beads, and so the old lady had to go
outside and collect a lot of pieces of wood and bamboo,
which she placed on the ground, and then going to one
of the girls, she helped her down and held her hand as
she stepped from one piece of wood to another until
she came near enough to get the beads I held out to

her.　I then went to inspect the inside of the cage out of which she had come, but could scarcely put my head inside of it, the atmosphere was so hot and stifling. It was clean and contained nothing but a few short lengths of bamboo for holding water.　There was only room for the girl to sit or lie down in a crouched position on the bamboo platform, and when the doors are shut it must be nearly or quite dark inside.　The girls are never allowed to come out except once a day to bathe in a dish or wooden bowl placed close to each cage.　They say that they perspire profusely.　They are placed in these stifling cages when quite young, and must remain there until they are young women, when they are taken out and have each a great marriage feast provided for them."[1]

In some parts of New Guinea "daughters of chiefs, when they are about twelve or thirteen years of age, are kept indoors for two or three years, never being allowed, under any pretence, to descend from the house, and the house is so shaded that the sun cannot

---

[1] The Rev. G. Brown, quoted by the Rev. B. Danks, "Marriage Customs of the New Britain Group," *Journ. Anthrop. Institute*, xviii. 284 *sq.*; cp. Rev. G. Brown, "Notes on the Duke of York Group, New Britain, and New Ireland," *Journ. Royal Geogr. Soc.* xlvii. (1877) p. 142 *sq.* Powell's description of the New Ireland custom is similar (*Wanderings in a Wild Country*, p. 249).　According to him the girls wear wreaths of scented herbs round the waist and neck; an old woman or a little child occupies the lower floor of the cage : and the confinement lasts only a month.　Probably the long period mentioned by Mr. Brown is that prescribed for chiefs' daughters.　Poor people could not afford to keep their children so long idle.　This distinction is sometimes expressly stated ; for example, among the Goajiras of Colombia rich people keep their daughters shut up in separate huts at puberty for periods varying from one to four years, but poor people cannot afford to do so for more than a fortnight or a month. F. A. Simons, "An exploration of the Goajira Peninsula," *Proceed. Royal Geogr. Soc.* N.S. vii. (1885) p. 791. In Fiji, brides who were being tattooed were kept from the sun.　Williams, *Fiji and the Fijians*, i. 170.　This was perhaps a modification of the Melanesian custom of secluding girls at puberty.　The reason mentioned by Mr. Williams, "to improve her complexion," can hardly have been the original one.

shine on them."[1]   Among the Ot Danoms of Borneo
girls at the age of eight or ten years are shut up in a
little room or cell of the house and cut off from all
intercourse with the world for a long time.   The cell,
like the rest of the house, is raised on piles above the
ground, and is lit by a single small window opening on
a lonely place, so that the girl is in almost total darkness.   She may not leave the room on any pretext
whatever, not even for the most necessary purposes.
None of her family may see her all the time she is shut
up, but a single slave woman is appointed to wait on
her.   During her lonely confinement, which often lasts
seven years, the girl occupies herself in weaving mats
or with other handiwork.   Her bodily growth is
stunted by the long want of exercise, and when, on
attaining womanhood, she is brought out, her complexion is pale and wax-like.   She is now shown the
sun, the earth, the water, the trees, and the flowers, as
if she were newly born.   Then a great feast is made,
a slave is killed, and the girl is smeared with his
blood.[2]   In Ceram girls at puberty were formerly shut
up by themselves in a hut which was kept dark.[3]

Amongst the Aht Indians of Vancouver Island,
when girls reach puberty they are placed in a sort
of gallery in the house "and are there surrounded
completely with mats, so that neither the sun nor any
fire can be seen.   In this cage they remain for several
days.   Water is given them, but no food.   The
longer a girl remains in this retirement the greater

---

[1] Chalmers and Gill, *Work and Adventure in New Guinea*, p. 159.

[2] Schwaner, *Borneo, Beschrijving van het stroomgebied van den Barito*, etc. ii. 77 *sq.*; Zimmerman, *Die Inseln des Indischen und Stillen Meeres*, ii.

632 *sq.*; Otto Finsch, *Neu Guinea und seine Bewohner*, p. 116.

[3] Riedel, *De sluik-en kroesharige rassen tusschen Selebes en Papua*, p. 138.

honour is it to the parents; but she is disgraced for life if it is known that she has seen fire or the sun during this initiatory ordeal."[1] Amongst the Thlinkeet or Kolosh Indians of Alaska, when a girl shows signs of womanhood she is shut up in a little hut or cage, which is completely blocked up with the exception of a small air-hole. In this dark and filthy abode she had formerly to remain a year, without fire, exercise, or associates. Her food was put in at the small window; she had to drink out of the wing-bone of a white-headed eagle. The time has now been reduced, at least in some places, to six months. The girl has to wear a sort of hat with long flaps, that her gaze may not pollute the sky; for she is thought unfit for the sun to shine upon.[2] Amongst the Koniags, an Esquimaux people of Alaska, girls at puberty were placed in small huts in which they had to remain on their hands and knees for six months; then the hut was enlarged enough to let them kneel upright, and they had to remain in this posture for six months more.[3]

When symptoms of puberty appeared on a girl for the first time, the Indians of the Rio de la Plata

---

[1] Sproat, *Scenes and Studies of Savage Life*, p. 93 *sq.*

[2] Erman, "Ethnographische Wahrnehmungen u. Erfahrungen an den Küsten des Berings-Meeres," *Zeitschrift f. Ethnologie*, ii. 318 *sq.*; Langsdorff, *Reise um die Welt*, ii. 114 *sq.*; Holmberg, "Ethnogr. Skizzen über die Völker d. russischen Amerika," *Acta Societatis Scientiarum Fennicae*, iv. (1856) p. 320 *sq.*; Bancroft, *Native Races of the Pacific States*, i. 110 *sq.*; Krause, *Die Tlinkit-Indianer*, p. 217 *sq.*; Rev. Sheldon Jackson, "Alaska and its Inhabitants," *American Antiquarian*, ii. 111 *sq.*; W. M. Grant, in *Journal of American Folk-lore*, i. 169. For caps, hoods, and veils worn by girls at such seasons, compare G. H. Loskiel, *History of the Mission of the United Brethren among the Indians*, i. 56; *Journal Anthrop. Institute*, vii. 206; G. M. Dawson, *Report of the Queen Charlotte Islands*, 1878 (Geological Survey of Canada), p. 130 B; Petitot, *Monographie des Dènè-Dindjié*, pp. 72, 75; *id.*, *Traditions indiennes du Canada Nord-Ouest*, p. 258.

[3] Holmberg, *op. cit.* p. 401; Bancroft, i. 82; Petroff, *Report on the Population*, etc. *of Alaska*, p. 143.

used to sew her up in her hammock as if she were dead, leaving only a small hole for her mouth to allow her to breathe. In this state she continued so long as the symptoms lasted.[1] In similar circumstances the Chiriguanos of Bolivia hoisted the girl in her hammock to the roof, where she stayed for a month; the second month the hammock was let half way down from the roof; and in the third month old women, armed with sticks, entered the hut and ran about striking everything they met, saying they were hunting the snake that had wounded the girl. This they did till one of the women gave out that she had killed the snake.[2] Amongst some of the Brazilian Indians, when a girl attained to puberty, her hair was burned or shaved off close to the head. Then she was placed on a flat stone and cut with the tooth of an animal from the shoulders all down the back, till she ran with blood. Then the ashes of a wild gourd were rubbed into the wounds; the girl was bound hand and foot, and hung in a hammock, being enveloped in it so closely that no one could see her. Here she had to stay for three days without eating or drinking. When the three days were over, she stepped out of the hammock upon the flat stone, for her feet might not touch the ground. If she had a call of nature, a female relation took the girl on her back and carried her out, taking with her a live coal to prevent evil influences from entering the girl's body. Being replaced in her hammock she was now allowed to get some flour, boiled roots, and water, but might not taste salt or flesh. Thus she continued to the end

---

[1] Lafitau, *Moeurs des Sauvages américuains*, i. 262 *sq.*

[2] *Lettres édifiantes et curieuses*, viii.

333. On the Chiriguanos see Von Martius, *Zur Ethnographie Amerika's zumal Brasiliens*, p. 212 *sqq.*

of the first monthly period, at the expiry of which she was gashed on the breast and belly as well as all down the back. During the second month she still stayed in her hammock, but her rule of abstinence was less rigid, and she was allowed to spin. The third month she was blackened with a certain pigment and began to go about as usual.[1]

Amongst the Macusis of British Guiana, when a girl shows the first signs of puberty, she is hung in a hammock at the highest point of the hut. For the first few days she may not leave the hammock by day, but at night she must come down, light a fire, and spend the night beside it, else she would break out in sores on her neck, throat, etc. So long as the symptoms are at their height, she must fast rigorously. When they have abated, she may come down and take up her abode in a little compartment that is made for her in the darkest corner of the hut. In the morning she may cook her food, but it must be at a separate fire and in a vessel of her own. In about ten days the magician comes and undoes the spell by muttering charms and breathing on her and on the more valuable of the things with which she has come in contact. The pots and drinking vessels which she used are broken and the fragments buried. After her first bath, the girl must submit to be beaten by her mother with thin rods without uttering a cry. At the end of the second period she is again beaten, but not afterwards. She is now " clean," and can mix again with people.[2] Other Indians of Guiana, after keeping the girl in her

---

[1] Thevet, *Cosmographie Universelle* (Paris, 1575) ii. 946 B *sq.* ; Lafitau, *op. cit.* i. 290 *sqq.*

[2] Schomburgk, *Reisen in Britisch Guiana*, ii. 315 *sq.* ; Martius, *Zur Ethnographie Amerika's*, p. 644.

hammock at the top of the hut for a month, expose
her to certain large ants, whose bite is very painful.[1]
The custom of stinging the girl with ants or beating
her with rods is intended, we may be sure, not as a
punishment or a test of endurance, but as a purification, the object being to drive away the malignant
influences with which a girl at such times is believed
to be beset and enveloped.   Examples of purification,
both by beating and by stinging with ants, have
already come before us.[2]   Probably, beating or scourging as a religious or ceremonial rite always originated
with a similar intention.   It was meant to wipe off
and drive away a dangerous contagion (whether
personified as demoniacal or not) which was supposed to be adhering physically, though invisibly,
to the body of the sufferer.[3]   The pain inflicted on

---

[1] Labat, *Voyage du Chevalier des
Marchais en Guinée, Isles voisines, et à
Cayenne*, iv. p. 365 *sq.* (Paris ed.), p. 17
sq. (Amsterdam ed.)

[2] Above, p. 213 *sq.*, vol. i. p. 153 *sq.*

[3] This interpretation of the custom
is supported by the fact that beating
or scourging is inflicted on inanimate
objects expressly for the purpose indicated in the text.   Thus the Indians
of Costa Rica hold that there are two
kinds of ceremonial uncleanness, *nya*
and *bu-ku-rú*.   Anything that has been
connected with a death is *nya*.   But
bu-ku-rú is much more virulent.   It
can not only make one sick but kill.
"The worst *bu-ku-rú* of all is that of
a young woman in her first pregnancy.
She infects the whole neighbourhood.
Persons going from the house where
she lives carry the infection with them
to a distance, and all the deaths or
other serious misfortunes in the vicinity
are laid to her charge.   In the old
times, when the savage laws and customs
were in full force, it was not an uncommon thing for the husband of such
a woman to pay damages for casualties

thus caused by his unfortunate wife. . . .
Bu - ku - rú emanates in a variety of
ways ; arms, utensils, even houses
become affected by it after long disuse,
and before they can be used again
must be purified.   In the case of
portable objects left undisturbed for a
long time, the custom is to beat them
with a stick before touching them.   I
have seen a woman take a long walking
stick and beat a basket hanging from
the roof of a house by a cord.   On
asking what that was for, I was told
that the basket contained her treasures,
that she would probably want to take
something out the next day, and that she
was driving off the *bu-ku-rú*.   A house
long unused must be swept, and then
the person who is purifying it must
take a stick and beat not only the
movable objects, but the beds, posts,
and in short every accessible part of
the interior.   The next day it is fit for
occupation.   A place not visited for a
long time or reached for the first time
is *bu-ku-rú*.   On our return from the
ascent of Pico Blanco, nearly all the
party suffered from little calenturas,

the person beaten was no more the object of the beating than it is of a surgical operation with us ; it was a necessary accident, that was all.   In later times such customs were interpreted otherwise, and the pain, from being an accident, became the prime object of the ceremony, which was now regarded either as a test of endurance imposed upon persons at critical epochs of life, or as a mortification of the flesh well pleasing to the god.   But asceticism, under any shape or form, is never primitive.   Amongst the Uaupes of Brazil a girl at puberty is secluded in the house for a month, and allowed only a small quantity of bread and water. Then she is taken out into the midst of her relations and friends, each of whom gives her four or five blows with pieces of *sipo* (an elastic climber), till she falls senseless or dead.   If she recovers, the operation is repeated four times at intervals of six hours, and it is considered an offence to the parents not to strike hard.   Meantime, pots of meats and fish have been made ready ; the *sipos* are dipped into them and then given to the girl to lick, who is now considered a marriageable woman.[1]

When a Hindoo maiden reaches maturity she is kept in a dark room for four days, and is forbidden to see the sun.   She is regarded as unclean ; no one is

---

the result of extraordinary exposure to wet and cold and want of food.   The Indians said that the peak was especially *bu-ku-rú*, since nobody had ever been on it before."   One day Mr. Gabb took down some dusty blow-guns amid cries of *bu - ku - rú* from the Indians. Some weeks afterwards a boy died, and the Indians firmly believed that the *bu-ku-rú* of the blow-guns had killed him.   "From all the foregoing, it would seem that *bu-ku-rú* is a sort of evil spirit that takes possession of the

object, and resents being disturbed ; but I have never been able to learn from the Indians that they consider it so.   They seem to think of it as a property the objects acquires."   W. M. Gabb, *Indian Tribes and Languages of Costa Rica* (read before the American Philosophical Society, 20th August 1875), p. 504 *sq.*

[1] A. R. Wallace, *Narrative of Travels on the Amazon and Rio Negro,* p. 496.

allowed to touch her.   Her diet is restricted to boiled
rice, milk, sugar, curd, and tamarind without salt.[1]
In Cambodia a girl at puberty is put to bed under
a mosquito curtain, where she should stay a hundred
days.   Usually, however, four, five, ten, or twenty
days are thought enough ; and even this, in a hot
climate and under the close meshes of the curtain, is
sufficiently trying.[2]   According to another account, a
Cambodian maiden at puberty is said to "enter into
the shade."   During her retirement, which, according
to the rank and position of her family, may last any
time from a few days to several years, she has to
observe a number of rules, such as not to be seen by
a strange man, not to eat flesh or fish, and so on.
She goes nowhere, not even to the pagoda.   But
this state of retirement is discontinued during eclipses ;
at such times she goes forth and pays her devotions to
the monster who is supposed to cause eclipses by
catching the heavenly bodies between his teeth.[3]   The
fact that her retirement is discontinued during an
eclipse seems to show how literally the injunction is
interpreted which forbids maidens entering on
womanhood to look upon the sun.

A superstition so widely diffused as this might be
expected to leave traces in legends and folk-tales.
And it has done so.   In a modern Greek folk-tale

---

[1] Bose, *The Hindoos as they are*, p.
86. Similarly, after a Brahman boy
has been invested with the sacred
thread, he is for three days strictly
forbidden to see the sun. He may not
eat salt, and he is enjoined to sleep
either on a carpet or a deer's skin,
without a mattress or mosquito curtain.
Ib. p. 186. In Bali, boys who have
had their teeth filed, as a preliminary
to marriage, are kept shut up in a dark
room for three days.   Van Eck,
"Schetsen van het eiland Bali,"
Tijdschrift voor Nederlandsch Indië,
N. S. ix. (1880) 428 *sq.*.

[2] Moura, *Royaume du Cambodge*, i.
377.

[3] Aymonier, "Notes sur les coutumes
et croyances superstitieuses des Cambodgiens," *Cochinchine Française, Excursions et Reconnaissances*, No. 16
(Saigon, 1883), p. 193 *sq.* Cp. *id.
Notice sur le Cambodge*, p. 50.

the Fates predict that in her fifteenth year a princess must be careful not to let the sun shine on her, for if this were to happen she would be turned into a lizard.[1] A Tyrolese story tells how it was the doom of a lovely maiden to be transported into the belly of a whale if ever a sunbeam fell on her.[2] In another modern Greek tale the Sun bestows a daughter upon a childless woman on condition of taking the child back to himself when she is twelve years old. So, when the child was twelve, the mother closed the doors and windows, and stopped up all the chinks and crannies, to prevent the Sun from coming to fetch away her daughter. But she forgot to stop up the key-hole, and a sunbeam streamed through it and carried off the girl.[3] In a Sicilian story a seer foretells that a king will have a daughter who, in her fourteenth year, will conceive a child by the Sun. So, when the child was born, the king shut her up in a lonely tower which had no window, lest a sunbeam should fall on her. When she was nearly fourteen years old, it happened that her parents sent her a piece of roasted kid, in which she found a sharp bone. With this bone she scraped a hole in the wall, and a sunbeam shot through the hole and impregnated her.[4]

---

[1] B. Schmidt, *Griechische Märchen, Sagen und Volkslieder*, p. 98.

[2] Schneller, *Märchen und Sagen aus Wälschtirol*, No. 22.

[3] J. G. von Hahn, *Griechische und albanesische Märchen*, No. 41.

[4] Gonzenbach, *Sicilianische Märchen*, No. 28. The incident of the bone occurs in other folk-tales. A prince or princess is shut up for safety in a tower and makes his or her escape by scraping a hole in the wall with a bone which has been accidentally conveyed into the tower ; sometimes it is expressly said that care was taken to let the princess have no bones with her meat. Hahn, *op. cit.* No. 15 ; Gonzenbach, Nos. 26, 27 ; *Pentamerone*, No. 23. From this we should infer that it is a rule with savages not to let women handle the bones of animals during their monthly seclusions. We have already seen the great respect with which the savage treats the bones of game (see above, p. 116 *sqq.*) ; and women in their courses are specially forbidden to meddle with the hunter or fisher, as their contact or neighbourhood would spoil his sport (see below, p. 238 *sqq.*) In folk-tales the hero who uses the bone

The old Greek story of Danae, who was confined by her father in a subterranean chamber or a brazen tower, but impregnated by Zeus, who reached her in the shape of a shower of gold, perhaps belongs to the same class of tales. It has its counterpart in the legend which the Kirgis of Siberia tell of their ancestry. A certain Khan had a fair daughter, whom he kept in a dark iron house, that no man might see her. An old woman tended her; and when the girl was grown to maidenhood she asked the old woman, " Where do you go so often ? "— " My child," said the old dame, "there is a bright world. In that bright world your father and mother live, and all sorts of people live there. That is where I go." The maiden said, " Good mother, I will tell nobody, but show me that bright world." So the old woman took the girl out of the iron house. But when she saw the bright world, the girl tottered and fainted; and the eye of God fell upon her, and she conceived. Her angry father put her in a golden chest and sent her floating away (fairy gold can float in fairyland) over the wide sea.[1] The shower of gold in the Greek story, and the eye of God in the Kirgis legend, probably stand for sunlight and the sun. The idea that women may be impregnated by the sun is not uncommon in legends,[2] and there are even traces of it in marriage customs.[3]

---

is sometimes a boy; but the incident might easily be transferred from a girl to a boy after its real meaning had been forgotten. Amongst the Hare-skin Indians a girl at puberty is forbidden to break the bones of hares. Petitot, *Traditions indiennes du Canada Nord-ouest*, p. 258. On the other hand, she drinks out of a tube made of a swan's bone (Petitot, *l.c.* and *id.*, *Monographie des Dènè-Dindjié*, p. 76), and we have seen that a Thlinkeet girl in the same circumstances used to drink out of the wing-bone of a white-headed eagle (Langsdorff, *Reise um die Welt*, ii. 114).

[1] W. Radloff, *Proben der Volks-litteratur der türkischen Stämme Süd-Sibiriens*, iii. 82 *sq.*

[2] Bastian, *Die Völker des östlichen Asien*, i. 416, vi. 25; Turner, *Samoa*, p. 200; *Panjab Notes and Queries*, ii. No. 797.

[3] Amongst the Chaco Indians of

The ground of this seclusion of girls at puberty lies
in the deeply engrained dread which primitive man
universally entertains of menstruous blood.   Evidence
of this has already been adduced,[1] but a few more facts
may here be added.   Amongst the Australian blacks
"the boys are told from their infancy that, if they see
the blood, they will early become gray-headed, and
their strength will fail prematurely."   Hence a woman
lives apart at these times ; and if a young man or boy
approaches her she calls out, and he immediately
makes a circuit to avoid her.   The men go out of
their way to avoid even crossing the tracks made
by women at such times.   Similarly the woman may
not walk on any path frequented by men, nor touch
anything used by men ; she may not eat fish, or go
near water at all, much less cross it ; for if she did, the
fish would be frightened, and the fishers would have
no luck ; she may not even fetch water for the camp ;
it is sufficient for her to say *Thama* to ensure her
husband fetching the water himself.   A severe beating, or even death, is the punishment inflicted on an
Australian woman who breaks these rules.[2]   The
Bushmen think that, by a glance of a girl's eye

South America a newly-married couple
sleep the first night on a skin with
their heads towards the west; "for the
marriage is not considered as ratified
till the rising sun shines on their feet
the succeeding morning."   T. J. Hutchinson, "The Chaco Indians," *Transact.
Ethnolog. Soc.* iii. 327.   At old Hindoo
marriages, the first ceremony was the
"Impregnation - rite" (*Garbhādhāna*).
"During the previous day the young
married woman was made to look
towards the sun, or in some way exposed to its rays."   Monier Williams,
Religious Life and Thought in India,
p. 354.   Amongst the Turks of Siberia
it was formerly the custom on the
morning after marriage to lead the
young couple out of the hut to greet
the rising sun.   The same custom is
said to be still practised in Iran and
Central Asia, the belief being that the
beams of the rising sun are the surest
means of impregnating the new bride.
Vambery, *Das Türkenvolk*, p. 112.

[1] Above, vol. i. p. 170.

[2] *Native Tribes of South Australia*,
p. 186 ; E. J. Eyre, *Journals*, ii. 295,
304 ; W. Ridley, *Kamilaroi*, p. 157 ;
Journ. Anthrop. Inst. ii. 268, ix. 459
sq. ; Brough Smyth, *Aborigines of Victoria*, i. 65, 236.   Cp. Sir George
Grey, *Journals*, ii. 344 ; J. Dawson,
Australian Aborigines, ci. *sq.*

at the time when she ought to be kept in strict
retirement, men become fixed in whatever position
they happen to occupy, with whatever they were
holding in their hands, and are changed into trees
which talk.[1] The Guayquiries of the Orinoco think
that, when a woman has her courses, everything
upon which she steps will die, and that if a man
treads on the place where she has passed, his legs
will immediately swell up.[2] The Creek and kindred
Indians of the United States compelled women at
menstruation to live in separate huts at some distance
from the village. There the women had to stay, at
the risk of being surprised and cut off by enemies.
It was thought "a most horrid and dangerous pollution" to go near the women at such times ; and the
danger extended to enemies who, if they slew the
women, had to cleanse themselves from the pollution
by means of certain sacred herbs and roots.[3] Similarly,
among the Chippeways and other Indians of the
Hudson Bay Territory, women at such seasons are
excluded from the camp, and take up their abode in
huts of branches. They wear long hoods, which
effectually conceal the head and breast. They may
not touch the household furniture nor any objects
used by men ; for their touch "is supposed to defile
them, so that their subsequent use would be followed
by certain mischief or misfortune," such as disease or
death. They may not walk on the common paths
nor cross the tracks of animals. They "are never
permitted to walk on the ice of rivers or lakes, or near
the part where the men are hunting beaver, or where

1 Bleek, *Brief Account of Bushman Folk-lore*, p. 14 ; cp. *ib.* p. 10.
2 Gumilla, *Histoire de l'Orénoque*, i. 249.
3 James Adair, *History of the American Indians*, p. 123 *sq.*

a fishing-net is set, for fear of averting their success. They are also prohibited at those times from partaking of the head of any animal, and even from walking in or crossing the track where the head of a deer, moose, beaver, and many other animals have lately been carried, either on a sledge or on the back. To be guilty of a violation of this custom is considered as of the greatest importance ; because they firmly believe that it would be a means of preventing the hunter from having an equal success in his future excursions."[1] So the Lapps forbid women at menstruation to walk on that part of the shore where the fishers are in the habit of setting out their fish.[2]

Amongst the civilised nations of Europe the superstitions which have prevailed on this subject are not less extravagant. In the oldest existing cyclopaedia— the *Natural History* of Pliny—the list of dangers apprehended from menstruation is longer than any furnished by savages. According to Pliny, the touch of a menstruous woman turned wine to vinegar, blighted crops, killed seedlings, blasted gardens, brought down the fruit from trees, dimmed mirrors, blunted razors, rusted iron and brass (especially at the waning of the moon), killed bees, or at least drove them from their hives, caused mares to miscarry, and so forth.[3] Similarly, in various parts of Europe, it is still believed that if a woman in her courses enters a brewery the beer will turn sour ; if she touches beer, wine, vinegar, or milk, it will go bad ; if she makes

---

[1] S. Hearne, *Journey to the Northern Ocean*, p. 314 *sq.* ; Alex. Mackenzie, *Voyages through the Continent of North America*, cxxiii. ; Petitot, *Monographie des Dènè-Dindjié*, p. 75 *sq.*

[2] C. Leemius, *De Lapponibus Fin-* *marchiae eorumque lingua vita et religione pristina* (Copenhagen, 1767), p. 494.

[3] Pliny, *Nat. Hist.* vii. § 64 *sq.*, xxviii. § 77 *sqq.* Cp. *Geoponica*, xii. c. 20, 5, and c. 25, 2 ; Columella, xi. 3, 50.

jam, it will not keep ; if she mounts a mare, it will miscarry ; if she touches buds, they will wither ; if she climbs a cherry-tree, it will die.[1]

Thus the object of secluding women at menstruation is to neutralise the dangerous influences which are supposed to emanate from them at such times. That the danger is believed to be especially great at the first menstruation appears from the unusual precautions taken to isolate girls at this crisis. Two of these precautions have been illustrated above, namely, the rules that the girl may not touch the ground nor see the sun. The general effect of these rules is to keep the girl suspended, so to say, between heaven and earth. Whether enveloped in her hammock and slung up to the roof, as in South America, or elevated above the ground in a dark and narrow cage, as in New Ireland, she may be considered to be out of the way of doing mischief, since, being shut off both from the earth and from the sun, she can poison neither of these great sources of life by her deadly contagion. In short, she is rendered harmless by being, in electrical language, insulated. But the precautions thus taken to isolate or insulate the girl are dictated by a regard for her own safety as well as for the safety of others. For it is thought that the girl herself would suffer if she were to neglect the prescribed

---

[1] A. Schleicher, *Volkstümliches aus Sonnenberg*, p. 134 ; B. Souché, *Croyances, Présages et Traditions diverses*, p. 11 ; V. Fossel, *Volksmedicin und medicinischer Aberglaube in Steiermark* (Graz, 1886), p. 124. The Greeks and Romans thought that a field was completely protected against insects if a menstruous woman walked round it with bare feet and streaming hair. Pliny, *Nat. Hist.* xvii. 266, xxviii. 78 ; Columella, x. 358 *sq.*, xi. 3, 64 ; Palladius, *De re rustica*, i. 35, 3 : *Geoponica*, xii. 8, 5 *sq.*; Aelian, *Nat. Anim.* vi. 36. A similar remedy is employed for the same purpose by North American Indians and European peasants. Schoolcraft, *Indian Tribes*, v. 70 ; Wiedemann, *Aus dem inneren und äussern Leben der Ehsten*, p. 484. Cp. Haltrich, *Zur Volkskunde der Siebenbürger Sachsen*, p. 280 ; Heinrich, *Agrarische Sitten und Gebräuche unter den Sachsen Siebenbürgens*, p. 14 ; Grimm, *Deutsche Mythologie*,[4] iii. 468.

regimen. Thus Zulu girls, as we have seen, believe that they would shrivel to skeletons if the sun were to shine on them at puberty, and in some Brazilian tribes the girls think that a transgression of the rules would entail sores on the neck and throat. In short, the girl is viewed as charged with a powerful force which, if not kept within bounds, may prove the destruction both of the girl herself and of all with whom she comes in contact. To repress this force within the limits necessary for the safety of all concerned is the object of the taboos in question.

The same explanation applies to the observance of the same rules by divine kings and priests. The uncleanness, as it is called, of girls at puberty and the sanctity of holy men do not, to the primitive mind, differ from each other. They are only different manifestations of the same supernatural energy which, like energy in general, is in itself neither good nor bad, but becomes beneficent or maleficent according to its application.[1] Accordingly, if, like girls at puberty, divine personages may neither touch the ground nor see the sun, the reason is, on the one hand, a fear lest their divinity might, at contact with earth or heaven, discharge itself with fatal violence on either ; and, on the other hand, an apprehension, that the divine being, thus drained of his ethereal virtue, might thereby be incapacitated for the future performance of those supernatural functions, upon the proper discharge of which the safety of the people and even of the world is believed to hang. Thus the rules in question fall under the head of the taboos which we examined in the second chapter ; they are intended to preserve the life

---

[1] For an example of the beneficent application of the menstrual energy, see note on p. 241.

of the divine person and with it the life of his subjects and worshippers. Nowhere, it is thought, can his precious yet dangerous life be at once so safe and so harmless as when it is neither in heaven nor in earth, but, as far as possible, suspended between the two.[1]

[1] The rules just discussed do not hold exclusively of the persons mentioned in the text, but are applicable in certain circumstances to other tabooed persons and things. Whatever, in fact, is permeated by the mysterious virtue of taboo may need to be isolated from earth and heaven. Mourners are taboo all the world over; accordingly in mourning the Ainos wear peculiar caps in order that the sun may not shine upon their heads. Bastian, *Die Völker des östlichen Asien*, v. 366. During a solemn fast of three days the Indians of Costa Rica eat no salt, speak as little as possible, light no fires, and stay strictly indoors, or if they go out during the day they carefully cover themselves from the light of the sun, believing that exposure to the sun's rays would turn them black. W. M. Gabb, *Indian Tribes and Languages of Costa Rica*, p. 510. On Yule night it has been customary in parts of Sweden from time immemorial to go on pilgrimage, whereby people learn many secret things and know what is to happen in the coming year. As a preparation for this pilgrimage, "some secrete themselves for three days previously in a dark cellar, so as to be shut out altogether from the light of heaven. Others retire at an early hour of the preceding morning to some out-of-the way place, such as a hayloft, where they bury themselves in the hay, that they may neither hear nor see any living creature; and here they remain, in silence and fasting, until after sundown; whilst there are those who think it sufficient if they rigidly abstain from food on the day before commencing their wanderings. During this period of probation a man ought not to see fire." L. Lloyd, *Peasant Life in Sweden*, p. 194. During the sixteen days that a Pima Indian is undergoing purification for killing an Apache he may not see a blazing fire. Bancroft, *Native Races of the Pacific States*, i. 553. Again warriors on the war-path are strictly taboo; hence Indians may not sit on the bare ground the whole time they are out on a warlike expedition. J. Adair, *History of the American Indians*, p. 382; *Narrative of the Captivity and Adventures of John Tanner*, p. 123. The holy ark of the North American Indians is deemed "so sacred and dangerous to be touched" that no one, except the war chief and his attendant, will touch it "under the penalty of incurring great evil. Nor would the most inveterate enemy touch it in the woods for the very same reason." In carrying it against the enemy they never place it on the ground, but rest it on stones or logs. Adair, *History of the American Indians*, p. 162 *sq*. The sacred clam shell of the Elk clan among the Omahas is kept in a sacred bag, which is never allowed to touch the ground. F. James, *Expedition from Pittsburgh to the Rocky Mountains*, ii. 47; J. Owen Dorsey, "Omaha Sociology," *Third Report of the Bureau of Ethnology* (Washington, 1884), p. 226. Newly born infants are strongly taboo; accordingly in Loango they are not allowed to touch the earth. Pechuel-Loesche, "Indiscretes aus Loango," *Zeitschrift für Ethnologie*, x. (1878) p. 29 *sq*. In Laos the hunting of elephants gives rise to many taboos; one of them is that the chief hunter may not touch the earth with his foot. Accordingly when he alights from his elephant, the others spread a carpet of leaves for him to step upon. E. Aymonier, *Notes sur le Laos*, p. 26. In some parts of Aberdeenshire, the last bit of standing corn (which, as we have seen, is very sacred) is not allowed to touch the ground; but as it is cut, it is placed on the lap

§ 2.—*Balder*

A god whose life might in a sense be said to be neither in heaven nor earth but between the two, was the Norse Balder, the good and beautiful god. The story of his death is as follows : Once on a time Balder dreamed heavy dreams which seemed to forebode his death. Thereupon the gods held a council and resolved to make him secure against every danger. So the goddess Frigg took an oath from fire and water, iron and all metals, stones and earth, from trees, sicknesses and poisons, and from all four-footed beasts, birds, and creeping things, that they would not hurt Balder. When this was done Balder was deemed invulnerable; so the gods amused themselves by setting him in their midst, while some shot at him, others hewed at him, and others threw stones at him. But whatever they did, nothing could hurt him ; and at this they were all glad. Only Loki, the mischief-maker, was displeased, and he went in the guise of an old woman to Frigg, who told him that the weapons of the gods could not wound Balder, since she had made them all swear not to hurt him. Then Loki asked, "Have all things sworn to spare Balder ?" She answered, "East of Walhalla grows a plant called mistletoe ; it seemed to me too

---

of the "gueedman." W. Gregor, "Quelques coutumes du Nord-Est du Comté d'Aberdeen," *Revue des Traditions populaires*, iii. (1888) 485 B. Sacred food may not, in certain circumstances, touch the ground. F. Grabowsky, "Der Distrikt Dusson Timor in Südost - Borneo und seine Bewohner," *Ausland* (1884), No. 24, p. 474 ; Ch. F. Hall, *Narrative of the Second Arctic Expedition*, edited by Prof. J. E. Nourse (Washington, 1879), p. 110 ; Gerard, *The Land beyond the Forest*, ii. 7. In Scotland, when water was carried from sacred wells to sick people, the water-vessel might not touch the ground. C. F. Gordon Cumming, *In the Hebrides*, p. 211. On the relation of spirits to the ground, compare Denzil Ibbetson in *Panjab Notes and Queries*, i. No. 5.

young to swear." So Loki went and pulled the mistletoe and took it to the assembly of the gods. There he
found the blind god Hödur standing at the outside of
the circle. Loki asked him, "Why do you not shoot
at Balder?" Hödur answered, "Because I do not
see where he stands; besides I have no weapon."
Then said Loki, "Do like the rest and show Balder
honour, as they all do. I will show you where he
stands, and do you shoot at him with this twig." Hödur
took the mistletoe and threw it at Balder, as Loki
directed him. The mistletoe struck Balder and pierced
him through and through, and he fell down dead. And
that was the greatest misfortune that ever befel gods
and men. For a while the gods stood speechless, then
they lifted up their voices and wept bitterly. They
took Balder's body and brought it to the sea-shore.
There stood Balder's ship; it was called Ringhorn,
and was the hugest of all ships. The gods wished to
launch the ship and to burn Balder's body on it, but
the ship would not stir. So they sent for a giantess
called Hyrrockin. She came riding on a wolf and gave
the ship such a push that fire flashed from the rollers
and all the earth shook. Then Balder's body was
taken and placed on the funeral pile upon his ship.
When his wife Nanna saw that, her heart burst for
sorrow and she died. So she was laid on the funeral
pile with her husband, and fire was put to it. Balder's
horse, too, with all its trappings, was burned on the
pile.[1]

The circumstantiality of this story suggests that it
belongs to the extensive class of myths which are in-

---

[1] *Die Edda*, übersetzt von K. Sim- length by Prof. Rhys, *Celtic Heathen-*
rock,[8] pp. 286-288, cp. pp. 8, 34, 264. *dom*, p. 529 *sqq.*
In English the Balder story is told at

vented to explain ritual. For a myth is never so graphic and precise in its details as when it is a simple transcript of a ceremony which the author of the myth witnessed with his eyes. At all events, if it can be made probable that rites like those described in the Balder myth have been practised by Norsemen and by other European peoples, we shall be justified in inferring that the ritual gave birth to the myth, not the myth to the ritual. For while many cases can be shown in which a myth has been invented to explain a rite, it would be hard to point to a single case in which a myth has given rise to a rite. Ritual may be the parent of myth, but can never be its child.[1]

The main incidents in the myth of Balder's death are two; first, the pulling of the mistletoe, and second, the death and burning of the god. Now both these incidents appear to have formed parts of an annual ceremony once observed by Celts and Norsemen, probably also by Germans and Slavs.

In most parts of Europe the peasants have been accustomed from time immemorial to kindle bonfires on certain days of the year, and to dance round them or leap over them. Customs of this kind can be traced back on historical evidence to the Middle Ages,[2] and their analogy to similar customs observed in antiquity goes with strong internal evidence to prove that their origin must be sought in a period long

---

[1] It is strange to find so learned and judicious a student of custom and myth as H. Usener exactly inverting their true relation to each other. After showing that the essential features of the myth of the marriage of Mars and Nerio have their counterpart in the marriage customs of peasants at the present day, he proceeds to infer that these customs are the reflection of the myth. "Italische Mythen," *Rheinisches Museum*, N. F. xxx. 228 *sq.* Surely the myth is the reflection of the custom. Men not only fashion gods in their own likeness (as Xenophanes long ago remarked) but make them think and act like themselves. Heaven is a copy of earth, not earth of heaven.

[2] See Grimm, *Deutsche Mythologie*,[4] i. 502, 510, 516.

prior to the spread of Christianity. Indeed the earliest evidence of their observance in Northern Europe is furnished by the attempts made by Christian synods in the eighth century to put them down as heathenish rites.[1] Not uncommonly effigies are burned in these fires, or a pretence is made of burning a living person in them; and there are grounds for believing that anciently human beings were actually burned on these occasions. A brief review of the customs in question will bring out the traces of human sacrifice, and will serve at the same time to throw light on their meaning.[2]

The seasons of the year at which these bonfires are most commonly lit are spring and midsummer, but in some places they are kindled at Hallow E'en (October 31st) and Christmas. In spring the first Sunday in Lent (Quadragesima) and Easter Eve are the days on which in different places the ceremony is observed. Thus in the Eifel Mountains, Rhenish Prussia, on the first Sunday in Lent young people used to collect straw and brushwood from house to house. These they carried to an eminence and piled them up round a tall, slim, beech-tree, to which a piece of wood was fastened at right angles to form a cross. The structure was known as the "hut" or "castle." Fire was set to it and the young people marched round the blazing "castle" bareheaded, each carrying a lighted torch and praying aloud. Sometimes a straw man was burned in the "hut." People observed the direction in which the smoke blew from the fire. If it blew towards the corn-fields, it was a sign that the

[1] Mannhardt, *Baumkultus*, p. 518 *sq.*
[2] In the following survey of these fire-customs I follow chiefly W. Mann-hardt, *Baumkultus*, kap. vi. p. 497 *sqq.* Compare also Grimm, *Deutsche Mythologie*,[4] i. 500 *sqq.*

harvest would be abundant. On the same day, in some parts of the Eifel, a great wheel was made of straw and dragged by three horses to the top of a hill. Thither the village boys marched at nightfall, set fire to the wheel, and sent it rolling down the slope. Two lads followed it with levers to set it in motion again, in case it should anywhere meet with a check.[1] About Echternach the same ceremony is called "burning the witch."[2] At Voralberg in the Tyrol on the first Sunday in Lent a slender young fir-tree is surrounded with a pile of straw and fire-wood. At the top of the tree is fastened a human figure called the "witch"; it is made of old clothes and stuffed with gunpowder. At night the whole is set on fire and boys and girls dance round it, swinging torches and singing rhymes in which the words "corn in the winnowing-basket, the plough in the earth" may be distinguished.[3] In Swabia on the first Sunday in Lent a figure called the "witch" or the "old wife" or "winter's grandmother" is made up of clothes and fastened to a pole. This is stuck in the middle of a pile of wood, to which fire is applied. While the "witch" is burning the young people throw blazing discs into the air. The discs are thin round pieces of wood, a few inches in diameter, with notched edges to imitate the rays of the sun or stars. They have a hole in the middle, by which they are attached to the end of a wand. Before the disc is thrown it is set on fire, the wand is swung to and fro, and the impetus thus communicated to the disc is augmented by dashing the rod sharply against a sloping board. The burning disc is thus thrown off, and mounting

[1] Schmitz, *Sitten und Sagen* etc. *des Eifler Volkes*, i. pp. 21-25 ; *B. K.* p. 501.

[2] *B. K.* p. 501.
[3] Vonbun, *Beiträge zur deutschen Mythologie*, p. 20 ; *B. K.* p. 501.

high into the air, describes a long curve before it reaches the ground. A single lad may fling up forty or fifty of these discs, one after the other. The object is to throw them as high as possible. The wand by which they are hurled must, at least in some parts of Swabia, be of hazel. Sometimes the lads also leap over the fire brandishing blazing torches of pine-wood. The charred embers of the burned "witch" and discs are taken home and planted in the flax-fields the same night, in the belief that they will keep vermin from the fields.[1] In the Rhön Mountains, Bavaria, on the first Sunday in Lent the people used to march to the top of a hill or eminence. Children and lads carried torches, brooms daubed with tar, and poles swathed in straw. A wheel, wrapt in combustibles, was kindled and rolled down the hill; and the young people rushed about the fields with their burning torches and brooms, till at last they flung them in a heap, and standing round them, struck up a hymn or a popular song. The object of running about the fields with the blazing torches was to "drive away the wicked sower." Or it was done in honour of the Virgin, that she might preserve the fruits of the earth throughout the year and bless them.[2]

It seems hardly possible to separate from these bonfires, kindled on the first Sunday in Lent, the fires in which, about the same season, the effigy called Death is burned as part of the ceremony of "carrying out Death." We have seen that at Spachendorf,

---

[1] E. Meier, *Deutsche Sagen, Sitten und Gebräuche aus Schwaben*, p. 380 *sqq.*; Birlinger, *Volksthümliches aus Schwaben*, ii. 59 *sq.*, 66 *sq.*; *Bavaria*, ii. 2, p. 838 *sq.*; Panzer, *Beitrag zur deutschen Mythologie*, i. p. 211, No. 232, *B. K.* p. 501 *sq.*

[2] Witzschel, *Sagen, Sitten und Gebräuche aus Thüringen*, p. 189; Panzer, *Beitrag zur deutschen Mythologie*, ii. 207; *B. K.* p. 500 *sq.*

Austrian Silesia, on the morning of Rupert's Day (Shrove Tuesday ?) a straw-man, dressed in a fur coat and a fur cap, is laid in a hole outside the village and there burned, and that while it is blazing every one seeks to snatch a fragment of it, which he fastens to a branch of the highest tree in his garden or buries in his field, believing that this will make the crops to grow better. The ceremony is known as the " burying of Death."[1] Even when the straw-man is not designated as Death, the meaning of the observance is probably the same ; for the name Death, as I have tried to show, does not express the original intention of the ceremony. At Cobern in the Eifel Mountains the lads make up a straw-man on Shrove Tuesday. The effigy is formally tried and accused of having perpetrated all the thefts that have been committed in the neighbourhood throughout the year. Being condemned to death, the straw-man is led through the village, shot, and burned upon a pyre. They dance round the blazing pile, and the last bride must leap over it.[2] In Oldenburg on the evening of Shrove Tuesday people used to make long bundles of straw, which they set on fire, and then ran about the fields waving them, shrieking, and singing wild songs. Finally they burnt a straw-man on the field.[3] In the district of Düsseldorf the straw-man burned on Shrove Tuesday was made of an unthreshed sheaf of corn.[4] On the first Monday after the spring equinox the urchins of Zurich drag a straw-man on a little cart through the streets, while at the same time the girls

---

[1] Th. Vernalcken, *Mythen und Bräuche des Volkes in Oesterreich*, p. 293 sq.; *B. K.* p. 498. See above, vol. i. p. 267.

[2] Schmitz, *Sitten, u. Sagen des*

Eifler Volkes, i. p. 20 ; *B. K.* p. 499.

[3] Strackerjan, *Aberglaube u. Sagen aus dem Herzogthum Oldenburg,* ii. 39, No. 306 ; *B. K.* p. 499.

[4] *B. K.* p. 499.

carry about a May-tree. When vespers ring, the
straw-man is burned.[1] In the district of Aachen on
Ash Wednesday a man used to be encased in peas-
straw and taken to an appointed place. Here he
slipped quietly out of his straw casing, which was then
burned, the children thinking that it was the man who
was being burned.[2] In the Val di Ledro (Tyrol) on
the last day of the Carnival a figure is made up of
straw and brushwood and then burned. The figure is
called the Old Woman, and the ceremony " burning
the Old Woman."[3]

Another occasion on which these fire-festivals are
held is Easter Eve, the Saturday before Easter Sunday. On that day it has been customary in Catholic
countries to extinguish all the lights in the churches,
and then to make a new fire, sometimes with flint and
steel, sometimes with a burning-glass. At this fire is
lit the Easter candle, which is then used to rekindle all
the extinguished lights in the church. In many parts
of Germany a bonfire is also kindled, by means of the
new fire, on some open space near the church. It is
consecrated, and the people bring sticks of oak, walnut,
and beech, which they char in the fire, and then take
home with them. Some of these charred sticks are
thereupon burned at home in a newly-kindled fire, with
a prayer that God will preserve the homestead from
fire, lightning, and hail. Thus every house receives
" new fire." Some of the sticks are placed in the
fields, gardens, and meadows, with a prayer that God
will keep them from blight and hail. Such fields and
gardens are thought to thrive more than others; the
corn and the plants that grow in them are not beaten

---

[1] *B. K.* p. 498 *sq.*   [2] *B. K.* p. 499.
[3] Schneller, *Märchen u. Sagen aus Wälschtirol*, p. 234 *sq.*; *B. K.* p. 499 *sq.*

down by hail, nor devoured by mice, vermin, and beetles, no witch harms them, and the ears of corn stand close and full. The charred sticks are also applied to the plough. The ashes of the Easter bonfire, together with the ashes of the consecrated palm-branches, are mixed with the seed at sowing. A wooden figure called Judas is sometimes burned in the consecrated bonfire.[1]

Sometimes instead of the consecrated bonfire a profane fire used to be kindled on Easter Eve. In the afternoon the lads of the village collected firewood and carried it to a corn-field or to the top of a hill. Here they piled it together and fastened in the midst of it a pole with a cross-piece, all wrapt in straw, so that it looked like a man with outstretched arms. This figure was called the Easter-man, or the Judas. In the evening the lads lit their lanterns at the new holy fire in the church, and ran at full speed to the pile. The one who reached it first set fire to it and to the effigy. No women or girls might be present, though they were allowed to watch the scene from a distance. Great was the joy while the effigy was burning. The ashes were collected and thrown at sunrise into running water, or were scattered over the fields on Easter Monday. At the same time the palm branches which had been consecrated on Palm Sunday, and sticks which had been charred in the fire and consecrated on Good Friday, were also stuck up in the fields. The object was to preserve the fields from hail.[2] In Münsterland, these Easter fires are always kindled upon

---

[1] *B. K.* pp. 502-505; Wuttke, *Der deutsche Volksaberglaube,*[2] § 81; Zingerle, *Sitten, Bräuche und Meinungen des Tiroler Volkes,*[2] p. 149, §§ 1286-1289; *Bavaria,* i. 1, p. 371.

[2] Panzer, *Beitrag zur deutschen Mythologie,* i. p. 212 *sq.,* ii. p. 78 *sq.;* *B. K.* p. 505.

certain definite hills, which are hence known as Easter
or Pascal Mountains. The whole community assembles
about the fire. Fathers of families form an inner circle
round it. An outer circle is formed by the young men
and maidens, who, singing Easter hymns, march round
and round the fire in the direction of the sun, till the
blaze dies down. Then the girls jump over the fire in
a line, one after the other, each supported by two
young men who hold her hands and run beside her.
When the fire has burned out, the whole assemblage
marches in solemn procession to the church, singing
hymns. They march thrice round the church, and
then break up. In the twilight boys with blazing
bundles of straw run over the fields to make them
fruitful.[1] In Holland, also, Easter fires used to be
kindled on the highest eminences, the people danced
round them, and leaped through the flames.[2] In
Schaumburg, the Easter bonfires may be seen blazing
on all the mountains around for miles. They are made
with a tar barrel fastened to a pine-tree, which is wrapt
in straw. The people dance singing round them.[3]
Easter bonfires are also common in the Harz Mountains
and in Brunswick, Hanover, and Westphalia. They
are generally lit upon particular heights and mountains which are hence called Easter Mountains. In
the Harz the fire is commonly made by piling brushwood about a tree and setting it on fire, and blazing
tar barrels are often rolled down into the valley. In
Osterode, every one tries to snatch a brand from
the bonfire and rushes about with it; the better it
burns, the more lucky it is. In Grund there are torch

---

[1] Strackerjan, *Aberglaube und Sagen aus dem Herzogthum Oldenburg*, ii. p. 43 *sq.*, No. 313; *B. K.* p. 505 *sq.*

[2] Wolf, *Beiträge zur deutschen Mythologie*, i. 75 *sq.*; *B. K.* p. 506.

[3] Grimm, *Deutsche Mythologie*,[4] i. 512; *B. K.* p. 506 *sq.*

races.[1] In the Altmark, the Easter bonfires are composed of tar barrels, bee-hives, etc., piled round a pole. The young folk dance round the fire; and when it has died out, the old folk come and collect the ashes, which they preserve as a remedy for the ailments of bees. It is also believed that as far as the blaze of the bonfire is visible, the corn will grow well throughout the year, and no conflagration will break out.[2] In some parts of Bavaria, bonfires were kindled at Easter upon steep mountains, and burning arrows or discs of wood were shot high into the air, as in the Swabian custom already described. Sometimes, instead of the discs, an old waggon wheel was wrapt in straw, set on fire, and sent rolling down the mountain. The lads who hurled the discs received painted Easter eggs from the girls.[3] In some parts of Swabia the Easter fires might not be kindled with iron or flint or steel; but only by the friction of wood.[4] At Braunröde in the Harz Mountains it was the custom to burn squirrels in the Easter bonfire.[5] In the Altmark, bones were burned in it.[6]

In the central Highlands of Scotland bonfires, known as the Beltane fires, were formerly kindled with great ceremony on the 1st of May, and the traces of human sacrifices at them were particularly clear and unequivocal. In the neighbourhood of Callander, in Perthshire, the custom lasted down to

---

[1] H. Pröhle, *Harzbilder*, p. 63; Kuhn und Schwartz, *Norddeutsche Sagen, Märchen und Gebräuche*, p. 373; *B. K.* p. 507.

[2] Kuhn, *Märkische Sagen und Märchen*, p. 312 *sq.*; *B. K.* p. 507.

[3] Panzer, *Beitrag zur deutschen Mythologie*, i. p. 211 *sq.*; *B. K.* p. 507 *sq.*

[4] Birlinger, *Volksthümliches aus Schwaben*, ii. p. 82, No. 106; *B. K.* p. 508.

[5] *B. K.* p. 508; cp. Wolf, *Beiträge zur deutsch. Myth.* i. 74; Grimm, *Deutsche Myth.*[4] i. 512. The two latter writers only state that before the fires were kindled it was customary to hunt squirrels in the woods.

[6] Kuhn, *l.c.*; *B. K.* p. 508.

the close of last century. The fires were lit by the
people of each hamlet on a hill or knoll round which
their cattle were pasturing. Hence various eminences
in the Highlands are known as "the hill of the fires,"
just as in Germany some mountains take their name
from the Easter fires which are kindled upon them.
On the morning of May Day the people repaired to
a hill or knoll and cut a round trench in the green
sod, leaving in the centre a platform of turf large
enough to contain the whole company. On this turf
they seated themselves, and in the middle was placed a
pile of wood or other fuel, which of old they kindled
with *tein-eigin*—that is, forced fire or need-fire. The
way of making the need-fire was this : "The night
before, all the fires in the country were carefully
extinguished, and next morning the materials for
exciting this sacred fire were prepared. The most
primitive method seems to be that which was used
in the islands of Skye, Mull, and Tiree. A well-
seasoned plank of oak was procured, in the midst of
which a hole was bored. A wimble of the same
timber was then applied, the end of which they fitted
to the hole. But in some parts of the mainland the
machinery was different. They used a frame of
green wood, of a square form, in the centre of which
was an axle-tree. In some places three times three
persons, in others three times nine, were required for
turning round, by turns, the axle-tree or wimble. If
any of them had been guilty of murder, adultery,
theft, or other atrocious crime, it was imagined either
that the fire would not kindle, or that it would be
devoid of its usual virtue. So soon as any sparks
were emitted by means of the violent friction, they
applied a species of agaric which grows on old birch-

trees, and is very combustible. This fire had the appearance of being immediately derived from heaven, and manifold were the virtues ascribed to it. They esteemed it a preservative against witchcraft, and a sovereign remedy against malignant diseases, both in the human species and in cattle; and by it the strongest poisons were supposed to have their nature changed." For many years, however, before the close of last century, the Beltane fires were kindled in the usual way. The fire being lit, the company prepared a custard of eggs and milk, which they ate. Afterwards they amused themselves a while by singing and dancing round the fire. Then "they knead a cake of oatmeal, which is toasted at the embers against a stone. After the custard is eaten up they divide the cake into so many portions, as similar as possible to one another in size and shape, as there are persons in the company. They daub one of these portions all over with charcoal until it be perfectly black. They put all the bits of cake into a bonnet. Every one, blindfold, draws out a portion. He who holds the bonnet is entitled to the last bit. Whoever draws the black bit is the devoted person who is to be sacrificed to *Baal*, whose favour they mean to implore, in rendering the year productive of the sustenance of man and beast." The victim thus selected "was called *cailleach bealtine—i.e.* the Beltane *carline*, a term of great reproach. Upon his being known, part of the company laid hold of him, and made a show of putting him into the fire; but, the majority interposing, he was rescued. And in some places they laid him flat on the ground, making as if they would quarter him. Afterwards he was pelted with egg-shells, and retained the odious appellation during the

whole year.   And, while the feast was fresh in people's
memory, they affected to speak of the *cailleach bealtine*
as dead."   He had to leap thrice through the flames,
and this concluded the ceremony.[1]

Another account of the Beltane festival, written in
the latter half of last century, is as follows : " On the 1st
of May the herdsmen of every village hold their Bel-
tien, a rural sacrifice.   They cut a square trench on the
ground, leaving the turf in the middle ; on that they
make a fire of wood, on which they dress a large caudle
of eggs, butter, oatmeal, and milk, and bring, besides the
ingredients of the caudle, plenty of beer and whisky ;
for each of the company must contribute something.
The rites begin with spilling some of the caudle on
the ground, by way of libation ; on that every one
takes a cake of oatmeal, upon which are raised nine
square knobs, each dedicated to some particular being,
the supposed preserver of their flocks and herds, or to
some particular animal, the real destroyer of them ;
each person then turns his face to the fire, breaks off a
knob, and, flinging it over his shoulder, says, ' This I
give to thee, preserve thou my horses ; this to thee,
preserve thou my sheep ; and so on.'   After that they
use the same ceremony to the noxious animals : ' This
I give to thee, O fox ! spare thou my lambs ; this to
thee, O hooded crow ! this to thee, O eagle !'   When
the ceremony is over they dine on the caudle ; and,
after the feast is finished, what is left is hid by two
persons deputed for that purpose ; but on the next
Sunday they reassemble, and finish the reliques of the

---

[1] Brand, *Popular Antiquities*, i. 224
sq., Bohn's ed., quoting Sinclair's
Statistical Account of Scotland, 1794,
xi. 620; *Scotland and Scotsmen in the*
Eighteenth Century, from the MSS. of
John Ramsay of Ochtertyre, edited by
Alex. Allardyce, ii. 439-445 ; *B. K.*
p. 508.

first entertainment." [1]   The 1st of May is a great
popular festival in the more midland and southern
parts of Sweden.   On the preceding evening huge
bonfires, which should be lighted by striking two
flints together, blaze on all the hills and knolls.
Every large hamlet has its own fire, round which the
young people dance in a ring.   The old folk notice
whether the flames incline to the north or to the south.
In the former case the spring will be cold and backward ; in the latter mild and genial. [2]

But the season at which these fire-festivals are
most generally held all over Europe is the summer
solstice, that is, Midsummer Eve (23d June) or Midsummer Day (24th June).   According to a mediæval
writer the three great features of this festival were
the bonfires, the procession with torches round the
fields, and the custom of rolling a wheel.   The writer
adds that the smoke drives away harmful dragons
which cause sickness, and he explains the custom of
rolling the wheel to mean that the sun has now reached
the highest point in the ecliptic, and begins thenceforward to descend. [3]   From his description, which is
still applicable, we see that the main features of the
midsummer fire-festival are identical with those which
characterise the spring festivals.   In Swabia lads and
lasses, hand in hand, leap over the midsummer bonfire,
praying that the hemp may grow three ells high, and
they set fire to wheels of straw and send them rolling
down the hill. [4]   In Lechrain bonfires are kindled on

---

[1] Pennant, "Tour in Scotland,"
Pinkerton's *Voyages and Travels*, iii.
49 ; Brand, *Popular Antiquities*, i.
226.

[2] L. Lloyd, *Peasant Life in Sweden*,
p. 233 *sq.*

[3] *B. K.* p. 509; Brand, *Pop. Antiq.*
i. 298 *sq.*; Grimm, *D. M.*[4] i. 516.

[4] Birlinger, *Volksthümliches aus
Schwaben*, ii. p. 96 *sqq.* No. 128, p.
103 *sq.* No. 129; E. Meier, *Deutsche
Sagen, Sitten und Gebräuche aus
Schwaben*, p. 423 *sqq.*; *B. K.* p. 510.

The Three Fates.

A couple leaping over a Bohemian bonfire.

the mountains on Midsummer Day ; and besides the bonfire a tall beam, thickly wrapt in straw, and surmounted by a cross-piece, is burned in many places. Round this cross, as it burns, the lads dance; and when the flames have subsided, the young people leap over the fire in pairs, a young man and a young woman together. It is believed that the flax will grow that year as high as they leap over the fire ; and that if a charred billet be taken from the fire and stuck in a flax field it will promote the growth of the flax.[1] At Deffingen, as they jumped over the midsummer bonfire, they cried out, "Flax, flax! may the flax this year grow seven ells high!"[2] In Bohemia bonfires are kindled on many of the mountains on Midsummer Eve ; boys and girls, hand in hand, leap over them ; cart-wheels smeared with resin are ignited and sent rolling down the hill; and brooms covered with tar and set on fire are swung about or thrown high into the air. The handles of the brooms or embers from the fire are preserved and stuck in gardens to protect the vegetables from caterpillars and gnats. Sometimes the boys run down the hillside in troops, brandishing the blazing brooms and shouting. The bonfire is sometimes made by stacking wood and branches round the trunk of a tree and setting the whole on fire.[3]

In old farm-houses of the Surenthal and Winenthal a couple of holes or a whole row of them may sometimes be seen facing each other in the door-posts of the barn or stable. Sometimes the holes are smooth and round; sometimes they are deeply burnt and blackened.

---

[1] Leoprechting, *Aus dem Lechrain*, p. 182 *sq.*; *B. K.* p. 510. Cp. Panzer, *Beitrag zur deutschen Mythologie*, i. 210 ; *Bavaria*, iii. 956.

[2] Panzer, *op. cit.* ii. 549.

[3] Reinsberg-Düringsfeld, *Fest - Kalender aus Böhmen*, pp. 306-311 ; *B. K.* p. 510. For the custom of burning a tree in the midsummer bonfires, see vol. i. p. 79.

The explanation of them is this. About midsummer, but especially on Midsummer Day, two such holes are bored opposite each other, into which the extremities of a strong pole are fixed. The holes are then stuffed with tow steeped in resin and oil; a rope is looped round the pole, and two young men, who must be brothers or must have the same baptismal name, and must be of the same age, pull the ends of the rope backwards and forwards so as to make the pole revolve rapidly, till smoke and sparks issue from the two holes in the door-posts. The sparks are caught and blown up with tinder, and this is the new and pure fire, the appearance of which is greeted with cries of joy. Heaps of combustible materials are now ignited with the new fire, and blazing bundles are placed on boards and sent floating down the brook. The boys light torches at the new fire and run to fumigate the pastures. This is believed to drive away all the demons and witches that molest the cattle. Finally the torches are thrown in a heap on the meadow and allowed to burn out. On their way back the boys strew the ashes over the fields : this is supposed to make them fertile. If a farmer has taken possession of a new house, or if servants have changed masters, the boys fumigate the new abode and are rewarded by the farmer with a supper.[1]

At Konz, on the Moselle, the midsummer fire-festival used to be celebrated as follows. A quantity of straw, contributed jointly by every house, was collected on the top of the Stromberg Hill. Here, towards evening, the men and boys assembled, while the women and girls took up their position at a certain well down below. On the top of the hill a huge wheel was completely covered with a portion of the

---

[1] Rochholz, *Deutscher Glaube und Brauch*, ii. 144 *sqq.*

collected straw, the remainder of which was made into torches.   The mayor of Sierk, who always received a basket of cherries for his services, gave the signal, the wheel was ignited with a torch, and sent rolling down the hill amid shouts of joy.   All the men and boys swung their torches in the air, some of them remained on the top of the hill, while others followed the fiery wheel on its course down the hillside to the Moselle. As it passed the women and girls at the well they raised cries of joy which were answered by the men on the top of the hill.   The inhabitants of the neighbouring villages also stood on the banks of the river and mingled their voices with the general shout of jubilation.   The wheel was often extinguished before it reached the water, but if it plunged blazing into the river the people expected an abundant vintage, and the inhabitants of Konz had the right to exact a waggon-load of white wine from the surrounding vineyards.[1]

In France the midsummer customs are similar.   In Poitou a wheel enveloped in straw is set on fire, and people run with it through the fields, which are supposed to be fertilised thereby ; also, the people leap thrice over the fire, holding in their hands branches of nut-trees, which are afterwards hung over the door of the cattle-stall.   At Brest torches are brandished, and hundreds of them flung up into the air together.[2]   In Britanny midsummer fires blaze on the hills, the people dance round them, singing and leaping over the glowing embers. The bonfire is made by piling wood round a pole which is surmounted by a nosegay or crown.[3]

---

[1] Grimm, *D. M.*[4] i. 515 *sq.*; *B. K.* p. 510 *sq.*

[2] Wolf, *Beiträge zur deutschen Mythologie*, ii. 393; Grimm, *D. M.*[4] i. 517; *B. K.* p. 511.

[3] Sébillot, *Coutumes populaires de la Haute Bretagne*, p. 193 *sq.*; Wolf, *op. cit.* ii. 392 *sq.*

Sometimes, instead of rolling fiery wheels, discs of wood are ignited in the midsummer fires and thrown into the air in the manner already described.[1] At Edersleben, near Sangerhausen, a high pole was planted in the ground and a tar barrel was hung from it by a chain which reached to the ground. The barrel was then set on fire and swung round the pole amid shouts of joy.[2]

In our own country the custom of lighting bonfires at midsummer has prevailed extensively. In the North of England these fires used to be lit in the open streets. Young and old gathered round them ; the former leaped over the fires and engaged in games, while the old people looked on. Sometimes the fires were kindled on the tops of high hills. The people also carried firebrands about the fields.[3] In Herefordshire and Somersetshire people used to make fires in the fields on Midsummer Eve " to bless the apples."[4] In Devonshire the custom of leaping over the midsummer fires was also observed.[5] In Cornwall bonfires were lit on Midsummer Eve and the people marched round them with lighted torches, which they also carried from village to village. On Whiteborough, a large tumulus near Launceston, a huge bonfire used to be kindled on Midsummer Eve ; a tall summer pole with a large bush at the top was fixed in the centre of the bonfire.[6] At Darowen in Wales small bonfires were lit on Midsummer Eve.[7] On the same

[1] Zingerle, *Sitten*, etc. *des Tiroler Volkes*,[2] p. 159, No. 1354 ; Panzer, *Beitrag*, i. 210 ; *B. K.* p. 511.

[2] Kuhn u. Schwartz, *Norddeutsche Sagen, Märchen und Gebräuche*, p. 390 ; *B. K.* 511.

[3] Brand, *Popular Antiquities*, i. 300

sq., 318, cp. pp. 305, 306, 308 *sq.*; *B. K.* p. 512.

[4] Aubrey, *Remaines of Gentilisme and Judaisme*, p. 96, cp. *id.* p. 26.

[5] Brand, *op. cit.* i. 311.

[6] *Id.* i. 303, 318, 319 ; Dyer, *British Popular Customs*, p. 315.

[7] Brand, *op. cit.* i. 318.

day people in the Isle of Man used to light fires to the windward of every field, so that the smoke might pass over the corn ; and they folded their cattle and carried blazing furze or gorse round them several times.[1]

In Ireland, "on the Eves of St. John Baptist and St. Peter, they always have in every town a bonfire late in the evening, and carry about bundles of reeds fast tied and fired ; these being dry, will last long, and flame better than a torch, and be a pleasing divertive prospect to the distant beholder ; a stranger would go near to imagine the whole country was on fire."[2] Another writer says of the South of Ireland : "On Midsummer's Eve, every eminence, near which is a habitation, blazes with bonfires ; and round these they carry numerous torches, shouting and dancing."[3] An author who described Ireland in the first quarter of last century says : "On the vigil of St. John the Baptist's nativity, they make bonfires, and run along the streets and fields with wisps of straw blazing on long poles to purify the air, which they think infectious by believing all the devils, spirits, ghosts, and hobgoblins fly abroad this night to hurt mankind."[4] Another writer states that he witnessed the festival in Ireland in 1782 : "Exactly at midnight the fires began to appear, and taking advantage of going up to the leads of the house, which had a widely extended view, I saw on a radius of thirty miles, all around, the fires burning on every eminence which the country afforded. I had a further satisfaction in learning, from undoubted authority, that the people *danced*

---

[1] J. Train, *Account of the Isle of Man*, ii. 120.

[2] Brand, i. 303, quoting Sir Henry Piers's *Description of Westmeath*.

[3] Brand, *l.c.*, quoting the author of the *Survey of the South of Ireland*.

[4] Brand, i. 305, quoting the author of the *Comical Pilgrim's Pilgrimage into Ireland*.

round the fires, and at the close went through these fires, and made their sons and daughters, together with their cattle, pass through the fire ; and the whole was conducted with religious solemnity." [1] That the custom prevailed in full force as late as 1867 appears from a notice in the *Liverpool Mercury*, 29th June 1867, which runs thus : " The old pagan fire-worship still survives in Ireland, though nominally in honour of St. John. On Sunday night bonfires were observed throughout nearly every county in the province of Leinster. In Kilkenny fires blazed on every hillside at intervals of about a mile. There were very many in the Queen's county, also in Kildare and Wexford. The effect in the rich sunset appeared to travellers very grand. The people assemble and dance round the fires, the children jump through the flames, and in former times live coals were carried into the corn-fields to prevent blight." [2]

In Scotland the traces of midsummer fires are few. In reference to the parish of Mongahitter it is said : " The Midsummer Eve fire, a relic of Druidism, was kindled in some parts of this country." [3] Moresin states that on St. Peter's Day (29th June) the Scotch ran about with lighted torches on mountains and high grounds ; [4] and at Loudon in Ayrshire it appears that down to the close of last century the custom still prevailed for herdsmen and young people to kindle fires on high grounds on St. Peter's Day. [5] In the Perthshire Highlands on Midsummer Day the cowherd used to go three times round the fold, according to the

---

[1] Brand, i. 304, quoting *The Gentleman's Magazine*, February 1795, p. 124.

[2] Quoted by Dyer, *British Popular Customs*, p. 321 *sq.*

[3] Brand, i. 311, quoting *Statistical Account of Scotland*, xxi. 145.

[4] *B. K.* p. 512.

[5] Brand, i. 337.

course of the sun, with a burning torch in his hand. This was believed to purify the flocks and herds and prevent diseases.[1]

In Slavonic countries also the midsummer festival is celebrated with similar rites. In Russia fires are lighted and young people, crowned with flowers, jump through them and drive their cattle through them. In Little Russia a stake is driven into the ground on St. John's Night, wrapt in straw, and set on fire. As the flames rise the peasant women throw birch-tree boughs into them, saying, " May my flax be as tall as this bough ! " [2] " In Ruthenia the bonfires are lighted by a flame procured from wood by friction, the operation being performed by the elders of the party, amid the respectful silence of the rest. But as soon as the fire is ' churned,' the bystanders break forth with joyous songs, and when the bonfires are lit the young people take hands, and spring in couples through the smoke, if not through the flames, and after that the cattle in their turn are driven through it." [3] In many parts of Prussia and Lithuania great fires are kindled on the Eve of St. John (Midsummer Eve). All the heights are ablaze with them, as far as the eye can see. The fires are supposed to be a protection against thunder, hail, and cattle disease, especially if next morning the cattle are driven over the places where the fires burned.[4] In some parts of Masuren it is the custom on the evening of Midsummer Day to put out all the fires in the village. Then an oaken stake is driven into the ground, a wheel is fixed on it as on an axle

---

[1] J. Ramsay and A. Allardyce, *Scotland and Scotsmen in the Eighteenth Century*, ii. 436.

[2] Ralston, *Songs of the Russian People*, p. 240 ; Grimm, *D. M.*[4] i. 519.

[3] Ralston. *l.c.*

[4] Tettau und Temme, *Die Volkssagen Ostpreussens, Litthauens und Westpreussens*, p. 277 ; Grimm, *D. M.*[4] i. 519.

and is made to revolve rapidly, till the friction produces
fire. Every one takes home a light from the new
fire and rekindles the fire on the domestic hearth.[1]
In Bohemia the cows used to be driven over the
midsummer fires to protect them from witchcraft.[2]
In Servia on Midsummer Eve herdsmen light torches
of birch bark and march round the sheepfolds and
cattle-stalls; then they climb the hills and there allow
the torches to burn out.[3]

In Greece the women light fires on St. John's Eve
and jump over them crying, "I leave my sins behind
me."[4]   Italy must also have had its midsummer bonfires, since at Orvieto they were specially excepted
from the prohibition directed against bonfires in
general.[5]   We have seen that they are still lighted in
Sardinia.[6]   In Corsica on the Eve of St. John the
people set fire to the trunk of a tree or to a whole
tree, and the young men and maidens dance round the
blaze, which is called *fucaraja*.[7]   Midsummer fires
are, or were formerly, lighted in Spain.[8]   Even the
Mohammedans of Algeria and Morocco are reported
to have kindled great midsummer bonfires of straw,
into which they kept throwing incense and spices
the whole night, invoking the divine blessing on their
fruit-trees.[9]

It remains to show that the burning of effigies
of human beings in the midsummer fires was not
uncommon. At Rottenburg in Würtemberg, down

---

[1] Töppen, *Aberglauben aus Masuren*,[2]
p. 71.
[2] Grimm, *l.c.*; Reinsberg-Düringsfeld, *Fest-Kalender aus Böhmen*, p. 307
note.
[3] Grimm, *l.c.*   [4] Grimm, *l.c.*
[5] Grimm, *D. M.*[4] i. 518.
[6] Above, vol. i. p. 291.

[7] Gubernatis, *Mythologie des Plantes*,
i. 185.
[8] Brand, *Popular Antiquities*, i. 317;
Grimm, *l.c.*
[9] G. Ferraro, *Superstizioni, usi e
proverbi Monferrini*, p. 34 *sq.*, referring
to Alvise da Cadamosto, *Relazion dei
viaggi d'Africa*, in Ramusio.

to the beginning of the present century, a ceremony was observed on Midsummer Day which was called "beheading the angel-man." A stump was driven into the ground, wrapt with straw, and fashioned into the rude likeness of a human figure, with arms, head, and face. This was the angel-man; round about him wood was piled up. The boys, armed with swords, assembled in crowds, covered the figure completely over with flowers, and eagerly awaited the signal. When the pile of wood was fired and the angel-man burst into a blaze, the word was given and all the boys fell upon him with their swords and hewed the burning figure in pieces. Then they leaped backwards and forwards over the fire.[1] In some parts of the Tyrol a straw-man is carted about the village on Midsummer Day and then burned. He is called the *Lotter*, which has been corrupted into Luther.[2] In French Flanders down to 1789 a straw figure representing a man was always burned in the midsummer bonfire, and the figure of a woman was burned on St. Peter's Day, 29th June.[3] At Grätz on the 23d June the common people used to make a puppet called the *Tatermann*, which they dragged to the bleaching-ground, and pelted with burning besoms till it took fire.[4] In some parts of Russia a figure of Kupalo is burned or thrown into a stream on St. John's Night.[5] The Russian custom of carrying the straw effigy of Kupalo over the midsummer bonfire has been already described.[6]

The best general explanation of these European

---

[1] Birlinger, *Volksthümliches aus Schwaben*, ii. 100 *sq.*; *B. K.* p. 513 *sq.*

[2] Zingerle, *Sitten*, etc., *des Tiroler Volkes*,[2] p. 159, No. 1353, cp. No. 1355; *B. K.* p. 513.

[3] Wolf, *Beiträge zur deutschen Mythologie*, ii. 392; *B. K.* p. 513.

[4] *B. K.* p. 513.

[5] Ralston, *Songs of the Russian People*, p. 240.

[6] Above, vol. i. p. 272 *sq.*

fire-festivals seems to be the one given by Mannhardt, namely, that they are sun-charms or magical ceremonies intended to ensure a proper supply of sunshine for men, animals, and plants. We have seen that savages resort to charms for making sunshine,[1] and we need not wonder that primitive man in Europe has done the same. Indeed, considering the cold and cloudy climate of Europe during a considerable part of the year, it is natural that sun-charms should have played a much more prominent part among the superstitious practices of European peoples than among those of savages who live nearer the equator. This view of the festivals in question is supported by various considerations drawn partly from the rites themselves, partly from the influence which they are believed to exert upon the weather and on vegetation. For example, the custom of rolling a burning wheel down a hillside, which is often observed on these occasions, seems a very natural imitation of the sun's course in the sky, and the imitation is especially appropriate on Midsummer Day when the sun's annual declension begins. Not less graphic is the imitation of his apparent revolution by swinging a burning tar-barrel round a pole.[2] The custom of throwing blazing discs, shaped like suns, into the air is probably also a piece of imitative magic. In these, as in so many cases, the magic force is supposed to take effect through mimicry or sympathy; by imitating the desired result you actually produce it; by counterfeiting the sun's progress through the heavens you really help the luminary to pursue his celestial journey with punctuality and despatch. The name " fire of heaven," by which the

---

[1] Above, vol. i. p. 22 *sqq.*   [2] Above, p. 262.

midsummer fire is sometimes popularly known,[1] clearly
indicates a consciousness of the connection between
the earthly and the heavenly flame.

Again, the manner in which the fire appears to have
been originally kindled on these occasions favours the
view that it was intended to be a mock-sun. For, as
various scholars have seen,[2] it is highly probable that
originally at these festivals fire was universally obtained
by the friction of two pieces of wood. We have seen
that this is still the case in some places both at the
Easter and midsummer fires, and that it is expressly
stated to have been formerly the case at the Beltane
fires.[3] But what makes it almost certain that this was
once the invariable mode of kindling the fire at these
periodic festivals is the analogy of the need-fires.
Need-fires are kindled, not at fixed periods, but on
occasions of special distress, particularly at the outbreak of a murrain, and the cattle are driven through
the need-fire, just as they are sometimes driven through
the midsummer fires.[4] Now, the need-fire has always
been produced by the friction of wood and sometimes
by the revolution of a wheel; in Mull, for example, it
was made by turning an oaken wheel over nine oaken
spindles from east to west, that is, in the direction of
the sun. It is a plausible conjecture that the wheel
employed to produce the need-fire represents the sun;[5]
and if the spring and midsummer fires were originally
produced in the same way, it would be a confirmation

---

[1] Birlinger, *Volksthümliches aus
Schwaben*, ii. 57, 97; *B. K.* p. 510;
cp. Panzer, *Beitrag*, ii. 240.

[2] Cp. Grimm, *D. M.*[4] i. 521; Wolf,
Beiträge zur deutschen Mythologie, ii.
389; Ad. Kuhn, *Herabkunft des
Feuers*,[2] pp. 41 *sq.*, 47; W. Mannhardt,
B. K. p. 521.

[3] See above, pp. 254, 255, 260, 265.

[4] On the need-fires, see Grimm,
D. M. i. 501 *sqq.*; Wolf, *op. cit.* i.
116 *sq.*, ii. 378 *sqq.*; Kuhn, *op. cit.*
p. 41 *sqq.*; *B. K.* p. 518 *sqq.*; Elton,
Origins of English History, p. 293 *sq.*;
Jahn, *Die deutschen Opfergebräuche
bei Ackerbau und Viehzucht*, p. 26 *sqq.*

[5] This is the view of Grimm, Wolf,
Kuhn, and Mannhardt.

of the view that they were originally sun-charms. In point of fact there is, as Kuhn has pointed out,[1] some evidence to show that the midsummer fire was originally thus produced. For at Obermedlingen in Swabia the "fire of heaven," as it was called, was made on St. Vitus's Day (15th June) by igniting a cart-wheel, which, smeared with pitch and plaited with straw, was fastened on a pole twelve feet high, the top of the pole being inserted in the nave of the wheel. This fire was made on the summit of the mountain, and as the flame ascended, the people uttered a set form of words, with eyes and arms directed heaven-ward.[2] Here the fact of a wheel being fixed on the top of a pole and ignited makes it probable that originally the fire was produced, as in the need-fire, by the revolution of a wheel. The day on which the ceremony takes place (15th June) is near midsummer; and we have seen that in Masuren fire is (or was) actually made on Midsummer Day by turning a wheel rapidly about an oaken pole, though it is not said that the new fire so produced is used to light a bonfire.

Once more, the influence which these bonfires are supposed to exert on the weather and on vegetation, goes to show that they are sun-charms, since the effects ascribed to them are identical with those of sunshine. Thus, in Sweden the warmth or cold of the coming season is inferred from the direction in which the flames of the bonfire are blown; if they blow to the south, it will be warm, if to the north, cold. No doubt at present the direction of the flames is regarded merely as an augury of the weather, not as a mode of influencing it. But we may be pretty sure that this is one of the cases in which magic has

---

[1] *Herabkunft des Feuers,*[2] p. 47.   [2] Panzer, *Beitrag,* ii. 240.

dwindled into divination. So in the Eifel Mountains, when the smoke blows towards the corn-fields, this is an omen that the harvest will be abundant. But doubtless the older view was, not merely that the smoke and flames prognosticated, but that they actually produced an abundant harvest, the heat of the flames acting like sunshine on the corn. Indeed, this older view must still have been held by people in the Isle of Man when they lit fires to windward of their fields in order that the smoke might blow over them. Again, the idea that the corn will grow well as far as the blaze of the bonfire is visible, is certainly a remnant of the belief in the quickening and fertilising power of the bonfires. The same belief reappears in the notion that embers taken from the bonfires and inserted in the fields will promote the growth of the crops, and again it plainly underlies the custom of mixing the ashes of the bonfire with the seed-corn at sowing, or of scattering the ashes by themselves over the field. The belief that the flax will grow as high as the people leap over the bonfire belongs clearly to the same class of ideas. Once more, we saw that at Konz, on the banks of the Moselle, if the blazing wheel which was trundled down the hillside reached the river without being extinguished, this was hailed as a proof that the vintage would be abundant. So firmly was this belief held that the successful performance of the ceremony entitled the villagers to levy a tax upon the owners of the neighbouring vineyards. Here the unextinguished wheel meant an unclouded sun, and this in turn meant an abundant vintage. So the waggon-load of white wine which the villagers received from the vineyards round about was in fact a payment for the sunshine which they had procured for the grapes.

The interpretation of these fire-customs as charms for making sunshine is confirmed by a parallel custom observed by the Hindoos of Southern India at the Pongol or Feast of Ingathering. The festival is cele- brated in the early part of January, when, according to Hindoo astrologers, the sun enters the tropic of Capricorn, and the chief event of the festival coin- cides with the passage of the sun. For some days previously the boys gather heaps of sticks, straw, dead leaves, and everything that will burn. On the morning of the first day of the festival the heaps are fired. Every street and lane has its bonfire. The young folk leap over the fire or pile on fresh fuel. This fire is an offering to Sûrya, the sun-god, or to Agni, the deity of fire; it "wakes him from his sleep, calling on him again to gladden the earth with his light and heat."[1] To say that the fires awaken the sun-god from his sleep is only a metaphorical and perhaps modernised expression of the belief that they actually help to rekindle the sun's light and heat.

The custom of leaping over the fire and driving cattle through it may be intended, on the one hand, to secure for man and beast a share of the vital energy of the sun, and, on the other hand, to purify them from all evil influences; for to the primitive mind fire is the most powerful of all purificatory agents. The latter idea is obviously uppermost in the minds of Greek women when they leap over the midsummer fire, saying, "I leave my sins behind me." So in Yucatan at a New Year's festival the people used to light a huge bonfire and pass through it, in the belief that this was a means of

---

[1] Ch. E. Gover, "The Pongol festival in Southern India," *Journ.* *Royal Asiatic Society*, N.S. v. (1870) p. 96 *sq.*

ridding themselves of their troubles.[1]   The custom
of driving cattle through a fire is not confined to
Europe.   At certain times the Hottentots make a
fire of chips, dry branches, and green twigs, so as to
raise a great smoke.   Through this fire they drive
their sheep, dragging them through by force, if
necessary.   If the sheep make their escape without
passing through the fire, it is reckoned a heavy
disgrace and a very bad omen.   But if they pass
readily through or over the fire, the joy of the
Hottentots is indescribable.[2]

The procession or race with burning torches,
which so often forms a part of these fire-festivals,
appears to be simply a means of diffusing far and
wide the genial influence of the bonfire or of the sunshine which it represents.   Hence on these occasions
lighted torches are very frequently carried over the
fields, sometimes with the avowed intention of fertilising them ;[3] and with the same intention live coals
from the bonfire are sometimes placed in the field
"to prevent blight."   The custom of trundling a
burning wheel over the fields, which is practised for
the express purpose of fertilising them, embodies
the same idea in a still more graphic form ; since
in this way the mock-sun itself, not merely its light
and heat represented by torches, is made actually to
pass over the ground which is to receive its quickening and kindly influence.   Again, the custom of
carrying lighted brands round the cattle is plainly

[1] Diego de Landa, *Relation des choses de Yucatan* (Paris, 1864), p. 233.

[2] Kolben, *Present State of the Cape of Good Hope*, i. 129 *sqq.*

[3] P. 253.   The torches of Demeter, which figure so largely in her myth and on the monuments, are perhaps to be explained by this custom.   To regard, with Mannhardt (*B. K.* p. 536), the torches in the modern European cus-toms as imitations of lightning seems unnecessary.

equivalent to driving the animals through the fire.
It is quite possible that in these customs the idea
of the quickening power of fire may be combined
with the conception of it as a purgative agent for the
expulsion or destruction of evil beings. It is certainly sometimes interpreted in the latter way by
persons who practise the customs; and this purgative
use of fire comes out very prominently, as we have
seen, in the general expulsion of demons from towns
and villages. But in the present class of cases this
aspect of it is perhaps secondary, if indeed it is more
than a later misinterpretation of the custom.

It remains to ask, What is the meaning of burning
an effigy in these bonfires? The effigies so burned,
as was remarked above, can hardly be separated from
the effigies of Death which are burned or otherwise
destroyed in spring; and grounds have been already
given for regarding the so-called effigies of Death
as really representations of the tree-spirit or spirit of
vegetation. Are the other effigies, which are burned
in the spring and midsummer bonfires, susceptible of
the same explanation? It would seem so. For just
as the fragments of the so-called Death are stuck in
the fields to make the crops grow, so the charred
embers of the figure burned in the spring bonfires
are sometimes placed in the fields in the belief that
they will keep vermin from the crop. Again, the
rule that the last married bride must leap over the
fire in which the straw-man is burned on Shrove
Tuesday, is probably intended to make her fruitful.
But, as we have seen, the power of blessing women
with offspring is a special attribute of tree-spirits;[1]
it is therefore a fair presumption that the burning

---

[1] Above, vol. i. p. 70 *sqq.*

effigy over which the bride must leap is a representative of the fertilising tree-spirit or spirit of
vegetation. This character of the effigy, as representative of the spirit of vegetation, is almost unmistakable when the effigy is composed of an unthreshed
sheaf of corn or is covered from head to foot with
flowers.[1] Again, it is to be noted that instead of an
effigy living trees are sometimes burned both in the
spring and midsummer bonfires.[2] Now, considering
the frequency with which the tree-spirit is represented
in human shape, it is hardly rash to suppose that
when sometimes a tree and sometimes an effigy is
burned in these fires, the effigy and the tree are
regarded as equivalent to each other, each being a
representative of the tree-spirit. This, again, is confirmed by observing, first, that sometimes the effigy
which is to be burned is carried about simultaneously
with a May-tree, the former being carried by the boys,
the latter by the girls ;[3] and, second, that the effigy
is sometimes tied to a living tree and burned with
it.[4] In these cases, we can scarcely doubt, the tree-
spirit is represented, as we have found it represented
before, in duplicate, both by the tree and by the
effigy. That the true character of the effigy as a
representative of the beneficent spirit of vegetation
should sometimes be forgotten, is natural. The custom of burning a beneficent god is too foreign to
later modes of thought to escape misinterpretation.
Naturally enough the people who continued to burn his
image came in time to identify it as the effigy of persons, whom, on various grounds, they considered objec-
tionable, such as Judas Iscariot, Luther, and a witch.

The general reasons for killing a god or his

[1] Pp. 250, 267.   [2] Pp. 247, 248, 253, 259, 266.   [3] P. 250 *sq.*   [4] Pp. 247, 248.

representative have been examined in the preceding chapter. But when the god happens to be a deity of vegetation, there are special reasons why he should die by fire. For light and heat are necessary to vegetable growth ; and, on the principle of sympathetic magic, by subjecting the personal representative of vegetation to their influence, you secure a supply of these necessaries for trees and crops. In other words, by burning the spirit of vegetation in a fire which represents the sun, you make sure that, for a time at least, vegetation shall have plenty of sun. It may be objected that, if the intention is simply to secure enough sunshine for vegetation, this end would be better attained, on the principles of sympathetic magic, by merely passing the representative of vegetation through the fire instead of burning him. In point of fact this is sometimes done. In Russia, as we have seen, the straw figure of Kupalo is not burned in the midsummer fire, but merely carried backwards and forwards across it.[1] But, for the reasons already given, it is necessary that the god should die ; so next day Kupalo is stripped of her ornaments and thrown into a stream. In this Russian custom, therefore, the passage of the image through the fire is a sun-charm pure and simple ; the killing of the god is a separate act, and the mode of killing him— by drowning—is probably a rain-charm. But usually people have not thought it necessary to draw this fine distinction ; for the various reasons already assigned, it is advantageous, they think, to expose the god of vegetation to a considerable degree of heat, and it is also advantageous to kill him, and they combine these advantages in a rough-and-ready way by burning him.

---

[1] Vol. i. p. 272.

Finally, we have to ask, were human beings formerly burned as representatives of the tree-spirit or deity of vegetation? We have seen reasons for believing that living persons have often acted as representatives of the tree-spirit, and have suffered death as such. There is no reason, therefore, why they should not have been burned, if any special advantages were likely to be attained by putting them to death in that way. The consideration of human suffering is not one which enters into the calculations of primitive man. It would have been surprising if it did, when we remember the record of Christian Europe. Now, in the fire-festivals which we are discussing, the pretence of burning people is sometimes carried so far that it seems reasonable to regard it as a mitigated survival of an older custom of actually burning them. Thus in Aachen, as we saw, the man clad in peas-straw acts so cleverly that the children really believe he is being burned. And at the Beltane fires the pretended victim was seized, and a show made of throwing him into the fire, and for some time afterwards people affected to speak of him as dead. In the following customs Mannhardt is probably right in recognising traces of an old custom of burning a leaf-clad representative of the spirit of vegetation. At Wolfeck, in Austria, on Midsummer Day, a boy completely clad in green fir branches goes from house to house, accompanied by a noisy crew, collecting wood for the bonfire. As he gets the wood he sings—

" Forest trees I want,
No sour milk for me,
But beer and wine,
So can the wood-man be jolly and gay."[1]

---

[1] *B. K.* p. 524.

In some parts of Bavaria, also, the boys who go from house to house collecting fuel for the midsummer bonfire envelop one of their number from head to foot in green branches of firs, and lead him by a rope through the whole village.[1] At Moosheim, in Würtemberg, the festival of St. John's Fire usually lasted for fourteen days, ending on the second Sunday after Midsummer Day. On this last day the bonfire was left in charge of the children, while the older people retired to a wood. Here they encased a young fellow in leaves and twigs, who, thus disguised, went to the fire, scattered it, and trod it out. All the people present fled at the sight of him.[2]

But it seems possible to go farther than this. Of human sacrifices offered on these occasions the most unequivocal traces, as we have seen, are those which, about a hundred years ago, still lingered at the Beltane fires in the Highlands of Scotland, that is, among a Celtic people who, situated in a remote corner of Europe, enjoying practical independence, and almost completely isolated from foreign influence, had till then conserved their old heathenism better than any other people in the West of Europe. It is significant, therefore, that human sacrifices by fire are known, on unquestionable evidence, to have been systematically practised by the Celts. The earliest description of these sacrifices is by Julius Caesar. As conqueror of the hitherto independent Celts of Gaul, Caesar had ample opportunity of observing the national Celtic religion and manners, while these were still fresh and crisp from the native mint and had not yet been fused in the melting-pot of Roman civilisation. With

---

[1] *Bavaria*, iii. 956 ; *B. K.* p. 524.   *Schwaben*, ii. 121 *sq.*, No. 146 ; *B. K.*
[2] Birlinger, *Volksthümliches aus*   p. 524 *sq.*

Hottentot in tribal dress.

A sacrifice by a Celt of Gaul.

his own notes Caesar appears to have incorporated the observations of a Greek explorer, by name Posidonius, who travelled in Gaul about fifty years before Caesar carried the Roman arms to the English Channel. The Greek geographer Strabo and the historian Diodorus seem also to have derived their descriptions of the Celtic sacrifices from the work of Posidonius, but independently of each other and of Caesar, for each of the three derivative accounts contains some details which are not to be found in either of the others. By combining them, therefore, we can restore the original account of Posidonius with some certainty, and thus obtain a picture of the sacrifices offered by the Celts of Gaul at the close of the second century B.C.[1] The following seem to have been the main outlines of the custom. Condemned criminals were reserved by the Celts in order to be sacrificed to the gods at a great festival which took place once in every five years. The more there were of such victims, the greater was believed to be the fertility of the land.[2] When there were not enough criminals to furnish victims, captives taken in war were sacrificed to supply the deficiency. When the time came the victims were sacrificed by the Druids or priests. Some were shot down with arrows, some were impaled, and some were burned alive in the following manner. Colossal images of wicker-work or of wood and grass were constructed; these were filled with live men, cattle, and animals of other kinds; fire was then applied to the images, and they were burned with their living contents.

---

[1] Caesar, *Bell. Gall.* vi. 15; Strabo, iv. 4, 5, p. 198 Casaubon; Diodorus, v. 32. See Mannhardt, *B. K.* p. 525 *sqq.*

[2] Strabo, iv. 4, 4, p. 197, τὰς δὲ φονικὰς δίκας μάλιστα τούτοις [*i.e.* the Druids] ἐπετέτραπτο δικάζειν, ὅταν τε φορὰ τούτων ᾖ, φορὰν καὶ τῆς χώρας νομίζουσιν ὑπάρχειν. On this passage see Mannhardt, *B. K.* p. 529 *sqq.*

Such were the great festivals held once every five years. But besides these quinquennial festivals, celebrated on so grand a scale and with, apparently, so large an expenditure of human life, it seems reasonable to suppose that festivals of the same sort, only on a lesser scale, were held annually, and that from these annual festivals are lineally descended some at least of the fire-festivals which, with their traces of human sacrifices, are still celebrated year by year in many parts of Europe. The gigantic images constructed of osiers or covered with grass in which the Druids enclosed their victims remind us of the leafy framework in which the human representative of the tree-spirit is still so often encased.[1] Considering, therefore, that the fertility of the land was apparently supposed to depend upon the due performance of these sacrifices, Mannhardt is probably right in viewing the Celtic victims, cased in osiers and grass, as representatives of the tree-spirit or spirit of vegetation. These wicker giants of the Druids seem to have still their representatives at the spring and midsummer festivals of modern Europe. At Douay a procession takes place annually on the Sunday nearest to the 7th of July. The great feature of the procession is a colossal figure made of osiers, and called "the giant," which is moved through the streets by means of rollers and ropes worked by men who are enclosed within the figure. The wooden head of the giant is said to have been carved and painted by Rubens. The figure is armed as a knight with lance and sword, helmet and shield. Behind him march his wife and his three children, all constructed of osiers on the same principle, but on a smaller scale.[2] At Dunkirk the giant is forty

---

[1] See vol. i. p. 88 *sqq.*   [2] *B. K.* p. 523, *note.*

to fifty feet high, being made of basket - work and
canvas, properly painted and dressed. It contains a
great many living men within it, who move it about.
Wicker giants of this sort are common in the towns of
Belgium and French Flanders ; they are led about at
the Carnival in spring. The people, it is said, are much
attached to these grotesque figures, speak of them with
patriotic enthusiasm, and never weary of gazing at
them.[1] In England artificial giants seem to have
been a standing feature of the midsummer festival. A
writer of the sixteenth century speaks of " Midsommer
pageants in London, where, to make the people wonder,
are set forth great and uglie gyants, marching as if
they were alive, and armed at all points, but within
they are stuffed full of browne paper and tow, which
the shrewd boyes, underpeeping, do guilefully discover,
and turne to a greate derision." [2] The Mayor of
Chester in 1599 " altered many antient customs, as the
shooting for the sheriff's breakfast ; the going of the
Giants at Midsommer, etc." [3] In these cases the giants
only figure in the processions. But sometimes they
are burned in the spring or summer bonfires. Thus
the people of the Rue aux Ours in Paris used annually
to make a great wicker-work figure, dressed as a soldier,
which they promenaded up and down the streets for
several days, and solemnly burned on the 3d of July,
the crowd of spectators singing *Salve Regina*. The
burning fragments of the image were scattered among
the people, who eagerly scrambled for them. The

---

[1] *B. K.* p. 523, *note*; John Milner,
*The History, Civil and Ecclesiastical, and
Survey of the Antiquities of Winchester*,
i. 8 *sq*. ; Brand, *Popular Antiquities*, i.
325 *sq*.; James Logan, *The Scottish Gael*,
ii. 358 (new ed.); Reinsberg-Düringsfeld,
Calendrier Belge, p. 123 *sqq*.

[2] Puttenham, *Arte of English Poesie*,
1589, p. 128, quoted by Brand, *Popular
Antiquities*, i. 323.

[3] King's *Vale Royal of England*, p.
208, quoted by Brand, *l.c.*

custom was abolished in 1743.[1] In Brie, Isle de France, a wicker-work giant, eighteen feet high, was annually burned on Midsummer Eve.[2]

Again, the Druidical custom of burning live animals, enclosed in wicker-work, has its counterpart at the spring and midsummer festivals. At Luchon in the Pyrenees on Midsummer Eve "a hollow column, composed of strong wicker-work, is raised to the height of about sixty feet in the centre of the principal suburb, and interlaced with green foliage up to the very top; while the most beautiful flowers and shrubs procurable are artistically arranged in groups below, so as to form a sort of background to the scene. The column is then filled with combustible materials, ready for ignition. At an appointed hour—about 8 P.M.—a grand procession, composed of the clergy, followed by young men and maidens in holiday attire, pour forth from the town chanting hymns, and take up their position around the column. Meanwhile, bonfires are lit, with beautiful effect, in the surrounding hills. As many living serpents as could be collected are now thrown into the column, which is set on fire at the base by means of torches, armed with which about fifty boys and men dance around with frantic gestures. The serpents, to avoid the flames, wriggle their way to the top, whence they are seen lashing out laterally until finally obliged to drop, their struggles for life giving rise to enthusiastic delight among the surrounding spectators. This is a favourite annual ceremony for the inhabitants of Luchon and its neighbourhood, and local tradition assigns to it a heathen origin."[3] In the midsummer

---

[1] Liebrecht, *Gervasius von Tilbury,* p. 212 *sq.*; *B. K.* p. 514.
[2] *B. K.* pp. 514, 523.

[3] *Athenaeum,* 24th July 1869, p. 115; *B. K.* p. 515 *sq.*

fires formerly kindled on the Place de Grève at Paris
it was the custom to burn a basket, barrel, or sack full
of live cats ; sometimes a fox was burned. The people
collected the embers and ashes of the fire and took
them home, believing that they brought good luck.[1]
At Metz midsummer fires were lighted on the Esplan-
ade, and six cats were burned in them.[2] In Russia a
white cock was sometimes burned in the midsummer
bonfire;[3] in Meissen or Thüringen a horse's head used
to be thrown into it.[4] Sometimes animals are burned
in the spring bonfires. In the Vosges cats were burned
on Shrove Tuesday ; in Elsass they were thrown into
the Easter bonfire.[5] We have seen that squirrels were
sometimes burned in the Easter fire.

If the men who were burned in wicker frames by
the Druids represented the spirit of vegetation, the
animals burned along with them must have had the
same meaning. Amongst the animals burned by the
Druids or in modern bonfires have been, as we saw,
cattle, cats, foxes, and cocks ; and all of these creatures
are variously regarded by European peoples as embodiments of the corn-spirit.[6] I am not aware of any certain
evidence that in Europe serpents have been regarded
as representatives of the tree-spirit or corn-spirit ;[7] as
victims at the midsummer festival in Luchon they may

---

[1] Wolf, *Beiträge zur deutschen Mythologie,* ii. 388 ; *B. K.* p. 515.

[2] *B. K.* p. 515.

[3] Grimm, *Deutsche Mythologie,*[4] i.
519 ; *B. K.* p. 515.

[4] *B. K.* p. 515.

[5] *Ib.*

[6] Above, vol. i. p. 408, vol. ii. p. 1 *sqq.*

[7] Some of the serpents worshipped
by the old Prussians lived in hollow
oaks, and as oaks were sacred among
the Prussians, the serpents may have
been regarded as genii of the trees.

Simon Grunau, *Preussische Chronik,*
ed. Perlbach, i. p. 89 ; Hartknoch, *Alt-
und Neues Preussen,* pp. 143, 163.
Serpents, again, played an important
part in the worship of Demeter, as we
have seen. But that they were regarded
as embodiments of her can hardly be
assumed. In Siam the spirit of the
takhien tree is believed to appear,
sometimes in the form of a woman,
sometimes in the form of a serpent.
Bastian, *Die Völker des östlichen Asien,*
iii. 251.

have replaced animals which really had this representative character. When the meaning of the custom was forgotten, utility and humanity might unite in suggesting the substitution of noxious reptiles as victims in room of harmless and useful animals.

Thus it appears that the sacrificial rites of the Celts of ancient Gaul can be traced in the popular festivals of modern Europe. Naturally it is in France, or rather in the wider area comprised within the limits of ancient Gaul, that these rites have left the clearest traces in the customs of burning giants of wicker-work and animals enclosed in wicker-work or baskets. These customs, it will have been remarked, are generally observed at or about midsummer. From this we may infer that the original rites of which these are the degenerate successors were solemnised at midsummer. This inference harmonises with the conclusion suggested by a general survey of European folk-custom, that the midsummer festival must on the whole have been the most widely diffused and the most solemn of all the yearly festivals celebrated by the primitive Aryans in Europe. And in its application to the Celts this general conclusion is corroborated by the more or less perfect vestiges of midsummer fire-festivals which we have found lingering in all those westernmost promontories and islands which are the last strongholds of the Celtic race in Europe — Britanny, Cornwall, Wales, the Isle of Man, Scotland, and Ireland. In Scotland, it is true, the chief Celtic fire-festivals certainly appear to have been held at Beltane (1st May) and Hallow E'en ; but this was exceptional.

To sum up : the combined evidence of ancient writers and of modern folk-custom points to the conclusion that amongst the Celts of Gaul an annual festival was celebrated at midsummer, at which living men, representing the tree-spirit or spirit of vegetation, were enclosed in wicker-frames and burned. The whole rite was designed as a charm to make the sun to shine and the crops to grow.

But another great feature of the Celtic midsummer festival appears to have been the gathering of the sacred mistletoe by the Druids. The ceremony has been thus described by Pliny in a passage which has often been quoted. After enumerating the different kinds of mistletoe he proceeds: "In treating of this subject, the admiration in which the mistletoe is held throughout Gaul ought not to pass unnoticed. The Druids, for so they call their wizards, esteem nothing more sacred than the mistletoe and the tree on which it grows, provided only that the tree is an oak. But apart from this they choose oak-woods for their sacred groves and perform no sacred rites without oak-leaves; so that the very name of Druids may be regarded as a Greek appellation derived from their worship of the oak.[1] For they believe that whatever grows on these trees is sent from heaven, and is a sign that the tree has been chosen by the god himself. The mistletoe is very rarely to be met with; but when it is found, they gather it with solemn ceremony. This they do especially in the sixth month (the beginnings of their months and years are determined by the moon) and after the tree has passed the thirtieth year of its age,

---

[1] Pliny derives the name Druid from the Greek *drūs*, "oak." He did not know that the Celtic word for oak was the same (*daur*), and that therefore Druid, in the sense of priest of the oak, was genuine Celtic, not borrowed from the Greek. See Curtius, *Griech. Etymologie*,[5] p. 238 *sq.*; Vaníček, *Griechisch-lateinisches etymolog. Wörterbuch*, p. 368 *sqq.*; Rhys, *Celtic Heathendom*, p. 221 *sqq.* In the Highlands of Scotland the word is found in place-names like Bendarroch (the mountain of the oak), Craigandarroch, etc.

because by that time it has plenty of vigour, though it has not attained half its full size. After due preparations have been made for a sacrifice and a feast under the tree, they hail it as the universal healer and bring to the spot two white bulls, whose horns have never been bound before. A priest clad in a white robe climbs the tree and with a golden[1] sickle cuts the mistletoe, which is caught in a white cloth. Then they sacrifice the victims, praying that God may make his own gift to prosper with those upon whom he has bestowed it. They believe that a potion prepared from mistletoe will make barren animals to bring forth, and that the plant is a remedy against all poison."[2]

In saying that the Druids cut the mistletoe in the sixth month Pliny must have had in his mind the Roman calendar, in which the sixth month was June. Now, if the cutting of the mistletoe took place in June, we may be almost certain that the day which witnessed the ceremony was Midsummer Eve. For in many places Midsummer Eve, a day redolent of a thousand decaying fancies of yore, is still the time for culling certain magic plants, whose evanescent virtue can be secured at this mystic season alone. For example, on Midsummer Eve the fern is believed to burst into a wondrous bloom, like fire or burnished gold. Who-

---

[1] It is still a folk-lore rule not to cut the mistletoe with iron; some say it should be cut with gold. Grimm, *Deutsche Mythologie*,[4] ii. 1001. On the objection to the use of iron in such cases, see Liebrecht, *Gervasius von Tilbury*, p. 103; and above, vol. i. p. 177 *sqq.*

[2] Pliny, *Nat. Hist.* xvi. § 249 *sqq.* On the Celtic worship of the oak, see also Maximus Tyrius, *Dissert.* viii. 8, Κελτοὶ σέβουσι μὲν Δία ἄγαλμα δὲ Διὸς Κελτικὸν ὑψηλὴ δρῦς. With this mode of gathering the mistletoe compare the following.

In Cambodia when a man perceives a certain parasitic plant growing on a tamarind-tree, he dresses in white and taking a new earthen pot climbs the tree at mid-day. He puts the plant in the pot and lets the whole fall to the ground. Then in the pot he makes a decoction which renders invulnerable. Aymonier, "Notes sur les coutumes et croyances superstitieuses des Cambodgiens," in *Cochinchine Française, Excursions et Reconnaissances*, No. 16, p. 136.

ever catches this bloom, which very quickly fades and falls off, can make himself invisible, can understand the language of animals, and so forth. But he must not touch it with his hand ; he must spread a white cloth under the fern, and the magic bloom (or seed) will fall into it.[1] Again, St. John's wort (*Hypericum perforatum*), a herb which is believed to heal all kinds of wounds and to drive away witches and demons, is gathered on Midsummer Eve (Eve of St. John), and is worn as an amulet or hung over doors and windows on that day.[2] Again, mugwort (*Artemisia vulgaris*) is believed to possess magic qualities provided it be gathered on St. John's Eve. Hence in France it is called the herb of St. John. People weave themselves a girdle of the plant, believing that it will protect them against ghosts, magic, misfortune, and disease, throughout the year. Or they weave garlands of it on St. John's Eve, and look through them at the midsummer bonfire or put them on their heads. Whoever does this will suffer no aches in his eyes or head that year. Sometimes the plant is thrown into the midsummer bonfire.[3] The superstitious association of fern-seed, St. John's wort, and mugwort with Midsummer Eve is widely diffused over Europe. The following associations seem to be more local. In England the orpine (*Sedum telephium*) is popularly called Midsummer

---

[1] Wuttke, *Der deutsche Volksaberglaube*,[2] § 123 ; Grohmann, *Aberglauben und Gebräuche aus Böhmen und Mähren*, §§ 673-677; Gubernatis, *Mythologie des Plantes*, ii. 144 *sqq.*; Friend, *Flowers and Flower Lore*, p. 362 ; Brand, *Popular Antiquities*, i. 314 *sqq.* ; Vonbun, *Beiträge zur deutschen Mythologie*, p. 133 *sqq.*; Burne and Jackson, *Shropshire Folklore*, p. 242. Cp. *Archaeological Review*, i. 164 *sqq.*

[2] Brand, *Popular Antiquities*, i. 307, 312 ; Dyer, *Folk-lore of Plants*, pp. 62, 286 ; Friend, *Flowers and Flower Lore*, pp. 147, 149, 150, 540 ; Wuttke, § 134.

[3] Grimm, *D. M.*[4] i. 514 *sq.*, ii. 1013 *sq.*, iii. 356 ; Grohmann, *op. cit.*, § 635-637; Friend, *op. cit.* p. 75 ; Gubernatis, *Myth. des Plantes*, i. 189 *sq.*, ii. 16 *sqq.*

Men, because it has been customary to gather it on Midsummer Eve for the purpose of using it to ascertain the fate of lovers ;[1] and in England sprigs of red sage are sometimes gathered on Midsummer Eve for the same purpose.[2] In Bohemia poachers fancy they can make themselves invulnerable by means of fir-cones gathered before sunrise on St. John's Day.[3] Again, in Bohemia wild thyme gathered on Midsummer Day is used to fumigate the trees on Christmas Eve, in order that they may grow well.[4] In Germany and Bohemia a plant called St. John's Flower or St. John's Blood (*Hieracium pilosella*) is gathered on Midsummer Eve. It should be rooted up with a gold coin. The plant is supposed to bring luck and to be especially good for sick cattle.[5]

These facts by themselves would suffice to raise a strong presumption that, if the Druids cut the mistletoe in June, as we learn from Pliny that they did, the day on which they cut it could have been no other than Midsummer Eve or Midsummer Day. This presumption is converted into practical certainty when we find it to be still a rule of folk-lore that the mistletoe should be cut on Midsummer Eve.[6] Further, the peasants of Piedmont and Lombardy still go out on Midsummer morning to search the oak-leaves for the "oil of St. John," which is supposed to heal all wounds made with cutting instruments.[7] Originally no doubt the "oil of St. John" was simply the mistletoe, or a decoction made

---

[1] Aubrey, *Remaines of Gentilisme and Judaisme*, p. 25 *sq.* ; Brand, *Pop. Ant.* i. 329 *sqq.*; Friend, p. 136.

[2] Brand, i. 333.

[3] Grohmann, § 1426.

[4] Grohmann, § 648.

[5] Grohmann, § 681; Wuttke, § 134; Rochholz, *Deutscher Glaube und Brauch*, i. 9; Gubernatis, *Mythologie des Plantes*, i. 190.

[6] Grimm, *D. M.*[4] iii. 78, 353.

[7] Gubernatis, *Mythologie des Plantes*, ii. 73.

from it.   For in Holstein the mistletoe, especially oak-mistletoe, is still regarded as a panacea for green wounds;[1] and if, as is alleged, "all-healer" is an epithet of the mistletoe in the modern Celtic speech of Britanny, Wales, Ireland, and Scotland,[2] this can be nothing but a survival of the name by which, as we have seen, the Druids addressed the oak, or rather, perhaps, the mistletoe.

Thus it appears that the two main features of the Balder myth—the pulling of the mistletoe and the burning of the god—were reproduced in the great midsummer festival of the Celts.   But in Scandinavia itself, the home of Balder, both these features of his myth can still be traced in the popular celebration of midsummer.   For in Sweden on Midsummer Eve mistletoe is "diligently sought after, they believing it to be, in a high degree, possessed of mystic qualities; and that if a sprig of it be attached to the ceiling of the dwelling-house, the horse's stall, or the cow's crib, the 'Troll' will then be powerless to injure either man or beast."[3]   And in Sweden, Norway, and Denmark huge bonfires are kindled on hills and eminences on Midsummer Eve.[4]   It does not appear, indeed, that any effigy is burned in these bonfires; but the burning of an effigy is a feature which might easily drop out after its meaning was forgotten.   And the name of Balder's bale-fires (*Balder's Bălar*), by which these midsummer fires were formerly known in Sweden,[5] puts their connection with Balder beyond the reach of doubt, and makes it certain that in

---

[1] Friend, *Flowers and Flower Lore*, p. 378.   Hunters believe that the mistletoe heals all wounds and brings luck in hunting.   Kuhn, *Herabkunft des Feuers*,[2] p. 206.

[2] Grimm, *D. M.*[4] ii. 1009.

[3] L. Lloyd, *Peasant Life in Sweden*, p. 269.

[4] Lloyd, *op. cit.* p. 259; Grimm, *D. M.*[4] i. 517 *sq.*   [5] Lloyd, *l.c.*

former times either a living representative or an effigy
of Balder must have been annually burned in them.
Midsummer was the season sacred to Balder, and the
fact that the Swedish poet Tegner, in his *Frithiofssaga*,
places the burning of Balder at midsummer[1] may perhaps be allowed as evidence of a Swedish tradition to
that effect. From this double coincidence of the
Balder myth, on the one hand with the midsummer
festival of Celtic Gaul and on the other with the midsummer festival in Scandinavia, we may safely conclude that the myth is not a myth pure and simple,
that is, a mere description of physical phenomena in
imagery borrowed from human life; it must undoubtedly be a ritualistic myth, that is a myth based
on actual observation of religious ceremonies and pur-
porting to explain them. Now, the standing explanation which myth gives of ritual is that the ritual in
question is a periodic commemoration of some remarkable transaction in the past, the actors in which may
have been either gods or men. Such an explanation
the Balder myth would seem to offer of the annual
fire-festivals which, as we saw, must have played so
prominent a part in the primitive religion of the Aryan
race in Europe. Balder must have been the Norse
representative of the being who was burnt in effigy or
in the person of a living mân at the fire-festivals in
question. But if, as I have tried to show, the being
so burnt was the tree-spirit or spirit of vegetation, it
follows that Balder also must have been a tree-spirit
or spirit of vegetation.

But it is desirable to determine, if we can, the

---

[1] Grimm, *D. M.*⁴ iii. 78, who adds,
" *Mahnen die Johannisfeuer an Baldrs
Leichenbrand?* " This pregnant hint,
which contains in germ the solution of
the whole myth, has been quite lost on
the mythologists who since Grimm's
day have enveloped the subject in a
cloud of learned dust.

particular kind of tree or trees, of which a personal
representative was burned at the fire-festivals. For
we may be quite sure that it was not as a representative of vegetation in general that the victim suffered
death.   The conception of vegetation in general is too
abstract to be primitive.   Most probably the victim at
first represented a particular kind of sacred tree.   Now
of all European trees none has such claims as the oak
to be considered as pre-eminently the sacred tree of
the Aryans.   Its worship is attested for all the great
branches of the Aryan stock in Europe. We have
seen that it was not only the sacred tree, but the
principal object of worship of both Celts and Slavs.[1]
According to Grimm, the oak ranked first among the
holy trees of the Germans, and was indeed their chief
god.   It is certainly known to have been adored by
them in the age of heathendom, and traces of its
worship have survived in various parts of Germany
almost to the present day.[2] Amongst the ancient
Italians, according to Preller, the oak was sacred above
all other trees.[3] The image of Jupiter on the Capitol
at Rome seems to have been originally nothing
but a natural oak-tree.[4] At Dodona, perhaps the
oldest of all Greek sanctuaries, Zeus was worshipped
as immanent in the sacred oak, and the rustling of
its leaves in the wind was his voice.[5] If, then, the
great god of both Greeks and Romans was represented in some of his oldest shrines under the form
of an oak, and if the oak was the principal object
of worship of Celts, Germans, and Slavs, we may

---

[1] Above, p. 285, and vol. i. pp. 58, 64.
[2] Grimm, *D. M.*[4] i. 55 *sq.*, 58 *sq.*,
ii. 542, iii. 187 *sq.*
[3] Preller, *Röm. Mythol.*[3] i. 108.
[4] Livy, i. 10.   Cp. C. Bötticher,

Der Baumkultus der Hellenen, p.
133 *sq.*
[5] Bötticher, *op. cit.* p. 111 *sqq.*;
Preller, *Griech. Mythol.*[4] ed. C. Robert,
i. 122 *sqq.*

certainly conclude that this tree was one of the chief, if not the very chief divinity of the Aryans before the dispersion ; and that their primitive home must have lain in a land which was clothed with forests of oak.[1]

Now, considering the primitive character and remarkable similarity of the fire-festivals observed by all the branches of the Aryan race in Europe, we may infer that these festivals form part of the common stock of religious observances which the various peoples carried with them in their wanderings from their original home. But, if I am right, an essential feature of those primitive fire-festivals was the burning of a man who represented the tree-spirit. In view, then, of the place occupied by the oak in the religion of the Aryans, the presumption is that the tree so represented at the fire-festivals must originally have been the oak. So far as the Celts and Slavs are concerned, this conclusion will perhaps hardly be contested. But both for them and for the Germans it is confirmed by a remarkable piece of religious conservatism. The most primitive method known to man of producing fire is by rubbing two pieces of wood against each other till they ignite ; and we have seen that this method is still used in Europe for kindling sacred fires such as the

---

[1] Without hazarding an opinion on the vexed question of the primitive home of the Aryans, I may observe that in various parts of Europe the oak seems to have been formerly more common than it is now. In Denmark the present beech woods were preceded by oak woods and these by the Scotch fir. Lyell, *Antiquity of Man*, p. 9 ; J. Geikie, *Prehistoric Europe*, p. 486 *sq.* In parts of North Germany it appears from the evidence of archives that the fir has ousted the oak. O. Schrader, *Sprachvergleichung und Urgeschichte*,[2] (Jena, 1890), p. 394. In prehistoric times the oak appears to have been the chief tree in the forests which clothed the valley of the Po ; the piles on which the pile villages rested were of oak. W. Helbig, *Die Italiker in der Poebene*, p. 25 *sq.* The classical tradition that in the olden time men subsisted largely on acorns is borne out by the evidence of the pile villages in Northern Italy, in which great quantities of acorns have been discovered. See Helbig, *op. cit.* pp. 16 *sq.*, 26, 72 *sq.*

need-fire, and that most probably it was formerly resorted to at all the fire-festivals under discussion. Now it is sometimes prescribed that the need-fire, or other sacred fire, must be made by the friction of a particular kind of wood ; and wherever the kind of wood is prescribed, whether among Celts, Germans, or Slavs, that wood is always the oak. Thus we have seen that amongst the Slavs of Masuren the new fire for the village is made on Midsummer Day by causing a wheel to revolve rapidly round an axle of oak till the axle takes fire.[1] When the perpetual fire which the ancient Slavs used to maintain chanced to go out, it was rekindled by the friction of a piece of oak-wood, which had been previously heated by being struck with a gray (not a red) stone.[2] In Germany the need-fire was regularly kindled by the friction of oak-wood ;[3] and in the Highlands of Scotland, both the Beltane and the need-fires were lighted by similar means.[4] Now, if the sacred fire was regularly kindled by the friction of oak-wood, we may infer that originally the fire was also fed with the same material. In point of fact, the perpetual fire which burned under the sacred oak at the great Slavonian sanctuary of Romove was fed with oak-wood ;[5] and that oak-wood was formerly the fuel

---

[1] Above, p. 265 *sq.*

[2] Praetorius, *Deliciae Prussicae*, 19 *sq.* Mr. Ralston states (on what authority I do not know) that if the fire maintained in honour of the Lithuanian god Perkunas went out, it was rekindled by sparks struck from a stone which the image of the god held in his hand. *Songs of the Russian People*, p. 88.

[3] Grimm, *D. M.*[4] i. 502, 503 ; Kuhn, *Herabkunft des Feuers*,[2] p. 43 ; Pröhle, *Harzbilder*, p. 75 ; Bartsch, *Sagen, Märchen und Gebräuche aus Mecklenburg*, ii. 150 ; Rochholz, *Deutscher Glaube und Brauch*, ii. 148.

The writer who styles himself Montanus says (*Die deutschen Volksfeste*, etc., p. 127) that the need-fire was made by the friction of oak and fir. Sometimes it is said that the need-fire should be made with nine different kinds of wood (Grimm, *D. M.*[4] i. 503, 505 ; Wolf, *Beiträge zur deutschen Mythologie*, ii. 380 ; Jahn, *Die deutschen Opfergebräuche*, p. 27) ; but the kinds of wood are not specified.

[4] John Ramsay, *Scotland and Scotsmen in the Eighteenth Century*, ii. 442 ; Grimm, *D. M.*[4] i. 506. See above, p. 255.

[5] Above, vol. i. p. 58.

burned in the midsummer fires may perhaps be inferred from the circumstance that in many mountain districts of Germany peasants are still in the habit of making up their cottage fire on Midsummer Day with a heavy block of oak-wood. The block is so arranged that it smoulders slowly and is not finally reduced to charcoal till the expiry of a year. Then upon next Midsummer Day the charred embers of the old log are removed to make room for the new one, and are mixed with the seed-corn or scattered about the garden. This is believed to promote the growth of the crops and to preserve them from blight and vermin.[1] It may be remembered that at the Boeotian festival of the Daedala, the analogy of which to the spring and mid-summer festivals of modern Europe has been already pointed out, the great feature was the felling and burn-ing of an oak.[2] The general conclusion is, that at those periodic or occasional ceremonies, of which the object was to cause the sun to shine, and the fruits of the earth to grow, the ancient Aryans both kindled and fed the fire with the sacred oak-wood.

But if at these solemn rites the fire was regularly made of oak-wood, it follows that the man who was burned in it as a personification of the tree-spirit could have represented no tree but the oak. The sacred oak was thus burned in duplicate; the wood of the tree was consumed in the fire, and along with it was consumed a living man as a personification of the oak-spirit. The conclusion thus drawn for the European Aryans in general is confirmed in its special application to the Celts and Scandinavians by the relation in which, amongst these peoples, the mistletoe stood to the burn-ing of the victim in the midsummer fire. We have

[1] Montanus, *Die deutschen Volksfeste*, etc., p. 127. [2] Above, vol. i. p. 100.

seen that among Celts and Scandinavians it has been
customary to gather the mistletoe at midsummer.   But
so far as appears on the face of this custom, there is
nothing to connect it with the midsummer fires in
which human victims or effigies of them were burned.
Even if the fire, as seems probable, was originally
always made with oak-wood, why should it have been
necessary to pull the mistletoe ?   The last link between
the midsummer customs of gathering the mistletoe
and lighting the bonfires is supplied by Balder's
myth, which certainly cannot be disjoined from the
customs in question.   The myth shows that a vital
connection must once have been believed to subsist
between the mistletoe and the human representative of
the oak who was burned in the fire.   According to the
myth, Balder could be killed by nothing in heaven or
earth except the mistletoe ; and so long as the mistletoe
remained on the oak, he was not only immortal, but
invulnerable.   Now, as soon as we see that Balder
was the oak, the origin of the myth becomes plain.
The mistletoe was viewed as the seat of life of the oak,
and so long as it was uninjured nothing could kill or
even wound the oak.   The conception of the mistletoe
as the seat of life of the oak would naturally be suggested to primitive people by the observation that
while the oak is deciduous, the mistletoe which grows
on it is evergreen.   In winter the sight of its fresh
foliage among the bare branches must have been hailed
by the worshippers of the tree as a sign that the divine
life which had ceased to animate the branches yet
survived in the mistletoe, as the heart of a sleeper
still beats when his body is motionless.   Hence when
the god had to be killed—when the sacred tree had
to be burnt—it was necessary to begin by breaking off

the mistletoe. For so long as the mistletoe remained intact, the oak (so people thought) was invulnerable; all the blows of their knives and axes would glance harmless from its surface. But once tear from the oak its sacred heart—the mistletoe—and the tree nodded to its fall. And when in later times the spirit of the oak came to be represented by a living man, it was logically necessary to suppose that, like the tree he personated, he could neither be killed nor wounded so long as the mistletoe remained uninjured. The pulling of the mistletoe was thus at once the signal and the cause of his death.

But since the idea of a being whose life is thus, in a sense, outside itself, must be strange to many readers, and has, indeed, not yet been recognised in its full bearing on primitive superstition, it will be worth while to devote a couple of sections to the subject. The result will be to show that, in assuming this idea as the explanation of the relation of Balder to the mistletoe, I assume a principle which is deeply engraved on the mind of primitive man.

§ 3.—*The external soul in folk-tales*

In a former chapter we saw that, in the opinion of primitive people, the soul may temporarily absent itself from the body without causing death. Such temporary absences of the soul are often believed to involve considerable risk, since the wandering soul is liable to a variety of mishaps at the hands of enemies, and so forth. But there is another aspect to this power of externalising the soul. If only the safety of the soul can be ensured during its absence from the body, there

Israelite sacrifice of the lamb.

Egyptian sacrifice of the bull.

is no reason why the soul should not continue absent
for an indefinite time ; indeed a man may, on a pure
calculation of personal safety, desire that his soul should
never return to his body.   Unable to conceive of life
abstractly as a "permanent possibility of sensation" or
a "continuous adjustment of internal arrangements to
external relations," the savage thinks of it as a concrete
material thing of a definite bulk, capable of being seen
and handled, kept in a box or jar, and liable to be
bruised, fractured, or smashed in pieces.   It is not
needful that the life, so conceived, should be in the
man ; it may be absent from his body and still continue to animate him, by virtue of a sort of sympathy
or "action at a distance."   So long as this object
which he calls his life or soul remains unharmed,
the man is well ; if it is injured, he suffers ; if it is
destroyed, he dies.   Or, to put it otherwise, when a
man is ill or dies, the fact is explained by saying that
the material object called his life or soul, whether it be
in his body or out of it, has either sustained injury or
been destroyed.   But there may be circumstances in
which, if the life or soul remains in the man, it stands
a greater chance of sustaining injury than if it were
stowed away in some safe and secret place.   Accordingly, in such circumstances, primitive man takes his
soul out of his body and deposits it for security in
some safe place, intending to replace it in his body
when the danger is past.   Or if he should discover
some place of absolute security, he may be content to
leave his soul there permanently.   The advantage of
this is that, so long as the soul remains unharmed in
the place where he has deposited it, the man himself
is immortal ; nothing can kill his body, since his life is
not in it.

Evidence of this primitive belief is furnished by a class of folk-tales of which the Norse story of "The giant who had no heart in his body" is perhaps the best-known example. Stories of this kind are widely diffused over the world, and from their number and the variety of incident and of details in which the leading idea is embodied, we may infer that the conception of an external soul is one which has had a powerful hold on the minds of men at an early stage of history. For folk-tales are a faithful reflection of the world as it appeared to the primitive mind ; and we may be sure that any idea which commonly occurs in them, however absurd it may seem to us, must once have been an ordinary article of belief. This assurance, so far as it concerns the supposed power of externalising the soul for a longer or shorter time, is amply corroborated by a comparison of the folk-tales in question with the actual beliefs and practices of savages. To this we shall return after some specimens of the tales have been given. The specimens will be selected with a view of illustrating both the characteristic features and the wide diffusion of this class of tales.

In the first place, the story of the external soul is told, in various forms, by all Aryan peoples from Hindustan to the Hebrides. A very common form of it is this : A warlock, giant, or other fairyland being is invulnerable and immortal because he keeps his soul hidden far away in some secret place ; but a fair princess, whom he holds enthralled in his enchanted castle, wiles his secret from him and reveals it to the hero, who seeks out the warlock's soul, heart, life, or death (as it is variously called), and, by destroying it, simultaneously kills the warlock. Thus a Hindoo story tells how a magician called Punchkin held a

queen captive for twelve years, and would fain marry
her, but she would not have him.   At last the queen's
son came to rescue her, and the two plotted together
to kill Punchkin.   So the queen spoke the magician fair,
and pretended that she had at last made up her mind
to marry him.   " 'And do tell me,' she said, 'are you
quite immortal?   Can death never touch you?   And
are you too great an enchanter ever to feel human
suffering?' . . . 'It is true,' he said, 'that I am not as
others.   Far, far away—hundreds of thousands of
miles from this—there lies a desolate country covered
with thick jungle.   In the midst of the jungle grows a
circle of palm-trees, and in the centre of the circle stand
six chattees full of water, piled one above another;
below the sixth chattee is a small cage, which contains
a little green parrot—on the life of the parrot depends
my life—and if the parrot is killed I must die.   It is,
however,' he added, 'impossible that the parrot should
sustain any injury, both on account of the inaccessibility
of the country, and because, by my appointment, many
thousand genii surround the palm-trees, and kill all
who approach the place.' "   But the queen's young
son overcame all difficulties, and got possession of
the parrot.   He brought it to the door of the magician's palace, and began playing with it.   Punchkin,
the magician, saw him, and, coming out, tried to
persuade the boy to give him the parrot.   " 'Give me
my parrot!' cried Punchkin.   Then the boy took hold
of the parrot and tore off one of his wings; and as he
did so the magician's right arm fell off.   Punchkin
then stretched out his left arm, crying, 'Give me my
parrot!'   The prince pulled off the parrot's second
wing, and the magician's left arm tumbled off.   'Give
me my parrot!' cried he, and fell on his knees.   The

prince pulled off the parrot's right leg, the magician's right leg fell off; the prince pulled off the parrot's left leg, down fell the magician's left. Nothing remained of him except the lifeless body and the head; but still he rolled his eyes, and cried, 'Give me my parrot!' 'Take your parrot, then,' cried the boy; and with that he wrung the bird's neck, and threw it at the magician; and, as he did so, Punchkin's head twisted round, and, with a fearful groan, he died!"[1] In another Hindoo tale an ogre is asked by his daughter, "'Papa, where do you keep your soul?' 'Sixteen miles away from this place,' said he, 'is a tree. Round the tree are tigers, and bears, and scorpions, and snakes; on the top of the tree is a very great fat snake; on his head is a little cage; in the cage is a bird; and my soul is in that bird.'" The end of the ogre is like that of the magician in the previous tale. As the bird's wings and legs are torn off, the ogre's arms and legs drop off; and when its neck is wrung he falls down dead.[2]

In another Hindoo story a princess called Sodewa Bai is born with a golden necklace about her neck, and the astrologer told her parents, "This is no common child; the necklace of gold about her neck contains your daughter's soul; let it, therefore, be guarded with the utmost care; for if it were taken off and worn by another person, she would die." So her mother caused it to be firmly fastened round the child's neck, and, as soon as the child was old enough to understand, she told her its value, and warned her never to let it be taken off. In course of time Sodewa Bai was married to a prince who had another wife living. The

---

[1] Mary Frere, *Old Deccan Days*, p. 12 *sqq.*

[2] Maive Stokes, *Indian Fairy Tales*, p. 58 *sqq.* For similar stories, see *id.* p. 187 *sq.*; Lal Behari Day, *Folk-tales of Bengal*, p. 121 *sq.*; F. A. Steel and R. C. Temple, *Wide-awake Stories*, p. 58 *sqq.*

first wife, jealous of her young rival, persuaded a negress to steal from Sodewa Bai the golden necklace which contained her soul. The negress did so, and, as soon as she put the necklace round her own neck, Sodewa Bai died. All day long the negress used to wear the necklace; but late at night, on going to bed, she would take it off and put it by till morning; and whenever she took it off, Sodewa Bai's soul returned to her and she lived. But when morning came, and the negress put on the necklace, Sodewa Bai died again. At last the prince discovered the treachery of his elder wife and restored the golden necklace to Sodewa Bai.[1] In another Hindoo story a holy mendicant tells a queen that she will bear a son, adding, " As enemies will try to take away the life of your son, I may as well tell you that the life of the boy will be bound up in the life of a big *boal*-fish which is in your tank in front of the palace. In the heart of the fish is a small box of wood, in the box is a necklace of gold, that necklace is the life of your son." The boy was born and received the name of Dalim. His mother was the Suo or younger queen. But the Duo or elder queen hated the child, and learning the secret of his life, she caused the *boal*-fish, with which his life was bound up, to be caught. Dalim was playing near the tank at the time, but " the moment the *boal*-fish was caught in the net, that moment Dalim felt unwell; and when the fish was brought up to land, Dalim fell down on the ground, and made as if he was about to breathe his last. He was immediately taken into his mother's room, and the king was astonished on hearing of the sudden illness of his son and heir. The fish was by the order of the physician taken into the room of the Duo queen, and

---

[1] *Old Deccan Days*, p. 239 *sqq.*

as it lay on the floor striking its fins on the ground, Dalim in his mother's room was given up for lost. When the fish was cut open, a casket was found in it; and in the casket lay a necklace of gold. The moment the necklace was worn by the queen, that very moment Dalim died in his mother's room." The queen used to put off the necklace every night, and whenever she did so, the boy came to life again. But every morning when the queen put on the necklace, he died again.[1]

In a Cashmeer story a lad visits an old ogress, pretending to be her grandson, the son of her daughter who had married a king. So the old ogress took him into her confidence and showed him seven cocks, a spinning wheel, a pigeon, and a starling. "These seven cocks," said she, "contain the lives of your seven uncles, who are away for a few days. Only as long as the cocks live can your uncles hope to live; no power can hurt them as long as the seven cocks are safe and sound. The spinning-wheel contains my life; if it is broken, I too shall be broken, and must die; but otherwise I shall live on for ever. The pigeon contains your grandfather's life, and the starling your mother's; as long as these live, nothing can harm your grandfather or your mother." So the lad killed the seven cocks and the pigeon and the starling, and smashed the spinning-wheel; and at the moment he did so the ogres and ogresses perished.[2] In another story from Cashmeer an ogre cannot die unless a particular pillar in the verandah of his palace be broken. Learning the secret, a prince struck the

[1] Lal Behari Day, *op. cit.* p. 1 *sqq.* For similar stories of necklaces, see *Old Deccan Days*, p. 233 *sq.*; *Wide-awake Stories*, p. 83 *sqq.*

[2] J. H. Knowles, *Folk-tales of Kashmir* (London, 1888), p. 49 *sq.*

pillar again and again till it was broken in pieces. And it was as if each stroke had fallen on the ogre, for he howled lamentably and shook like an aspen every time the prince hit the pillar, until at last, when the pillar fell down, the ogre also fell down and gave up the ghost.[1]   In another Cashmeer tale an ogre is represented as laughing very heartily at the idea that he might possibly die.   He said that "he should never die.   No power could oppose him; no years could age him; he should remain ever strong and ever young, for the thing wherein his life dwelt was most difficult to obtain."   It was in a queen bee, which was in a honeycomb on a tree.   But the bees in the honeycomb were many and fierce, and it was only at the greatest risk that any one could catch the queen.   But the hero achieved the enterprise and crushed the queen bee; and immediately the ogre fell stone dead to the ground, so that the whole land trembled with the shock.[2]   In some Bengalee tales the life of a whole tribe of ogres is described as concentrated in two bees.   The secret was thus revealed by an old ogress to a captive princess who pretended to fear lest the ogress should die.   " Know, foolish girl," said the ogress, " that we ogres never die.   We are not naturally immortal, but our life depends on a secret which no human being can unravel.   Let me tell you what it is that you may be comforted.   You know yonder tank; there is in the middle of it a crystal pillar, on the top of which in deep water are two bees.   If any human being can dive into the water and bring up the two bees from the pillar in one breath, and destroy them so that not a drop of their

---

[1] J. H. Knowles, *Folk-tales of Kashmir* (London, 1888), p. 134.
[2] *Id.* p. 382 *sqq.*

blood falls to the ground, then we ogres shall certainly die ; but if a single drop of blood falls to the ground, then from it will start up a thousand ogres. But what human being will find out this secret, or, finding it, will be able to achieve the feat? You need not, therefore, darling, be sad; I am practically immortal." As usual, the princess reveals the secret to the hero, who kills the bees, and that same moment all the ogres drop down dead, each on the spot where he happened to be standing.[1] In another Bengalee story it is said that all the ogres dwell in Ceylon, and that all their lives are in a single lemon. A boy cuts the lemon in pieces, and all the ogres die.[2]

In a Siamese or Cambodian story, probably derived from India, we are told that Thossakan or Ravana, the King of Ceylon, was able by magic art to take his soul out of his body and leave it in a box at home, while he went to the wars. Thus he was invulnerable in battle. When he was about to give battle to Rama, he deposited his soul with a hermit called Fire-eye, who was to keep it safe for him. So in the fight Rama was astounded to see that his arrows struck the king without wounding him. But one of Rama's allies, knowing the secret of the king's invulnerability, transformed himself by magic into the likeness of the king, and going to the hermit asked back his soul. On receiving it he soared up into the air and flew to Rama, brandishing the box and squeezing it so hard that all the breath left the King of Ceylon's body, and he died.[3] In a Bengalee

---

[1] Lal Behari Day, *op. cit.* p. 85 *sq.*, cp. *id.* p. 253 *sqq.*; *Indian Antiquary*, i. (1872) 117. For an Indian story in which a giant's life is in five black bees, see Clouston, *Popular Tales and Fictions*, i. 350.

[2] *Indian Antiquary*, i. 171.

[3] A. Bastian, *Die Völker des östlichen Asien*, iv. 340 *sq.*

story a prince going into a far country planted with his
own hands a tree in the courtyard of his father's
palace, and said to his parents, " This tree is my life.
When you see the tree green and fresh, then know
that it is well with me ; when you see the tree fade in
some parts, then know that I am in an ill case ; and
when you see the whole tree fade, then know that I
am dead and gone."[1]   In another Indian tale a prince,
setting forth on his travels, left behind him a barley
plant with instructions that it should be carefully
tended and watched, for if it flourished, he would be
alive and well, but if it drooped, then some mischance
was about to happen to him.   And so it fell out.   For
the prince was beheaded, and as his head rolled off,
the barley plant snapped in two and the ear of barley
fell to the ground.[2]   In the legend of the origin of
Gilgit there figures a fairy king whose soul is in the
snows and who can only perish by fire.[3]

In Greek tales, ancient and modern, the idea of
an external soul is not uncommon.   When Meleager
was seven days old, the Fates appeared to his mother
and told her that Meleager would die when the brand
which was blazing on the hearth had burnt down.   So
his mother snatched the brand from the fire and kept
it in a box.   But in after years, being enraged at her
son for slaying her brothers, she burnt the brand in
the fire and Meleager at once expired.[4]   Again, Nisus
King of Megara, had a purple or golden hair on the
middle of his head, and it was fated that whenever
the hair was pulled out the king should die.   When
Megara was besieged by the Cretans, the king's

[1] Lal Behari Day, *op. cit.* p. 189.
[2] *Wide-awake Stories*, pp. 52, 64.
[3] G. W. Leitner, *The Languages and Races of Dardistan*, p. 9.

[4] Apollodorus, i. 8 ; Diodorus, iv. 34 ; Pausanias, x. 31, 4 ; Aeschylus, *Choeph.* 604 *sqq.*

daughter Scylla fell in love with Minos, their King, and pulled out the fatal hair from her father's head. So he died.[1] Similarly Poseidon made Pterelaus immortal by giving him a golden hair on his head. But when Taphos, the home of Pterelaus, was besieged by Amphitryon, the daughter of Pterelaus fell in love with Amphitryon and killed her father by plucking out the golden hair with which his life was bound up.[2] In a modern Greek folk-tale a man's strength lies in three golden hairs on his head. When his mother pulls them out, he grows weak and timid and is slain by his enemies.[3] In another modern Greek story the life of an enchanter is bound up with three doves which are in the belly of a wild boar. When the first dove is killed, the magician grows sick, when the second is killed, he grows very sick, and when the third is killed, he dies.[4] In another Greek story of the same sort an ogre's strength is in three singing birds which are in a wild boar. The hero kills two of the birds, and then coming to the ogre's house finds him lying on the ground in great pain. He shows the third bird to the ogre, who begs that the hero will either let it fly away or give it to him to eat. But the hero wrings the bird's neck and the ogre dies on the spot.[5] In a variant of the latter story the

[1] Apollodorus, iii. 15, 8; Aeschylus, *Choeph.* 612 *sqq.* ; Pausanias, i. 19, 4. According to Tzetzes (*Schol. on Lycophron*, 650) not the life but the strength of Nisus was in his golden hair ; when it was pulled out, he became weak and was slain by Minos. According to Hyginus (*Fab.* 198) Nisus was destined to reign only so long as he kept the purple lock on his head.

[2] Apollodorus, ii. 4, §§ 5, 7.

[3] Hahn, *Griechische und Alban-* *esische Märchen*, i. p. 217 ; a similar story, *id.* ii. p. 282.

[4] Hahn, *op. cit.* ii. p. 215 *sq.*

[5] *Id.* ii. p. 275 *sq.* Similar stories, *id.* ii. pp. 204, 294 *sq.* In an Albanian story a monster's strength is in three pigeons, which are in a hare, which is in the silver tusk of a wild boar. When the boar is killed, the monster feels ill ; when the hare is cut open, he can hardly stand on his feet ; when the three pigeons are killed, he expires. Dozon, *Contes albanais*, p. 132 *sq.*

monster's strength is in two doves, and when the hero kills one of them, the monster cries out, "Ah, woe is me! · Half my life is gone. Something must have happened to one of the doves." When the second dove is killed, he dies.[1] In another Greek story the incidents of the three golden hairs and the three doves are artificially combined. A monster has three golden hairs on his head which open the door of a chamber in which are three doves; when the first dove is killed, the monster grows sick, when the second is killed, he grows worse, and when the third is killed, he dies.[2] In another Greek tale an old man's strength is in a ten-headed serpent. When the serpent's heads are being cut off, he feels unwell, and when the last head is struck off, he expires.[3] In another Greek story a dervish tells a queen that she will have three sons, that at the birth of each she must plant a pumpkin in the garden, and that in the fruit borne by the pumpkins will reside the strength of the children. In due time the infants are born and the pumpkins planted. As the children grow up the pumpkins grow with them. One morning the eldest son feels sick, and on going into the garden they find that the largest pumpkin is gone. Next night the second son keeps watch in a summer-house in the garden. At midnight a negro appears and cuts the second pumpkin. At once the boy's strength goes out of him and he is unable to pursue the negro. The youngest son, however, succeeds in slaying the negro and recovering the lost pumpkins.[4]

Ancient Italian legend furnishes a close parallel to the Greek story of Meleager. Silvia, the young wife

[1] Hahn, *op. cit.* ii. p. 260 *sqq.*   [2] *Id.* i. p. 187.   [3] *Id.* ii. p. 23 *sq.*
[4] Legrand, *Contes populaires grecs*, p. 191 *sqq.*

of Septimius Marcellus, had a child by the god Mars. The god gave her a spear, with which he said that the fate of the child would be bound up. When the boy grew up he quarrelled with his maternal uncles and slew them. So in revenge his mother burned the spear on which his life depended.[1] In one of the stories of the *Pentamerone* a certain queen has a twin brother, a dragon. The astrologers declared at her birth that she would live just as long as the dragon and no longer, the death of the one involving the death of the other. If the dragon were killed, the only way to restore the queen to life would be to smear her temples, breast, pulses, and nostrils with the blood of the dragon.[2] In a modern Roman version of "Aladdin and the Wonderful Lamp," the magician tells the princess whom he holds captive in a floating rock in mid-ocean that he will never die. The princess reports this to the prince her husband, who has come to rescue her. The prince replies, "It is impossible but that there should be some one thing or other that is fatal to him; ask him what that one fatal thing is." So the princess asked the magician and he told her that in the wood was a hydra with seven heads; in the middle head of the hydra was a leveret, in the head of the leveret was a bird, in the bird's head was a precious stone, and if this stone were put under his pillow he would die. The prince procured the stone and the princess laid it under the magician's pillow. No sooner did the enchanter lay his head on the pillow than he gave

---

[1] Plutarch, *Parallela*, 26. In both the Greek and Italian stories the subject of quarrel between nephew and uncles is the skin of a boar, which the nephew presented to his lady-love and which his uncles took from her.

[2] Basile, *Pentamerone*, ii. p. 60 *sq.* (Liebrecht's German trans.)

three terrible yells, turned himself round and round three times, and died.[1]

Stories of the same sort are current among Slavonic peoples. Thus in a Russian tale a warlock called Koshchei the Deathless is asked where his death is. "My death," he answered, "is in such and such a place. There stands an oak, and under the oak is a casket, and in the casket is a hare, and in the hare is a duck, and in the duck is an egg, and in the egg is my death." A prince obtained the egg and squeezed it, whereupon Koshchei the Deathless bent double. But when the prince shivered the egg in pieces, the warlock died.[2] "In one of the descriptions of Koshchei's death, he is said to be killed by a blow on the forehead inflicted by the mysterious egg—that last link in the magic chain by which his life is darkly bound. In another version of the same story, but told of a snake, the fatal blow is struck by a small stone found in the yolk of an egg, which is inside a duck, which is inside a hare, which is inside a stone, which is on an island."[3] In another variant the prince shifts the fatal egg from one hand to the other, and as he does so Koshchei rushes wildly from side to side of the room. At last the prince smashes the egg, and Koshchei drops dead.[4] In another Russian story the death of an enchantress is in a blue rose-tree in a blue forest. Prince Ivan uproots the rose-tree, whereupon the enchantress straightway sickens. He brings the rose-tree to her house and finds her at the point of death. Then he throws it into the cellar, crying, " Behold her death!" and at once the whole building

[1] R. H. Busk, *Folk-lore of Rome*, p. 164 *sqq.*
[2] Ralston, *Russian Folk-tales*, p.
103 *sq.*; so Dietrich, *Russian Popular Tales*, p. 23 *sq.*
[3] Ralston, *op. cit.* p. 109.   [4] *Ib.*

shakes, "and becomes an island, on which are people who had been sitting in Hell, and who offer up thanks to Prince Ivan."[1]   In another Russian story a prince is grievously tormented by a witch who has got hold of his heart, and keeps it seething in a magic cauldron.[2] In a Bohemian tale a warlock's strength lies in an egg, which is in a duck, which is in a stag, which is under a tree.   A seer finds the egg and sucks it. Then the warlock grows as weak as a child, "for all his strength had passed into the seer."[3]   In a Serbian story a fabulous being called True Steel declares, " Far away from this place there is a very high mountain, in the mountain there is a fox, in the fox there is a heart, in the heart there is a bird, and in this bird is my strength."   The fox is caught and killed and its heart is taken out.   Out of the fox's heart is taken the bird, which is then burnt, and that very moment True Steel falls dead.[4]   In a South Slavonian story a dragon tells an old woman, " My strength is a long way off, and you cannot go thither. Far in another empire under the emperor's city is a lake, in that lake is a dragon, and in the dragon a boar, and in the boar a pigeon, and in that is my strength."[5]

Amongst peoples of the Teutonic stock stories of the external soul are not wanting.   In a tale told by the Saxons of Transylvania it is said that a young man shot at a witch again and again.   The bullets went clean through her but did her no harm, and she only laughed and mocked at him.   " Silly earthworm,"

---

[1] Ralston, *Russian Folk-tales*, p. 113 *sq.*
[2] *Id.*, p. 114.   [3] *Id.*, p. 110.
[4] Mijatovics, *Serbian Folk-lore*, edited by the Rev. W. Denton, p. 172;

F. S. Krauss, *Sagen und Märchen der Südslaven*, i. (No. 34) p. 168 *sq.*
[5] A. H. Wratislaw, *Sixty Folk-tales from exclusively Slavonic sources* (London, 1889), p. 225.

she cried, "shoot as much as you like. It does me no harm. For know that my life resides not in me but far, far away. In a mountain is a pond, on the pond swims a duck, in the duck is an egg, in the egg burns a light, that light is my life. If you could put out that light, my life would be at an end. But that can never, never be." However, the young man got hold of the egg, smashed it, and put out the light, and with it the witch's life went out also.[1] In a German story a cannibal called Soulless keeps his soul in a box, which stands on a rock in the middle of the Red Sea. A soldier gets possession of the box and goes with it to Soulless, who begs the soldier to give him back his soul. But the soldier opens the box, takes out the soul, and flings it backward over his head. At the same moment the cannibal drops down stone dead.[2] In an Oldenburg story a king has three sons and a daughter, and for each child there grows a flower in the king's garden. Each of the flowers is a life flower; it blooms and flourishes while the child lives, but when the child dies it withers away.[3] In another German story an old warlock lives with a damsel all alone in the midst of a vast and gloomy wood. She fears that being old he may die and leave her alone in the forest. But he reassures her. "Dear child," he said, "I cannot die, and I have no heart in my breast." But she importuned him to tell her where his heart was. So he said, "Far, far from here in an unknown and lonesome land stands a great church. The church is well secured with iron doors, and round about it flows

[1] Haltrich, *Deutsche Volksmärchen aus dem Sachsenlande in Siebenbürgen,*[4] No. 34 (No. 33 of the first ed.), p. 149 *sq.*

[2] J. W. Wolf, *Deutsche Märchen und Sagen,* No. 20, p. 87 *sqq.*

[3] Strackerjan, *Aberglaube und Sagen aus dem Herzogthum Oldenburg,* ii. p. 306 *sq.*

a broad deep moat. In the church flies a bird and in the bird is my heart. So long as that bird lives, I live. It cannot die of itself, and no one can catch it; therefore I cannot die, and you need have no anxiety." However the young man, whose bride the damsel was to have been before the warlock spirited her away, contrived to reach the church and catch the bird. He brought it to the damsel, who stowed him and it away under the warlock's bed. Soon the old warlock came home. He was ailing, and said so. The girl wept and said, "Alas, daddy is dying; he has a heart in his breast after all." "Child," replied the warlock, "hold your tongue. I *can't* die. It will soon pass over." At that the young man under the bed gave the bird a gentle squeeze; and as he did so, the old warlock felt very unwell and sat down. Then the young man gripped the bird tighter, and the warlock fell senseless from his chair. "Now squeeze him dead," cried the damsel. Her lover obeyed, and when the bird was dead, the old warlock also lay dead on the floor.[1]

In the Norse tale of "the giant who had no heart in his body," the giant tells the captive princess, "Far, far away in a lake lies an island, on that island stands a church, in that church is a well, in that well swims a duck, in that duck there is an egg, and in that egg there lies my heart." The hero of the tale obtains the egg and squeezes it, at which the giant screams piteously and begs for his life. But the hero breaks the egg in pieces and the giant at once bursts.[2] In another Norse story a hill-ogre tells the captive princess that she will never be able to return home unless she finds the

---

[1] K. Müllenhoff, *Sagen, Märchen und Lieder der Herzogthümer Schleswig-Holstein und Lauenburg*, p. 404 *sqq.*

[2] Asbjörnsen og Moe, *Norske Folke-Eventyr*, No. 36; Dasent, *Popular Tales from the Norse*, p. 55 *sqq.*

grain of sand which lies under the ninth tongue of the ninth head of a certain dragon ; but if that grain of sand were to come over the rock in which the ogres live, they would all burst " and the rock itself would become a gilded palace, and the lake green meadows." The hero finds the grain of sand and takes it to the top of the high rock in which the ogres live. So all the ogres burst and the rest falls out as one of the ogres had foretold.[1] In an Icelandic parallel to the story of Meleager, the spae-wives or sybils come and foretell the high destiny of the infant Gestr as he lies in his cradle. Two candles were burning beside the child, and the youngest of the spae-wives, conceiving herself slighted, cried out, " I foretell that the child shall live no longer than this candle burns." Whereupon the chief sybil put out the candle and gave it to Gestr's mother to keep, charging her not to light it again until her son should wish to die. Gestr lived three hundred years ; then he kindled the candle and expired.[2]

In a Celtic tale a giant says, " There is a great flagstone under the threshold. There is a wether under the flag. There is a duck in the wether's belly, and an egg in the belly of the duck, and it is in the egg that my soul is." The egg is crushed, and the giant falls down dead.[3] In another Celtic tale, a sea beast has carried off a king's daughter, and an old smith declares that there is no way of killing the beast but one. " In the island that is in the midst of the loch is Eillid Chaisthion—the white-footed hind, of the

---

[1] Asbjörnsen og Moe, *Norske Folke-Eventyr*, Ny Samling, No. 70 ; Dasent, *Tales from the Fjeld*, p. 229 (" Boots and the Beasts.")

[2] Mannhardt, *Germanische Mythen*, p. 592 ; Jamieson, *Dictionary of the Scottish Language, s.v.* " Yule."

[3] J. F. Campbell, *Popular Tales of the West Highlands*, i. p. 10 *sq.*

slenderest legs, and the swiftest step, and, though she should be caught, there would spring a hoodie out of her, and though the hoodie should be caught, there would spring a trout out of her, but there is an egg in the mouth of the trout, and the soul of the beast is in the egg, and if the egg breaks, the beast is dead." As usual the egg is broken and the beast dies.[1] In a Breton story there figures a giant whom neither fire nor water nor steel can harm. He tells a princess whom he has just married. "I am immortal, and no one can hurt me, unless he crushes on my breast an egg which is in a pigeon, which is in the belly of a hare; this hare is in the belly of a wolf, and this wolf is in the belly of my brother, who dwells a thousand leagues from here. So I am quite easy on that score." A soldier gets the egg and crushes it on the breast of the giant, who immediately expires.[2] In another Breton tale a giant is called Body-without-Soul because his life does not reside in his body. It resides in an egg, the egg is in a dove, the dove is in a hare, the hare is in a wolf, and the wolf is in an iron chest at the bottom of the sea. The hero kills the animals one after another, and at the death of each animal the giant grows weaker, as if he had lost a limb. When at last the hero comes to the giant's castle bearing the egg in his hand, he finds Body-without-Soul stretched on his bed at the point of death. So he dashes the egg against the giant's forehead, the egg breaks, and the giant straightway dies.[3]

The notion of an external soul has now been traced in folk-tales told by Aryan peoples from India to

---

[1] J. F. Campbell, *Popular Tales of the West Highlands*, i. p. 80 *sqq.*

[2] Sébillot, *Contes populaires de la Haute-Bretagne* (Paris, 1885), p. 63 *sqq.*

[3] F. M. Luzel, *Contes populaires de Basse-Bretagne* (Paris, 1887), i. 445-449.

Brittany and the Hebrides. We have still to show that the same idea occurs commonly in the popular stories of non-Aryan peoples. In the first place it appears in the ancient Egyptian story of " The Two Brothers." This story was written down in the reign of Rameses II, about 1300 years B.C. It is therefore older than our present redaction of Homer, and far older than the Bible. The outline of the story, so far as it concerns us here, is as follows : Once upon a time there were two brethren ; the name of the elder was Anupu and the name of the younger was Bitiu. Now Anupu had a house and a wife, and his younger brother dwelt with him as his servant. It was Anupu who made the garments, and every morning when it grew light he drove the kine afield. As he walked behind them they used to say to him, " The grass is good in such and such a place," and he heard what they said and led them to the good pasture that they desired. So his kine grew very sleek and multiplied greatly. One day when the two brothers were at work in the field the elder brother said to the younger, " Run and fetch seed from the village." So the younger brother ran and said to the wife of his elder brother, " Give me seed that I may run to the field, for my brother sent me saying, tarry not." She said, " Go to the barn and take as much as you desire." He went and filled a jar full of wheat and barley, and came forth bearing it on his shoulders. When the woman saw him her heart went out to him, and she laid hold of him and said, " Come, let us rest an hour together." But he said, " Thou art to me as a mother, and my brother is to me as a father." So he would not hearken to her, but took the load on his back and went away to the field. In the evening, when the elder brother was returning from the field,

his wife feared for what she had said. So she took
soot and made herself as one who has been beaten.
And when her husband came home, she said, "When
thy younger brother came to fetch seed, he said to me,
Come, let us rest an hour together. But I would not,
and he beat me." Then the elder brother became like
a panther of the south; he sharpened his knife and
stood behind the door of the cow-house. And when
the sun set and the younger brother came laden
with all the herbs of the field, as was his wont every
day, the cow that walked in front of the herd said to
him, " Behold, thy elder brother stands with a knife to
kill thee. Flee before him." When he heard what
the cow said, he looked under the door of the cow-house
and saw the feet of his elder brother standing behind
the door, his knife in his hand. So he fled and his
brother pursued him with the knife. But the younger
brother cried for help to the Sun, and the Sun heard
him and caused a great water to spring up between
him and his elder brother, and the water was full of
crocodiles. The two brothers stood, the one on the
one side of the water and the other on the other, and
the younger brother told the elder brother all that had
befallen. So the elder brother repented him of what
he had done and he wept aloud. But he could not
come at the farther bank by reason of the crocodiles.
His younger brother called to him and said, " Go home
and tend the cattle thyself. For I will dwell no more
in the place where thou art. I will go to the Valley of
the Acacia. But this is what thou shalt do for me.
Thou shalt come and care for me, if evil befalls me, for
I will enchant my heart and place it on the top of the
flower of the Acacia; and if they cut the Acacia and
my heart falls to the ground, thou shalt come and seek

it, and when thou hast found it thou shalt lay it in a
vessel of fresh water.   Then I shall come to life again.
But this is the sign that evil has befallen me ; the pot
of beer in thine hand shall bubble."   So he went away
to the Valley of the Acacia, but his brother returned
home with dust on his head and slew his wife and cast
her to the dogs.

For many days afterwards the younger brother
dwelt alone in the Valley of the Acacia.   By day
he hunted the beasts of the field, but at evening he
came and laid him down under the Acacia, on the
top of whose flower was his heart.   And many days
after that he built himself a house in the Valley of the
Acacia.   But the gods were grieved for him ; and the
Sun said to Khnum, " Make a wife for Bitiu, that he
may not dwell alone."   So Khnum made him a woman
to dwell with him, who was perfect in her limbs more
than any woman on earth, for all the gods were in her.
So she dwelt with him.   But one day a lock of her
hair fell into the river and floated down to the land of
Egypt, to the house of Pharaoh's washerwomen.   The
fragrance of the lock perfumed Pharaoh's raiment, and
the washerwomen were blamed, for it was said, " An
odour of perfume in the garments of Pharaoh ! "   So
the heart of Pharaoh's chief washerman was weary of
the complaints that were made every day, and he went
to the quay, and there in the water he saw the lock of
hair.   He sent one down into the river to fetch it, and,
because it smelt sweetly, he took it to Pharaoh.   Then
Pharaoh's magicians were sent for and they said, "This
lock of hair belongs to a daughter of the Sun, who has
in her the essence of all the gods.   Let messengers go
forth to all foreign lands to seek her."   So the woman
was brought from the Valley of the Acacia with chariots

and archers and much company, and all the land of
Egypt rejoiced at her coming, and Pharaoh loved her.
But when they asked her of her husband, she said to
Pharaoh, " Let them cut down the Acacia and let them
destroy him." So men were sent with tools to cut
down the Acacia. They came to it and cut the flower
upon which was the heart of Bitiu; and he fell down
dead in that evil hour. But the next day, when the
elder brother of Bitiu was entered into his house and
had sat down, they brought him a pot of beer and it
bubbled, and they gave him a jug of wine and it grew
turbid. Then he took his staff and his sandals and
hied him to the Valley of the Acacia, and there he found
his younger brother lying dead in his house. So he
sought for the heart of his brother under the Acacia.
For three years he sought in vain, but in the fourth
year he found it in the berry of the Acacia. So he
threw the heart into a cup of fresh water. And when
it was night and the heart had sucked in much water,
Bitiu shook in all his limbs and revived. Then he
drank the cup of water in which his heart was, and his
heart went into its place, and he lived as before.[1]

In the story of Seyf-el-Mulook in the Arabian
Nights, the Jinnee declares, "When I was born, the
astrologers declared that the destruction of my soul
would be effected by the hand of one of the sons of the
human kings. I therefore took my soul, and put it
into the crop of a sparrow, and I imprisoned the sparrow
in a little box, and put this into another small box, and
this I put within seven other small boxes, and I put
these within seven chests, and the chests I put into a
coffer of marble within the verge of this circumambient
ocean ; for this part is remote from the countries of

---

[1] Maspero, *Contes populaires de l'Égypte ancienne* (Paris, 1882), p. 5 *sqq.*

mankind, and none of mankind can gain access to it."
But Seyf-el-Mulook got possession of the sparrow and
strangled it, and the Jinnee fell upon the ground a
heap of black ashes.[1] In a modern Arabian tale a
king marries an ogress, who puts out the eyes of the
king's forty wives. One of the blinded queens gives
birth to a son whom she names Mohammed the Prudent.
But the ogress queen hated him and compassed his
death. So she sent him on an errand to the house of
her kinsfolk the ogres. In the house of the ogres he
saw some things hanging from the roof, and on asking
a female slave what they were, she said, "That is the
bottle which contains the life of my lady the queen,
and the other bottle beside it contains the eyes of the
queens whom my mistress blinded." A little afterwards he spied a beetle and rose to kill it. "Don't
kill it," cried the slave, "for that is my life." But
Mohammed the Prudent watched the beetle till it
entered a chink in the wall ; and when the female slave
had fallen asleep, he killed the beetle in its hole, and so
the slave died. Then Mohammed took down the two
bottles and carried them home to his father's palace.
There he presented himself before the ogress queen
and said, "See, I have your life in my hand, but I will
not kill you till you have replaced the eyes which you
took from the forty queens." The ogress did as she
was bid, and then Mohammed the Prudent said,
"There, take your life." But the bottle slipped from
his hand and fell, the life of the ogress escaped from
it, and she died.[2]

---

[1] Lane's *Arabian Nights*, iii. 316 *sq.*

[2] G. Spitta - Bey, *Contes arabes modernes* (Leyden and Paris, 1883), No. 2, p. 12 *sqq.* The story in its main outlines is identical with the Cashmeer story of "The Ogress Queen" (J. H. Knowles, *Folk-tales of Kashmir*, p. 42 *sqq.*) and the Bengalee story of "The Boy whom Seven Mothers Suckled" (Lal Behari Day, *Folk-tales*

In a Kabyl story an ogre declares that his fate is
far away in an egg, which is in a pigeon, which is in a
camel, which is in the sea.   The hero procures the egg
and crushes it between his hands, and the ogre dies.[1]
In a Magyar folk-tale, an old witch detains a young
prince called Ambrose in the bowels of the earth.   At
last she confided to him that she kept a wild boar in a
silken meadow, and if it were killed, they would find a
hare inside, and inside the hare a pigeon, and inside
the pigeon a small box, and inside the box one black
and one shining beetle : the shining beetle held her
life, and the black one held her power ; if these two
beetles died, then her life would come to an end also.
When the old hag went out, Ambrose killed the wild
boar, took out the hare, from the hare he took the
pigeon, from the pigeon the box, and from the box the
two beetles ; he killed the black beetle, but kept the
shining one alive.   So the witch's power left her
immediately, and when she came home, she had to
take to her bed.   Having learned from her how to
escape from his prison to the upper air, Ambrose
killed the shining beetle, and the old hag's spirit left
her at once.[2]   In another Hungarian story the safety

---

of Bengal, p. 117 sqq.; Indian Antiquary, i. 170 sqq.)   In another Arabian
story the life of a witch is bound up
with a phial ; when it is broken, she
dies. W. A. Clouston, A Group of
Eastern Romances and Stories, p. 30.
A similar incident occurs in a Cashmeer
story. Knowles, op. cit. p. 73.   In
the Arabian story mentioned in the
text, the hero, by a genuine touch of
local colour, is made to drink the milk
of an ogress's breasts and hence is
regarded by her as her son. Cp. W.
Robertson Smith, Kinship and Marriage
in Early Arabia, p. 149 ; and for the
same mode of creating kinship among
other races, see D'Abbadie, Douze ans

dans la Haute Ethiopie, p. 272 sq.;
Tausch, "Notices of the Circassians,"
Journ. Royal Asiatic Soc. i. (1834) p.
104 ; Biddulph, Tribes of the Hindoo
Koosh, pp. 77, 83 (cp. Leitner, Lan-
guages and Races of Dardistan, p. 34) ;
Denzil Ibbetson, Settlement Report of
the Panipat, Tahsil, and Karnal Par-
ganah of the Karnal District, p. 101 ;
Moura, Royaume du Cambodge, i. 427 ;
F. S. Krauss, Sitte und Brauch der
Südslaven, p. 14.

[1] Rivière, Contes populaires de la
Kabylie du Djurdjura, p. 191.

[2] W. H. Jones and L. L. Kropf,
The Folk-tales of the Magyar (London,
1889), p. 205 sq.

Congolese witch doctor.

Jupiter (or Zeus, to the Greeks) worshipped as immanent in
the sacred oak.

of the Dwarf-king resides in a golden cockchafer, inside a golden cock, inside a golden sheep, inside a golden stag, in the ninety-ninth island. The hero overcomes all these golden animals and so recovers his bride, whom the Dwarf-king had carried off.[1] A Samoyed story tells how seven warlocks killed a certain man's mother and carried off his sister, whom they kept to serve them. Every night when they came home the seven warlocks used to take out their hearts and place them in a dish, which the woman hung on the tent-poles. But the wife of the man whom they had wronged stole the hearts of the warlocks while they slept, and took them to her husband. By break of day he went with the hearts to the warlocks, and found them at the point of death. They all begged for their hearts; but he threw six of their hearts to the ground, and six of the warlocks died. The seventh and eldest warlock begged hard for his heart, and the man said, "You killed my mother. Make her alive again, and I will give you back your heart." The warlock said to his wife, "Go to the place where the dead woman lies. You will find a bag there. Bring it to me. The woman's spirit is in the bag." So his wife brought the bag; and the warlock said to the man, "Go to your dead mother, shake the bag and let the spirit breathe over her bones; so she will come to life again." The man did as he was bid, and his mother was restored to life. Then he hurled the seventh heart to the ground, and the seventh warlock died.[2]

In a Tartar poem two heroes named Ak Molot and Bulat engage in mortal combat. Ak Molot pierces his foe through and through with an arrow, grapples

---

[1] R. H. Busk, *The Folk-lore of Rome*, p. 168.

[2] Castren, *Ethnologische Vorlesungen über die Altaischen Völker*, p. 173 *sqq.*

with him, and dashes him to the ground, but all in vain, Bulat could not die. At last when the combat has lasted three years, a friend of Ak Molot sees a golden casket hanging by a white thread from the sky, and bethinks him that perhaps this casket contains Bulat's soul. So he shot through the white thread with an arrow, and down fell the casket. He opened it, and in the casket sat ten white birds, and one of the birds was Bulat's soul. Bulat wept when he saw that his soul was found in the casket. But one after the other the birds were killed, and then Ak Molot easily slew his foe.[1] In another Tartar poem, two brothers going to fight two other brothers take out their souls and hide them in the form of a white herb with six stalks in a deep pit. But one of their foes sees them doing so and digs up their souls, which he puts into a golden ram's horn, and then puts the ram's horn in his quiver. The two warriors whose souls have thus been stolen know that they have no chance of victory, and accordingly make peace with their enemies.[2] In another Tartar poem a terrible demon sets all the gods and heroes at defiance. At last a valiant youth fights the demon, binds him hand and foot, and slices him with his sword. But still the demon is not slain. So the youth asked him, "Tell me, where is your soul hidden? For if your soul had been hidden in your body, you must have been dead long ago." The demon replied, "On the saddle of my horse is a bag. In the bag is a serpent with twelve heads. In the serpent is my soul. When you have killed the serpent, you have killed me also." So the youth took the saddle-bag from the horse and killed the twelve-headed serpent, whereupon the demon

---

[1] Schiefner, *Heldensagen der Minussinschen Tataren*, pp. 172-176.
[2] Schiefner, *op. cit.* pp. 108-112.

expired.[1] In another Tartar poem a hero called Kök
Chan deposits with a maiden a golden ring, in which is
half his strength. Afterwards when Kök Chan is
wrestling long with a hero and cannot kill him, a
woman drops into his mouth the ring which contains
half his strength. Thus inspired with fresh force he
slays his enemy.[2]

In a Mongolian story the hero Joro gets the
better of his enemy the lama Tschoridong in the
following way. The lama, who is an enchanter, sends
out his soul in the form of a wasp to sting Joro's
eyes. But Joro catches the wasp in his hand, and by
alternately shutting and opening his hand he causes
the lama alternately to lose and recover consciousness.[3]
In a Tartar poem two youths cut open the body of an
old witch and tear out her bowels, but all to no purpose, she still lives. On being asked where her soul
is, she answers that it is in the middle of her shoe-sole
in the form of a seven-headed speckled snake. So
one of the youths slices her shoe-sole with his sword,
takes out the speckled snake, and cuts off its seven
heads. Then the witch dies.[4] Another Tartar poem
describes how the hero Kartaga grappled with the
Swan-woman. Long they wrestled. Moons waxed
and waned and still they wrestled ; years came and
went, and still the struggle went on. But the piebald
horse and the black horse knew that the Swan-woman's

---

[1] Schiefner, *op. cit.* pp. 360-364 ;
Castren, *Vorlesungen über die finnische
Mythologie*, p. 186 *sq.*

[2] Schiefner, *op. cit.* pp. 189-193.
In another Tartar poem (Schiefner, *op.
cit.* p. 390 *sq.*) a boy's soul is shut up
by his enemies in a box. While the
soul is in the box, the boy is dead ;
when it is taken out, he is restored to
life. In the same poem (p. 384) the
soul of a horse is kept shut up in a box,

because it is feared the owner of the
horse will become the greatest hero on
earth. But these cases are, to some
extent, the converse of those in the text.

[3] Schott, "Ueber die Sage von
Geser Chan," *Abhandlungen d. Königl.
Akad. d. Wissensch. zu Berlin*, 1851, p.
269.

[4] W. Radloff, *Proben der Volks-
litteratur der türkischen Stämme Süd-
Sibiriens*, ii. 237 *sq.*

soul was not in her. Under the black earth flow
nine seas ; where the seas meet and form one, the sea
comes to the surface of the earth. At the mouth of
the nine seas rises a rock of copper ; it rises to the
surface of the ground, it rises up between heaven and
earth, this rock of copper. At the foot of the copper
rock is a black chest, in the black chest is a golden
casket, and in the golden casket is the soul of the
Swan-woman. Seven little birds are the soul of the
Swan-woman ; if the birds are killed the Swan-woman
will die straightway. So the horses ran to the foot of
the copper rock, opened the black chest, and brought
back the golden casket. Then the piebald horse
turned himself into a bald-headed man, opened the
golden casket, and cut off the heads of the seven birds.
So the Swan-woman died.[1] In a Tartar story a chief
called Tash Kan is asked where his soul is. He
answers that there are seven great poplars, and under
the poplars a golden well ; seven *Maralen* (?) come to
drink the water of the well, and the belly of one of
them trails on the ground ; in this *Maral* is a golden
box, in the golden box is a silver box, in the silver
box are seven quails, the head of one of the quails
is golden and its tail silver ; that quail is Tash
Kan's soul. The hero of the story gets possession
of the seven quails and wrings the necks of six of
them. Then Tash Kan comes running and begs the
hero to let his soul go free. But the hero wrings the
quail's neck, and Tash Kan drops dead.[2] In another
Tartar poem the hero, pursuing his sister who has
driven away his cattle, is warned to desist from the
pursuit because his sister has carried away his soul in
a golden sword and a golden arrow, and if he pursues

---

[1] W. Radloff, *op. cit.* ii. 531 *sqq.*   [2] *Id.*, iv. 88 *sq.*

her she will kill him by throwing the golden sword or shooting the golden arrow at him.[1]

A Malay poem relates how once upon a time in the city of Indrapoera there was a certain merchant who was rich and prosperous, but he had no children. One day as he walked with his wife by the river they found a baby girl, fair as an angel. So they adopted the child and called her Bidasari. The merchant caused a golden fish to be made, and into this fish he transferred the soul of his adopted daughter. Then he put the golden fish in a golden box full of water, and hid it in a pond in the midst of his garden. In time the girl grew to be a lovely woman. Now the King of Indrapoera had a fair young queen, who lived in fear that the king might take to himself a second wife. So, hearing of the charms of Bidasari, the queen resolved to put her out of the way. So she lured the girl to the palace and tortured her cruelly; but Bidasari could not die, because her soul was not in her. At last she could stand the torture no longer and said to the queen, "If you wish me to die, you must bring the box which is in the pond in my father's garden." So the box was brought and opened, and there was the golden fish in the water. The girl said, "My soul is in that fish. In the morning you must take the fish out of the water, and in the evening you must put it back into the water. Do not let the fish lie about, but bind it round your neck. If you do this, I shall soon die." So the queen took the fish out of the box and fastened it round her neck; and no sooner had she done so, than Bidasari fell into a swoon. But in the evening, when the fish was put back into the water, Bidasari came to herself again. Seeing that she thus

---

[1] W. Radloff, *op. cit.* i. 345 *sq.*

had the girl in her power, the queen sent her home to her adopted parents. To save her from further persecution her parents resolved to remove their daughter from the city. So in a lonely and desolate spot they built a house and brought Bidasari thither. Here she dwelt alone, undergoing vicissitudes that corresponded with the vicissitudes of the golden fish in which was her soul. All day long, while the fish was out of the water, she remained unconscious; but in the evening, when the fish was put into the water, she revived. One day the king was out hunting, and coming to the house where Bidasari lay unconscious, was smitten with her beauty. He tried to waken her, but in vain. Next day, towards evening, he repeated his visit, but still found her unconscious. However, when darkness fell, she came to herself and told the king the secret of her life. So the king returned to the palace, took the fish from the queen, and put it in water. Immediately Bidasari revived, and the king took her to wife.[1]

The last story of an external soul which I shall notice comes from Nias, an island to the west of Sumatra, which we have visited more than once in the course of this book. Once on a time a chief was captured by his enemies, who tried to put him to death but failed. Water would not drown him nor fire burn him nor steel pierce him. At last his wife revealed the secret. On his head he had a hair as hard as a copper wire; and with this wire his life was bound up. So the hair was plucked out, and with it his spirit fled.[2]

---

[1] G. A. Wilken, "De Simsonsage," *De Gids*, 1888, No. 5, p. 6 *sqq.* (of the separate reprint). Cp. Backer, *L'Archipel Indien*, pp. 144-149.

[2] Nieuwenhuisen en Rosenberg, "Verslag omtrent het eiland Nias," *Verhandel. van het Batav. Genootsch. v. Kunsten en Wetenschappen*, xxx. p. 111; Sundermann, "Die Insel Nias," *Allgemeine Missions - Zeitschrift*, xi. (1884) p. 453.

§ 4.—*The external soul in folk-custom*

Thus the idea that the soul may be deposited for a longer or shorter time in some place of security outside the body, or at all events in the hair, is found in the popular tales of many races.   It remains to show that the idea is not a mere figment devised to adorn a tale, but is a real article of primitive faith, which has given rise to a corresponding set of customs.

We have seen that in the tales the hero, as a preparation for battle, sometimes removes his soul from his body, in order that his body may be invulnerable and immortal in the combat.   With a like intention the savage removes his soul from his body on various occasions of real or imaginary danger. Thus we have seen that among the Minahassa of Celebes, when a family moves into a new house, a priest collects the souls of the whole family in a bag, and afterwards restores them to their owners, because the moment of entering a new house is supposed to be fraught with supernatural danger.[1]   In Southern Celebes when a woman is brought to bed the messenger who fetches the doctor or the midwife always carries with him a piece of iron, which he delivers to the doctor.   The doctor must keep it in his house till the confinement is over, when he gives it back, receiving a fixed sum of money for doing so.   The piece of iron represents the woman's soul, which at this critical time is believed to be safer out of her body than in it.   Hence the doctor must take great care of

---

[1] Above, vol. i. p. 134.

the piece of iron ; for if it were lost, the woman's soul would assuredly, it is supposed, be lost with it.[1]

Again, we have seen that in folk-tales a man's soul or strength is sometimes represented as bound up with his hair, and that when his hair is cut off he dies or grows weak. So the natives of Amboina used to think that their strength was in their hair and would desert them if it were shorn. A criminal under torture in a Dutch Court of that island persisted in denying his guilt till his hair was cut off, when he immediately confessed. One man who was tried for murder endured without flinching the utmost ingenuity of his torturers till he saw the surgeon standing with a pair of shears. On asking what this was for, and being told that it was to cut his hair, he begged they would not do it, and made a clean breast. In subsequent cases, when torture failed to wring a confession from a prisoner, the Dutch authorities made a practice of cutting off his hair.[2] In Ceram it is still believed that if young people have their hair cut they will be weakened and enervated thereby.[3] In Zacynthus people think that the whole strength of the ancient Greeks resided in three hairs on their breasts, and vanished whenever these hairs were cut ; but if the hairs were allowed to grow again, their strength returned.[4]

Again, we have seen that in folk-tales the life of a person is sometimes so bound up with the life of a plant that the withering of the plant will immediately follow or be followed by the death of the person.[5] Similarly among the M'Bengas in Western Africa, about the

---

[1] B. F. Matthes, *Bijdragen tot de Ethnologie van Zuid-Celebes*, p. 54.

[2] F. Valentyn, *Oud en Nieuw Oost-Indiën*, ii. 143 *sq.*; G. A. Wilken, *De Simsonsage*, p. 15 *sq.*

[3] Riedel, *De sluik-en kroesharige rassen tusschen Selebes en Papua*, p. 137.

[4] B. Schmidt, *Das Volksleben der Neugriechen*, p. 206.

[5] Above, pp. 305, 307, 309, 311.

Gaboon, when two children are born on the same day, the people plant two trees of the same kind and dance round them. The life of each of the children is believed to be bound up with the life of one of the trees ; and if the tree dies or is thrown down, they are sure that the child will soon die.[1] In the Cameroons, also, the life of a person is believed to be sympathetically bound up with that of a tree.[2] Some of the Papuans unite the life of a new-born child sympathetically with that of a tree by driving a pebble into the bark of the tree. This is supposed to give them complete mastery over the child's life; if the tree is cut down, the child will die.[3] After a birth the Maoris used to bury the navel-string in a sacred place and plant a young sapling over it. As the tree grew, it was a *tohu oranga* or sign of life for the child; if it flourished, the child would prosper; if it withered and died, the parents augured the worst for their child.[4] In Southern Celebes, when a child is born, a cocoa-nut is planted, and is watered with the water in which the after-birth and navel-string have been washed. As it grows up, the tree is called the " contemporary " of the child.[5] So in Bali a cocoa-palm is planted at the birth of a child. It is believed to grow up equally with the child, and is called its " life-plant."[6] On certain occasions the Dyaks of Borneo plant a palm-tree, which is believed to be a complete index of their fate. If it flourishes, they reckon on good fortune ; but if it withers or dies, they

[1] *Revue d Ethnographie*, ii. 223.
[2] Bastian, *Die deutsche Expedition an der Loango-Küste*, i. 165.
[3] Bastian, *Ein Besuch in San Salvador*, p. 103 *sq.*; *id.*, *Der Mensch in der Geschichte*, iii. 193.
[4] R. Taylor, *Te Ika a Maui ; or, New Zealand and its Inhabitants*,[2] p.

184 ; Dumont D'Urville, *Voyage autour du monde et à la recherche de La Pérouse sur la corvette Astrolabe*, ii. 444.
[5] Matthes, *Bijdragen tot de Ethnologie van Zuid-Celebes*, p. 59.
[6] Van Eck, "Schetsen van het eiland Bali," *Tijdschrift voor Nederlandsch Indië*, N. S. ix. (1880) p. 417 *sq.*

expect misfortune.[1]   It is said that there are still families in Russia, Germany, England, France, and Italy who are accustomed to plant a tree at the birth of a child.   The tree, it is hoped, will grow with the child, and it is tended with special care.[2]   The custom is still pretty general in the canton of Aargau in Switzerland; an apple-tree is planted for a boy and a pear-tree for a girl, and the people think that the child will flourish or dwindle with the tree.[3]   In Mecklenburg the after-birth is thrown out at the foot of a young tree, and the child is then believed to grow with the tree.[4]   In England persons are sometimes passed through a cleft tree as a cure for rupture, and thenceforward a sympathetic connection is believed to exist between them and the tree.   " Thomas Chilling-worth, son of the owner of an adjoining farm, now about thirty-four years of age, was, when an infant of a year old, passed through a similar tree, now perfectly sound, which he preserves with so much care that he will not suffer a single branch to be touched, for it is believed that the life of the patient depends on the life of the tree; and the moment that it is cut down, be the patient ever so distant, the rupture returns, and a mortification ensues."[5]   When Lord Byron first visited his ancestral estate of Newstead " he planted, it seems, a young oak in some part of the grounds, and had an idea that as *it* flourished so should *he*."[6]

But in practice, as in folk-tales, it is not merely

---

[1] G. A. Wilken, *De Simsonsage*, p. 26.

[2] Gubernatis, *Mythologie des Plantes*, i. xxviii. *sq.*

[3] W. Mannhardt, *B. K.* p. 50; Ploss, *Das Kind*,[2] i. 79.

[4] K. Bartsch, *Sagen, Märchen und*

Gebräuche aus Mecklenburg, ii. 43, No. 63.

[5] *Gentleman's Magazine*, October 1804, p. 909, quoted by Brand, *Popular Antiquities*, iii. 289 ; W. G. Black, *Folk-medicine*, pp. 31 *sq.*, 67.

[6] Moore's *Life of Lord Byron*, i. 101.

with trees and plants that the life of an individual is
occasionally believed to be united by a bond of physical
sympathy. The same bond, it is supposed, may
exist between a man and an animal or a thing,
so that the death or destruction of the animal or
thing is immediately followed by the death of the
man. The Emperor Romanus Lecapenus was once
informed by an astronomer that the life of Simeon
prince of Bulgaria was bound up with a certain column
in Constantinople, so that if the capital of the column
were removed Simeon would immediately die. The
Emperor took the hint and removed the capital, and at
the same hour, as the emperor learned by inquiry,
Simeon died of heart disease in Bulgaria.[1] Amongst
the Karens of Burma " the knife with which the navel-
string is cut is carefully preserved for the child. The
life of the child is supposed to be in some way connected with it, for if lost or destroyed it is said the child
will not be long-lived." [2] The Malays believe that
" the soul of a person may pass into another person
or into an animal, or rather that such a mysterious
relation can arise between the two that the fate of the
one is wholly dependent on that of the other." [3] In
the Banks Islands " some people connect themselves
with an object, generally an animal, as a lizard or a
snake, or with a stone, which they imagine to have a
certain very close natural relation to themselves. This,
at Mota, is called tamaniu—likeness. This word at
Aurora is used for the ' atai ' [*i.e.* soul] of Mota. Some
fancy dictates the choice of a tamaniu ; or it may be

[1] Cedrenus, *Compend. Histor.* p.
625 B, vol. ii. p. 308, ed. Bekker.
[2] F. Mason, " Physical Character of
the Karens," *Journal of the Asiatic
Society of Bengal*, 1866, pt. ii. p. 9.

[3] Matthes, *Makassarsch - Hollandsch
Woordenboek, s.v. soemáñgá,* p. 569 ;
G. A. Wilken, " Het animisme bij de
volken van den Indischen Archipel,"
De Indische Gids, June 1884, p. 933.

found by drinking the infusion of certain herbs and
heaping together the dregs.   Whatever living thing is
first seen in or upon the heap is the tamaniu.   It is
watched, but not fed or worshipped.   The natives
believe that it comes at call.   The life of the man is
bound up with the life of his tamaniu.   If it dies, gets
broken or lost, the man will die.   In sickness they
send to see how the tamaniu is, and judge the issue
accordingly.   This is only the fancy of some."[1]

But what among the Banks Islanders and the
Malays is irregular and occasional, among other
peoples is systematic and universal.   The Zulus
believe that every man has his *ihlozi*, a kind of
mysterious serpent, " which specially guards and helps
him, lives with him, wakes with him, sleeps and travels
with him, but always under ground.   If it ever makes
its appearance, great is the joy, and the man must seek
to discover the meaning of its appearance.   He who has
no *ihlozi* must die.   Therefore if any one unintention-
ally kills an *ihlozi* serpent, the man whose *ihlozi* it was
dies, but the serpent comes to life again."[2]   Amongst
the Zapotecs of Central America, when a woman was
about to be confined, her relations assembled in the
hut, and began to draw on the floor figures of different
animals, rubbing each one out as soon as it was completed.   This went on till the moment of birth, and
the figure that then remained sketched upon the
ground was called the child's *tona* or second self.
"When the child grew old enough he procured the
animal that represented him and took care of it, as it

---

[1] R. H. Codrington, "Notes on the
Customs of Mota, Banks Islands"
(communicated by the Rev. Lorimer
Fison), *Transactions of the Royal Society
of Victoria*, xvi. 136.

[2] F. Speckmann, *Die Hermannsburger Mission in Afrika* (Hermanns-
burg, 1876), p. 167.

was believed that health and existence were bound up with that of the animal's, in fact that the death of both would occur simultaneously," or rather that when the animal died the man would die.[1] Among the Indians of Guatemala the *nagual* or *naual* is an "animate or inanimate object, generally an animal, which stands in a parallel relation to a particular man, so that the weal and woe of the man depend on the fate of the animal." Among the Chontal Indians who inhabit the part of Honduras bordering on Guatemala and in point of social culture stand very close to the Pipil Indians of Guatemala, the *nagual* used to be obtained as follows. The young Indian went into the forest to a lonely place by a river or to the top of a mountain, and prayed with tears to the gods that they would vouchsafe to him what his forefathers had possessed before him. After sacrificing a dog or a bird he laid himself down to sleep. Then in a dream or after awakening from sleep there appeared to him a jaguar, puma, coyote (prairie-wolf), crocodile, serpent, or bird. To this visionary animal the Indian offered blood drawn from his tongue, his ears, and other parts of his body, and prayed for an abundant yield of salt and cacao. Then the animal said to him, "On such and such a day you shall go out hunting, and the first animal that meets you will be myself, who will always be your companion and *nagual*." A man who had no *nagual* could never grow rich. The Indians were persuaded that the death of their *nagual* would entail their own. Legend affirms that in the first battles with the Spaniards on

---

[1] Bancroft, *Native Races of the Pacific Coast*, i. 661. The words quoted by Bancroft (p. 662, *note*) "*Consérvase entre ellos la creencia de que su vida está unida à la de un animal, y que es forzoso que mueran ellos cuando éste muere*," are not quite accurately represented by the statement of Bancroft in the text.

the plateau of Quetzaltenango the *naguals* of the Indian chiefs fought in the form of serpents. The *nagual* of the highest chief was especially conspicuous, because it had the form of a great bird, resplendent in green plumage. The Spanish general Pedro de Alvarado killed the bird with his lance, and at the same moment the Indian chief fell dead to the ground.[1]

In many of the Australian tribes each sex regards a particular species of animals in the same way that a Central American Indian regards his *nagual*, but with this difference, that whereas the Indian apparently knows the individual animal with which his life is bound up, the Australians only know that each of their lives is bound up with some one animal of the species, but they cannot say with which. The result naturally is that every man spares and protects all the animals of the species with which the lives of the men are bound up ; and every woman spares and protects all the animals of the species with which the lives of the women are bound up ; because no one knows but that the death of any animal of the respective species might entail his or her own ; just as the killing of the green bird was immediately followed by the death of the Indian chief, and the killing of the parrot by the death of Punchkin in the fairy tale. Thus, for example, the Wotjobaluk tribe of South Eastern Australia " held that ' the life of Ngŭnŭngŭnŭt (the Bat) is the life of a man and the life of Yártatgŭrk (the Nightjar) is the life of a woman,' and that when either of these creatures is killed the life of some man or of some woman is shortened. In such a case every man or every woman

---

[1] Otto Stoll, *Die Ethnologie der Indianerstämme von Guatemala* (Leyden, 1889), p. 57 *sq.*; Bancroft, *Native* *Races of the Pacific States*, i. 740 *sq.*; Bastian, *Die Culturländer des alten Amerika*, ii. 282.

in the camp feared that he or she might be the victim, and from this cause great fights arose in this tribe. I learn that in these fights, men on one side and women on the other, it was not at all certain which would be victorious, for at times the women gave the men a severe drubbing with their yamsticks while often women were injured or killed by spears."[1] The particular species of animals with which the lives of the sexes were believed to be respectively bound up varied somewhat from tribe to tribe. Thus whereas among the Wotjobaluk the bat was the animal of the men, at Gunbower Creek on the lower Murray the bat seems to have been the animal of the women, for the natives would not kill it for the reason that "if it was killed, one of their lubras [women] would be sure to die in consequence."[2] But the belief itself and the fights to which it gave rise are known to have extended over a large part of South Eastern Australia, and probably they extended much farther.[3] The belief is a very serious one, and so consequently are the fights which spring from it. Thus where the bat is the men's animal they "protect it against injury, even to the half-killing of their wives for its sake;" and where the fern owl or large goatsucker (a night bird) is the women's animal, "it is jealously protected by them. If a man kills one, they are as much enraged as if it was one of their children, and will strike him with their long poles."[4]

The jealous protection thus afforded by Australian men and women to bats and owls respectively (for bats

---

[1] A. W. Howitt, "Further Notes on the Australian Class Systems," *Journ. Anthrop. Inst.* xviii. 58.

[2] Gerard Krefft, "Manners and Customs of the Aborigines of the Lower Murray and Darling," *Transact. Philos. Soc. New South Wales*, 1862-65, p. 359 *sq.*

[3] A. W. Howitt, *l.c.*

[4] Dawson, *Australian Aborigines*, p. 52.

and owls seem to be the creatures usually allotted to men and women respectively) is not based upon purely selfish considerations. For each man believes that not only his own life, but the lives of his father, brothers, sons, etc., are bound up with the lives of particular bats, and that therefore in protecting the bat species he is protecting the lives of all his male relations as well as his own. Similarly, each woman believes that the lives of her mother, sisters, daughters, etc., equally with her own, are bound up with the lives of particular owls, and that in guarding the owl species she is guarding the lives of all her female relations in addition to her own. Now, when men's lives are thus supposed to be contained in certain animals, it is obvious that the animals can hardly be distinguished from the men, or the men from the animals. If my brother John's life is in a bat, then, on the one hand, the bat is my brother as well as John; and, on the other hand, John is in a sense a bat, since his life is in a bat. Similarly, if my sister Mary's life is in an owl, then the owl is my sister and Mary is an owl. This is a natural enough conclusion, and the Australians have not failed to draw it. When the bat is the man's animal, it is called his brother; and when the owl is the woman's animal, it is called her sister. And conversely a man addresses a woman as an owl, and she addresses him as a bat.[1] So with the other animals allotted to the sexes respectively in other tribes. For example, among the Kurnai all Emu Wrens were "brothers" of the men, and all the men were Emu Wrens; all Superb Warblers were "sisters" of the women, and all the women were Superb Warblers.[2]

---

[1] *Journ. Anthrop. Inst.* xiv. 350, xv. 416, xviii. 57 (the "nightjar" is apparently an owl).

[2] Fison and Howitt, *Kamilaroi and Kurnai*, pp. 194, 201 *sq.*, 215; *Journ. Anthrop. Inst.* xv. 416, xviii. 56 *sq.*

But when a savage names himself after an animal,
calls it his brother, and refuses to kill it, the animal is
said to be his totem.   Accordingly the bat and the owl,
the Emu Wren and the Superb Warbler, may properly
be described as totems of the sexes.   But the assig-
nation of a totem to a sex is comparatively rare, and
has hitherto been discovered nowhere but in Australia.
Far more commonly the totem is appropriated not to
a sex, but to a tribe or clan, and is hereditary either in
the male or female line.   The relation of an individual
to the tribal totem does not differ in kind from his
relation to the sex totem ; he will not kill it, he speaks
of it as his brother, and he calls himself by its name.[1]
Now if the relations are similar, the explanation which
holds good of the one ought equally to hold good of
the other.   Therefore the reason why a tribe revere a
particular species of animals or plants (for the tribal
totem may be a plant) and call themselves after it, must
be a belief that the life of each individual of the tribe is
bound up with some one animal or plant of the species,
and that his or her death would be the consequence
of killing that particular animal, or destroying that
particular plant.   This explanation of totemism squares
very well with Sir George Grey's definition of a totem
or *kobong* in Western Australia.   He says, " A certain
mysterious connection exists between a family and its
kobong, so that a member of the family will never kill
an animal of the species to which his *kobong* belongs,
should he find it asleep ; indeed he always kills it
reluctantly, and never without affording it a chance to
escape.   This arises from the family belief that some
one individual of the species is their nearest friend, to

---

[1] The chief facts of totemism have   a little work, *Totemism* (Edinburgh, A.
been collected by the present writer in   and C. Black, 1887).

kill whom would be a great crime, and to be carefully avoided. Similarly, a native who has a vegetable for his *kobong* may not gather it under certain circumstances, and at a particular period of the year."[1] Here it will be observed that though each man spares all the animals or plants of the species, they are not all equally precious to him ; far from it, out of the whole species there is only one which is specially dear to him ; but as he does not know which the dear one is, he is obliged to spare them all from fear of injuring the one. Again, this explanation of the tribal totem harmonises with the supposed effect of killing one of the totem species. "One day one of the blacks killed a crow. Three or four days afterwards a Boortwa (crow) [*i.e.* a man of the Crow clan or tribe] named Larry died. He had been ailing for some days, but the killing of his wingong [totem] hastened his death."[2] Here the killing of the crow caused the death of a man of the Crow clan, exactly as, in the case of the sex totems, the killing of a bat causes the death of a Bat man, or the killing of an owl causes the death of an Owl woman. Similarly, the killing of his *nagual* causes the death of a Central American Indian, the killing of his *ihlozi* causes the death of a Zulu, the killing of his *tamaniu* causes the death of a Banks Islander, and the killing of the animal in which his life is stowed away causes the death of the giant or warlock in the fairy tale.

Thus it appears that the story of " The giant who had no heart in his body " furnishes the key to the religious aspect of totemism, that is, to the relation which is supposed to subsist between a man and his totem. The totem, if I am right, is simply the recep-

---

[1] (Sir) George Grey, *Journals of Two Expeditions of Discovery in North-West and Western Australia*, ii. 228 *sq.*

[2] Fison and Howitt, *Kamilaroi and Kurnai*, p. 169.

tacle in which a man keeps his life, as Punchkin kept
his life in a parrot, and Bidasari kept her soul in a
golden fish.   It is no valid objection to this view that
when a savage has both a sex totem and a tribal totem
his life must be bound up with two different animals,
the death of either of which would entail his own.   If
a man has more vital places than one in his body, why,
the savage may think, should he not have more vital
places than one outside it ?   Why, since he can exter-
nalise his life, should he not transfer one portion of it
to one animal and another to another?   The divisi-
bility of life, or, to put it otherwise, the plurality of
souls, is an idea suggested by many familiar facts,
and has commended itself to philosophers like Plato
as well as to savages.   It is only when the notion
of a soul, from being a quasi-scientific hypothesis,
becomes a theological dogma that its unity and indi-
visibility are insisted upon as essential.   The savage,
unshackled by dogma, is free to explain the facts of
life by the assumption of as many souls as he thinks
necessary.   Hence, for example, the Caribs supposed
that there was one soul in the head, another in the
heart, and other souls at all the places where an artery
is felt pulsating.[1]   Some of the Hidatsa Indians explain
the phenomena of gradual death, when the extremities
appear dead first, by supposing that man has four
souls, and that they quit the body, not simultaneously,
but one after the other, dissolution being only complete
when all four have departed.[2]   The Laos suppose that
the body is the seat of thirty spirits, which reside in
the hands, the feet, the mouth, the eyes, etc.[3]   Hence,

---

[1] De la Borde, " Relation de
l'Origine, etc. des Caraïbes," p. 15, in
*Recueil de divers Voyages faits en Afri-
que et en l'Amérique* (Paris, 1684).

[2] Washington Matthews, *The Hidatsa
Indians*, p. 50.

[3] Bastian, *Die Völker des östlichen
Asien*, iii. 248.

from the primitive point of view, it is perfectly possible that a savage should have one soul in his sex totem, and another in his tribal totem. However, as I have observed, sex totems occur nowhere but in Australia ; so that as a rule the savage who practises totemism need not have more than one soul out of his body at a time.

If this explanation of the totem as a receptacle in which a man keeps his soul or one of his souls is correct, we should expect to find some totemistic tribes of whom it is expressly stated that every man amongst them is believed to keep at least one soul permanently out of his body, and that the destruction of this external soul is supposed to entail the death of its owner. Such a tribe are the Battas of Sumatra. The Battas are divided into exogamous clans (*margas*) with descent in the male line ; and each clan is forbidden to eat the flesh of a particular animal. One clan may not eat the tiger, another the ape, another the crocodile, another the dog, another the cat, another the dove, another the white buffalo. The reason given by members of a clan for abstaining from the flesh of the particular animal is either that they are descended from animals of that species, and that their souls after death may transmigrate into the animals, or that they or their forefathers have been under certain obligations to the animals. Sometimes, but not always, the clan bears the name of the animal.[1] Thus the Battas have

---

[1] I. B Neumann, "Het Pane- en Bila - stroomgebied op het eiland Sumatra," *Tijdschrift van het Nederlandsch Aardrijks. Genootsch.*, Tweede Serie, dl. iii. Afdeeling : meer uitgebreide artikelen, No. 2, p. 311 *sq.*; *id.*, dl. iv. No. 1, p. 8 *sq.*; Van Hoëvell, "Iets over 't oorlogvoeren der Batta's," *Tijdschrift voor Nederlandsch Indië*, N. S. vii. (1878) p. 434 ; G. A. Wilken, *Over de verwantschap en het huwelijks-en erfrecht bij de volken van het maleische ras*, pp. 20 *sq.*, 36 ; *id.*, *Iets over de Papoewas van de Geelvinksbaai*, p. 27 *sq.* (reprint from *Bijdragen tot de Taal-Land-en Volkenkunde van Ned.-Indië*, 5e Volgreeks ii.) ; *Journal Anthrop. Inst.* ix. 295 ; Backer, *L'Archipel Indien*, p. 470.

totemism in full. But, further, each Batta believes that he has seven or, on a more moderate computation, three souls. One of these souls is always outside the body, but nevertheless whenever it dies, however far away it may be at the time, that same moment the man dies also.[1] The writer who mentions this belief says nothing about the Batta totems; but on the analogy of the Australian and Central American evidence we can scarcely avoid concluding that the external soul, whose death entails the death of the man, must be housed in the totem animal or plant.

Against this view it can hardly be thought to militate that the Batta does not in set terms affirm his external soul to be in his totem, but alleges other, though hardly contradictory, grounds for respecting the sacred animal or plant of his clan. For if a savage seriously believes that his life is bound up with an external object, it is in the last degree unlikely that he will let any stranger into the secret. In all that touches his inmost life and beliefs the savage is exceedingly suspicious and reserved; Europeans have resided among savages for years without discovering some of their capital articles of faith, and in the end the discovery has often been the result of accident. Above all, the savage lives in an intense and perpetual dread of assassination by sorcery; the most trifling relics of his person—the clippings of his hair and nails, his spittle, the remnants of his food, his very name—all these may, he fancies, be turned by the sorcerer to his destruction, and he is therefore anxiously careful to conceal or destroy them. But if in matters such as

---

[1] B. Hagen, "Beiträge zur Kenntniss der Battareligion," *Tijdschrift voor Indische Taal-Land-en Volken-kunde*, xxviii. 514. J. B. Neumann (*op. cit.* dl. iii. No. 2, p. 299) is the authority for the seven souls.

these, which are but the outposts and outworks of his life, he is shy and secretive to a degree, how close must be the concealment, how impenetrable the reserve in which he enshrouds the inner keep and citadel of his being! When the princess in the fairy tale asks the giant where he keeps his soul, he generally gives false or evasive answers, and it is only after much coaxing and wheedling that the secret is at last wrung from him. In his jealous reticence the giant resembles the timid and furtive savage; but whereas the exigencies of the story demand that the giant should at last reveal his secret, no such obligation is laid on the savage; and no inducement that can be offered is likely to tempt him to imperil his soul by revealing its hiding-place to a stranger. It is therefore no matter for surprise that the central mystery of the savage's life should so long have remained a secret, and that we should be left to piece it together from scattered hints and fragments and from the recollections of it which linger in fairy tales.

This view of totemism throws light on a class of religious rites of which no adequate explanation, so far as I am aware, has yet been offered. Amongst many savage tribes, especially such as are known to practise totemism, it is customary for lads at puberty to undergo certain initiatory rites, of which one of the commonest is a pretence of killing the lad and bringing him to life again. Such rites become intelligible if we suppose that their substance consists in extracting the youth's soul in order to transfer it to his totem. For the extraction of his soul would naturally be supposed to kill the youth or, at least, to throw him into a death-like trance, which the savage hardly distinguishes from death. His recovery would then be attributed either

to the gradual recovery of his system from the violent
shock which it had received, or, more probably, to the
infusion into him of fresh life drawn from the totem.
Thus the essence of these initiatory rites, so far as
they consist in a simulation of death and resurrection,
would be an exchange of life or souls between the
man and his totem.   The primitive belief in the possibility of such an exchange of souls comes clearly out
in the story of the Basque hunter who affirmed that
he had been killed by a bear, but that the bear had,
after killing him, breathed its own soul into him, so
that the bear's body was now dead, but he himself was
a bear, being animated by the bear's soul.[1]   This
revival of the dead hunter as a bear is exactly analogous to what, if I am right, is supposed to take place
in the totemistic ceremony of killing a lad at puberty
and bringing him to life again.   The lad dies as a
man and comes to life again as an animal ; the animal's
soul is now in him, and his human soul is in the
animal.   With good right, therefore, does he call himself a Bear or a Wolf, etc., according to his totem ;
and with good right does he treat the bears or the
wolves, etc., as his brethren, since in these animals are
lodged the souls of himself and his kindred.

Examples of this supposed death and resurrection
at initiation are the following.   Among some of the
Australian tribes of New South Wales, when lads are
initiated, it is thought that a being called Thuremlin
takes each lad to a distance, kills him, and sometimes
cuts him up, after which he restores him to life and
knocks out a tooth.[2]   In one part of Queensland the

---

[1] Th. Benfey, *Pantschatantra*, i. 128
sq.

[2] A. L. P. Cameron, " Notes on

some Tribes of New South Wales,"
Journ. Anthrop. Instit. xiv. 358.

humming sound of the Bullroarer, which is swung at the initiatory rites, is said to be the noise made by the wizards in swallowing the boys and bringing them up again as young men. "The Ualaroi of the Upper Darling River say that the boy meets a ghost which kills him and brings him to life again as a man."[1] This resurrection appears to be represented at the initiatory rites by the following ceremony. An old man, disguised with stringy bark fibre, lies down in a grave, and is lightly covered up with sticks and earth, and as far as possible the natural appearance of the ground is restored, the excavated earth being carried away. The buried man holds a small bush in his hand; it appears to be growing in the soil, and other bushes are stuck in the soil to heighten the effect. The novices are then brought to the edge of the grave, and a song is sung, in which the only words used are the "class-name" of the buried man and the word for stringy bark fibre. Gradually, as the song continues, the bush held by the buried man begins to quiver and then to move more and more, and finally the man himself starts up from the grave.[2] Similarly, Fijian lads at initiation were shown a row of apparently dead men, covered with blood, their bodies seemingly cut open, and their entrails protruding. But at a yell from the

---

[1] A. W. Howitt, "On Australian Medicine Men," *Journ. Anthrop. Inst.* xvi. 47 *sq.* On the Bullroarer (a piece of wood fastened to a cord or thong and swung round so as to produce a booming sound), see A. Lang, *Custom and Myth*, p. 29 *sqq.* The religious use of the Bullroarer is best known in Australia, but in the essay just referred to Mr. Andrew Lang has shown that the instrument has been similarly employed not only in South Africa and by the Zunis of New Mexico, but also by the ancient Greeks in their religious mysteries. As a sacred instrument it also occurs in Western Africa (R. F. Burton, *Abeokuta and the Cameroons Mountains*, i. 197 *sq.*; Bouche, *La Côte des Esclaves*, p. 124), and in New Guinea (J. Chalmers, *Pioneering in New Guinea*, p. 85).

[2] A. W. Howitt, "On some Australian ceremonies of initiation," *Journ. Anthrop. Inst.* xiii. 453 *sq.* The "class-name" is the name of the totemic division to which the man belongs.

priest the pretended dead men sprang to their feet and ran to the river to cleanse themselves from the blood and entrails of pigs with which they had been besmeared.[1]

In the valley of the Congo initiatory rites of this sort are common. In some places they are called Ndembo. "In the practice of Ndembo the initiating doctors get some one to fall down in a pretended fit, and in that state he is carried away to an enclosed place outside the town. This is called 'dying Ndembo.' Others follow suit, generally boys and girls, but often young men and women. . . . They are supposed to have died. But the parents and friends supply food, and after a period varying, according to custom, from three months to three years, it is arranged that the doctor shall bring them to life again. . . . When the doctor's fee has been paid, and money (goods) saved for a feast, the *Ndembo* people are brought to life. At first they pretend to know no one and nothing; they do not even know how to masticate food, and friends have to perform that office for them. They want everything nice that any one uninitiated may have, and beat them if it is not granted, or even strangle and kill people. They do not get into trouble for this, because it is thought that they do not know better. Sometimes they carry on the pretence of talking gibberish, and behaving as if they had returned from the spirit-world. After this they are known by another name, peculiar to those who have 'died Ndembo.' . . . We hear of the custom far along on the upper river, as well as in the cataract region."[2] The following account of

[1] L. Fison, "The Nanga, or sacred stone enclosure of Wainimala, Fiji," *Journ. Anthrop. Inst.* xiv. 22.

[2] W. H. Bentley, *Life on the Congo* (London, 1887), p. 78 *sq.*.

the rites, as practised in this part of Africa, was given to Bastian by an interpreter. " In the land of Ambamba every one must die once, and when the fetish priest shakes his calabash against a village, all the men and lads whose hour is come fall into a state of lifeless torpidity, from which they generally awake after three days. But if the fetish loves a man he carries him away into the bush and buries him in the fetish house, often for many years. When he comes to life again, he begins to eat and drink as before, but his understanding is gone and the fetish man must teach him and direct him in every motion, like the smallest child. At first this can only be done with a stick, but gradually his senses return, so that it is possible to talk with him, and when his education is complete, the priest brings him back to his parents. They would seldom recognise their son but for the express assurances of the fetish priest, who moreover recalls previous events to their memory. He who has not gone through the ceremony of the new birth in Ambamba is universally looked down upon and is not admitted to the dances." During the period of initiation the novice is sympathetically united to the fetish by which his life is henceforward determined.[1] The novice, plunged in the magic sleep or death-like trance within the sacred hut, " beholds a bird or other object with which his existence is thenceforward sympathetically bound up, just as the life of the young Indian is bound up with the animal which he sees in his dreams at puberty." [2]

---

[1] A. Bastian, *Ein Besuch in San Salvador*, pp. 82 *sq.* 86.

[2] Bastian, *Die deutsche Expedition an der Loango-Küste*, ii. 183 ; cp. *id.*, pp. 15-18, 30 *sq.* On these initiatory rites in the Congo region see also H. H. Johnston in *Proceed. Royal Geogr. Soc.* N. S. v. (1883) p. 572 *sq.*, and in *Journ. Anthrop. Inst.* xiii. 472 ; E. Delmar Morgan, in *Proceed. Royal Geogr. Soc.* N. S. vi. 193.

Rites of this sort were formerly observed in Quoja, on the west coast of Africa, to the north of the Congo. They are thus described by an old writer :—" They have another ceremony which they call Belli-Paaro, but it is not for everybody. For it is an incorporation in the assembly of the spirits, and confers the right of entering their groves, that is to say, of going and eating the offerings which the simple folk bring thither. The initiation or admission to the Belli-Paaro is celebrated every twenty or twenty-five years. The initiated recount marvels of the ceremony, saying that they are roasted, that they entirely change their habits and life, and that they receive a spirit quite different from that of other people and quite new lights. The badge of membership consists in some lines traced on the neck between the shoulders ; the lines seem to be pricked with a needle. Those who have this mark pass for persons of spirit, and when they have attained a certain age they are allowed a voice in all public assemblies ; whereas the uninitiated are regarded as profane, impure, and ignorant persons, who dare not express an opinion on any subject of importance. When the time for the ceremony has come, it is celebrated as follows : By order of the king a place is appointed in the forest, whither they bring the youths who have not been marked, not without much crying and weeping ; for it is impressed upon the youths that in order to undergo this change it is necessary to suffer death. So they dispose of their property, as if it were all over with them. There are always some of the initiated beside the novices to instruct them. They teach them to dance a certain dance called *killing*, and to sing verses in praise of Belli. Above all, they are very careful not to let them die of hunger, because if they did so, it is much to be feared that the spiritual resurrection would profit them nothing. This manner of life lasts five or six years, and is comfortable enough, for there is a village in the forest, and they amuse themselves with hunting and fishing. Other lads are brought thither from time to time, so that the last comers have not long to stay. No woman or uninitiated person is suffered to pass within four or five leagues of the sacred wood. When their instruction is completed, they are taken from the wood and shut up in small huts made for the purpose. Here they begin once more to hold communion with mankind and to talk with the women who bring them their food. It is amusing to see their affected simplicity. They pretend to know no one, and to be ignorant of all the customs of the country, such as the customs of washing themselves, rubbing themselves with oil, etc. When they enter these huts, their bodies are all covered with the feathers of birds, and they wear caps of bark which hang down before their faces. But after a time they are dressed in clothes and taken to a great open place, where all the people of the neighbourhood are assembled. Here the novices give the first proof of their capacity by dancing a dance which is called the dance of Belli. After the dance is over, the novices are taken to the houses of their parents by their instructors."[1]

Among the Indians of Virginia, an initiatory ceremony, called *Huskanaw*, took place every sixteen or twenty years, or oftener, as the young men happened to grow up. The youths were kept in solitary confinement in the woods for several months,

---

[1] Dapper, *Description de l'Afrique*, p. 268 *sq.* Dapper's account has been abbreviated in the text.

receiving no food but an infusion of some intoxicating roots, so that they went raving mad, and continued in this state eighteen or twenty days. " Upon this occasion it is pretended that these poor creatures drink so much of the water of Lethe that they perfectly lose the remembrance of all former things, even of their parents, their treasure, and their language. When the doctors find that they have drank sufficiently of the Wysoccan (so they call this mad potion), they gradually restore them to their senses again by lessening the intoxication of their diet ; but before they are perfectly well they bring them back into their towns, while they are still wild and crazy through the violence of the medicine. After this they are very fearful of dis-covering anything of their former remembrance ; for if such a thing should happen to any of them, they must immediately be *Huskanaw'd* again ; and the second time the usage is so severe that seldom any one escapes with life. Thus they must pretend to have forgot the very use of their tongues, so as not to be able to speak, nor understand anything that is spoken, till they learn it again. Now, whether this be real or counterfeit, I don't know ; but certain it is that they will not for some time take notice of any body nor any thing with which they were before acquainted, being still under the guard of their keepers, who constantly wait upon them everywhere till they have learnt all things perfectly over again. Thus they unlive their former lives, and commence men by forgetting that they ever have been boys." [1]

Among some of the Indian tribes of North America there are certain religious associations which are only open to candidates who have gone through a pretence

---

[1] (Beverley's) *History of Virginia* (London, 1722), p. 177 *sq.*

of being killed and brought to life again. Captain Carver witnessed the admission of a candidate to an association called " the friendly society of the Spirit " among the Naudowessies. The candidate knelt before the chief, who told him that " he himself was now agitated by the same spirit which he should in a few moments communicate to him ; that it would strike him dead, but that he would instantly be re-stored again to life. . . . As he spoke this, he appeared to be greatly agitated, till at last his emotions became so violent that his countenance was distorted and his whole frame convulsed. At this juncture he threw something that appeared both in shape and colour like a small bean at the young man, which seemed to enter his mouth, and he instantly fell as motionless as if he had been shot." For a time the man lay like dead, but under a shower of blows he showed signs of conscious-ness, and finally, discharging from his mouth the bean, or whatever it was the chief had thrown at him, he came to life.[1] In other tribes the instrument by which the candidate is apparently slain is the medicine-bag. The bag is made of the skin of an animal (such as the otter, wild cat, serpent, bear, racoon, wolf, owl, weasel), of which it roughly preserves the shape. Each mem-ber of the society has one of these bags, in which he keeps the odds and ends that make up his " medicine " or charms. "They believe that from the miscellaneous contents in the belly of the skin bag or animal there issues a spirit or breath, which has the power, not only to knock down and kill a man, but also to set him up and restore him to life." The mode of killing a man with one of these medicine-bags is to thrust it at him ;

---

[1] J. Carver, *Travels through the Interior Parts of North America*, pp. 271-275.

he falls like dead, but a second thrust of the bag restores him to life.[1]

A ceremony witnessed by Jewitt during his captivity among the Indians of Nootka Sound doubtless belongs to this class of customs. The Indian king or chief "discharged a pistol close to his son's ear, who immediately fell down as if killed, upon which all the women of the house set up a most lamentable cry, tearing handfuls of hair from their heads, and exclaiming that the prince was dead ; at the same time a great number of the inhabitants rushed into the house armed with their daggers, muskets, etc., inquiring the cause of their outcry. These were immediately followed by two others dressed in wolf skins, with masks over their faces representing the head of that animal. The latter came in on their hands and feet in the manner of a beast, and taking up the prince, carried him off upon their backs, retiring in the same manner as they entered."[2] In another place Jewitt mentions that the young prince—a lad of about eleven years of age—wore a mask in imitation of a wolf's head.[3] Now, as the Indians of this part of America are divided into totem clans, of which the Wolf clan is one of the principal, and as the members of each clan are in the habit of wearing some portion of the totem animal about their person,[4] it is probable that the prince belonged to the Wolf clan, and that the ceremony described by Jewitt represented the killing

[1] Carver, *op. cit.* p. 277 *sq.*; Schoolcraft, *Indian Tribes*, iii. 287, v. 430 *sqq.*; Kohl, *Kitschi-Gami*, i. 64-70.

[2] *Narrative of the Adventures and Sufferings of John R. Jewitt* (Middletown, 1820), p. 119.

[3] *Id.*, p. 44. For the age of the prince, see *id.*, p. 35.

[4] Holmberg, "Ueber die Völker des russischen Amerika," *Acta Soc. Scient. Fennicae*, iv. (Helsingfors, 1856) pp. 292 *sqq.*, 328 ; Petroff, *Report on the Population, etc. of Alaska*, p. 165 *sq.*; A. Krause, *Die Tlinkit-Indianer*, p. 112 ; R. C. Mayne, *Four years in British Columbia and Vancouver Island*, p. 257 *sq.*, 268.

of the lad in order that he might be born anew as a wolf, much in the same way that the Basque hunter supposed himself to have been killed and to have come to life again as a bear. The Toukaway Indians of Texas, one of whose totems is the wolf, have a ceremony in which men, dressed in wolf skins, run about on all fours, howling and mimicking wolves. At last they scratch up a living tribesman, who has been buried on purpose, and putting a bow and arrows in his hands, bid him do as the wolves do—rob, kill, and murder.[1] The ceremony probably forms part of an initiatory rite like the resurrection from the grave of the old man in the Australian rites.

The people of Rook, an island east of New Guinea, hold festivals at which one or two disguised men, their heads covered with wooden masks, go dancing through the village, followed by all the other men. They demand that the circumcised boys who have not yet been swallowed by Marsaba (the devil) shall be given up to them. The boys, trembling and shrieking, are delivered to them, and must creep between the legs of the disguised men. Then the procession moves through the village again, and announces that Marsaba has eaten up the boys, and will not disgorge them till he receives a present of pigs, taro, etc. So all the villagers, according to their means, contribute provisions, which are then consumed in the name of Marsaba.[2] In New Britain all males are members

---

[1] Schoolcraft, *Indian Tribes*, v. 683. In a letter dated 16th Dec. 1887, Mr. A. S. Gatschet, of the Bureau of Ethnology, Washington, writes to me : "Among the Toukawe whom in 1884 I found at Fort Griffin [?], Texas, I noticed that they never kill the big or gray wolf, *hatchukunän*, which has a mythological signification, 'holding the earth' (*hatch*). He forms one of their totem clans, and they have had a dance in his honor, danced by the males only, who carried sticks."

[2] Reina, "Ueber die Bewohner der Insel Rook," *Zeitschrift für allgemeine Erdkunde*, N. F. iv. (1858) p. 356 *sq.*

The Bat, venerated by the Wotjobaluk.

The dance of the Duk-duk.

of an association called the Duk-duk. The boys are
admitted to it very young, but are not fully initiated
till their fourteenth year, when they receive from the
Tubuvan a terrible blow with a cane, which is supposed to kill them. The Tubuvan and the Duk-duk
are two disguised men who represent cassowaries.
They dance with a short hopping step in imitation of
the cassowary. Each of them wears a huge hat like
an extinguisher, woven of grass or palm-fibres; it is
six feet high, and descends to the wearer's shoulders,
completely concealing his head and face. From the
neck to the knees the man's body is hidden by a crino-
line made of the leaves of a certain tree fastened on
hoops, one above the other. The Tubuvan is regarded
as a female, the Duk-duk as a male. No woman may
see these disguised men. The institution of the Duk-
duk is common to the neighbouring islands of New
Ireland and the Duke of York.[1]

Amongst the Galela and Tobelorese of Halmahera,
an island to the west of New Guinea, boys go through
a form of initiation, part of which seems to consist in a
pretence of begetting them anew. When a number of
boys have reached the proper age, their parents agree
to celebrate the ceremony at their common expense,
and they invite others to be present at it. A shed is
erected, and two long tables are placed in it, with

---

[1] R. Parkinson, *Im Bismarck
Archipel*, pp. 129-134; Rev. G.
Brown, "Notes on the Duke of York
Group, New Britain, and New Ire-
land," *Journ. Royal Geogr. Soc.* xlvii.
(1878) p. 148 *sq.*; H. H. Romilly,
"The Islands of the New Britain
Group," *Proceed. Royal Geogr. Soc.*
N. S. ix. (1887) p. 11 *sq.*; Rev. G.
Brown, *ib.* p. 17; W. Powell, *Wanderings in a Wild Country*, pp. 60-66;
C. Hager, *Kaiser Wilhelm's Land und*
der Bismarck Archipel, pp. 115-128.
The inhabitants of these islands are
divided into two exogamous classes,
which in the Duke of York Island have
two insects for their totems. One of
the insects is the *mantis religiosus ;* the
other is an insect that mimicks the leaf
of the horse-chestnut tree very closely.
Rev. B. Danks, "Marriage customs of
the New Britain Group," *Journ. Anthrop. Inst.* xviii. 281 *sq.*

benches to match, one for the men and one for the women. When all the preparations have been made for a feast, a great many skins of the rayfish, and some pieces of a wood which imparts a red colour to water, are taken to the shed. A priest or elder causes a vessel to be placed in the sight of all the people, and then begins, with significant gestures, to rub a piece of the wood with the ray-skin. The powder so produced is put in the vessel, and at the same time the name of one of the boys is called out. The same proceeding is repeated for each boy. Then the vessels are filled with water, after which the feast begins. At the third cock-crow the priest smears the faces and bodies of the boys with the red water, which represents the blood shed at the perforation of the *hymen*. Towards daybreak the boys are taken to the wood, and must hide behind the largest trees. The men, armed with sword and shield, accompany them, dancing and singing. The priest knocks thrice on each of the trees behind which a boy is hiding. All day the boys stay in the wood, exposing themselves to the heat of the sun as much as possible. In the evening they bathe and return to the shed, where the women supply them with food.[1]

In the west of Ceram boys at puberty are admitted to the Kakian association.[2] Modern writers

---

[1] J. G. F. Riedel, "Galela und Tobel- oresen," *Zeitschrift f. Ethnologie*, xvii. (1885) p. 81 *sq.*

[2] The Kakian association and its initiatory ceremonies have often been described. See Valentyn, *Oud en nieuw Oost - Indiën*, iii. 3 *sq.*; Von Schmid, "Het Kakihansch Verbond op het eiland Ceram," *Tijdschrift v. Neêrlands Indië*, v. dl. ii. (1843) 25-38; Van Ekris, "Het Ceramsche Kakianverbond," *Mededeelingen van wege het Nederland. Zendelinggenoot- schap*, (1865) ix. 205 - 226 (repeated with slight changes in *Tijdschrift v. Indische Taal - Land - en Volkenkunde*, xvi. 1866, pp. 290-315); F. Fournier, "De Zuidkust van Ceram," *Tijdschrift v. Indische Taal-Land- en Volkenkunde*, xvi. 154 *sqq.*; Van Rees, *Die Pion- niers der Beschaving in Neêrlands Indië*, pp. 92-106; Van Hoëvell, *Ambon en meer bepaaldelijk de Oeliasers*, p. 153 *sqq.*; Schulze, "Ueber Ceram und seine Bewohner," *Verhandl. d. Berliner Gesell. f. Anthropologie*, etc. (1877) p. 117; W. Joest, "Beiträge zur Kenntniss der Eingebornen der

have commonly regarded this association as primarily
a political league instituted to resist foreign domina-
tion.   In reality its objects are purely religious and
social, though it is possible that the priests may have
occasionally used their powerful influence for political
ends.   The society is in fact merely one of those
widely-diffused primitive institutions, of which a chief
object is the initiation of young men.   In recent years
the true nature of the association has been duly recognised by the distinguished Dutch ethnologist, J. G. F.
Riedel.   The Kakian house is an oblong wooden
shed, situated under the darkest trees in the depth of
the forest, and is built to admit so little light that it is
impossible to see what goes on in it.   Every village
has such a house.   Thither the boys who are to be
initiated are conducted blindfolded, followed by their
parents and relations.   Each boy is led by the hand
by two men, who act as his sponsors or guardians,
looking after him during the period of initiation.
When all are assembled before the shed, the high
priest calls aloud upon the devils.   Immediately a
hideous uproar is heard to proceed from the shed.   It
is made by men with bamboo trumpets, who have been
secretly introduced into the building by a back door,
but the women and children think it is made by the
devils, and are much terrified.   Then the priests enter
the shed, followed by the boys, one at a time.   As
soon as each boy has disappeared within the precincts,
a dull chopping sound is heard, a fearful cry rings out,
and a sword or spear, dripping with blood, is thrust

Insel Formosa und Ceram," *id.* (1882),
p. 64; Rosenberg, *Der Malayische
Archipel*, p. 318; Bastian, *Indonesien*,
i. 145-148; Riedel, *De sluik-en kroesharige rassen tusschen Selebes en Papua*,
pp. 107-111. The best accounts are
those of Valentyn, Von Schmid, Van
Ekris, Van Rees, and Riedel, which
are accordingly followed in the text.

through the roof of the shed. This is a token that the
boy's head has been cut off, and that the devil has
carried him away to the other world, there to regener-
ate and transform him. So at sight of the bloody
sword the mothers weep and wail, crying that the
devil has murdered their children. In some places, it
would seem, the boys are pushed through an opening
made in the shape of a crocodile's jaws or a cassowary's
beak, and it is then said that the devil has swallowed
them. The boys remain in the shed for five or nine
days. Sitting in the dark, they hear the blast of the
bamboo trumpets, and from time to time the sound of
musket shots and the clash of swords. Every day
they bathe, and their faces and bodies are smeared
with a yellow dye, to give them the appearance of
having been swallowed by the devil. During his stay
in the Kakian house each boy has one or two crosses
tattooed with thorns on his breast or arm. When they
are not sleeping, the lads must sit in a crouching posture without moving a muscle. As they sit in a row
cross-legged, with their hands stretched out, the chief
takes his trumpet, and placing the mouth of it on the
hands of each lad, speaks through it in strange tones,
imitating the voice of the spirits. He warns the lads,
under pain of death, to observe the rules of the Kakian
society, and never to reveal what has passed in the
Kakian house. The novices are also told by the
priests to behave well to their blood relations, and are
taught the traditions and secrets of the tribe.

Meantime the mothers and sisters of the lads have
gone home to weep and mourn. But in a day or two
the men who acted as guardians or sponsors to the
novices return to the village with the glad tidings that
the devil, at the intercession of the priests, has restored

the lads to life. The men who bring this news come in a fainting state and daubed with mud, like messengers freshly arrived from the nether world. Before leaving the Kakian house, each lad receives from the priest a stick adorned at both ends with cock's or cassowary's feathers. The sticks are supposed to have been given to the lads by the devil at the time when he restored them to life, and they serve as a token that the lads have been in the spirit-land. When they return to their homes they totter in their walk, and enter the house backward, as if they had forgotten how to walk properly ; or they enter the house by the back door. If a plate of food is given to them, they hold it upside down. They remain dumb, indicating their wants by signs only. All this is to show that they are still under the influence of the devil or the spirits. Their sponsors have to teach them all the common acts of life, as if they were new-born children. Further, upon leaving the Kakian house the boys are strictly forbidden to eat of certain fruits until the next celebration of the rites has taken place. And for twenty or thirty days their hair may not be combed by their mothers or sisters. At the end of that time the high priest takes them to a lonely place in the forest, and cuts off a lock of hair from the crown of each of their heads. After these initiatory rites the lads are deemed men, and may marry ; it would be a scandal if they married before.

The simulation of death and resurrection or of a new birth at initiation appears to have lingered on, or at least to have left traces of itself, among peoples who have advanced far beyond the stage of savagery. Thus, after his investiture with the sacred thread — the symbol of his order — a Brahman is called "twice-born." Manu says, "According to the injunction of the revealed texts the first birth of an Aryan is from his natural mother, the second happens on the tying of the girdle of Muñga grass, and the third on the initiation to the performance of a Ṣrauta sacrifice."[1] A pretence of killing the candidate appears to have formed part of the initiation to the Mithraic mysteries.[2]

Thus, if I am right, wherever totemism is found, and wherever a pretence is made of killing and bringing to life again at initiation, there must exist or have existed not only a belief in the possibility of permanently depositing the soul in some external object— animal, plant, or what not—but an actual intention of so depositing it. If the question is put, why do men desire to deposit their life outside their bodies? the answer can only be that, like the giant in the fairy tale, they think it safer to do so than to carry it about with them, just as people deposit their money with a banker rather than carry it on their persons. We have seen that at critical periods the life or soul is sometimes temporarily deposited in a safe place till the danger is past. But institutions like totemism are not resorted to merely on special occasions of danger; they are systems into which every one, or at least every male, is obliged to be initiated at a certain period of life. Now the period of life at which initiation takes place is regularly puberty; and this fact suggests that the special danger which totemism and systems like it are intended to obviate is supposed not to arise till sexual maturity has been attained, in fact, that the danger

[1] *Laws of Manu*, ii. 169, trans. by Bühler; Dubois, *Moeurs, Institutions et Cérémonies des Peuples de l'Inde*, i. 125; Monier Williams, *Religious Life and Thought in India*, pp. 360 *sq.* 366 *sq.*

[2] Lampridius, *Commodus*, 9; C. W. King, *The Gnostics and their Remains*,[2] pp. 127, 129.

Initiatory ceremonies among the Indians of Virginia.

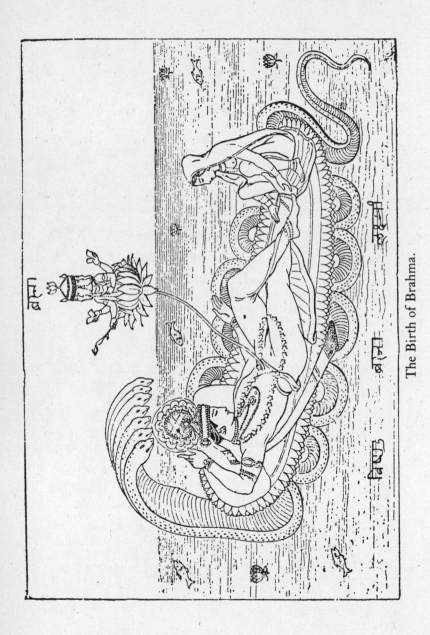

The Birth of Brahma.

apprehended is believed to attend the relation of the sexes to each other. It would be easy to prove by a long array of facts that the sexual relation is associated in the primitive mind with many supernatural perils; but the exact nature of the danger apprehended is still obscure. We may hope that a more exact acquaintance with savage modes of thought will in time disclose this central mystery of primitive society, and will thereby furnish the clue, not only to the social aspect of totemism (the prohibition of sexual union between persons of the same totem), but to the origin of the marriage system.

§ 5.—*Conclusion*

Thus the view that Balder's life was in the mistletoe is entirely in harmony with primitive modes of thought. It may indeed sound like a contradiction that, if his life was in the mistletoe, he should nevertheless have been killed by a blow from it. But when a person's life is conceived as embodied in a particular object, with the existence of which his own existence is inseparably bound up, and the destruction of which involves his own, the object in question may be regarded and spoken of indifferently as the person's life or as his death, as happens in the fairy tales. Hence if a man's death is in an object, it is perfectly natural that he should be killed by a blow from it. In the fairy tales Koshchei the Deathless is killed by a blow from the egg or the stone in which his life or death is;[1] the ogres burst when a certain grain of sand—doubtless containing their life or death—is carried over their

---

[1] Above, p. 309.

heads ; [1] the magician dies when the stone in which his life or death is contained is put under his pillow ; [2] and the Tartar hero is warned that he may be killed by the golden arrow or golden sword in which his soul has been stowed away. [3]

The idea that the life of the oak was in the mistletoe was probably suggested, as I have said, by the observation that in winter the mistletoe growing on the oak remains green, while the oak itself is leafless. But the position of the plant—growing, not from the ground, but from the trunk or branches of the tree—might confirm this idea. Primitive man might think that, like himself, the oak-spirit had sought to deposit his life in some safe place, and for this purpose had pitched on the mistletoe, which, being in a sense neither on earth nor in heaven, was as secure a place as could be found. At the beginning of this chapter we saw that primitive man seeks to preserve the life of his human divinities by keeping them in a sort of intermediate position between earth and heaven, as the place where they are least likely to be assailed by the dangers that encompass the life of man on earth. We can there-

---

[1] Above, p. 312 *sq.* [2] Above, p. 308 *sq.*
[3] Above, p. 324 *sq.* In the myth the throwing of the weapons and of the mistletoe at Balder and the blindness of Hödur who slew him remind us of the custom of the Irish reapers who kill the corn-spirit in the last sheaf by throwing their sickles blindfold at it. (See above, vol. i. p. 339). In Mecklenburg a cock is sometimes buried in the ground and a man who is blindfolded strikes at it with a flail. If he misses it, another tries, and so on till the cock is killed. Bartsch, *Sagen, Märchen und Gebräuche aus Mecklenburg,* ii. 280. In England on Shrove Tuesday a hen used to be tied upon a man's back, and other men blindfolded struck at it with branches till they killed it. Dyer,

British Popular Customs, p. 68. Mannhardt (*Die Korndämonen,* p. 16 *sq.*) has made it probable that such sports are directly derived from the custom of killing a cock upon the harvest-field as a representative of the corn-spirit (see above, p. 9). These customs, therefore, combined with the blindness of Hödur in the myth suggest that the man who killed the human representative of the oak-spirit was blindfolded, and threw his weapon or the mistletoe from a little distance. After the Lapps had killed a bear —which was the occasion of many superstitious ceremonies — the bear's skin was hung on a post, and the women, blindfolded, shot arrows at it. Scheffer, *Lapponia,* p. 240.

fore understand why in modern folk - medicine the
mistletoe is not allowed to touch the ground; if it
touches the ground, its healing virtue is supposed to
be gone.[1]   This may be a survival of the old superstition that the plant in which the life of the sacred tree
was concentrated should not be exposed to the risk
incurred by contact with the ground.   In an Indian
legend, which offers a parallel to the Balder myth, Indra
promised the demon Namuci not to kill him by day or
by night, nor with what was wet or what was dry.   But
he killed him in the morning twilight by sprinkling
over him the foam of the sea.[2]   The foam of the sea
is just such an object as a savage might choose to put
his life in, because it occupies that sort of intermediate
or nondescript position between earth and sky or sea
and sky in which primitive man sees safety.   It is
therefore not surprising that the foam of the river
should be the totem of a clan in India.[3]   Again, the
view that the mistletoe owes its mystic character partly
to the fact of its not growing on the ground is confirmed
by a parallel superstition about the mountain-ash or
rowan-tree.   In Jutland a rowan that is found growing
out of the top of another tree is esteemed " exceedingly
effective against witchcraft : since it does not grow on
the ground witches have no power over it ; if it is to
have its full effect it must be cut on Ascension Day." [4]
Hence it is placed over doors to prevent the ingress of
witches.[5]   Similarly the mistletoe in Germany is still

---

[1] Grimm, *Deutsche Mythologie*,[4] ii.
1001, 1010.

[2] *Folk-lore Journal*, vii. 61.

[3] Col. E. T. Dalton, " The Kols of
Chota-Nagpore," *Trans. Ethnol. Soc.*
vi. 36.

[4] Jens Kamp, *Danske Folkeminder*
(Odense, 1877), pp. 172, 65 *sq.* referred
to in Feilberg's *Bidrag til en Ordbog*

over *Jyske Almuesmål*, Fjerde hefte
(Copenhagen, 1888), p. 320. For a
sight of Feilberg's work I am indebted
to the kindness of the Rev. Walter
Gregor, M.A., Pitsligo, who pointed
out the passage to me.

[5] E. T. Kristensen, *Iydske Folkeminder*, vi. 380_{262}, referred to by
Feilberg, *l.c.*

universally considered a protection against witchcraft, and in Sweden, as we saw, the mistletoe which is gathered on Midsummer Eve is attached to the ceiling of the house, the horse stall, or the cow's crib, in the belief that this renders the Troll powerless to injure man or beast.[1]

The view that the mistletoe was not merely the instrument of Balder's death, but that it contained his life, is countenanced by the analogy of a Scottish superstition. Tradition ran that the fate of the family of Hay was bound up with the mistletoe of a certain oak.

" While the mistletoe bats on Errol's oak,
And that oak stands fast,
The Hays shall flourish, and their good gray hawk
Shall not flinch before the blast.

" But when the root of the oak decays,
And the mistletoe dwines on its withered breast,
The grass shall grow on the Earl's hearthstone,
And the corbies craw in the falcon's nest."

"A large oak with the mistletoe growing on it was long pointed out as the tree referred to. A piece of the mistletoe cut by a Hay was believed to have magical virtues. 'The oak is gone and the estate is lost to the family,' as a local historian says."[2] The idea that the fate of a family, as distinct from the lives of its members, is bound up with a particular plant or tree, is no doubt comparatively modern. The older view probably was that the lives of all the Hays were in this particular mistletoe, just as in the Indian story the lives of all the ogres are in a lemon; to break a twig of the mistletoe would then have been to kill one

---

[1] Wuttke, *Der deutsche Volksaberglaube*,[2] § 128 ; L. Lloyd, *Peasant Life in Sweden*, p. 269.

[2] Extract from a newspaper, copied and sent to me by the Rev. Walter Gregor, M.A., Pitsligo. Mr. Gregor does not mention the name of the newspaper.

of the Hays. Similarly in the island of Rum, whose
bold mountains the voyager from Oban to Skye
observes to seaward, it was thought that if one of
the family of Lachlin shot a deer on the mountain of
Finchra, he would die suddenly or contract a dis-
temper which would soon prove fatal.[1] Probably the
life of the Lachlins was bound up with the deer on
Finchra, as the life of the Hays was bound up with
the mistletoe on Errol's oak.

It is not a new opinion that the Golden Bough
was the mistletoe.[2] True, Virgil does not identify but
only compares it with the mistletoe. But this may be
only a poetical device to cast a mystic glamour over
the humble plant. Or, more probably, his description
was based on a popular superstition that at certain
times the mistletoe blazed out into a supernatural golden
glory. The poet tells how two doves, guiding Aeneas
to the gloomy vale in whose depth grew the Golden
Bough, alighted upon a tree, "whence shone a
flickering gleam of gold. As in the woods in winter
cold the mistletoe—a plant not native to its tree—is
green with fresh leaves and twines its yellow berries
about the boles ; such seemed upon the shady oak the
leafy gold, so rustled in the gentle breeze the golden
leaf."[3] Here Virgil definitely describes the Golden
Bough as growing on an oak, and compares it with the
mistletoe. The inference is almost inevitable that the
Golden Bough was nothing but the mistletoe seen
through the haze of poetry or of popular superstition.

Now grounds have been shown for believing that

[1] Martin, "Description of the
Western Islands of Scotland," in
Pinkerton's *Voyages and Travels*, iii.
661.

[2] Rochholz, *Deutscher Glaube und
Brauch*, i. 9.

[3] Virgil, *Aen.* vi. 203 *sqq.*, cp. 136
sqq. On the mistletoe (*viscum*) see
Pliny, *Nat. Hist.* xvi. 245 *sqq.*

the priest of the Arician grove — the King of the Wood—personified the tree on which grew the Golden Bough.[1] Hence, if that tree was the oak, the King of the Wood must have been a personification of the oak-spirit. It is, therefore, easy to understand why, before he could be slain, it was necessary to break the Golden Bough. As an oak-spirit, his life or death was in the mistletoe on the oak, and so long as the mistletoe remained intact, he, like Balder, could not die. To slay him, therefore, it was necessary to break the mistletoe, and probably, as in the case of Balder, to throw it at him. And to complete the parallel, it is only necessary to suppose that the King of the Wood was formerly burned, dead or alive, at the midsummer fire festival which, as we have seen, was annually celebrated in the Arician grove.[2] The perpetual fire which burned in the grove, like the perpetual fire under the oak at Romove, was probably fed with the sacred oak-wood ; and thus it would be in a great fire of oak that the King of the Wood formerly met his end. At a later time, as I have suggested, his annual tenure of office was lengthened or shortened, as the case might be, by the rule which allowed him to live so long as he could prove his divine right by the strong hand. But he only escaped the fire to fall by the sword.

Thus it seems that at a remote age in the heart of Italy, beside the sweet lake of Nemi, the same fiery tragedy was annually enacted which Italian merchants and soldiers were afterwards to witness among their rude kindred, the Celts of Gaul, and which, if the

---

[1] Virgil (Aen. vi. 201 *sqq.*) places the Golden Bough in the neighbourhood of Lake Avernus. But this was probably a poetical liberty, adopted for the convenience of Aeneas's descent to the infernal world. Italian tradition, as we learn from Servius, placed the Golden Bough in the grove at Nemi.

[2] See above, vol. i. p. 4 *sq.*

Roman eagles had ever swooped on Norway, might have been found repeated with little difference among the barbarous Aryans of the North. The rite was probably an essential feature in the primitive Aryan worship of the oak.[1]

It only remains to ask, Why was the mistletoe called the Golden Bough ? The name was not simply a poet's fancy, nor even peculiarly Italian ; for in Welsh also the mistletoe is known as " the tree of pure gold."[2] The whitish-yellow of the mistletoe berries is hardly enough to account for the name. For Virgil says that the Bough was altogether golden, stem as well as leaves,[3] and the same is implied in the Welsh name, "the tree of pure gold." A clue to the real meaning of the name is furnished by the mythical fern-seed or fern-bloom.

We saw that fern-seed is popularly supposed to bloom like gold or fire on Midsummer Eve. Thus in Bohemia it is said that " on St. John's Day fern-seed blooms with golden blossoms that gleam like fire."[4] Now it is a property of this mythical fern-seed that whoever has it, or will ascend a mountain holding it in his hand on Midsummer Eve, will discover a vein of gold or will see the treasures of the earth shining with a bluish flame.[5] And if you place fern-

---

[1] A custom of annually burning a human representative of the corn-spirit has been noted among the Egyptians, Pawnees, and Khonds. See above, vol. i. pp. 382, 387, 401 *sq.* In Semitic lands there are traces of a practice of annually burning a human god. For the image of Hercules (that is, of Baal) which was periodically burned on a pyre at Tarsus, must have been a substitute for a human representative of the god. See Dio Chrysostom, *Orat.* 33, vol. ii. p. 16, ed. Dindorf ; W. R. Smith, *The Religion of the Semites*, i. 353 *sq.* The Druids seem to have eaten portions of the human victim. Pliny, *Nat. Hist.* xxx. § 13. Perhaps portions of the flesh of the King of the Wood were eaten by his worshippers as a sacrament. We have seen traces of the use of sacramental bread at Nemi. See above, p. 82 *sq.*

[2] Grimm, *Deutsche Mythologie*,[4] ii. 1009, *pren puraur.*

[3] Virgil, *Aen.* vi. 137 *sq.*

[4] Grohmann, *Aberglauben und Gebräuche aus Böhmen und Mähren*, § 673.

[5] Grohmann, *op. cit.* § 676 ; Wuttke, *Der deutsche Volksaberglaube*, § 123.

seed among money, the money will never decrease,
however much of it you spend.[1]　Sometimes the
fern - seed is supposed to bloom at Christmas, and
whoever catches it will become very rich.[2]　Thus, on
the principle of like by like, fern-seed is supposed to
discover gold because it is itself golden ; and for a
similar reason it enriches its possessor with an un-
failing supply of gold.　But while the fern-seed is
described as golden, it is equally described as glowing
and fiery.[3]　Hence, when we consider that two great
days for gathering the fabulous seed are Midsummer
Eve and Christmas—that is, the two solstices (for
Christmas is nothing but an old heathen celebration of
the winter solstice)—we are led to regard the fiery
aspect of the fern - seed as primary, and its golden
aspect as secondary and derivative.　Fern - seed, in
fact, would seem to be an emanation of the sun's fire
at the two turning-points of its course, the summer
and winter solstices.　This view is confirmed by a
German story in which a hunter is said to have
procured fern-seed by shooting at the sun on Midsummer Day at noon ; three drops of blood fell
down, which he caught in a white cloth, and these
blood-drops were the fern-seed.[4]　Here the blood
is clearly the blood of the sun, from which the fern-
seed is thus directly derived.　Thus it may be
taken as certain that fern - seed is golden, because
it is believed to be an emanation of the sun's golden
fire.

　　Now, like fern-seed, the mistletoe is gathered

[1] Zingerle, *Sitten, Bräuche und Meinungen des Tiroler Volkes,*[2] § 882.

[2] Zingerle *op. cit.* § 1573.

[3] Grohmann, *op. cit.* § 675.;

Ralston, *Songs of the Russian People,* p. 98.

[4] L. Bechstein, *Deutsches Sagenbuch* No. 500 ; *id., Thüringer Sagenbuch* (Leipzig, 1885), ii. No. 161.

either at Midsummer or Christmas[1]—that is, at the summer and winter solstices—and, like fern-seed, it is supposed to possess the power of revealing treasures in the earth. On Midsummer Eve people in Sweden make divining-rods of mistletoe or of four different kinds of wood, one of which must be mistletoe. The treasure-seeker places the rod on the ground after sundown, and when it rests directly over treasure, the rod begins to move as if it were alive.[2] Now, if the mistletoe discovers gold, it must be in its character of the Golden Bough; and if it is gathered at the solstices, must not the Golden Bough, like the golden fern-seed, be an emanation of the sun's fire? The question cannot be answered with a simple affirmative. We have seen that the primitive Aryans probably kindled the midsummer bonfires as sun-charms, that is, with the intention of supplying the sun with fresh fire. But as this fire was always elicited by the friction of oak wood,[3] it must have appeared to the primitive Aryan that the sun was periodically recruited from the fire which resided in the sacred oak. In other words, the oak must have seemed to him the original storehouse or reservoir of the fire which was from time to time drawn out to feed the sun. But the life of the oak was conceived to be in the mistletoe; therefore the mistletoe must have contained the seed or germ of the

---

[1] For gathering it at midsummer, see above, p. 289. The custom of gathering it at Christmas still survives among ourselves. At York "on the eve of Christmas Day they carry mistletoe to the high altar of the cathedral, and proclaim a public and universal liberty, pardon, and freedom to all sorts of inferior and even wicked people at the gates of the city, towards the four quarters of heaven." Stukeley, *Medallic History of Carausius*, quoted by Brand, *Popular Antiquities*, i. 525. This last custom is of course now obselete.

[2] Afzelius, *Volkssagen und Volkslieder aus Schwedens älterer und neuerer Zeit*, i. 41 *sq.*; Grimm, *Deutsche Mythologie*,[4] iii. 289; L. Lloyd, *Peasant Life in Sweden*, p. 266 *sq.*

[3] Above, p. 293.

fire which was elicited by friction from the wood of the
oak. Thus, instead of saying that the mistletoe was
an emanation of the sun's fire, it would be more
correct to say that the sun's fire was regarded as an
emanation of the mistletoe. No wonder, then, that
the mistletoe shone with a golden splendour, and was
called the Golden Bough. Probably, however, like
fern-seed, it was thought to assume its golden aspect
only at those stated times, especially midsummer,
when fire was drawn from the oak to light up the
sun.[1] At Pulverbatch, in Shropshire, it was believed
within living memory that the oak-tree blooms on Midsummer Eve and the blossom withers before daylight.[2]
This fleeting bloom of the oak, if I am right, could
originally have been nothing but the mistletoe in its
character of the Golden Bough. As Shropshire
borders on Wales, the superstition may be Welsh in
its immediate origin, though probably the belief is a
fragment of the primitive Aryan creed. In some
parts of Italy, as we saw,[3] peasants still go out on
Midsummer morning to search the oak-trees for the
"oil of St. John," which, like the mistletoe, heals all
wounds, and is doubtless the mistletoe itself in its
glorified aspect. Thus it is easy to understand how a
title like the Golden Bough or the "tree of pure gold,"
so little descriptive of the real appearance of the plant,
should have held its ground as a name for the mistletoe
in Italy and Wales, and probably in other parts of the
Aryan world.[4]

---

[1] Fern-seed is supposed to bloom at Easter as well as at midsummer and Christmas (Ralston, *Songs of the Russian People*, p. 98 *sq.*); and Easter, as we have seen, is one of the times when sun-fires are kindled.

[2] Burne and Jackson, *Shropshire Folk-lore*, p. 242.

[3] P. 288.

[4] The reason why Virgil represents Aeneas as taking the mistletoe with him to Hades is perhaps that the mistletoe was supposed to repel evil spirits (see above, p. 362). Hence when Charon is disposed to bluster at

Now, too, we can fully understand why Virbius came to be confounded with the sun. If Virbius was, as I have tried to show, a tree-spirit, he must have been the spirit of the oak on which grew the Golden Bough ; for tradition represented him as the first of the Kings of the Wood. As an oak-spirit he must have been supposed periodically to rekindle the sun's fire, and might therefore easily be confounded with the sun itself. Similarly we can explain why Balder, an oak-spirit, was described as " so fair of face and so shining that a light went forth from him,"[1] and why he should have been so often taken to be the sun. And in general we may say that in primitive society, when the only known way of making fire is by the friction of wood, the savage must necessarily conceive fire as a property stored away, like sap or juice, in trees, from which he has laboriously to extract it. Thus all trees, or at least the particular sorts of trees whose wood he employs in fire-making, must be regarded by him as reservoirs of hidden fire, and it is natural that he should describe them by epithets like golden, shining, or bright. May not this have been the origin of the name, " the Bright or Shining One " (Zeus, Jove) by which the ancient Greeks and Italians designated their supreme god ?[2] It is at least highly significant that, amongst

---

Aeneas, the sight of the Golden Bough quiets him (*Aen.* vi. 406 *sq.*) Perhaps also the power ascribed to the mistletoe of laying bare the secrets of the earth may have suggested its use as a kind of " open Sesame " to the lower world. Compare *Aen.* vi. 140 *sq.*—

" *Sed non ante datur telluris operta subire, Auricomos quam qui decerpserit arbore fetus.*"

[1] *Die Edda*, übersetzt von K. Simrock,[8] p. 264.

[2] On the derivation of the names Zeus and Jove from a root meaning " shining," " bright," see Curtius, *Griech. Etymologie*,[5] p. 236 ; Vaniček, *Griech.-Latein. Etymolog. Wörterbuch*, p. 353 *sqq.* On the relation of Jove to the oak, compare Pliny, *Nat. Hist.* xii. § 3, *arborum genera numinibus suis dicata perpetuo servantur, ut Jovi aesculus* ; Servius on Virgil, *Georg.* iii. 332, *omnis quercus Jovi est consecrata.* Zeus and Jupiter have commonly been regarded as sky gods, because their names are etymologically connected with the Sanscrit word for sky. The reason seems insufficient.

both Greeks and Italians, the oak should have been the tree of the supreme god, that at his most ancient shrines, both in Greece and Italy, this supreme god should have been actually represented by an oak, and that so soon as the barbarous Aryans of Northern Europe appear in the light of history, they should be found, amid all diversities of language, of character, and of country, nevertheless at one in worshipping the oak as the chief object of their religious reverence, and extracting their sacred fire from its wood. If we are to judge of the primitive religion of the European Aryans by comparing the religions of the different branches of the stock, the highest place in their pantheon must certainly be assigned to the oak. The result, then, of our inquiry is to make it probable that, down to the time of the Roman Empire and the beginning of our era, the primitive worship of the Aryans was maintained nearly in its original form in the sacred grove at Nemi, as in the oak woods of Gaul, of Prussia, and of Scandinavia; and that the King of the Wood lived and died as an incarnation of the supreme Aryan god, whose life was in the mistletoe or Golden Bough.

If, in bidding farewell to Nemi, we look around us for the last time, we shall find the lake and its surroundings not much changed from what they were in the days when Diana and Virbius still received the homage of their worshippers in the sacred grove. The temple of Diana, indeed, has disappeared, and the King of the Wood no longer stands sentinel over the

Golden Bough.   But Nemi's woods are still green,
and at evening you may hear the church bells of
Albano, and perhaps, if the air be still, of Rome itself,
ringing the Angelus.   Sweet and solemn they chime
out from the distant city, and die lingeringly away
across the wide Campagnan marshes.   *Le roi est mort,
vive le roi !*

NOTE

Offerings of first-fruits

WE have seen (vol. ii. p. 68 *sqq.*) that primitive peoples often partake of the new corn sacramentally, because they suppose it to be instinct with a divine spirit or life. At a later age, when the fruits of the earth are conceived as produced rather than as animated by a divinity, the new fruits are no longer partaken of sacramentally as the body and blood of a god; but a portion of them is presented as a thank-offering to the divine beings who are believed to have produced them. Sometimes the first-fruits are presented to the king, probably in his character of a god. Till the first-fruits have been offered to the deity or the king, people are not at liberty to eat of the new crops. But, as it is not always possible to draw a sharp line between the sacrament and the sacrifice of first-fruits, it may be well to round off this part of the subject by appending some miscellaneous examples of the latter.

Among the Basutos, when the corn has been threshed and winnowed, it is left in a heap on the threshing-floor. Before it can be touched a religious ceremony must be performed. The persons to whom the corn belongs bring a new vessel to the spot, in which they boil some of the grain. When it is boiled they throw a few handfuls of it on the heap of corn, saying, " Thank you, gods; give us bread to-morrow also! " When this is done the rest is eaten, and the provision for the year is considered pure and fit to eat.[1] Here the sacrifice of the first-fruits to the gods is the prominent idea, which comes out again in the custom of leaving in the threshing-floor a little hollow filled with grain, as a thank-offering to the gods.[2]

---

[1] Casalis, *The Basutos*, p. 251 *sq.*   [2] *Ib.* p. 252.

Still the Basutos retain a lively sense of the sanctity of the corn in itself; for, so long as it is exposed to view, all defiled persons are carefully kept from it.   If it is necessary to employ a defiled person in carrying home the harvest, he remains at some distance while the sacks are being filled, and only approaches to place them upon the draught oxen.   As soon as the load is deposited at the dwelling he retires, and under no pretext may he help to pour the corn into the baskets in which it is kept.[1]

In Ashantee a harvest festival is held in September when the yams are ripe.   During the festival the king eats the new yams, but none of the people may eat them till the close of the festival, which lasts a fortnight.   During its continuance the grossest liberty prevails; theft, intrigue, and assault go unpunished, and each sex abandons itself to its passions.[2]   The Hovas of Madagascar present the first sheaves of the new grain to the sovereign.   The sheaves are carried in procession to the palace from time to time as the grain ripens.[3]   So in Burma, when the *pangati* fruits ripen, some of them used to be taken to the king's palace that he might eat of them; no one might partake of them before the king.[4]

Every year, when they gather their first crops, the Kochs of Assam offer some of the first-fruits to their ancestors, calling to them by name and clapping their hands.[5]   In August, when the rice ripens, the Hos offer the first-fruits of the harvest to Sing Bonga, who dwells in the sun.   Along with the new rice a white cock is sacrificed; and till the sacrifice has been offered no one may eat the new rice.[6]   Among the hill tribes near Rajamahall, in India, when the *kosarane* grain is being reaped in November or early in December, a festival is held as a thanksgiving before the new grain is eaten.   On a day appointed by the chief a goat is sacrificed by two men to a god called Chitariah Gossaih, after which the chief himself sacrifices a fowl.   Then the vassals repair to their fields, offer thanksgiving, make an oblation to Kull Gossaih (who is described as the Ceres of these mountaineers), and then return to their houses to eat of the new *kosarane*.   As soon as the

[1] Casalis, *The Basutos*, p. 252 *sq.*

[2] A. B. Ellis, *The Tshi-speaking Peoples of the Gold Coast*, p. 229 *sq.*; T. E. Bowdich, *Mission to Ashantee*, p. 226 *sq.* (ed. 1873.)

[3] J. Cameron, "On the Early Inhabitants of Madagascar," *Antana-narivo Annual and Madagascar Magazine*, iii. 263.

[4] Bastian, *Die Völker des östlichen Asien*, ii. 105.

[5] Dalton, *Ethnology of Bengal*, p. 91.

[6] Dalton, *op. cit.* p. 198.

inhabitants have assembled at the chief's house—the men sitting on one side and the women on the other—a hog, a measure of *kosarane*, and a pot of spirits are presented to the chief, who in return blesses his vassals, and exhorts them to industry and good behaviour; "after which, making a libation in the names of all their gods, and of their dead, he drinks, and also throws a little of the *kosarane* away, repeating the same pious exclamations." Drinking and festivity then begin, and are kept up for several days. The same tribes have another festival at reaping the Indian corn in August or September. Every man repairs to his fields with a hog, a goat, or a fowl, which he sacrifices to Kull Gossaih. Then, having feasted, he returns home, where another repast is prepared. On this day it is customary for every family in the village to distribute to every house a little of what they have prepared for their feast. Should any person eat of the new *kosarane* or the new Indian corn before the festival and public thanksgiving at the reaping of these crops, the chief fines him a white cock, which is sacrificed to Chitariah.[1] In the Central Provinces of India the first grain of the season is always offered to the god Bhímsen or Bhím Deo.[2] In the Punjaub, when sugar-cane is planted, a woman puts on a necklace and walks round the field, winding thread on to a spindle;[3] and when the sugar-cane is cut the first-fruits are offered on an altar, which is built close to the press and is sacred to the sugar-cane god. Afterwards the first-fruits are given to Brahmans. Also, when the women begin to pick the cotton, they go round the field eating rice-milk, the first mouthful of which they spit upon the field toward the west; and the first cotton picked is exchanged at the village shop for its weight in salt, which is prayed over and kept in the house till the picking is finished.[4]

In the island of Tjumba, East Indies, a festival is held after harvest. Vessels filled with rice are presented as a thank-offering to the gods. Then the sacred stone at the foot of a palm-tree is sprinkled with the blood of a sacrificed animal; and rice, with some of

---

[1] Thomas Shaw, "The Inhabitants of the Hills near Rajamahall," *Asiatic Researches*, iv. 56 *sq.*

[2] *Panjab Notes and Queries*, i. No. 502.

[3] This is curiously unlike the custom of ancient Italy, in most parts of which women were forbidden by law to walk on the highroads twirling a spindle, because this was supposed to injure the crops. Pliny, *Nat. Hist.* xxviii. § 28.

[4] D. C. J. Ibbetson, *Outlines of Panjab Ethnography* (Calcutta, 1883), p. 119.

the flesh, is laid on the stone for the gods. The palm-tree is hung with lances and shields.[1] The Dyaks of Borneo hold a feast of first-fruits when the paddy (unhusked rice) is ripe. The priestesses, accompanied by a gong and drum, go in procession to the farms and gather several bunches of the ripe paddy. These are brought back to the village, washed in cocoa-nut water, and laid round a bamboo altar, which at the harvest festivals is erected in the common room of the largest house. The altar is gaily decorated with white and red streamers, and is hung with the sweet-smelling blossom of the areca palm. The feast lasts two days, during which the village is tabooed; no one may leave it. Only fowls are killed, and dancing and gong-beating go on day and night. When the festival is over the people are free to get in their crops.[2]

The pounding of the new paddy is the occasion of a harvest festival which is celebrated all over Celebes. The religious ceremonies which accompany the feast were witnessed by Dr. B. F. Matthes in July 1857. Two mats were spread on the ground, each with a pillow on it. On one of the pillows were placed a man's clothes and a sword, on the other a woman's clothes. These were seemingly intended to represent the deceased ancestors. Rice and water were placed before the two dummy figures, and they were sprinkled with the new paddy. Also dishes of rice were set down for the rest of the family and the slaves of the deceased. This was the end of the ceremony.[3] The Minahassa of Celebes have a festival of "eating the new rice." Fowls or pigs are killed; some of the flesh, with rice and palm-wine, is set apart for the gods, and then the eating and drinking begin.[4] The people of Kobi and Sariputi, two villages on the north-east coast of Ceram, offer the first-fruits of the paddy, in the form of cooked rice, with tobacco, etc., to their ancestors, as a token of gratitude. The ceremony is called "feeding the dead."[5] In the Tenimber and Timorlaut Islands, East Indies,

[1] Fr. Junghuhn, *Die Battaländer auf Sumatra*, ii. 312.

[2] Spenser St. John, *Life in the Forests of the Far East*, i. 191. On taboos observed at agricultural operations, see *id.* i. 185; R. G. Woodthorpe, "Wild Tribes Inhabiting the so-called Naga Hills," *Journ. Anthrop. Inst.* xi. 71; *Old New Zealand*, by a Pakeha Maori (London, 1884), p. 103 *sq.*; R. Taylor, *Te Ika a Maui; or, New Zealand and its Inhabitants*,[2] p.

165 *sq.*; E. Tregear, "The Maoris of New Zealand," *Journ. Anthrop. Inst.* xix. 110.

[3] B. F. Matthes, *Beknopt Verslag mijner reizen in de Binnenlanden van Celebes, in de jaren 1857 en 1861*, p. 5.

[4] N. Graafland, *De Minahassa*, i. 165.

[5] J. G. F. Riedel, *De sluik-en kroesharige rassen tusschen Selebes en Papua*, p. 107.

the first-fruits of the paddy, along with live fowls and pigs, are offered to the *matmate*.   The *matmate* are the spirits of their ancestors, which are worshipped as guardian-spirits or household gods.   They are supposed to enter the house through an opening in the roof, and to take up their abode temporarily in their skulls, or in images of wood or ivory, in order to partake of the offerings and to help the family.   They also take the form of birds, pigs, crocodiles, turtles, sharks, etc.[1]   In Amboina, after the rice or other harvest has been gathered in, some of the new fruits are offered to the gods, and till this is done, the priests may not eat of them.   A portion of the new rice, or whatever it may be, is boiled, and milk of the cocoa-nut is poured on it, mixed with Indian saffron.   It is then taken to the place of sacrifice and offered to the god.   Some people also pour out oil before the deity; and if any of the oil is left over, they take it home as a holy and priceless treasure, wherewith they smear the forehead and breast of sick people and whole people, in the firm conviction that the oil confers all kinds of blessings.[2]   The Irayas and Catalangans of Luzon, tribes of the Malay stock, but of mixed blood, worship chiefly the souls of their ancestors under the name of *anitos*, to whom they offer the first-fruits of the harvest.   The *anitos* are household deities; some of them reside in pots in the corners of the houses; and miniature houses, standing near the dwelling-house, are especially sacred to them.[3]

In certain tribes of Fiji "the first-fruits of the yam harvest are presented to the ancestors in the Nanga [sacred stone enclosure] with great ceremony, before the bulk of the crop is dug for the people's use, and no man may taste of the new yams until the presentation has been made.   The yams thus offered are piled in the Great Nanga, and are allowed to rot there.   If any one were impiously bold enough to appropriate them to his own use, he would be smitten with madness.   The mission teacher before mentioned told me that when he visited the Nanga he saw among the weeds with which it was overgrown numerous yam vines which had sprung up out of the piles of decayed offerings.   Great feasts are made at the presentations of the first-fruits, which are times of public rejoicing, and the Nanga itself is frequently spoken of as the *Mbaki*, or Har-

[1] Riedel, *op. cit.* pp. 281, 296 *sq.*
[2] Fr. Valentyn, *Oud en nieuw Oost-Indiën*, iii. 10.
[3] C. Semper, *Die Philippinen und ihre Bewohner*, p. 56.

vest." [1]   In other parts of Fiji the practice with regard to the first-fruits seems to have been different, for we are told by another observer that "the first-fruits of the yams, which are always presented at the principal temple of the district, become the property of the priests, and form their revenue, although the pretence of their being required for the use of the god is generally kept up." [2]   In Tana, one of the New Hebrides, the general name for gods appeared to be *aremha*, which meant "a dead man."   The spirits of departed ancestors were among the gods of the people.   Chiefs who reached an advanced age were deified after their death, addressed by name, and prayed to on various occasions.   They were supposed to preside especially over the growth of the yams and fruit-trees.   The first-fruits were presented to them.   A little of the new fruit was laid on a stone, or on a shelving branch of the tree, or on a rude temporary altar, made of a few sticks lashed together with strips of bark, in the form of a table, with its four feet stuck in the ground.   All being quiet, the chief acted as high priest, and prayed aloud as follows : "Compassionate father! here is some food for you ; eat it ; be kind to us on account of it."   Then all the people shouted.   This took place about noon, and afterwards the assembled people feasted and danced till midnight or morning. [3]

In some of the Kingsmill Islands the god most commonly worshipped was called Tubuériki.   He was represented by a flat coral stone, of irregular shape, about three feet long by eighteen inches wide, set up on one end in the open air.   Leaves of the cocoa-nut palm were tied about it, considerably increasing its size and height. The leaves were changed every month, that they might be always fresh.   The worship paid to the god consisted in repeating prayers before the stone, and laying beside it a portion of the food prepared by the people for their own use.   This they did at their daily meals, at festivals, and whenever they specially wished to propitiate the favour of the god.   ·The first-fruits of the season were always offered to him.   Every family of distinction had one of these stones which was considered rather in the light of a family altar than as an idol. [4]

---

[1] Rev. Lorimer Fison, "The Nanga, or sacred stone enclosure, of Wainimala, Fiji," *Journ. Anthrop. Inst.* xiv. 27.

[2] J. E. Erskine, *Journal of a Cruise among the Islands of the Western Pacific*, p. 252.   [3] Turner, *Samoa*, p. 318 *sq.*

[4] Horatio Hale, *United States Exploring Expedition, Ethnology and Philology*, p. 97.

The following is a description of the festival of first-fruits as it was celebrated in Tonga in the days when a European flag rarely floated among the islands of the Pacific. "*Inachi*. This word means literally a share or portion of any thing that is to be, or has been, distributed out : but in the sense here mentioned it means that portion of the fruits of the earth, and other eatables, which is offered to the gods in the person of the divine chief Tooitonga, which allotment is made once a year, just before the yams in general are arrived at a state of maturity ; those which are used in this ceremony being planted sooner than others, and, consequently, they are the first-fruits of the yam season. The object of this offering is to insure the protection of the gods, that their favour may be extended to the welfare of the nation generally, and in particular to the productions of the earth, of which yams are the most important.

"The time for planting most kinds of yams is about the latter end of July, but the species called *caho-caho*, which is always used in this ceremony, is put in the ground about a month before, when, on each plantation, there is a small piece of land chosen and fenced in, for the purpose of growing a couple of yams of the above description. As soon as they have arrived at a state of maturity, the *How* [King] sends a messenger to Tooitonga, stating that the yams for the *inachi* are fit to be taken up, and requesting that he would appoint a day for the ceremony ; he generally fixes on the tenth day afterwards, reckoning the following day for the first. There are no particular preparations made till the day before the ceremony ; at night, however, the sound of the conch is heard occasionally in different parts of the islands, and as the day of the ceremony approaches, it becomes more frequent, so that the people of almost every plantation sound the conch three or four times, which, breaking in upon the silence of the night, has a pleasing effect, particularly at Vavaoo, where the number of woods and hills send back repeated echoes, adding greatly to the effect. The day before the ceremony the yams are dug up, and ornamented with a kind of ribbon prepared from the inner membrane of the leaf of a species of pandanus, and dyed red. . . .

"The sun has scarcely set when the sound of the conch begins again to echo through the island, increasing as the night advances. At the Mooa [capital] and all the plantations the voices of men and women are heard singing *Nòfo bòa tegger gnaobe, bòoa gnaobe*, Rest thou, doing no work ; thou shalt not work. This increases till midnight, men generally singing the first part of the sentence, and the women the last : it then subsides for three or four hours, and again increases as the sun rises.   Nobody, however, is seen stirring out in the public roads till about eight o'clock, when the people from all quarters of the island are seen advancing towards the Mooa, and canoes from all the other islands are landing their men ; so that all the inhabitants of Tonga seem approaching by sea and land, singing and sounding the conch.   At the Mooa itself the universal bustle of preparation is seen and heard ; and the different processions entering from various quarters of men and women, all dressed up in new *gnatoos*, ornamented with red ribbons and wreaths of flowers, and the men armed with spears and clubs, betoken the importance of the ceremony about to be performed.   Each party brings in its yams in a basket, which is carried in the arms with great care by the principal vassal of the chief to whom the plantation may belong.   The baskets are deposited in the *malái*[1] (in the *Mooa*), and some of them begin to employ themselves in slinging the yams, each upon the centre of a pole about eight or nine feet long, and four inches diameter.   The proceedings are regulated by attending matabooles.[2]   The yams being all slung, each pole is carried by two men upon their shoulders, one walking before the other, and the yam hanging between them, orna-mented with red ribbons.   The procession begins to move towards the grave of the last Tooitonga (which is generally in the neighbour-hood, or the grave of one of his family will do), the men advancing in a single line, every two bearing a yam, with a slow and measured pace, sinking at every step, as if their burden were of immense weight.   In the meantime the chiefs and matabooles are seated in a semicircle before the grave, with their heads bowed down, and their hands clasped before them."   The procession then marched round the grave twice or thrice in a great circle, the conchs blowing and the men singing.   Next the yams, still suspended from the poles, were deposited before the grave, and their bearers sat down beside them.   One of the *matabooles* of Tooitonga now addressed the gods generally, and afterwards particularly, mentioning the late Tooitonga, and the names of several others.   He thanked them for their divine bounty in favouring the land with the prospect of so good a harvest, and prayed that their beneficence might be continued in future.

---

[1] The *malái* is "a piece of ground, generally before a large house, or chief's grave, where public ceremonies are principally held."   Mariner, *Tonga Islands, Vocabulary*.

[2] The *mataboole* is "a rank next below chiefs or nobles."   *Ib.*

When he had finished, the men rose and resumed their loads, and after parading two or three times round the grave, marched back to the *maláì*, singing and blowing the conchs as before. The chiefs and *matabooles* soon followed to the same place, where the yams had been again deposited. Here the company sat down in a great circle, presided over by Tooitonga. Then the other articles that formed part of the *Inachi* were brought forward, consisting of dried fish, mats, etc., which, with the yams, were divided into shares. About a fourth was allotted to the gods, and appropriated by the priests; about a half fell to the king; and the remainder belonged to Tooitonga. The materials of the *Inachi* having been carried away, the company set themselves to drink *cava*, and a *mataboole* addressed them, saying that the gods would protect them, and grant them long lives, if they continued to observe the religious ceremonies and to pay respect to the chiefs.[1]

The Samoans used to present the first-fruits to the spirits (*aitus*) and chiefs.[2] For example, a family whose god was in the form of an eel presented the first-fruits of their taro plantations to the eel.[3] In Tahiti "the first fish taken periodically on their shores, together with a number of kinds regarded as sacred, were conveyed to the altar. The first-fruits of their orchards and gardens were also *taumaha*, or offered, with a portion of their live stock, which consisted of pigs, dogs, and fowls, as it was supposed death would be inflicted on the owner or the occupant of the land from which the god should not receive such acknowledgment."[4] In Huahine, one of the Society Islands, the first-fruits were presented to the god Tani. A poor person was expected to bring two of the earliest fruits gathered, of whatever kind; a *raatira* had to bring ten, and chiefs and princes had to bring more, according to their rank and riches. They brought the fruits to the temple, where they threw them down on the ground, with the words, "Here, Tani, I have brought you something to eat."[5] The chief gods of the Easter Islanders were Make-Make and Haua. To these they offered the first of all the produce of the ground.[6] Amongst the Maoris the offering of the first-fruits of the

---

[1] W. Mariner, *Account of the Natives of the Tonga Islands* (London, 1818), ii. 196-203.

[2] Ch. Wilkes, *Narrative of the United States Exploring Expedition*, ii. 133.

[3] Turner, *Samoa*, p. 70 *sq.*

[4] Ellis, *Polynesian Researches*, i. 350.

[5] Tyerman and Bennet, *Journal of Voyages and Travels*, i. 284.

[6] Geiseler, *Die Oester-Insel* (Berlin, 1883), p. 31.

sweet potatoes to Pani, son of Rongo, the god of sweet potatoes, was a solemn religious ceremony.[1]

It has been affirmed that the old Prussians offered the first-fruits of their crops and of their fishing to the god Curcho, but doubt rests on the statement.[2]   The Romans sacrificed the first ears of corn to Ceres, and the first of the new wine to Liber; and until the priests had offered these sacrifices, the people might not eat the new corn nor drink the new wine.[3]

The chief solemnity of the Natchez, an Indian tribe on the Lower Mississippi, was the Harvest Festival or the Festival of New Fire. When the time for the festival drew near, a crier went through the villages calling upon the people to prepare new vessels and new garments, to wash their houses, and to burn the old grain, the old garments, and the old utensils in a common fire.   He also proclaimed an amnesty to criminals.   Next day he appeared again, commanding the people to fast for three days, to abstain from all pleasures, and to make use of the medicine of purification.   Thereupon all the people took some drops extracted from a root which they called the "root of blood."   It was a kind of plantain and distilled a red liquor which acted as a violent emetic.   During their three days' fast the people kept silence.   At the end of it the crier proclaimed that the festival would begin on the following day.   So next morning, as soon as it began to grow light in the sky, the people streamed from all quarters towards the temple of the Sun.   The temple was a large building with two doors, one opening to the east, the other to the west.   On this morning the eastern door of the temple stood open.   Facing the eastern door was an altar, placed so as to catch the first beams of the rising sun.   An image of a *chouchouacha* (a small marsupial) stood upon the altar; on its right was an image of a rattlesnake, on its left an image of a marmoset.   Before these images a fire of oak bark burned perpetually.   Once a year only, on the eve of the Harvest Festival, was the sacred flame suffered to die out.   To the right of the altar, on "this pious morn," stood the great chief, who took his title and traced his descent from the Sun.   To the

---

[1] E. Tregear, "The Maoris of New Zealand," *Journ. Anthrop. Inst.* xix. 110.

[2] Hartknoch, *Alt und neues Preussen*, p. 161; *id.*, *Dissertationes historicae de variis rebus Prussicis*, p. 163 (appended to his edition of Dusburg's *Chronicon Prussiae*).   Cp. W. Mannhardt, *Die Korndämonen*, p. 27.

[3] Festus, *s.v. sacrima*, p. 319, ed. Müller; Pliny, *Nat. Hist.* xviii. § 8.

left of the altar stood his wife.   Round them were grouped, according
to their ranks, the war chiefs, the sachems, the heralds, and the young
braves.   In front of the altar were piled bundles of dry reeds, stacked
in concentric rings.

The high priest, standing on the threshold of the temple, kept his
eyes fixed on the eastern horizon.   Before presiding at the festival he
had to plunge thrice into the Mississippi.   In his hands he held two
pieces of dry wood which he kept rubbing slowly against each other,
muttering magic words.   At his side two acolytes held two cups filled
with a kind of black sherbet.   All the women, their backs turned to
the east, each leaning with one hand on her rude mattock and
supporting her infant with the other, stood in a great semicircle at
the gate of the temple.   Profound silence reigned throughout the
multitude while the priest watched attentively the growing light in
the east.   As soon as the diffused light of dawn began to be shot
with beams of fire, he quickened the motion of the two pieces of
wood which he held in his hands ; and at the moment when the
upper edge of the sun's disc appeared above the horizon, fire flashed
from the wood and was caught in tinder.   At the same instant the
women outside the temple faced round and held up their infants
and their mattocks to the rising sun.

The great chief and his wife now drank the black liquor.   The
priests kindled the circle of dried reeds ; fire was set to the heap
of oak bark on the altar, and from this sacred flame all the hearths
of the village were rekindled.   No sooner were the circles of reeds
consumed than the chief's wife came forth from the temple and
placing herself at the head of the women marched in procession
to the harvest fields, whither the men were not allowed to follow
them.   They went to gather the first sheaves of maize and returned
to the temple bearing them on their heads.   Some of the sheaves
they presented to the high priest, who laid them on the altar.
Others they used to bake the unleavened bread which was to be
eaten in the evening.   The eastern door of the sanctuary was now
closed, and the western door was opened.

When the day began to decline, the multitude assembled once
more at the temple, this time at its western gate, where they formed
a great crescent, with the horns turned toward the west.   The
unleavened bread was held up and presented to the setting sun,
and a priest struck up a hymn in praise of his descending light.

When darkness had fallen the whole plain twinkled with fires, round which the people feasted ; and the sounds of music and revelry broke the silence of night.[1]

---

[1] Chateaubriand, *Voyage en Amérique*, pp. 130-136 (Michel Lévy, Paris, 1870). Chateaubriand's description is probably based on earlier accounts, which I have been unable to trace. Compare, however, Le Petit, "Relation des Natchez," in *Recueil de voiages au Nord*, ix. 13 *sq.* (Amsterdam edition) ; De Tonti, "Relation de la Louisiane et du Mississippi," *ib.* v. 122 ; Charlevoix, *Histoire de la Nouvelle France*, vi. 183 ; *Lettres édifiantes et curieuses*, vii. 18 *sq.*

INDEX